Transcultural Diplomacy and International Law in Heritage Conservation

Olimpia Niglio · Eric Yong Joong Lee
Editors

Transcultural Diplomacy and International Law in Heritage Conservation

A Dialogue between Ethics, Law, and Culture

Forewords by Francesco Francioni and Francesco Follo

Springer

Editors
Olimpia Niglio
Graduate School of Humanities and Human Sciences
Hokkaido University
Sapporo, Japan

Eric Yong Joong Lee
YIJUN Institute of International Law
Seoul, Korea (Republic of)

ISBN 978-981-16-0308-2 ISBN 978-981-16-0309-9 (eBook)
https://doi.org/10.1007/978-981-16-0309-9

This Springer imprint is published by the registered company Springer Nature Singapore Pte Ltd.
The registered company address is: 152 Beach Road, #21-01/04 Gateway East, Singapore 189721, Singapore

[...] No government policy and legality without culture

—Otto Morales Benítez (Colombia), El Pais, July 2010

[...] Culture means measure, thoughtfulness, circumspection

—Norberto Bobbio (Italy), Politica e Cultura, 1955

[…] A society without culture, without respect, without the pathos, paves the way for the society of scandal.

—Byung-Chul Han (Republic of Korea), In the Swarm, 2017

To

Our Parents

Foreword by Francesco Francioni: Culture, Heritage and International Law

Culture Between Universalism and Relativism

Culture and cultural heritage have not been prominent topics in the historical development of international law. The tradition of legal positivism has always considered the State as the centre of gravity of international law and relegated culture and cultural heritage within the horizon of state sovereignty. This tendency has been reinforced by the conceptualisation of material heritage as an element to be considered part of the State territory and of the nation. Today, cultural heritage in its broadest sense—thus including both material and intangible heritage—remains part of the territory of every state and part of the Nation in the legal system of many states. But there is no doubt that starting from the second part of the twentieth century, culture and heritage have started to play an increasing role as an element of the general interest of humanity and of international law. The creation of UNESCO as the world organisation for culture, science and education in 1945 was predicated on the fundamental belief that culture is inextricably linked to peace because "wars begin the minds of men" and therefore "it is in the minds of men that the defenses of peace must be construed". These words, taken from the Preamble of the UNESCO Constitution indicate that culture and education are not only indispensable conditions for the respect of human dignity and for the building of cohesive and stable societies, but are also the foundation of a "moral and intellectual solidarity of mankind", the ultimate guarantee of a lasting peace among the peoples of the world.

These words of the UNESCO Constitution, coined in the immediate aftermath of World War 2 and of the catastrophe of genocide, acquire today the value of a prophetic message at the present stage of development of international law. The process of globalisation that opened the new millennium, with the elimination or reduction of State barriers to the free circulation of goods, services and ideas, has marked profoundly international law as a system traditionally based on the centrality of the State. It has contributed to the overcoming of the ideological divide between the West and the East that had characterised the long period of the cold war; it has created the conditions for the economic development of millions of peoples and the reduction of poverty in many regions of the world. Non state actors—including individuals, communities and business corporations—have become holders of rights and bearers of duties under international law. At the same time globalisation and its project of universalism, free market and liberal capitalism has been accompanied by mounting backlash, rising nationalism and cultural fragmentation. Ethnic and religious conflicts have re-emerged with unprecedented violence in the Middle East, Africa, Asia—as they had earlier exploded in Yugoslavia—resulting in mass atrocities and the deliberate destruction of cultural heritage and of symbols marking the religious and cultural identity of the enemies. In recent times we have seen the re-emergence of xenophobia and the spreading of the new ideology of "national sovranism", which builds upon the distrust towards international institutions and even towards international law as a system of rules and values constraining State power and supporting cooperation and reconciliation among nations. This phenomenon is exemplified by the unfortunate decision of some states to walk out of UNESCO,[1] from the World Health Organization, and, in the case of Brexit, from the European Union.

In this context culture and identity politics have a profound effect on international law because they tend to break the relationship between the "self" and the "others" under the impulse of a perceived unrenounceable group characteristics that resist integration, or even coexistence, in a larger community of shared values and interests. This attitude builds on cultural specificity to oppose a cosmopolitan project based on pluralism, international law and human rights. In its most extreme and pathological forms it gives rise to a cultural and religious fundamentalism which refuses any concept of mutual respect and equal liberty of the "others" and rejects any form of dialogue based on reason. The most pathological and violent manifestations of this attitude have been the rise of the so-called Islamic State in Syria and Iraq and its pursuit of a universal order based on terror and the assassination or enslavement of the "others". This has resulted in one of the most horrific forms of "cultural genocide" of our epoch with the extermination and persecution of the cultural minority of the Yazidis and with countless acts of terrorism that cost the life of thousands of innocent victims and the intentional destruction of cultural treasures of outstanding universal importance.

Culture in the Theories of International Law

Mainstream international law scholarship and especially human rights thinking have continued to affirm the universality of international law and its primacy over the cultural, social and political specificity of national societies and other human communities throughout the world. On the opposite side, "cultural relativists" have challenged the concept of universality of international law and have given precedence to the particularity of different cultures, all entitled to equal dignity and respect. Similar

[1] The United States and Israel have withdrawn from UNESCO because of fundamental differences with the cultural policies of the Organization.

conclusions, albeit on different theoretical premises, are reached by the views from the "Global South", which tend to look at international law, and especially international human rights, as a sort of a colonial legacy of the West and as an "imperial global state in the making" (Chimni, 2004).

Little contribution to the identification of the place of culture in international law comes from the post-modern "deconstructivist" theories, such as the "critical legal studies" developed in the United States in the second part of the last century (Unger, 1983). At the heart of this theory is the aim of showing how under the guise of seemingly objective values, such as liberalism and human rights, international law can well be used to conceal a political agenda of promotion of special interests of the powerful. Beyond the unquestionable merit of this theory in showing the limits of international law in a particular historical moment, its weakness is in its approaching a nihilistic position with regard to the objective existence of the whole international legal order. If law is just an aggregate argumentation, an ensemble of strategies of persuasion, then how can we save its objective existence as a system of norms, limited and imperfect as they may be but necessary to permit the coexistence, interaction and cooperation among members of a culturally plural and diverse international society? This question remains unanswered even in the most sophisticated elaborations of the deconstructivist theory (Koskenniemi, 2006).

Another important school of thought developed in the United States, the anti-formalistic New Haven international law jurisprudence, places individual liberty and human dignity at the centre of international law, which is seen as a continuing process of deliberation capable of approximating "… the optimum access by all human beings to all things they cherish: power, health, enlightenment, skill, well-being, affection, respect and rectitude" (Reisman, 2007). This manifesto of liberalism is important in counter-balancing the State-centred tradition of legal positivism. But it leaves little room for the role of culture in international law. The idea of international law and international justice is concentrated on individuals, on the fulfillment of their aspirations and the flourishing of their human potential. Little space is left for the collective interests of society, such as public health, environmental security and especially for the role of culture as a unifying element of a community in which the individual self-realisation is anchored, be it the family, the local community, the nation or even a supranational entity founded on a common cultural heritage.

Other contemporary theories have attempted to overcome the limits of the above doctrines, as well as the traditional rule based approach of legal positivism, by developing a "value based" method (Iovane, 2000) and a "constitutional law" perspective ultimately appealing to the human dimension of international law. These are innovative and generous approaches premised on the centrality of human dignity and peoples' rights in the making, interpretation and implementation of international law. But their limit remains in the belief that the transformative process leading to the "constitutionalisation" of international law may occur by some magical internal force of the system, a force capable of establishing a hierarchical legal order based on inalienable legal principles of constitutional character such as safeguarding peace, basic human rights and prohibiting the destruction of natural and cultural heritage of great importance to humanity. This is certainly part of a progressive project of modernisation of international law. But this project, though it has achieved important results at a normative level with the emergence of concepts such as *Jus cogens* and obligations *erga omnes*, still finds obstacles in the lack of a centralised system of judicial review and in the reality of a pluralistic world with a variety of cultures and different ideas of the public good. These obstacles are all the more apparent today with the declining sense of collective purpose at the international level and the persistent deficit of a cosmopolitan "demos".

"Culturalising" International Law

If international law cannot be reduced to a simple aggregate of arguments to advance naked power, or a to sterile ensemble of rules, it is obvious that the its reality must be found in the actual existence of an international community, comprising the states and the peoples of the world, each one of them with a district political and cultural tradition and specific national or community interests. In spite of this cultural and political pluralism, States and human communities need to interact one with another, and in the absence of a world government, they need international law to avoid chaos and to ensure a minimum of order, of peaceful coexistence and cooperation. Since besides the community of States there is also humanity, the totality of the peoples of the world with their common needs, shared interests and an emerging sense of international justice, the contemporary development of international law and its modernisation are marked by the increasing role that general interests of humanity play in the making, interpretation and implementation of international norms that transcend the regulation of reciprocal interests of the States. Actually, some of these interests are antithetic to the purely governmental interests of the States. This is the case with the international law of human rights, which is meant to limit States powers in order to guarantee respect for human dignity and individual liberty. It is the case with humanitarian law, which is meant to limit the freedom of belligerents to resort to violence in armed conflicts. It is also the case with international environmental law which by and large consists of limits to the sovereign right of every State to use the natural resources of their territory and of the planet in the pursuit of sometimes unsustainable projects of economic development.

It is in this general context that we can place the phenomenon of what I have called "culturalisation of international law". That is, the growing relevance that culture and cultural heritage are playing in the development of international law. This phenomenon has two faces. On the one hand it entails the development of multilateral treaties, sometimes with universal membership, whose objective is the safeguarding of different types of cultural heritage, sometimes building on already formed customary norms and general principles developed in the practice of States and of national courts. Today we can count six cultural heritage treaties of very widespread or even universal application (the 1954 Hague Convention, with its two Protocols; the 1970 UNESCO Convention on illicit traffic; the 1995 UNIDROIT Convention on Stolen and Illegally Exported Cultural Objects; the 2001 Underwater

Cultural Heritage Convention; the 2003 Convention on the Safeguarding of Intangible Cultural Heritage; and the 2005 Convention on cultural diversity). To this list one should add the many instruments dealing with culture at the regional level, and the many recommendations and declarations adopted by UNESCO and other relevant organisations as instruments of "soft law".[2] On the other hand, the process of culturalisation of international law consists in the pervasive impact that the specific international cultural heritage law has had on other branches of international law. Cultural treaties and general principles of cultural heritage protection have infiltrated the area of international economic law, both trade law and investment law (Vadi, 2020; Voon, 2020: 483–531), resulting in the adoption of the 2005 UNESCO Convention on the Protection and Promotion of the Diversity of Cultural Expressions,[3] in the application of cultural heritage norms to economic disputes or in the utilisation of cultural heritage law as relevant criteria for the interpretation of the applicable rules of international economic law, so as to bring the two branches of law into a relationship of mutual support. Cultural heritage law has pervaded the field of international human rights law, both in the sense of supporting the recognition of cultural human rights, especially the right to participate in cultural life, and in the sense of defining the boundaries of a comprehensive and inclusive cultural pluralism in opposition to cultural nationalism and policies of exclusion (Francioni & Scheinin, 2008). Modern developments of cultural heritage have increasingly impacted on international environmental law and have helped to bridge the traditional gap between nature and culture (Boer, 2020: 318–346). This is made evident by the emergence of the concept of "landscape" as a cultural object resulting from the impact of human labour and creativity on the natural environment and the attribution of transcendental cultural or religious values to specific features of the natural environment (Strecker, 2018). In a broader sense, the idea that humans, with their infinite variety of cultures, are an integral part of the natural ecosystem underlies the 1972 UNESCO Convention on the protection of world heritage. This convention, now in force for 193 States, brings together cultural and natural heritage under a common system of international cooperation for the identification and protection of cultural and natural sites of "outstanding universal value" (Francioni, 2020: 250–272).

In this general overview of the various forms of impact that culture and cultural heritage have had on the fabric of international law we must include also the recent developments regarding the role of culture and cultural heritage in the maintenance of peace and security. In this field there has been a synergic effort by the United Nations and UNESCO towards the objective of linking respect of cultural heritage and protection of cultural pluralism to the preservation of peace and security at the international level. On the one hand the Security Council has consistently held that attacks on, and deliberate destruction of cultural heritage may constitute a threat to peace and therefore may trigger the adoption of mandatory measures for the maintenance of peace under Chapter VII of the UN Charter.

[2]For a complete list of these soft law instruments, see *Standard Setting in UNESCO*, Vol. II, UNESCO Publishing, 2007, Part II and III.

[3]Text reprinted in *Standard Setting in UNESCO*, Vol. II, cit. p. 326ff.

This is made evident by a series of binding resolutions that include Resolution 1483 of 2003, concerning measures to enforce the respect of the cultural heritage of Iraq in the wake of the United States led invasion of the country, which had resulted *inter alia* in a mass scale looting of museums and heritage sites[4]; Resolution 2199 of 2015, and Resolution 2347 of 2017, which is entirely devoted to the measures to be taken to prevent the destruction and looting of cultural heritage in the context of conflicts and terrorism.[5] On the other hand, the increasing frequency of cases of intentional destruction of cultural heritage as a means of ethnic and cultural cleansing has resulted in the recognition at the level of international law of a close nexus between mass atrocities and deliberate destruction of cultural heritage.

This recognition is implicit in several provisions of treaties criminalising the intentional destruction of cultural heritage, such as Articles 15–18 of the Second Protocol to the 1954 Hague Convention, Article 8 of the Rome Statute establishing the International Criminal court (reflecting Article 3 d. of the Statute of the International Criminal Tribunal for Yugoslavia), and Article 10 of the 2017 Council of Europe Convention on Offences Relating to Cultural Property.[6] But, most important, it is confirmed by the abundant jurisprudence developed by international courts and tribunals, including the International Criminal Tribunal for Yugoslavia, the International Criminal court and the International court of Justice, that have consistently found that intentional destruction of cultural heritage can constitute a war crime, a crime against humanity and even the evidence of the *mens rea* of genocide (Lenzerini, 2020: 75–100).

Conclusion

In spite of the limited role played by culture in the traditional inter-state paradigm of international law, there is no doubt that contemporary developments show a constant progress towards the elaboration of a coherent body of "international cultural heritage law". This body is not only the product of the expanding nucleus of cultural treaties of universal and regional application; it is the also the result of the emergence of customary norms and general principles of international law that directly or indirectly aim at ensuring respect for cultural heritage and for cultural diversity as an essential element for the maintenance of peace, respect for human dignity and socio-economic sustainability.

The progressive development of international law in this field is supported by the jurisprudence if international courts and tribunals that in the past twenty five years have contributed to the criminalisation of assaults on cultural property and

[4]Resolution 1483, 2003 "stressing the need for respect for the archaeological, historical, cultural and religious heritage of Iraq, and for the continued protection of archaeological, historical, cultural and religious sites, museums, libraries and monuments".

[5]Resolution 2347 was adopted by unanimous vote on 24 March 2017.

[6]CETS No. 221.

to the enforcement of the responsibility of individuals and States for the intentional destruction of cultural heritage. But also domestic courts have contributed to the progressive development of this field of international law by an innovative case law informed by the awareness of the importance of a close cooperation in view of preventing and suppressing looting and illicit traffic of cultural heritage (Shyllon, 2020: 227 ff.; Gerstenblith, 2020: 200 ff.). As in other areas of international law, such as human rights, the protection of the environment and the maintenance of peace, respect and protection of the infinite variety of cultures and of cultural heritage are slowly becoming an international public good and a common concern of humankind.

Francesco Francioni
Emeritus Professor
International Law
European University Institute
Florence, Italy
Francesco.Francioni@eui.eu

References

Boer, B. (2020). The environment and cultural heritage. In F. Francioni & A. F. Vrdoljak (Eds.), *The Oxford handbook of international cultural heritage law* (pp. 318–336). Oxford: Oxford University Press.

Chimni, B. S. (2004). International institutions today: An imperial global state in the making. *EJIL, 15*(1), 1–37.

Francioni, F. (2020). World cultural heritage. In F. Francioni & A. F. Vrdoljak (Eds.), *The Oxford handbook of international cultural heritage law* (pp. 250–272). Oxford: Oxford University Press.

Francioni, F., & Scheinin, M. (Eds.). (2008). *Cultural human rights.* Leiden and Boston: Martinus Nijhoff Publishers.

Gerstenblith, P. (2020). Theft and illegal excavations: Legal principles for protection of archaeological heritage. In F. Francioni & A. F. Vrdoljak (Eds.), *The Oxford handbook of international cultural heritage law* (p. 200ff.). Oxford: Oxford University Press.

Iovane, M. (2000). *La tutela dei valori fondamentali nell'ordinamento internazionale.* Napoli: Editoriale Scientifica.

Koskenniemi, M. (2006). *From apology to Utopia. The structure of international legal argument.* Cambridge: Cambridge University Press.

Lenzerini, F. (2020). Intentional destruction of cultural heritage. In F. Francioni & A. F. Vrdoljak (Eds.), *The Oxford handbook of international cultural heritage law* (pp. 75–100). Oxford: Oxford University Press.

Reisman, M. (2007). The New Haven school: A brief introduction. *Yale Journal of International Law*, 575 ff. at 576.

Shyllon, F. (2020). Grasping the nettle of illicit export, import and transfer of ownership of cultural objects. In F. Francioni & A. F. Vrdoljak (Eds.), *The Oxford handbook of international cultural heritage law* (p. 227 ff.). Oxford: Oxford University Press.

Strecker, A. (2018). *Landscape protection in international law.* Oxford: Oxford University Press.

Unger, R. M. (1983). The critical legal studies movement. *Harvard Law Review*, 96, 561–675.

Vadi, V. (2020). Cultural heritage in international investment law. In F. Francioni & A. F. Vrdoljak (Eds.), *The Oxford handbook of international cultural heritage law* (pp. 483–531). Oxford: Oxford University Press.

Voon, T. (2020). National treasures at the intersection between cultural heritage and international trade law. In F. Francioni & A. F. Vrdoljak (Eds.), *The Oxford handbook of international cultural heritage law* (pp. 483–531). Oxford: Oxford University Press.

Foreword by Francesco Follo: Education, Globalisation and Intercultural Dialogue

Everyone, or at least everyone who has studied the Greek classics, will be familiar with the apologue about the father who wanted to have his son educated by sending him to the school of a "Sophist". Finding the cost of the lessons exorbitant, he asked what would be the practical use to which such a great expenditure might be put. The "Sophist" replied "when your son goes to the theatre to see a tragedy performed, he will not be a stone sitting on another stone." By thus responding to a question that focused on utility and demanded "specifics", the Sophist referred it to what is true and good, i.e. to knowledge of the "universal" and the desire for it.

That is one of the most important "legacies" that Hellenic speculation has transmitted to us. The natural desire to know, which Aristotle discusses in the first pages of*Metaphysics*, relates to the acquisition of a disinterested knowledge of Being by searching for its cause, i.e. seeking the invisible that explains the visible (*Metaphysics*, Book 1, section 980a). That disinterested knowledge, with its "discoveries", will then create the conditions for the "inventions" that will transform Man's being alive into his being in the world, whilst also creating new opportunities for his well-being.

But in 1983 when the American economist Theodore Levitt coined the term "globalisation", I do not believe he was referring to disinterested knowledge of that kind; he was simply inventing an expression to describe the new international economic environment (*cf*. *Les racines de la mondialisation: De Rome a New York, L'Histoire*, November 2002, p. 33). In historical terms we can date globalisation back to the fifteenth century, the time of the European conquests and mercantilism; but following J. A. Scholte's argument in*Globalisation, A critical Introduction,* (pp. 15–16) we can also take "globalisation" to mean internationalisation, liberalisation, universalisation, modernisation and supra-territoriality.

Whilst others use the term "glocalisation" or define the "global" as "the local without walls", let us not forget that the globalisation of media (televisions, computers, tablets and smartphones) does not necessarily mean that their content is globalised.

In any case none of those terms is sufficient to embody the full meaning of globalisation; what is more they reflect a tendency to evaluate the policies and practices of "other" civilisations depending on whatever principles and ideals are current in the "West" (which to give it a geo-cultural indication we should specify as "Atlantic").

Indeed as is increasingly evident there are many non-Western, i.e. non-Atlantic versions of this modernisation that have to be taken into account, which for the sake of intellectual honesty we should try to include in our analyses of globalisation, knowing as we do how those Others (in China, India, the Islamic countries and Africa) view the West; not least because from their standpoint our "Western" principles, far from being universally valid, are anything but convincing. In fact, due to some behaviour by the West that is less than consistent with some of "our" most widely proclaimed ideals, in practice these are "trampled underfoot" and lose their credibility. Indeed, in the practice of Western geopolitics, the values of which our Western postmoderns are so enamoured (otherness, difference, sense of identity) are very often forgotten.

Further: whilst at the end of the twentieth century, the implosion of the Soviet Union and the economic opening up of China, did indeed accelerate and intensify a globalisation that accorded with the Western neoliberal model—and which is actually pushing towards a compression and simultaneity of space/time across the planet (a time of homogenisation, uniformisation and standardisation)—it is also the case now, in the second decade of the twenty-first century, that China, India, Southeast Asia and the Islamic world are challenging the universality of "our" values and are proclaiming not one, but multiple trajectories for modernisation. Asian values are now very much in vogue, and non-Western versions of modernisation (in China. India and Malaysia) are experiencing the kind of economic success that is attracting the attention of investors.

As an effect of this multifaceted globalisation of neoliberal inspiration, our age is also experiencing the challenge to that hegemonic scheme according to which Western modernity was to be the arrival point for all historical development (an "Atlantic" modernity extending from Rome to New York or, if we prefer, Athens to Seattle, although today perhaps the question of "from where to where" needs to be made clearer—because to me it seems far from easy to indicate where the centre of the West is now, or what its peripheries are; added to which the term "globalisation" can no longer be used to implicitly mean "Americanisation"). In the Islamic countries their culture and religion have once again become points of reference whilst the two Asian giants, China and India, which are emerging as "othernesses" crowned with economic success—albeit less conspicuously now—also intend to use it as a means to exert their cultural influence (for instance in the Confucius Institutes set up by the Chinese, or the dissemination by Prime Minister Modi of the Indian practice of yoga).

The affirmation by China and India of their own clear identities, and of their own projects, is now demanding that everyone, including we "Atlantic" Westerners, take a more open-minded attitude. More than ever, the human race is now called upon to situate itself within the perspective of a fullness that this plurality and difference are bringing to completion.

As is increasingly evident, in fact, globalisation today is not the product of any one culture or the ideas and values that typify any one civilisation, and does not equate to homogeneity or conformity. It has become a much more complex process generated by multiple circumstances, interests and forces (*cf*. Rajaee, *La mondialisation au banc des accusés: La condition humaine et la civilisation*, 2001). Far from being a uniform phenomenon, globalisation now is characterised by the movement of ideas and values that confront and push against one another: pulling back, developing, spreading, crystallising and transforming again. What is more, the ideas and values that underlie this new globalisation are not emerging from the globalisation itself, which by now has taken on its own regional and polycentric dimension. This is demonstrated by the fact that any of those ideas and values can be expelled from the process without thereby calling into question the idea of globalisation itself which, as I am saying, is more and more "regional". Furthermore, alongside the geography of globalisation we also need to consider historical globalisation, i.e. an interculturality that is not only geographical but also has a history.

So, to be realistic, any project for world governance must be orchestrated respecting the cultural integrity of local communities, a process that can only be effective if those communities themselves are committed to discussing and constructing a concerted, shared world culture (*The Ethics of Globalisation*, 2002).

As humanity uncovers this human face of globalisation the Church is close at hand, not only by underlining the urgent need to ensure that solidarity, too, is globalised, but that charity is also global: constructing a civilisation of love (an expression originally used by Paul VI and often then adopted by his successors John Paul II, Benedict XVI, and today Pope Francis).

On this subject Pope Saint John Paul II said (among other things): "in undertaking the process of globalisation, humanity can no longer do without a common code of ethics. This does not mean a single dominant socio-economic system or a single culture that would impose its own values and criteria on ethics. These norms for social life must be sought in man himself: in a universal humanity that springs from the hand of God. This search is indispensable if globalisation is not to become just another word for the absolute relativisation of values and the homogenisation of lifestyles and cultures". (27 April 2001).

In that sense there is much that education can do; an education—obviously—that trains people to be "citizens of the world". St. John Paul II also taught us that "belonging to the human family confers a kind of world citizenship on all people, giving them both entitlements and duties; and since all human beings are united by a community of origin and a supreme destiny, […] the condemnation of racism, the protection of minors, assistance for refugees, and the mobilisation of international solidarity towards the most needy. These are nothing more than simple and consistent applications of the principle of world citizenship." (*Message for World Day of Peace*, 1 January 2005).

His teaching puts into question the objectives and content of teaching and education. In the "ancient" system of Western values, the idea of personal identity reverberated with notions of national supremacy, presumed superiority and otherness as compared to the nationality of the foreigner, who was seen as inferior or threatening. But in our new system of values, "identity" and "otherness" are recognised as complementary and constitutive factors in human development.

This introduction of "identity" and "otherness" into the development of the human person also brings "time" and "space" into consideration. We can use archery as a metaphor to describe it: as a person develops and grows, he draws his bow back and then releases the arrow. The more he has pulled back on the "educational" bowstring towards "the past" and "the other place", the farther his arrow will fly towards the "future", beyond the "here and now". With this image we can infer that in the future prospect of "globality" and "plurality" the human person should be educated to welcome cultural diversity and complexity.

An education of that kind should be based on imparting knowledge about the cultural heritage of the world, with particular reference to

- the specificity and diversity of the religions,
- interculturality, understood as a meeting of cultures and reciprocal fertilisation,
- knowledge of atheism and agnosticism,
- physical, political and economic geography,
- the general outlines of the histories and cultures of peoples and nations,
- the evolution of science and technology,
- the linguistic and cultural learning of languages,
- the discovery of universal codes and languages,
- the discovery of the rights of the integral human being,
- and, above all, the tendency to arrive at a "coherence of knowledge" or—to use an expression dear to the Catholic world that dates back to the origins of the Universities—for a "unity of knowledge" that brings together the scientific and the humanistic (for UNESCO, cf. the World Humanities Conference, Liège, 6–12 August 2017 and for the Church, the STOQ Foundation, which the Pontifical Council for Culture has been promoting for some time along with a number of Pontifical Universities in Rome: Science, Theology, and the Ontological Quest.

As an outline of school subjects, the foregoing list will certainly need to be revised in view of the last item, which calls for a disciplinarity that is both *trans* and *inter* at the same time. But I would go so far as to hope that when any subject is taught for the purpose of imparting an education that is global, those two perspectives will give full meaning and value to what is taught.

In expressing that hope, it is not my intention to propose the continuance of some updated version of encyclopaedic culture; what I would like to encourage, rather, is an education that enables the individual to encounter different cultures every day, with different mentalities: to prepare individuals who have the ability to "think catholic" or as Paul Claudel would put it, with a Catholic soul i.e. who know how to grasp whatever fragments of truth, regardless of where they come from, that enable the person to open themselves to an ever more inclusive embrace with Truth. Whilst this does not mean the renunciation of an encyclopaedic, global opening up, it should above all concentrate on offering a point of synthesis. At present, in almost every case, our schools tend to impart an understanding of reality in general by strongly compartmentalising it into discrete initiatives, bodies of knowledge, and ambits, giving the impression that it is all determined by a centrifugal principle: many skills, many disciplines and many interests. In my view that will not suffice. We need to propose meaning that is global: a unity of knowledge that makes possible a unity of the person. At first the student will tend to categorise whatever he is being taught into pigeonholes of his own. Instead he should be educated to understand that what he is learning relates not only to the human condition as it is lived in the world, but also to his personal search for meaning. If we do not do this we will be educating individuals who are competent but ignorant. We therefore require teachers who are capable of imparting not only notions, but also the meaning of life (understood as its sense and direction). And these teachers cannot—must not—explain it via some philosophical "metadiscourse", but by putting themselves forward as a paragon so that the scholar can develop and resolve the hypothesis of life's work via their own critical and systematising ability. Putting forward proposals is not enough; it is necessary to educate with reference to an exemplar: to teach "*come l'uom s'eterna*" (Dante, *Inferno*, XV, 84).

To seek the Infinite through the finite, to seek the Eternal through the temporal, to seek the Truth by taking the path among many partial truths: this, it seems to me, is the educational pathway that every human being knows he should complete.

To arrive at this he should be taught how to look at "things", to find eternal reality "by way of" contingent reality. Permit me to explain by quoting Blaise Pascal in one of his delightful letters to M.lle de Roannez: "All things cover some mystery; all things have veils that cover God. Christians ought to recognise Him in every thing. Temporal afflictions cover eternal goods to which they lead. Temporal joys cover eternal ills that they cause." In other words, whatever appears as a metaphor to the eyes of sensitised experience is, rather, the "reality" to which education must be an introduction. Putting it another way: whatever appears to our "carnal" gaze as reality only reveals itself as a "sign" or a symbol when it is seen with the gaze of eternity, serving to make us glimpse the authentic reality that remains invisible to our merely physical eyes. Eventually, whatever seems to be the evanescent dream of a single day will manifest itself as an eternal reality and whatever seemed to be a tangible "thing" will vanish, swallowed up by the passage of time.

The mission of the teacher thus encompasses this great task, and the heavy responsibility, of opening the eyes of "beginners" so that they learn how to recognise and distinguish "imaginary" metaphors from "real" things: "removing" the blindfold that makes disciples unable to see, and doing whatever is necessary to open their eyes, just as the eyes of the disciples were opened at Emmaus (*cf*. *Luke* 24: 13–53), to see that which "really is". The teacher is therefore he who helps the disciple to open his eyes and free himself from illusions, trying to see the signs that will help him to glimpse the reality that does not fade away.

So rather than transmitting truths as a function of a global system, the teacher must teach the student how to "think" and "reason" in a global way so that he himself can walk the path towards the discovery of it; he must enrich his soul, filling his heart with a wisdom capable of "amazement" which, according to the words of the great Masters (from Aristotle onwards), is the first root of all knowledge. He who does not possess this wisdom will condemn himself to the insignificant and amorphous greyness of repetitive mediocrity.

To conclude, I think it is important to bear in mind the role of the university, which from the very beginning was conceived as universal as an institution open to all wishing to cultivate every form of knowledge and to study the truth in all its expressions: scientific, philosophical and theological. So the university has the responsibility to seek after truth in every field, and to communicate it using teaching as a form of dialogue that seeks not only to impart notions but also to transmit the meaning and truth of life. And—in my opinion—this is the true form of a dialogue which, as in Plato's Socratic dialogues, is always a search for truth.

"Hence the urgency for the university, every university, that intends to renew itself and rediscover its true mission, to shed light on its main purpose, which is to study truth in all its aspects" (Pope Francis,*Meeting with Students and the Academic World*, Bologna, 01 October 2017) referencing the teaching of St. Dominic who said we should study the "book of charity".

The role of the university is to forge peace and a new humanism, working to found a "*ius pacis*", in which the Church is not neutral (*cf*. Pope Francis, *ibid.*). The Church is on the side of peace and promotes an "integral humanism that comes from the centrality of Christ" (Pope Francis, Florence, 10/11/2015), which is the Word of God, the only Word from which all things have their being and that all things say is the one Word, which is the beginning that speaks in us.

The original sentence in Latin is "*Ex uno Verbo omnia et unum loquuntur omnia, et hoc est Principium quod et loquitur nobis*" (Imitatio Christi, Book 1, 3, 2).

We could translate it as follows: From one Word come all things, and one Word speaks all things of Him; and this Word is the Beginning that speaks within us. Or to offer a broader citation:

From that one Word all things descend, and all things proclaim that one Word; it is "the Beginning" that continues to speak to men (John 8:25). Without that Word no one understands, and no one can make a correct judgement. Only he who feels all things as one thing only, brings them towards 'unity' and sees them all in unity, can have inner tranquillity and dwell in God, in peace.

Francesco Follo
Permanent Observer Holy See (Vatican)
UNESCO
Paris, France

Acknowledgments

The editors are grateful to a number of professors, colleagues, friends and others in writing this research project. First to all we wish to express the deepest gratitude to Mgr. Francesco Follo, Permanent Observer Holy See UNESCO (France), and to Professor Grazia Marchianó, University of Siena (Italy) who were important mentors in the project. The dialogue and the sharing have helped to development of the ideas and to realise new perspectives. We also wish to extend our gratitude to Professor Ulrich Petersmann, European University Institute at Florence (Italy), and to Professor Atsushi Okada, Kyoto University (Japan) because their researches are been important references for us. Our gratitude also to Professor Hisashi Yakou, Hokkaido University (Japan), Professor Bernard Baeyens, Universidad de Ibagué, President IAESTE, (Colombia) and Dr. Gildo Zuccarini, Vice President Italian Chamber of Commerce in Colombia.

We wish to extend all our happiness and appreciation to the authors of this research; many important scholars from many countries in the world, from Orient to Occident, that have dedicated time and commitment during all period of this international project.

Special thanks must go to friends and colleagues in the world that in these years have built with us new cultural paradigms, fundamental to start this international research project and for opening new dialogues among cultures.

Special gratitude to Professor Francesco Francioni, European University Institute (Italy) for the support and the preface to this book very important for us.

Deep in our hearts, we sincerely wish to acknowledge the presence and the constant support of our parents and without their encouragement and patience, this book could not have seen the light of day.

We wish all readers and colleagues a good reading because your comments will help us to continue this international road in the future.

Olimpia Niglio
Eric Yong Joong Lee

About This Book

This book provides a substantial contribution to understanding the international legal framework for the protection and conservation of cultural heritage. It offers a range of perspectives from well-regarded contributors from different parts of the world on the impact of law in heritage conservation. Through a holistic approach, the authors bring the reader into dialogue around the intersection between the humanities and legal sciences, demonstrating the reciprocity of interaction in programmes and projects to enhance cultural heritage in the world. This edited volume compiles a selection of interesting reflections on the role of cultural diplomacy to address intolerances that often govern international relations, causing damage to human and cultural heritage. The main purpose of this collection of essays is to analyse the different cultural paradigms that intervene in the management of heritage, and to advocate for improvements in international laws and conventions to enable better cultural policies of individual nations for the protection of human rights. The editors submit that it is only through open dialogue between the humanities and jurisprudence that the international community will be able to better protect and value sovereignty and promote cultural heritage for the development of a better world. This collection is relevant to scholars working in areas relating to law, management and policies of cultural heritage conservation and protection.

Africa	Algeria
America	Canada, Colombia, Mexico, Peru
Asia	India, Iran, Japan, Jordan, Korea, Lebanon, Nepal, Syria, Turkey
Europe	Austria, Belgium, France, Greece, Italy, Poland, Romania, Spain, Sweden
Oceania	Australia

Contents

Heritage and Law

Heritage and Community

Heritage and Conflicts

Contributors

Bindu Adhikari Pokharel Findings Nepal, Kathmandu, Nepal

Giovanni Fontana Antonelli United Nations Senior Consultant (UNESCO, UN Habitat, 2013–2020), Jordan, Syria

Daniela Antonescu Center of Mountain Economy, Vatra Dornei, Romania

Graziella Bernardo Department of European and Mediterranean Cultures (DiCEM), Basilicata University, Campus Universitario, Potenza, Italy

Kaouther Bouchemal Paris Nanterre University (Paris 10), Nanterre, France

Kalliopi Chainoglou Department of International and European Studies, University of Macedonia, Thessaloniki, Greece

Keshav Raj Chalise Nepal Sanskrit University, Bijauri, Nepal

Andrea Cocco University of Cagliari—Studio Legale Cocco, Cagliari, Italy

Tommaso Cossu United Nations Consultant (UN Habitat, 2018–2020), Milan, Italy

Marie-Sophie de Clippele Fonds national de la recherche scientifique, Université Saint-Louis, Bruxelles, Belgium;
ICLAFI Expert Member, Bruxelles, Belgium

Antoine Dib Universidad Nacional Autónoma de México, Mexico City, Mexico

José Antonio González Zarandona History, CIDE, Mexico, Mexico

Nora Gueliane Mouloud Mammeri University, Tizi Ouzou (UMMTO), Tizi Ouzou, Algeria

Hans Thomas Hakl Octagon Library, Graz, Austria

Milagros Aurora Revilla Izquierdo Pontificia Universidad Catolica del Peru, Lima, Peru

Alessandra Lanciotti Department of Law, University of Perugia, Perugia, Italy

Eric Yong Joong Lee Dongguk University College of Law, YIJUN Institute of International Law, Seoul, Republic of Korea

Henrik Lindblad ICOMOS PRERICO and Future for Religious Heritage (FRH), Uppsala University, Uppsala, Sweden

Cristina Lull Noguera Higher Polytechnic School of Gandia, Universitat Politècnica de València, Valencia, Spain

Alberto Martorell Factor Cultura, Lima, Peru

Olimpia Niglio Graduate School of Humanities and Human Sciences, Hokkaido University, Sapporo, Japan

Luis Manuel Palmero Iglesias Polytechnic University of Valencia, Valencia, Spain

Navaraj Pokharel Patan College, Tribhuvan University, Lalitpur, Nepal

Francisca Ramón Fernández Department of Urbanism, Universitat Politècnica de València, Valencia, Spain

Pravin S. Rana Banaras Hindu University, Varanasi, India

Francisco J. Rufián Fdez Member of a Law Enforcement Agency, Madrid, Spain

Isber Sabrine Heritage for Peace, Barcelona, Spain

Tullio Scovazzi University of Milano-Bicocca, Milan, Italy

Rana P. B. Singh Banaras Hindu University, Varanasi, India

Małgorzata Ślarzyńska WNH Uniwersytet Kardynała Stefana Wyszyńskiego, Warsaw, Poland

Hamidreza Solaymani Osbooei Forest, Range, and Watershed Management, Organization of Iran—FRWO, Tehran, Iran

John Jairo Uribe Sarmiento Facultad de Derecho y Ciencias Políticas, Universidad de Ibagué, Ibagué, Colombia

Meltem Vatan Faculty of Architecture and Design, Bahçeşehir University, Istanbul, Turkey

César Augusto Velandia Silva Facultad de Humanidades, Artes y Ciencias Sociales, Universidad de Ibagué, Ibagué, Colombia

Marko Živković Department of Anthropology, University of Alberta, Edmonton, AB, Canada

Carla Zuddas University of Cagliari, Cagliari, Italy

Introduction

Structure of the Research: Toward Transculturality

Olimpia Niglio and Eric Yong Joong Lee

Abstract This research project meets the premises at the different studies and academic experiences realized by two editors between Orient and Occident.

> Cultures are not self-enclosed or static entities. They overlap and interact, if only to distinguish themselves from one another. "Cultures are like clouds, their confines ever changing, coming together or moving apart […] and sometimes merging to produce new forms arising from those that preceded them yet differing from them entirely" (UNESCO, 2007)

This research project meets the premises at the different studies and academic experiences realized by two editors between Orient and Occident.

The concept of culture is deeply changed. Having undergone a dramatic transformation over the course of at least two centuries, the notion of culture is ubiquitous in political discourse yet conceptually elusive. Core debates revolve around the content of culture, its relationship to society and civilization as well as its function and role in the human condition. However, it is very difficult to meet a good cultural policy in the governmental programs in the world. Perhaps we must first ask ourselves what culture means: what does culture do? and what *should* culture do?

Historically, the notion of culture was explicitly normative. This concept represented, more often than not, the eighteenth- and nineteenth-century humanistic understandings. Matthew Arnold's *Culture and Anarchy* analyzed this belief. Arnold held that culture is

> […] a pursuit of our total perfection by means of getting to know, on all the matters which most concern us, the best which has been thought and said in the world; and through this knowledge, turning a stream of fresh and free thought upon our stock notions and habits; the culture we recommend is, above all, an inward operation. (Arnold, 1993: 190)

O. Niglio
Graduate School of Humanities and Human Sciences, Hokkaido University, Sapporo, Japan
e-mail: olimpia.niglio@gmail.com

E. Y. J. Lee (✉)
Dongguk University College of Law, Seoul, Republic of Korea
e-mail: grotian@hotmail.com

O. Niglio and E. Y. J. Lee (eds.), *Transcultural Diplomacy and International Law in Heritage Conservation*, https://doi.org/10.1007/978-981-16-0309-9_1

For Arnold culture was a remedy to such human failings as *the want of sensitiveness of intellectual conscience, the disbelief in right reason, and the dislike of authority*. The goal of culture was, therefore, to overcome barbarity and realize higher goods, such as intellectual conscience, reason, and deference to authority, encapsulated in a broad, neoclassical understanding of civility and civilization. Culture became thus associated with products which were seen to embody these goods—classical music, opera, art, literature, and haute cuisine.

Obviously, this idealized the understanding of culture carried with it both ethnocentric and elitist connotations. If it were restricted to elite, Western social circles, then the vast majority of human beings were bereft of culture. Fortunately, the development of the interdisciplinary dialogue among scientists toward the end of the nineteenth century changed this particular trend and this vision.

In the twentieth century, many scholars recognized that every member of any society should have a culture which has to be respected and valorized.

While this was certainly a step forward, the totalizing nature of the concept of culture has been proved problematic, providing, in the first instance, a great deal of interpretations. This is indicated, as Clifford Geertz notes in the account of culture as:

> (1) "the total way of life of a people"; (2) "the social legacy the individual acquires from his group"; (3) "a way of thinking, feeling, and believing"; (4) "an abstraction from behaviour"; (5) a theory on the part of the anthropologist about the way in which a group of people in fact behave; (6) a "storehouse of pooled learning"; (7) "a set of standardized orientations to recurrent problems"; (8) "learned behaviour"; (9) a mechanism for the normative regulation of behaviour; (10) "a set of techniques for adjusting both the external environment and to other men"; (11) "a precipitate of history"; and turning, perhaps in desperation, to similes, as a map, as a sieve, and as a matrix. (Geertz 1973: 10–12)

Geertz's observation seems equally applicable to this concept also to other disciplines interested in the study of culture, including international law, history, applied sciences, ecology, and human rights (Lystra, 1983).

This vision introduces an important opportunity: the dialogue among different disciplines on the concept of culture that had an important evolution in the transculturality as this international research intends to demonstrate.

In this regard, culture meets on the idealism of science whose reference has opened the doors and new interpretations of the world, to new cultural paradigms. Further, this has laid the foundations for the development of new critical thinking importantly in the research project.

This critical thinking accepts the value of culture. If so, what does culture mean? Let's analyze the etymology of the word.

The word "culture" comes from the Greek language. Its root is found in the term Παιδεία, education, ethical and moral training of young people and citizens.

The culture constitutes the set of intellectual knowledge that, acquired through study, reading, experience, the influence of the environment and reworked in a subjective, critical, and autonomous way, becomes a building block of personality. Culture contributes to enriching the spirit, developing and improving individual ability to judge.

So, culture represents the set of intellectual knowledge that each individual acquires during his life through study and experience (Cassirer, 1997). This knowledge must be reworked through personal ideas and converted into useful moral and ethical actions for the community. Each action has a spiritual and aesthetic component that is fundamental to be able to appreciate and enhance the world in which we live. Culture is, therefore, a fundamental component to building important projects based on a "humanistic conception" of the world (Lee & Niglio, 2019).

Ernst Cassirer says that Culture is not a speculative issue. Culture is often regarded as a complex system of theories; different culture requires only a simple system of actions.

> […] Culture means an organic set of verbal and moral activities: activities that are not conceived in purely abstract terms but show the constant tendency to realize. This realization – this construction and reconstruction of the empirical world – is an integral part of the very concept of culture and constitutes one of the essential and most characteristic traits. (Cassirer, 1981: 73–74)

Culture is the progressive objectification of human experiences including our feelings, thoughts, emotions, ideas, and intuitions. The specific result of cultural creation is the construction of a world of thoughts and feelings—a world of humanity that pretends to be a common world, rather than each individual dream. This concept also comes from a humanistic vision of the world.

If we then analyze all this with respect to the different cultural forms present in the world, then it is easy to guess that preconceived patterns cannot help to understand the different realities. Differently, preconceptions only contribute to the slow and unproductive development of the human world.

For this evolved concept of culture, the international project *Transcultural Diplomacy and International Law in Heritage Conservation*, introduces several themes analyzed in more detail by important scholars from different countries and cultures. Given the range of questions and complexities surrounding heritage and his/her dialogue with the law, we have considered different perspectives and disciplinary visions in order to open a new route.

In fact, this research stems from the direct and indirect observation of many cultural realities that in recent years have been affected by events such as social balances, diplomatic dialogues, well-being of people, and the respect for human rights. Addressing the issue through a *transcultural* vision and with the support of *international law*, this research project aimed to carry out a dialogue between different disciplines and cultures to reexamine the very concept of "heritage" within evolutionary aspects that can no longer be considered. Therefore, this research project opens a new disciplinary and academic path aimed at the analysis of "cultural heritage" according to a multicentric and multicultural vision.

The very term "diplomacy" generally appears in the foreign policy practice of nation-states. In this research, however, we take account of a new and fundamental connotation for the dialogue between cultures (Ang et al., 2015). In fact, there is often a lack of clarity in the way that the notion is used: what exactly its practice involves? why is it important? or how it works?

Human beings relate to one another through society and express that relationship through culture. All our actions, thoughts, behavior, attitudes, and material or intellectual creations imply a cultural relationship. Even the natural world that we name, describe, and analyze may be said to be informed by human culture, to be invested with "inward meaning". In this fundamental sense, our similarities are more profound than just cultural differences. These differences, moreover, embody a positive potential, because we complement one another through them in devising novel solutions for living together in our social and natural settings. Cultural diversity represents the sum of these solutions, and dialogue is the bridge between them. In fact, if we are to respond to the challenges inherent in a culturally diverse world, we must develop new approaches to intercultural dialogue, going beyond the limitations of the "dialogue among civilizations" paradigm. The prerequisites for such a dialogue include consideration of the ways in which cultures relate to one another, awareness of cultural commonalities and shared goals, and identification of the challenges to be met in reconciling cultural differences and identities.

This project research has opened an intercultural dialogue and has favored the meeting between humanities, law, ecology, geography, history, cultural policies, anthropology, human rights, and religions.

This book is organized in four parts. After the preface by Francesco Francioni, Emeritus Professor at the European University Institute (Florence, Italy), the post-preface by Francesco Follo, Permanent Observer of the Holy See to the UNESCO (France), and the chapter on the main topic of the research realized by editors, the first part, *Heritage and Culture*, approaches important contributions on humanistic topics analyzed by Marko Zivkovic from Canada, Hans Thomas Hakl from Austria, Henrik Lindblad from Sweden, Malgorzata Slarzynska from Poland, Luis Manuel Palmero Iglesias from Spain, Graziella Bernardo from Italy, Keshav Raj Chalise from Nepal, Daniela Antonescu from Romania, and Navaraj Pokharel from Nepal.

The second part, *Heritage and Law*, with the important support of Tullio Scovazzi from Italy, Marie-Sophie de Clippele from Belgium, Alessandra Lanciotti, Andrea Cocco, and Carla Zuddas from Italy, analyzes a fundamental topic for this project: the dialogue between law and protection of the cultural heritage, following an international and innovative approach that has allowed to reflect on this important collaboration between an expert in law and expert in cultural policies.

The third part, *Heritage and Community*, introduces another important topic which has, since a few years ago, encouraged communities to appropriate their own cultural heritage while respecting local identities. A theme that is particularly felt today also for the strong migratory processes that are destabilizing communities and cultures. These topics are been analyzed very well by Rana P.B. Singh and Pravin S. Rana from India, Nora Gueliane from Algeria (France), Meltem Vatan from Turkey, and Alberto Martorell from Peru.

The last and fourth part, *Heritage and Conflicts*, makes important contributions reflecting actual topics which show how the lack of valid educational systems aimed at strengthening the cultural heritage, are generators of phenomena against humanity itself. We must turn our attention to these issues to build a better and sustainable world. Thanks for the contributions César Augusto Velandia Silva and John

Jairo Uribe Sarmiento from Colombia, Francisca Ramón Fernández and Cristina Lull Noguera from Spain, Kalliopi Chainoglou from Greece, Antoine Dib from Lebanon (Mexico), Milagros Aurora Revilla Izquierdo from Peru, Giovanni Fontana Antonelli and Tommaso Cossu from Italy, Francisco J. Rufián Fdez from Spain, Isber Sabrine from Syria, José Antonio González Zarandona from Australia, and Hamidreza Solaymani from Iran.

The editors thank all scholars for their friendship, collaboration, and the emotions that has been conveyed during the research with their texts and images.

Lucca and Seoul, October 17, 2020

References

Ang, I., Raj Isar, Y., & Mar, P. (2015). Cultural diplomacy: Beyond the national interest? *International Journal of Cultural Policy, 21*(4), 365–381.

Arnold, M. (1993). *Culture and anarchy and other writings*. Cambridge: University of Cambridge.

Cassirer, E. (1981). *Simbolo, mito e cultura* (pp. 73–74). Bari-Roma: Laterza.

Cassirer, E. (1997). I concetti di spazio e tempo dell'idealismo critico e la teoria della relatività (cap. V). In Id., *Teoria della relatività di Einstein* (pp. 111–137). Roma: Newton Compton.

Geertz, C. (1973). *The interpretation of cultures*. New York: Basic Books.

Lee, E. Y. J., & Niglio, O. (2019). *cultural diplomacy & heritage*. Roma: Tab Edizioni.

Lystra, K. (1983). Clifford Geertz and the concept of culture. *Prospects, 8,* 31–47. https://doi.org/10.1017/S0361233300003690.

UNESCO. (2007, May 21–23). *Mainstreaming principles of cultural diversity and intercultural dialogue in policies for sustainable development*. Final Communiqué of the Meeting of Experts, Paris. Paris: UNESCO.

Transcultural Diplomacy and International Law in Heritage Conservation

Olimpia Niglio and Eric Yong Joong Lee

Abstract "Cultural heritage" stands for the sum total of our fundamental knowledge of human creativity. It incorporates different identities of man's existence on the Earth. Throughout the history of the world, this knowledge has combined man's own reason with empirical rules whilst constantly questioning existence. This cultural heritage, which is both tangible and intangible, then assumed a transcultural value that has enhanced diversities and increased fruitful dialogue in the different regions of the Earth, regulated by the laws of nature alone. This *transcultural diplomacy* has an ethical value at the world level, and today more than ever is a fundamental reference for rethinking all together with the continuation of the existence of man on Earth. This paper aims to holistically analyse all activities related to creativity and the enhancement of cultural heritage, to create dialogues, enhancement projects, and *transcultural studies* for the progress of humanity in respect of international law.

Those who build a castle, they will be ruined.
Those who break through the road will prosper.
Oriental wisdom

1 Introduction

If we observe the world from above, we see no boundaries. The Earth is not regulated by any administrative norms other than the laws of nature; "everything"—water, air, earth, human beings, animals, and plants—coexists along with external elements such as the sun and the planets, all as a living whole.

O. Niglio
Graduate School of Humanities and Human Sciences, Hokkaido University, Sapporo, Japan
e-mail: olimpia.niglio@gmail.com

E. Y. J. Lee (✉)
Dongguk University College of Law, Seoul, Republic of Korea
e-mail: grotian@hotmail.com

O. Niglio and E. Y. J. Lee (eds.), *Transcultural Diplomacy and International Law in Heritage Conservation*, https://doi.org/10.1007/978-981-16-0309-9_2

The first traces of Greek philosophy were based precisely on the four fundamental elements of existence: Water, Earth, Air, and Fire. At that time the philosophers wondered about the *arché*, which they thought of as the origin of life. Those Greek thinkers considered that all things are born and die in this "Everything"; at the end of life they do not go to occupy spaces beyond the boundaries of this "Everything" but remain within it, albeit transformed. Philosophers continued to think about the principles that differentiated one thing from another, and from there began the search for the "*identities of the different*" (Severino, 1997).

Needless to say, all of this has undergone significant evolutions throughout the history of the world. However, the elements that the world continues to excel in are always the same, and despite their evolutionary diversity, they have gone on to produce different systems of sharing. Meanwhile, following the affirmation of the *lógos,* man has questioned his very own existence, leading the world back to a system of paradigms that are important for his affirmation, but these paradigms often abandoned research into the truth of the world. The rules of nature, as proclaimed by Orpheus, are contrasted by the will of Prometheus, considered a friend of humanity because it helps man to dominate nature in favour of his progress (Assunto, 1997).

This attitude, however, has led man to embark on a path that has gradually distanced him from the founding principles of the Whole to foster an increasingly homologating vision in which the identity of the different has given way to conformity. Under these principles, which then came to dominate certain aspects of human life on Earth, other paths have developed that, unlike the latter, have continued to question the *arché*, the founding values of life, the laws of nature, and hypotheses that are not always resolved. These are the activities that have led man to re-establish a dialogue with the laws of nature and therefore guided by Orpheus who, with the captivating sound of his lyre, has wanted to accompany human beings in the construction of doctrines and thoughts that have constituted a fundamental basis of the evolution of our existence. We talk about literature, law, music, philosophy, art, and therefore *human creativity.*

This heritage, which we commonly call "cultural heritage", constitutes that corpus of knowledge that is fundamental for in-depth analysis of the origins of human life on Earth. In history, that cognitive process has often been questioned but today has taken on *transcultural value* that can promote the enhancement of diversity and increasingly fruitful dialogue within the different geographies. So today more than ever transcultural heritage, because of its high ethical value worldwide, is a fundamental reference for objectively rethinking the continuation of man's existence on Earth.

Based on these premises, international law is essential for activating projects whose aim is to enhance the transculturality of human ideas and thus establish dialogues for the progress of humanity in accordance with the laws of nature. This interdisciplinary approach also favours comparative studies whose purpose is to structure points of tangency between the different areas of knowledge; because it is precisely at those points that it is possible to hope for fruitful developments and innovative approaches for the future of humanity.

2 Culture and Transculturality

Culture is at hand wherever practices in life are shared.
The basic task is … interaction with foreignness.
Ludwig Wittgenstein (1889–1951)

The word *Culture* comes from the Greek language. The root of this word is found in the term Παιδεία: education, ethical, and moral formation. Until the nineteenth century the concept of culture was always associated with the analysis of a specific and individual community. In *Ideas on the Philosophy of the History of Mankind*, Johann Gottfried Herder confirmed this traditional single value of culture which, however, did not address dialectical relationships with other realities (Herder, 1966).

This traditional concept of culture, as an expression of the individual, is a concept of homogenisation and separation at the same time. This, in fact, incites the concept of purity and a forced appeal of cultural identity which, as the Indian economist Amartya Sen put it, risks producing separatism and paving the way for political conflicts and wars (Sen, 2007). Although during the twentieth century the concept of culture produced harsh forms of xenophobia, it then underwent interesting evolutions that enabled networks and dialogues to be constructed between cultural diversities. So the classical model of culture is normatively dangerous and untenable.

In general, today, the culture constitutes a corpus of intellectual knowledge that builds a block of single personality. Culture contributes to enriching the spirit, developing and improving individual characteristics, and the ability to form judgements.

Today this knowledge must be reworked through personal thinking and converted into useful moral and ethical actions for the community. Each action has a spiritual and aesthetic component that is fundamental for appreciating and enhancing the world in which we live. Culture is therefore a fundamental component in the construction of important projects based on a "humanistic conception" of the world (Lee & Niglio, 2019). In particular, the German philosopher Ernst Cassirer states that culture is not a speculative subject. It is often thought that culture is a complex system of theories; culture demands only a simple system of action (Cassirer, 1981).

In fact, culture means an organic set of verbal and moral activities which are not conceived in purely abstract terms but show the constant tendency to achieve. This is realised by constructing and reconstructing the empirical world, which is an integral part of the very concept of culture and characteristic traits (Cassirer, 1981: 73–74).

Thus, Ernst Cassirer sees culture as a symbolic universe created by man to develop his very existence. In this way cultural references become symbolic; they do not present a real existence in the physical world but help to create a "value" to this world (Paetzold, 2002: 22–33).

One example could be the realisation of a work of art that involves the transformation of matter. The use of a block of marble transforms matter into a work of art. This transformation is only determined by a symbolic will of man, who transforms the marble into a sculpture. Thus its cultural value depends on man, although its original and natural existence does not change. Therefore, *culture is a system of symbolic forms* where every element does not enjoy autonomy except by way of a close relationship with the other elements that make up this system.

The world of culture is therefore built up by a system of forms that are an expression of the spirit of each individual (Cassirer, 1979: 194–195). Culture is therefore the progressive objectivity of our human experience: the objectivity of our feelings, thoughts, emotions, ideas, and intuitions. The specific result of cultural creation is the construction of thoughts and feelings—a world of humanity that aspires to be a common world, rather than the individual dream of each individual. A *humanistic vision* of the world also comes from this concept.

If all this is analysed in relation to the different cultural forms present in the world, it is easy to surmise that preconceived patterns cannot help to understand symbolic reality. Differently, preconceptions only contribute to the slow and unproductive development of the human world. Respecting the different cultures, we are all invited to know the symbolic forms and archetypal cultural phenomena that define our existence: language, history, science, art, and religion (Niglio, 2019: 67–86).

All of these symbolic forms contribute to realising that which cannot be universal, whilst, on the contrary, these symbolic forms sometimes help to create a world that relates to the needs of man. But the concept of culture has stimulated many studies, in different disciplines. In that context it is very interesting to briefly transcribe an interesting reflection by the British historian Peter Burke, who responds as follows to the question "what is culture":

> The term "culture" is even more problematic than the term "popular". As Burckhardt remarked in 1882, cultural history is "a vague concept". It used to refer to "high" culture. It was extended "downwards", to continue the metaphor, to include "low" or popular culture. More recently, it has expanded sideways as well. The term culture used to refer to the arts and sciences. Then it was used to describe the popular equivalents to the arts and sciences – folk music, folk medicine and so on. In the last generation, the word has come to refer to a wide range of artefacts (images, tools, houses and so on) and practices (conversation, reading, playing games). This new usage is not, strictly speaking, new at all. In 1948, in his *Notes Towards the Definition of Culture*, T. S. Eliot, an American observing England with an anthropological eye, had described its culture as including, among other elements, 'Derby Day… the dart board… boiled cabbage cut into sections, beetroot in vinegar, nineteenth-century Gothic churches and the music of Elgar'. The anthropologist Bronisław Malinowski was already defining culture in a broad way, in the article on the subject that he contributed to the *Encyclopaedia of the Social Sciences* in 1931, as comprising "inherited artefacts, goods, technical processes, ideas, habits and values".
>
> Indeed, in 1871, in his *Primitive Culture*, another anthropologist, Edward Tylor, had offered a similar definition of culture "taken in its wide ethnographic sense", as "that complex whole which includes knowledge, belief, art, morals, law, custom and any other capabilities and habits acquired by man as a member of society". The anthropological concern with the everyday, and with societies in which there was relatively little division of labour, encouraged the employment of the term "culture" in a wide sense.
>
> It is this anthropological notion that cultural historians – and other members of their culture – have made their own in the last generation, the age of 'historical anthropology' and "the new cultural history". (Burke, 2008: 29–30)

From an anthropological aspect, the concept of culture leads us not only to appreciate the differences of individual territories, but also to relate these differences to give principle to the transcultural dimension of knowledge that cannot be other in relation to nature and man.

In fact, the knowledge that is articulated in the intercultural field must have the ability to question itself much more than on the uncertain coexistence between traditions and scientific knowledge and on the survival of ideas that would otherwise be as definitively eclipsed as a comet. In this complex reality, we cannot hide the fact that even the contribution of new technologies announces the advent of new algorithms through which, however, knowledge based on the principles of "nature" risks being set aside like an old mask of the comedy of the Italian writer Luigi Pirandello.

This anthropological dimension helps to introduce a new perspective on the concept of culture by introducing two adjectives that have become widely used in recent decades: interculturality and multiculturalism. In that regard, it is interesting to refer to the studies of the German philosopher Wolfgang Welsch, who notes that both terms still retain a singularity that does not help us to understand the true value of culture. In fact, he writes:

> The conception of interculturality seeks ways in which such cultures could nevertheless get on with, understand and recognize one another. But the deficiency in this conception originates in that it drags along with it unchanged the premise of the traditional conception of culture. It still proceeds from a conception of cultures as islands or spheres. For just that reason it is unable to arrive at any solution since the intercultural problems *stem* from the island-premise. The classical conception of culture *creates* by its primary trait - the separatist character of cultures - the secondary problem of a structural inability to communicate between theses cultures. Therefore, this problem can, of course, not be solved on the basis of this very conception. The recommendations of interculturality, albeit well-meant, are fruitless. The concept does not get to the root of the problem. (Welsch, 1999: 196)

Again, on multiculturalism he goes on:

> The concept of multiculturality is surprisingly similar to the concept of interculturality. It takes up the problems which different cultures have living together *within one society*. But there with the concept basically remains in the duct of the traditional understanding of culture; it proceeds from the existence of clearly distinguished, in themselves homogenous cultures - the only difference now being that these differences exist within one and the same state community. (Welsch, 1999: 196)

All of which shows us how the concept of culture developed as so many islands or closed spheres which, for the whole of the twentieth century, did not relate to each other. Individual cultures have only apparently established diplomatic relations whilst remaining internally isolated. This is demonstrated by many projects, including projects that have been conceived within the diplomatic offices of individual countries, that have always affirmed the culture of origin without ever relating and amalgamating with the host territory. Even today, in fact, the different diplomatic offices tend to affirm the culture of origin but not to create synergies.

It is only with the new millennium and following the *Convention on the Protection and Promotion of the Diversity of Cultural Expressions* (Unesco, 2005) that the concept of culture has established itself in its international dimension, assuming a wider and less circumscribed connotation and meaning. The boundaries of the classical definition of culture have thus been torn down. Instead, the concept of transculturality has been introduced. Generically the word *transculturality* is, in the first place, a consequence of the inner differentiation and complexity of modern cultures. These encompass a number of ways of life and cultures, which also interpenetrate or emerge out of one another (Welsch, 1999: 197).

This transcultural dimension has undoubtedly been fostered by the spread of technologies that have changed the way we know in the world. Each nation is interconnected with others and the global network enables us to receive information at any point on the planet, in real time. Most people live interconnected with other cultures, and this makes us very hybrid. Let us consider the work of the writer. The writer once talked about his own territory but today, he has no single homeland and has many references to the different cultures he has been able to study, know, and deepen, thanks to travel and technological networks. For that reason, scholars have the ability to establish relationships, for example, between a North American culture and an Indonesian culture. This means that such scholars have a transcultural attitude. Certainly, future generations will be even more so.

The concept of transculturality is aimed at inclusion rather than separation, dialogue rather than the isolation of culture. It is not separated but united. But as yet it is not easy to understand the concept of transculturality because doing so implies a change of our inner compass that must ward off any preconception as to the unknown. Instead it is essential to establish dialogue with this unknown and to encourage the meeting between different cultures to build new syncretisms. This concept of transculturality, although it is theoretically understandable, finds no practical application other than in small niches such as those of scientific research. Indeed, the events we have witnessed in these first two decades of the new millennium have certainly not been rewarding from the point of view of cultural diplomacy.

In the meantime, transculturality will develop more in different ways. If we are not able to recognise the qualities and values that this new cultural interaction can make available to the new generations, there is a risk that even this form of culture can generate homologating systems. There is, in fact, a risk of equating transculturality with uniformity; were this to happen, it would bring with it the risk of returning to forms of exclusion rather than inclusion. In such an eventuality, a new kind of culture would take shape of the different but would have nothing to do with transculturality.

In this context it is interesting to note that unlike globalisation and particularisation, transculturality is an opportunity because it is the system that enhances diversity, mixing cultures and thereby creating new cultural forms that are the expression of inclusion and not exclusion (Garcia Canclini, 1999).

A good transcultural attitude shows that it is possible to harmoniously incorporate both globalisation and particularisation. In fact, transculturality is able to develop complex social systems by making dialogue both globally and locally without any prevarication. The aim, in fact, is to create new identities that are cosmopolitan but also well aware of their roots of belonging. A person is transcultural to the extent that acknowledging his roots adapts to new cultures, creating new identities (Hannerz, 1992).

If we then analyse this concept in cultural contexts marked by long colonisation that have often erased local cultural roots, it becomes easy to understand how the theme of transculturality finds other important assumptions.

In an interesting research paper published in 2010 Afef Benessaieh, a professor at CEIM (*Centre d'études sur l'intégration et la mondialisation*) in Montreal affirmed:

> The concept most often confused with transculturality is that of *transculturation*, coined by Cuban anthropologist Fernando Ortiz in the 1940s (Ortiz, 1947/1995) to offer an important alternative to "acculturation", and study the processes of resistance, exchange and appropriation that occur between culturally differentiated populations that have come into close contact with one another in the context of Cuban slaver economy since colonial times.
> More recently, post-colonialist anthropologists, sociologists and commentators (such as Pratt 1992; Butz and Besio 2004; and Millington 2007) have updated the concept in order to study "zones of contact", mostly in developing countries, where groups and communities from dominant and non-dominant cultures interact. (Benessaieh, 2010: 16)

Transculturality implies mutual influence between cultures without a form of prevarication but of dialogue. It is associated with transculturation, which considers all dynamic and adaptive cultures but all distinctly one from the other. Transculturation therefore analyses how diversity also interacts for the purpose of supremacy (Mirzoeff, 2002: 477–480). For example, metropolitan culture, as an expression of the interaction between different cultures, often dominates local ethnic cultures and considers them as minority cultures. This trend is common in those countries that have undergone long-lasting foreign colonisation as, for example, in Latin America or Australia. Alongside transculturation, the concept of multiculturalism is often confused with cosmopolitanism, which studies the cultural diversity of societies mainly affected by significant migratory flows. So also, the transculturation is often associated with the concept of multiculturalism but is confused with cosmopolitanism (UNESCO, 2003a, 2003b, 2008).

This research on transculturality requires multidisciplinary studies that include sociologists, anthropologists, urban planners, historians, international lawyers, and political scientists who can interact to study the essence of a community whilst respecting its diversity. All of which makes such research extraordinarily complex and far from simple to implement in a highly interactive world whose dynamics of change are very rapid. Nevertheless it is essential that we analyse these issues in order to understand how cultural heritage will be passed on to future generations.

The term "transculturality" thus replaces "interculturality" and "multiculturalism" because it opens more prospects towards an identity that transcends administrative boundaries and social permeations (Kymlicka, 2003: 147–161). Transculturality relates fluidly to the world whilst not identifying with the individual or with monolithic culture. Transculturality is the world. All of which implies a remarkably close dialogue with the disciplines that govern relations between different cultures, such as international law and the rules of diplomacy.

In fact, it is not possible to continue this extraordinary research without constant and synergistic collaboration with the studies that govern international treaties and agreements amongst different countries.

So transculturality and international law represent the main skills for constructing a better world. Certainly, transculturality and international law do not preclude the possibility of conflict, but they do constitute an important reference for knowing that we can reduce the distance from what we perceive as different.

3 International Law and Cultural Diplomacy

> *A man cannot govern a nation if he cannot govern a city; he cannot govern a city if he cannot govern a family; he cannot govern a family unless he can govern himself; and he cannot govern himself unless his passions are subject to reason.*
>
> Hugo Grotius (1583–1645)

International law expresses the establishment of a world system based almost exclusively on the idea that independent sovereign states are the only relevant players in the international system.

The Greeks first introduced the concept of *natural law*, which the Romans then turned into *jus gentium* or law of nations. Although the Romans were the first, along with the peoples of the Middle East, to draw up laws governing dialogue with territories of different cultures, there is no doubt that the essential structure of international law was mapped out during the European Renaissance.

Early writers who dealt with questions of governance and relations between nations included the Italian lawyers Bartolo da Sassoferrato (1313–1357), regarded as the founder of the modern study of private international law, and Baldo degli Ubaldi (1327–1400), a celebrated teacher, papal adviser, and authority on Roman and feudal law. In 1598 the Italian jurist Alberico Gentili (1552–1608), who is considered the originator of the secular school of thought in international law, published *De jure belli libri tres*, which included a comprehensive discussion of the laws of war and treaties. After Gentili, the Dutch jurist Hugo Grotius (1583–1645) influenced the development of the field to an extent unequalled by any other theorist. Hugo Grotius excised theology from international law and organised it into a comprehensive system, particularly in his famous book *De Jure Belli ac Pacis*, published in 1625.

> Such writers and professors as Gentili had sought to establish a higher standard of political ethics, but it was reserved to Grotius to combine all the wise and humane teaching of past ages in one great work, the result of his vast learning and his exalted ideas of right and justice. He made the teachings of the Bible and the law of nature the basis of his work. (Foster, 1909: 152)

Grotius was a towering figure in philosophy, political theory, law, and associated fields during the seventeenth century and afterwards. His writings have been fundamental because they gave rise to new theories about the identity conditions of states. These theories conceive of states as existing not in a pre-social or antisocial condition, but rather in an "international society" governed by a system of norms. These norms form the basis for activating a system of international laws regulating relations between different states (Edwards, 1981; Asser Institute, 1985). Grotius's primary contribution to international law lies in his suggestion that international relations are governed by a rational system. He began his analysis with natural law. Unlike brute creation, he reasoned, human nature is characterised by the desire for a peaceful and orderly society. From that basic observation we can comprehend the sources of the laws that govern both individual behaviour and the conduct of nations (Bull et al., 1990).

> The law of nature is a dictate of right reason, which points out that an act, according as it is or is not in conformity with rational nature, has in it a quality of moral baseness or moral necessity; and that, in consequence, such an act is either forbidden or enjoined by the author of nature, God. (Grotius, 1925: 38)

From this foundation Grotius developed his system of international law. He claimed that just as the desire for community necessitates certain laws and principles to hold society together for mutual benefit, so the community of nations is held together by certain natural principles. Consequently, the only justification for war is the enforcement of rights, although Grotius excluded "total" war. The execution of hostilities is itself limited, according to Grotius, by natural law. In fact the law functions as a kind of feedback loop that allows human society to rationalise and sustain the violence and failures of its past and present, as the necessary limitations of human understanding, whilst holding on to the belief that its principles are fundamentally sound and coherent, a veritable standard for understanding oneself in the world (Haskell, 2011).

Grotius' prediction was also realised in the centuries that followed up until the twentieth century, when the two World Wars certainly marked a major change in contemporary international relations.

Meanwhile, the principles have become increasingly established that although states are neither the only entities with international legal standing, nor the exclusive international actors, they are the primary subject of international law with the greatest range of rights and obligations. Unlike states—which possess rights and obligations automatically—international organisations, individuals, and others derive their rights and duties in international law directly from instruments. Individuals may, for example, assert their rights under international law through the International Covenant on Economic, Social, and Cultural Rights and the International Covenant on Civil and Political Rights, both of which entered into force in 1976 (Einar Fife, 2019).

In the meantime, however, the events that have dramatically characterised the entire second half of the twentieth century are well known, despite the good intentions of the United Nations and the many international organisations whose work is based on the principles of peace. Nevertheless, in many countries around the world there are numerous, no less serious conflicts still active every day.

These conflicts are involved in the nullification of personal identities and consequently of cultural identities as well. In that area, the dialogue between culture, transculturality, and international law comes into play. For that reason, the principles of the Dutch jurist Hugo Grotius shall be reassessed focusing on the issue of the protection of cultural heritage around the world.

Meanwhile, as is well known, the protection of cultural heritage, especially during armed conflicts, is based on a variety of treaties that are firmly anchored in the principles of international law. These treaties commit states to implement all the provisions to adequately protect cultural heritage and therefore also implement all those decisions that also play a key role in diplomacy.

Already Article 5 of the Hague Convention (IX) *concerning Bombardment by Naval Forces in time of War* of 18 October 1907 which are applicable in international armed conflict, provides that "in sieges and bombardments *all necessary steps* must be taken to spare, *as far as possible*, buildings dedicated to religion, art, science, or charitable purposes, historic monuments, hospitals, and places where the sick and wounded are collected, provided they are not being used at the time for military purposes".

All of these principles were then taken up in The Hague Convention in 1954, the UNESCO Convention of 1972, and again in the most recent UNESCO Conventions published in 2003. Even today, however, the preservation of cultural heritage is linked to cultural rights as a form of human rights insofar as "cultural property may be seen as an essential dimension of human rights when it reflects the spiritual, religious and cultural specificity of minorities and groups" (Francioni, 2011: 10).

Meanwhile, many conflicting situations around the world are demonstrating that governments are not organised to address the protection of cultural heritage. Despite the conventions, international norms, and good intentions, there is still a great deal of uncertainty in international law, which still fails to outline procedures to prevent the loss of cultural heritage in the world; and since cultural heritage is for everyone, the problem no longer lies in individual countries but in global society. This situation is common, and is increasingly difficult to regiment because hitting local identities mean implementing actions of supremacy that are the basis of the choices for intervening in the planning of conflicts.

However, international law increasingly plays a fundamental role in defining the most appropriate norms and behaviour for implementing actions aimed at protecting cultural heritage. Certainly, in these first two decades of the new millennium, it has been understood that the value of *human heritage*, even before material heritage, is the result of man's work. In fact, the actions to be strengthened primarily concern the humanitarian component, which is still very weak (Niglio, 2016: 47–51).

In this cultural context, international law plays an important diplomatic role. What, then, do we mean by cultural diplomacy? Cultural diplomacy can best be described as a course of actions that are based on, and make use of, the exchange of ideas, values, traditions, and other aspects of culture or identity, whether to strengthen relationships, enhance sociocultural cooperation, promote national interests, and beyond. Cultural diplomacy can be practised either by the public sector, the private sector, or civil society (Lee & Niglio, 2019).

> The term "cultural diplomacy" looms large today in the foreign policy practice of nation-states as well as in cultural discourse. Yet there is often a distinct lack of clarity in the way the notion is used, on exactly what its practice involves, on why it is important, or on how it

> works. Much of this indeterminateness stems from the conflation of cultural diplomacy *stricto* sensu, which is essentially interest-driven governmental practice, with cultural relations, which tends to be driven by ideals rather than interests and is practiced largely by non-state actors. Given the present-day intrications between trans-national cultural connections and cultural practice within nations, this phenomenon should be an important concern of the cultural disciplines. Yet so far, they have paid scant attention to cultural diplomacy as a key component of the contemporary cultural policy landscape. (Ang et al., 2015: 365)

Thus, the lack of attention to the issues of culture as an instrument of international dialogue is reflected precisely in the inadequacy of foreign policies applied by individual states that still have difficulty in understanding the great opportunities that cultural diplomacy can make available.

Over the past decade, there has been a strong interest in this subject and numerous specialist publications have also been evidenced by research activities aimed at studying cultural policies that are still non-existent in many countries (Manton, 2003). However, it is important to point out that cultural diplomacy is not simply a matter of providing activities aimed at making one's cultural identities known within other cultures, stating this as "soft power" (Hayden, 2011; Holden, 2013). Rather, cultural diplomacy has the task of implementing all the conditions that are favourable for dialogue between different social, political, and ideological contexts and to create the right conditions for collaboration and sharing on projects of international interest. Unlike today, cultural diplomacy operates beyond the interests of the nation it represents and is therefore an instrument of international dialogue. Thus, the concept for which cultural diplomacy has always been regarded as a "noble" tool at the service of diplomats to shape the interests of their nation, is now outdated and currently there is no longer any concrete evidence that, as we have previously demonstrated, has assumed a transcultural value.

Transculturality precisely sets the stage for a stable dialogue between culture and international law, a fundamental dialogue to build correct cultural policies.

Unfortunately, cultural diplomacy has so far developed within a very messy and poorly structured landscape, where far-sighted skills and strategies for social and political development have been lacking. Cultural diplomacy has been practised in a fragmented, ambiguous, and superficial way, without planning on the actions of international cultural policies. This lack of coherence has undermined the objectives of a proper cultural policy exploited by the institutional forums it represents. Indeed, the lack of cultural policies within individual states makes it difficult to enhance cultural diplomacy as an action of dialogue and international development. (Lee & Niglio, 2019).

However, it is no longer possible to delay major reforms in order to give cultural diplomacy the correct role in building international relations. For that reason, it is essential to focus on the transcultural value of society and the institutional task of international law, as a means of linking programmes and actions for a profitable dialogue between nations in favour of the development of humanity.

4 Towards International Law in a Time of Transculturality

Sapere aude
Dare to think for yourself!
Immanuel Kant (1724–1804)

In a hyper-connected society, transcultural value is an important basis for reflection on building future communities. Under the circumstance, the authors are promoting an interesting international research project entitled *The Marco Polo Platform: An Eurasian Law and Culture Highway* to connect Orient and Occident via the valorisation of local cultures and academies of law. The aim of this research project is to realise a first important initiative in order to restart from the valorisation of history and culture to identify the reasons and guidelines for the development of international law between Orient and Occident.

The Roman Empire tried to spread its political, economic, and cultural ideas to the whole world. In order to expand its dominion to the other side of the Eurasian continent, Romans needed to understand the Far East and finally made contact with the Han dynasty of China in the early second century (A.D.). At that time, they both traded goods and information, mainly along the Silk Road. These simple and sporadic communications continued onward to the Eastern Roman Empire without having meaningful information with each other. A turning point came in the thirteenth century when the Venetian-born merchant Marco Polo released his explorations of the Yuan (Mongolian) dynasty of China. His travels spanning over ten years were contained in a written report entitled "The Travels of Marco Polo" (Polo, 2006). Despite a few omissions and exaggerations, this was the first written record by a westerner about the Far East. His story promoted understanding of a world that was largely unknown to Europeans.

In the eighteenth century, however, the Silk Road was interrupted because the Europeans invaded Asia, colonised it, and brutally exploited its peoples. The restoration of the Silk Road was proposed by China in 2013 as the Belt and Road Initiative ("BRI"). The BRI is a grand project to rebuild the former Silk Road routes on both land and sea. This ambitious plan is for the construction of a new Sino-centred economic sphere covering the Eurasian continent. Notwithstanding the "openness, harmony, inclusiveness and mutual benefits" of the initiative, neighbouring states would fear a "hegemonic China (Pax Sinica)". This is because most of the regional cooperation projects under the BRI appear to be orientated towards promoting trade, investment, and finance led by China, insinuating a kind of political supremacy (Zhao, 2018). A necessity, now, is to set up an alliance of institutions to study the legal cultures of the cities corresponding to the BRI.

A genuine partnership cannot be built without a real underlying cultural coalition. In that regard, this research would propose to establish the "Marco Polo Platform" (hereinafter The Platform) by paving the Eurasian Law and Culture Highway.

The Marco Polo Platform envisions a virtual library "jukebox" designed to contain information on the different legal cultures of municipal jurisdictions along the Marco

Polo routes. Further, the legal scholarship of those jurisdictions is connected with each other academically.

The plan is to pave a "Law and Culture Highway" along the Marco Polo routes. The Highway will connect leading law schools of the cities with each other from Europe (Bologna–Venice–Leiden–Leuven–Salamanca–Heidelberg–Geneva) to the Far East (Seoul–Pyongyang–Harbin–Shanghai–Beijing–Vladivostok) via Central Asia (Samarkand–Kashgar–Karakorum), Russia (Moscow–St. Petersburg), and the Middle East (Istanbul–Akko–Baghdad). This academic research will finally provide the way for co-prosperity between different legal cultures, rather than confrontation.

The cultural relevance of legal studies is also meaningful with this project. It will be clarified by comparing and categorising the legal cultures of participating cities in connection to each law school there, which represents the legal studies and culture of its city, as a hub of such a network. Along the Highway, the individual legal culture of the city will be interpreted through contemporary legal principles such as common good, self-determination, civic democracy, human rights, tolerance, sovereign equality, social diversity, mutuality, and the digital revolution. Once implemented, such a law and culture network will act as a firm basis for reciprocal interaction between the different jurisdictions.

The "consilience" approach would be the most appropriate for understanding different legal cultures across the Platform. The research will therefore be conducted in an interdisciplinary manner, sharing the proactive viewpoints of law, politics, economics, humanities, and cultural studies. Information and Communication Technology will be also applied. The "consilience" approach will help to build a cosmopolitan legal network. It will also act to promote specific comparative legal culture across the cities in which the Platform is embedded.

The Platform will design a scheme to revitalise the "ancient vision" of Roman law for free and equal communication between civilisations "through roads". This research will reinterpret the Justinian Law of the Roman Empire from a Eurasian perspective. Each law school will share its legal studies and legal culture to identify their practical significance today. Each city, and its leading law school, will be encouraged to participate in The Platform under the national coordination, uniting ideologies, religions, economies, political opinions, etc. The Highway will correspond to the Belt and Road University Alliance which is under construction. The Platform can be imagined as a cabinet with many drawers. In the cabinet, the individual drawers are the cities and law schools representing different legal cultures and studies. Each drawer would thus represent a law school containing information and scholarship about its legal culture. Each drawer will freely communicate with others within the cabinet. When all the drawers are finally complete, the Law and Culture Highway will be ready.

So the international research project hopes to represent an important reference of the transcultural dialogues, where the culture of the people becomes the basis for building the future society, whilst the laws define norms and methods for establishing constructive relations (Cotterrell, 2006; Berg, 2011). Together, they define the new cultural diplomacy. But it will only be possible to build everything if we apply free and wise thinking.

5 Conclusion

In 1784, in his thesis on "What is Enlightenment?" the German philosopher Immanuel Kant, laid claim to the phase "Sapere Aude" (*Dare to be wise*) as the motto for the entire period of the Enlightenment and used it to develop his theories of the application of Reason in the public sphere of human affairs.

Kant answers the question citing the Roman poet Horace (*Epistulae*, I, 2, 40): "Enlightenment is man's emergence from his self-incurred immaturity". He argues that immaturity is self-inflicted not from a lack of understanding, but from a lack of courage to use one's reason, intellect, and wisdom without the guidance of another. Kant argued that using one's reason is considered dangerous by most men and all women.

For that reason, it is important to understand the value of "critical thinking". This critical thinking approach is fundamental for appreciating all the paths that we have realised in this chapter to analyse the value of transculturality and the dialogue between culture and law. Applying this critical thinking we can recognise the needs of the community to find the best solutions for a better world. The transcultural approach is the result of this free-thinking based on wisdom.

As Kant taught us, we must use two thinking methods. One is "theoretical" thinking—the law of thought. It is subjective but must be established to prevent us from falling into chaos. The other is "practical" thinking: the application of theoretical thinking to our thoughts. By putting both together, we can ensure the basis of moral laws through the concepts of freedom, the highest good, and happiness (Marini, 2007).

This freedom to use one's own reason is an important social advantage because knowing and making one's own knowledge available means guaranteeing progress not only for present-day society but also for future generations. It is therefore not only a personal priority, but also a collective priority.

In this project on transculturality and internationalisation we intend to apply critical and operational reflections to create innovative paths that can be a reference for future generations and for an equitable development of the world. The reflections of this chapter have only intended to open a path with which we must now build together for a new Humanism and a new Enlightenment capable of projecting us towards a more sustainable world.

So we open this new path remembering the wise thinking of Michel Foucault, the French philosopher who, in 1977, in his preface to the book *Anti-Oedipus*, written by Félix Guattari and Gilles Deleuze, affirms:

> [...] *Develop action, thought, and desires by proliferation, juxtaposition, and disjunction, and not by subdivision and pyramidal hierarchisation.*
>
> [...] *Prefer what is positive and multiple, difference over uniformity, flows over unities, mobile arrangements over systems. Believe that what is productive is not sedentary but nomadic.* (Deleuze & Guattari, 1993: 13)

References

Ang, I., Isar, Y. R., Mar, P. (2015). Cultural diplomacy: Beyond the national interest? *International Journal of Cultural Policy, 21*(4), 365–381. https://doi.org/10.1080/10286632.2015.1042474.

Asser Institute (Eds.). (1985). *International Law and the Grotian Heritage*. The Hague: T.M.C. Asser Institute.

Assunto, R. (1997). *La città di Anfione e la città di Prometeo*. Milano: Editoriale Jaca Book.

Benessaieh, A. (2010). *Transcultural Americas/Amériques transculturelles*. Ottawa: Presses de l'Université d'Ottawa.

Berg, W. (2011). *Transcultural areas*. Wiesbaden: Springer VS Verlag für Sozialwissenschaften.

Bull, H., et al. (Eds.). (1990). *Hugo Grotius and international relations*. Oxford: Clarendon Press.

Burke, P. (2008). *What is cultural history?*. Malden: Polity.

Cassirer E. (1979). Language and art II. In E. Cassirer (Ed.), *Symbol, myth and culture: Essays and lectures, 1935–1945* (pp. 194–201). New Haven: Yale University.

Cassirer, E. (1981). *Simbolo, mito e cultura* (Trans. D. Phillip Verene). Bari-Roma: Laterza.

Cotterrell, R. (2006). *Law, culture and society: Legal ideas in the mirror of social theory*. London: Taylor & Francis Ltd.

Deleuze, G., & Guattari, F. (Eds.). (1993). *Anti-Oedipus: Capitalism and schizophrenia*. Minneapolis: University of Minnesota Press.

Edwards, C. (1981). *Hugo Grotius*. Chicago: Nelson-Hall.

Einar Fife, R. (2019). Creative forces and institution building in international law. In A. Ciampi (Ed.), *History and international law* (pp. 2–21). Cheltenham: Edward Elgar.

Foster, J. W. (1909). The evolution of international law. *The Yale Law Journal, 18*(3), 149–164.

Francioni, F. (2011). The human dimension of international cultural heritage law: An introduction. *The European Journal of International Law, 22*(1), 9–16.

Garcia Canclini, N. (1999). *La globalización imaginada*. Mexico/Buenos Aires/Barcelona: Paidos.

Grotius, H. (1925). *On the law of war and peace*. Indianapolis: Bobbs-Merrill.

Hannerz, U. (1992). *Cultural complexity. studies in the social organization of meaning*. New York: Columbia University Press.

Haskell, J. D. (2011). Hugo Grotius in the contemporary memory of international law: Secularism, liberalism, and the politics of restatement and denial. *Emory International Law Review, 25*(1), 269–298.

Hayden, C. (2011). *The rhetoric of soft power: public diplomacy in global contexts*. Lanham, MD: Lexington Books.

Herder, J. G. (1966). *Outlines of a philosophy of the history of man*. New York: Bergman.

Holden, J. (2013). *Influence and attraction: Culture and the race for soft power in the 21st century*. London: British Council.

Kymlicka, W. (2003). Multicultural states and intercultural citizens. *Theory and Research in Education, 1*(2), 147–161.

Lee, E. Y. J., & Niglio, O. (2019). *Cultural diplomacy & heritage*. Roma: Tab edizioni.

Manton, N. (2003). *Cultural relations: The other side of the diplomatic coin*. Phillip: Homo Sapiens Books.

Marini, G. (2007). *La filosofia cosmopolitica di Kant*. Roma-Bari: Laterza.

Mirzoeff, N. (2002). *The visual culture reader*. London: Routledge.

Niglio, O. (2016). Il Patrimonio Umano prima ancora del Patrimonio dell'Umanità. *Cities of Memory, 1*(1), 47–51.

Niglio, O. (2019). The creativity and the culture in the critical idealism of the philosopher Ernst Cassirer. *DIAFANESU Diaphanes Art and Philosophy, 7*(1), 67–86.

Ortiz, F. (1947/1995). The social phenomenon of transculturation and its importance. In F. Ortiz (Ed.), *Cuban counterpoint: Tobacco and sugar* (pp. 97–103). New York: Alfred A. Knopf.

Paetzold, H. (2002). Symbol and culture: Cassirer's concept. In G. Foss & E. Kasa (Eds.), *Forms of knowledge and sensibility: Ernst Cassirer and the human sciences* (pp. 22–33). Oslo: Norwegian Academic.

Polo, M. (2006). *Il Milione*. Milano: Fabbri edizioni.

Sen, A. (2007). *Identity and violence: The illusion of destiny*. London: Penguin.

Severino, E. (1997). *La filosofia antica*. Milano: Rizzoli.

UNESCO. (2003a). Multiculturalism and political integration in modern nation-states. *International Journal on Multicultural Societies (IJMS), 5*(1), 1–103.

UNESCO. (2003b). Pluralism and multiculturalism in colonial and post-colonial societies. *International Journal on Multicultural Societies (IJMS), 5*(2), 104–192.

UNESCO. (2005). *Convention on the protection and promotion of the diversity of cultural expressions*. Also available at: https://en.unesco.org/creativity/sites/creativity/files/passeport-convention2005-web2.pdf. Accessed 3 July 2020.

UNESCO. (2008). Acts of the international seminar. *New stakes for intercultural dialogues* (Paris, UNESCO, June 6–7, 2006). Also available at: https://unesdoc.unesco.org/ark:/48223/pf0000158389. Accessed 3 Aug 2020.

Welsch, W. (1999). Transculturality—The puzzling form of cultures today. In M. Featherstone & S. Lash (Eds.), *Spaces of culture: City, nation, world* (pp. 194–213). London: Sage.

Zhao, Y. (2018). *International governance and the rule of law in China under the Belt and Road Initiative*. Cambridge: Cambridge University Press.

Heritage and Culture

Academic Disciplines as Transcultural Heritage: In Defence of Culture as Cultivation

Marko Živković

Abstract This chapter will focus on academic disciplines as intangible institutions for the systematic transmission of accumulated knowledge. Academic disciplines will be presented as one of the forms in which humankind has preserved, developed and transmitted not just factual knowledge, but the more comprehensive project of human cultivation. I will show that arts, humanities and sciences share this fundamental aim of cultivation, what in Goethe's terms might be called the "metamorphosis of the scientist," and that these aims are comparable to the aims of such great systems of cultivation as Chinese Calligraphy. While not threatened in the same way tangible cultural heritage is threatened by wars, these institutionalized ways of cultivation are besieged by what is often labelled as neoliberalism and its utilitarian ethos. I will argue for the fundamental unity of arts and sciences and defend them as transcultural systems for transmitting accumulated knowledge, memory and cultivation that are in need of protection.

1 Introduction: We Will Build an Even Older and More Beautiful One

In 1993 the Old Bridge (Stari Most) in Mostar, Bosnia succumbed to repeated shelling and fell into the emerald waves of River Neretva it has been gracefully spanning since 1567. Bridges had a special aura in the former Yugoslavia, my home country. Our only Nobel Laureate in literature, Ivo Andrić's most famous book was about another Ottoman-era Bosnian bridge—the Višegrad Bridge over Drina (Andrić, 1959) and the writers of the report on the Mostar Old Bridge successful rebuilding were quite right to put a quote from Ivo Andrić as an epigraph to their account (Armaly et al., 2004). In addition to memorizing such quotes about bridges in school, the Bridge metaphor—the idea that in the Balkans we are East to the West and West to the East, thus a Crossroads and a Bridge was also a contributor to the aura of actual bridges.

M. Živković (✉)
Department of Anthropology, University of Alberta, Edmonton, AB, Canada
e-mail: zivkovic@ualberta.ca

O. Niglio and E. Y. J. Lee (eds.), *Transcultural Diplomacy and International Law in Heritage Conservation*, https://doi.org/10.1007/978-981-16-0309-9_3

The Mostar Old Bridge was perhaps the most the iconic prototype of all bridges in Yugoslavia and thus condensed in itself all the manifold auras of the archetypal Bridge. When it was destroyed by the Croatian Army during the war in Bosnia, it became one of the most painfully poignant symbols of the horrors of the Yugoslav wars.

Destruction of objects can sometimes affect us more powerfully than the loss of human life. Inanimate objects can accumulate collective memories over multiple generations and the "charge" of condensed group values they get to embody can easily exceed that of any single human. And when they suffer damage we may be stricken with a particular grief that we reserve for objects (as well as animals) that unlike humans are "innocent" (see Živković, 2014a on why small cars can make us cry). It must have been these powerful collective sentiments concentrated in this particular bridge, that energized a "coalition of the committed" (the World Bank, UNESCO, Aga Khan Trust for Culture and World Monuments Fund) that, together with the government of Bosnia and Herzegovina, Turkey, France and the European Union, as well as other donors—Italy, the Netherlands, Croatia and the Council of Europe Development Bank provided financial and technical support to restore it (Armaly et al., 2004).

The outrage and disbelief surrounding the destruction of the innocent Old Bridge was immediately compounded by a proclamation, reputedly coming from the bridge destroyers, that if need be, they will "build an even older and more beautiful one." This outrageous oxymoron, whose ironic intention is undecidable (were destroyers of the bridge that fantastically stupid, ignorant and primitive not to understand what they were saying, or were they deliberately mocking the sentiments of educated urbanites so concerned about the preservation of the Mostar Bridge?) Whether ironic or not, it certainly demonstrated the disdain of the destroyers for the values of culture, history and memory embodied in the cities, monuments, houses of worship and other objects of material culture that were important for the identity of the ethnic other. In fact, it was precisely such objects that were systematically targeted during the 1990s' Yugoslav wars.

Rebuilt in 2004, the Old Bridge was inscribed into the World Heritage list in 2005. I started with its destruction, rebuilding and achievement of World Heritage status because I want to use it to cross from tangible to intangible heritage. And indeed the inscription of the Old Bridge on the World Heritage List does provide an interesting test case for the evolving notions of what it is that is worthy of preservation and protection. Christina Cameron (2008), for instance, traced this change spanning the historic city centre of Warsaw, first considered for listing in 1978, and ending with the Old Bridge inscription as the end point. The trend she documents started with concrete monuments and ended up increasingly embracing the intangible aspects of heritage.

What Warsaw and Mostar both tested was the entrenched view of replicas as inauthentic, and of authenticity as residing in the identity of building materials. Between Warsaw and Mostar, however, another test case stands out as perhaps the most crucial to the shift away from the tangible monuments, with their material continuity, towards the intangible heritage as central to preservation and protection—the Ise Shrine in Japan.[1] A central temple for the cult of the Japanese Imperial Family, Ise has been rebuilt every twenty years since it was first built in 690 AD. As Kirshenblatt-Gimblett put it in 2004 in her contribution to the special issue of *Museum International* devoted to protection of intangible heritage, "As long as there are people who know how to build the shrine, it is not necessary to preserve a single material manifestation of it, but it is necessary to support the continuity of knowledge and skill" (Kirshenblatt-Gimblett, 2004: 61).

Here we have an uncanny convergence of Mostar Bridge and Ise Shrine—on the one hand, a promise of destroyers to build an even older bridge if need be; on the other, a thirteen centuries-old shrine that is both ever-new and ever-old at the same time, verily a temporal "duck-rabbit figure" as Sand wittily put it (Sand, 2015: 138).

Both the perpetually repeating replicas of Ise and the one-time (we hope) replication of the Old Bridge owe at least a part of their imagined continuity, that shimmering oldness-in-newness, to the continuity of the craft knowledge employed in their rebuilding. The Old Bridge "was rebuilt according to traditional methods the accurate reconstruction of which was made possible by the existence of a wealth of documents, photos and surveys from the past." Engineers and architects were consulted and the work was done with the help of several Turkish companies (see Armaly et al., 2004).

Ise Shrine, acting as a powerful metaphor both inside Japan and globally, has implied a romantic image of unbroken continuity of unspoken craft knowledge, of the kind that could be only passed from master to apprentice. "Although the plans exist for every structure, the master carpenters must remember and pass on to apprentices their expert knowledge of how to put together the complex joints, using ancient and unfamiliar tools" (Kirshenblatt-Gimblett, 2004: 59).

Some of the same mystique hangs over the Old Bridge builder, the "renowned Ottoman architect Mimar Hayruddin, a student of the celebrated Sinan" and the Ottoman building craft. It is important to the argument I am building to be aware of the nature of this craft continuity. In the case of Ise, there was at least one documented hiatus in the 20-year rhythm of rebuilding between the late fifteenth and late sixteenth century—long enough to break the "continuity of patronage and craft" so that the "builders in the late sixteenth and early seventeenth-century renewals were compelled to reconstruct the shrines on the basis of past documents" (Sand, 2015: 129).

In both cases, rebuilding relies, at least in part, on the existing plans, drawings and documents including photography. The unstated problem is that if that was all that was needed for building replicas of Ise or Old Bridge, how would these replicas differ

[1]Ise Metaphor, as Jordan Sand calls it, as well as Japan in general, "played a key role in a global rethinking of the definition and boundaries of 'cultural heritage,'" serving as a "general antithesis to European conceptions of the monument." There is an irony about Ise, however, that he points out: "while it has become the icon of a broad reconception of cultural heritage associated with Japan and embraced by countless conservationists worldwide, the shrine itself is neither listed as a world heritage site nor even protected by the Japanese government under the country's cultural properties law. The shrine's custodians have vigorously defended it from the intervention of any branch of the secular state" (Sand, 2015: 128, 145, 150–151).

from any object "mechanically reproduced?" And if reproduction does not require intangible human skill would we still recognize the transmission of authenticity from the original to the copy?

In other words, even if the world heritage institutions have come a long way from the "fetichism of materials" towards embracing intangible heritage as primary object of protection, would we extend the awe we need to feel towards an object in order to list it as World Heritage site to anything reproducible by an algorithm, however complex? Or is it that the awe, the aura of things that makes them objects of art or worthy of preservation, comes from something in them that we sense as irreducibly intangible, that is, resistant to exhaustively complete explicit description?

Anthropologist Alfred Gell famously formulated his definition of art object as that which enchants because it exhibits technical virtuosity that transcends the ability of the beholder to cognitively master it—the skill embodied in the object is seen as magical. In short, the cognitive difficulty of figuring out how the object came to be produces the enchantment that endows objects with mana, magical power, or in our modern world, with aesthetic appeal (see Gell, 1992, 1998 as well as Živković, 2014b). I would like to propose that the aura of Ise or the Mostar Bridge, objects that command not only a common person's awe, but quite enormous amounts of money and effort to rebuild and maintain them, must have at its core our belief that the human skills they necessitate and embody are ultimately indescribable and incomprehensible. Or, and now we need to be precise, these skills need to be technically speaking "tacit"—obviously known to someone (the artisan), but in a way where they can do it perfectly, but cannot tell how.

In our two cases, the contrast is between the existing plans and descriptions, on the one hand, and the skill needed to actually build the bridge or the shrine even if the builders have the plans. It is the distinction between explicit rules and personal judgement needed to apply them, between the map and finding your way, a musical score and a competent performance, a recipe and the craft of a great chef. These different ways of knowing are often referred to as "knowing how" versus "knowing that" (Ryle, 1984), or as "tacit" versus "explicit" knowledge (Polanyi, 1962, 1974; see also Collins, 2010 and Gascoigne & Thornton, 2013).

2 What If a Library Burns?

Plans and documents needed for rebuilding artefacts such as the Mostar Bridge, Warsaw old city or the Ise Shrine typically reside in archives and libraries. Somehow we consider this repository of knowledge about valued artefacts safe, even if their use in actual rebuilding may call for embodied, concrete artisanal skills that cannot be likewise codified and kept in the library. The tangible crucially depends on the intangible, and the intangible may be much more fragile. And indeed, the debates about the preservation of the intangible heritage often feature the pronouncement that the famous Malian writer, historian and ethnologist Amadou Hampaté Bâ made at UNESCO in 1960: "In Africa, when an old person dies a library burns down." It is worth examining this powerful and poignant statement because it will lead us directly to the issue of academic disciplines by sharpening the issue of variable vulnerability of written documents and knowledge inextricably bound in living persons.

Library stands precisely for the explicit knowledge in Polanyi's terms. Books and documents, together with maps, diagrams, manuals and recipes are precisely the knowledge that could be transported or transmitted "without loss of meaning." The knowledge of an old person in Africa, and Hampaté Bâ, probably had traditional bards (griots)[2] in mind, are idiosyncratic, unique human beings whose knowledge is by definition not reducible even to the largest library because they integrate this knowledge in a personal, unrepeatable way. The rhetorical force of Hampaté Bâ's pronouncement comes from talking about a loss of personal, oral knowledge, that his culture values highly, in terms of the kind of knowledge that our literate, computerized world of mechanical reproduction tends to value most—written down and neatly classified in a library. This saying thus does two things: it boosts up what is for the modern Westerners an inferior mode of knowledge up to what they consider the superior mode; and simultaneously boosts up a single human to the order of a mass of accumulated human knowledge represented by the library. The appeal to the programmes for protecting intangible heritage is obvious: just as cultivated Westerners should be horrified by libraries being burned, they should be horrified at the loss of knowledge other cultures consider as valuable as we consider libraries.[3] What is important to note here is that cultural transmission could indeed be broken and "die" if their carriers, in one way or another, fail to transmit it to the next generation.

After these observations on the irreducible magic of Master Hayruddin, or the nameless Japanese carpenters with their intricate joinery, which led us from tangible into intangible heritage, we are ready to make the jump that I intended to make in this chapter—the jump of considering contemporary academic disciplines, from natural and social sciences to humanities and fine arts as equivalents of intangible cultural heritage in need of protection. I would now want to throw Hampaté Bâ's powerful appeal back at us, modern globalized citizens, and suggest that the kinds of knowledge we consider secure, partly because they are supposedly contained in libraries, are in fact as vulnerable as an old African bard.

---

[2]Traditional Griots of West Africa belonged to a specialized caste and combined the roles of oral historians and praise singers. Ben-Ami Scharfstein mentions that Hampaté Bâ made a sharp distinction between "serious guardians of tradition" and "minstrels who sing of the past in order to entertain," and that the public never confused the two. As a champion of oral tradition, Hampaté Bâ extolled the meticulous adherence to strict rules of transmission of these guardians of tradition (Scharfstein 2009: 75). We can then assume that it is these oral historians that Hampaté Bâ had in mind. For shortness, I will thereafter refer to them as "bards."

[3]Matthew Crawford undertakes to challenge this hierarchy of two modes of knowing: "If you know that something is the case, then this proposition can be stated from anywhere … It can be transmitted through speech or writing without loss of meaning and expounded by a generic self that need not have any prerequisite experiences. Occupations based on universal, propositional knowledge are more prestigious, but they are also the kind that face competition from the whole world as book learning becomes more widely disseminated in the global economy. Practical know-how, on the other hand, is always tied to the experience of a particular person. It can't be downloaded; it can only be lived" (Crawford 2009: 161–162).

This is a surprising claim: the prototypical cases of intangible cultural heritage in need of protection tend to belong to those we identify with First Nations, oral cultures, craft knowledge (tacitly or explicitly assuming that it is endangered by the industrial, mass production). But to claim that modern academic disciplines, including those involved with the very project of cultural heritage protection, such as history, archaeology, museum studies, anthropology, folklore studies, etc., are themselves endangered and in need of protection may sound counterintuitive. And indeed, as we will see, there are strong arguments about the robustness, resilience and power of disciplines. I would, however, venture to say that what we may consider dominant forms of knowledge transmission are in fact as fragile as those traditional ones we keep thinking as perpetually vanishing and in need of legal, international protection.

To see a scientist as Hampaté Bâ's old bard, and the African bard as a scientist may have the benefits of "turning the tables" and seeing something in a novel way. This is one of the ways anthropologists practice their trade—by turning the strange into familiar and the familiar into strange. Going in this way back and forth may further illuminate issues of heritage preservation by raising, in a new light and perhaps more sharply, some nuances in the question of what is worth preserving (and legally protecting).

So how are academic disciplines under threat or in need of protection? Aren't universities widely accepted as trusted institutions with legitimate authority in matters of accumulated human knowledge? Even supreme, unchallengeable authority? Where else does our civilization situate the highest levels of its knowledge production and transmission? And don't we all accept the supreme value of our accumulated knowledge? How is it possible that such a powerful institution which in the West has about eight centuries of continuous existence could come to be as fragile as an antique craft or oral traditions?

I would be happy to be mistaken, but I don't think we can take such widespread popular and government support for institutions of higher learning for granted. In my oil-addicted Canadian province of Alberta, for instance, arguments are widespread that put social science and humanities, and perhaps even the "pure sciences" as "economically unviable" since they don't contribute in some obvious and simple-minded way to the oil-addicted provincial economics. In this, our current government is but a small replica of the world's most powerful nation's government with its rampant mistrust and denial of science and expertise, and its crude attacks on higher education (quite literally deadly in the current COVID19 pandemic). This type of right-wing populist authoritarianism that actively fosters anti-scientific sentiments from the top is by now a recognized pattern that reoccurs across the planet. And one of its hallmarks is indeed a more or less concerted attack on the higher education.

Even more importantly, the undermining of academic disciplines is not just a matter of current right-wing regimes, but a process that even though less overtly apocalyptic, is still sufficiently relentless and powerful as to constitute and abiding trend and a clear danger. More insidious than the current upsurge of authoritarian populism is the much longer process of devaluing and defunding higher education underwritten by the ideology of neoliberalism, To simplify matters, this is the trend that combines the following general components that are linked and mutually reinforcing:

1. Pressure on the academia to produce "value for taxpayer's money." In practice this is the call for the arts and sciences to produce "deliverables" of utilitarian value to the particular locality, region or the state where they are situated, sometimes phrased as delivering employable students with skills demanded by local employers, or as applied research resulting in marketable products.
2. Increased auditing. This is the pressure on the academia and scholarly community to justify its existence by providing increasingly more onerous detailed self-accounting (see Power, 1997; Strathern, 2000). In practice, this resolves into accounting regimes that rely on particular quantifications of academic output, and directly contribute to the administrative bloat at the universities. Again, the mythical taxpayer is invoked who supposedly demands that these professors in their ivory towers account for every cent they spend.
3. Increasing and open favouring of the so-called STEM education (science, technology, engineering and mathematics) over social sciences, humanities, arts—the liberal arts disciplines.
4. An aspect of these pressures, intertwined with them but worthy of listing separately, is the pressure to speed up, especially the process of graduate education. This is seen in the increasing importance of "time to graduation" as a metric for judging higher education's performance and thus the doling out of the public funds. This is moreover, the metric that the university administrations then strongly reinforce and it becomes a guiding ethos of the institution. I will focus on this time-pressure in particular in what follows.

So here is the outline of my argument.

First, I have to show that a range of academic disciplines, especially the ones that don't "deliver jobs to students" and are not "good value for money for the taxpayer" are indeed in danger.

Second, I need to show what kind of danger it is. Since that danger relies on some sort of danger to transmission, reproduction and development of intangible knowledge, I have to demonstrate that disciplines in question do indeed crucially depend for their reproduction and flourishing on intangible, tacit knowledge transmission. For if the knowledge they produce is codifiable in a context-free way without loss or reminder, then it would be hard to make the argument that this knowledge is in danger of perishing. This is analogous to the situation explored through the cases of the Old Bridge in Mostar and the Ise Shrine, as well as the African elders who hold libraries in their heads. In our metaphor, lest all the libraries in the world burn down simultaneously together with all books and digital files, our scholarly, academic knowledge seems to be safe. Thus I have to argue that academic disciplines are not essentially different from Hampaté Bâ's old African bards.

Since I am arguing for the protection of academic disciplines in particular, I also need to address some persistent criticisms levelled at them that, while often not intended as such, do in practice tend to lend arguments to restructurers of higher education and aid them in the wreckage they intend to visit on it. I will therefore deal with the accusations that disciplines are too conservative and rigid, hermetic and closed, as well as too esoteric and unresponsive to the needs of society.

Interdisciplinarity, often explicitly in the form of problem-driven research clusters, is then offered as the remedy for disciplinary vices. However, even though interdisciplinarity is as old as disciplines itself, in all this time it has failed to significantly change the disciplinary ecology of academia. I will indicate some reasons why this is so that will serve to further illuminate the function of disciplines and why they are to be defended.

3 How Are Academic Disciplines Endangered?

By academic disciplines, I primarily mean those who comprise what is still called in the Anglo-American world, the "liberal arts" or "liberal education" together with the pure or fundamental sciences. In short, complex systems of knowledge accumulation and transmission such as modern academic disciplines are in danger when the foundation of their legitimacy is eroded. Simply put, if society doesn't see them as valuable, it will not sustain them. Since we are by now thoroughly trained to think only in market terms, this question all too easily appears in the following guise: why shouldn't whatever doesn't have market value just be let to die? If academic disciplines cannot sell themselves, they should disappear. This way of thinking is possible once the very notion of public or common good is erased, and where the state is not seen as a guarantor of public good, but just one of the market players. Moreover, and this is crucial to my argument, this is a world in which the value of individual self-refinement or cultivation, what was neatly encapsulated by the German word, *bildung*, is not even seen as quaint and outmoded, but disappears as a social value altogether. And this is precisely the world of neoliberalism which Wendy Brown defines as "not simply as economic policy, but as a governing rationality that disseminates market values and ... formulates everything, everywhere, in terms of capital investment and appreciation, including and especially humans themselves." In such a world, "public goods of any kind are increasingly difficult to speak of or secure" (Brown, 2015: 176).

Liberal education was always an elite thing, but especially in North America where it dramatically expanded after WWII, it opened the door "through which descendants of workers, immigrants, and slaves entered onto the main stage of the society to whose wings they were historically consigned" (Brown, 2015: 180). And while a few top elite universities will continue to "market prestige and alumni networks," it is the public university liberal education and its promise of both social mobility and education for democracy that are increasingly forced into the role of vocational schools and for-profit colleges (ibid.: 182). The very value of democracy (and I would add, personal cultivation), Brown points out, relies on citizenry educated to value them. Once they are not, they, ordinary people, will not even see why one needs such "luxuries." It is in such circumstances that liberal education and the academic disciplines that comprise it can face serious threats of extinction. When voters, governments and the university administrations no longer even recognize these values, the professoriate, one sure group who nurtures them, will be too weak to stop the tide.

Why is it pernicious to academic disciplines to be subjected to the neoliberal logic? There is a growing volume of work written on the subject, but here I want to focus my argument on intangible knowledge (i.e. Readings, 1996; Ginsberg, 2011).

There is a wide consensus in the social studies of sciences today that even the hardest of sciences have to rely on the kind of tacit, craft knowledge that could never be fully codified in textbooks or documents of any sort. The facts that sciences generate are arguably fully codified, explicit and transparent, but the process by which they are arrived at is full of inexplicable hunches, inspired groping, and laboratory jerry-rigging done by irreplaceable technicians. A well-established literature exists on numerous ways in which scientists rely on knowledge they cannot or need not fully codify (Kuhn's paradigms are a good example). As a testament to the existence of such inexplicable knowledge at the heart of all sciences, consider that each discipline recognizes legendary practitioners who have a special knack neophytes lack. It is not just the fabled intuition of an archaeologist who knows exactly where to dig, but also the ability of a molecular modeller to recognize when the model clicks or not (Myers, 2015). The very fact that sciences from molecular biology to astrophysics (Uzelac, 2019) recognize that fundamental research skills require time and practice that no amount of written instruction can replace attests to the ineradicable presence of tacit, craft knowledge in sciences, no less than among the Ise Shrine carpenters.

What applies to hard sciences then, has to apply with even more force to the softer disciplines, especially the kind of idiographic, conjectural ones, described brilliantly by Carlo Ginzburg (1984), of which he lists the three illustrious avatars—Freud, Morelli and Sherlock Holmes. Uniting hunters, diviners and connoisseurs of all kinds with modern medical diagnostics, forensics, palaeontology, archaeology, history or anthropology, conjectural paradigm of reconstructing wholes from fragments with uncodifiable but reliable and testable skills actually permeates all disciplines, hard or soft. Just to mention one example, anthropologist Natasha Myers (2015) demonstrated how in the molecular modelling lab she studied, scientists use their bodies to dance their molecules, are playful and even superstitious. The clues to the molecular structure they are given by x-ray crystallography are as hard to read as the traces of a pray animal, fragments of pottery or symptoms of a complicated disease. Explicit knowledge of molecular forces, atomic distances, etc., is helpful but cannot alone lead to the solution. What is also quite striking in her lab, is that graduate students working on their molecules need long months of staring at their computers before they can acquire almost miraculous skills of their lab director who can figure out whether the molecular model feels right or wrong at a glance! What I want to emphasize here is something that is often overlooked. The labs, such as these, do not only produce molecular models; they also, crucially, forge the new generation of scientists. Many ingredients enter into such daily metamorphoses of neophytes into fully fledged practising scientists, the most important of them being their motivation, ample (funded) time and the physical presence of living, breathing models of excellence. In that sense, a modern lab is no different from a medieval guild workshop or the cultivation systems such as Chinese calligraphy (see for instance, Jean François Billeter's [1990] magisterial study, *The Chinese Art of Writing*).

This brings me to the crux of my argument about intangible skills at the root of all the academic disciplines that are now endangered by the neoliberal rationality. The core issue in the survival of these disciplines is in the nature of graduate education. The disciplines cannot reproduce themselves if they cannot cultivate scientists. And scientists, or scholars in general, cannot be cultivated unless certain minimal conditions exist for them.

I was tempted at first to extend the analogy from the craft workshop to all the scholarly disciplines and insist on the indispensability of actual master–apprentice relationship in the transmission of disciplinary craft knowledge. One of my models was the case of Stradivarius as examined by Richard Sennett in *The Craftsman.*

4 The Stradivari Syndrome

Stradivari's Workshop is interesting for my argument as precisely the famous case of ineffable, tacit skills failing to reproduce—Stradivari's secrets died with him! Moreover, with all our modern technology, at least as of the time Sennett wrote (2008), "mountains of cash and endless experiments have failed to prize out the secrets of these masters" (Sennett, 2008: 75). For Sennett, Stradivari's workshop is serving as an example of dangers to tacit transmission of craft, and he explicitly likens it to modern labs, "run by idiosyncratic geniuses" such as Enrico Fermi, whose secrets "can't be fathomed by poring over the minutiae of his lab procedures" (ibid.: 78). Sennett even identifies the "Stradivari Syndrome" as "the conviction that one's expertise is ineffable" (ibid.: 248).

Apart from the cases where craft secrets are deliberately withheld, however, I don't think that modern sciences and academic disciplines are really threatened in such a simple manner. For one, Gascoigne and Thornton (2013) devote their whole book to meticulously arguing that while not fully codifiable, tacit knowledge, summarized by Polanyi as "what we know but cannot tell," need not be something ineffable. For them the contrast between tacit and explicit, or knowing *how* and knowing *that* resolves into the contrast between *articulation*, which is context-dependent, and *codification* which is context-free. In short then, tacit knowledge is fully articulable but not codifiable without a loss.

"We live in an age of explicit rules and guidelines; of aims and objectives; of benchmarks and performance indicators," Gascoigne and Thornton say, under the pressure "to obviate dependence on the skillful judgements of individuals by formalizing the knowledge and making explicit the rules that experts purportedly employ in making them" (Gascoigne & Thornton, 2013: 1–2).

Even though there should be nothing baffling, ineffable or surprising about tacit knowledge, it remains, they say,

> [...] surprising and even subversive in a culture in which explicit codification is taken increasingly to be the norm … even if there are no principled barriers to the transmission of tacit knowledge, its personal nature can sometimes make its transfer difficult. Particular demands may be made on an audience who may need to have particular educated sensitivities and skills … while tacit knowledge can be articulated without reminder, it cannot be codified without loss. That fact can seem threatening in a culture that assumes that knowledge and expertise can be fully accounted for in a manual or a guideline. In that context, a defence of tacit knowledge is both a contribution to the rebalancing of views of knowledge and a defence of the exercises of good judgement. (Gascoigne & Thornton, 2013: 192)

If we agree that both Stradivari and Fermi, even though their knowledge was personal and tacit, could have transmitted it successfully, we still have to take into account that such transmission needs favourable conditions in order to occur and that it could indeed be threatened if these conditions are missing.

If this is the exact analogue, then one could argue that scholarly disciplines may be equally exposed to the danger of certain types of mastery being lost forever. The analogy between Stradivari's and modern disciplinary "workshops" is not perfect, but it could still be illuminating. While certain disciplinary skills may indeed be transmitted in one-to-one master–student relationships, this is by no means the most prevalent or even the indispensable requirement for the transmission of tacit craft knowledge. An example will bring this to fore.

I asked a good friend, a recently retired professor of history, the following hypothetical question. Remembering that he told me about the special skill of reading medieval German handwriting, I asked him what would it take for that knowledge to fail to be transmitted to the next generation? "The example of reading medieval German manuscripts is perhaps a bit far-fetched," he replied. "Hundreds, probably thousands of Germans can do it. So it can't really die out. And my superpower really consists of being able to read (decipher and understand) pretty much any manuscript written in Latin as well as any text written after, say, 1000 in German, Low German/Netherlandish, French, English, Spanish, or Italian. And that's not so much a set of skills that might be taught or passed on, as a mastery that requires years to acquire, and has to be acquired actively rather than learned from someone." And he was able to develop this expertise, he added, because he had "*the time and government funding* (Canadian, German, French, largely) to do so. It is hardly conceivable that any of our students might be in a position to do so now [emphasis mine]." In this he echoed what he wrote in 2007 about the "Automatic University":

> [...] how can the humanities disciplines now under populist, utilitarian and administrative siege in western societies reproduce themselves, given the intensive and extensive training needed to learn the necessary languages, methods and methodology, source criticism, and varied skills in ancillary disciplines for the study of history, literature, religion, art, music, film or other forms of culture? …. I take it as given that traditional, admittedly often oppressive forms of university training and production are facing numerous challenges (some deserved) from the corporate and managerial culture of business efficiency, financial accountability with its attendant logic of automation, efficiency, predictability, closure certainty … Curiosity-driven, scholarship/research, speculative thought, exploratory and experimental publication, and painstaking erudition do not conform to the formulae of such evaluative regimes and are thus rendered marginal – not by conscious processes, usually; but by the seductively

> efficient automatisms that makes those evaluative regimes so desirable in environments of accountabillity-obsession and micro-management. (Gow, 2007: 6, 14)

So, in short, the most fundamental requirement for the reproduction of disciplines, such as history in this case, is what we could call *ample funded time*. To which I will add that the presence of those who embody the craft skill is also necessary, even if what happens is not a literal master-to-apprentice transmission. A novice, at the very least, needs to know that such skills exist, and that they are demonstrable and attainable. It is also crucial, of course, that the student is cultivated enough to understand why such skills, even if they require a lot of time and effort, are worthy of acquiring. Having a living model is indispensable.

To come back to what is actually threatening academic disciplines: in order to reproduce themselves, and transmit their tacit crafts to neophytes, these neophytes need ample funded time and I would now add—space. By space I mean a convivial space that like a draft workshop that brings masters, journeymen, apprentices and beginners under one roof and protects them from the immediate demands extraneous to the acquiring of the skill. A family, a crucible, a cradle/creche, this is what disciplines need to be in order to incubate and then hatch the new generations who will continue the work. Having such funded time and autonomous space, however, is not free and needs support. In the past, this support came from wealthy patrons, then private foundations, and finally from the public in the form of government funding. To justify the funding, the public needs to trust that scientists and scholars should be left to themselves and well supported to produce something lay public cannot understand. When that trust erodes, so will the public support. In such circumstances, what looked like a robust system of disciplines may indeed fail to reproduce.

So far, I talked only about the danger to the very survival of academic disciplines or liberal education, that is, to their ability to reproduce. But we trust science and scholarship not only to preserve and transmit a fund of accumulated knowledge (and craft) but to constantly improve, develop and enrich it. While disciplines, as we will see for good reason, have to rely on tradition, they are also built to be engines of innovation and even periodic revolutions (Kuhn, 1996). In 1962, Michael Polanyi published his "Republic of Science" as a Manifesto for the "speculative autonomy" of sciences, and I would add, by extension to all university disciplines.

Formulated in response to the initiatives to introduce central planning in the post-WWII England in order to make sciences more accountable and useful to the society, Polanyi starkly claimed that "You can kill or mutilate the advancement of science, you cannot shape it. For it can advance only by essentially unpredictable steps, pursuing problems of its own, and the practical benefits of these advances will be incidental and hence doubly unpredictable." (Polanyi, 1974: 59). And here are the words that still resonate today amidst government efforts to make Universities servants of industry.

> The only justification for the pursuit of scientific research in universities lies in the fact that the universities provide an intimate communion for the formation of scientific opinion, free from corrupting intrusions and distractions. For though scientific discoveries eventually diffuse into all people's thinking, the general public cannot participate in the intellectual milieu in which discoveries are made. Discovery comes only to a mind immersed in its pursuit. For such work the scientist needs a secluded place among like-minded colleagues who keenly

> share his aims and sharply control his performances. The soil of academic science must be *exterritorial* in order to secure its rule by scientific opinion [emphasis mine]. (Polanyi, 1974: 64)

At the heart of Polanyi's argument for the autonomy of science is what he called the "unaccountable element" in all scientific inquiry and it is to this that he devoted his major work, of which his *Personal Knowledge* (Polanyi, 1962) is the magnum opus. For our purposes, his key insight is that "methods of scientific inquiry cannot be explicitly formulated and hence can be transmitted only in the same way as an art, by the affiliation of apprentices to a master. The authority of science is essentially *traditional*" [emphasis mine] (Polanyi, 1974: 64).

To summarize:

1. No scientific discovery without immersion in a convivial community of scientists free from outside interference by politics or business. Utility may guide scientists but they should ultimately be the only judges of where to take their research.
2. University science has the right to demand "exterritoriality" from the local funders since leaving scientists in peace to pursue science as they see fit is the very precondition to having science at all. Public good, in terms of knowledge and yes, useful technology will flow from sciences but not because scientists attend to such "deliverables" on purpose.[4]
3. Science crucially depends on scientists accepting its authority on faith. In that they don't differ significantly from crafts where apprentices have to accept the authority of masters. Science thus holds in balance tradition, discipline and discovery. But no discovery without tradition!

If we look at modern academic disciplines from hard sciences to social sciences, humanities and fine arts as Medieval guilds, we will immediately notice that, like guilds, they all have their hierarchies, arcane jargons, ceremonies and ritual gatherings, even coats of arms and tribal lore (of which insider's jokes are a major genre). It is time now to address some of the common complaints against academic disciplines—that they are too conservative and rigid, hermetic and closed, as well as too esoteric and unresponsive to the needs of society.

[4]Scientists often respond to such pressures by pretending their research will have practical utility. But such doctoring of grant applications is time-consuming, chilling to curiosity-driven research and frankly demoralizing (since scientists are implicitly not trusted to set their own research agenda). On the other hand, there is no reason that pure and applied should not freely exchange; like another prominent philosopher of science, William Wimsatt (ref), Polanyi would argue that the pure or theoretical and applied fields fundamentally enrich each other. He is only against non-scientists, applied or pure, telling scientists what to do.

5 The Burden of Tradition

It is jarring how modern sciences understand themselves to tell them that they are dependent on tradition and rely on tacit sensibilities they cannot explain. The revolutionary impact of Kuhn's *Structure of Scientific Revolution* (Kuhn, 1996) is partly due to such insights into the nature of scientific endeavour (that he, with hardly an acknowledgement, picked up from Polanyi). One of the effects of modernity, in fact, its very definition, is its mistrust of tradition. Since this modern impulse to destroy tradition is at its most glaring in modern art, I want to briefly introduce Ben-Ami Scharfstein's discussion of the tensions between the tradition and the cult of the new in arts since it will help us see more clearly why tradition is necessary and how it tends to include its own mechanisms for change and escape from stasis. For tradition tends to be equated with stasis, rigidity and obstinate refusal to change. As a champion of comparative philosophy and aesthetics, moreover, Scharfstein usefully ranges over Chinese, Indian, and other artistic traditions, not only the Western ones.

The young artist can no longer rely on the old guild model of "long apprenticeship and slow long-term improvement leading to mastery," but is instead compelled to invest in "short-lived, dramatic projects that promise a quick return" (Scharfstein, 1988: 4). Ever since the Impressionist rebellion against the old Academic art, the cult of the new and the explicit destruction of tradition became the rallying cry of every new movement, proclaimed ever more fervently in proliferating manifestos—think of Futurists and Dada as the most glaring examples. "The desire to cut themselves off from the past has been characteristic of all the arts, though only visual art shows so prolonged, merciless, and publicly successful an attack on the means and ends of traditional art, on everything but the need to be somehow interesting," writes Scharfstein (ibid.: 8).

The often-noticed paradox involved in any wholesale effort to destroy all previous tradition, however, is that in order to rebel against old standards, they must be first assimilated and invoked. Any such gesture remains meaningless if it doesn't in some way reference what is being destroyed and thus recall it. Rebellion is always against something; absolutely new beginnings are an oxymoron.

More interesting for academic disciplines, whose modes of rebellion against tradition, as we will see, are of a less spectacular sort, is the case of traditional Chinese art. Here, more than anywhere, we can see what Scharfstein calls the "burden of tradition." In China especially, with its long unbroken continuity, the burden refers to the sheer weight of accumulated knowledge that, at least by the sixteenth century has become almost unbearable." It threatened art's vitality by … "giving the feeling that everything worthwhile has already been done." The great collections of calligraphy, painting and bronzes, for instance, compounded by the increasingly elaborate efforts of scholars and critics, themselves often both connoisseurs and artists, "confronted artists with a problem of competition with this extremely rich past … There was simply too much to be assimilated … The responses ranged from deliberate eclecticism to conscious eccentricity" (Scharfstein, 1988: 13–14).

What is instructive in Scharfstein's account is how such a burden creates internal mechanisms of change. What happens, Scharfstein writes,

> […] is that the known number of remembered small variations grows so numerous that additional small variations lose their ability to stimulate. They drown in the sea of past variations … then tradition shows itself to be a heavy drain on memory, ingenuity, and above all spontaneity … such *involution* then acts as a spur for internal change … A successful tradition radiates into divergent paths, each drawing a particular group together by making strangers of the other, related groups. *Hybridization* with members of another tradition may both add vigour and increase the distance from the mother-tradition … all this interplay between the relative fixity of tradition and the changes it undergoes can be regarded … a prolonged demonstration of the need to create, disrupt and recreate order [emphasis mine]. (Scharfstein, 1988: 180–181)

6 Flexible Disciplines Surrounded by the Buzz of Interdisciplinarity

In his *Chaos of Disciplines*, sociologist Andrew Abbott (2001) demonstrated precisely this dynamic for academic disciplines. With Abbott we will tackle the previous accusations against disciplines, and mount their defence, especially in view of the criticism they receive from the standpoint of "interdisciplinarity."

Abbott persuasively argues that there is a fractal or recursive logic that underlies the process by which disciplines change internally and interact among themselves in the larger ecology of disciplines. In short, oppositions such as idiographic–nomothetic, culture–social structure, nature–nurture, explanation vs. interpretation, synchrony–diachrony, etc., tend to reproduce themselves on ever larger or smaller scales both within and among disciplines. Within disciplines, fractal cycles often take the form of incoming generation "killing" their elders by taking a radical swing to one of the poles of the discipline-relevant polarity. In Anthropology, for instance, at some point synchrony (how actual societies work) replaced diachrony (cultural evolution); at another point interpretation (Geertz's interpretative turn) replaced positivist explanation, and so on.

Abbott demonstrates no less than four rediscoveries of "social construction" in sociology starting in the 1920s:

> The insight that social reality is produced by practice rather than given ex ante has made at least four separate appearances in this century's social science … there are different *wrinkles* to these appearances, and of course there is a new terminology in each case. But there is no real progress, no fundamentally new concept. We simply keep recalling a good idea. It makes one think that …. social science … consists mainly of *rediscovering the wheel.* A generation triumphs over its elders, then calmly resurrects their ideas, pretending all the while to advance the cause of knowledge [emphasis mine]. (Abbott, 2001: 17)

Neither Abbott nor Scharfstein, it has to be said, believe that either art traditions (East or West) or academic disciplines are doomed to everlasting stasis or "rediscovering the wheel"—they both believe that traditions contain their own mechanism for change and adaptation to the changing world. What saves these "wrinkles" attending every new cycle of rediscovery from being ever more minute and trivial, the situation analogous to the "involution" of Chinese artistic tradition, is among other things, the kind of mutual "hybridization" that occurs among the disciplines.

Mutual hybridization, however, seems to be obstructed by the notorious "reciprocal ignorance" or blindness that exists among the disciplines. Social sciences, for instance, tend to overlap because they are mostly undifferentiated when it comes to subject matter, but that overlap is combined with "extraordinary reciprocal ignorance" (Abbott, 2001: 142). As Abbott demonstrates through a number of examples, studying the same social reality from different perspectives, disciplines tend to arrive at similar solutions, but they are seldom aware of what the neighbours have been up to. There is a reason why disciplines are accused of insularity. They are insular indeed. And not only are they trapped inside their own worlds defined by their own canons, journals and professional organizations, but their own internal fractal swings (or rather, spiral cycles) make the communication even more difficult. Sociology may rediscover something that anthropology discovered in its previous fractal cycle and vice versa. Combined with the reciprocal ignorance, however, there is also a widespread poaching among disciplines. In a process that recalls Ben-Ami Scharfstein's hybridization … "disciplines rejuvenate each other by a system of reciprocal theft that is facilitated by disciplinary overlap" (ibid.: 143).

In sum, for sound structural and cultural reasons which I cannot go in here, disciplines are robust and enduring social formations, prone to internal swings but metastable in the long run.[5] They are not static, but rather internally buzzing with revolutions that tend to reproduce them—making them ever-new, ever-old structures not dissimilar to the Ise Shrine. And the ecology of disciplines, especially in the American academia, tends to be metastable as well. Disciplines are expansionist but their expansion is checked by the imperialism of their neighbours and their mutual settlement seems to hold.

Perhaps the most prominent modality of criticizing disciplines comes from the standpoint of "interdisciplinarity." Jacobs (2014: 14–18) distils these criticisms into five: "Disciplines, it is charged, inhibit communication, stifle innovation, thwart the search for integrated solutions to social problems, inhibit the economic contributions of universities, and provide a fragmented education for undergraduates." The central complaint is that disciplines have become isolated "silos" (a term that apparently spilled over from the business world to academia sometime between 1995 and 2000).

Disciplines are also likened to ethnocentric, chauvinistic tribes engaged in turf wars. The fundamental problem with them seems that they don't communicate well because of their inward-oriented insularity. Consequently, they ignore developments in other disciplines and leave large swaths of territory unexplored.

Both Abbott and Jacobs pursue similar strategies in defending disciplines from the criticisms coming from interdisciplinary ideology. They show why there are good reasons that disciplines dominate our intellectual inquiries, and why they are

[5]In short, what props them up is the extremely enduring system of undergraduate majors combined with the exchange of disciplinary Ph.Ds among departments, that is, the structure of the academic labour market.

indispensable despite the flaws of the disciplinary ecology. They moreover, show that while there is plenty to criticize the disciplinary universe for, most critiques are unfounded, superficial and flawed. In short, disciplines are less insular, conservative, and esoteric as they are seen to be, the evidence, for instance, indicating "that communication across fields is not only common but is remarkably rapid" (Jacobs, 2014: 3). Finally, they both examine the problems overly facile calls for wholesale interdisciplinarity fail to take into account.

To summarize what are often complex arguments, disciplines are, with all their shortcomings, a reasonable modality of dealing with the unavoidable "intellectual specialization in the face of the daunting volume of contemporary scholarship," and thus reflect "a rough and admittedly imperfect response to the need to divide intellectual domains" (Jacobs, 2014: 4). Their "reciprocal ignorance" is precisely a necessary corollary of their need to delimit the field of inquiry in order to enable inquiry that is deep, sustained, and yes, "esoteric."[6]

Disciplinary boundaries exist for very good reasons. To be trained in a given discipline, in Carlo Ginzburg's words, "means after all (if not above all) to learn which questions, which methods, which answers must be regarded as inadmissible by its practitioners" (Ginzburg et al., 1995: 534). In fact, this is exactly one of the core functions of scientific paradigms, which for Kuhn (1996) enable the practice of "normal science."

The idea that the total field of possible knowledge is a *Flatland* sparsely populated with isolated disciplinary blobs leaving large areas of *terra incognita* is a very misleading one. Hard sciences, for one, divide their turf "vertically," so to speak, along the levels of complexity—subatomic, atomic, molecular, organic, genetic, whole organisms, ecologies, etc.—each level with its own discipline or subdiscipline. Social sciences and humanities, on the other hand, are not organized in that fashion, but rather around a very diverse set of "axes of cohesion" (Abbott, 2001: 139) that combine subject matter and approach in no systematic way. History is about diachrony, anthropology gathers around the ethnographic method, political science and economics study supposedly isolatable domains of modern societies (the political and economic sphere), and so on. In short, the principle of classification that rules the domain of disciplines is as bewilderingly incoherent as Borges's (1999) Chinese classification of animals, made famous by Foucault in *The Order of Things* (Foucault, 1994).

Rather than a Flatland, the domain of inquiry is probably better described as a hyperdimensional city that various disciplines, driven by their own fractal cycles, reciprocal theft, and the demands of the changing world systematically explore. The stress is on systematic and disciplined inquiry. Such inquiry does have to be constrained in order to be rigorous and reliable. We have not figured out a better way

[6]In his brilliant and prescient *Genesis and Development of a Scientific Fact*, Ludwik Fleck (1981) already in 1935 talked about esoteric and exoteric circles in sciences. A precursor of Kuhn and Polanyi, Fleck is worth consulting for precisely the difficulties in communication among "thought collectives" as he called them, that I am discussing here.

of insuring this rigour than disciplinary communities, and if we want that hyperdimensional city of knowledge to be thoroughly explored, we need to let disciplines follow their grooves. There are ways of making such interstitial exploration cover more ground between the core domains of strength that each discipline has.[7] In doing so, however, we run into some real problems of human limitation.

If we agree that discoveries happen primarily in small esoteric circles (that we need esoteric science for significant discoveries Kuhn, 1996; Polanyi, 1962; Fleck, 1981, etc.) and if training in such esoteric inquiry necessitates a great deal of time and effort, this puts limits on how many such domains a single human being could master sufficiently well to make fruitful exchange between them viable. This is what facile calls for interdisciplinarity often overlook—"some ideas may be too distant from others to serve as useful points of connection" (Jacobs, 2014: 21), and even with those that are "ripe for development," the expertise needed to bridge esoteric domains, may in practice be extremely hard to obtain.

Collins and Evans (2002), in an influential article actually formalize these requirements. They distinguish "contributory expertise" of the "core-set" (what Fleck would call "esoteric" science)—of those recognized as capable of genuine contribution to their field's knowledge (what we sometimes call "cutting-edge") from the "interactional expertise"—"enough to interact interestingly with participants" (ethnographers would say, when you get their jokes and get them to laugh at yours).

They furthermore distinguish "referred expertise"—that required to manage a field where one lacks contributory expertise, and the expertise of translators among expert communities. The managers then need to know what it is to have contributory experience in a related field "which puts them in a position to understand what is involved in making a contribution to the fields of the scientists they are leading at one remove" (Collins & Evans, 2002: 257). Translators, and this is what I am interested in, need to have at least interactional expertise in both fields they translate between (ibid.: 258).

The point I want to make is this. Contributory expertise is essential. What qualifies for contributory level is extended experience within a core group that is ineradicably informal (tacit). Formulated as an imperative it commands: Thou shalt acquire protracted, not quite definable and informal experience in a group before you are granted the trust of having the highest, contributory expertise. Translation among such core groups then also requires, if not this most specialized type of knowledge, then at least the level of knowledge sociologists of science require (demand of themselves) when they are investigating other sciences.

This is all to say, that communication among sciences, paradigms or epistemic communities is not an easy matter. Acquiring contributory expertise is difficult and time-consuming. A lifetime may not be enough to acquire more than perhaps two. The level of knowledge to communicate among core groups likewise is not trivial

[7] Abbott actually uses such a city of fractal paths as a model for exploring mechanisms of knowledge change and the best ways to "saturate the space of possible epistemologies," that is, the gaps between disciplinary islands. The hyperdimensional implications of this model do not escape Abbott, who incidentally, shares his last name with Edwin A. Abbott (Abbott & Stewart, 2002), the author of *Flatland: A Romance of Many Dimensions*.

either. Proponents of interdsciplinarity are right about the need for communication and cross-fertilization of fields, but often not mindful of how difficult this is in practice.

Jacobs and Abbott converge on their evaluation of the system we have now, esp. in the American academia: "flexibly stable disciplines, surrounded by a perpetual hazy buzz of interdisciplinarity" is fine by Abbott, while Jacobs argues that the system of discipline-based departments coupled with interdisciplinary research centres already accomplishes the objectives of those who criticize disciplines (Jacobs, 2014: 125). Disciplines are prior and more fundamental in the sense that interdisciplinarity depends on them, builds on them, and should not replace them. In a word, interdisciplinarity answers to a real need, and a real shortcoming of disciplines, but it should not be engaged in prematurely nor is it a replacement. It should rather emerge out of established disciplines.

There have been great interdisciplinary geniuses even within academia, Abbott remarks, "Gregory Bateson is an obvious example (I would add, Elémire Zolla). But they have no obvious mode of reproduction. They simply arise, revolutionize two or three disciplines, and leave magical memories behind" (Abbott, 2001: 130).

7 Conclusion: On Homes and Bridges

The aim of this chapter was to use shrines and bridges to think about other types of heritage that are fragile and in need of recognition. The Mostar Bridge is particularly instructive to think with. As Armaly et al. (2004) report, the citizens of Mostar (unlike some heritage specialists) don't seem to mind that the new bridge is a replica of old. What matters is that rebuilding it recreated some important part of what a sense of home for the Mostar citizens was. After all, the very name of their city derives from *most* (bridge); the city is literally a "bridge-keeper." The physical structure was a peg to hang your memories on, whether of crossing it daily, watching the breathtakingly dangerous divers jump into Neretva twenty-four metres below, or even making the jump yourself (the tradition of Old Bridge diving apparently goes back to the seventeenth century). Both tangibly and intangibly, the Old Bridge was at once a home and a way to cross to the other side. And somehow it managed to shimmer, in the notorious Mostar summer heat, as both new and old. It is also both fragile and resilient. A few shells could topple it into the river, but its intangible power could bring it back to life.

Disciplines too are both old and new, both fragile and resilient, both homes and bridges to the other side. They protect and nurture, and in the end prepare inquirers to depart and explore other, more distant fields. It is this nurturing that is a fundamental function of disciplines—to produce not only disembodied knowledge but the metamorphosis of scholars themselves. "Disciplines provide dreams and models both of reality and of learning." Abbott says.

> They give images of coherent discourse. They create models of knowledge that seem, to the participants, uniquely real … Disciplines in fact provide the core of identity for the vast majority of intellectuals in modern America … even those who are most critical of disciplines turn out to have been profoundly shaped by them… They define what is permissible not to know and thereby limit the body of books one must have read. They provide a specific tradition and lineage. (Abbott, 2001: 130–131)

Just as guilds, disciplines are homes for cultivating ultimately ineffable, unanalysable craft skills of research and inquiry. In this all sciences and humanities, across the spectrum of hard to soft, share some of the "elastic rigour" that Ginzburg (1984) identified as the paradoxical core of his "conjectural sciences"—there is something of a hunter reading the pray's tracks, an archeologist reconstructing past life from shards, or a diagnostician (or Sherlock Holmes) in every scientist (i.e. Myer's protein modellers). These skills are precious, hard to develop and easy to lose. The collectivities that are set up (and yes, financed) in order to insure the orderly transmission of such perishable cultivation, are themselves, ultimately, our most precious heritage in need of preservation. Not so much a protection from the shells of bridge destroyers, but of neoliberal managers whose collective interest is in downplaying or outright elimination of hard-to-acquire skills while at the same time mystifying their managerial magic and the latest management fad (Birnbaum, 2000) they are selling to their masters.

Disciplines are homes that are extraterritorial and local at the same time. Governments (in the Canadian case, provincial) should take care not to be heavy-handed in forcing disciplines into local relevance. Academics tend to have their own motivation to contribute to their immediate surrounding and it is safe to let them do it on their own. Their contribution to public good is rarely immediate, direct and obvious and it comes, in a large part, precisely from the fact that they are "exterritorial"—that is to say, translocal and transnational.

In some ways like Stradivari's workshop that produces not just the finest violins but violin makers, in some ways repositories of tradition like Hampaté Bâ's bards, like Japanese carpenters who can rebuild the Ise Shrine every twenty years, or the Mostar Bridge, disciplines are ever-old, ever-new structures that seem solid today, but may melt into the air if we don't value what they stand for. Like Chinese calligraphy, they are systems of cultivation that stretch over centuries, and protected spaces where eccentrics and recluses are left free to play their Glass Bead Games. Finally, they are architectonic marvels of accumulated human knowledge twisted by numerous fractal spirals into Gaudi-like cathedrals. Perhaps it is not too far-fetched to think of safeguarding them as Intangible Cultural Heritage.

References

Abbott, A. (2001). *The chaos of disciplines*. Chicago and London: The University of Chicago Press.

Abbott, E. A., & Stewart, I. (2002). *The annotated flatland: A romance of many dimensions*. Cambridge, MA: Perseus Publishing.

Andrić, I. (1959). *The bridge on the Drina*. New York: Macmillan.

Armaly, M., Blasi, C., & Hannah, L. (2004). Stari Most: Rebuilding more than a historic bridge in Mostar. *Museum International, 56*(4), 6–17.
Billeter, J. F. (1990). *The Chinese art of writing*. New York: Skira Rizzoli.
Birnbaum, R. (2000). *Management fads in higher education: Where they come from, what they do, why they fail*. San Francisco: Jossey-Bass.
Borges, J. L. (1999). John Wilkins' analytical language (E. Weinberger, Trans.). In E. Weinberger (Ed.), *Selected nonfiction*. Penguin Books.
Brown, W. (2015). *Undoing the demos: Neoliberalism's stealth revolution*. New York: Zone Books.
Cameron, C. (2008). From warsaw to Mostar: The world heritage committee and authenticity. *APT Bulletin: Journal of Preservation Technology, 39*(2–3), 19–22.
Collins, H. M. (2010). *Tacit and explicit knowledge*. Chicago: The University of Chicago Press.
Collins, H. M., & Evans, R. (2002). The third wave of science studies: Studies of expertise and experience. *Social Studies of Science, 32*(2), 235–296.
Crawford, M. B. (2009). *Shop class as soulcraft: An inquiry into the value of work*. Penguin.
Fleck, L. (1981). *Genesis and development of a scientific fact* (F. Bradley & T. J. Trenn, Trans.). Chicago: The University of Chicago Press.
Foucault, M. (1994). *The order of things: An archaeology of the human sciences*. New York: Vintage Books.
Gascoigne, N., & Thornton, T. (2013). *Tacit knowledge*. Durham, UK: Acumen.
Gell, A. (1992). The technology of enchantment and the enchantment of technology. In J. Coote & A. Shelton (Eds.), *Anthropology, art, and aesthetics* (pp. 40–63). Oxford: Clarendon Press.
Gell, A. (1998). *Art and agency: An anthropological theory*. Oxford: Clarendon Press.
Ginsberg, B. (2011). *The fall of the faculty: The rise of the all-administrative university and why it matters*. Oxford: Oxford University Press.
Ginzburg, C. (1984). Clues: Morelli, freud, and sherlock holmes. In U. Eco & A. S. Thomas (Eds.), *The sign of three: Dupin, holmes, peirce* (pp. 81–118). Bloomington: Indiana University Press.
Ginzburg, C., Herbert, J. D., Mitchell, W. J. T., Reese, T. F., & Spitz, E. H. (1995). Inter/disciplinarity. *The Art Bulletin, 77*(4), 534–552.
Gow, A. C. (2007). The future of the humanities and humanities-history in the automatic university. In A. C. Gow (Ed.), *Hyphenated histories: Articulations of Central European Bildung and slavic studies in the contemporary academy* (pp. 3–18). Leiden: Brill.
Jacobs, J. A. (2014). *In defense of disciplines: Interdisciplinarity and specialization in the research university*. Chicago: University of Chicago Press.
Kirshenblatt-Gimblett, B. (2004). Intangible heritage as metacultural production. *Museum International, 56*(1–2), 52–65.
Kuhn, T. S. (1996). *The structure of scientific revolutions*. Chicago: The University of Chicago Press.
Myers, N. (2015). *Rendering life molecular: Models, modelers, and excitable matter*. Durham and London: Duke University Press.
Polanyi, M. (1962 [1958]). *Personal knowledge: Towards a post-critical philosophy* (Corrected edition ed.). Chicago: The University of Chicago Press.
Polanyi, M. (1974 [1969]). The republic of science: Its political and economic theory. In M. Grene (Ed.), *Knowing and being: Essays by Michael Polanyi* (pp. 49–72). Chicago: The University of Chicago Press.
Power, M. (1997). *The audit society: Rituals of verification*. Oxford: Oxford University Press.
Readings, B. (1996). *The university in ruins*. Cambridge, MA: Harvard University Press.
Ryle, G. (1984). *The concept of mind*. Chicago: University of Chicago Pres.
Sand, J. (2015). Japan's monument problem: Ise Shrine as metaphor. *Past & Present, 226*, 126–152.
Scharfstein, Ben-Ami. (1988). *Of birds, beasts, and other artists: An essay on the universality of art*. New York and London: New York University Press.
Scharfstein, Ben-Ami. (2009). *Art without borders: A philosophical exploration of art and humanity*. Chicago and London: University of Chicago Press.
Sennett, R. (2008). *The craftsman*. New Haven: Yale University Press.

Strathern, M. (Ed.). (2000). *Audit cultures: Anthropological studies in accountability, ethics, and the academy*. London: Routledge.
Uzelac, M. (2019). *Life on the Stargazing Hill: Belgrade astronomical observatory at the intersection of gender, science and culture in post-socialist Serbia*. Ph.D. dissertation. University of Alberta, Edmonton, Alberta.
Živković, M. (2014a). Little cars that make us cry: Yugoslav Fića as a vehicle for social commentary and ritual restoration. In D. Lipset & R. Handler (Eds.), *Vehicles: Cars, canoes, and other metaphors of moral imagination* (pp. 111–132). New York and Oxford: Berghahn Books.
Živković, M. (2014b). Entry on Alfred Gell. In M. Kelly (Ed.), *Oxford encyclopedia of aesthetics* (2nd ed.). New York: Oxford University Press.

Octagon: The Quest for Wholeness

Hans Thomas Hakl

Abstract An octagon is an eight-sided polygon. According to traditional teachings it symbolizes resurrection, perfection, and fulfillment, hence baptisteries are so often octagonal. That is also why I chose it as the denomination for my own multilingual collection of books and magazines on philosophy, psychology, religions, spirituality, and esotericism. The idea behind it was to form a humanistic and spiritual stronghold against the rampant materialistic and often purely mechanistic trends of these days. After fifty years a library of nearly 50.000 books and 20.000 magazines has resulted. Octagon is regarded as one of the largest specialized collections in this field in Europe.

1 Octagon

It was in my twelfth year that I happened to stumble across a book called *The Third Eye* by Lobsang Rampa, the invented story of a fake Tibetan monk. It immediately excited my juvenile phantasy and left a strong impression in my memory, reinforced by later readings of Far Eastern literature, philosophy, religion, and secret doctrines. Ramana Maharshi became a major influence on me. Further studies of Theosophy, Yoga, Tantrism, and Taoism led me to comparative religion and psychology, mainly Carl Gustav Jung. He in turn acquainted me with Gnosticism, alchemy, and mysticism. Curiosity made me approach parapsychology, occultism, and magical doctrines. There was only one further step: to meet distinguished members of Freemasonry, "secret" societies and orders like Rosicrucianism. Prof. Dr. Adolf Hemberger, a German university professor of Sociology, Politology, Methodology and Scientific Theories, himself a Freemason and member of numerous occult groups, was my main contact. Besides, he was an important book collector and had himself authored works on societies practicing barely known doctrines. So, I became acquainted with all sorts of strange but also intelligent and educated people, who were at the same

H. T. Hakl (✉)
Octagon Library, Graz, Austria
e-mail: ht.hakl@a1.net
URL: https://www.hthakl-octagon.com/

O. Niglio and E. Y. J. Lee (eds.), *Transcultural Diplomacy and International Law in Heritage Conservation*, https://doi.org/10.1007/978-981-16-0309-9_4

time also avid collectors of rare books and manuscripts, through whom I often got hold of precious material. In order to become somewhat of an expert in this field it was of paramount importance to be multilingual, not infrequently demanding some knowledge of Latin, Greek, Sanskrit, and Hebrew. That is why Octagon contains so much literature in foreign languages.

Through Prof. Hemberger I got to know numerous famous collectors like the German émigré Oskar Schlag in Zürich, whose c.25.000 books are now housed in the famous Zürcher Zentralbibliotek. Mr. Schlag was also the owner of one of the largest collections of Tibetan Thangkas, sold at Sotheby's after his death. Another book collector was Karl Worel, who lived right in my hometown. One thing I learned from him was that you will never be lonely if you possess an important library. Interesting people continue to visit you, if only to hold one or another rare book in their hands. This was also the case for Oskar Schlag. Through Prof. Hemberger I also made friends with Ellic Howe, the expert of the most renowned magical order in the English-speaking world, namely the Golden Dawn. Knowing several languages perfectly, he worked as "master forger" in the psychological warfare against the Third Reich. On top of this he was also an expert in German Occultism during that period, which was of great help in his work.

Another very rich library I was able to visit and use freely was the one owned by the Swiss O.T.O. (Ordo Templi Orientis), a magical society inspired by the famous English magician Aleister Crowley, who influenced many modern esotericists but also well-known pop musicians. There too I was able to study the internal works and rituals of the most interesting German magical order, the Fraternitas Saturni whose leading members I had already known personally through Prof. Hemberger. The holdings of the Swiss O.T.O. are now housed in the public library of the Canton of Appenzell-Ausserrhoden near St. Gallen.

What made all these libraries especially precious was that they also contained the books of the main philosophers and psychologists.

After my university studies I established an export-import company with Swiss partners, enabling me to travel extensively. In this way I became acquainted with many collectors and specialist bookshops all over the world. Probably the most famous library in my field, the Biblioteca Philosophica Hermetica based in Amsterdam and founded by Joseph Ritman, I only visited for the first time however, in the early 1990s. But of equal importance as meeting points with knowledgeable people were bookstores like Watkins in London, Samuel Weiser in New York, Caves Book Shop in Taipei, La Table d'Eméraude, Librairie du Graal, Dervy Livres, all in Paris, as well as Libreria Aseq and Edizioni Mediterranee, both in Rome. I must also add dozens of mail-order bookshops, whose owners helped me very much in my search.

The specialty of my library besides the sector of religions (mainly from the Far East) is, as you can easily guess from what I have written so far, the field of esotericism (alchemy, occultism, magic, secret societies, ancient mysteries, paganism, mysticism, kabbala, etc.) which has grown into a respectable academic field since Antoine Faivre, Jean-Pierre Brach, Jean-Pierre Laurant, Joscelyn Godwin, Arthur Versluis, and especially Wouter Hanegraaff as prominent professors have laid the groundwork of these sectors in their respective universities (Sorbonne, Colgate, Michigan State and Amsterdam). Esotericist associations organizing regular academic conferences like the ESSWE (European Society for the Study of Esotericism with numerous branches in various countries) and ASE (Association for the Study of Esotericism) have given the field a wider reputation. The Warburg Institute in London, incidentally, was one of the first academic facilities to promote esotericism.

In 1989, I sold my part of the shares of the export-import company that my partners and I had built, and which had meanwhile spread to thirteen countries. Having earned a fair amount of money, I decided to go back to my home country with the intention of gathering all my books in one place and enlarging my collection. Soon the idea arose of assembling as many first editions of the fundamental works in this sector as I could.

However, in order to acquire truly rare and ancient books you must have personal contacts with booksellers who specialize in the so-called art of book hunting. They travel continuously around the world to visit auctions and bookshops, as well as their old clients, to find the treasures they are searching for. Because I owe them so much, I will name a couple of them, although most of them have gone out of business in this modern world of the Internet. The most renowned of them was probably Nick Schors of Amsterdam, who to a great extent is responsible for the richness of the libraries of the likes of Joseph Ritman, C.G. Jung, Antoine Faivre, and Gershom Scholem. These book-hunters had an enormous knowledge in their field and consequently I learnt a lot from them. Besides Nick I just name a few others out of pure gratitude.

There was Todd Pratum from Oakland, USA, who found for me not only manuscripts from secret societies but also mimeographed lectures of C.G. Jung and first editions of Robert Fludd and Athanasius Kircher. In the UK I recall Robert Gilbert of Bristol (a specialist in Freemasonry and occult orders). In Germany there were Wolfgang Kistemann (Gold-and Rosicrucianism and Alchemy) and Volker Lechler. In France one must name Dervy Livres, La Table d'Eméraude and Alain Marchiset, and in Italy both Bruno Bertozzi of Genoa and Laszlo Toth of Milan. Some of them have done me the favor of writing biographical sketches of their activities, which I have published in my four volume collection (written in four languages) under the title: *Octagon. The Quest for Wholeness.*

Naturally, tens of thousands of books plus hundreds of very often complete runs of exceedingly rare esoteric magazines require enormous space. Although my nineteenth century house is large, it was not built to carry all this weight. Therefore, I was obliged to build an annex in 1993. Looking for an inspiration I chose one of Italy's most spectacular monuments: the Castel del Monte in Apulia built by Emperor Frederick II of Hohenstaufen, known as "The Wonder of the World," which has an octagon as its basic form. The number eight is the symbol of resurrection and perfection. That is why it symbolizes the heaven of the fixed stars, once the seven ancient planets have been conquered on the path of old mysteries, and why, as the fairytale of Snow White teaches, the land of magic lies behind the seven mountains.

What is the point of collecting so many books? To get the reputation of being an educated person? That is partly true, for sure. But just owning such a library does not make you any wiser by itself. My main reason for collecting the books was primarily to preserve the sort of wisdom I regard as important in our modern world, where technology and materialism reign supreme and which needs a compensatory balance of humanity and spiritual knowledge. This may now come from indigenous cultures, from the Far East or from ancient times. Its rarity made my endeavors even more urgent and important. Many professionals in these fields strengthened my conviction and also confirmed this in writing. That is how the four volumes of *Octagon -The Quest for Wholeness* came into being, where about 90 professors and other academics collaborated to produce new and, in some cases, even revolutionary studies in their special fields.

Although I do not regard myself as someone who has enough knowledge to be a "teacher" of "spirituality," I nevertheless feel the urge to pass on to future generations the valuable literature I have been collecting all my life. For quite some time I thought of letting the University of Amsterdam be the beneficiary, as it is the only one offering a complete curriculum of esotericism with an academic master's diploma as final degree. But this was not possible, because I wanted to keep the library intact in my house until my death in order to write my own books. So I contacted the Zentralbibliothek (University of Zürich), being very grateful to Switzerland for enabling me to have the financial standing I enjoyed. But for other reasons this did not materialize either.

Finally, I concluded a very satisfactory deal with the Cini Foundation in Venice (Italy), which owns the greater part of the island of San Giorgio opposite San Marco Square. (Further information in Wikipedia under Cini Foundation).

This renowned foundation, known for its art treasures (not least a church built by the Renaissance architect Andrea Palladio), already possesses numerous legacies but mainly coming from painters, musicians, and writers. It is however also the home of the legacy of Alain Daniélou, who besides being an expert in Indian music had extensively studied Shivaism and Tantrism. The Cini Foundation sponsors not only numerous concerts, exhibitions, and academic conferences on its premises, but also publishes books and magazines. Not long ago the Foundation created a new department "Center for Comparative Studies on Civilizations and Spiritualities" run by the sociologist Francesco Piraino, whom I got to know during an ESSWE Conference in Erfurt, Germany three years ago. He told me that the Cini was looking for an adequate library, and I replied that I could probably provide it. A short time later I got an invitation to Venice for formal talks with the leading management, especially with Prof. Pasquale Gagliardi, its General Secretary. The talks were very fruitful and an appraisal of the contents of my library was launched, to be done by five professors from various universities specializing in religion and esotericism. As their approval was unanimous, we were quick to establish a contract to hand over the books after my death. In spite of the high investment cost due to transportation of the large library to Venice, plus the adaptation of the necessary building and the acquisition of new storage furniture, Prof. Gagliardi's efforts gained the approval of the majority of the directors, including the Patriarch of Venice, representatives of the city of Venice and the province of the Veneto, and also of important industries and banks. On October 3, 2019, the agreement was formally legalized by a public notary in Venice. As the Cini Foundation also provides funds for grants, I sincerely hope that a great number of students will use my books, which according to our agreement are to be exhibited freely in reading rooms. Thus, the collection will take on a life of its own, in a city already incomparable for its cultural treasures and magnetic attraction.

2 Octagon: The Quest for Wholeness

by Jafe Arnold[1]

Any cursory glance at the four volumes—in German, English, Italian and French—of Hans Thomas Hakl's *Octagon: The Quest for Wholeness, mirrored in a library dedicated to religious studies, philosophy and esotericism in particular* is sure enough to leave the impression that these tomes belong to that category of exhibitive anthologies which are irreducible to any single level of surveying, and to that category of books which cannot be confined to any one section of shelves—with the exception, of course, of the Octagon Library itself. Being simultaneously an account and testimony to the life work of Hans Thomas Hakl, a creative series of insights into the shelves, authors, visitors, themes, and inspirations of his Octagon Library in Graz, Austria, and as an unprecedentedly diverse collection of perspectives on the study of esotericism and related fields, the very subtitle of these volumes and its nuanced alternative rendering across four European languages—*La recherche de perfection, Die Suche nach Vollkommenheit, The Quest for Wholeness, La ricerca della totalità*—highlights the original, unique scopes of the 91 original contributions that have been integrated to form the four volumes of *Octagon*.

The immense swathes and depths of biographical, historical and philosophical ground explored by several dozen authors across the nearly 2000 total pages of the *Octagon* series are prefaced altogether modestly in Hakl's introduction, which opens all four volumes, entitled "'There once was a young man…': The History of a Library and the Personal Reflections of a Collector." Sharing the personal and intellectual journey behind the founding, expansion, and particular concentrations of the Octagon Library, its contents, and the researchers and fields of research drawn together into these volumes, Hakl nonetheless issues a certain disclaimer: "Some readers will also search in vain for the unity that underlies this collection. That unity does not exist, for if anything I am 'polytheistically' disposed, and the only coherence exists within my own person. And I am manifold" (p. 9). In addition to this "personal equation," Hakl explains that "narrow scholarly criteria were not the first priority in the selection of contributions"; rather, alongside studies of an academic character, the *Octagon* volumes feature contributions of what the editor calls a "'literary' tone that stimulates the imaginative faculties" as well as a number of personal and philosophical reflections which "do not conform to what is commonly described as the mainstream" (p. 9). On the one hand, this is qualified by the editor as reflecting "my belief in regard to the humanities that today's (academic) world all too often marginalises

[1] Published in French in *Politica Hermetica* 33 (2019): pp. 290–301.

intellectual diversity and potentially conflicting value judgements from other epochs, peoples and individuals, or often heedlessly venerates instrumental rationality and conceptions of linear progress" (p. 9). On the other hand, this proposed heterodox, "polyphonic" approach to the *Octagon* volumes' composition and the motivating "quest for wholeness" reflects the much larger area of study to which the Octagon Library is "particularly dedicated" and, in Hakl's words, "truly significant," namely, the study of esotericism and its many relevant intellectual contexts (p. 19). To a considerable extent, it is the importance and vitality of reconstructing the breadth and depth of the legacy of the latter, embodied in the unique holdings of the Octagon, which the *Octagon* volumes seek to exemplify with a diverse series of original texts by both established and new voices, many of whom have experienced and drawn upon the Octagon Library first hand. Indeed, it might be said that one of the main qualities which strikes the reader of the *Octagon* series is the creative demonstration, through numerous historical, personal, and intellectual examples, of the rigorous development of the study of esotericism in all directions and the invaluable role played in such by the approximately "40,000 books and perhaps 200 shelf metres of periodicals" (p. 21) as well as the many manuscripts and objects preserved by Hakl for study in the Octagon Library.

Faced with attempting to review such a massive concentration of knowledge, analyses, and impressions as has been condensed from the many corners of the Octagon Library into these four volumes, one cannot help but recall how Hakl's seminal study, *Eranos: An Alternative Intellectual History of the Twentieth Century*, frequently appraised by many authors across the *Octagon* volumes, qualified its immense scope as "a mosaic where the pattern emerges slowly out of a mass of tesserae laid out on the ground" (Hakl, 2014). As is justifiable in the case of the immensity of the materials of Eranos, we can only hope to introduce and stimulate further treatment of the "wholeness" of the "mosaic" of *Octagon* with the brief presentation and tracing of some of the key threads which run across the *Octagon* volumes with selected mentions of various contributions. Nevertheless, even if such cannot claim to do justice to all the accounts offered in these volumes, a brief overview of some of the most pertinent themes that run across *Octagon*, in a sense a kind of initial surveying of the "topography" of the *Octagon* books, can in the very least promise broader appreciation and stimulation of the further study of the horizons of the study of esotericism as such have been preserved and expanded around the Octagon.

The first, German volume of *Octagon*, published in 2015, *Die Suche nach Vollkommenheit*, opens by situating the series' context with creative elaborations of the significance of libraries, the preservation of books, and the particular qualities of Hakl's Octagon Library, and the intellectual currents that cross through it. Quotable in this respect from the first contribution by Julia Iwersen, "Library Geniuses and Hidden Spirits - the Reader as a Shaman" ("Bibliotheksgenien und verborgene Geister – Der Leser als Schamane"), is the allusion that "The Octagon provides an example of how a library devoted primarily to esotericism also especially exhibits a tendency to infinity" ["Das Octagon liefert ein Beispiel dafür, dass auch und gerade eine Bibliothek, die sich vorrangig der Esoterik widmet, eine Tendenz zur Unendlichkeit aufweist"] (pp. 34–35). The latter remark is made in the context of an extensive, poetic pondering by Iwersen on the experiential and metaphysical dimensions of reading, which she compares to shamanic trances, and on the relationship between libraries such as the Octagon and what she conceptualizes as "esoteric religiosity":

> Esotericism has a particularly close relationship with the Library, and not only to one single or typical such institution, but with the principle of the Library itself. One mark of the arbitrariness of which Esotericism is accused of here and there—its "syncretism," "eclecticism," or even its "tolerance" —is that it emits books of any type of content, be it established holy scriptures alongside modern revelatory texts, edifying tracts, philosophical treatises, world literature, formula fiction, as well as rubbish. The method underlying esoteric religiosity is the same as the principle of any book collection: just like a library, and almost always with the help of such, esotericism thereby seeks to trace truth by juxtaposing sundry truths.
>
> [die Esoterik ein besonders enges Verhältnis zur Bibliothek, und zwar nicht nur zu einer einzelnen oder typischen solchen Institution, sondern zum Prinzip der Bibliothek schlechthin. Ein Merkmal der Beliebigkeit, die der Esoterik hier und da zum Vorwurf gemacht wird – ihres ‚Synkretismus'oder ‚Eklektizismus'oder auch zu ihrer Toleranz – ist, dass sie sich mit Büchern jeden Inhalts abgibt: etablierten heiligen Schriften neben modernen Offenbarungstexten, Erbauungstraktätchen, philosophischen Abhandlungen, Ratgebern für alle Lebenslagen, Weltliteratur, Trivialliteratur und Schund. Auch die esoterischer Religiosität zu Grunde liegende Methode ist dieselbe wie das Prinzip einer jeden Büchersammlung: Ebenso wie die Bibliothek und fast immer mit ihrer Hilfe will die Esoterik der Wahrheit dadurch auf die Spur kommen, dass sie verschiedene Wahrheiten nebeneinander stellt.]. (p. 35)

The bibliographical meditations of the latter are situated before what might be one of the highlights of the German volume, also concerned with the many dimensions of books and libraries: Karl Baier's contribution, "On Biblio-Magic, Magical Language, and Script" ("Über Bibliomagie, magische Sprache und Schrift"). In the latter, Baier examines how the concepts of spoken language, written language, and magic are deeply intertwined in the history of magical texts, practices, and "linguistic units." Baier develops and explores the notion of *Bibliomagie* to refer to the "wider context of written magic and the magical use of spoken language" ["im weiteren Kontext schriftgestützter Magie und magischem Gebrauch gesprochener Sprache dargestellt"] (p. 53). Baier's particularly conceptually stimulating essay also pays homage to the Octagon, referring to the latter as a "model magical library" (p. 67), and remarking:

> "Here the only concern is to point to the raison d'être of the collection of magic books: the Chaosmos of the magical world, and therefore an important part of our cultural history, only becomes a little clearer if one can research in a skimming, wandering yet purposeful manner in such a wonderful library in the likes of that of Hans Thomas Hakl."
>
> "[Es geht hier nur darum, auf einen Sinngrund der Sammlung magischer Bücher hinzuweisen: darauf, dass sich der Chaosmos der magischen Welt und damit ein wichtiger Bereich unserer Kulturgeschichte nur dann ein Stück weit lichtet, wenn man in wunderbaren Bibliotheken wie der von Hans Thomas Hakl querlesend, streunend und zugleich zielgerichtet forschen darf.]". (p. 71)

Impressions of and homage to the Octagon Library and Hakl's scholarship are also paired with reflections on the centrality of esotericism and gnosis in the milestones of Occidental literature in the contribution of Joseph Strelka. Although issue can be taken with Strelka's distinction between "serious" and "pseudo-esotericism," he nevertheless appreciates "Hans Thomas Hakl's legitimate wish to include the entire esotericism of the world in his library" with the "the greatest possible completeness and this is precisely where the high value of this collection lies" [als den legitimen Wunsch Hans Thomas Hakls, die gesamte Esoterik der Welt in seine Bibliothek aufzunehmen…Es ging ihm um größtmögliche Vollständigkeit und gerade auch darin liegt der hohe Wert dieser Sammlung] (p. 77).

The variety of possible experiences and interpretations of such bibliographical encounters articulated in the first selections perhaps also serves as preparation for the decisively heterogenous contributions which *Die Suche nach Vollkommenheit* comprises, and which are highly characteristic of the *Octagon* series. Indeed, in the German edition alone, such range widely from emic accounts comparing traditional Chinese medicinal and spiritual traditions with Western practices, to Monika Antes' study of the Italian poet Dino Campana (1885–1932), "A Port of Postmodernity" ("Ein Dichter der Postmoderne"), from an interview between Hakl and Marc Melchert on psychotherapy to an essay on "Traditional Spirituality and Scientific Philosophy" [Traditionelle Spiritualität und wissenschaftliche Philosophie] by Ralf Liedtke. At the same time, one conspicuous theme which will be present in the other volumes, and one which reflects a significant corner of the Octagon Library and, indeed, the history of many of the currents examined throughout, is the meeting of East and West. Janos Darvas offers an overview of Henry Corbin's phenomenological approach to Islamic mysticism and traces the scholar's biography. In addition, Gino Poosch presents a history of the discourse and reception of mysticism and Sufism in the thought of the historian of religions Annemarie Schimmel (1922–2003). The German *Octagon* is also concluded with an article by Birgit Zotz, "Western Esotericism and Buddhism in the works of Anagarika Govinda" ["Westliche Esoterik und Buddhismus bei Anagarika Govinda."]

The second, English edition of *Octagon* from 2016 is opened with a spirited assessment by Wouter Hanegraaff of the present challenges confronting the sustainability of libraries and the academic study of esotericism, identified as the conditions increasingly imposed by neo-liberal policies, the "valorization of universities," and the long-armed legacy of the "grand narratives" and "eclecticist historiography" of the Enlightenment. In his contribution, "*Ad loca secretoria:* Rejected Knowledge and the Future of Libraries," Hanegraaff warns:

> esoteric libraries find themselves in a very special situation that makes them even more vulnerable than non-esoteric libraries. The reason is that they focus on the domain of 'rejected knowledge', that is to say, they are concerned precisely with those traditions of thought and practice that have been dumped into the dustbin of history since the age of the Enlightenment. (p. 27)

Quite appropriately, Hanegraaff's considerations resonate with Hakl's remarks in the introduction, but also venture further to articulate an epistemological and historiographical case for the study of esotericism and the preservation of such "rejected knowledge." Most forwardly, Hanegraaff formulates: "We are not just dealing here with yet another domain of research that happens to be of interest to only a minority of scholars - in addition, and crucially for our concerns, what sets this field apart is the fact that it happens to represent the structural 'Other' of the modern academy and its basic values" (pp. 27–28). While the thought-provoking critical reflection on the situation of the study of esotericism provided by Hanegraaff is by all means a valuable contribution to the *Octagon* in itself, also noteworthy is Hanegraaff's emphasis: "If the Humanities do survive, in one form or another, and the study of esotericism survives with them, then esoteric libraries and archives will remain essential…the library created by Thomas Hakl is undoubtedly the most important and wide-ranging of them all" (p. 33). Following Hanegraaff's perspective, the rigorous, objective and unprejudiced scholarly study of esotericism, as a living alternative, depends upon the very accessibility to empirical research of such safe havens of "rejected knowledge" as the Octagon Library, whose potential, in Hanegraaff's words, "remains largely untapped" (p. 34).

This uniqueness of the Octagon Library's holdings to the study of the history of esoteric and related currents, or, in Hanegraaff's words, this "massive memory bank of rejected knowledge, with many materials that are simply impossible to find anywhere else" (p. 33), is exemplified and explored in the ensuing contributions devoted to Octagon findings, such as Hereward Tilton's "The Urim and Thummim and the Origins of the Gold- und Rosenkreuz," Peter Forshaw's "Unexpected in the Octagon: Heinrich Khunrath's Presentation Copy to Erasmus Wolfart," and Henrik Bogdan's "The Hermetic Order of the Golden Dawn and the George E.H. Slater Collection." The ensuing "Walk Through the Speculative Music Section" by Joscelyn Godwin briefly tours a number of "esoteric musicologies" to be found in the Octagon collection, followed by another "wandering tour" by Christopher McIntosh: "Searching for the Gods in the Octagon." In the latter account, McIntosh offers a brief tracing of some of the key sources and intellectual history of European paganism as strung along the corridors and shelves of the Octagon. Most illustratively, McIntosh concludes: "For the Octagon, like the I Ching, is an oracle of inexhaustible combinations, as its visionary creator, Hans Thomas Hakl, no doubt intended it to be" (p. 124). Hakl's own connection of one of the major foci of the Octagon in his study of Eranos is highlighted and complemented with an extensive review of the historiography of Eranos by Riccardo Bernardini. This bloc of contributions underscores one of the key aspects of the *Octagon* series, namely, the wide-ranging reconstruction of the intellectual legacy of esotericism on the basis of otherwise inaccessible source materials uniquely assembled in the Octagon Library. Also noteworthy in this respect is the homage to this field paid in Jeffrey Kripal's personal account: "How I Came to the Study of Western Esotericism: And Why I Think It Is So Important." The English edition of *Octagon*'s reflections on this legacy are complemented by a number of specialized studies, such as Aaron Cheak's into the alchemical metaphysics of Schwaller de Lubicz (1887–1961), Konstantin Burmistrov's "Kabbalah in the Doctrine of the Order of the Asiatic Brethren," and Christian Guidice's study of the significance of Theosophy in the legacy of Arturo Reghini (1878–1946). The English volume is concluded with the lively account of Todd Pratum, "Dark Impressions: 35 Years as a Dealer in Books on the Occult."

Among the ever growing number of more thematically focused and specialized anthologies in the field of esotericism, the English volume of *Octagon* offers a diversity of case studies interspersed with original perspectives and critical reflections which tie the larger picture of this domain into a whole, demonstrating its relevance and expansiveness, and highlighting the node represented by the Octagon Library and its particular store of knowledge. Indeed, *Octagon: The Quest for Wholeness*' array of contributors and contributions renders this volume a unique "collectible" of insights by explicitly showing the diversity of perspectives in this field of study.

If the English volume's studies are mostly preoccupied with the early modern and modern periods, then the Italian volume from 2017, *La ricerca della totalità*, refreshingly visits a wider range of temporal and spatial zones and fields of research. In the first part of the volume, two articles deal with premodern case studies. In "Ritual hunting and initiatic models in archaic Greece" ["*Caccia rituale e modelli iniziatici nella Grecia arcaica*"], Nuccio d'Anna highlights how the act of hunting was charged with a high symbolic value, a sort of initiatic ritual in which "the *kouroi* intended to ritually reproduce the cosmic principle of the daily victory of light over darkness, of the celestial order over disorder" ["*i kouroi intendevano riprodurre ritualmente il principio cosmico della vittoria quotidiana della luce sulle tenebre, dell'ordine celeste sul disordine*"] (p. 103). Edi Minguzzi's article in turn deals with Dante Alighieri's famous fourteenth-century masterpiece, *The Divine Comedy*. Minguzzi aims to show how the structure of Dante's work can be read in a Neoplatonic key. Of particular interest is the fact that, in this attempt to decipher the contradictions and shadows of the *Commedia*, Minguzzi also discusses questions of methodology. The author believes that it is the "tools of semiology and of structural and comparative linguistics" ["*strumenti della semiologia e della linguistica strutturale e comparativa*"] that allow us to "identify the systems of thought that provided a model for the poem" ["*identificare i sistemi di pensiero che fornirono un modello al poema*"] (p. 105).

Together with Minguzzi's contribution, the Italian volume features other proposals for methodological reflection on the history of religions, such as Giovanni Casadio's article "The View of Anthropology and Archaeology from the History of Religions" ["*Lo sguardo della storia delle religioni sull'antropologia e l'archeologia*,"] which aims to focus on the question of the method of research by listing the differences in requirements between archeology, anthropology and the history of religions. Casadio's argues that "the historical method of religions is, like that of any other historian, an empirical-philological method that pays due attention to the perspectives of the so-called social sciences (sociology, socio-psychology, socio-biology and, precisely, anthropology)." ["*il metodo storico delle religioni è, come quello di ogni altro storico, un metodo empirico-filologico che presta le debite attenzioni alle prospettive delle cosiddette scienze sociali (la sociologia, la socio-psicologia, la socio-biologia e, appunto l'antropologia*)." (p. 25) Thus, the article examines some of the contributions of the publication curated by Valentino Nizzo e Luigi La Rocca, *Antropologia e archeologia a confronto. Rappresentazioni e pratiche del sacro*. These contributions render the Italian *Octagon* the most theoretico-methodologically engaged of the series.

Beyond these more theoretically driven articles, in an attempt to outline the main topics that innervate the Octagon, the Italian volume gives particular prominence to the study of two Italian esotericists, Julius Evola (1898–1974) and Giuliano Kremmerz (1861–1930), of whom the Octagon library has a large documentary archive and on whom Hakl's extensive scholarship and translations are well-renowned. Gaetano lo Monaco, in his expansive article (numbering 86 pages) analyzes the role that French occultism played in Kremmerz's thought and "his hermetic school" ["*scuola ermetica*"] (p.372). Further, Oscar Maganza ventures to explain the "Sense and Meaning of Kremmerzian 'Inheritance'" ["*Senso e significato dell' 'Eredità' Kremmerziana*"]. As far as Evola is concerned, the Italian *Octagon* boasts multiple articles, in particular focusing on the role that Evola played in the greater context of Italian culture, as well as the complex relationship between the Roman philosopher and Rudolf Steiner (1861–1925), which is reconstructed in Stefano Arcella's article: "The relationship between Evola and Steiner and the contemplation of the 'Midnight Sun': Philosophical antagonism and 'operative' convergences" ["Il rapporto Evola – Steiner e la contemplazione del 'Sole di Mezzanotte'. Antagonismo filosofico e convergenze 'operative'"].

La ricerca della totalità is also enriched by previously unpublished documents. For example, the unpublished letters between Eranos-founder Olga Fröbe-Kapteyn (1881–1962) and Mircea Eliade (1907–1986) are presented in Giovanni Sorge's "The Round Table or the 'Center' of Eranos. From an exchange of letters between Olga Fröbe-Kapteyn and Mircea Eliade" ["La Table Ronde o del 'Centro' di Eranos. Da uno scambio epistolare tra Olga Fröbe-Kapteyn e Mircea Eliade"]. Equally of interest are the correspondences, presented by Marco Pasi in his article "Antonio Fogazzaro and the Theosophical Movement. A survey on the basis of new unpublished documents," ["*Antonio Fogazzaro e il movimento teosofico. Una ricognizione sulla base di nuovi documenti inediti,*"], between the writer and poet from Vicenza, Antonio Fogazzaro (1842–1911), Aimée Blech (1862–1930), and Decio Calvari (1863–1937). These correspondences form the basis for Pasi's analysis of the relationship between Fogazzaro and the Theosophical movement. Fogazzaro's presence between *Octagon's* pages represents another "unexpected connection," as Pasi emphasizes:

> "Although he was very interested in the presence of esoteric currents and alternative spirituality in contemporary Italian culture, I do not know that H.T. Hakl has ever paid particular attention to the figure of Fogazzaro. Being a specialist of Julius Evola (1898-1974) you can understand why. In many ways, Fogazzaro represents a figure that is antithetical to that of Evola. In fact, Fogazzaro embodies a certain bourgeois world of the period prior to the First World War that Evola, and with him the whole generation of young people who had emerged from the trenches of the immense conflict, viscerally detests."
>
> ["*Pur essendosi interessato molto alla presenza delle correnti esoteriche e della spiritualità alternativa nella cultura italiana contemporanea, non mi risulta che H.T. Hakl abbia mai dedicato particolare attenzione alla figura di Fogazzaro. Essendo egli uno specialista di Julius Evola (1898-1974) si potrà capire perché. Per molti versi Fogazzaro rappresenta una figura antitetica rispetto a quella di Evola. Fogazzaro infatti incarna un certo mondo borghese del periodo anteriore alla prima guerra mondiale che Evola, e con lui tutta la generazione di giovani usciti dalle trincee dell'immane conflitto, detesta visceralmente.*"]. (p. 231)

The Italian volume is also rich in biographical journeys through the lives and thoughts of scholars and esoteric and occult exponents. For example, Massimo Introvigne presents an intellectual biography of the anthropologist and sociologist Gilbert Durand (1921–2012) in "Gilbert Durand, the explorer of the imaginary," ["Gilbert Durand, l'esploratore dell'immaginario"]. Also noteworthy is the bio-bibliographical sketch that Michele Olzi traces of the francophone Russian occultist Maria de Naglowska (1883–1936). Olzi retraces the steps of Naglowska's intellectual life, showing the places and crucial meetings of the famous organizer of the "Luciferian religion," the *Confrérie de la Fléche d'Or*.

The most recent volume of *Octagon*, the French edition, comprises a number of seminal studies and documentary overviews. A newly compiled bibliography of the works of Antoine Faivre between 2001 and 2018 is offered, and additional bibliographical insight is presented in PierLuigi Zoccatelli's bibliography of Louis Charbonneau-Lassay (1871–1946), which promises: "It is no longer right, as has often been the case, for the contribution of Charbonneau-Lassay to be considered subordinate to the personality and works of the Franco-Egyptian esotericist René Guénon (1886-1951)" ["Il n'en reste pas moins vrai que l'apport de Charbonneau-Lassay est souvent considéré comme subordonné à la personnalité et à l'oeuvre de l'ésotériste franco-égyptien René Guénon (1886-1951)"] (p. 371). The reconstruction of the legacy of Guénon is also furthered in Jean-Pierre Laurant's study "For a thematic typology of the correspondences of René Guénon: the case of the exchange with Vasile Lovinescu (1934-1940)" ("Pour une typologie thématique de la correspondance de René Guénon: l'exemple de l'échange avec Vasile Lovinescu (1934-1940)," as well as in David Bisson's article, "The notion of 'secret' in the esoterism of René Guénon" ("La notion de 'secret' dans l'ésotérisme de René Guénon"). These studies are particularly relevant in light of recent heightened media and academic attention to the legacy of Traditionalism, as well as reflect the fact that, in Hakl's words, "René Guénon and the 'traditionalist school'...and the 'integral tradition' still forms one of its [the Octagon Library's] focal points today" (p. 14). An overview of rare works of French Masonry is offered by Alain Marchiset, and the topic of "anti-Judeo-Masonism" in the turbulent history of the *Revue internationale des sociétés secrètes* (*R.I.S.S.*) is examined in the contribution of Emmanuel Kreis. The latter sheds light on a particularly salient chapter and region in the history of esotericism and "conspiracy" and connects with the contributions of Laurant and Bisson. Also noteworthy in this context, *La recherche de perfection* features the exclusive autobiography of Laszlo Toth and the history of his Arché publishing house, whose special mention in Hakl's introduction is made clear by this unparalleled glimpse into the world of esoteric publishing in the twentieth century, an account which remembers encounters with many of the currents and personalities present across the *Octagon* series (especially the French and Italian volumes).

Outside of this nineteenth-twentieth century French context, the French *Octagon* features a study by Jean-Pierre Brach into the intellectual birthmarks of Christian Kabbalah, alluringly titled "A practice of the book...or library(-ies)?" ("Une pratique du livre...ou de bibliothèque(s)?"). Quite resonantly with the "bibliographic" considerations of Baier's contribution, Jean-Pierre Brach submits:

"Book activities and practical results ought not to be conventionally contrasted like two sides which are foreign to one another or are supposed to be mutually exclusive. In fact, Christian Kabbalah has most often been considered to be above all a typically humanist exercise cultivated for this reason by scholars and theologians, whether lay or religious, devoted to the production of works of an essentially speculative or exegetical scope, dominated by a strong apologetic concern, and aimed at renovating the study of biblical text with the help of Jewish philosophical and religious literature."

"Il ne faut pas se contenter d'opposer conventionnellement activité livresque et résultats pratiques, comme deux versants étrangers l'un à l'autre ou supposés mutuellement exclusifs. De fait, pourtant, la kabbale chrétienne a le plus souvent été considérée avant tout comme un exercice typiquement humaniste, cultivé pour cette raison par des érudits et des théologiens, laïcs ou religieux, et dévolu à la production d'ouvrages de portée essentiellement spéculative ou exégétique, dominés par un fort souci apologétique et visant à rénover l'étude du texte biblique en s'aidant de la littérature philosophique et religieuse juive." (p. 68)

The intellectual legacy of Kabbalah, which Brach calls "very well represented in the collection of the 'sacred Octagon'" (p. 67), is also treated in Benjamin Barret's contribution, "The 'Kabbalistic science' of Lazare Lenain (1793-1877" ("La 'science cabalistique' de Lazare Lenain (1793-1877)."

The contribution of perhaps the longest *durée* in the history of ideas is represented by Thierry Zarcone's "Le voyage oriental du Rose-Croix," which traces the key intellectual sources, themes, and lines of transmission and transformation characterizing the history of the myth of the initiatic journey to the East of Christian Rosenkreuz. Surveying the components, sources, and conceptualizations of this myth from the ancient wisdom narratives of Hellenistic philosophy all the way up to the thought of Rudolf von Sebottendorf (1875–?), Zarcone postulates a key distinction between the two accounts of Christian Rosenkreuz's Eastern pilgrimage: the one derived from Valentinus Andreae's *Fama fraternitatis* of 1614, whose visit to the East is interpreted as a "search for a universal knowledge which is to be found above the established religions and which is therefore not the property of Christians alone" ("recherche d'un savoir universel qui se trouve au-dessus des religions instituées et qui n'est donc pas le partage des seuls chrétiens"), that is, the chain of the "Torlaquis d'Allemagne"; and the other Rosenkreuz, derived from *Les Noces Chymiques*, who "forgets the geographical Orient, replaced by an interior Orient which leads to Christ but does not exceed such" ("oublie l'Orient géographique remplacé par un Orient intérieur qui conduit au Christ, mais ne le dépasse pas"), and is therefore the root inspiration of French Masonry and "its rank of the Rosicrucian which puts the Paschal mystery into ritual" ("son grade de rose-croix qui met en rituel le mystère Pascal") (p. 192).

The unique study between East and West and between French and German accents put forth by Zarcone renders it even further appropriate that the constantly accompanying thread of Eranos is also extended in the French volume by Barbara Sturnega, whose article examines the complex intellectual exchange between Louis Massignon (1883–1962) and Carl Gustav Jung (1875–1961) at Eranos between 1937 and 1951. In particular, Sturnega discusses Jung and Massignon's interpretations of the Koranic figure al-Khidr and the Biblical and Koranic plot of the Seven Sleepers, a collaboration which Sturnega highlights as an invitation to dig deeper into the relationships and ideas that "matured around the round table of Eranos" ["mûrie autour de la table ronde d'Eranos"] (p. 165). This Eranos context and the Islamic thread are referenced and explored in the contribution of Pierre Lory, "Herny Corbin and the history of Islamic thought" ("Henry Corbin et l'histoire de la pensée islamique").

In the spirit of Christopher McIntosh's remark, an "inexhaustible combination" of perspectives and threads could be expected from any potential volume centered around the many dimensions of the Octagon Library and the work of Hans Thomas Hakl. The preceding thematic "meandering" through the *Octagon* volumes can only hope to have demonstrated that these volumes indeed live up to these anticipations, especially on the "condition" that the reader and scholar take heed of the disclaimer in the preface as to the "polytheistic" and "manifold" range of the series' "whole." The far-ranging diversity of contributing authors and perspectives is the strength of the *Octagon* series, as it is the originality and unique voices and scopes of the many contributions that render such at once a fitting testimony to both Hakl's Octagon Library, a mosaic-like panorama of the many threads and angles of the study of esotericism, and as the *Octagon* volumes clearly illustrate, an homage to the close intertwinement and inspirations joining these enterprises that has culminated in the present *Octagon* series. From the standpoint of the scholarly study of esotericism, the *Octagon* volumes are uniquely inter-generational, multilingual, and provide a unique collection of secondary and primary source materials. The *Octagon* series, as well as the greater legacy of Hakl's Octagon Library, deserve further attention.

References

Hakl, H. T. (2014). *Eranos: An alternative intellectual history of the twentieth century* (C. McIntosh, Trans., p. 3). New York: Routledge).

Hakl, H. T. (Ed.). (2015). *Octagon: Die Suche nach Vollkommenheit, im Spiegel einer religionswissenschaftlichen, philosophischen, und im besonderen Maße esoterischen Bibliothek*. Gaggenau: Scientia Nova.

Hakl, H. T. (Ed.). (2017). *Octagon: La ricerca della totalità, riflessa in una biblioteca dedicata alla Storia delle religioni, alla filosofia e, soprattutto, all'esoterismo*. Gaggenau: Scientia Nova.

Hakl, H. T. (Ed.). (2018). *Octagon: La recherche de perfection, dans une collection d'ouvrages dédiée, en particulier, aux travaux sur la religion, la philosophie et surtout l'ésotérisme*. Gaggenau: Scientia Nova.

Ecclesiastical Heritage as a Human Right

Henrik Lindblad

Abstract In several documents, the Church of Sweden has expressed that participation in the Church's cultural heritage is a common right. According to the Church of Sweden's cultural heritage goals, "the ecclesiastical cultural heritage belongs to all". In the Church's report to the government 2014, this is expressed as "Everyone who lives in Sweden is entitled to the history previous generations have created" and "access to the ecclesiastical cultural heritage is a right". The article discusses what this "right" means and on what grounds it is based. It investigates the right to participate in ecclesiastical heritage on the basis of common cultural rights, according to international conventions and, more specifically, on the basis of rights to the ecclesiastical heritage according to national cultural policies. The article states that not only demolition but also closure, privatization, or otherwise inaccessibility of common and public ecclesiastical heritage may mean that people's rights are not fulfilled and therefore neither conventions nor legislation are followed. Finally, it also discusses the right to assess ecclesiastical heritage values and the development of methods to increase participation in this work.

1 Introduction

This article was originally published in Swedish as a chapter in the 2017 printed publication *Between heaven and earth – the Church of Sweden's cultural heritage in the future (Mellan himmel och jord – Svenska kyrkans kulturarv i framtiden).* This version has been revised and translated into English by the author.

The following article addresses the right to participate in the Church of Sweden's ecclesiastical heritage, partly on the basis of common rights to cultural heritage and, more specifically, on the basis of rights to the ecclesiastical heritage. The right to participate in ecclesiastical cultural heritage is primarily addressed in two aspects: the right to take part in church heritage sites, buildings and interiors by their

H. Lindblad (✉)
ICOMOS PRERICO and Future for Religious
Heritage (FRH), Uppsala University, Uppsala, Sweden
e-mail: lindbladresearch@gmail.com

O. Niglio and E. Y. J. Lee (eds.), *Transcultural Diplomacy and International Law in Heritage Conservation*, https://doi.org/10.1007/978-981-16-0309-9_5

being open and accessible to everyone, and the right to participate in the work with church heritage, for example in the form of identification and valuation processes that precede decisions by ecclesiastical bodies and government agencies. These rights, ideologically and politically, from the standpoint of the Church of Sweden and the state, may seem relatively unproblematic, but have, in part, proved difficult to implement in practice. How can all churches be kept open to the public when congregations merge into larger units with even more churches and the economy is in decline? How should more than professional experts be included in the work with heritage assessments, when support for this is lacking in the *Historic Environment Act* and tools for participation have not yet been developed?

Parts of the article are based on one of the reports for the project *Evaluation and Development of Characterizations and Priorities*, carried out by the Church of Sweden's national level in 2007–2010. The project resulted in three interim reports and a final report that was referred to all dioceses, the National Heritage Board and the County Administrative Boards, responsible for the regional implementation of the *Historic Environment Act* (Lindblad, 2010a–d). The final report's recommendations on participation in the ecclesiastical cultural heritage have been indicative of the formulation of the Church of Sweden's goals for the Church Heritage Compensation, funded by the state, and for several of the Church's responses on the referrals of governmental and other public investigations and reports concerning the Church's cultural heritage. A summary of the project's results with a focus on public participation has also been published in *De kyrkliga kulturarven* (The Cultural Heritages of the Church, Lindblad, 2014).

In several documents, the Church of Sweden has expressed that participation in the Church's cultural heritage is a common right. According to cultural heritage goals, "the ecclesiastical cultural heritage belongs to all". In the Church's report to the government 2014, this is expressed as "Everyone who lives in Sweden is entitled to the history previous generations have created" and "access to the ecclesiastical cultural heritage is a right" (*Ett rum öppet för alla. Svenska kyrkans redovisning till regeringen angående de kyrkoantikvariska frågorna inför kontrollstationen*, 2014). The right to participate in the Church's cultural heritage has also been raised in connection with the government's assignment to the National Heritage Board to investigate a Swedish ratification of the Council of Europe's Faro Convention. The work with the Church of Sweden's response to the National Heritage Board's remittance of the report *The Faro Convention - the Council of Europe's Framework Convention on the Social Value of Cultural Heritage* has added more perspectives to the Church's national cultural heritage work and thus has been significant for this text as well.

2 Luxury Renovated Cultural Heritage

In the online edition of the interior and design magazine Sköna Hem (Beautiful Homes) from 15 May 2015, is an article with the title "Wonderful chapel for sale - this is how we want to live (do not miss the kitchen)". The article is about a church that has been renovated to become "a real dream home" and is for sale for just under SEK 4 million. Pictures show how the church's interior has been transformed into a light and airy living room and a "lovely country kitchen" with "gas stove and place-built interior" can be found instead of the chancel. About where the altar was located, there is now a kitchen island, filled with cookbooks and wine bottles (Underbart kapell till salu, 2015).

The church building is Normannebo chapel in Gothenburg diocese, which was sold to a private person in 2013, since it was considered redundant and the parish was lacking resources to take care of it. The sale was illustrated by Swedish television in a feature on 14 January 2013, marked by the parish's sadness at having to leave the church (Kyrkor säljs ut, 2013).

Normannebo chapel was inaugurated in 1919 and is, as all churches that were built before 1940 and was owned by the Church of Sweden in the year of 2000 when Church and state split, protected with a duty of permission according to Chapter 4. 3§ the *Historic Environment Act*. As the law is designed, the chapel is also covered by the same protection after the sale and the new owners need to apply for permission from the county administrative board for virtually any change they wish to make. Although the church has been secularized and privatized, according to the law it is still a church building and an ecclesiastical cultural heritage. But it has gone from being a public building, which should in principle be open to everyone, to a private residence that is closed to the public and where the county administrative board obviously approved major changes to the church space. Another sold church is Caroli church in central Malmö, built 1879–1880, which the parish sold a few years ago to a real estate company. The new owner was granted permission by the County Administrative Board to change the church space by, among other things, removing parts of the permanent interior. The purpose was to increase the usability of the building by adapting the premises to different event activities and increasing the opportunities to rent and use the building. The National Heritage Board decided to appeal the decision of the County Administrative Board, as the measures would lead to a reduction in the cultural heritage values of the church building and therefore should not be allowed under the *Historic Environment Act* (Överklagande av beslut angående tillstånd till ändring av Caroli kyrka i Malmö, 2014). However, the Malmö Administrative Court rejected the appeal and during the work with the Swedish version of this article it was still unclear whether the case would proceed to the District Court. While waiting for the legal process to be decided, the church space was unused, and the building and surrounding environment gave an increasingly desolate impression. The case was proceeded to the District Court, who finally ruled in favour of the owner. However, due to the long time span of the legal process, the plans for reusing the church were cancelled and still in 2020, the building is still closed and in a quite miserable condition.

The case can illustrate how the Historic Environment Act's intention to safeguard the public interest in keeping the cultural heritage accessible by preserving it, can have an opposite effect if the law is applied too strictly.

The question must be raised if the churches as cultural heritage still belong to everyone if they change owners and are privatized and it is no longer possible to enter them? If cultural heritage is seen as something that people create or do, instead of being material objects such as buildings or objects, the question becomes even more complicated than just about physical accessibility. In principle, it can be expressed that the right to participate in the cultural heritage process (see below) becomes more difficult to fulfil if the cultural heritage and the church space itself are no longer accessible and open to all.

3 Churches and Cultural Heritage Open to All

The churches have long been regarded as public buildings. Already in the 1571 Church Ordinance, it is stated that they are "public houses and as schools where Christian people can congregate" (*Then Swenska Kyrkeordningen*, 1571). Today's church ordinance states that they "are part of the public space" and that they should be made available to the public (*Kyrkoordning för Svenska kyrkan*, 2015, p. 152). The state has also emphasized the importance of public accessibility in one of the government proposals that preceded the change of relationship between the state and the Church of Sweden in 2000: "The Church of Sweden is responsible for making the church's cultural heritage accessible to everyone in the future - regardless of, for example, church affiliation - at least to the same extent as before the relationship change" (*Staten och trossamfunden - begravningsverksamheten, kulturminnena, personalen, avgiftsbetalningen, m.m.*, p. 149). This was part of the agreement between church and state where the Church of Sweden promised to take care of the churches and keep them open to the public. Against these commitments and as compensation for the strict protection of the law, the Church of Sweden would receive the state church heritage compensation (*Överenskommelse mellan staten och Svenska kyrkan i frågor som rör de kulturhistoriska värdena inom Svenska kyrkan*, 2000). Access to the churches is thus formally regulated in the Church of Sweden's own regulations and in agreement with the state. In addition to the practical difficulty of keeping churches open in sparsely populated areas and in parishes with weak finances, the question of physical accessibility today seems rather unproblematic in principle and ideologically. So it is, at least for the churches that are still owned by the Church of Sweden. For those legally protected churches that have other owners, accessibility requirements may be more difficult to maintain for both practical and financial reasons, as they are not entitled to church heritage compensation.

The Swedish legislation regulates the tangible cultural heritage in the *Historic Environment Act 1988: 950*. The introductory provisions of the law state that "responsibility for cultural heritage is shared by all" and that "the provisions of this law are intended to ensure current and future generations' access to a variety of historic environments". The aim of the provisions in this Act is to ensure current and future generations have access to a diverse range of cultural heritage. The following sections of the law regulate the issue of responsibility in detail, while the purpose of the law, which is to ensure current and future generations' access to a variety of historic environments, is not further addressed. The question is what does it mean to have access to historic environments? Formulations on the purpose were introduced following proposals in the report of the *Historic Environment Investigation* (*Kulturmiljöarbete i en ny tid*, 2012), where it was found that the *Historic Environment Act* lacked an explicit provision on what the law aims to regulate (Ibid., 2012, p. 152 f.). The fact that responsibility but not the right to cultural heritage is regulated in the statutory clauses is not in itself so strange as the *Historic Environment Act* is a distinct obligation or protection law, which was also emphasized in the report: "It is important that the protection aspect comes to the forefront when the purpose of the law is formulated" (*Kulturmiljöarbete i en ny tid*, 2012, p. 153). However, the fact that it is now stated in the law that historic environments should be accessible to everyone can be perceived as not only the public being responsible for the historic environments, but also having the right to access them. As can be seen above, the Church of Sweden has, on its own initiative, decided that everyone is entitled to the church's cultural heritage.

4 Participation According to International Documents and Conventions

The right to participate in the valuation, management and use of cultural heritage can today be said to be a paradigm in the international heritage community. This has been expressed in research, in politics and also in cultural heritage practice, where a number of conventions, charters and other documents have been indicative.

In 1979, principles, both theoretical and practical, for the management of cultural-historical sites were presented in a document called *The Burra Charter* (*The Burra Charter, The Australia ICOMOS Charter for Places of Cultural Significance*) created by the Australian National Committee of the International Council on Monuments and Sites (ICOMOS, an expert organization affiliated with UNESCO). *The Burra Charter* has over time become a national standard for heritage management in Australia and has also had an international impact, although in Sweden it was relatively unknown in cultural heritage work for many years. In 1998, the charter was supplemented by the *Code on the Ethics of Co-existence in Conserving Significant Places*, where a number of articles discuss in more detail the rights of different groups for e.g. identify, access and manage culturally significant places. The 1999 issue of the charter was provided with a special article on participation, which has essentially the same text in the latest version from 2013:

> Conservation, interpretation and management of a place should provide for the participation of people for whom the place has significant associations and meanings, or who have social, spiritual or other cultural responsibilities for the place.

The Burra Charter was created in response to a need for a cultural charter in a multicultural country with an indigenous population that defines and values its cultural heritage in a different and more intangible way than the cultural heritage expertise has done or has failed to do. With its democratic principles and process-oriented view on heritage planning and management, *The Burra Charter* has become even more relevant in a societal development where more and more social, cultural, ethnic and religious groups are added and recognized (See for example the Swedish National Heritage Board's Environmental Scanning Report *Towards Future Heritage Management* 2006, pp. 51–53). In particular, it has had an impact in Anglo-Saxon countries such as the United Kingdom, the United States, Canada and New Zealand, but has also gained importance in countries in South America and Asia. However, *The Burra Charter* has also been criticized for being less democratic than it seems. It is said to be aimed primarily at cultural heritage experts, who still have the preference to interpret in valuing and managing cultural heritage. Nor does the document indicate what participation really means in practice (Waterton et al. 2006). This may be justified criticism; the choice of certain words in the charter can be regarded as a way to exclude the public or at least to reduce its role in conservation work. However, as stated above, *Code on the Ethics* (…) and the later article on participation compensate some of the shortcomings in the original document.

The Burra Charter is a guiding document created by a national professional organization and is thus not formally internationally accepted or legally binding. But there are also international declarations and conventions that raise the right to participate in culture and heritage. The United Nations' *Universal Declaration of Human Rights* (1948) states in Article 22 that "Everyone (…) is entitled to realization (…) of the economic, social and cultural rights indispensable for his dignity and the free development of his personality". Cultural rights have since been developed, inter alia, in the *International Covenant on Economic, Social and Cultural Rights*, which was adopted by the UN General Assembly in 1966 and entered into force in 1976, which states in the fifteenth article of the Covenant that the States Parties recognize the right of everyone "To take part in cultural life". This applies to culture in general, but it is reasonable to interpret the Covenant's writings that cultural heritage is included (see below).

All people's rights to cultural heritage have recently been specified in the Council of Europe's *Framework Convention on the Value of Cultural Heritage for Society*, the so-called *Faro Convention* (2005). The Convention's definition of cultural heritage states that cultural heritage is defined and redefined by people and their actions and that it should not be perceived as static or impossible to change. In this Convention cultural heritage is defined as:

> […] a group of resources inherited from the past which people identify, independently of ownership, as a reflection and expression of their constantly evolving values, beliefs, knowledge and traditions. It includes all aspects of the environment resulting from the interaction between people and places through time.

After 15 years, the writing of *The Faro Convention* still stands as perhaps the broadest and most dynamic definition of cultural heritage that can be quoted in an official document. Even regarding the right to cultural heritage and to participate in cultural heritage work, the convention can be seen as progressive. Already in the introduction, it is stated that the Member States that have signed the Framework

Convention are "Convinced of the need to involve everyone in society in the ongoing process of defining and managing cultural heritage". Furthermore, according to the first article, the parties agree to "recognise that rights relating to cultural heritage are inherent in the right to participate in cultural life, as defined in the Universal Declaration of Human Rights". *The Faro Convention* thus defines the right to cultural heritage as part of the right to participate in cultural life according to the UN Declaration and the fifteenth article of the *International Covenant on Economic, Social and Cultural Rights* (see above). In the Explanatory report, which complements the *Faro Convention*, the above article is commented on as "the existence of rights relating to cultural heritage, deriving as an unavoidable consequence of the internationally accepted right to participate in cultural life" (*Explanatory Report to the Council of Europe Framework Convention on the Value of Cultural Heritage for Society* 2005, p. 5). In the 12th article of *The Faro Convention*, "Access to cultural heritage and democratic participation", more detailed explanations are given of participation in such a way that everyone is encouraged to participate in "the process of identification, study, interpretation, protection, conservation and presentation of the cultural heritage". The concept of Heritage Community is also introduced here, which can be considered as a new way of defining stakeholders to the cultural heritage, regardless of geography or other belonging as a class, gender or ethnicity. Compared with *The Burra Charter*, *The Faro Convention* is, by further reducing the authority of the experts, even more far-reaching in the principle of everyone's right to value and manage the cultural heritage. However, it is important to note that *The Faro Convention* is a framework convention with broad commitments without details, which means that is not so clear how the principles should be implemented in practice. At the time of writing the Swedish version of this article (2016), work was underway on a possible Swedish ratification of *The Faro Convention*. The Swedish National Heritage Board was commissioned by the Government to investigate the conditions and consequences of joining the Convention and to assess what constitutional changes would be required for ratification. In its report to the government, the agency recommends the Government to ratify the convention and claims that no constitutional changes are needed in connection with ratification (*The Faro Convention. Report from the Swedish National Heritage Board*, 2014). However, after receiving this report, the Government has still (2020) not ratified the Convention (the reason for this is unknown to the author). In June 2020, the number of countries that had ratified the convention was 19, out of 47 member states. *The Faro Convention's* innovative view of cultural heritage regarding its importance in society and as human right is emphasized by several authors in the publication *Heritage and Beyond* published by the Council of Europe in 2009. Gabi Dolff-Bonekämper, Professor of Cultural Heritage at the Technische Universität Berlin, claims that cultural heritage has never before appeared so high up on the list of fundamental human rights and values in a universal context. According to Dolff-Bonekämper, a consequence of this is that the "right to heritage is, like the other human rights, declared to be an individual right, to be exercised either alone or jointly" (Dolff-Bonekämper, 2012, p. 69).

However, the notion of cultural heritage as a human right is hardly uncomplicated or uncontroversial, as evidenced in the comments made by the Swedish national agency Diskriminerings-ombudsmannen (DO, the Equality Ombudsman) in its referral response on the National Heritage Board's report. DO claims that there is no analysis of the consequence of *The Faro Convention's* view on the right to culture and the concept of culture to the human rights of individuals, minorities and indigenous peoples, as expressed in the human rights conventions ratified by Sweden (*Yttrande över Riksantikvarieämbetets rapport Farokonventionen,* 2015). Another referral body, the County Administrative Board of Stockholm County, welcomes a strengthened participation, but also emphasizes the "danger of letting trends or small or large resource-rich groups influence the definition and interpretation of cultural heritage". The County Administrative board believes that this could risk "counteracting long-term work with a diversified and meaningful historic environment" (*Remiss avseende Riksantikvarieämbetets rapport om Farokonventionen*, 2015).

A critical review of the concept of cultural heritage as a human right is made by Diane Barthel-Bouchier, professor of sociology at Stony Brook University, New York. Barthel-Bouchier refers to critics who believe that it is not obvious that cultural heritage should be perceived as a human right. Rather, cultural heritage can be seen as a value (not necessarily a universal value) or as a social resource (a social good), which is appreciated for providing some benefits but without costing too much (Barthel-Bouchier 2014, p. 27).

In this chapter there is no room to further discuss the arguments about participation in the cultural heritage as a human right. But one possible conclusion could be that since both the Church of Sweden and the state regard the ecclesiastical cultural heritage as a public heritage belonging to all, at least it would not be negative for the church if the ecclesiastical heritage—apart from being regarded as valuable and a societal resource—also was regarded as a human right. From a legal point of view, the protection according to the *Historic Environment Act* means considerably greater restrictions on the Church of Sweden's ownership of church properties, interior decorations, movable objects than the restrictions an international convention could entail. Sweden has ratified other conventions that are relevant in this context. In 2010, the UNESCO *Convention for the Safeguarding of the Intangible Cultural Heritage* (2003) was ratified. This Convention also emphasizes participation in cultural heritage and in particular in Article 15, "Participation of communities, groups and individuals", which declares that "(…) each State Party shall endeavour to ensure the widest possible participation of communities, groups and, where appropriate, individuals that create, maintain and transmit such heritage, and to involve them actively in its management". The *European Landscape Convention*, established in 2000 and ratified by the Swedish Government in 2011, also has a clear democratic aspect because it emphasizes the social importance of the landscape as well as the importance of people being able to participate in the assessment and management of the landscape (*Explanatory Report to the European Landscape Convention. European Treaty Series—No. 176*). The very definition of landscape, in the first article of the Convention, has a democratic and social appropriation, where the landscape is described as "an area, as perceived by people, whose character is the result of the action and interaction of natural and/or human factors". As a conclusion, it can be noted that regardless of whether the government decides to ratify *The Faro Convention* or not, Sweden has committed itself to involving the public in the parts of the cultural heritage that comprise (cultural) landscapes and intangible cultural heritage.

5 Cultural Policy and Participation

In recent decades, the public's right to transparency and participation in social planning has been increasingly emphasized in politics, which is also reflected in the cultural heritage area. However, the view of the right to participation in a broad cultural heritage process as defined in the 12th article of *The Faro Convention* has developed slowly in Sweden. Already in the 1997 cultural policy bill, it was emphasized that the tasks of preserving and communicating heritage are central to the work on cultural heritage and that cultural policy must create interest in and participation in cultural heritage through a dialogue with citizens (*Kulturpolitik*, p. 127). However, several writings in the bill can be interpreted as that increased participation is required to legitimize the preservation of cultural heritage, i.e. participation is for the sake of preservation.

In the bill *Cultural Heritage—historic environments and cultural objects* (1998) the government proposed a number of overall goals for the activities in the historic environment field. One of the goals is formulated as "everyone's understanding, participation and responsibility for their own cultural environment" and was justified with "everyone has the right to respect for their historic environment and to participate in its use and its design (*Kulturarv – kulturmiljöer och kulturföremål*, p. 28). However, the two government proposals (1997, 1998) do not mention who have the right to be involved in the evaluation of the historic environment. This can be interpreted as being understood that it is the experts who are to determine the historic environments and their values and that the public is then entitled to use the environments that the experts have pointed out. In the bill *Time for culture* (SOU, 2009: 16) that followed the Cultural Investigation report, the overall cultural heritage goal is formulated as: "Cultural policy should promote a living cultural heritage that is preserved, used and developed". The government presented its considerations as follows: "Citizens' involvement and participation is an important prerequisite for the cultural heritage to live and develop. It is therefore important to ensure that people are increasingly able to access, use and further develop the cultural heritage" (*Tid för kultur*, 2009, pp. 30–31). Finally, in *Time for Culture*, one of the proposed historic environmental goals, which are based on the cultural policy goals of 2009, is fully focused on participation. The state historic environment work shall thus promote "people's participation in the historic environment work and the opportunity to understand and take responsibility for the historic environment". According to the Government's justification of the goal, everyone should have the right to be inspired and enriched by the historic environment. Furthermore, the public historic environment work shall strengthen the opportunity for everyone's participation, whatever background and conditions, and contribute to making the historic environment accessible and possible to interpret (*Kulturmiljöns mångfald*, 2012, *Kulturmiljöarbete i en ny tid*, 2012). With the formulation on the right to interpret the historic environment, which can also be understood as identifying and valuing the historic environments, the government goes further than before. The political intentions regarding the benefit of and also the right to public and civil society participation in cultural heritage work have thus increased over time. However, as previously mentioned in this article, this is so far hardly reflected in current legislation, except in the brief description of the purpose of *The Historic Environment Act.*

6 Participation in Theory and Practice

At the international ICOMOS conference *Finding the spirit of place—between the tangible and the intangible* in 2008, the American architect and heritage consultant Ned Kaufmann presented a method for documentation and value assessment of historic environments. The method is called storyscapes and can be briefly explained as when a (historical) place and its values are to be investigated, residents and other stakeholders are first interviewed about how they perceive and value the place, about the local stories that exist and how the place is used. Only after this is a more conventional cultural heritage documentation performed. The idea is that the local stakeholders' frame of reference and knowledge provide a platform for the experts' description and evaluation, rather than the other way around.

Krister Olsson, Ph.D. in regional planning, recommends a quantitative survey-based methodology for increased participation in the physical planning of the historic environments (Olsson, 2003). In the project Citizens, Historic Environment and Planning, the method is further investigated and in the introduction to the project report, Krister Olsson and his colleague Elin Berglund note that physical planning has traditionally been regarded as a rational business, where the planner is an expert with the ability to make objective and value-free considerations (Olsson and Berglund, 2012, pp. 5–6). However, this view has become increasingly questioned and replaced by a communicative planning ideal, where different interests, including those of the citizens, should be given the same space and equal opportunities to participate in planning and decision-making. But, according to the authors, comments are as a rule only made from a few, those directly affected by planned measures, while the wider circle of citizens and companies in general is hardly prominent in the planning process (ibid., p. 9). In practice, the notion that planning is and should be an expert-controlled rational activity still dominates. The communicative ideal thus appears mostly like rhetoric and the fundamental question remains: how should citizens' influence in physical planning be organized? (ibid., p. 6.). In the report, a quantitative method is proposed, where everyone can participate with the help of surveys that are sent out to citizens. The method is justified by the fact that the urban environment is characterized by properties that can be described as public goods, i.e. services and goods that everyone can use without having to pay for them. In order to define this public good, surveys are required from the perspective of all citizens (ibid., p. 15). An example in the area of ecclesiastical heritage is the survey of the great church of Åtvid (see below).

The method of surveys to get opinions from citizens would, according to this reasoning, be suitable for the public cultural heritage, which can be considered a collective or public good. Since all citizens can be considered stakeholders to the public cultural heritage, a certain part of their taxes goes to maintain it. But not all taxpayers can be assumed to have the opportunity to participate in the workshops or other meetings that are arranged. Can even a church be described as a collective good? All Swedish citizens contribute to the care of the legally protected churches, primarily through the tax-based church heritage compensation. Furthermore, it is the intention of both the state and the Church of Sweden that everyone should have access to the church buildings and most of the churches have automatic legal protection. The church building itself and the church space should thus be perceived as a public good, with the restriction that the parish owns and disposes of the building.

Concerning surveys of the attitudes to the use of an individual church, at the time of writing this article, there is only one known Swedish case. It is a questionnaire that in 2010 was sent out to all households in Åtvidaberg municipality about the significance of Åtvid's great church. The future of the church was uncertain because the adjacent old church had long served as the parish's main church and the newer church was used to a small extent. The survey was designed by architect Catarina Sternudd at Lund University in collaboration with the parish, Linköping diocese, the county administrative board, the County Museum in Östergötland and the Church of Sweden at the national level. The response rate can be measured in different ways, but of the urban residents over the age of 20, 40 percent had answered the survey, which appears to be a relatively high frequency (Sternudd, 2010, p. 8). According to Sternudd, the survey clearly showed that the respondents are involved in the church building and want it to remain in place. The church in its surroundings and with its location is valued as a great asset.

A study that shows that the management of an individual church may be deficient in terms of public participation is *Local voices and local values* by Wera Grahn, at the time of the study senior researcher (associate professor) at the state research organization NIKU in Norway. In Norwegian Ålgård, there had been a struggle for some years as to whether the local chapel church should be demolished or not. The study examines why people, who rarely or never go to church, suddenly struggle for its preservation when it is threatened with demolition, what the church means to them and what values those who are not believers or active in church life attribute to it. The study was conducted using a qualitative method in the form of in-depth interviews with ten people. The interviews revealed a variety of meanings and local values in the material cultural heritage that are rarely expressed by the heritage experts who usually establish value assessments. According to Grahn, these values are not considered important in professional assessments, as only expert knowledge counts. But by avoiding problematizing the cultural heritage processes, one ignores the fact that the construction of historic environments is basically social. According to Grahn, if cultural heritage is to be important to a wider public, local values must be actively included and made visible in the assessments (Grahn, 2007, p. 23 f).

Similar conclusions are reached by Michael Turnpenny, Museum Development Manager at York Museums Trust:

> There is an implicit assumption within the system that significance is inherent in the fabric of the place. This approach presumes that assessments of significance can or should be entirely detached from the communities in which features are located. (Turnpenny, 2004, p. 297)

Turnpenny believes that in the cultural heritage sector it is often assumed that the cultural-historical value is materially inherent in the historic environment and that the value assessments can thus be presented as scientific or objective. Thus, the local, subjective and non-professional values are not recognized as true or authentic by the experts, nor are they integrated into the assessments. According to Turnpenny, this is reinforced by the fact that the local actors' participation in the valuation and management process is not regulated by law. The result is that the value assessments, rather than being "objective" assessments of the total value, become accounts of the professionals' own values and ideologies. The attitude towards cultural heritage management is therefore exclusive instead of inclusive, which can lead to the public becoming alienated from cultural heritage (ibid., pp. 295– 307).

The studies of Wera Grahn and Michael Turnpenny provide a rather pessimistic picture of the possibility of finding working models and increasing participation in cultural heritage work. But there may be solutions. During the years 1998–2005, the *Research on the Values of Heritage* project at the Getty Conservation Institute, USA, was performed, with Marta de la Torre, then head of the institute's Training Program, as project manager. In a project report, Randall Mason, now Professor of Historic Preservation at the University of Pennsylvania, described the conditions for a broader and more democratic assessment of cultural heritage and historic environments (places of cultural significance). The management of the environments is based on the cultural values that have been assessed and Mason's method can be seen as a modernization and further development of the principles in *The Burra Charter*. The model has influenced the Church of Sweden's national evaluation of the church heritage characterizations (Mason, 2002, especially Figs. 1 and 2, pp. 6–7, which have been translated and modified somewhat in Lindblad, 2010d, pp. 14, 19, and in Lindblad, 2014, p. 291).

7 Participation in the Church's Cultural Heritage Work

As stated above, during the years 2007–2010, the Church of Sweden's national level carried out the project *Evaluation and development of characterizations and priorities*. One purpose was to compile and evaluate the cultural-historical characterizations and values assessments made of the Church of Sweden's church buildings and historic environments. However, the final goal of the project was more far-reaching, namely, to establish recommended, established and implemented models of the Church of

Sweden's national level for assessment and prioritization of ecclesiastical cultural historic values. Furthermore, the value assessments "should be living documents with the parish involved in the valuation work" and the cultural values "integrated in the management of the ecclesiastical cultural heritage" (Lindblad, 2010c, p. 3).

The first report of the evaluation project focuses on the cultural-historical characterizations carried out by the majority of the Church of Sweden's churches and on the scope, accessibility, structure, content and usability of the characterizations.

The second report provides a review and comparative analysis of a number of principles and models for valuation, ranking and prioritization of cultural heritage. It states that the different steps of the value assessments are insufficiently defined and that there are shortcomings in the participation of different actors, both in the production of the value assessments and in their use.

Therefore, the project's third report provides a review and analysis of principles and methods for a more holistic perspective and increased public participation in value assessments and management planning. The interim report also discusses methods for integrating defined values in the management process.

A probable reason for the lack of participation in the examined characterizations is that, by analogy with Michael Turnpenny's reasoning, it is the traditional expert-assessed, usually materially based art and architectural historical values that are considered important. Local and intangible values that may be related to the church environment and church spaces have not been considered sufficiently "scientific" or "objective". It also seems likely that many of the heritage experts did not have knowledge of them.

Why were the characterizations designed in this way? One reason is that it is usually art historians or historic building officers who have carried out the work with the characterizations, which has led to other perspectives or subject areas such as aesthetics, ethnology, theology and sociology being partially or completely absent. When the work with characterizations of Church of Sweden's churches began around 2002, there was also no developed Swedish methodology that focused on a broader cultural heritage assessment, where for example social values were included or where different stakeholders were expected to participate in the valuation work. It is also probable that the issue of participation had not had a sufficient impact on the authorities and institutions that prepared and applied guidelines for cultural heritage valuation. It may have been about insufficient knowledge, lack of time and commitment to the issue and also about a fear of sharing the work with value assessments—and thus diminishing the professional authority and power of the heritage expert. The project's final report therefore proposes a methodology that aims to increase participation in the valuation and management of cultural heritage and historic environments. The most important steps in this work process are stakeholder analysis, inclusive value assessments, communication and integration of the values in the heritage management (Lindblad, 2010d, p. 9).

Several of the consultative bodies that commented on the project's reports expressed that they were too academic in their approach and that the reasoning was too theoretical to be used in daily activities. Therefore, the church office aimed to develop a practically useful method based on the principles developed in the evaluation project, which in turn are based on the Burra Charter and Randall Mason's models. However, the project was closed before it was completed and the guidelines were never published. The reason for this failure is complex, but it is likely to be, at least partially, due to insufficient professional resources and competence and even lack of will of the Church's national level to invest time and staff resources in the project. However, the main reason might be the harsh criticism expressed by the Swedish National Heritage board, which simultaneously was developing a clearly more expert driven method for assessing heritage values. By reducing and finally closing the project, the Church's National level avoided a conflict with an important organization in the heritage sector, which also had the ambition to be leading actor and expert body in assessing heritage values (Lindblad and Wetterberg, 2017).

After the closure of the national project, other development projects have been initiated, inspired by the national project but managed at diocese and local levels. Being closer to the daily life and activities of the parishes, these projects seem to have been more successful with useful recommendations for assessing and managing values by the core communities and other stakeholders in order to keep the ecclesiastical heritage living, useful and accessible for all citizens (Lindblad, 2019).

8 Conclusion

The right to participate in cultural heritage work can be regarded as an aspect of cultural heritage as a human right, expressed in the European Council's *Faro Convention* of 2005. This view of the cultural heritage is based on the *International Covenant on Economic, Social and Cultural Rights* (1966) and ultimately on the United Nations' *Universal Declaration of Human Rights* (1948), which states that everyone has the right to take part in the cultural life of society.

The protection and preservation of cultural heritage is a prerequisite for the fulfilment of people's right to cultural heritage. It is about managing resources that benefit society and the individual. The *Historic Environment Act* and the church heritage compensation, both of which are primarily focused on the protection and preservation of the ecclesiastical cultural heritage values, can thus be seen as tools for the goal that everyone can take part in the Church's cultural heritage. This is valid providing that the law is not applied so strictly that the churches become too difficult to use and thus inaccessible or impossible to preserve. A few years ago, a declaration of purpose was introduced in the introduction of the *Historic Environment Act*: "The aim of the provisions in this Act is to ensure current and future generations have access to a diverse range of cultural heritage". This could be regarded as a first step in a development where, in addition to being a protection or obligation law, the *Historic Environment Act* is regarded as a rights law. A reasonable consequence of *The Faro Convention* and the *International Covenant on Economic, Social and Cultural Rights* could be that the ecclesiastical cultural heritage, which, by being protected by the *Historic Environment Act*, could be considered as common cultural heritage, needs to be accessible so that everyone can take part in it. The closure, privatization, demolition or otherwise inaccessibility of common and public ecclesiastical heritage may mean that people's right to this cultural heritage is not fulfilled. Although not contrary to current legislation, it hardly seems compatible with the perception of culture and heritage expressed in international conventions and the purpose of the *Historic Environment Act*. It is thus possible to conclude that the best prerequisite for the ecclesiastical cultural heritage to be accessible and that all who wants can participate in the work of preserving, using and developing them is that they are still owned by the Church of Sweden or by other public actors.

Participation in the church's cultural heritage is not only about the right to access the churches but also to participate in a broader cultural heritage process that includes managing cultural heritage values. The Church of Sweden's evaluation of cultural-historical characterizations, or statements of significance, found that parishes and other stakeholders were not sufficiently involved in the identification and management of ecclesiastical cultural values. Consequently, the characterizations and the values described in them are not seen as resources for the Church's activities or as a basis for decisions. The failure of providing national guidelines for valuing ecclesiastical cultural heritage demonstrates the complexity of the issue and also the ongoing struggle for power of the rights to heritage assessment and management. If the Swedish government ultimately decides to ratify the *Faro Convention*, it can provide a strong support for the work with increased participation in the ecclesiastical cultural heritage as well as in the country's other historic environments. Whether this work will be led by the state agencies or by the different levels at the Church of Sweden, is still an open question. Hopefully and if these actors can ignore their prestige, it can be performed by all parties together.

References

Barthel-Bouchier, D. (2014). *Cultural heritage and the challenge of sustainability*. Walnut Creek, CA: Left Coast Press.

The Burra Carter. The Australia ICOMOS Charter for Places of Cultural Significance. (2013). Australia ICOMOS Incorporated International Council on Monuments and Sites. http://australia.icomos.org/wp-content/uploads/The-Burra-Charter-2013-Adopted-31.10.2013.pdf. Accessed 30 July 2020.

Code on the Ethics of Co-existence in Conserving Significant Places. (1998). Australia ICOMOS. https://australia.icomos.org/wp-content/uploads/Code-on-the-Ethics-of-Co-existence.pdf. Accessed 30 July 2020.

Convention for the Safeguarding of the Intangible Cultural Heritage. (2003). UNESCO. https://ich.unesco.org/en/convention. Accessed 30 July 2020.

Council of Europe Framework Convention on the Value of Cultural Heritage for Society. Faro, *27.X.2005.* https://www.coe.int/en/web/conventions/full-list/-/conventions/rms/0900001680083746. Accessed 30 July 2020.

Dolff-Bonekämper, Gabi (2012). "The social and spatial frameworks of heritage-What is new in the Faro Convention?". In *Heritage and Beyond*, pp 69–74. Strasbourg: Council of Europe Publishing.

Ett rum öppet för alla. Svenska kyrkans redovisning till regeringen angående de kyrkoantikvariska frågorna inför kontrollstationen 2014 (2013). Uppsala: Trossamfundet Svenska kyrkan.

European Landscape Convention. (2000). Council of Europe. https://www.coe.int/en/web/conventions/full-list/-/conventions/rms/0900001680080621. Accessed 30 July 2020.

Europeiska landskapskonventionen. Riksantikvarieämbetet. http://www.raa.se/om-riksantikvarieambetet/vart-internationel-la-arbete/europaradet/europeiska-landskapskonventionen/. Accessed 11 March 2016.

Explanatory Report to the Council of Europe Framework Convention on the Value of Cultural Heritage for Society. (2005). Council of Europe. https://rm.coe.int/16800d3814. Accessed 30 July 2020.

The Faro Convention. Report from the Swedish National Heritage Board (2014). https://historicengland.org.uk/content/docs/research/faro-conventionpdf/. Accessed 30 July 2020.

Grahn, W. (2007). *Lokala röster och lokala värden. En studie av Ålgårds kyrkas betydelse för ickekyrkogängare. [NIKU Rapport 20], Oslo: Stif-telsen Norsk institutt for kulturminneforskning.*

Historic Environment Act. (1988: 950). https://www.raa.se/in-english/cultural-heritage/historic-environment-laws/historic-environment-act-1988950/. Accessed 30 July 2020.

Kulturmiljöarbete i en ny tid. (2012). [SOU 2012:37]. Kulturmiljöutredningen. Stockholm: Fritze.

Kulturmiljöns mångfald. Regeringens proposition 2012/13:96. Stock-holm: Regeringen. https://www.riksdagen.se/sv/dokument-lagar/dokument/proposition/kulturmiljons-mangfald_H00396. Accessed 30 July 2020.

Kulturpolitik. Regeringens proposition 1996/97:3. https://www.regeringen.se/contentassets/e1620c6c381145c5adf8a1dedf4cdfaa/kulturpolitik. Accessed 30 July 2020.

Kyrkoordning för Svenska kyrkan. (2015). Svenska kyrkan. http://www.svenskakyrkan.se/kyrkoordningen. Accessed 30 July 2020.

"Kyrkor säljs ut". (2013). *SVT Väst* 2015-05-14. http://www.svt.se/nyheter/regionalt/vast/kulturarv-till-hogstbjudande. Accessed 30 July 2020.

Lindblad, H. (2010a). *Utvärdering och utveckling av karaktäriseringar och prioriteringar. Delrapport 1.* [Dnr Ks 2010/0633], Uppsala: Svenska kyrkan 2009, 2010.

Lindblad, H. (2010b). *Värderingar och prioriteringar. Delrapport 2.* [Dnr Ks 2010/0633], Uppsala: Svenska kyrkan 2009, 2010.

Lindblad, H. (2010c). *Delaktighet i värdering och förvaltning av det kyrkliga kulturarvet. Delrapport 3.* [Dnr Ks 2010/0633], Uppsala: Svenska kyrkan.

Lindblad, H. (2010d). *Slutsatser och rekommendationer. Slutrapport till projektet Utvärdering och utveckling av karaktäriseringar och pririteringar.* Uppsala: Svenska kyrkan 2009, 2010.

Lindblad, H. (2014). Delaktighet och förvaltning av det kyrkliga kulturarvet. In E. Karlsmo, J. Lindblad, & H. Widmark (Eds.), *De kyrkliga kulturarven. Aktuell forskning och pedagogisk utveckling* (pp. 287–293). [Arcus sacri 1], Uppsala: Acta Univer-sitatis Upsaliensis.

Lindblad, H. (2019). *Preserve, use and develop—International conference on ecclesiastical heritage and its future challenges Conference report,* Diocese of Lund. https://www.frh-europe.org/cms/wp-content/uploads/2019/01/Conference-Report_PUD.pdf. Accessed 30 July 2020.

Lindblad, H., & Wetterberg, O. (2017). Delat ansvar (Shared Responsibility). In M. Hillström, E. Löfgren, O. Wetterberg (eds), *Alla dessa kyrkor. Kulturvård, religion och politik* (pp. 183–202). Göteborgs universitet.

Mason, R. (2002). Assessing values in conservation planning: Methodological issues and choices. In M. de la Torre (Ed.), *Assessing the values of cultural heritage. Research report* (pp. 5–30). Los Angeles: The Getty Conservation Institute.

Olsson, K. (2003). *Från bevarande till skapande av värde. Kulturmiljövården i kunskapssamhället.* Stockholm: KTH.

Olsson, K., & Berglund, E. (2012). *Medborgare, kulturmiljö och planering. Ett kvantitativt arbetssätt på medborgardeltagande.* Stockholm: Riksantikvarieämbetet.

Överenskommelse mellan staten och Svenska kyrkan i frågor som rör de kulturhistoriska värdena inom Svenska kyrkan (2000). [Ku2000/470/Ka]. Regeringskansliet: Kulturdepartementet.

Överklagande av beslut angående tillstånd till ändring av Caroli kyrka i Malmö, fattat av länsstyrelsen i Skåne län den 10 december 2014 i ärende med diarienummer 433-2859-2014 (2014). Riksantikvarieämbetet.

Remiss avseende Riksantikvarieämbetets rapport om Farokonventionen – Europarådets ramkonvention om kulturarvets samhälleliga värde. (2015). [Dnr. 101-6296-2015]. Länsstyrelsen Stockholm. https://www.regeringen.se/49db84/contentassets/b7b4a2a20b9e424dbee0f1bedf58c6c5/lansstyrelsen-i-stockholms-lan.pdf. Accessed 30 July 2020.

Staten och trossamfunden – begravningsverksamheten, kulturminnena, personalen, avgiftsbetalningen, m.m. (1998). Regeringens proposition 1998/99:38. https://www.regeringen.se/49bb8e/contentassets/c4fd748e806c47df87ff9e736e3ee3fe/staten-och-trossamfunden—begravningsverksamheten-kulturminnena-personalen-avgiftsbetalningen-m.m. Accessed 30 July 2020.

Sternudd, C. (2010). *Vad ska hända med Åtvids stora kyrka? Rapport från enkätundersökning 2010.* Lund: Lunds universitet.

Towards Future Heritage Management. The Swedish National Heritage Board's Environmental Scanning Report (2006). http://samla.raa.se/xmlui/bitstream/handle/raa/54/9789172094581.pdf?sequence=1&isAllowed=y. Accessed 30 July 2020.

Tid för kultur. (2009). Regeringens proposition 2009/10:3. https://www.regeringen.se/contentassets/5afd813ffae94dae91e9db0f8725c3b6/tid-for-kultur-prop.-2009103. Accessed 30 July 2020.

Turnpenny, M. (2004). Cultural Heritage, an Ill-defined Concept? A Call for Joined-up Policy. *International Journal of Heritage Studies, 10*(3), 295–307.

Underbart kapell till salu – exakt så här vill vi bo (missa inte köket). (2015). *Sköna hem*, 15 May 2015. https://skonahem.com/inredning/badrum/norrmannebo-610-underbart-kapell-till-salu/. Accessed 30 July 2020.

The Universal Declaration of Human Rights. (1948). United Nations. https://www.un.org/en/universal-declaration-human-rights/. Accessed 30 July 2020.

International Covenant on Civil and Political Rights (1966). United Nations. https://www.ohchr.org/EN/ProfessionalInterest/Pages/CCPR.aspx. Accessed 20 February 2021.

Waterton, E., Smith, L., & Campbell, G. (2006). The utility of discourse analysis to heritage studies: The Burra charter and social inclusion. *International Journal of Heritage Studies, 12*(4), 339–355.

Yttrande över Riksantikvarieämbetets rapport Farokonventionen – Europarådets ramkonvention om kulturarvets samhälleliga värde. [LED 2015/88]. DO, Diskrimineringsombudsmannen. https://www.regeringen.se/49db83/contentassets/b7b4a2a20b9e424dbee0f1bedf58c6c5/diskrimineringsombudsmannen.pdf. Accessed 30 July 2020.

Yttrande över Riksantikvarieämbetets rapport Farokonventionen – Europarådets ramkonvention om kulturarvets samhälleliga värde. [Ks 2015/0281]. Svenska kyrkan. https://www.regeringen.se/49cb50/contentassets/b7b4a2a20b9e424dbee0f1bedf58c6c5/svenska-kyrkan.pdf. Accessed 30 July 2020.

Curzio Malaparte's War Novels in Poland: Then and Now

Małgorzata Ślarzyńska

Abstract The paper analyses the reception of Curzio Malaparte's novels *Kaputt* (1944) and *La pelle* (*The Skin*; 1949) in Poland and its relation to the problem of war and cultural heritage. Firstly, it describes the impact of the political situation in the 1960s in Poland on the reception of *Kaputt* and it examines the late reception of *The Skin* in Poland. Secondly, it focuses on the recent reception of Malaparte's novels in a spectacle *Capri—the Island of the Fugitives* (*Capri – wyspa uchodźców*; 2019) by a Polish stage director Krystian Lupa and shows how Malaparte's novels reread today in the light of new cultural paradigms can contribute to the analysis of the problem of war and conflict in a broader contemporary perspective.

1 Introduction

Curzio Malaparte's presence in Poland can be traced back to 1919 when he came to Warsaw as a member of Italian diplomatic mission (Bruni, 2017; Serra, 2012). For a year he had an opportunity to observe the political formation of a country that had just regained its independency after more than 100 years of being partitioned, as well as stay in contact with Polish and Italian cultural and political circles. The Tuscan writer came back to Poland for the second time in 1942 as a war correspondent and Italian officer, and that visit became crucial to his novel *Kaputt* (1944), a big part of which he dedicated to Poland under Nazi occupation.

Kaputt was a fundamental point of reference in world literature after the World War II and gained popularity in many countries, translated e.g. into English, German, French, Spanish, Dutch, Estonian, Romanian and Japanese. Similarly, his other novel *La pelle* (1949; *The Skin*), dedicated to American presence in Italy in the final years of the World War II, proved its importance by numerous translations and its significant presence in other countries. To these novels and their presence in the Polish context will be dedicated this article. One, however, must remember that Malaparte

M. Ślarzyńska (✉)
WNH Uniwersytet Kardynała Stefana Wyszyńskiego, Warsaw, Poland
e-mail: m.slarzynska@uksw.edu.pl

O. Niglio and E. Y. J. Lee (eds.), *Transcultural Diplomacy and International Law in Heritage Conservation*, https://doi.org/10.1007/978-981-16-0309-9_6

confronted the subject of war also in his other writings, such as *Viva Caporetto!* (1921) written after World War I (on this subject see: De Paulis, 2019).

In *Kaputt* and *The Skin* Malaparte introduces the theme of war as an apocalyptical situation that signalled the end of a certain epoque and involved in its destructive theatre all living creatures, from human beings to animals and nature. Malaparte had a direct experience of war, when as a young man he took part in the battles of the World War I, and then worked as a correspondent on Eastern front during World War II (Serra, 2012; Martellini, 1997). Throughout his life he never remained indifferent to political questions, assuming a defined attitude to the surrounding reality, although his political stand varied.

In the early years he adhered to the fascist movement and became an important person in Mussolini's circle, with whom he subsequently entered in an open conflict and was confined to the island of Lipari. Although during the World War II he initially worked for fascist journals, later his political position changed, and he started to criticize the regime. His war reports from Eastern Europe may be considered of fundamental importance among others published in Italy (Bruni, 2018: 315). After the war, he returned to his modernistic mansion in Capri where he finished his novels *Kaputt* and *The Skin* which brought him international fame and, in case of the latter, caused scandal in Italy. Tired of the constant accuses of his fascist past in Italy, he moved for several years to France, in the same time trying to work in the field of theatre and cinema. Finally, he adopted a communist point of view, after a trip to China before his death in 1957.

In Poland, although Malaparte in the 1960s became an object of literary debate due to the publication of *Kaputt*, it was not until recently that he re-emerged, and his novels once again attracted attention, as did his life (Ślarzyńska, 2019). The reason for this situation was a monumental spectacle by Krystian Lupa *Capri—the Island of Fugitives* (*Capri – wyspa uciekinierów*), staged in 2019 in Warsaw, based on the two novels: *Kaputt* and *The Skin*. The spectacle was widely commented not only for its high artistic merit but also for the way it incorporates Malaparte's texts, by application of a modern theoretical perspective. Nevertheless, along with reintroducing the novels of the Tuscan writer in Poland, it also promotes a strong and universal anti-war message that stems from Malaparte's experience of World War II in Europe. The war that posed into question our qualities as human beings, as we proved to be capable of any kind of cruelty against one another and against the nature. The war, at last, that cannot be forgotten, since its basic matrix can be traced in many other contemporary experiences.

This article will examine Malaparte's presence in Poland from the perspective of cultural value of his war novels *Kaputt* and *The Skin* that when read in the light of new cultural paradigms, become the heritage of all people.

2 *Kaputt* and *the Skin* in Poland

Studying translation and its history can be illuminating not only by showing what there is, but also by bringing to the light what there is not. As Jeroen Vandaele said: "translation allows us to study what does *not* exist in a given system, although it could in principle have existed. Translation is a means to study the *non-dit*, the cultural unsaid" (Vandaele, 2010: 89). In this perspective, in the case of *Kaputt* and *The Skin*, it is interesting to see both what, where and when *was* published, just as what, where and when *was not* published and remained unsaid. It is also worth to ask why.

A part of the novel *Kaputt*, particularly the chapters "The Mice": "God shave the king" and "Forbidden Cities", was dedicated to the situation in Poland under Nazi occupation. These fragments were found so important by their first Polish readers that their Polish translation was published even a few months before the first Italian edition of the book (Malaparte, 1944b), in 1944, in *Orzeł Biały* [White Eagle], a Polish periodical published abroad (Malaparte, 1944a). However, a long time had to pass until the integral translation of *Kaputt* was released in Poland.

After the end of the World War II Poland passed under Soviet influence and thus an institutionalized censorship was introduced in Poland in 1945 (Romek, 2000; Łęcicki, 2016: 152–153). Censorship affected not only press and information but also literary fiction, written in Polish, as well as translations. Although the Polish parts of *Kaputt* could have been highly interesting for a Polish reader, Malaparte was not particularly welcomed in the post-war Poland. One of the reasons was the cultural line introduced by the Polish United Workers' Party (PZPR), according to which there was a strong predilection towards literature from the USSR and the Eastern Bloc while the Western literature was valued mainly if it denigrated the Western world. The other reason might be the fascist past of Malaparte that influenced his image in the country where after the War all possible references to Nazism and fascism were strictly forbidden. A relatively important opening towards the Western literature took place in 1956 along with the October crisis and so-called Polish thaw (Granville, 2001; Kemp-Welch, 2006; Orłowski, 1988: 270–286; Lasowy-Pudło, 2010: 88; Ślarzyńska, 2017: 51–63). The other factor that increased interest in Malaparte's writings in that time was his death in 1957 which was commented in Polish press and literature (Szwarcenberg-Czerny, 1957: 5; Breza, 1960). It was in those years that fragments of *Kaputt* in Polish translation started to be published frequently in the press, mostly in a very popular magazine *Przekrój*. The growing interest in the novel resulted finally in its first publication as a book, in 1962 (Malaparte, 1962), translated by Barbara Sieroszewska. *Kaputt* soon became an object of a heated debate in Poland.

The book was immediately commented in the official press of the PZPR, in a weekly newsmagazine *Polityka* (Michałowska, 1963). The key point underlined in the generally highly favourable article was Malaparte's detachment from fascism (Michałowska, 1963: 1) that rendered his works publishable. *Kaputt* was seen as the essence of war. War, in the first place, was interpreted as an event that could be related to the experience of a given nation, and in this perspective *Kaputt* seemed to be closer to Polish experience than the books of "the Americans" (Michałowska,

1963: 6) that were not seen particularly well even after the thaw. Secondly, war was interpreted as an experience universal to all humanity, and Malaparte turned out to present it in a compelling and broad way, capable to see the war "in the landscape, in the women's smile, in the cruelty and the happiness, he sees how the war embrace all the human life and transforms it in a new quality that conceals abysses which can be looked at by a human's eye only in a short flash, as long as there is no indifference and inertia that turn a man of peace into a man of war"[1] (Michałowska, 1963: 6). The titles of Malaparte's texts are cited in Polish or in French (even *La Peau*) which might be a sign of French mediation in the reception of *Kaputt*. Michałowska (1963: 7) calls the publication of *Kaputt* "a great event in Polish culture". The review in an opinion-forming magazine was important but did not spare the book some critique (Koźniewski, 1963: 5; Linowska-Marchocka, 1963: 1). After all, though, the first edition of *Kaputt* in Poland was a great success and had a very high circulation of over 20,000 copies sold out almost immediately (Zieliński, 1963: 322). It became a source of a heated debate in the press and a must-read position for numerous readers for whom the memory of hideous war experiences was still fresh. The readers could not be fully aware of some changes in the body of the book, the effect of the censorship that eliminated certain fragments that could not be accepted for political reasons.

The translation was republished in 1983, in the same version. The 1983 edition did not raise as vast an interest as the previous one but still attracted some attention. Another factor that spurred the interest in Malaparte's text in that time was the Italian film *La pelle* by Liliana Cavani that also in Poland some critics managed to watch (Kydryński, 1983: 10; Mętrak, 1983: 5).

Only in 2000 a new and integral edition of *Kaputt* was published. It was its first integral publication without intervention of censorship: the institutionalized system of control was eliminated as a consequence to the general change of political system in 1989. The book composed of the earlier translation of Barbara Sieroszewska was combined with the parts previously absent, translated by Joanna Ugniewska. The passages previously eliminated varied in its length and importance but nonetheless their former absence could be explained by political reasons. On that basis one can see how the extratextual questions related to the current geopolitical situation of Poland influenced the content of this novel that, given its subject, should have been treated with particular attention. One of the fragments cut out entirely in the first and second editions of *Kaputt* referred to ideological questions related to Marxism (conf. Malaparte, 1962; 2000: 251). It might have been perceived as denigrating and problematic, since it might have been read as showing possible criminal consequences of radical interpretation of Marxist thought:

> And he told us what had occurred a little time ago in Turku, the Finnish city on the Gulf of Bothnia. A Soviet parachutist who had dropped near the city was captured and locked up in the Turku prison. He was about thirty years old, a workman in a factory in Kharkov and a fervid communist. Being of a thoughtful turn of mind, he seemed not only interested in but also well informed about many subjects, particularly ethics. He was obviously better read than most *udarniki* or *stakhanovtzi*. In his cell the prisoner read extensively, choosing books on religious subjects that the governor of the prison, who was interested in so strange and

[1] All translations hereafter are mine, if not stated otherwise.

> complex a human specimen, allowed him to take out of his private library. Naturally, the prisoner was a materialist and an atheist.
>
> After a time he was given work as a mechanic in the prison factory. One day he asked to have a talk with a clergyman. A young Lutheran pastor, highly esteemed for his learning and piety, and famous as a preacher, went to the prison and was taken into the cell of the Soviet paratrooper. For nearly two hours the two men were locked up together alone in the cell. At the end of this long talk, when the pastor rose to leave, the prisoner placed his hands on the pastor's shoulders and, after a moment of hesitation, embraced him. Later, these details were printed in the Turku papers.
>
> A few weeks went by, and the prisoner, who for days had appeared to be tortured by secret and painful thoughts, asked again to be allowed to see the pastor, who went to the prison and, as on the previous occasion, was locked up with the communist in his cell. About half an hour went by, when a jailer walking outside heard a shriek and a call for help. He unlocked the cell and saw the prisoner standing against the wall and the pastor lying at his feet in a pool of blood. Before he died, the pastor revealed that at the end of their conversation the prisoner had embraced him and, while his arms were around him, had stabbed him in the back with a sharp iron file. In the course of the trial the murderer declared during his examination that he had killed the pastor because his communist and atheist mind was troubled by the weight of the clergyman's reasonings. He was sentenced to death and shot.
>
> "He had tried", concluded Bengt von Törne, "to kill God in the pastor".
>
> The story of that murder, which appeared in all the Finnish papers, had deeply stirred public opinion. Lieutenant Gummerus, the son of a former Minister of Finland in Rome told me that the commander of the firing squad, a Turku officer who was a friend of his, had been greatly impressed by the murderer's serenity.
>
> "He had made peace with his conscience", said de Foxá.
>
> "But this is horrible!" exclaimed Countess Mannerheim. "How can anyone conceive of the idea of killing God?" (Malaparte, 2005)

In Polish wide-read first version of the novel this fragment is omitted, and the dialogue of the characters swiftly goes on, covering the void by uniting the lines that originally come before and after the fragment:

> – Największym problemem współczesnym jest jednak wciąż jeszcze problem religijny – rzekł Bengt von Törne. – *On ne peut pas tuer Dieu*, Boga nie da się zabić.
>
> – Cały świat współczesny usiłuje zabić Boga – odezwał się Agah Aksel. (Malaparte, 1962; conf. Malaparte, 2000: 305–306)
>
> "The greatest problem of modern days is still the religious problem", said Bengt von Törne. "*On ne peut pas tuer le dieu*— God cannot be killed". [...]
>
> "The entire modern world is trying to kill God", said Agah Aksel. (Malaparte, 2005)

Thus, the intervention actually changes the plot, not only by mere elimination of the part that created problems from ideological point of view, but also by introduction of a dialogue between the characters that originally did not exchange those lines. The procedure of creating a version from the remaining parts into a kind of a seamless patchwork was common in those years when censorship was active (on interventions in Italian literature translations in Poland see Ślarzyńska, 2017). It is worth noting, though, that rarely any formal and institutional explanation of such elimination can be found, and nowadays we face nothing more than texts that differ. As Kuhiwczak (2009: 55) indicates, the instructions followed by the censors were never clear nor transparent. It is also good to remember that censorial cuts, caused by political systemic requirements, are not the only factor that can be interpreted as censorship (Looby, 2015: 7–12; Tymoczko, 2009: 30–38; Wolf, 2002: 45). Eliminations in translated text could be substantial, like the one described above, but they could also be minute and concern a structure of a sentence. For example, in the part dedicated to Poland from the chapter "The Mice" Bichette Radziwillowa has to flee from the occupied country during the war and by doing so, she has to wait for a train on a demolished station. In the meantime, she is talking with her friends telling them about her recent experiences "during her Odyssey across the territories occupied by the Russians and the Germans" (Malaparte, 2005). In Polish version the territories are simply "occupied", without specifying the aggressor: "niedole swojej wędrówki przez tereny okupowane" (Malaparte, 1962: 81). Historical narration in those time did not let the possibility to perceive Russians as aggressors. Censorship was also very aware not to let any possibility of comparison between the Germans and the Russians. Just as it was forbidden to compare in any way Nazism or fascism with communism, and Hitler or Mussolini with Stalin (see also Ślarzyńska, 2017: 178–189).

As far as the Polish reception of *The Skin* is concerned, fragments in Polish translation were published in the late 1950s and the 1960s in the press, particularly in *Przekrój*. Even though the public found the novel interesting and some of the critics from time to time emphasized the urgent need to translate it (Kydryński, 1983: 10), the novel was not published in Poland until the late 90s. In 1998 the book was translated by Jarosław Mikołajewski (Malaparte, 1998). As it was said, due to general political change in 1989 and abolishment of institutionalized censorship, literature in the 1990s ceased to depend on systemic political decisions. The text of *The Skin* in translation remained intact, as far as its content is concerned. The publication of *The Skin* however, did not attract as much attention as the preceding *Kaputt*. As one of the few contemporary commentators noted, it was no more the time when people were interested in Malaparte (Szczęsna, 1997: 10). Recently, though, *The Skin*, along with *Kaputt*, have come into light from the oblivion, and the war narrated by Malaparte once again has become an important point of reference.

3 Malaparte's War Novels in *Capri: The Island of the Fugitives*

In the autumn of 2019 in Warsaw, the spectacle *Capri—the Island of the Fugitives* based on Malaparte's novels *Kaputt* and *The Skin* and directed by a famous stage director Krystian Lupa was introduced in Powszechny Theatre in Warsaw. The spectacle is a unique proof of contemporary reception of Malaparte's *ouvre*. It was realized in a monumental form, with splendid scenography and six-hour duration, and as an important cultural event it attracted massive attention of spectators and theatrical critics (among many texts dedicated to the spectacle one can find e.g. Kopciński, 2019; Kuziak, 2020; Baniewicz, 2019; Katafiasz, 2020; Obarska, 2019).

In the programme of the spectacle the translation of Boyd Tonkin's *Self-love among the ruins* is included (Tonkin, 2019). The fact of choosing an English-language text to present the figure of Malaparte could be seen as a proof that once again Malaparte does not enter into Polish culture directly from Italy, but through a mediating culture, this time Anglo-American. The author of the text represents important literary circles and the text proves the international interest in the figure of Malaparte that could have been observed recently. Still, though, the information contained in the article is imprecise when it says that there is no accessible English edition of *Technique du coup d'état* (it would be worth noting that the book was translated into English and released in America in 1932). The presence of the article by Tonkin and the absence of a direct commentary from the field of Malaparte studies or from an Italian source shows also that the choice of his novels as a base for the spectacle was conditioned by the generally growing interest in his writings in the international context, and not by some individual inquiries in the field of Italian literature or a kind of a maverick act. Tonkin (2019: 23) himself points to the recent attention that Malaparte got from Margaret Atwood (2005) and Edmund White (2020) who expressed their admiration, sometimes mixed with abomination. Atwood's words, cited frequently as a praise of the book, efficiently render the intertwined emotions of appreciation and horror provoked by it: "*Kaputt* is a sad, astonishing, horrifying and lyrical book. It shows us the results of ideological fanaticism, racism, twisted values masquerading as spiritual purity, and the hatred of life, in their most personal and shameful aspects. It is essential for any human understanding of World War II" (Atwood, 2005).

Along with Lupa's habitual practice of providing various commentaries of his plays (Godlewski, 2019), also this time the spectacle is accompanied with his personal commentary in the form of diaries written during rehearsals, included in the programme. As he wrote in his diary in 2018, when the works on the spectacle were in progress (partially also on the Capri island), he was not sure where the evolving elaboration of the theme will finally take it and what will be the final structure of the play (Lupa, 2019: 16; Bollin & Lupa, 2019: 44–45).

Thus, the strange coil of emotions and of paths one can choose while reading and interpreting *Kaputt* and *The Skin* can also be observed in the way Lupa approached the novels in his play. However, one can find at least a few paths that seem to constitute the message of *Capri* and a few themes of Malaparte's novels that are accentuated in the play. Malaparte's war novels turn out to be useful to confront the themes of fascism, home, homosexuality, ecology and apocalypse.

4 Fascism Revisited

One of the major themes that seems to be a starting point for the artistic reflection in *Capri*, is the question of fascism (Lupa, 2019: 9; Cieślak and Lupa, 2019). As Lupa said, after the work in progress shows (the spectacle was shown to the public in an uncomplete form in July 2019, before its completion in autumn 2019): "Will this spectacle be a treatise on fascism, or will it have also other spaces? It is good when an artistic work has such spaces which are not recognized even by its author" (Bollin & Lupa, 2019: 45). The director underlines the necessity to remind about fascism constantly, to awake awareness of the fascist crimes—since fascism has never gone away, has never disappeared. It is a perspective still active in our times, it is "not a philosophical stand, nor a social ideology. Fascism may dress up various ideologies that depend on current social or political fashion" (Lupa, 2019: 19); "fascism as a Frankenstein" (Lupa, 2019: 16). That is why in this vision staging Malaparte's war novels nowadays should bring into question actual political issues, since the director does not conceal his deliberate gesture towards current situation in Poland and in Europe. Fascism is understood in this perspective widely, as an attitude of general intolerance of otherness, a climate of excessive regularity without respect to other viewpoints and other (human) beings. This general atmosphere, that can be easily overlooked by people living in it and gradually accustomed to its aggravation, is seen as the factor underlying and heralding any war situation.

Even though some Lupa's spectacles used to be criticized for a lack of precise timing and "genericness" of his adaptation (Błoński in Godlewski, 2019), this time the play is rather visibly contextualized in the World War II settings. The main part of the spectacle takes place in the World War II decorations, actors wearing the costumes reminding military uniforms and scenography vaguely referring to the war reality, e.g. in the scene taken from the second chapter of *Kaputt* ("The Mice") in ghetto in Warsaw in "Szczury – tryptyk Hansa Franka" ("The Mice – Hans Frank's Triptych"). In the same time, on the wall present in the scene one can read phrases referring to actual politics. While on the screen in one of the further episodes, scenes of war destruction in Aleppo are displayed. Thus, the time perspective regarding war in the spectacle oscillates and changes, and nothing remains linear.

The lack of linearity is one of the Lupa's main decisions as to the form of the play. He decides to focus rather on "situational stains" (Lupa, 2019: 16), stains of thought associated together by the reflection on fascist mentality. These non-linear units are based on *Kaputt* and *The Skin* but go beyond these textual limits and involve the mythical Malaparte's mansion on Capri Island as a text of culture. This perspective lets focus the attention on other works of art related to this object and, thus, the spectacle begins with a reference to the film *Le Mépris* (*Contempt*) by Jean-Luc Godard. Godard and Fritz Lang become the characters in the scene and open citations from the film (with Odysseus pointing into clear horizon and claiming to see Ithaca, and with Prokosh and Camille killed in a car accident) are shown on the screen.

5 Jungian Archetypes: Home and Warrior

Various interpretational paths that are activated through different associations with Casa Malaparte and Malaparte's novels involve two other major areas that in this perspective emerge from assuming war as a subject. The first one is the destruction and various attempts of reconstruction of home: as a concept that organizes the reality and as a material structure. The second one, is the archetype of man as a warrior that Lupa tries to deconstruct and that is blamed for bringing the catastrophe to the world.

War is a situation when all structures that organize life get subverted, questioned and destroyed. Home is a basic and fundamental structure that provides shelter and gives stability. From the beginning of the spectacle one can assume that this structure will be taken into question, which is visually confirmed by a video of Casa Malaparte, a cold and strange construction that is far from a standard image of a cozy house. In the same time the same construction can be perceived as a new kind of shelter, the only possible shelter for the outcasts that try to hide from the permanent war outside: "Island and house on the island. Sanctuary, refuge. We are running away from the state, from the religion, from the dictatorship [...]. Outside there is an indefinite war, it is hard to tell if it is first, second or third war" (Lupa, 2019: 7). As Lupa points out, Capri was the place that attracted those who sought isolation: from Tiberius to Axel Munthe and Malaparte (Lupa, 2019: 7; Bollin & Lupa, 2019: 45). This perspective harmonizes with Lupa's previous spectacles in which he created situations of exile and asylum (Kopciński, 2019: 9).

Home can be interpreted as one of the Jungian archetypes, as an element related to the spiritual development of man, "opus magnum alchemicum" (Lupa, 2019: 29). The search for home, search of the mode to organize the reality from the beginning after the destruction, is also related in the spectacle with the initial figure of Odysseus in Godard's film. Odysseus, the great mythical figure of Warrior, gazes into the clear horizon claiming to see Ithaca. Perhaps the Warrior will no longer be able to be an efficient leader and to set the frames for a new safe home. The figure proved his inadequateness and is no longer able to respond to the needs of the new reality.

The figure of a Warrior can be read also in a Jungian key, as an archetype representing masculinity. The perspective assumed in the spectacle focuses on the negative traits of the figure (even though in Jung's interpretation this figure bore also constructive and positive traits). The Warrior is the one who represents masculinity in its aggressive and destructive aspect. Lupa connects it with the civilization prior to the World War II and in some way accuses the ethos of unrestrained aggressive masculinity ("ethos of a knight") of having caused the war. After the war comes the time of the death of this ethos: "the death of the ethos of a man-knight that applied to the entire Jung's month (the Era of Pisces → before passing to the Era of Aquarius) → that is, during the period of Christian formation" (Lupa, 2019: 22). The world created according to the ethos of knight, of a warrior, in this perspective ended up with all the cruelties and degeneration of war. Through the horror of the World War II it proved itself to be full of lies, and ethical mistakes (Lupa, 2019: 22). Thus, the war might be interpreted as the final crisis of a wrongly perceived man formation, of culture based on masculine aggressiveness.

6 New Era and a New Man

The death of civilization that was called into question by Malaparte in *Kaputt* ("I prefer starting anew, rather than accepting everything as if it were an immutable heritage. Let us hope that the new era will really be new and that writers will enjoy liberty and respect", Malaparte, 2005), in the perspective adopted in *Capri* could be understood as the death of the Warrior/knight model and the beginning of a new world organized according to a new cultural paradigm, the formation of a "new man". The image of a new man, as Lupa perceives it, could be related to homosexuality (Lupa, 2019: 33). The programme of the spectacle encourages to reflect on the figure of *feminiello* and combines a citation from Malaparte's *The Skin* regarding *figliata* ritual with a translation of a fragment of Achille della Ragione's text "I feminielli" (Della Ragione, 2019).

Thus, homosexuality becomes an important theme explored in *Capri*, congruously with the positions already taken by Lupa in his previous spectacles (Godlewski, 2019; Kopciński, 2019: 9; Kościelniak 2015). The exploration of the theme of homosexuality has its basis in Malaparte's works. The writer associates it with the theme of war not only in *The Skin*, but also in *Mamma marcia*. According to his reflections, after the time of virile men that fought in war, the post-war period is the time of effeminate men. The narrator of *The Skin* critically observes the young effeminate men debating about communism in bourgeois surroundings (in the chapter "The Rose of Flesh"):

> And I asked myself in amazement how on earth my own robust, courageous, virile generation, a generation of men who had been moulded by war, by civil strife, by their resistance as individuals to the tyranny of dictators and of the mob, a masculine generation, not resigned to death and certainly not conquered, in spite of the humiliation and suffering of its defeat, had fathered a generation so corrupt, cynical and effeminate, so calmly and amiably despairing, a generation of which young men like Jeanlouis represented the flower, which bloomed on the extreme fringe of the consciousness of our time. (Malaparte, 1954: 86)

While in *Mamma marcia* Malaparte states:

> È un fatto che le generazioni che avevan venti anni nel 1900 o venti anni nel 1920 erano, sessualmente parlando, più sane, più normali, di quelle attuali. Nel 1900 l'omosessualità era circoscritta agli omosessuali. Nel 1920, essa era diventata un atteggiamento, una moda. Nel 1950 appare come uno spirito di rivolta, come un fatto sociale positivo, non negativo, come un'affermazione di vita, non come una negazione, come un'esigenza morale, insomma. [...] Il problema attuale dell'omosessualità giovanile mi ha preoccupato, e mi preoccupa, ed è uno tra i problemi moderni che mi attira e mi assorbe. (Malaparte, 1959: 259)
>
> [It's a fact that the generations that were twenty in the 1900 or twenty in the 1920 were, in the terms of sexuality, saner, more normal, than those actual. In the 1900 homosexuality was limited to the homosexuals. In the 1920 it became an attitude, a fashion. In the 1950 it appears to be a spirit of a rebellion, a positive social fact, not negative, an affirmation of life, not its negation, a moral exigence, in short. [...] I was, and I am preoccupied with the actual problem of homosexuality among the young, and it is one of the modern problems that attracts me and absorbs me.]

In *Mamma marcia* one can find a lot of Malaparte's reflections on this question, along with a whole chapter dedicated to the relation between sex and liberty (Malaparte, 1959: 281–322). Although it is difficult to define the writer's final view of the problem, even though he is surely interested in it and it becomes an object of his writings, for sure he does not take an openly favourable position. Lupa in his interpretation of *The Skin* associates the "new man", possibly homosexual (Lupa, 2019: 33), that would come after the war with the end of the myth of warrior and the subsequent positive change of the mankind (Mrozek & Lupa, 2019). Malaparte sees in the fall of the virile warrior model the end of the world he knew and even though rebuilding from the beginning after destruction is seen in a positive way, this particular change is something that he cannot fully understand or appreciate.

In Lupa's *Capri* the attention is brought to the homosexuality especially in the act entitled "Roses of flesh" (named after one of the chapters of *The Skin*, dedicated to Naples as a post-war capital of European homosexuality). One of the highly pictorial scenes presents a group of gays sit in the station of Naples. Another scene frequently commented in critical texts is dedicated to the ritual of *figliata*, described by Malaparte in *The Skin*. The ritual, which is derived traditionally from the Uranian secret cult, consists in staged childbirth by a man, namely by a *feminiello*. A man, accompanied by a group of witnessing *feminielli* deeply emotionally involved in the process, gives "birth" to a dysmorphic wooden figure of a boy with an enormous phallus. In the context of contemporary popular art, the ritual has recently attracted the attention of Ferzan Özpetek in his Italian film *Napoli velata* (*Naples in Vails*, 2017). Malaparte in *The Skin* (in the chapter "The Son of Adam") described his presumed taking part in the ritual as a witness together with his American friend Jack Hamilton. What is interesting in the light of our former reflections on the censorship of Malaparte's works, in the English translation the description of this ritual of "queer maternity" was censored (which has been already indicated, e.g. in Iovino, 2014: 107; Escolar, 2011; see Malaparte, 1954: 124–129; the first unexpurgated edition: Malaparte, 2013). The possibility of finding these passages too drastic to be published in the English version shows how the selection of this part may be perceived as controversial.

In Lupa's spectacle, the scene is very pronounced, and some read it even as its crucial part (Kopciński, 2019: 11). One of the characters incarnates a man that after painful labour gives birth to a wooden figure, sculptured in the form that exactly imitates the one described in *The Skin* (the sculpture was prepared for the use in *Capri* by Albert Kozak). It is worth noticing that the phallic element of the figure was censored in the English version of the novel:

> It had a very small, shapeless head, its arms were short, like those of a skeleton, with a swollen stomach. (Malaparte, 1954: 126)
>
> Il capo aveva piccolissimo e informe, le braccia corte e scheletriche, il ventre gonfio, enorme, e dal basso del ventre sporgeva un fallo di grossezza e di forma mai viste, quasi la testa di un fungo velenoso, rossa e sparsa di macchioline bianche. (Malaparte, 2010: 151)

Just as were the reactions of the "father" of the child (conf. Malaparte, 1954: 126; 2010: 151), and the scene of homosexual orgy (conf. Malaparte, 1954: 128; 2010: 153–154).

In Lupa's *Capri* the scene of *figliata* is staged with great emotions applied from the actors' part and with a careful representation of the elements accentuated in the novel. However, in one of the comments of the spectacle the scene is criticized for not following the Malaparte's factual description of the ritual which takes a rather distanced and analytical position towards the event: "Lupa excellently caught Malaparte's ironic allusions of to the evangelical description of Jesus's birth, however the same things that surprised the narrator of *The Skin*, fascinated him" (Kopciński, 2019: 11). The critic also points out that there is an added material in the scene (such as the verse: "They will kill us, old faggots") that was absent in Malaparte's novel. Thus, the scene might be perceived as a direct commentary on the current political situation in Poland where the question of gender and homosexuality has become a theme of actual political debate. Kopciński (2019: 11) questions the sense of the selection of the scene if it was meant to serve as a means to manifest the fear of fascistization of contemporary society. In this perspective, Lupa's interpretation could be read as his version of Malaparte's theme that distances itself from its original counterpart in *The Skin*, as far as its message is concerned. Such procedure would be nonetheless congruous with Lupa's own words that he hopes that *Capri* will not remain only "a reserve for the fragments from Malaparte" (Bollin & Lupa, 2019: 45). A different attitude towards the scene is adopted by Michał Kuziak who observes that the final of the scene can still be read as ironic. The scene of *figliata* is in fact broken by an abrupt abandonment of the ritual for the sake of spaghetti (Kuziak, 2020: 11), which is congruous with the scene presented in the novel. And thus, *spaghettata* takes place of *figliata*. In this perspective the ritual scene finally loses its solemnity and becomes less univocal.

7 Ecology and Nature

Irony as an important element of construction takes part in the negotiation of the spectacle meaning. War in Malaparte's novels is described in its full horror but at the same time, as it was said, the writer adopts a perspective of constructive possibilities that are offered by a new world that comes after the destruction of the old one. The question, related also with the possible general interpretation of *Capri*, is whether one is more prone to accept its positive or negative aspect. It is not so much the problem of accentuating the positive in this apocalyptical vision but of choosing the mere possibility of any constructive proposal. Otherwise, the message of the spectacle can as well be read as devoid of any possible positive project to humanity. As Kuziak (2020: 11) indicates, almost all ideological perspectives that can be seen as potentially constructive are in the end broken in *Capri* by their ironic echo. After *figliata* comes *spaghettata*, after seriously pronounced leftist ideological discourses comes *Mambo Italiano* song. The only voice that seems to sound clearly and is devoid of its ironical echo is the nature suffering and systematically destroyed by human actions.

In fact, one of the problems this spectacle tackles is the destruction of nature during the war that can be interpreted not only as World War II but as a general and incessant war that men wage against nature. Thus, ecology becomes another big theme raised in *Capri*. This decision may be perceived as perfectly harmonizing with the important role that animals and nature play in Malaparte's novels. The writer in fact entitled the chapters in *Kaputt* with the names of different kinds of animals. Horses, mice, dogs, birds, reindeers, flies serve as a great metaphor of narrated events and become thematized in the novel's plot.

In the spectacle none of the monumental episodes dedicated to animals in Malaparte's novels can be found, that is e.g. the horrifying scene of hundreds of horses frozen in the waters of Lake Ladoga (*Kaputt*) or dog Febo dying in a cruel experiment in an academical clinic (*The Skin*). However, the relation between men and nature reappears as one of its leading problems. Men's thoughtless cruelty towards nature unveils itself in various scenes, among which there can be found a narrated story of salmon hunting (the episode "Siegfried and the Salmon" from *Kaputt*) and numerous scenes of eating. Malaparte himself in his novels ahead of his times had given material to this modern interpretation of the problem of cruelty related to eating animals. *Capri* pulls this possible thread and stages the dinner by general Cork (*The Skin*) during which a particular dish is served: a fish that has visual traits of a siren or a little girl. The original silicone sculpture of siren was prepared for the use of the spectacle by Marta Mojanowska. The ethical question of eating the human body, that makes one on the characters ask a decent funeral for this poor cooked being, extends here on the ethical question of devouring other body in general. War causes extermination of men and animals, but incessant cruelty characterizes also the apparently peaceful post-war world.

In the light of contemporary paradigms of posthumanism can be read the fierce statement that concludes the extensive reflection on human cruelty in *Capri*. One of the female characters (previously incarnating Brigitte Bardot) in the final scene "Muzeum Czasu" ["Museum of Time"] claims that she no longer wants to be a part of human species. The apocalyptical perspective activated in this phrase is global: war not only brings the end of an old paradigmatic man-warrior but in the final outcome forces to ask the question of general sense of the survival of cruel mankind.

8 Apocalypse in the Global and Personal Perspective

Apocalyptical aspect in *Kaputt* and *The Skin* activates as the novels narrate the final of the old prewar world. Apocalyptical in *Capri* can be interpreted as representing both the end, the ruins of the world (war, material destruction) and of the end, the ruins of a man (senility). Apocalyptical in Malaparte can be related with "the end" understood in a more profound and extensive meaning, as the war he presents is a part of destiny, related to a mystery of existence (Turra, 2019: 39).

Kaputt used to be interpreted in this perspective also in a now-forgotten article of Stanisław Grochowiak, one of the most renowned twentieth-century Polish poets. Grochowiak (1963: 3) emphasizes dramatical potential of *Kaputt*, accentuating the dialogue between Principe Ruffo e Ministo Mameli in the third part of the novel "The Dogs":

> "È la fine del mondo" disse il secondo segretario, Principe Ruffo.
>
> "È un vero inferno" disse il Ministro Mameli accendendo una sigaretta.
>
> "Tutte le forze della natura si sono scatenate contro di noi" disse il primo segretario Guidotti. "Anche la natura è impazzita".
>
> "Non c'è nulla da fare" disse il Conte Fabrizio Franco. (Malaparte, 2009: 256)

The world described by Malaparte is the Shakespearian tragic world that went "out of joint", the world that lost its frames and is dying. Grochowiak compares it to a "Hitlerian lazarette" into which we are led by a guide that might be contagious himself. *Kaputt* makes him think of another Italian novel that became popular in Poland in those times: *Il gattopardo* (*The Leopard*) by Giuseppe Tomasi di Lampedusa. The comparison seems to be important as long as it also draws the possible reading of *Kaputt* out of the strict war perspective and shows its universal value as a book about the End.

The same mechanism is activated in *Capri*, which in some way becomes a play about the end of the world and the end of a man. Lupa in his diary mentions the post-war landscape of *The Skin* that transmits to the writer an enigmatic apocalyptic message (Lupa, 2019: 22). He also writes about the gradual atrophy of the world, perceived as a premonition before the arrival of the physical end, contained in the vision of dead bodies that pulls Malaparte together with them into a grave (Lupa, 2019: 35). The gradual fading away of the world, before it will finally fade away materially, is a general vision contained in *Kaputt* and *La pelle*.

Fading away relates to the theme of aging and senility that in the spectacle is introduced on the formal level: by involving, next to Malaparte (played once by Julian Świeżewski, once by Grzegorz Artman), the figure of Narrator (Piotr Skiba). The Narrator, "a tired phantom on the verge of life and death that haunts Casa Malaparte" (Obarska, 2019), in some scenes may also be interpreted as the "old" Malaparte. Such a procedure efficiently alludes to the theme of memory and activates the poetics of dream and recollection that serves well in the light of the fact that *The Skin* and the great part of *Kaputt* were written on Capri Island after the war. The contrasting spaces and times: the horror of the war recollected from the perspective of picturesque Tyrrhenian Sea view, seem to thematize well the theme of memory and oneiric reminiscence.

In the final scene of the spectacle, one can observe a particular rendition of the theme of memory and passing of time. The Narrator/old Malaparte assists a protracted scene in which characters that one after another enter through a door in the back of the scene that at the same time leads to Casa Malaparte interior screened on the screen. In the same moment of closing the door, the character starts to be one's own projection on the screen. Thus, their material bodies change, and they become a part of a projected memory/dream. As for its counterpart in the novels, the scene has its far origins in *Kaputt*, in the second chapter "The Mice" when in an oneiric scenery of narrator's dream enters "young" Malaparte and the friends that sit in silence (Malaparte, 2009). One can find also other numerous oneiric, atemporal sequences in both novels. Recurring reflection on the living and the death, on the winners and the losers is also a constant point in Malaparte's war novels, to finally arrive at the motif of "the living" and "the death" at the end of *The Skin* (Malaparte, 2010: 341–342). Malaparte in the dialogue in *The Skin* locates himself among "the death" and refuses to join Jimmy and "the living". The horrible images of the war described in *Kaputt* and *The Skin* very often assume this spectral asset, far from a regular non-fiction reportage, as if the narration regarded some spectral vision. Just as the days of Warsaw of the 1920s recollected in *Kaputt*, "that landscape was rising before my eyes again with the worn-out realness of an old faded photograph. [...] I, too, was certainly a ghost, a dull ghost of a remote age" (Malaparte, 2005). The method of description used by Malaparte towards sometimes has some dead aspects in itself, "there was something dead about the scene, and at the same time, something too precise, as in a photograph; I would have believed that I was facing a ghostly photographic backdrop" (Malaparte, 2005). In *Capri*, this potential of Malaparte's novels is efficiently explored.

9 Conclusions

Curzio Malaparte's war novels *Kaputt* and *The Skin* resulted interesting to the post-war international public and demonstrated their cultural and universal potential also in their reception in recent years. Malaparte's writing serves to answer the big questions on human nature in the light of war, on the essence of war as a hideous and unexplainable carnival of cruelty, on the effects of war and possible construction of a new paradigm on the ruins of the old world.

The recent theatrical adaptation of Malaparte's war novels *Kaput* and *The Skin* proves that the subject can still be elaborated with reference to modern paradigms and through asking new questions prove its cultural value. The spectrum of topics and the range of perspectives confronted in *Capri—the Island of Fugitives* through war theme is very wide and the spectacle does not offer clear answers nor closes all the doors it opens. Just as Krystian Lupa himself said in one of the interviews, "the theatre is one of these branches of arts where we can, in a painful way, drop a certain problem in front of a spectator, show some conflict, but in a way that the spectator could not disentangle himself too easily" (Maciejewski & Lupa, 2005). Malaparte's narration on the war seems to be a perfect material to create an entangled mass of horrifying, multi-significant scenes that can become a starting point for reflection on the modern cultural issues. *Capri* spectacle is also a perfect mixture of casual and universal, of politics and mysticism. Just as Malaparte in his war novels mixed political and factual narration with a unique artistic and poetical interpretation, Lupa manages to create an artistic vision of war narration in a universal perspective. Thus, *Capri—the Island of Fugitives* allows us to focus on archetypes and problems common to all mankind, and to reflect on war as a tragic existential experience of all people.

References

Atwood, M. (2005). Comment on the back cover of Curzio Malaparte's *Kaputt*. In C. Malaparte (Ed.), *Kaputt* (C. Foligno, Trans.). New York: New York Review of Books.

Baniewicz, E. (2019). Capri – wyspa uciekinierów. *Twórczość, 12,* 132–137.

Bollin, P., & Lupa, K. (2019). Trzy lata narodowego dyskursu doprowadziły do eskalacji nienawiści [Three years of national discourse have led to the escalation of hatred; Interview with Krystian Lupa]. In *Capri – wyspa uciekinierów* [Programme of the spectacle] (pp. 37–46). Warszawa: Teatr Powszechny im. Zygmunta Hübnera.

Breza, T. (1960). *Spiżowa brama*. Warszawa: Czytelnik.

Capri – wyspa uciekinierów [Programme of the spectacle]. (2019). Warszawa: Teatr Powszechny im. Zygmunta Hübnera.

Bruni, R. (2017). La Polonia occupata nel racconto di Curzio Malaparte: dalle cronache giornalistiche a *Kaputt*. In L. Masi, E. Nicewicz-Staszowska, J. Pietrzak-Thébault, & M. Woźniewska-Działak (Eds.), *Polska i Włochy w dialogu kultur / La Polonia e l'Italia nel dialogo tra le culture* (pp. 141–152). Warszawa: Wydawnictwo Naukowe UKSW.

Bruni, R. (2018). Malaparte, *Kaputt* e l'ombra dell'olocausto (con una testimonianza inedita di Alceo Valcini su Malaparte nel ghetto di Varsavia). *La Rassegna della Letteratura Italiana*, 315–330.

Cieślak, J., & Lupa, K. (2019). Gdy zło urządza świat. Z Krystianem Lupą rozmawia Jacek Cieślak [When the evil organizes the world. Jacek Cieślak interviews Krystian Lupa]. *Rzeczpospolita*, 237. Online http://www.e-teatr.pl/pl/artykuly/281064.html?josso_assertion_id=8773E531E27B495D. Accessed 15 July 2020.

De Paulis, M. P. (2019). *Curzio Malaparte. Il trauma infinito della Grande Guerra*. Firenze: Cesati.

Della Ragione, A. (2019). I femminielli. In *Capri – wyspa uciekinierów*. [Programme of the spectacle]. Warszawa: Teatr Powszechny im. Zygmunta Hübnera, 32.

Granville, J. (2001). Hungarian and Polish reactions to the events of 1956: New archival evidence. *Europe-Asia Studies, 53*(7), 1051–1076.

Godlewski, S. (2019). Devotional articles and a unicorn: Queer aspects in the work and bibliography of Krystian Lupa. *Polish Theatre Journal, 1–2*(7–8). https://www.polishtheatrejournal.com/index.php/ptj/article/view/189/979. Accessed 15 July 2020.

Grochowiak, S. (1963). *Leprozorium. Współczesność, 9*(3), 15–23.

Escolar, M. A. (2011). *Contaminating conversions: Narrating censorship, translation, fascism*. PhD dissertation, UC Berkeley. https://escholarship.org/uc/item/0r7943w7. Accessed 15 July 2020.

Iovino, S. (2014). Bodies of Naples: Stories, matter, and the landscapes of porosity. In S. Iovino & S. Oppermann (Eds.), *Material Ecocriticism* (pp. 97–113). Bloomington: Indiana University Press.

Katafiasz, O. (2020). Awaria narracji. *Didaskalia,* 155. https://didaskalia.pl/pl/artykul/awaria-narracji. Accessed 15 July 2020.

Kemp-Welch, T. (2006). Dethroning Stalin: Poland 1956 and its legacy. *Europe-Asia Studies, 58*(8), 1261–1284.

Kopciński, J. (2019). Koniec ze wstydem. *Teatr, 12,* 8–12.

Koźniewski, K. (1963). Paszkwil na Malapartego [List do redakcji]. *Polityka, 13,* 5.

Kościelniak, M. (2015). Poza wspólną wiarą [Beyond a common faith. Marcin Kościelniak interviews Krystian Lupa]. *Didaskalia, 125,* 48–55.

Kuhiwczak, P. (2009). Censorship as a collaborative project: A systemic approach. In E. N. Chuilleáin, C. Ó. Cuilleanáin, & D. Parris (Eds.), *Translation and censorship: Patterns of communication and interference* (pp. 46–56). Dublin: Four Cuorts Press.

Kuziak, M. (2020). Ja jestem uzależniony od Capri… *Dialog, 5,* 1–13.

Kydryński, J. (1983). Malaparte w Warszawie. *Dziennik Polski*, 220, 10.

Lasowy-Pudło, M. (2010). *Recepcja literatury NRD w Polsce w latach 1949–1990*. Wrocław: PWN.

Linowska-Marchocka, H. (1963). Malaparte. *Polityka*, 16, 1.

Looby, R. (2015). *Censorship, translation and English language fiction in people's Poland*. Leiden and Boston: Brill Rodopi.
Lupa, K. (2019). Dzienniki Capri. In *Capri – wyspa uciekinierów* [Programme of the spectacle]. Warszawa: Teatr Powszechny im. Zygmunta Hübnera.
Łęcicki, G. (2016). Censorship in people's Poland. *Journalism Research, 10,* 147–175.
Maciejewski, Ł., & Lupa, K. (2005). Koniec świata wartości [The end of the world of values]. *Notatnik Teatralny,* 35. http://encyklopediateatru.pl/artykuly/8682/koniec-swiata-wartosci. Accessed 15 July 2020.
Malaparte, C. (1944a). Szczury. *Orzeł Biały* 25, 4; 26, 8; 27, 8; 28, 6; 29, 8; 30, 8–9.
Malaparte, C. (1944b). *Kaputt*. Firenze: Casella.
Malaparte, C. (1954). *The skin* (D. Moore, Trans.). New York: The New American Library [reprint of the first edition (1952) by Boston: Houghton Mifflin Company].
Malaparte, C. (1959). *Mamma marcia*. Firenze: Valecchi.
Malaparte, C. (1962). *Kaputt* (B. Sieroszewska, Trans.). Warszawa: Czytelnik.
Malaparte, C. (1998). *Skóra* (J. Mikołajewski, Trans.). Wrocław: Wydawnictwo Dolnośląskie.
Malaparte, C. (2000). *Kaputt* (B. Sieroszewska, Trans.) passages formerly censored translated by J. Ugniewska. Warszawa: Czytelnik.
Malaparte, C. (2005). *Kaputt* (C. Foligno, Trans.). New York: New York Review of Books [e-book].
Malaparte, C. (2009). *Kaputt*. Milano: Adelphi.
Malaparte, C. (2010). *La pelle*. Milano: Adelphi.
Malaparte, C. (2013). *The Skin* (D. Moore, Trans.). New York: New York Review of Books.
Martellini, L. (1997). Cronologia. In C. Malaparte, *Opere scelte* (L. Martellini, Ed., pp. LXXIX–CII). Milano: Mondadori.
Mętrak, K. (1983). Osobliwa historia. *Express Wieczorny, 157,* 5.
Michałowska, B. (1963). Pisarz wojny narodów. *Polityka, 1*(1), 6–7.
Mrozek, W., & Lupa, K. (2019, June 13). Malaparte był faszystą, przyjacielem Mussoliniego. A zmieniał się w wędrującą po świecie wrażliwość [Malaparte was a fascist, Mussolini's friend. And still he transformed himself in a sensitivity wandering through the world. Interview with Krystian Lupa]. *Gazeta Wyborcza.*
Obarska, M. (2019). Capri: The Island of Fugitives – Krystian Lupa. *culture.pl.* https://culture.pl/en/work/capri-the-island-of-fugitives-krystian-lupa.
Orłowski, H. (1988). Distributive Rezeption. Deutschsprachige Literatur in Polen 1945–1985. In H. Kneip & H. Orłowski (Eds.), *Die Rezeption der polnischen Literatur im deutschsprachigen Raum und die der deutschsprachigen in Polen 1945–1985.* Darmstadt: Deutsches–Polen Institut.
Romek, Z. (Ed.). (2000). *Cenzura w PRL. Relacje historyków.* Warszawa: Neriton.
Serra, M. (2012). *Malaparte. Vite e leggende* (A. Folin, Trans.). Venezia: Marsilio.
Ślarzyńska, M. (2017). *Obraz literatury włoskiej w Polsce lat 70. i 80. XX wieku.* Warszawa. Wydział Polonistyki Uniwersytetu Warszawskiego.
Ślarzyńska, M. (2019). Spotkanie po latach na Capri (on Curzio Malaparte's life and works). *Teatr,* 13–16.
Szczęsna, J. (1997). Pod skórą wojny. *Gazeta Wyborcza, 264,* 10.
Szwarcenberg-Czerny, K. (1957). Curzio Malaparte. Autor Techniki zamachu stanu. *Za i Przeciw,* 27, 5.
Tonkin, B. (2019) Samouwielbienie wśród ruin (A. Nowacki, Trans.). In *Capri – wyspa uciekinierów* [Programme of the spectacle]. Warszawa: Teatr Powszechny im. Zygmunta Hübnera.
Turra, G. (2019). "Come un Angelo, gridando". Fine e oltrepassamento della fine in *Kaputt* di Curzio Malaparte. *Nuova Corrente, 163,* 39–50.
Tymoczko, M. (2009). Censorship and self-censorship in translation: Ethics and ideology, resistance and collusion. In E. N. Chuilleáin, C. Ó. Cuilleanáin, & D. Parris (Eds.), *Translation and censorship: Patterns of communication and interference* (pp. 24–45). Dublin: Four Cuorts Press.
Vandaele, J. (2010). It Was What It Wasn't: Translation and Francoism. In Ch. Rundle, & K. Sturge (Eds.), *Translation under Fascism* (pp. 84–116). New York: Palgrave Macmillan.

White, E. (2020). Reading the eccentric Italian writer who tried to cover up his fascism. *Lithub*. https://lithub.com/reading-the-eccentric-italian-writer-who-tried-to-cover-up-his-fascism/. Accessed 12 July 2020.

Wolf, M. (2002). Censorship as cultural blockage: Banned literature in the late Habsburg monarchy. *TTR: traduction, terminologie, rédaction, 15*(2), 45–61.

Zieliński, S. (1963). W kostiumie lwa. *Nowe Książki, 6*, 322–324.

A Living Heritage: The Villa E.1027 by the Sea

Luis Manuel Palmero Iglesias and Graziella Bernardo

Abstract The work tells the story of a holiday home with a mysterious code name E.1027. The house is in one of the most beautiful places on the French Riviera, Roquebrune-Cap-Martin, a few kilometers from the Italian border. The villa was designed in 1926 by Eileen Gray in collaboration with her lover of the time, Jean Badovici. The name of the villa is an alphanumeric code with the initials of their names. Gray planned every little detail of the house, from the garden to the furnishing, and built a place where guests or permanent resident can relax and feel comfortable. Gray claimed that "Entering a house should be like the sensation of entering a mouth which will close behind you." The Villa E.1027 is a masterpiece of modern architecture that overcomes the cold rationalism of Le Corbusier with the passion of a clever woman. Between 1938 and 1939, Le Corbusier wanted to take revenge on this woman by painting obscene sexist murals on every white wall in the house and he spent his life to control the villa's fate. Today, after a long period of neglect and memory loss, we can finally visit the house, which has been restored to its original beauty and intimacy by a critical restoration that preserved also the Le Corbusier's murals.

L'invitation au voyage
Mon enfant, ma sœur,
Songe à la douceur
D'aller là-bas vivre ensemble!
Aimer à loisir,
Aimer et mourir
Au pays qui te ressemble!

L. M. Palmero Iglesias (✉)
Polytechnic University of Valencia, Valencia, Spain
e-mail: lpalmero@csa.upv.es

G. Bernardo
Department of European and Mediterranean Cultures (DiCEM), Basilicata University, Campus Universitario, Potenza, Italy
e-mail: graziella.bernardo@unibas.it

O. Niglio and E. Y. J. Lee (eds.), *Transcultural Diplomacy and International Law in Heritage Conservation*, https://doi.org/10.1007/978-981-16-0309-9_7

The invitation to travel
My child, my sister,
Think of the sweetness
To go over there and live together!
To love at leisure,
Love and die
To the country that looks like you!

Charles Baudelaires, Les fluers du mal, 1857

1 A Journey Through the Architecture of the Last Century

Every place we visit leaves permanent signs, emotions, echoes, and whispers, that we can continue to feel when the journey is over. Architecture with its volumes, shapes, colors, odours, is both container and content of memory. The smell of mothballsthe, the scent of real wood, the crack in the wall, the dust on the floor, the heavy curtains that turn off the sun, the silent piano, all this things are just waiting us to came back. And that's where we will return to see what we couldn't see at the moment. It will be a glance, a color, a smell that itches suddenly to keep alive the desire to enjoy those opulent containers of life, designed by someone even for us, unaware travelers. Architecture is history told with the powerful language of objects created by human ingenuity at a certain time and in a certain moment of one's life.

The last century was full of unimaginable changes and cultural and social controversy. What society has ever been capable of seizing the opportunities of the industrial revolution, advancing with courage and losing everything in a war, and then survive and fall back after a few years into another war even more devastating than the first one? While all this was happening, Modern architecture developed with a plurality of expressions that translated the prolific drive toward the future of positivism, coining a new language with a close dialogue between science and art (Read, 2002). This was the time of a culture revolution that lead to a modern humanism with a new aestetics, involving all fields of arts, that we define with our own neologism as the epoch of the *archi-revoluculture*.

In 1908, Adolf Loos theorized the fundamentals of the new aesthetics in his essay Ornament and Crime, an invective against what he called the ornament epidemy. He spurred people to appreciate and enjoy the beauty of the essentiality of all usefull objects, not just of the buildings (Canales & Herscher, 2005). During a sumptuous dinner with pompously decorated dishes, the Austrian architect could have shouted *take the decorations of turkey and pheasant off this plate because I can't tell what I'm eating*! Architecture was taking off his sumptuous clothes, leaving behind the superfluous and the "false luxuries" (Loos, 1908). The aesthetics of the ornament had contaminated without mercy all the social, cultural, and architectural contingencies of the time, but its days had numbered. It was borning the aesthetic of essentiality of the raw architectural component, without coatings, without additions or camouflaging, in which the reinforced concrete, the most innovative material of the time, had its maximum expression.

On February 20, 1909, the multifaceted Filippo Tommaso Marinetti published in the Parisian newspaper Le Figaro the Manifesto of Futurism. This avant-garde artistic movement rejected tradition and celebrated the new beauty of the speed, machinery, and industry. "We declare that the splendor of the world has been enriched by a new beauty: the beauty of speed. A racing automobile with its bonnet adorned with great tubes like serpents with explosive breath … a roaring motor car which seems to run on machine-gun fire" (Marinetti, 1909).

In the second decade of the last century, the most primitive rationalism began to spread with quite a few doubts and criticisms. This new architecture exalted the purity of straight lines without decorations in a formal coherence dictated by the function of the spaces, focusing for the first time on the interior design. A new design approach based on technical principles rather than on conventions and empirical rules of the past spread all over Europe, giving architecture the tools for a freedom of expression that would satisfy the aesthetic canons of the modern industrialized world.

Rationalism in its conceptual genesis of defending function finds its unexpected roots in the book "Histoire d'une maison" published in 1873 by Eugène Emmanuel Viollet-le-Duc. He is known as a restoration theorist, but his theories have also made a great contribution to modern design. He proposes an ideal model of home that should be "neither stately nor monumental," reflecting the personality of its inhabitant who finds his happiness there (Viollet-le-Duc, 1873). He describes the construction materials and their function. He also stresses that decoration must be an integral part of architecture and not a mere addition, sometimes helping to solve structural construction challenges.

Between the two world wars, architecture contributed to overcoming the social conflicts exacerbated by the serious economic crisis with a remarkable development of social housing and urban planning. In this dramatic and yet so prolific historical moment, the *archi-revoluculture* led to a naked architecture, devoid of ornaments and classical symmetry. In this period, the avant-garde of figurative arts greatly influenced rationalism, which gave rise to a bold architectural language that went far beyond the mere search for functionality. As in cubism and the neoplastic movement, rationalist architecture expanded into a fourth dimension where geometrical forms without symmetry are suspended in a dynamic balance (Read, 2002). Modern architecture designs the construction from the inside out, giving paradigmatic models in which the principles of classical architecture, *utilitas*, *firmitas*, and *venustas*, are achieved by means technological innovations and new materials. Many rationalist architectures have been private homes that tell the personality and intimacy of their creators, becoming material and immaterial testimony of a great page in the history of architecture.

In many cases, modern architecture is catalogued as a worthless contemporaneity and not recognized as heritage. Fortunately, some abandoned and forgotten modern buildings have been restored and protected, reaching us unaware travelers. This is the case of the Villa E.1027, which is the testimony of the genius of a woman who has long remained unknown.

2 A Brave and Silent Woman. Eileen Gray

Eileen Gray was born in Enniscorthy, County Wexford, in the southeast of Ireland, on August 9, 1878. She spent a happy childhood with her four siblings in a simple house surrounded by greenery. She missed her father who spent long periods of time in France and Italy as an amateur painter. It was thanks to him that she had a passion for art since her early age. Her mother, always close to her shyness and fears (*I am afraid of spirits and people*, Eileen said), gave her calm and values that will accompany her throughout her life. *Never falling into self-pity*, she told her mother repeatedly, forming a personality with a strong-willed temperament (Adam, 2009). When Eileen was fifteen, her mother inherited a noble title from an uncle and became Baroness Gray.

The Baroness Gray decided that the new social rank required a new way of life and a new home. In 1895, the bucolic house where Eileen had spent her childhood was demolished and, in its place, the luxurious red brick Tudor-style house was built as new residence of the Gray family. Our protagonist was sorry to leave a magical and welcoming world for her. She lived without enthusiasm the new social status and continued to think silently about the world she would have wanted with a fervent mind and a brave heart. The wealth of her family and her restless and curiosity allowed her to travel a lot. In 1900, she visited with her mother the Universal Exhibition of Paris. Eileen dazzled by the allure of the trendy city as well as by the striking innovations of the Paris Universal Exhibition. This trip had a considerable influence on her life's destiny (Adam, 2009).

In 1901, she attended in London the Slade School of Fine Arts, a painting school for high society youngsters. In 1902, she went to Paris to study drawing and enrols at the Atelier Colarossi and later the Académie Jullian (Cap Modern Association, 2014). She learned the art of lacquering by the Japanese Seizo Sugawara.[1] She mastered this technique of great patience and skill that gave her fame as a creator and designer of lacquered furniture. Her activity began with refined and elegant screens and lampshades, such as the famous Via Lactea, and continued with original and modern furniture.

In 1907 he went to live in the apartment at 21 rue Bonaparte in Paris where she died after a long life on 31 October 1976.

In 1909, after a trip to Morocco with the cellist Evelyn Wyld, Eileen's chatty love, she decided to make rugs. Her fervent mind led her to start new trades and entrepreneurial initiatives, an attitude she maintained throughout her life.

In 1913, she exhibited her creations at the Salon des Artistes Décorateurs (SAD) where she met the couturier Jacques Doucet who ordered a major supply of furniture with the clear intention of being her only customer.

The beginning of his career as creator designer was awfully hard. Critics ignored the promising work of a young female artist. The turning point arrived in 1917,

[1]Seizo Sagawara (1884 Sakata–1937 Machi, Japan). Artist of Japanese origin, nationalized in France, who had the merit of spreading the ancient Asian lacquering technique in Europe. With Jean Dunand and Eileen Gray, he was a key figure in the plastic arts of the early twentieth century.

when Madame Mathieu Lévy gave her the task of designing the interior of the whole apartment on rue de la Lota. Eileen dedicated a lot of time and all her creativity to this first important commitment (Constant, 1994). It gave her the success she deserved. Eileen managed to gain notoriety as designer at a time when a woman could at most aspire to become a weaver or decorator. Eileen's creations had a *new look*. They were elegant and useful and often surprising. Eileen used new materials, such as aluminum, introducing teamwork methods and collaboration between different skills, never seen before.

In 1922, she opened the Galerie Jean Désert, a non-existent name born of his fervent imagination, where she exhibited screens, rugs, and modern furniture with a clear influence of the Dutch avant-garde De Stijl.

In 1924, Eileen met Jean Badovici, a young and brilliant architect of Romanian origin known in the fashionable circles of Paris and Jean began a professional collaboration, and they fell madly in love. Eileen was attracted by the ambitious character and strong personality of the young architect, fifteen years younger than her. On the other hand, Jean was fascinated by Eileen's notoriety and wealth, which could have helped him realize his dreams and projects. In the same year, Eileen began to frequent Adrianne Gorska, one of the first female architects, who introduced her to architectural design (Loye & Raynaud, 1984).

From this moment on, Eileen will have a long and extraordinary career as designer and architect. Unfortunately, this visionary, modern woman has not had the honors and notoriety she deserved. Perhaps because history is still written by blind and arrogant men, while clever women remain silent when they should scream, and mediocre women speak when they should be silent.

3 The Villa E.1027 by the Sea

Eileen Gray spent several months and several travel to the French Riviera to choose a place to build a holiday home. When she arrived in Roquebrune Cap Martin, a few kilometers from the Italian frontier, she found what she was looking for, a place to live with her lover, Jean Badovici.

The place is a natural oasis of peace and quiet. You could get there by only one street and once you get there you never come out. The smell of pines and lemon trees numb your senses and you stay there motionless looking at the sea which has a shade of blue like nowhere else.

In 1926, Eileen in collaboration with Jean designed their holiday home that she called E.1027. The name of the villa was a coded message and a proof of the intimate complicity of the couple: E for Eileen, 10 for the J of Jean, 2 for the B of Badovici, 7 for the G of Gray.

Jean had a friendly relationship with the Master Le Corbusier, already famous at the time, who often wrote in the magazine L'Architecture Vivante published by Badovici.

Now we have all the protagonists of our story: Eileen Gray, Jean Badovici, and Le Corbusier. But what makes the intricate feelings between them and a villa by the sea so worthy of attention?

The design of the house was an exciting challenge for Eileen. She spent hours and hours analyzing every single line and corner of the future construction, planning every detail of both the interior furnishings and the open spaces with the magnificent garden. She defined the compositional distribution of the spaces according to their function, the orientation of solar radiation, and the view of the sea that should be always present in that house.

Eileen head every phase of the villa construction, sharing the entire day's work with the workers at the construction site. Her practical vocation mocked prejudices and began the revolutionary path of women's independence. Eileen put into practice the wise motto that ensures the success of any work, the boss must always be an additional member of work team (Espegel Alonso, 2013).

The construction of the Villa E.1027 ended in 1929. Under French law at the time, Eileen, unmarried and foreigner, could not be the owner of the house that she entirely financed with her money. So, Eileen decided to donate the holiday home to her lover Jean.

The silent Eileen designed a masterpiece of modern architecture. The housing model of Eileen can be defined *le theatre à habiter*, as opposite to *la machine à habiter* theorized by Le Corbusier (1923). Eileen Gray's seaside house is a place for human entertainment, where the inhabitants dialogue with a permanent stage set consisting of live objects that hide their usefulness in sinuous and elegant forms. Her design philosophy was full of passion and opposed to the cold intellectualism of the aesthetics of the machine that that blurs the wonders of life. "The poverty of modern architecture stems from the atrophy of sensuality," Eileen said in an interview in 1929 for L'Architecture Vivante (Willette, 2017).

The villa E.1027 with a total area of 120 square meters stands through columns on an artificial terrace. The front façade broken up by a series of balconies and verandas has an amazing view of the sea that is right down there (Fig. 1). You can believe that are not in a house, but you are crossing the ocean with a transatlantic liner. The doubt is more than founded looking at the sea from there. It is one of the special effects of the *theatre à abiter*.

The large windows with a screen-like opening system allow natural lighting and ventilation of the building (Fig. 2). This design solution allows conditions of internal comfort without wasting energy and without the use of the too obvious brise-soleil shielding. The *stage-house* has an open curtain and the actors-roommates will live a new adventure every day with the blue sea as a background.

The villa in reinforced concrete has the typical appearance of modern building with cantilevered elements and plain blank solid walls (Espegel Alonso, 2016). The white color of the villa stands out among the lush greenery and the blue sea of the French Riviera (Fig. 3).

Everyone must be able to feel free and independent. This is the dogma that guides the project of the interior of the villa (Espegel Alonso, 2016). Each room has its own balcony with access to the outside and a guest or permanent resident

Fig. 1 View from the sea of the Villa E.1027, Roquebrune-Cap-Martin (Gray & Badovici, 1929)

could have privacy, comfort, and peace. As Eileen explained on the special issue of L'Architecture Vivante, "Entering a house should be like the sensation of entering a mouth which will close behind you" (Gray & Badovici, 1929). The garden extends the intimacy of the villa on the seaside, hosting an outdoor drawing room sheltered from the wind by maritime pines on the southwest side and an outdoor kitchen surrounded by citrus fruits on the north side.

Throughout the home, from room to room, there is comfort and a meticulous attention to detail. Every complement and piece of furniture of the house is works of arts of Eileen's creativity, like the famous Bibendum and Transat chairs (Fig. 4). Eileen designs every component of the interior of the house, considering not only its function, but also its ease of use and using the most suitable materials.

Fig. 2 Detail of ribbon windows with a screen-like opening system, Villa E.1027, Roquebrune-Cap-Martin. Picture by Kasper Akhøj (Akhøj, 2017)

Fig. 3 Back of the Villa E.1027, Roquebrune-Cap-Martin. Picture by Kasper Akhøj (Akhøj, 2017)

Fig. 4 The Bibendum Chair (left) and the Transat Chair (right). Villa E.1027, Roquebrune-Cap-Martin (Willette, 2017)

4 The Story of un Obsession

It was the summer of 1938. Gray and Badovici were no longer a couple, their love had ended a few years earlier. Eileen had left the house she had lived with Jean. The couple kept in touch with each other as well as with their famous friends of yesteryear. That summer the Master Le Corbusier accepted the invitation of Badovici to spend a few days of vacation at his holiday home in Roquebrune-Cap-Martin. We wonder if the Master noticed that the Villa E.1027 had all the five points of modern architecture that he had theorized: the pylons, the free plan, the roof garden, the ribbon windows, the free façade (Le Corbusier, 1923) (Fig. 5).

All we know for sure is that Le Corbusier wrote a letter of congratulations to Eileen. "I am so happy to tell you how much those few days spent in your house have made me appreciate the rare spirit which dictates all the organization inside and outside. A rare spirit which has given the modern furniture and installations such a dignified, charming, and witty shape" (Adam, 2009).

These words certainly flattered our silent lady. The most famous architect of the moment Le Corbusier praised her work. But something serious was about to happen.

Between 1938 and 1939, the Master went back to the Villa E.1027 and painted obscene sexist murals on every blank wall he could find on the inside of the home One of the murals covered also the message of welcome in the entrance, *entrez lentement*, painted by Eileen to invite guests on a journey into the intimacy of her home. Le

Fig. 5 Murals by Le Corbusier. Villa E.1027, Roquebrune-Cap-Martin. Picture by Kasper Akhøj (Akhøj, 2017)

Corbusier also had himself photographed naked while he was painting the murals, taking pleasure in his brutal rape (Fig. 6). It was an awfully hard blow to Eileen, another one inflicted on what remained of her great love story. Now even the house was no longer hers and no longer represented her. The Villa E.1027 has just become the desecrated container of a betrayal. Eileen's never setting foot in it again.

Le Corbusier took revenge on a woman who had that had made the cold rationalism vibrate with a great passion and love for life. The villa E.1027 was a masterpiece and it was not his work. In addition, it was designed by a woman. The great Le Corbusier had to remedy what was an unacceptable affront to him. And he found the remedy by painting obscene murals, putting together the acrimony for a woman smarter than him and another one frustration, the painting. He wanted to be a great painter, but he was just recognized as one of the greatest architects of the time.

From this moment on, the relationship between Le Corbusier and Gray will be broken forever. Le Corbusier raped the intact whiteness of the Villa E.1027 and invaded the whole scene of the *house-stage*. Badovici allowed this violence and was pleased. The murals of the great Le Corbusier had increased the value of his home.

During the war, the Germans occupied and vandalized the house. At the end of the war, Badovici was quick to inform Le Corbusier that his murals were safe. But Gray wanted Le Corbusier to take those hideous murals off her house. In a letter dated December 30, 1949, which according to Peter Adam was written by Gray herself, Badovici asked the Master to repair the damage he had done. "You luck generosity toward me. A correction from you seems necessary, if not, I will be forced to do it myself to re-establish the original spirit of the house by the sea" (Adam, 2009).

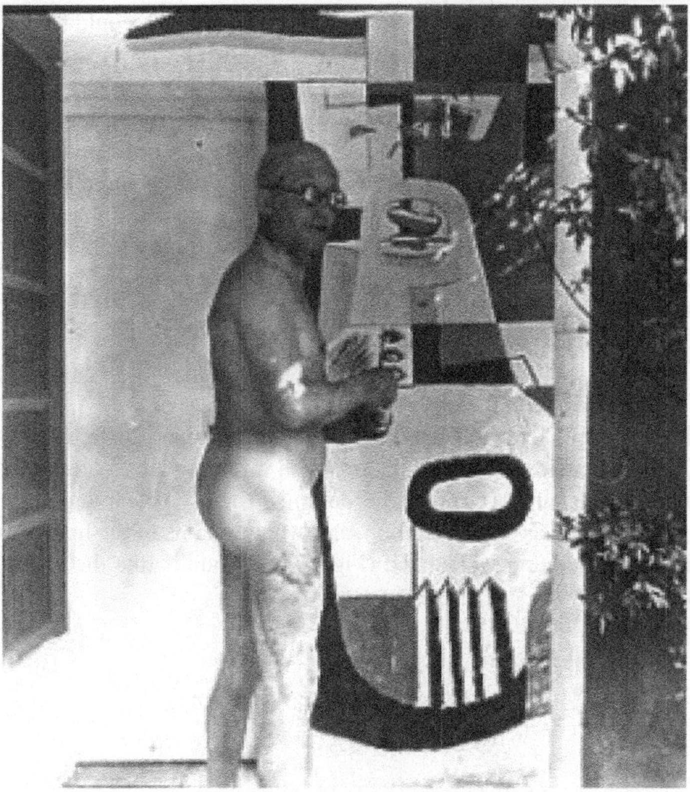

Fig. 6 Le Corbusier in the Villa E.1027 (Willette, 2017)

Le Corbusier refused to remove his murals and carried out a smear campaign against Gray's work. His anger toward that woman did not subside and that villa by the sea was a real obsession he could not get away from (Colomina, 2018).

Probably for this reason, in the year 1952 he designed Le Cabanon, a small refuge a few meters from the villa adjacent to the restaurant L'etoile de mer by the Italian Roberto Rebutato (Prelorenzo, 2013). According to Le Corbusier's biographers, Le Cabanon was simply a birthday present for his wife, but Beatriz Colomina tells another terrible truth. "By imposing his vision from above, he established his domain on the site of Gray's house. The cabanon was just an observation platform, a kind of house for watchdogs" (Colomina, 2018).

In that small house, so naif made of tree trunks, the perfect antithesis of his model of the *machine à habiter*, also without bathrooms, he spent his time painting, his other obsession. And he also spent a lot of time in Gray's house, even for long periods, especially after his wife's death (Prelorenzo, 2013).

The villa by the sea that Le Corbusier wanted to hide from the whole world soon became famous for its murals. A strange twist of fate that was preparing the final counterpoint. The house was considered a cult object, a heritage to be preserved, which many attributed to Le Corbusier himself. After all, who could have designed a house like this in 1926? Gray's name always remained unknown, just as Le Corbusier wanted it to be.

When Badovici died in 1956, E.1027 was inherited by an aunt nun living in Romania who had to give up it. A great opportunity then presented itself for Le Corbusier who continued to be obsessed with the villa. Among international intrigues that even involved the wealthy shipowner Onassis, the great manipulator Le Corbusier arranged for the villa to be bought at auction by one of his admirers, Madame Schelbert. The new owner believed that the villa E.1027 was one of the works of the great Master and Le Corbusier never denied it.

But the sea, that blue sea of southern France, knew the truth of the story of Gray, Badovici, and Le Corbusier. In 1965, Le Corbusier died while swimming near the Villa E.1027 that had been the obsession of his life.

After Le Corbusier's death, the Villa E.1027 continued to be haunted by bad fortune. The villa carries a troubled history with it for decades to come. A dissolute owner arrived to turn it into a crime scene, ending up dead on the living room floor. All the original furniture was sold at auction, and what remains of the house, abandoned and in ruins, is looted and vandalized (Figs. 7–8). Sounds like the end of the line, but it was not.

Fig. 7 House entrance of the Villa E.1027. Picture by Kasper Akhøj (Akhøj, 2017)

Fig. 8 Drawing room of the Villa E.1027. Picture by Tim Benton (Benton, 2016)

5 A Happy Ending Travel

Since the 1970s, the French Government has considered that the villa should be preserved thanks to the presence of Le Corbusier's murals. In 1999, the house has been included in the list of the architectural heritage of France.

From 2004 to 2012, the Regional Directorate of Cultural Affairs of Provence and the Conservatory of the coast have carried out restoration work to prevent the house from suffering further serious irreparable damage. These preliminary works have left visible the marks of history in accordance to the conservative restoration. In 2014, the non-profit organization Cap Moderne has started a long critical restoration that now, after 6 years of work, had restored the villa to its original state (Cap Modern Association, 2014; Benton, 2016). The restoration has involved the reinforced concrete structure and facades of the building, the reconstruction and remake in the form of copies of all the furnishings, and the restoration of the garden.

Finally, the Villa E.1027 can be visited and seen just as Eileen Gray had carefully designed it in every little detail. One hundred years after its construction, the house is a living heritage that fascinates and welcomes us with its warming rational and sensual grace. The Villa E.1027 has been restored to its original beauty, except for one single, not insignificant detail, those rough murals that still disfigure it. However, we believe that it is right they are still there. The obscene murals will be a warning against human stupidity and will tell us, unaware travelers, the story of a woman that was a great architect and the story of a man that was hostage of his wicked narcissism. But to understand the story all the way through, you must go to French Riviera, look at

Fig. 9 View by the see of the Villa E.1027. Roquebrune-Cap-Martin. Painting by the author (Palmero Iglesias, June 2020)

Eileen's house from the sea and experience the intimacy of a masterpiece of modern architecture (Fig. 9).

Acknowledgements The authors wish to thank the Cap Moderne Association for the great effort dedicated to the preservation of the original beauty and intimacy of the Villa E.1027. A special thanks to Tim Benton for the generous concession of some of his photos.

References

Adam, P. (2009). *Eileen Gray her life and work*. London: Thames and Hudson Ltd.

Akhøj, K. (2017). *Welkome (to The Teknival) E-1027*. Monaco, Zurich: Nouveau Musée National de Monaco and b.frank books GmbH.

Benton, T. (2016). *E-1027 Restauration de la maison en bord de mer d'Eileen Gray et Jean Badovici*. Paris: Cap Moderne.

Canales, J., & Herscher, A. (2005). Criminal skins: Tattoos and modern architecture in the work of Adolf Loos. *Architectural History, 48*, 235–256. https://doi.org/10.1017/S0066622X00003798.

Cap Modern Association. (2014). https://capmoderne.com/en/. Accessed 21 June 2020.

Colomina, B. (2018). *La obsesión de Le Corbusier con E.1027*. https://www.march.es/videos/?p0=11504. Accessed 23 March 2020.

Constant, C. (1994). E. 1027: The nonheroic modernism of Eileen Gray. *Journal of the Society of Architectural Historians, 53*(3), 265–279. https://doi.org/10.2307/990937.

Espegel Alonso, C. (2013). Aires Modernos: E.1027: Maison en bord de mer. Eileen Gray y Jean Badovici, 1926–1929. *BAc Boletín Académico: Revista De investigación Y Arquitectura contemporánea, 3*, 75–76. https://doi.org/10.17979/bac.2013.3.0.1000.

Espegel Alonso, C. (2016). *Heroínas del espacio: mujeres arquitectos en el movimiento moderno.* Ciudad Autonoma de Buenos Aires: Diseño.

Gray, E., & Badovici, J. (1929). E. 1027: Maison en bord de mer, L'architecture vivante. Septième année, numéro 26. Paris: Éditions Albert Morance. Re-edition. Rayon, J. P., Bonillo, J. L., & Gatier, P. A. (Eds.). (2006). Marseille: Éd. Imbernon.

Le Corbusier. (1923). Vers une architecture. Collection L'Esprit Nouveau. Paris: Les Editions G. Cres et Cie.

Loos, A. (1908). *Ornament and crime: Selected essays: Studies in Austrian literature, culture, and thought: Translation series.* Editor Opel, A. (M. Mitchell, Trans.). Riverside, CA: Ariadne Press.

Loye, B., & Raynaud, M. (1984). *Eileen Gray 1879–1976: Architecture design.* Paris: Analeph/J.P. Viguier.

Marinetti, F. T. (1909). Le Futurisme. 20 February 1909. No. 51. Le Figaro. Gallica, Bibliothèque nationale de France. Retrieved November 1, 2018. https://gallica.bnf.fr/ark:/12148/bpt6k2883730/f1.image. Accessed 2 April 2020.

Prelorenzo, C. (2013). *Eileen Gray L'Étoile de mer, Le Corbusier, Three mediterranean adventures.* Paris: Archibooks.

Read, A. (2002). *Architecturally speaking: Practices of art, architecture and the everyday.* London: Routlege Edit. U.K.

Viollet-le-Duc, E. E. (1873). *Histoire d'une maison.* https://gallica.bnf.fr/ark:/12148/bpt6k6567176q/f317.image.texteImage. Accessed 20 May 2020.

Willette, J. (2017). *Eileen Gray, architect: The E.1027 house.* https://arthistoryunstuffed.com/author/jeanne/. Accessed 21 June 2020.

Jitiya: Tharu Inherence to Eco-Culture

Keshav Raj Chalise

Abstract Having their physical and psychological struggle with frequently happening pandemics like malaria for many centuries until the new settlement plan from the government, Tharus, the indigenous people of central Nepal, Chitwan, have long attachment, recognition, and consideration to nature; and despite the issues of cultural hegemony over nature in environmental studies, they have the eco-culture to respect, preserve, implore, and eulogize nature. Now, after the formal migration, they live with cultural diaspora among many cultural values, but they have their own cultural values, distinct from non-Tharus, however, majorities of their religious functions resemble with traditional Hindu culture. Jitiya festival, distinct from rest of Hindu communities, is an example on how Tharu people, especially, women stay Vrata, and primarily worship nature and identify nature as the source of harmonizing all human and nonhuman environment. Their cultural respect to nature signifies their belief on the value and greatness of nature. The paper analyzes Tharu patterns of eco-culture in Jitiya, the cultural festival, and *Jitiya Pawani*, their Mythical literature.

1 Introduction

Are "Nature" and "Culture" two distinct ontological provinces? The distinction deepens as Taylor finds, "Culture is placed in opposition to nature in a variety of ways" (Taylor, 2018: 798). Thinking this way means we are separating the pole of human beings and culture from the pole of non-humans and nature. Culture, associated with all human product and nature, having automatic and external environment, have certain distinctions in the way they function, and they inherit their modes. It means culture and nature appear to be different from each other as if they were two separate realms of reality, hence with symmetry. At the same time, culture with its variety, does not remain the same everywhere and every when. This difference, with the reality of natural and man-made is not always the difference in value as oppositely existing, struggling, and surviving. They may be different, but it does not mean

K. R. Chalise (✉)
Nepal Sanskrit University, Bijauri, Nepal
e-mail: Keshav.chalise@nsu.edu.np

O. Niglio and E. Y. J. Lee (eds.), *Transcultural Diplomacy and International Law in Heritage Conservation*, https://doi.org/10.1007/978-981-16-0309-9_8

that they are necessarily opposite, and they can exactly be complementary to each other. This allows alternative interpretations as to what the character of their mutual relationship is, or should be. Culture is traditionally viewed as an agent that actively strives for domination over nature, or as a malicious tumor that tends to grow and exceed the limits set by nature, and nature is regarded as a source of adversities and calamity that needs to be conquered by human rational action or, alternatively, as benevolent providence that offers advice. Because the nature consciousness in humans has taken a new strength and this mode of cultural hegemony over nature does not subsist today in the way it did.

With reference to nature and culture relation, this study tries to examine Tharu cultural patterns of celebrating Jitiya festival and their mythical folk narrative *Jitiya Pawani* on the way Tharus, "under the shared ethnonym Tharu inhabit in the region of Nepal, of which they account themselves the aboriginal inhabitants" (Guneratne, 2002: 20), response to nature, either as worshipping it or as generating harmony in human-nature relationship. Though the concept of nature as biological diversity, and humans as cultural diversity was not properly developed when Jitiya culture was introduced, Tharus follow their cultural pattern as if they are intrinsically and inextricably linked with nature and natural patterns. This study, based on the observation of the cultural patterns and interviewing with Tharu people of Chitwan (names of interviewees indicated), and the theoretical analysis of the mythical narratives, aims to examine on how Tharus value to natural patterns during the cultural festival, Jitiya and how they keep nature at priority in their mythical literature, *Jitiya Pawani*.

2 Cultural Ecology: Culture, Nature, and Jitiya

Cultures are human products. They are rooted in a time and place. They are not nature products, but they show human attachment or detachment to nature because they define how people relate to nature and their physical environment, to the earth and to the cosmos, and they express our attitudes to and beliefs in other forms of life, both animal and plant. Cultures tend to make roots in and adapt to the particularity of a specific environment and geo-historical context. This is because, at a fundamental level, biological and cultural diversities are co-dependent. Cultures, as the social norms, are developed over time through mutual adaptation between humans and the environment. Therefore, rather than existing in separate and parallel realms, nature and culture interact with and affect one another in complex ways in a sort of co-evolutionary process-nature is the part of culture, and culture should help to grow and strengthen the nature.

Culture refers to a set of distinctive spiritual, material, intellectual, and emotional features of society or a social group and it includes art and literature, lifestyles, ways of living together, value systems, tradition, and beliefs. The cultural lifestyle includes the activities of human beings related to humans and non-humans, or humans, plants, and animals at a time. No culture can be understood ignoring the nature and the environment, however, the advancement in culture can have greater problem in the environmental preservation as, "simpler cultures are more directly conditioned by the environment than advanced ones" (Steward, 2006: 8). With ancient origin and having no advancement in the patterning, Jitiya culture is conditioned environmentally in the mode of ecological culture.

Is ecology different from culture? Since culture is human lifestyle and lifestyle is balance between humans and nonhuman nature, ecology is the combination of culture and nature, "Ecology is the study of the interaction between living things and their environment. Human ecology is the study of the relationships and interactions among humans, their biology, their cultures, and their physical environments" (Sutton & Anderson, 2010: 3). Having the complete life in nature, Tharus, the original inhabitants of Terai, born with nature, live with nature and die with nature and have the real sense of natural upbringing being close to the surrounding environment and the proper adaptation of nature in the mode of eco-culture. Surrounding with nature does not necessarily refer to the positive attachment, as many cultures in other societies do not show affinity to nature in the way Tharu culture presents. Tharu culture has the real affinity to nature and environment; hence their culture is environmental culture.

A large Tharu community of central Terai observes Jitiya as an important festival celebrated "mainly by Nepali married women of Mithilanchal and Tharu woman of all castes" (Khanal, 2071 BS: 45). Many of the festivals in Hindu culture show and express the good-wish and well-being of others, such as *Guru Purnima* is a festival for the praise and respect to guru. Jitiya festival shows some similarity with *Teej*, in which married women stay *Vrata* for the well-being of their husbands. Likewise, Tharu women perform this festival for the well-being and long life of their sons. It has a special day to celebrate the whole function. It is performed on *Aswin Krishna Ashtmi* usually during *Pradosh* time. Nepali Tharu women observe *Nirjala* fast (even without water) on this day and break the fast next day on the end of *Ashtami*. Sometimes, they have to make two-day Vrata when *Ashtami tithi* (day) does not begin from the morning, especially the beginning of the day and *Tithi* may not match sometimes.

As women do not eat anything, and even it becomes stronger when they stay *Nirahara Vrata*, they name it as *Khar Jitia*. They have the belief that, Mangal Tharu (68) says, "staying *Khar Jitiya* is the way to save the children even from severe accidents and misfortunes," and most of the married Tharu women prefer to stay this type of *Vrata*. It means children who escape severe accidents are believed to have the blessings of their mother having performed this *Vrata*. They have the tradition of feast the night before the Vrata, "we eat roti and other delicious food on the day before we observe the Vrata" (Kalli Tharu 42). It is their trend or tradition to eat fish and chapatti (roti, bread) made of millet (Marua) the previous day. In the night prior to fast they take a meal just before the beginning of *Ashtami*. This is peculiar to this fasting only. Often children are awoken and fed the preparations. This feasting is known as *Ongthan*.

This cultural origin of Jitiya Parwa has its geographical connection. It is not the *Vrata* for Tharus of all Nepal: rather it is observed only by Tharus of Chitwan, Nawalparasi, and surrounding geographic locations. Similar appears the difference between Tharus of Chitwan and the Tharus of Dang; Tharus of Chitwan celebrate

Jitiya Parwa as their culturally important festival, whereas Tharus of Dang celebrate *Maghi Parwa* as their central cultural festival. It means Jitiya Parwa, being celebrated only by Chitwania Tharus, has its geo-cultural value to generate the social and cultural lifestyle of Tharus of Chitwan. Jitiya has specific geographical characteristics especially among the Tharus of Chitwan and surrounding locations, Parveni Chaudhari (36) says, "we only Chitwanian Tharus celebrate this Festival." Also they have their geo-cultural norm, the language they speak becomes different from the Tharus of other locations, such as Dang. So, their culture is Chitwanian Tharu culture and their language is Chitwanian Tharu language.

Tharus are the original residents of Chitwan. Being the ethnic group of people, they possess their culture, cultural celebrations, functions of life and their own literature, especially in the mode of folk stories. Jitiya festival is one of their cultural festivals celebrated especially by Tharu women. This cultural festival resembles to other Hindu cultural festivals. Not only this festival is celebrated, but also, there is a folk story behind this celebration as the mythical text in Tharu language.

3 Jitiya: Conserving Both Culture and Nature

Tharus of Chitwan do not feel contrast between culture and nature, but they have realized that nature is helpful to shape their lifestyle, "nature teaches children essential life lessons" (Hull, 2018: 69). They are the indigenous group of people in Chitwan district. They have been following their own culture from the very beginning. By religion, most of them are Hindus, however, some people seem to be adopting Christianity in the recent situation. Basudev Chaudhary (63) claims, "Hinduism is our original religion and most of our cultural practices are exactly similar to those of Hindus and other casts." Tharus' religious and cultural celebrations, "the religion of Tharus is traditionally animistic" (Webster, 1993: 4) and they have the nature as the part of their life, and therefore, have the closeness to Hindu celebrations and their responses to nature follow the same. It does not mean that Tharus do not have their separate cultural functions. They celebrate major annual festivals of Hindus: Dashain, Tihar, Shivaratri, Fagupurnima, and others. Basudev shows slight difference in the trend of celebrating Fagupurnima from other group of people, "we born Chir on the first day at Fagupurnima and we celebrate it on the next day, but other people celebrate Fagupurnima and born Chir on the first day." (Sharma and Malla, 1990: 19) This difference is not on the belief of the cultural value, but the difference is on the manner or way of following the same culture.

One of the characteristics Tharus are identified distinctly is their cultural link with nature and natural phenomena; they are rich in their culture and they primarily focus on the worshipping of nature and natural elements. Yamosa and Jitiya are two strongly observed festivals by the Tharus. Yamosa is the day; Pitri Amabasya, when they remember their fore fathers (Pitris). Basudev Chaudhary says, "It is the single day all Tharus worship and remember their own Pitris." Jitiya is another purely

Tharu-based cultural function celebrated only among the Chitwanian Tharus, the Tharus of Chitwan and surrounding districts.

Tharu women celebrate Jitiya ritual for three days. Etymologically, Jitiya has a symbolic meaning to *jit* or victory. Jitiya falls on the month of *Ashwin* (September–October). It is celebrated for three days on *Saptami* (the seventh day of dark fortnight), *Astami* (the eighth day of dark fortnight), and *Navami* (the ninth day of dark fortnight). They take *Vrata* (fasting) for the good sign for their family and children. They do not only pray for the health, prosperity, and long life of their children and family but also they pray for collective well fare. During the period, women worship to lord Bishnu, Shiva, and Sun. However, Jitabahan is the main deity of Jitiya. The main part of the ritual is that women worship the nature. Women take *Vrata* and do not eat anything for a whole day. Women celebrate Jitiya by singing songs and dancing.

The different ethnic groups of people are gathered to listen songs and see dance. They call it as *Jhamata*. The celebration of Jitiya makes good relationship between each other, one ethnic group to another ethnic group and creates harmony in humans of society and environment. And it creates social solidarity helping to function the society properly.

The first day of the Jitiya is called *Lahakhai*. On this day, as Budhan Chaudhary (29) says, "women take bath in a river early in the morning and formally start their *Vrata*." They suppose nature (river) as the purifying agent for them, especially mental and physical purification, "The river Ganga, in the Hindu religious vision, takes the form of a goddess who possesses the power to purify all sorts of human and worldly impurities" (Alley, 1998: 299). Taking bath has a process too. All the women follow the same process. Before taking bath they put *Khari* (oil-seed-cake) on the leaf of plant and let it flow on the river. It has a purpose. Budhan explains, "this *Khari* is flown for legendary figure *Chilo* (Eagle) and *Shero* (Fox) wishing them to take *Vrata* (fasting) of Jitiya." It is their invoking to Ganga in the way Hindu culture teaches them to invoke, "Hindu residents and pilgrims invoke the purifying power of 'Ma Ganga' (Mother Ganga) through ritual ablution, meditation, and worship" (299). This connection of their purification in river, offering *Khari* to eagle and fox through the river has connected humans, rivers and birds and animal relation.

Another part of nature-connected ritual behind the preparation of Jitiya is the purification of the house with cow dung. On this day Tharu women brush and clean their house with cow dong to make their house pure. Sushila Chaudhary (45) thinks, "the cow dung is supposed to make the whole surrounding clean and pure." In this day, they eat only vegetable items. On the mid night they prepare *Datkhat\dar* (special food) and eat *Datkhat\dar* before cockcrow. Again they remember and respect the nature symbolically as they offer the food to animals, *Chilo* and *Shero* before they eat. They offer their festive meal to the eagle and fox which is their indication of their respect to animal and birds zone.

Another important mode of their cultural respect to nature is seen when they take bath on the day of real *Vrata*. After taking a bath they go to pluck some leaves of *Bel* (Wooden apple) for *Pooja* or worshipping. During that time, they sing a song, which is called *Phool Lorhoni* (song sung before plucking leaf of *Bel*). Budhan (29) says, "They have to respect and inform the owner of the *Bel* plant with the song." This song especially sings for owner of garden to inform before they pluck the leaf of *Bel*. It is what the greater respect to nature, especially the plant. They don't directly pluck the leaves of the tree; rather they want to ask a kind of permission. This song is the sense of excuse for plucking the leaves to the tree. This particular event shows that Tharus have the sense of personification toward the plants. Furthermore, they appear to be sensible for the destruction they happen to make in the nature.

And second importance of this song for *Bel* tree is the wish to make it pure and preserved. Budhan (29) says, "*Bel* is goof for both man and gods." Bel as the representative of all plant zones, they believe that *Bel* (tree) is the purifying agent for humans and the divine both. After this song women can pluck *Bel* leaf. *Phool* refers to flower and *Lorhoni* refers to pluck the flower. The leaves of *Bel* are used in *Pooja* not as the leaf but as the flower. After plucking the leaf of *Bel* they come back home. Then women get ready to sing and dance all over the day. They come together to sing songs and they perform a group dance, which is called *Jhamta* (a kind of group dance). Tharu women sing Tharu folk song and perform *Jhamta* in a group. The songs they sing during the day carry some kind of Tharu ancient story and history.

The place of worshipping and the manner of their worshipping also exhibit Tharu cultural inheritance to nature. They have really realized the role of nature significant higher than the position of men. Their worshipping begins at the mid-day. They prepare a worshiping place known as *Brahmathan*. Every place cannot be the *Brahmathan*. *Brahmathan* is a big tree. Basudev (63) opines that "they select a tree as *Brahmathan* and worship under the tree and suppose the tree as *Brahma*." In the middle of the day they go to *Brahmathan* to worship god *Brahma*. This process of worshipping Brahma through the tree has a great value. It is a *Yajna* and the *yajna* is important for the nature and universe, "yajñas were performed to maintain the ṛtam of the universe" (Jain, 2011: 107). The worship in the *Brahmathana* is not just a culture; it is their cultural *yajna* and offering to Brahma. Brahma is the god of creation in Hindu myth and belief. It is Tharu belief that they suppose the tree as the source of creation. There is the logic behind this belief that women follow this cultural pattern for the betterment, health, well-being, and prosperity of their children and they worship the image of Brahma, the tree or the creator. They inherit from the very core of the culture that nature is the prime force of creation, protection, health, and prosperity in their lives.

The real *Vrata*, known as *Upavasa* takes place on the second day, the day of *Astami*. The real *Vrata* day begins with the pray to dawn. Binu Chaudhari (38) says, "Tharu women wake up early in the morning and gather together at a time, if possible all women from the community at a place at a time and sing *Badahaw*." *Badaha* is a song especially wishing for a good dawn. *Badahaw*; this song is sung during the dawn so it is also called *Bhinsaharuwa* (song of dawn). All aged women and girls sing this song together. The next step is their bath in the river. They go to the river and bathe as in the first day. They think it as the means of purification for the day of real *Vrata*. Staying fasting all the day does not end their *Varta*. After the *Nirahara Vrata* the whole day, they listen to the sermon (a story about Jitiya) at night.

Historically and culturally, Tharu people do not make any concrete temple as the place to worship rather they worship the nature, most often trees and river. Tharu people have the real sense of "intersection of human, natural, and supernatural worlds" (Jain, 2011: 115). In *Brahmathan* women sing a song that is called *Jatsari*. Budhan believes, "It is the song for water god". This song of worshipping water is sung to make lord *Bishnu* happy. They believe that Lord Vishnu dwells in water, in the river, and they worship water on this occasion. This song is especially about asking for god and goddess to relief, peace, and wealth as well as protection of life, nature, and village.

Similarly, they have the high respect to the animal kingdom. Their respect to *Chilo* (eagle) from the sky zone and *Shero* (fox) from the earthly zone shows their intertwined relationship of spirituality, ethics, and ecology. When they come back from *Brahmathan*, they go to cut a branch of *Peepal* and *Pakadi* to make an artificial tree to make a nest of eagle (*Chilo*) during the time of sermon. *Chilo* is the most honest and loyal, hardworking legendary figure. Some boys help them to cut the branch of *Peepal* and *Pakadi*. Again, the women sing the song while cutting the *Peepal* branch for the permission. Mangal Tharu says this song "*Darkatoni*, and makes the tree happy listening this song". This song has another symbolic attachment that they believe *Peepal* tree as the form of Lord Vishnu, "Some associate the pipal tree particularly with VISHNU, who is said to have been born under one" (Jones & Ryan, 2007: 329), and also a tree "that Buddha reached his enlightenment" (329) with the belief of "foremost among the sacred trees" (629). This song is intended to make Lord Vishnu happy and asking god to give them the best daughter, son, father in law, and mother in law in their marital life.

The branch of *Peepal* and plant of paddy are brought at the center of the village to make *Thaat* of *Chilo* and *Shero*. *Thaat* is the nest or secret place for *Chilo* and *Shero* to stay. The place of the *Thaat* is scrubbed by cow dung to make it pure and holly. After making it Tharu women go to a river to worship *Jarahari* (goddess of water). In this time they also sing a song, which is about the goddess *Ganga, Jamuna*, and *Saraswati*. Again, they suppose the river as the symbol of the goddesses, *Ganga, Jamuna*, and *Saraswati*. They have the trend not to throw any waste in the river because they think that the river must be preserved, and it must be clean. After finishing this song, they go to their home. Tharu women bring the fruits and leaf of *Bel* in basket made from bamboo and put it around the artificial tree *Thaat*. They sit around it to listen the story of Jitiya that is told by a good narrator or headman of the village. Woman can also tell the story of Jitiya if she is a good narrator.

The whole day of Jitiya *Vrata* passes with their close affinity with nature and natural elements: river, plant, animal, and birds. They stay fasting, take bath frequently, worship plants like *Bel* and *Peepal*, worship the dawn and the river and water, worship the tree, *Brahmathana*, and find the sense of purification with nature and offer food, fruits and prepare nest to the animals and birds, eagle, and fox. All these events take place one after another as their cultural patterning to the respect and preservation of nature is their cultural procedure. These natural elements are just the icons representing their trend of how they keep the nature in their cultural patterning.

Their Jitiya *Vrata* is not complete on the second day. They have to perform some cultural function on the third day too. The Third day or last day of Jitiya is called *Paran*. Tharu women wake up early in the morning and go to the river to take bath. They bring soil and *Bel* leaf with them. They bring soil to make idol. Women bring *Bel* leaf to cover the idol that is made by soil because *Bel* leaf is sacred. At the time of bathing they make a pair of idols from soil. These idols stand for their children, one for son and another for daughter. They cover it from leaf of *Bel*. Tharu women believe that if they make good idol, they have good and beautiful child. After finishing it they offer milk to sun. Then they come back at their home and scrub their house with cow dung. Tharu women burn *Guietha*, firewood made by cow's dung, and put *Dhup*, wood of aloes on the fire. They offer some fruits, milk, and curd on the fire for the god before they eat. Then only they can eat food and drink water. After all this, Tharu women complete their Vrata and whole day they sing and dance.

Hence, the essence behind the Jitiya culture, not "as cultural and imperial dominance" (Mangan, 1990: 18), has to do with the friendly and co-operative handling, taking care of, and worshipping nature. Culture for Tharus is "an ideal bridge signifying ethics, virtues, duties, and cosmic order" (Jain, 2011: 115), because Jitiya helps to bring moral ethics, shape the life style, respect and love others and preserve and respect nature. All the activities they perform from beginning to the end of the festival show that they enhance nature preservation "further by combining religion, ethics, and ecology" (118). For them environment, ethics, and theology and culture are not separate. The nature comes as often as human socialization to them.

Tharus, the aboriginal people of Chitwan and surrounding locations have understood the importance of ecology. Known as the Bhumiputras (sons of the earth), Tharus have been worshipping water, dawn, plants and animals as the icons of divine with greater value in human life. It has created efforts to kindle a sense of reverence toward nature. Being conscious not to hurt nature, Tharus have shown ample respect with the sense that "humans and their cultures are an integral part of the environment. Human activity affects the environment, which is then altered, in turn affecting human activities" (Sutton & Anderson, 2010: 2). Jitiya culture regards nature to be always sacred phenomenon in the mode of pantheism. They adopt culture "as a combination of ethics (in the human world), ecology (in natural world), and theology (in the spiritual world)" (Jain, 2011: 118). Ethics, especially the cultural ethics, ecology, the nature, and natural phenomena, and theology, their cultural religion exist as predominant part of their culture, Jitiya.

They have sense of "connection" and "belonging" to earth, its living systems, or the universe as a whole with their belief that "natural objects are shot through with sticky notions of sacrality embedded within and through them" (Nagarajan, 1998: 278). They, "have been living in the Terai for centuries, were reputed to have innate resistance to malaria" (Terrenato, 2018: 115) with their nature of being natural, have close attachment to earth and other natural elements with a faith that "the natural world is a divine being" (277) and perceive nature with spirituality. For them religion is the spiritualities of connections. This culture has to do with belonging or being bound to forces greater than the self. Following the culture is their dharma, the great religion, "dharma" is based on "Vedic monism," a holistic idea that means virtue (in the human world), cosmic order (in the ecological world), and rituals (in the spiritual world), (Jain 120). Such spiritualties usually are accompanied by kinship feelings and ethical obligations toward nonhuman life. They appear to be likely to play an important role in the human religious future, perhaps in part because such cultural associations can be apprehended through the senses.

4 Myths of *Jitiya Pawani*: Eco-Rereading

The success of *Jitiya Parwa* or *Jitiya Vrata* has to do with the myths and religious stories recited on its occasion. The culture of Jitiya Parwa is strongly connected with the myth and the literature of *Jitiya Pawani*. Reciting *Jitiya Pawani*, listening to the stories related to Jitabahana and other mythical events is a compulsory activity of the *Parwa or Vrata*. Otherwise, the *Vrata* is supposed to remain incomplete. Originally transmitted to the large Tharu communities, "Jitiya Pawani is a religious story with social value passing from Satya Yuga" (Sharma, 2071: 37). The beginning of the narration shows its ancient, religious, and social value with reference to the gods and goddesses.

The direct connection of the story is with a central character, Jitabahana, "a character distinct from the imagined communities of modern nations" (Anderson, 1983: 13), having his link with the myth of far past, but the reflective understanding of the story goes to the base level of worshipping Lord Krishna, Lord Vishnu, Lord Shiva, Surya, Goddess Maha Laxmi, and Goddess Saraswati. There is a single plot of the mythical story, but it consists of many mythical references. There are mainly three mythical stories found in oral tradition, and the recitation takes place as a matured, usually the old and respected one in the society, man or woman telling the stories by heart, purely in oral form.

5 Myth of She-Hawk and She-Jackle[1]

Long ago, Kanchanawati was the city near Narmada River. Malayaketu ruled this city that time. There was a large Pakar tree and a "she-hawk" would live on the branch and a "she-jackal" would live in its trunk hole. They were fast friends. They saw women were staying fasting and doing *Vrata* and performing *pooja*. Also, they decided to observe the fasting and perform the puja of Jimutabahan, son of Shalibahan. It was the same day when the son of the richest trader of that city died. He was cremated nearby. In the night there was terrific rain and thunderstorm. The jackal could not resist the temptation of eating the remains, but the hawk continued with her fasting.

[1]Originally these myths are found in Tharu oral traditions. After centuries of their oral foundation, Kalanath Adhikari wrote them in Tharu language, and Babu Ram Pandey translated into Nepali. The myths are presented in synopsis modes and these translations are my translations.

Next day after the women folks broke the fasting, she also broke it. In the next birth, they were born as sisters in the house of a Brahmin named Bhaskar. The elder sister, (hawk in previous birth) was named Sheelawati and was married to Buddhisen and the younger sister, (jackal in previous birth) was named Karpoorawati and was married to the king, Malayketu. Due to the blessings of Jimootbahan, Sheelwati was blessed with seven sons. But all the sons of Karpoorawati died just after birth. She was very sad.

When the seven sons of Sheelawati came of young age, they applied for and got service with the king. When Karpoorawati saw them, she turned blue with envy. With her wicked design, she persuaded the king to get the seven youths killed and sent the heads in seven containers covered with red cloth to her elder sister. Jimootbahan knew about this and he made heads of clay, fixed them on the trunk and scattered elixir (*amrit*) to make them alive. The sons returned to their home. The wives had received the heads, but they turned to palm fruits.

Karpoorawati, all day, waited to hear the screams of the women folk of the house of Buddhisen. When nothing happened, she sent her maid to that house. The maid reported that the sons are all rejoicing in their house. The queen first suspected her husband of fooling her, but he told that there must be God's blessing on that family.

Karpoorawati went to her sister and told her everything and enquired how her sons could not die. Sheelawati, due to her penance, remembered every details of previous life. She took Karpoorawati to the tree and narrated the events of previous life. Hearing all these Karpoorawati fell unconscious and died. The king performed her last ritual. It is the time that people have believed on the power of Vrata and Pooja not only in life but also after life.

6 Human Nature Bonding in the Myth of "She-Hawk" and "She-Jackal"

At its surface level, this story appears just as a myth, and an imagination. It consists of many unbelievable connections. How do the animal and the bird know the essence of human ritual and culture? How such idea of staying *Vrata* come to them? How was it possible that they get birth in the same family as sisters in their next life? These and so many other questions are unanswered if looked into scientific logic. But, the major aspect of understanding the text is on "how the concept of human and nature connection has passed through" (Acharya, 2074 BS: 32) for many generations.

It is believed that "this event took place ages ago, before *Kali Yuga*, even in *Treta Yuga*" (Pandey, 2074 Bs: 43). The story shows how humans and animals had the mutual communication. As the story is a part of the myth, the intention of the story is to say that human and nonhuman beings were having the same sense and understanding, and should follow the same even today though not the same in condition. Another point is that it was the time that birds and animals could do the same as humans could. This very information exposes that "essentially humans, birds, and animals have common essence-life" (Pokharel, 2016: 33), desire, emotion, feeling, hunger, and many others. This information may be surrealistic, but the main massage is to show the connection between human nature and nonhuman nature from the common base.

Similarly, another mode of bonding is the birth of "she hawk" and "she jackal" as the sisters. As a myth, the main aspect of the story is not to dissect the truth and untruth, but it intends to generate faith in the people today. Humans are born as animals and birds and other forms of life after death, and these nonhuman beings are born as humans after death. It shows the eternal connection between human nature and nonhuman naturethe connection is not only lifelong connection, it has the eternal and endless connection. Ultimately, this way of mythopoeia of humans and nonhuman inter-birth relation encourages people from the same culture to respect nonhuman nature with the faith that they could take birth in the same zone in any cycle of life.

7 Myth of Jitabahana and His Adventure

Another story recited at Jitiya festival is the story of adventurous life of Jitabahana. Long ago there were two monsters named Uchcharinga and Musari Dan. Uchcharinga killed Musari Dan for not bringing the woods for him. The earth was created from the skin, bones, and the flesh of Musari Dan. Slowly the life got started on earth. One of the rulers was King Parikchit who had two sons named Haradatta and Shubhadatta with very short life. As the part of their tradition, the citizens had to manage the materials for the death rituals (*Fachhaka*) of the princes. A lady, Maswami could not manage such materials because of her poverty. She prayed to lord Krishna and he, being happy with her worshiping, visited her house, but she had gone to her neighbour's house that night.

Lord Krishna became angry with her because she had prayed him and called him but she had left the house. He defecated outside of her house out of which the green vegetable was green up on the same single night. She found the green vegetable in her backyard and she became happy and ate it. She gave birth to a son because she had eaten the vegetable grown out of his excretion. The son grew up and people began to call the boy without the father. As per the instruction of her mother, the boy went in search of his father. He found Lord Krishna, his father and Krishna gave him his name as Jitabahana and blessed him for his good, social, and prosperous life. The boy had to go to long and difficult journey to find his father.

Jitabahana, with the help of the blessing of lord Krishna and his good works, is known as the divine figure and is worshipped as the incarnated form of Lord Krishna among the Tharu community, especially in Chitwan district and surrounding areas. It is the main story of the creation of earth, birth of Jitbahan, struggle of Jitbahana and the social service and the good will of Jitabahana for many generations in the past and expected to be continued for many generations to come as the part of the culture.

8 Enriching Eco-Culture Through the Myth of Jitabahana

Jitabahana, as the "characters once relocated, often lose their problematic status" (Arata, 2010: 107), is a heroic figure in the mythical story. His birth has raised questions on his mysterious birth without the biological contact. The mysteries are also found on how he travels a long and immeasurable distance from earth to the heaven. He has also met different gods and goddesses in the heaven. And he has returned back to earth, to his village, and has undergone a common and successful life, but with the success for the betterment of the whole human beings. His birth and his travel have delivered the eco-cultural message to Tharu people.

His birth has the messages to impart to the people of Tharu culture. Though Jitbahana's birth is a mysterious and incredible, its ecological message is that Jitabahana has been birth basically from the green plant. Maswami woman has eaten the green plant grown at the back of her house, and she has become pregnant. This reference has mystery cum nature-human message. Though it seems as unnatural at its surface level, his birth has connected human-plant contact and the consequent creation. Having the divine intention, his birth has justified human-plant nexus, hence the message for human-nature harmony.

Jitabahana, name from the word, "*jit*" victory, has struggling life from the very birth. He has to answer all the questions about his birth and father. Troubled with many nuisance questions, he has set an infinite journey to heaven. His journey has properly addressed ecological concern at different modes of his journey. He has met with many animals having some problems each on his infinite journey. Their problems are finite ones, but they are expecting the solutions from his infinite journey. He has met a tiger suffering from his throat; especially the bones of animals have blocked his throat, which had made him difficult to eat and even to breathe. The tiger shares this problem and requests to find the solution from the Lord Krishna if he met. Similarly, in another step, he met an elephant sunk into the quicksand, neither it could move ahead nor go the back. The elephant requested in the same manner. Likewise, a crocodile was suffering from stomach pain for long. It requested him to come with the solution from Lord Krishna. He has carried the message of those animals to Lord Krishna, and has brought the solutions. These solutions have become the remedies for each of these animals. Jitabahana has become a helping agent to reduce their problems. It examines the idea that originally humans are not the destroyer of plant and animal kingdom. They must help preserve the animals and nature.

9 Jitiya, Creation Myth and Human-Nonhuman Equality

Jitiya culture also includes the creation myth included in Jitiya myth. The myth transmits the idea of the world creation from the bones of monster. The myth says that there were two monsters named Uchcharinga and Musari Dan. Musari was a hardworking and earning the livelihood by hard work. One day, Uchcharinga killed

Musari Dan for not bringing the woods for him. It is believed the earth was created from the skin, bones, and the flesh of Musari Dan. Slowly the life got started on earth.

This belief of the creation does not make any distinction between human creation and other forms of natural creation. The earth, life, both human and nonhuman including plants had the same process of creation. This shows that, the origin of the humans, and other forms is the same, and the distinction as humans as superior and other animals and plants as inferior has no logic. Based on this principle, Tharus respect every form of life in nature, they live with nature, they get help to nature preservation and they get help from the nature. They have immense love to the earth, and they are also known as *Bhumiputra*—the children of the earth.

10 Conclusion

Human behavior is strictly guided by the hidden instinct, and also by the cultural pattern one is born and brought up. If the culture provides the lesson of living with nature, man learns it as the same, and if the culture teaches the man to exploit nature and live in the extreme destruction of nature, he/she does the same. Culture is the guiding principle for humans to treat to nature and the environment. The "tabula rasa" view held that humans learned most from their culture, and so does it happen in the case of Tharus. They are born in nature on earth as the sons/daughters of the earth (*Bhumiputra*), and they learn to live with nature, but not against nature. They respect the eagle, the fox, the Bel tree, the Peepal tree, the river, the dawn, the earth, the soil, and other natural elements with equal respect to human beings and the divine sources. All of their divine icons are from the nature. They tell and retell the stories of the nature, their life in nature to their children to make them aware of the role of nature in their lives.

Their worship to nature in the mode of pantheism does not mean that they do not make use of the nature. But it means they share equal responsibility to nature as much as they do to other human beings. Plucking the Bel leaf for the purification does not happen messily, but they sing a song of regret and pluck it with a kind of permission. They offer food to animals, wild ones and the tamed ones for the sake of equality. They have not understood the theory of human and natural harmony, but they provide the culture of natural harmony through their culture, especially Jitiya.

Furthermore, both the mythical stories—"She hawk" and "She jackal" and the story of Jitabahana, have shown strong connectivity between human being and animal life. These stories not only provide them the pleasure, but also they give them the moral on the equality between humans and nonhuman nature. They expect and have the wish that their son/daughter would be like Jitabahan, would follow all the cultural patterns and would keep a good relationship with other beings. Therefore, Jitiya culture, unlike other cultures, violates the culture/nature binary and destroys the cultural hegemony over nature. It is an eco-friendly culture (Figs. 1 and 2).

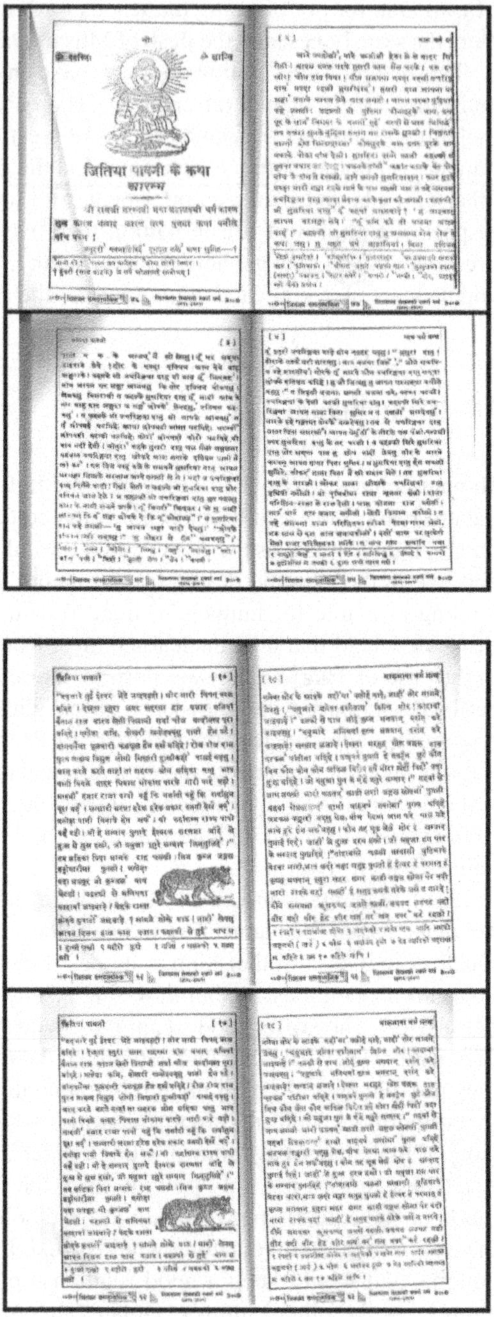

Fig. 1 Jitiya Pawani in Tharu Language (author's archive)

Fig. 2 Dialogue with community and rituals (author's archive)

Glossary

Amrit**:** elixir
Ashmin Krishna asthami**:** a day in the month of Ashwin (September–October)
Badahaw**:** a Tharu song
Bel**:** wooden apple
Bhinsaharuwa**:** song of the dawn
Bhumiputra sons of the earth
Chitwania/n**:** of Chitwan
Fagupurnima**:** a Hindu cultural festival
Guietha**:** wood made out of cow dung
Janai Purnima**:** a Hindu cultural festival
Jhamata**:** a Tharu dance
Jit**:** victory
Khar Jitiya**:** strong Vrata of Jitiya
Lahakai**:** first day of Jitiya
Mithilanchal**:** a place of Mithila region
Nirjala**:** without even taking water
Paran**:** last day of Jitiya
Parwa**:** festival
Peepal**:** a kind of tree
Phool Lorhoni**:** song for plucking Bel
Pradosh**:** faulty time
Raptodun**:** a government commission
Tharu**:** aboriginal caste living in different places of Tarai
Upabas**:** fasting
Vrata**:** fasting
Yamosa**:** the festival of Tharus to remember their forefathers.

References

Acharya, H. (2074 BS). *Kalanath Adhikari: Byakti ra Kriti*. Hetauda: Kalanath Adhikari Smriti Pratisthan.

Alley, K. D. (1998). *Idioms of degeneracy: Assessing Ganga's purity and pollution: Purifying the earthly body of god: Religion and ecology in Hindu India*. New York: SUNY Press.

Anderson, B. (1983). *Imagined communities: Reflections on the origins and spread of nationalism*. London: Verso.

Arata, S. (2010). *Fictions of loss in the Victorian Fin de Siècle*. Cambridge: Cambridge University Press.

Guneratne, A. (2002). *Many tongues, one people: The making of Tharu identity in Nepal*. Ithaca: Cornell UP.

Hull, R. B. (2018). Nature. *Companion to environmental study* (Eds.), Noel Castree, Mike Hulme, & James D. Proctor. New York: Routledge.

Jain, P. (2011). *Dharma and ecology of Hindu communities: Sustenance and sustainability*. England: Ashgate.

Jones, C. A., & Ryan, J. D. (Eds.). (2007). *Encyclopedia of Hinduism*. New York: Facts on File.

Khanal, N. P. (Ed.). (2071 BS). *Chitwan Samasamayik*. Chitwan: Chitwan Samasamayik Patrika.

Khanal, N. P. (Ed.). (2073 BS). *Chitwan Samasamayik*. Chitwan: Chitwan Samasamayik Patrika.

Mangan, J. A. (1990). Introduction: Making imperial mentalities. *Making Imperial Mentalities: Socialisation and British Imperialism*. Manchester/New York: Manchester University Press.

Nagarajan, V. R. (1998). The earth as goddess Bhu Devi: Toward a theory of "embedded ecologies" in Folk Hinduism. *Purifying the earthly body of god: Religion and ecology in Hindu India*. New York: SUNY Press.

Pandey, B. (2074 BS). *Mera Aasthaka Dharohar*. Nawalparasi: Triveni Sahitya Parisad.

Pokharel, D. R. (2016). *Jitiya Pawani: Chitwan Samasamayik*. Chitwan: Samasamayik Patrika.

Sharma, M. R. (2071 BS). Kabi Kalanath Adhikari ra Jitiya Pawani Katha: Ek Adhyan. *Vivek*. 31. 10. TUTA: Birendra Multiple Campus.

Sharma, J., & Malla, K. (1990). A study on educationally disadvantaged population groups. *Rapti Valley*. CERID TU.

Steward, J. (2006). The concept and method of cultural ecology. In N. Haenn & Richard R. Wilk (Eds.), *The environment in anthropology*. New York/London: New York.

Taylor, P. J. (2018). Nature and nurture. In N. Castree, M. Hulme, & J. D. Proctor (Eds.), *Companion to environmental study*. New York: Routledge.

Terrenato, L. (2018). Decreased Malaria Morbidity in the Tharu people compared to sympatric population in Nepal. *Annals of tropical medicine and parasitology: The popular science monthly*, Vol. 46.

UP. Sutton, M. Q., & Anderson, E. N. (2010). *Introduction to cultural ecology* (2nd ed.). New York: Altamira Press.

Webster, J. (1993). *A Sociolinguistic profile of the Tharu Dialects of the Western Indo-Nepal Tarai*. A Survey Report. https://www.sil.org/resources/publications/entry/70672.

Importance and Perspectives of Natural Heritage in Romania

Daniela Antonescu

Abstract Romania has more than 24.8% of its land designated as protected area under different directives and regulations. A significant part is covered by primeval forests. Despite the significant share of natural landscapes, different pressures and amenities are continually increasing. Logging of forests, modifications of wild rivers, and decreasing numbers of wildlife threaten natural heritage in Romania. The biodiversity losing is the result of intensive agricultural and forestry activities, partially industrialized, advanced fragmentation of natural habitats by infrastructure and urbanization, water, air pollution and tourism development. This paper analyses the main aspects regarding to evolution, SWOT evaluation, general vision regarding to the field of protected areas and the main aspects of conservation of biodiversity and natural heritage, in Romania.

1 Introduction

The natural heritage is the system for life supporting, the base of economic and social activities, and the development process, ensuring the survival of life. Eco-natural systems are those that determine the specific conditions which require exchanges of energy, materials, and information, contributing to adaptability, resilience, and productivity. The relations established between different ecosystems are very complex, difficult to estimate the importance of each person, but also the potential consequences of losing an individual or group.

Organizing and conducting different economic activities generate environmental pressures related to land use, changing landscapes and ecosystems, destruction of natural spaces, irrational use of land, the overconcentration activities on a very sensitive space and high environmental value, etc. Population growth, agricultural development, and economy determined an increase in anthropogenic activities.

D. Antonescu (✉)
Center of Mountain Economy, Vatra Dornei, Romania
e-mail: daniela.antonescu25@gmail.com

O. Niglio and E. Y. J. Lee (eds.), *Transcultural Diplomacy and International Law in Heritage Conservation*, https://doi.org/10.1007/978-981-16-0309-9_9

In the last three decades, the diversification of human activities, accelerating globalization, and chronic pollution are the dominant traits of environmental deterioration. The damage of natural capital is a real process extremely complex, lengthy, and evolving strictly dependent on the pace, forms and forces of socio-economic development systems (Antonescu, 2013).

To protect biodiversity and for ensuring public access to outstanding natural areas for recreation and tourism, it has been proposed Protected Areas (PA). Whatever the definitions in each country and in international organizations, it is certain that they provide environmental, scientific, educational, recreational, economic, and cultural benefits, while the coverage of Protected Areas is an indicator of the degree to which biodiversity components are protected.

Given that, actually, we are witness of visible degradation of biodiversity, with irreversible effects and major imbalances on the environment, which make it necessary to establish an inventory of all-natural and biodiversity resources in Romania.

2 The Main Components of National Natural Heritage

Located in Central Europe, at an equal distance between the North Pole and the Equator, and between the Atlantic Ocean and the Ural Mountains, the Danube river and the Black Sea, Romania has balanced climatic and landscape regime: 28% mountains; 42% hills and plateaus; 30% plains and high biological diversity. Romania's geographical location and radial natural distribution determined the existence of a wide range of meso-microclimate and soil conditions.

Romania owns 54% of the Carpathians and almost 97.8% of the national rivers flowing into the Danube. The Black Sea region includes coastal platform and territorial waters, plus exclusive economic zone under the Strategy of Marine Net-works (Directive 2008/56/EC).

To maintain and preserve species and habitats, in European Union there are seven statutes of preservation, covered by: Directive 2009/147/EC (Birds Directive); Council Directive 92/43/EEC on the conservation of natural habitats and of wild fauna and flora (Habitats Directive). These directives are implemented in Romania through the following projects:

- Monitoring the conservation status of species and habitats (Art.17 Habitats Directive);
- National System of birds monitoring (Art. 12 Birds Directive).

The concept of "natural habitat" is defined by the Habitats Directive no. 92.43/EEC on the conservation of natural habitats and wildlife: terrestrial or aquatic areas, which are distinguished by comprehensive geographic features, abiotic and biotic, natural and semi-natural, similar with the concept of ecosystem (Bălteanu et al., 2006).

At national level, protected areas represent 24.84% of the country (protected areas of national interest—7%, Natura 2000 to 17.84%). Meanwhile, natural ecosystems represent 47% of the country, agricultural ecosystems hold 45% and construction/infrastructure around 8% of the territory.

The great diversity of Romanian natural heritage is determined, mainly, by the very high number of them, as it follows:

- 357 habitat types, the most of them having equivalent in major classification systems used at European level;
- 199 habitats—equivalent in Natura 2000;
- 213 habitats—Emerald equivalent;
- 170 habitats—Corine Program;
- 357 habitats—Palearctic Program;
- 263 habitats—EUNIS (European Nature Information System).

After Romanian's to EU, at national level there was an increase of protected natural areas (number and size). Thus, the national protected area network has gradually expanded by a series of Government Decision, in the period 2004–2010 (GD no. 2151/2004, no. 1581/2005, no. 1143/2007, no. 1066/2010, no. 1217/2010). Currently, in Romania, there are 998 protected areas, namely: 79 scientific reserves; 13 national parks; 230 nature monuments; 661 nature reserves; 15 natural parks; three biosphere reserves: Delta (1991), Retezat (1979), Pietrosul Rodnei (1979); 19 Ramsar Sites and one World Heritage Site: the Danube Delta.

3 Evolution of Protected Area, in Romania

Due to the growing interest for Protected Area in Romania, the number of these increased in recent years, from 1384 (2008) to 1503 areas (2013) (8.6%), thus: the wetlands of international importance with a growth rate of 280%, followed by the protected areas of Community Importance with a growth rate of 40.3% in 2013 compared to 2008. However, there are two categories of Protected Areas that did not follow the general trend, recording a numerical reduction: scientific reservations and natural monuments (Fig. 1).

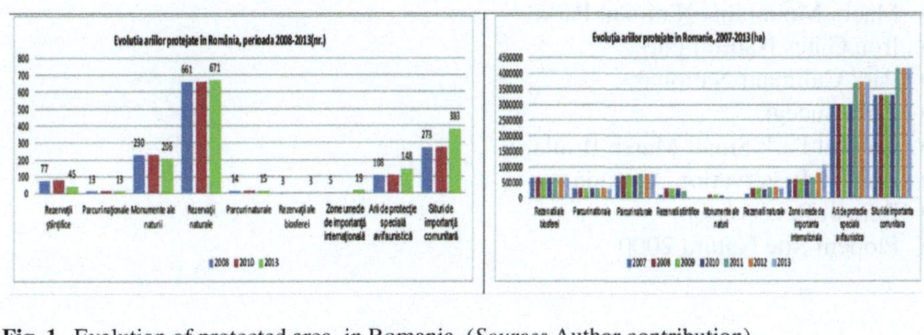

Fig. 1 Evolution of protected area, in Romania (*Sources* Author contribution)

Table 1 Central institutions involved in managing protected areas, in Romania

Ministry of Environment, Water and Forests	Developing national strategies on environmental protection (Romania's National Strategy on climate change—2050); LIFE + Program
Environment Fund Administration	The main institution that provides financial support to environmental protection program; It is coordinated by the Ministry of Environment
Ministry of European Funds	Develops and manages the Operational Program Large Infrastructure for period 2014–2020
Ministry of Regional Development and Public Administration (Territorial Development) National Agency for Cadastre and Land	Spatial Development Strategy of Romania; Coordinate integrated strategy for sustainable development of the Danube Delta; Implement National and Regional Spatial Program (RSP); Provides documentation endorsement landscaping, according to the competencies established by law
Ministry of Agriculture	National Program for Rural Development 2014–2020

Sources Author's contribution

Authorities responsible for protecting natural areas in Romania are those who develop strategies and programs, and legislation to domain (Table 1).

Management of protected natural areas is carried out according to OUG no. 57/2007 on the regime of protected natural areas, conservation of natural habitats, wild flora and fauna, approved by Law 49/2011, with HG 1000/2012 regarding the reorganization and functioning of the National Agency for Environmental Protection and subordinate public institutions.

At the end of 2013 there are ten approved management plans:

- Natural Park Grădiştea Muncelului,
- Cioclovina National Park,
- Macin Mountains National Park,
- Iron Gates Natural Park,
- Park Calimani National,
- Park Bucegi,
- Natural Park Small Marsh Braila,
- Blindly Rezervation Apahida,
- Beresti Rezervation,
- Plopeni Site Natura 2000.

4 SWOT Analysis of Romania's Biodiversity

A comprehensive SWOT analysis for the protected area was undertaken as part of the evaluation process and this identified the following opportunities and threats.

Strong points:

- Romania has a high biodiversity (about 3,700 plant species and almost 33,800 animal species), including species of Community interest and/or are on different lists of world heritage protection;
- The existence of adequate legislation and institutions empowered to act in this area;
- Romania has continuously participated in international environmental policy, signing and ratifying international conventions regarding the protection of World Heritage (cultural and natural);
- The existence of major natural areas 31 (3 biosphere reserves, 13 national parks, 15 nature parks) and 671 nature reserves;
- Significant growth area nationally protected natural areas mainly through setting up network covering about 23% of the country;
- The existence of an integrated GIS database at national level (catastre of protected areas, national parks zoning, creating the database in accordance with Natura 2000) and available free on the website of the Ministry of Environment;
- The existence of Natural Monuments Commission of the Romanian Academy, founded in 1950 and its involvement in the decision making process on protected areas;
- A large number of NGOs in environmental protection associations;
- The existence of national programs directly aimed at protected areas;
- Heritage diversity built under some protected areas (monasteries, archaeological sites, churches, etc.).

Weaknesses:

- Lack of management plans and effective protection for most of natural reservation and site Natura 2000;
- The increasing anthropogenic pressure on protected natural areas (deforestation, tourism, mining, overgrazing, etc.);
- Large area of Natura 2000 sites which include different land uses that are contrary to the objectives of protection;
- Lack rules for the application of laws aimed at protected areas and their management;
- Lack of funds for implementing the objectives of management protected natural areas;
- Lack of staff (or lack of) employee for activities for implementing the objectives of protection and management;
- The localities in the vicinity of protected areas are generally underdeveloped and have limited growth/development; they have limited access to infrastructure, and the population is in a continuous migration process;

- Irrational use of natural resources (e.g., forestry);
- Excessive use of coastal areas, without considering the ecological balance; gradual erosion and steep coastal zone and reducing the areas of the beach;
- The management of protected areas does not result in a correlation of economic and social development objectives with conservation, given that communities are fragile protected areas (mountain areas, border isolated).

Opportunities:

- The existence of important European sources of funding to the elaboration of management plans and public awareness to the importance of protected areas;
- Implementation of projects through the effective management of protected natural areas (ex., SINCRON);
- Increase the involvement of NGOs, educational institutions and research on issues related to protected areas and their management;
- Provision of grants to reduce human pressure on natural protected areas.

Threats:

- Habitat loss and fragmentation of habitat due to urbanization, infrastructure development, exploitation of natural resources, especially the forest;
- Uncontrolled and illegal logging in protected natural areas;
- The draining of wetlands for cultivation or use and for obtain economic profits;
- The abandonment of use traditional land, especially for pastures and meadows; the incineration; overgrazing;
- The overexploitation of ecosystems and species through various economic activities;
- Penetration and expansion of invasive species;
- Environmental pollution and uncontrolled waste effects the biodiversity (acid rain, eutrophication, etc.);
- Wind farms build especially on migration routes of migratory birds;
- Global environmental changes, climate change through extreme weather events (droughts, floods, heat waves or cold, windy intensification, etc.).

SWOT analysis is the main instrument for evaluating the threats for protected areas, in Romania. The local and regional authorities play a important role in the process of protecting biodiversity by providing advice on how to:

- strengthen the adaptive management and monitoring the whole process;
- enhance organizational and development learning;
- enable informed decision—making and enhance the long-term sustainability of the different program achievements.

5 The Vision of Protected Areas Development

By comparing internal and external factors of SWOT analysis acceptable vision and perspectives were formulated which are as follows. Thus, the general vision regarding to the field of protected areas: until 2035, Romania biodiversity, including ecosystem services it provides (natural capital), will be protected, valued and restored. It will take account of the intrinsec value of biodiversity and the vital contribution of the services provided by nature to human wellbeing and economic prosperity. The vision proposed is consistent with the EU and national objectives and strategies: EU Strategy for biodiversity and Strategy Europe 2020; National Strategy of territorial development of Romania—2035 (Horizon 2050); Sustainable Millennium Development Goals; Romania's National Strategy 2013–2020–2030; The National Sustainable Development Strategy for the agri-food sector and rural areas in the period 2014–2020–2030; the priority-action (Prioritized Action Frameworks)—Habitats Directive Natura 2000 sites.

In the author' opinion, the main actions which will support this vision are:

- Inventory of all species to determine measures for maintaining/improving their conservation status;
- Elaboration of studies to assess and monitor the conservation status of species and habitats;
- Economic and social analysis on the impact of human activity on Natura 2000 sites and the species of community interest or internationally.
- Prioritization of actions depending on the seriousness of the situation.
- Implementation and follow up of management plans;
- Identifying and prioritizing invasive species and ways to strike; control/eradication of invasive species with potentially higher;
- Maintaining ecological corridors, for migratory species, maintaining, and/or improving the connectivity network of protected areas, including Natura 2000;
- Ecological reconstruction of degraded ecosystems on the surface of protected areas, including Natura 2000 sites

6 Possible Scenarios for 2035 Horizon

Regardless of the time to which they relate, territorial planning scenarios should consider the nature and the environment, among other factors. From this perspective, we propose further four spatial planning scenarios, which can be applied to individual regions and can provide an overview of the evolution and status of biodiversity and protected areas in Romania.

Scenario 1: Knowledge-regions according to Europe 2020)—regions turn to modern technology, exchange of information, and modern systems of communication in order to identify new solutions to environmental issues. In parallel, it relies on good information to citizens and their effective participation in the management of the ecosystem in which they live. In this scenario, research and new technologies are the main driving forces that let a sustainable use of natural capital throughout the region. Increase the dissemination of information will allow better awareness of residents about the natural living environment and for society as a whole will become more involved in the management area. The three sectors that contribute significantly to the environmental concerns—urbanization, tourism, and agriculture—will benefit from a number of inventions and innovations that will help protect the environment and maintain or restore biodiversity.

Scenario 2: Regions based on endogenous potential (New Economic Geography)—relying on the local resources and traditions, in pursuit of a regional economy flexible, able to adapt to the outdoor environment. This scenario is specific to regions that promote long-term programs and capitalizing on regional strengths, including natural. Scenario opposes market liberalization trend (trend promoted by the European Union) and the recovery at any price, endogenous potential by large international companies. The effects of climate change and unsustainable agricultural policies, which seek to maximize the benefits, affecting biodiversity in protected areas. Part of the local population will migrate from the affected area due to the worsening environmental conditions, while the differences between rich and poor will increase. The inhabitants of these regions want to live in a sustainable environment in terms of environmental quality and social.

Scenario 3: Regions so-called red-zone (with the important environmental problems), which have clear signs of environmental damage as a result of uncontrolled human action: continuously increasing temperature, precipitation will decrease or flooding occurs. In this scenario, the region, together with an environmental crisis and the economic and social one. Biodiversity is increasingly threatened, more water use is strictly controlled, agriculture returns to dry crop varieties, tourism activity decreases, urbanization is increasing, etc. As a result, it is necessary to invest increasingly funds in research for clean technologies (green). Researchers and NGOs will become key members of the local community. This will result in a new paradigm of sustainability.

Scenario 4: Adaptive-region—covers the main features of each described above scenario. The main principle of this scenario is: global knowledge will support the development and application of new technologies in the context of the economic-social-ecological system. Under this scenario, the region will develop sectors of agriculture/forestry and eco-basic tourism and urbanization will take account of landscape and land use conditions in protected areas. In this regard, these regions will attract inhabitants, companies, NGOs, public institutions, etc., maintaining territorial and social at a high level of cohesion.

Because human activities (economic, social, cultural, etc.) can't be separated from nature, it is necessary to promote a model of thought on the development of protected areas based on the principle of conservation framework for development. Besides, in areas with many natural landscapes, future practices have to en-force both economic and social services, in parallel with the protection of ecosystems. The stimulation of economic activities must respect the environment unconditional and promoting human welfare.

7 Conclusions

In Romania, natural heritage influenced in particular by inaction and depletion of financial and intern resources. Threats to biodiversity are both quantitative and, especially, qualitative, which entails a need for better knowledge of the current situation. Moreover, there are many strategic documents and action plans, remaining in statements that have reported negative effects of human activities on nature: wild species threatened with extinction (fourth EU), many ecosystems degraded habitats modified as a result of increasing urbanization, overexploitation of natural resources, introduction and spread of invasive species, climate change, extreme, landslides, floods, etc.

Given the capital, global, and dramatic environmental changes, conservation of protected areas is a strategic priority at the national and international levels. In this respect, Romania should promote and implement urgently a strategy for the conservation of natural areas based on the reality of information on policies and measures integrated development on a sustainable approach horizontal trans-disciplinary and involve both of all its inhabitants.

Protected areas represent 24.84% of the total national surface. These protected areas are under the coordination of national and county authorities. The research has shown that local factors have a very important role in implementing strategies for protecting biodiversity. Taking into account the low financing resources available it is important the wise management of available funds allocated and establishing clear priorities in the short and long run. As well important is the stability in a time of these priorities and not to be allowed conjectural modifications for the sake of short term interests.

References

Antonescu, D. (2013). *The regional development policy of Romania in the post-accession period.* Postdoctoral Research. www.ince.ro.

Bălteanu, D., Dumitraşcu, M., Ciupitu, D., & Geacu, S. (2006). Protected natural areas. In *Romania. Space. Society. Environment.* Bucureşti: The Publishing House of the Romanian Academy.

EU Strategy for biodiversity and Strategy Europe 2020. National Strategy of territorial development of Romania—2035 (Horizon 2050).

Hotărâre nr. 2151/2004 privind instituirea regimului de arie naturală protejată pentru noi zone. https://lege5.ro/Gratuit/guydqnbu/hotararea-nr-2151-2004-privind-instituirea-regimului-de-arie-naturala-protejata-pentru-noi-zone. Accessed 10 August 2020.

Hotărârea Guvernului nr. 1581/2005 privind instituirea regimului de arie naturală protejată pentru noi zone. https://lege5.ro/Gratuit/hazdgmru/hotararea-nr-1581-2005-privind-instituirea-regimului-de-arie-naturala-protejata-pentru-noi-zone. Accessed 10 August 2020.

Hotărârea Guvernului nr. 1143/2007 privind instituirea de noi arii naturale protejate. https://lege5.ro/Gratuit/geydkmzqg4/hotararea-nr-1143-2007-privind-instituirea-de-noi-arii-naturale-protejate. Accessed 10 August 2020.

Hotărârea Guvernului nr. 1066 /2010 privind instituirea regimului de arie naturală protejată asupra unor zone din Rezervaţia Biosferei Delta Dunării şi încadrarea acestora în categoria rezervaţiilor ştiinţifice. https://lege5.ro/Gratuit/geztqnjsge/hotararea-nr-1066-2010-privind-instituirea-regimului-de-arie-naturala-protejata-asupra-unor-zone-din-rezervatia-biosferei-delta-dunarii-si-incadrarea-acestora-in-categoria-rezervatiilor-stiintifice. Accessed 10 August 2020.

Legea nr. 5 din 6 martie 2000 privind aprobarea planului de amenajare a teritoriului naţional, secţiunea III – zone protejate, Bucureşti. https://lege5.ro/Gratuit/gi3donbu/legea-nr-5-2000-privind-aprobarea-planului-de-amenajare-a-teritoriului-national-sectiunea-a-iii-a-zone-protejate. Accessed 10 August 2020.

Ordinul Ministrului Mediului şi Pădurilor nr. 2387/2011 pentru modificarea Ordinului ministrului mediului şi dezvoltării durabile nr. 1964/2007 privind instituirea regimului de arie naturală protejată a siturilor de importanţă comunitară, ca parte integrantă a reţelei ecologice europene Natura 2000 în România. https://lege5.ro/Gratuit/gi3dimrsgq/ordinul-nr-2387-2011-pentru-modificarea-ordinului-ministrului-mediului-si-dezvoltarii-durabile-nr-1964-2007-privind-instituirea-regimului-de-arie-naturala-protejata-a-siturilor-de-importanta-comunitar. Accessed 10 August 2020.

Strategia Naţională privind Schimbările Climatice 2013–2020, Ministerul Mediului şi Schimbărilor Climatice. http://www.mmediu.ro/categorie/strategia-nationala-privind-schimbarile-climatice-rezumat/171. Accessed 10 August 2020.

Strategia Naţională pentru Conservarea Biodiversităţii 2013–2020. Ministerul Mediului şi Schimbărilor Climatice.

Sustainable Millennium Development Goals. Romania's National Strategy 2013–2020–2030.

The National Sustainable Development Strategy for the agri-food sector and rural areas in the period 2014–2020–2030. The priority-action (Prioritized Action Frameworks)—Habitats Directive Natura 2000 sites.

A Relationship Between Plants and Their Hindu and Buddha Cultures: An Analysis Ficus Religiosa (Pipal)

Navaraj Pokharel and Bindu Adhikari Pokharel

Abstract Ficus religiosa or the sacred fig is a common tree found in the South Asian area having a cultural value. This study examines the environmental and cultural value of Ficus religiosa in the context of Nepal and Hindu and Buddha religious culture. This tree is found in the tropical, subtropical, and temperate region of Nepal (80 m–1600 m elevation range). Physically this species reaches a height of up to 30 m in Nepal. As per the study this tree has a life span of 1500 years. The longevity of the trees have the proof of various changes that occur in the earth system. Culturally this species is taken as one of the symbols of the Hindu mythical 'Bishnu' who is the people saver god in Hindu myth. Gautam Buddha got the knowledge sitting below the Ficus religiosa tree. So, Hindus and Buddhists both give more importance to this tree. Beside that scientific proof is there about having the highest rate of oxygen release during the daytime. This study gives the detail of the mythical aspects and scientific approach of the Ficus religiosa in Nepal, Hindu and Buddha culture.

1 Introduction

Ficus religiosa or sacred fig is a species of fig native to Nepal, India, and China, that belongs to *Moraceae* family. This is also known as pipal in Nepal, Bodhi Tree in Buddhism, Pipalaa tree in India and somewhere *ashwattha* tree. The sacred fig is considered to have a religious significance in three major religions that originated on the Indian subcontinent, Hinduism, Buddhism, and Jainism. Hindu and Jain ascetics consider the tree to be sacred and often meditate under them and it is the tree under which Gautama Buddha is believed to have attained enlightenment. Some area of India like Odisha this tree is designated as the state tree also.

N. Pokharel (✉)
Patan College, Tribhuvan University, Lalitpur, Nepal

B. Adhikari Pokharel
Findings Nepal, Kathmandu, Nepal

O. Niglio and E. Y. J. Lee (eds.), *Transcultural Diplomacy and International Law in Heritage Conservation*, https://doi.org/10.1007/978-981-16-0309-9_10

The word 'Ficus' is originally from the Latin word 'Fig' which means the fruit of the tree whereas 'religiosa' refers to 'religion' that reflects sacredness of the plant in both Hinduism and Buddhism and by which is very frequently planted in temples.

Genus Ficus has 750 species of woody plants, from which Ficus religiosa is one of the important and usable species (Sharma et al., 2016; Joseph and Justin Raj, 2010). Ficus religiosa, commonly known as pipal is one of the oldest trees in Indian literature (Gautam et al., 2014). Its existence can be traced back to the Indus valley civilization (300–1700 BC) where it was embarked on the currency of that time (Pandey & Pandey, 2016). The tree finds its documentation in the holy books of Hinduism such as Arthasastra, Puranas, Upanishads, Ramayana, Mahabharata, Bhagavad Gita, and Buddhist literature. It belongs to the family Moraceae and genus Ficus. It derived its botanical name from two words i.e., 'Ficus' a Latin word for 'fig' and 'Religiosa' refers to 'religion' indicating its importance in Hindu and Buddhist religions (Bhalerao & Sharma, 2014). The detailed classification of tree has been presented in Table 1. The tree is native to Nepal and India and is believed to originate mainly in Nepal, and Northern and Eastern India. (Bhalerao & Sharma, 2014) and some of the common names of F. religiosa are as pipal in Nepali, Hindi, ashwatha in Sankrit (Gautam et al., 2014) Because of its contribution in historical events it has an important place in medicinal, mythological, and religious systems of India and hence this tree is mostly seen near religious places (Rutuja et al., 2015). The fig or pipal tree is foremost among the sacred trees of Indian tradition. This lush tree can grow to a huge size with a large canopy. It has large, rather thin leaves that make a rustling sound in a breeze, which tradition compares to the sound of the lute or veena. No one is allowed to cut down, remove branches, or tear off leaves from a pipal tree.

Some associate the pipal tree particularly with VISHNU, who is said to have been born under one. Often a pipal tree is officially 'married' to a margosa tree when they are planted together.

Table 1 Scientific classification of Ficus Religiosa

Kingdom:	Plantae
Subkingdom:	Viridaeplantae
Phylum:	Tracheophyta
Subphylum:	Euphyllophytina
Infraphylum:	Radiatopses
Class:	Magnoliopsida
Subclass:	Dilleniidae
Superorder:	Urticanae
Order:	Urticales
Family:	Moraceae
Genus:	Ficus
Species	Ficus religiosa

Fig. 1 A Full F. religiosa Tree, Nepal. Dinesh Valke, 2016

The tree plays a role in certain Brahminical rituals, and sometimes in marriage ceremonies. Branches of pipal wood were used in the VEDIC fire ritual. It was under a pipal tree that BUDDHA reached his enlightenment. Many legends, myths, and stories in Indian literature refer to events and occurrences that take place under this, the most sacred of Indian trees (Encyclopedia of Hinduism, 329) (Fig. 1).

2 Physical Appearance of *Ficus Religiosa*

The tree grows large in size with wide spreading branches and brown colored bark. It has thin shiny leaves and the fruit is compressed and circular in shape. New immature leaves are reddish pink in color which turns into deep green at the stage of maturity (Panchawat, 2012). Flowering occurs in February, onset of fruits start in summers, and ripening is complete before the onset of rainy season (Bhalerao & Sharma, 2014). Fruits grow in pairs together to form a single mass. Immature fruits are green in color which changes to blackish purple after ripening (Dharmender et al., 2010). All parts of this tree are rich in phytochemicals and are used in various food and medicinal preparations. The ripe fruits of F. religiosa are edible and rich source of proteins and minerals (Ruby et al., 2000). Fruits are rich in phytochemicals like flavonoids, terpenoids, glycosides, etc. which are known to cure diseases like asthma and digestive disorders (Makhija et al., 2010). The leaves contain phytochemicals such as flavonoids, terpenoids, tannins, etc., which are effective in curing ailments like hiccups, vomiting, gonorrhea, etc. (Bhalerao & Sharma, 2014) (Fig. 2).

Branchlets are grayish brown, sparsely pubescent when young. Stipules ovate, small, apex acute. Petiole slender, as long as or longer than leaf blade, articulate; leaf

Fig. 2 The leaves of the F. Religiosa. Blake C. Willson, 2002

blade triangular-ovate, 9–17 × 8–12 cm, leathery, abaxially green, adaxially dark green and shiny, base broadly cuneate to ± cordate, margin entire or undulate, apex acute to caudate with a 2–5 cm cauda; basal lateral veins 2, secondary veins 5–7 on each side of mid-vein.

Figs axillary on leafy branchlets, paired or solitary, red when mature, globose to depressed globose, 1–1.5 cm in diameter, smooth; peduncle 4–9 mm; involucral bracts ovate. Male, gall, and female flowers within same fig. Male flowers: few, near apical pore, sessile; calyx 2- or 3-lobed, margin revolute; stamen 1; filament short.

Gall flowers: pedicellate; calyx 3- or 4-lobed; ovary globose, smooth; style short; stigma enlarged, 2-lobed. Female flowers: sessile; calyx 4-lobed, broadly lanceolate; ovary globose, smooth; style thin; stigma narrow.

2.1 Distribution

This species is originally found in Nepal, India, and China. Moreover, the distribution is found over the following countries as per the literature:

In Africa this species is found: Chad, Egypt, Libya, and Madagascar.

Asia: Bangladesh, Bhutan, China, Fuijan, Guangdong, Yunnana, India, Hongkong, Andaman, and Nicobar Island, Israel, Laos, Myanmar, Nepal, Pakistan, the Philippines, Singapore, Sri lanka, Thailand, and Vietnam.

North America; Costa Rica, Cuba, Dominican Republic, Haiti, Panama, Nicaragua, Puerto Rico, United States, Oceania, Australia, Fiji, Paraguay, Venezuela, etc.

2.2 Habitat

F. religiosa occurs naturally in the submontane forest and is grown as an ornamental both within its native range and in places where it has been introduced. In the Middle East, the species is planted as an avenue or roadside tree and is held sacred and commonly planted by Hindus in India near temples. In the Philippines and in Nicaragua the species is cultivated in parks and along roadsides and pavements (Madulid, 1995), while in Paraguay it occurs in forests at lower elevations. *Ficus religiosa* is known to be a native Indian tree and thought to be originating mainly in Northern and Eastern India, where it widely found in uplands and plane areas and grows up to about 1650 m or 5000 ft in the mountainous areas. It is also found growing elsewhere in India and throughout the subcontinent and Southern Asia, especially in Buddhist countries, wild or cultivated. It is a familiar sight in Hindu temples, Buddhist monasteries and shrines, villages, and at roadsides. People also like to grow this sacred tree in their gardens. Ficus religiosa has also been widely planted in many hot countries all over the world from South Africa to Hawaii and Florida but it is not able to naturalize away from its Indian home, because of its dependence on its pollinator wasp, Blastophaga quadraticeps. An exception to this rule is Israel where the wasp has been successfully introduced 12. The available information on F. religiosa has been divided into four sections, which are ethnopharmacology, morphology, phytochemistry, and pharmacological studies (Table 2).

2.3 Traditional Uses

Traditionally, the leaf juice was used in the treatment of asthma, cough, sexual disorders, diarrhoea, haematuria, earache, toothache, migraine, eye troubles, gastric problems, and scabies. The leaf decoction was used as in toothache. The fruits were used in the treatment of asthma and other respiratory disorders and scabies. The stem

Table 2 Plant characteristic. Plant type

Characteristics	Broadleaved
	Perennial
	Seed propagated
	Shrub Tree
	Vegetative propagated
	Vine/climber
	Woody

bark was used in gonorrhea, bleeding, paralysis, diabetes, diarrhea, bone fracture, as antiseptic, astringent, and antidote.

Vedic History

Ficus religiosa, is the most popular member of the Moraceae family. *Ficus religiosa* has mythological, religious, and medicinal importance in Indian culture. References to *Ficus religiosa* are seen in numerous ancient holy texts like Arthasastra, Puranas, Upanishads, Ramayana, Mahabharata, Bhagavad Gita, and Buddhistic literature, etc. (Prasad et al., 2006). According to Vedic archives cited in the Brahma Purana, Padma Purana, and Skanda Purana, the pipal is a representative of Lord Vishnu. It also believed that all Trimurti's are born under this tree (Panchawat, 2012; Rutuja et al., 2015). As a mythological assumption, the root of pipal is devoted as a figure of Brahma, the trunk is Lord Vishnu and the leaves are regarded as Maha Shiva. The tree propagates very fast and roots are appended with trunk and seem like supportive pillars. It is sometimes also called kalpvriksha. Thus, the basis of different historical beliefs; pipal tree is distinguished with various vernacular names.

Hinduism and F. Religiosa

For antiquity and veneration, the *Ficus religiosa* (Aswattha) is unrivalled throughout the world. There is a mention of the tree from Vedic time onward. The tree is mentioned in the Bhagavad Gita as *Aswattha* or the 'one that is not the same tomorrow,' with reference perhaps, to this world which is ever changing. There is a superstitious belief that the plant gives off oxygen at night, but this belief is not supported by any scientific fact. The sacredness of the *Ficus religiosa* is mentioned in the Mahabharata: '*Aswattha*, having its roots above and branches below is eternal. Its leaves are the Chhandas. He who knows it, knows the vedas. Downwards and upwards are stretched its branches which are enlarged by the qualities; its sprouts are the objects of sense. Downwards, its roots leading to action are extended to this world of men.' According to the footnotes given by Roy in his translation of the Mahabharata: 'upwards and downwards means from the highest to the lowest of created things. Enlarged by the qualities i.e., the qualities appearing as the body, the senses, etc. The sprouts are the objects of sense, being attached to the senses themselves as sprouts to branches. The roots extending downwards are the desires for diverse enjoyments.' Detailing the sacredness of *Ficus religiosa*, it is said that its form cannot be known or its end, or its beginning, or its support.

Hindus associate the tree with the three gods Brahma, Vishnu, and Siva. The tree is considered to be a Brahman and worshipped daily after the morning bath. If an elderly member of the family dies, special offerings are made to it during the full thirteen days of mourning. If a boy dies during his thread ceremony, he is supposed to haunt the *Ficus religiosa* tree. The *Ficus religiosa* springs from the godhead.

In the Gita, the tree is supposed to typify the universe. This perhaps is because the figs of the tree are eaten by birds and its, seeds pass through the alimentary canal of the birds unharmed and take root at most unimaginable places like the roof or walls of a house or even on another tree.

The tree is considered to be Vishnu himself and at the same time Vishnu is believed to have been born under it. That is the reason why the tree or its branches are never cut unless it is for worship. A ceremony called Pratishta or the consecration of the *Ficus religiosa* is performed to transform the tree into a divinity by inducing Vishnu into it. Brahmins believe that untold blessings will be showered upon anyone who performs this ceremony.

According to the Mahabharata, the man who worships *Ficus religiosa* daily worships the whole universe. When Krishna stole the clothes of the maidens, he took them to a *Ficus religiosa* tree. Even though the tree is mainly associated with Vishnu, some consider Siva as the patron deity of the tree.

Brahmins worship the *Ficus religiosa* during their daily evening prayer. They go to the tree and facing east repeat a prayer and sing hymns in praise of the tree which says, you arc a God.

Buddhism

- The name Bodhi tree was given to a specific tree of the species *Figus religiosa (pipal tree)* under which, it is said, the Buddha first attained enlightenment. The name has subsequently been used for other members of the same species.
- *bodh gaya*—means *realized* in Hindi (bodh—sense | gaya—style) is a religious site and place of pilgrimage associated with the Mahabodhi (maha—big) Temple Complex in Gaya district in the Indian state of Bihar. It is famous as it is the place where Gautama Buddha is said to have obtained Enlightenment (Pali: bodhi) under what became known as the Bodhi Tree.
- A banyan is a tree in the same genus (*Ficus*) which starts as an epiphyte. It is often used to refer to the species *Ficus benghalensis*, the Indian banyan, but can refer to any of a number of other species, not including *Ficus religiosa.*

The Bodhi Tree in Lumbini Nepal is in the premises of the Maya Devi Temple complex right next to the shrine on the banks of the serene Maya Devi Pond. Buddhist monks often sit under the tree meditating and chanting spiritual scripts. The tree is an age-old pipal tree or *Ficus Religiosa* clad in colourful prayer flags, Locals believe that wishes made while tying a colorful prayer flag are often granted.

The significance of this tree is because of Bodhi Tree in Bodh Gaya where Buddha attained enlightenment and liberation from delusions, anger, and self-indulgence. The entire journey of Buddha's life is often associated with the tree—right from the time he abdicated his throne, became an ascetic, achieved enlightenment and taught about his observations till his death. The Bodhi Tree is, therefore, considered immensely significant in Buddhism.

Nowhere is the ignorance of and confusion about Buddhism better illustrated than in the widespread inability to distinguish between Bodhi trees and Banyan trees. I thought everyone knew that the Buddha was enlightened while sitting under the Bodhi tree, otherwise known as *assattha* in Pali, *asvattha* in Sanskrit, *bo* in Sinhala, *po* in Thai, *bawdi* in Burmese, *pipple* in Hindi, Bodhi Tree or Sacred Fig in English, *Ficus religios*a in botanical writings; and that a Bodhi tree is one thing and a Banyan is another. The Bodhi tree has thin bright-green leaves with the characteristic long pointed tip.

2.4 Botanical Description

F. religiosa is a long life span tree with an average life ranging between 900–1,500 years. It grows at sea plain heights ranging from 33 ft up to 4,990 ft. Ficus religiosa is cultivated by specialty tree plant nurseries for use as an ornamental tree, in gardens and parks in tropical and subtropical climates. Habitually, the Bodhi tree is semi-evergreen tree that has up to 98 ft tall and a trunk of about 9.8 ft. It is usually epiphytic with the drooping branches having long-petiole, ovate, cordate shiny leaves. Leaves are bright green, 10–17 cm long and 8–12 cm broad, with a 6–10 cm petiole. The apex dropped into a linear-lanceolate end as the foremost portion of the leaf. The bark is flat or slightly curved, varying from 5 to 8 mm in thickness. The outer cover is grey or ash with membranous layers and oftentimes it is also covered with crustose lichen brown or ash colored surface. The fruits are small figs, in paired, 1–1.5 cm in diameter, green to purple during ripening. Flowers are positioned as axillary sessile and are unisexual. With morphological characteristics, Banyans is distinguished as male and female trees.

F religiosa is a tree with high importance in terms of cultural and ecological perspectives. Each organs of this species are useful for the human beings. The ecosystem maintenance is one of the aspects of this tree. Beside it, Hindu culture is taking this tree as a form of God. While the Buddha religion is also taken this as an important Bodhi Tree. Ecologically this species is important due to its nature of the long-life span. This species originated from Nepal and India of the Asian continent. This species is named in varieties of names as per different locations. This ecologically important tree species is equally important for the cultural value also. Specially, Hindu culture and Buddha Culture requires this species on each of cultural event of human beings.

References

Bhalerao, S. A., & Sharma, A. S. (2014). Ethenomedicinal, phytochemical and pharmacological profile of Ficus religiosa Roxb. *International Journal of Current Microbiology and Applied Sciences, 3*(11), 528–538.

Dharmender, R., Permender, R., Sushila, R., & Deepti, R. (2010). Pharmacognostical standardization of Ficus religiosa fruits. *Pharmacogn Journal, 2*(17), 10–16.

Gautam, S., Meshram, A., Bhagyawant, S. S., & Srivastava, N. (2014). Ficus religiosa-potential role in pharmaceuticals. *International Journal of Pharmaceutical Sciences and Research, 5*(5), 1616–1623.

Joseph, B., & Justin Raj, S. (2010). Phytopharmacological and phytochemical properties of three ficus species: An overview. *International Journal of Pharma and Bio Sciences, 1,* 246–253.

Madulid, D. A. (1995). *A pictorial cyclopedia of philippine ornamental plants* (pp. 214–217). Metro Manilla: Bookmark, Inc.

Makhija, I. K., Sharma, I. P., & Khamar, D. (2010). Phytochemistry and pharmacological properties of Ficus religiosa: An overview. *Annals of Biological Research, 1*(4), 171–180.

Panchawat, S. (2012). Ficus religiosa Linn. (Peepal): A phyto-pharmacological review. *International Journal of Pharmaceutical and Chemical Sciences, 1*(1), 435–446.

Pandey, D., & Pandey, V. C. (2016). Sacred plants from ancient to modern era: Traditional worshipping towards plants conservation. *Tropical Plant Research, 3*(1), 136–141.

Prasad, P. V., Subhakttha, P. K., Narayan, A., & Rao, M. M. (2006). Medico-histotical study of "asvattha" (sacred fig tree). *Bulletin of the Indian Institute of History of Medicine (Hyderabad), 36,* 1–20.

Ruby, J., Nathan, P. T., Balasingh, J., & Kunz, T. H. (2000). Chemical composition of fruits and leaves eaten by short-nosed fruit bat, Cynopterus sphinx. *Journal of Chemical Ecology, 26*(12), 2825–2841.

Rutuja, R.S., Shivsharan, U., & Shruti, A.M. (2015). Ficus religiosa (Peepal): A phytochemical and pharmacological review. *International Journal of Pharmacy and Chemical Sciences, 4*(3), 360–370.

Sharma, D., Dangi, C., & Kaur, M. (2016). A Review on Pharmacological Activities and Therapeutic Potentials of Ficus Religiosa (Pipal). Life Science. *Indian Journal of Applied Research, 623,* 624–626.

Heritage and Law

International Legal Instruments as a Means for the Protection of Cultural Heritage

Tullio Scovazzi

Abstract The international legal instruments concluded to date in the field of culture, especially within the framework of UNESCO, aim at bringing two fundamental messages. First, culture contributes to the maintenance of international peace and security. Second, the protection and promotion of culture is a general interest of humankind as a whole. The paper reviews the main objectives pursued by the UNESCO "cultural conventions", relating, respectively, to the protection of cultural property during armed conflicts, illicit export of cultural property, world cultural and natural heritage, underwater cultural heritage, intangible cultural heritage, and diversity of cultural expressions.

1 The Link Between Cultural Heritage and Peace

The States that on 26 June 1945 adopted in San Francisco the Charter of the United Nations (UN) agreed that the purposes of the new organization, besides the main responsibility to maintain international peace and security, included also the achievement of international cooperation in solving international problem of a "cultural character" (Art. 1, para. 3). This was also considered as a condition to ensure the establishment of a viable peace among nations (Goodrich & Hambro, p. 319).

The UN was established to save succeeding generations from the untold sorrow brought by the scourge of war and to reaffirm faith in fundamental human rights (preamble of the UN Charter). It is important to remark in this regard that the destruction of the culture of a given group is the first step toward genocide. This crime is directed against a group as an entity and against individuals not in their personal capacity, but as members of this group. It was understood by Raphaël Lemkin, who was the first to use the word "genocide" in his seminal book published in 1944, as

T. Scovazzi (✉)
University of Milano-Bicocca, Milan, Italy
e-mail: tullio.scovazzi@unimib.it

O. Niglio and E. Y. J. Lee (eds.), *Transcultural Diplomacy and International Law in Heritage Conservation*, https://doi.org/10.1007/978-981-16-0309-9_11

> [...] a coordinated plan of different actions aiming at the destruction of essential foundations of the life of national groups, with the aim of annihilating the groups themselves. The objectives of such a plan would be disintegration of the political and social institutions, of culture, language, national feelings, religion, and the economic existence of national groups, and the destruction of the personal security, liberty, health, dignity, and even the lives of the individuals belonging to such groups. (Lemkin, 1944, 79)[1]

The United Nations Educational Scientific and Cultural Organization (UNESCO) was established in 1945 to contribute to peace and security by promoting collaboration among the nations through education, science, and culture in order to further universal respect for justice, the rule of law, human rights, and fundamental freedoms (Art. I, para. 1, of the UNESCO Constitution).[2] UNESCO is linked to the UN by a relationship agreement concluded in 1946.

The preamble of the UNESCO Constitution points out very clearly the links existing between culture and peace, as well as, conversely, between ignorance and war. It also stresses that political and economic cooperation is not sufficient to ensure a long-lasting peace, because intellectual and moral solidarity is also needed. The UNESCO member States declare

> that since wars begin in the minds of men, it is in the minds of men that the defenses of peace must be constructed;
>
> that ignorance of each other's ways and lives has been a common cause, throughout the history of mankind, of that suspicion and mistrust between the peoples of the world through which their differences have all too often broken into war; (...)
>
> that a peace based exclusively upon the political and economic arrangements of governments would not be a peace which could secure the unanimous, lasting and sincere support of the peoples of the world, and that the peace must therefore be founded, if it is not to fail, upon the intellectual and moral solidarity of mankind.

The building of peace remains one of the fundamental objectives of the organization. In 2013, when approving the medium-term strategy for the period 2014–2021, the UNESCO General Conference endorsed the following mission statement:

> As a specialized agency of the United Nations, UNESCO – pursuant to its Constitution – contributes to the building of peace, the eradication of poverty, and sustainable development and intellectual dialogue through education, the sciences, culture, communication and information.[3]

In the first years of this century, cooperation between the UN and UNESCO has been strengthened in view of the threats posed by the practice of targeting or looting cultural properties in situations of crisis or conflict, as a means to exacerbate tensions and finance illegal activities.

By Resolution 1483 (2003), relating to reconstruction in Iraq, the UN Security Council stressed "the need for respect for the archaeological, historical, cultural, and

[1] However, the Convention on the Prevention of the Crime of Genocide (New York, 1948) does not include cultural genocide in the definition of "genocide" (Art. II).

[2] 193 States are today members of UNESCO. Israel and the United States withdrew from it as from 31 December 2018.

[3] UNESCO doc. 37 C/4 of 2014, p. 13.

religious heritage of Iraq, and for the continued protection of archaeological, historical, cultural, and religious sites, museums, libraries, and monuments". Accordingly, UN member States were bound to return all cultural properties illegally removed from Iraq and a prohibition on trade in or transfer of such items was established. UNESCO, the International Criminal Police Organization (Interpol), and other international organizations were called upon to assist in the implementation of such action. Resolution 1483 was adopted on the basis of Chapter VII (Action with respect to threats to the peace, breaches of the peace, and acts of aggression) of the UN Charter.

By Resolution 2199 (2015), also adopted under Chapter VII, the Security Council condemned the destruction of cultural heritage in Iraq and Syria, particularly by the Islamic State in Iraq and the Levant (ISIL) and the Al-Nusrah Front (ANF), whether such destruction was incidental or deliberate, including targeted destruction of religious sites and objects. It also noted with concern that the looting and trafficking of cultural properties was a means to finance terrorist activities. The Security Council confirmed, as regards Iraq, and extended to Syria its ban on the trade of removed cultural properties and renewed its call upon relevant international organizations to assist in the implementation of the relevant measures.

The acknowledgment that the protection of cultural heritage is required not only to preserve the traces of human civilization, but also to ensure international security and restore peace, culminated in UN Security Council Resolution 2347 (2017), which addressed the subject in a general perspective. Welcoming the central role played by UNESCO in protecting cultural heritage and promoting culture as an instrument to bring people closer together and foster dialogue, the Security Council emphasized that

> […] the unlawful destruction of cultural heritage, and the looting and smuggling of cultural property in the event of armed conflicts, notably by terrorist groups, and the attempt to deny historical roots and cultural diversity in this context can fuel and exacerbate conflict and hamper post-conflict national reconciliation, thereby undermining the security, stability, governance, social, economic and cultural development of affected States. (preamble)

The Security Council added that the mandate of United Nations peacekeeping operations may encompass assisting relevant authorities, upon their request, in the protection of cultural heritage from destruction, illicit excavation, looting, and smuggling in the context of armed conflicts, in collaboration with UNESCO (para. 9).

The first time that a peacekeeping mission had been entrusted with functions relating to the protection of the cultural heritage was by Resolutions 2100 (2013) and 2295 (2016), whereby the Security Council, inter alia, authorized the UN Multidimensional Integrated Stabilization Mission in Mali (MINUSMA) to assist "the Malian authorities, as necessary and feasible, in protecting from attack the cultural and historical sites in Mali, in collaboration with UNESCO" (respectively, paras. 16, *f*, and 20, *c*).

In keeping with the Security Council resolutions are the considerations developed by the UNESCO General Conference in a policy document prepared in 2015, which explains how attacks on cultural heritage today contribute to creating hatred and fragmentation and, consequently, instability and conflict. There is an evident need to integrate the protection of cultural heritage in peace-building processes:

> There is today growing recognition that the protection of cultural diversity and the promotion of cultural pluralism, through the safeguarding of the tangible and intangible heritage of communities and the protection of human rights and fundamental freedoms, is more than a cultural emergency. It is a security and humanitarian imperative in conflict and transition situations, and an essential element in ensuring sustainable peace and development. Participation and access to culture and its living expressions, including intangible heritage can help strengthen people's resilience and sustain their efforts to live through and overcome crisis. A new approach is urgently required at both international and national levels to operationalize the link between protection of cultural heritage and diversity on the one hand; and, on the other hand, humanitarian action, peace-building processes and security policies. In defining this new approach, another significant development must be considered, namely the emergence of a number of new actors, at all levels, governmental and non-governmental, international and regional.[4]

2 The Broad Concept of Cultural Heritage

The concept of "cultural heritage" can be understood in different meanings. A quite narrow notion, referring only to monuments, works of art, and books, can be found in Art. I, para. 2, *c*, of the UNESCO Constitution. It provides that, to realize its purposes, UNESCO is called, inter alia, to maintain, increase, and diffuse knowledge "by assuring the conservation and protection of the world's inheritance of books, works of art and monuments of history and science, and recommending to the nations concerned the necessary international conventions".

However, in the Declaration adopted by the World Conference on Cultural Policies, convened by UNESCO and held in Mexico City in 1982, States agreed to give the concepts of culture and cultural heritage a quite broader meaning, as any form of expression of the spirituality and creativity of single men and peoples as a whole:

> In its widest sense, culture may now be said to be the whole complex of distinctive spiritual, material, intellectual and emotional features that characterize a society or social group. It includes not only the arts and letters, but also modes of life, the fundamental rights of the human being, value systems, traditions and beliefs". (preamble)
>
> "The cultural heritage of a people includes the works of its artists, architects, musicians, writers and scientists and also the work of anonymous artists, expressions of the people's spirituality, and the body of values which give meaning to life. It includes both tangible and intangible works through which the creativity of that people finds expression: languages, rites, beliefs, historic places and monuments, literature, works of art, archives and libraries. (para. 23)

Other thought-provoking ideas find a place in the Mexico City Declaration. The cultures of all single peoples compose the common cultural heritage of mankind and grow rich through intercultural dialogue:

---

[4]*Reinforcement of UNESCO's Action for the Protection of Culture and the Promotion of Cultural Pluralism in the Event of Armed Conflict*, UNESCO doc. 38 C/49 of 2 November 2015, para. 10.

> All cultures form part of the common heritage of mankind. The cultural identity of a people is renewed and enriched through contact with the traditions and values of others. Culture is dialogue, the exchange of ideas and experience and the appreciation of other values, and traditions; it withers and dies in isolation. (para. 4)

This explains why, in the case of culture, identity and diversity become almost the same thing:

> The universal cannot be postulated in the abstract by any single culture: it emerges from the experience of all the world's peoples as each affirms its own identity. Cultural identity and cultural diversity are inseparable". (para. 5)

The Mexico City Declaration also points out that the cultural heritage suffers damage because of many reasons, including some that are more intolerable than others:

> The cultural heritage has frequently suffered damage or destruction as a result of thoughtlessness as well as of the processes of urbanization, industrialization and technological penetration. But even more intolerable is the damage caused to the cultural heritage by colonialism, armed conflict, foreign occupation and the imposition of alien values. All these have the effect of severing a people's links with and obliterating the memory of its past. Preservation and appreciation of its cultural heritage therefore enable a people to defend its sovereignty and independence, and hence affirm and promote its cultural identity. (para. 25)

Besides the values of spirituality and creativity that have been stressed in the Mexico City Declaration, it is well known that cultural heritage has also an economic dimension, becoming an asset for individuals and societies and offering opportunities for generating sustainable development through commercial activities and tourism. A fair balance between the intrinsic and the economic aspects of cultural heritage is difficult to strike. For instance, commercialization of elements of the cultural heritage is not a priori a disqualifying factor, highlighting the role of this heritage as a factor for the economic development of some communities. However, processes of excessive commercialization could distort traditional cultural customs or expressions and it should be required that such processes remain under the control of the communities that create and transmit the heritage.[5]

[5]See Subsidiary Body for the Examination of Nominations to the Representative List of the Intangible Cultural Heritage of Humanity, *Report by the Rapporteur*, UNESCO doc. ITH/09/4.COM/CONF.209/INF.6 of 26 August 2009, p. 6.

3 The Protection of the Cultural Heritage as a General Interest of the International Community

The adoption of six so-called "cultural conventions" within the framework of UNESCO is a sign of a continued trend toward the strengthening of the protection of cultural heritage in many of its components.[6] These conventions are based on the assumption that the protection and promotion of cultural properties is not only an obligation for the State in whose territory they are located but also constitutes a general interest of the international community as a whole. What represents the history and identity of a single people can also become the heritage of humankind (Hoffman, 2006; Yusuf, 2007; Nafziger & Scovazzi, 2008; Nafziger & Nicgorski, 2009; Kono, 2010; Borelli & Lenzerini, 2012; Francioni & Gordely, 2013).

The UNESCO cultural convention has contributed toward the forming of a rule of general international law with regard to the obligation to respect and protect cultural heritage of significant importance (Francioni, p. 25). The review made hereunder will focus on this general aspect of cultural heritage, as it is manifested in the relevant cultural conventions.

3.1 Protection of Cultural Property During Armed Conflict

The parties to the Convention for the Protection of Cultural Property in the Event of Armed Conflict (The Hague, 1954)[7] recognize that cultural property has suffered grave damage during armed conflicts and that, by reason of the developments in the technique of warfare, it is in increasing danger of destruction. They also emphasize that the preservation of the cultural heritage is of great importance for all peoples of the world and declare themselves convinced "that damage to cultural property belonging to any people whatsoever means damage to the cultural heritage of all mankind, since each people makes its contribution to the culture of the world" (preamble).

Art. 4, para. 1, shows that any party is bound to protect the cultural property situated within its own territory as the cultural property situated within the territory of another party, which in many cases is the enemy State:

> The High Contracting Parties undertake to respect cultural property situated within their own territory as well as within the territory of the other High Contracting Parties by refraining from any use of the property and its immediate surroundings or of the appliances in use for its protection for purposes which are likely to expose it to destruction or damage in the event of armed conflict; and by refraining from any act of hostility directed against such property.

[6] The concept of culture becomes broader if a seventh treaty concluded within UNESCO, the International Convention against Doping in Sport (Paris, 2005), is considered. Sport is seen in this convention "as a means to promote education, health, development and peace" (preamble). 189 States are today parties to the convention.

[7] 133 States are today (July 2020) parties to the 1954 Convention.

No form of theft, pillage, misappropriation, and vandalism of cultural property is allowed. The First Protocol (The Hague, 1954)[8] prohibits the export of cultural properties from an occupied territory and binds parties to return such properties at the close of hostilities, if they have been exported.

The obligation to refrain from any act of hostility directed against cultural property may be waived only in cases where military necessity imperatively requires such a waiver. Special protection is granted to a limited number of refuges intended to shelter movable cultural property in the event of armed conflict and of centers containing monuments and other immovable cultural property of very great importance, provided that they have been entered in the International Register of Cultural Property under Special Protection, held by UNESCO. States parties are required to ensure the immunity of cultural property under special protection from any act of hostility. Such immunity may be withdrawn only in exceptional cases of unavoidable military necessity and only for such time as that necessity continues. An enhanced protection—although not amounting to absolute immunity from acts of warfare—is granted to properties that have been included in the List of Cultural Property under Enhanced Protection, as established under the Second Protocol (The Hague, 1999).[9] The conceptual nuances between "protection", "special protection", and "enhanced protection" show the difficulties in finding a balance between the needs of cultural heritage, on one hand, and those of military necessity, on the other.

3.2 *Illicit Export of Cultural Property*

The preamble of the Convention on the Means of Prohibiting and Preventing the Illicit Import, Export and Transfer of Ownership of Cultural Property (Paris, 1970)[10] recalls that these kinds of illicit activities are an obstacle to the understanding between nations which is part of the UNESCO's mission. It adds that "cultural property constitutes one of the basic elements of civilization and national culture, and that its true value can be appreciated only in relation to the fullest possible information regarding its origin, history and traditional setting".

This is particularly true for archaeological properties, as their looting implies the destruction of the site where they have been found, the loss of information, and the dispersion of irreplaceable and finite artifacts. Even where the object is taken away intact, it is uprooted from the context in which it belongs, losing its identity and real meaning and making it impossible to reconstruct a whole context that has been altered in its original composition.

---

[8] 110 States are today parties to the First Protocol.

[9] 83 States are today parties to the Second Protocol, which was concluded "considering that the rules governing the protection of cultural property in the event of armed conflict should reflect developments in international law".

[10] 140 States, including both States of origin and States of destination of cultural properties, are today parties to the Convention.

In order to avert the dangers posed by theft, clandestine excavation, and illicit export of cultural properties, the parties emphasize that "it is essential for every State to become increasingly alive to the moral obligations to respect its own cultural heritage and that of all nations".

Regrettably, for a number of restrictions in their scope of application, the substantive provisions of the 1970 Convention do not correspond to the ambitious objectives set forth in the preamble (Scovazzi & Ferri, p. 198). In 2015 the parties adopted by consensus a set of Operational Guidelines for the implementation of the 1970 Convention. They are intended "to identify ways and means to further the achievement of the goals of the 1970 Convention through strengthened international cooperation" and provide advanced interpretations to the most important provisions of the latter. However, the Guidelines, although useful as a means of understanding the spirit and the objectives of the 1970 Convention, do not have a binding character.

The 1970 Convention is complemented by the UNIDROIT[11] Convention on Stolen or Illegally Exported Cultural Objects (Rome, 1995), which primarily deals with the private law aspects of illegal movements of cultural properties. However, the UNIDROIT Convention has so far been ratified by a limited number of States.[12]

3.3 *World Cultural and Natural Heritage*

According to the preamble of the Convention Concerning the Protection of the World Cultural and Natural Heritage (Paris, 1972),[13] the cultural and natural heritage are increasingly threatened with destruction not only by the traditional causes of decay, but also by changing social and economic conditions. However, "the deterioration or disappearance of any item of the cultural or natural heritage constitutes a harmful impoverishment of the heritage of all the nations of the world".

For this reason, "in view of the magnitude and gravity of the new dangers threatening them, it is incumbent on the international community as a whole to participate in the protection of the cultural and natural heritage of outstanding universal value, by the granting of collective assistance which, although not taking the place of action by the State concerned, will serve as an effective complement thereto".

The 1972 Convention has a selective character, applying only to properties that have an "outstanding universal value". As pointed out in the Operational Guidelines for its implementation, the 1972 Convention "is not intended to ensure the protection of all properties of great interest, importance or value, but only for a select list of the most outstanding of these from an international viewpoint" (Op. Guid. 52).

---

[11]The acronym refers to the International Institute for the Unification of Private Law, within the framework of which this Convention was negotiated.

[12]48 States are today parties to this Convention.

[13]193 States are today parties to the 1972 Convention, which applies to both cultural and the natural heritage. The former is defined as including only immovable properties, such as monuments, groups of buildings, and sites.

The concept of outstanding universal value is understood as "cultural and/or natural significance which is so exceptional as to transcend national boundaries and to be of common importance for present and future generations of all humanity" (Op. Guid. 49).

The 1972 Convention sets forth two lists, namely the World Heritage List and the List of World Heritage in Danger.[14] On the basis of a decision of the World Heritage Committee,[15] properties of outstanding universal value can be entered on either of the two lists if they meet a number of criteria established by the World Heritage Committee, comply with the conditions of authenticity and integrity, and have an adequate protection and management system. The properties which may be entered on the List of World Heritage in Danger are those threatened by the serious dangers that are specified in the 1972 Convention (Art. 11, para. 4). The 1972 Convention has established a World Heritage Fund to be used for purposes determined by the World Heritage Committee, with priority given to those properties included in the List of World Heritage in Danger.

The 1972 Convention strikes a balance between the interest of individual States and the interest of humankind. On the one hand, the inclusion of a property in the World Heritage List requires the consent of the State on the territory of which it is located. On the other, the inclusion of a property on the List of the World Heritage in Danger and the removal of it from either of the two lists can be decided by the World Heritage Committee even without the consent of the territorial State.

The inscription of a property on the World Heritage List entails the responsibility of the State where it is located to adequately protect it. The World Heritage Committee monitors the actions taken by States parties in application of the 1972 Convention and the state of conservation of listed properties through the review of periodic reports that States parties are required to submit. A special process of so-called reactive monitoring is also provided for in the Operational Guidelines. In fact, the removal from the World Heritage List can be seen as a moral sanction in cases where it is the consequence of an action by the State in whose territory it is located that deliberately affects the outstanding universal value of the property.[16]

The inclusion of a property in the World Heritage lists may also have effect on the gravity of the sentences imposed by international criminal courts on individuals for war crimes. This was the case of Miodrag Jokić and Pavle Strugar, convicted by the International Criminal Tribunal for the former Yugoslavia for the bombing of the

---

[14]To date 1121 properties have been entered on the lists (869 cultural, 213 natural, and 39 mixed), 53 of which are on the List of World Heritage in Danger. As the records of its activities shows, the World Heritage Committee faces a significant challenge in establishing and maintaining a World Heritage List that is adequately representative, balanced, and credible.

[15]The World Heritage Committee is composed of 21 States parties to the 1972 Convention.

[16]So far, the World Heritage Committee removed two properties from the World Heritage List, namely the natural property "Arabian Oryx Sanctuary" (Oman), in 2007, due to the reduction of the size of the protected area by 90%, and the cultural property "Dresden Elbe Valley" (Germany), in 2009, due to the construction of a four-lane bridge within it.

Old City of Dubrovnik in Croatia,[17] and of Ahmad Al Faqi Al Mahdi, convicted by the International Criminal Court for the destruction of mausoleums in Timbuktu in Mali.[18]

3.4 Underwater Cultural Heritage

The Convention on the Protection of the Underwater Cultural Heritage (Paris, 2001) acknowledges in the preamble the importance of underwater cultural heritage as an integral part of the cultural heritage of humanity and a particularly important element in the history of peoples, nations, and their relations with each other concerning their common heritage. The 2001 Convention applies to "all traces of human existence having a cultural, historical or archaeological character which have been partially or totally under water, periodically or continuously, for at least 100 years" (Art. 1, para. 1, *a*).

The responsibility of preserving and protecting this heritage, including where it is located on the seabed of the high seas, rests with all States. According to Art. 2, para. 3, of the 2001 Convention,

> States Parties shall preserve underwater cultural heritage for the benefit of humanity in conformity with the provisions of this Convention.

According to the 2001 Convention, "underwater cultural heritage shall not be commercially exploited" (Art. 2, para. 7), as this is fundamentally incompatible with the protection and proper management of it (Rule 2 of the Annex). In order to facilitate decision-making on how best to protect the heritage, the 2001 Convention sets forth a procedural mechanism that seeks to ensure cooperation among those States with a verifiable link to the heritage, involving three steps (reporting, consultations, and urgent measures).

Regrettably, the message of cooperation for the protection of an endangered cultural heritage coming from the 2001 Convention is not yet shared by a sufficiently high number of States.[19]

---

[17] *Prosecutor v. Jokić*, judgements of 18 March 2004 (Trial Chamber) and 30 August 2005 (Appeals Chamber); *Prosecutor v. Strugar*, judgements of 31 January 2005 (Trial Chamber) and 17 July 2008 (Appeals Chamber).

[18] *Prosecutor v. Al Mahdi*, judgment of 27 September 2016 and order of 7 August 2017.

[19] The 2001 Convention is today in force for 64 States.

3.5 *Intangible Cultural Heritage*

The Convention for the Safeguarding of the Intangible Cultural Heritage (Paris, 2003)[20] was negotiated to fill a gap within the UNESCO legal instruments in the cultural field. It places due emphasis on an aspect of cultural heritage that, although not as "tangible" as buildings or natural sites, is equally important "as a mainspring of cultural diversity and a guarantee of sustainable development" and deserves to be safeguarded in the "general interest to humanity" (preamble). The heritage in question is composed of "the practices, representations, expressions, knowledge, skills – as well as the instruments, objects, artefacts and cultural spaces associated therewith – that communities, groups and, in some cases, individuals recognize as part of their cultural heritage" (Art. 2, para. 1). It is manifested in a number of domains, such as oral traditions and expressions, including language as a vehicle of the intangible cultural heritage, performing arts, social practices, rituals and festive events, knowledge and practices concerning nature and the universe, and traditional craftsmanship (Art. 2, para. 2). Notably, the 2003 Convention takes into consideration solely the heritage that "is compatible with existing international human rights instruments, as well as with the requirements of mutual respect among communities, groups and individuals, and of sustainable development" (Art. 2, para. 1).

The parties to the 2003 Convention recognize that the processes of globalization and social transformation, while creating conditions for renewed dialogue among communities, "also give rise, as does the phenomenon of intolerance, to grave threats of deterioration, disappearance and destruction of the intangible cultural heritage" (preamble). Apart from its cultural dimension, the intangible cultural heritage also involves other fundamental values, such as the respect of human rights of the communities that create, maintain, and transmit the heritage and the preservation of the natural environment.

The 2003 Convention establishes two lists, namely the Representative List of the Intangible Cultural Heritage of Humanity and the List of Intangible Cultural Heritage in Need of Urgent Safeguarding. A third list is also drawn up to include the national, subregional, and regional programs, projects, and activities for the safeguarding of the heritage which best reflect the principles and objectives of the 2003 Convention (so-called "best practices"). The 2003 Convention sets forth the Intergovernmental Committee for the Safeguarding of the Intangible Cultural Heritage with responsibility for deciding on the proposals submitted by States Parties for addition to the lists.[21]

---

[20]The 2003 Convention is today in force for 178 States.

[21]The Committee has so far entered 549 elements in the lists (463 in the representative list, 64 in the urgent safeguarding list, and 22 in the best practices list).

3.6 Diversity of Cultural Expressions

The Convention on the Protection and Promotion of the Diversity of Cultural Expressions (Paris, 2005)[22] is based on the assumptions that "cultural diversity forms a common heritage of humanity and should be cherished and preserved for the benefit of all" and that "cultural diversity creates a rich and varied world, which increases the range of choices and nurtures human capacities and values, and therefore is a mainspring for sustainable development for communities, peoples and nations" (preamble). The process of globalization, while facilitating the rapid development of information and communication technologies and affording unprecedented conditions for enhanced interaction between cultures, also represents "a challenge for cultural diversity, namely in view of risks of imbalances between rich and poor countries". For these reasons, the States parties to the 2005 Convention recognize "the need to take measures to protect the diversity of cultural expressions, including their contents, especially in situations where cultural expressions may be threatened by the possibility of extinction or serious impairment".

According to the 2005 Convention, "cultural diversity" refers to the manifold ways in which the cultures of groups and societies find expressions that are passed on within and among groups and societies. Cultural diversity is made manifest not only through the varied ways in which the cultural heritage of humanity is expressed, augmented, and transmitted, but also through diverse modes of artistic creation, production, dissemination, distribution, and enjoyment, whatever the means and technologies used (Art. 4, para. 1). All cultures have an equal dignity and must be respected:

> The protection and promotion of the diversity of cultural expressions presuppose the recognition of equal dignity of, and respect for, all cultures, including the persons belonging to minorities and indigenous peoples. (Art. 2, para. 3)

The 2005 Convention tries to strike a balance between the two main "souls" (cultural and commercial) of its subject matter. Cultural activities, goods, and services must not be treated as solely having a commercial value, as they also convey identities, values, and meanings. Under Art. 8, if there are special situations where cultural expressions on the territory of a State party are at risk of extinction, under serious threat, or otherwise in need of urgent safeguarding, the State concerned is allowed to take "all appropriate measures" to protect and preserve such cultural expressions. The 2005 Convention does not specify in what such measures may consist.

4 Conclusive Considerations

Some gaps can be noticed among the subject matters covered by UNESCO cultural conventions. For instance, no treaty has so far been negotiated with respect to the

[22]The 2005 Convention is today in force for 148 States.

preservation of languages in danger of disappearance. In other cases, where the adoption of a treaty has not proven feasible, soft-law instruments have been approved. This is the case of the Declaration concerning the Intentional Destruction of Cultural Heritage, adopted in 2003 by the UNESCO General Conference, which recalls the tragic destruction of the Buddhas of Bamiyan, Afghanistan, that affected the international community as a whole. According to the Declaration, "the international community recognizes the importance of the protection of cultural heritage and reaffirms its commitment to fight against its intentional destruction in any form so that such cultural heritage is transmitted to the succeeding generations" (Principle I).

However, these gaps in the mandatory legal regime should not obscure the two fundamental messages that can clearly be drawn from the treaties of global scope adopted within the framework of UNESCO. First, culture substantially contributes to the maintenance of peace. Second, the protection and promotion of culture is a general interest of the international community as a whole.

References

Borelli, S., & Lenzerini, F. (Eds.). (2012). *Cultural heritage, cultural rights, cultural diversity*. Leiden: Martinus Nijhoff Publishers.

Francioni, F. (2012). The evolving framework for the protection of cultural heritage in international law. In S. Borelli & F. Lenzerini (Eds.), *Cultural heritage, cultural rights, cultural diversity* (pp. 3–25). Leiden: Martinus Nijhoff Publishers.

Francioni, F., & Gordely, J. (Eds.). (2013). *Enforcing international cultural heritage law*. Oxford: Oxford University Press.

Goodrich, L. M., & Hambro, E. (1949). *Charter of the United Nations—commentary and documents*. London: Stevens & Sons Limited.

Hoffman, B. (Ed.). (2006). *Art and cultural heritage*. Cambridge: Cambridge University Press.

Kono, T. (Ed.). (2010). *The impact of uniform laws on the protection of cultural heritage and the preservation of cultural heritage in the 21st century*. Leiden: Martinus Nijhoff Publishers.

Lemkin, R. (1944). *Axis rule in occupied Europe: Law of occupation, analysis of government, proposals for redress*. New York: Columbia University Press.

Nafziger, J., & Nicgorski, A. M. (Ed.). (2009). *Cultural heritage issues: The legacy of conquest, colonization, and commerce*. Leiden: Brill—Nijhoff.

Nafziger, J., & Scovazzi, T. (Eds.). (2008). *Le patrimoine culturel de l'humanité* [The cultural heritage of mankind]. Leiden: Martinus Nijhoff Publishers.

Scovazzi, T., & Ferri, P. G. (2015). Recent developments in the fight against the illicit export of archaeological objects: The operational guidelines to the 1970 UNESCO convention. *Art Antiquity and Law, 20*(3), 195–227.

Yusuf, A. (Ed.). (2007). *Standard-setting in UNESCO*. Paris, Leiden: UESCO Publishing, Martinus Nijhoff Publishers.

International and European Obligations on the Belgian State to Protect Cultural Heritage

Marie-Sophie de Clippele

Abstract Since the second half of the last century an increasing number of international and European rules have been adopted for the protection of cultural heritage. This transnational legal framework is applied by the Belgian State, even though the degree of applicability varies according to two criteria: the immediacy of application and the direct effect (also called direct applicability). The cross-cutting question through the analysis of this panel of rules imposing regulatory duties on States is how these rules have been applied in Belgian law and whether the burden required of the competent public authorities has increased in this area. It is important to note at this stage that most of these conventions are weak in terms of concrete implementation mechanisms and often have few binding monitoring bodies (except for the European Union). The obligations set out in these are not always precise but have nevertheless generally exerted some influence on Belgian legislators. The aim is therefore not to list every obligation contained in each ratified convention, but rather to measure the impact of the convention and the degree of constraint (notably through direct effect) that accompanies it.

1 Introduction

Belgium is a Federal State with three regions (Brussels-Capital, Flemish and Walloon Regions) and three communities (Flemish, French and German Communities). Following a complex distribution of powers from 1970 until 2014, cultural heritage is, quite artificially, split between immovable heritage (monuments, sites and archaeology) in the hands of the three regions and the German Community; and movable (cultural goods) and intangible heritage, falling within the three communities and partly of the Brussels Region (de Clippele, 2020). The Federal State remains competent for the ratification of international instruments and for a few national museums

M.-S. de Clippele (✉)
Fonds national de la recherche scientifique, Université Saint-Louis, Bruxelles, Belgium
e-mail: marie-sophie.declippele@usaintlouis.be

ICLAFI Expert Member, Bruxelles, Belgium

O. Niglio and E. Y. J. Lee (eds.), *Transcultural Diplomacy and International Law in Heritage Conservation*, https://doi.org/10.1007/978-981-16-0309-9_12

and cultural institutions. The federated States (regions and communities) have also international competence for the areas falling within their powers.

Belgium is part of a wide array of international and European conventions for the protection of cultural heritage, shaping its responsibility as a steward, albeit divided among the regions and communities, according to their competence. However, the degree of implementation of these texts varies according to two criteria, that of immediacy of application and that of direct effect (also called direct applicability).

The immediacy of application of an international convention means that it enters into the domestic legal order without any formalities. Belgium recognises immediate application of international law but still requires a formal assent law for these rules to enter into the Belgian legal system (Article 167 of the Constitution).

The second aspect is whether the international rule can be applied directly. This means that it confers subjective rights on its addressees who can invoke it directly before the judge. This is the direct effect in the narrow sense, which is privileged in doctrine (Hachez, 2008) as well as in this chapter. In a broad sense, direct effect would refer to the ability of a rule to be invoked in court, without necessarily having to rely on a subjective right. To measure this direct effect, objective criteria of precision and clarity are predominantly used. If the norm contained in the Convention is sufficiently clear and precise (and unconditional according to the interpretation of direct effect in European Union law), it does not require transposition into national law and can be applied directly in the national legal order. The direct effect also constitutes a lever of constraint against a State that does not comply with its international obligations and may be held accountable for it by its citizens.

The cross-cutting question is how these international (1), regional (2) and European Union (3) rules for cultural heritage have been applied in Belgian law and whether the burden required of the competent public authorities has increased in this area. Most of these conventions are weak in terms of concrete implementation mechanisms and often have few binding monitoring bodies (except for the European Union). The obligations set out in these are not always precise, but have nevertheless generally exerted some influence on Belgian legislators (Draye, 2007). The aim is therefore not to list every obligation contained in each ratified convention, but rather to measure the impact of the convention and the degree of constraint (notably through direct effect) that accompanies it. In other words, this paper will analyse how Belgium implements those transnational rules and further develops its cultural heritage policies.

2 International UNESCO Conventions Without Direct Effect in Belgian Law

The desire to protect cultural heritage is expressed in many sources of international law, mainly under the auspices of UNESCO, reflecting the desire to respect the cultural identity of peoples through their heritage.

The first rules were taken from conventions in armed conflicts, where the "right to plunder" of the victors in wartime was to be regulated. The numerous destructions of cultural properties have gradually prompted States to agree on the need to protect, at a minimum level, the heritage of countries in conflict. In that context, the first Convention was adopted in 1954, laying the foundation stone in international treaty law for cultural heritage (1).

The second stone was also established in response to a cultural scourge: illicit trafficking in cultural property. It is among the largest trafficking in the world, after drugs and weapons, despite the difficulty of obtaining data to measure its extent (European Commission and Directorate-General for Education, 2019). Once again, UNESCO was the forerunner in establishing the first convention on the subject to regulate the market in works of art in order to reduce illicit trafficking (2).

The third series of conventions aims at protecting cultural heritage in a more thematic manner (3).

2.1 The 1954 Convention Inspired Belgian Law

Since the dawn of time, war has been destroying not only human lives, but also works of art and monuments close to people's soul. The sacking of a city, such as ancient Carthage, or a place of worship, such as the historic site of Palmyra or the Buddhas of Bamyan (Négri, 2014), reaches at its roots a civilization and its collective identity. Such looting and ransacking of monuments, cultural property and places of worship, often deliberate and sometimes systematic, is part of the will of a war that has sometimes become total (R. O'Keefe, 2010).

But at all times, too, measures have been taken to temper the destructive rage of the belligerents. The first rules favoured places of worship, where the sacred was to be spared, lest the gods be angry (Toman, 1994). In ancient Greece, medieval Europe, in the world of Islam or Hinduism, rules were adopted to preserve certain shrines, churches, monasteries and other places of worship, as well as works of art therein (Bugnion, 2004). Renaissance Europe would have been a pioneer in the protection of works of art for their cultural rather than religious character.

At the start of the twentieth century, The Hague Conventions of 1899 and 1907 prohibit "to destroy or seize the enemy's property, unless such destruction or seizure be imperatively demanded by the necessities of war" (Article 23 (g) of the Regulations Respecting the Laws and Customs of War on Land, annexed to the Hague Convention (IV) Respecting the Laws and Customs of War on Land of 18 October 1907), or "the attack or bombardment, by whatever means, of towns, villages, dwellings or buildings which are undefended" or "the pillage of a town or place, even when taken by assault" (Articles 25 and 28 of the Regulations Respecting the Laws and Customs of War on Land, annexed to the Hague Convention (IV) Respecting the Laws and Customs of War on Land of 18 October 1907).

However, the general protection offered by these early conventions—treating monuments and cultural property as civilian property—was not sufficient, especially regarding the devastation of the Second World War. Out of the ashes of war, States drafted the Convention for the Protection of Cultural Property in the Event of Armed Conflict, signed at The Hague on 14 May 1954 and ratified by 133 Member States to date, including Belgium. Two Protocols were added, in 1954 and 1999. The 1954 Convention gives a broad definition of cultural property, including both movable and immovable property, unlike other multilateral texts. Advocating a principle of safeguarding and respect for cultural heritage, the text also enshrines the sign of the "blue shield" in Article 16, which is still widely used today.

The 1954 Convention concerns only cases of international armed conflict and does not govern the protection of cultural property in the event of internal conflicts or in peacetime.

Moreover, States that have not ratified the 1954 Hague Convention are nevertheless bound by the rules contained in the Geneva Conventions of 12 August 1949 and their two Additional Protocols of 8 June 1977 (Articles 52 and 53), or at least by customary humanitarian law, crystallised in the Geneva Conventions in particular.

This broad set of rules compels States to take measures to preserve their cultural property in the event of armed conflict. States are collectively responsible for this "endangered heritage" (Négri, 2014, pp. 137–138), including an obligation of reparation. However, the control of State coercion remains limited in so far as the means of action against the State not fulfilling its obligations remain limited, all the more so if these obligations cannot be invoked directly by claimants.

The situation is different with regard to the recent recognition in international law of a form of individual criminal responsibility, a kind of "new generation" responsibility, in addition to traditional State responsibilities (Négri, 2014, p. 145). On 27 September 2016, the International Criminal Court sentenced for the first time the Malian jihadist Ahmad Al-Faqi Al-Mahdi to nine years in prison for intentionally directing attacks against World Heritage monuments in Timbuktu, recognising the destruction of heritage as a war crime. Moreover, on 24 March 2017, the United Nations Security Council adopted a resolution with the sole objective of protecting cultural heritage against looting and destruction, sending a strong signal to EIIL terrorists, particularly in Syria (Resolution 2347 (2017), Adopted by the Security Council at its 7907th meeting, on 24 March 2016).

Belgium ratified the 1954 Convention and its Protocol by an assent law of 10 August 1960.[1] The Second Protocol of 1999 was ratified on 13 October 2010, after having received the assent of all the federate parliaments, since the text affects both community and regional matters. The 1954 Convention does not have direct effect because it requires measures to transpose it into domestic law, leaving a wide margin to the State while reducing the possibilities of compelling it (Casier, 2014). The various authorities responsible for protecting cultural property (understood in the broadest sense, covering both movable and immovable property) adopted legislation

[1]Law of 10 August 1960 approving the following international acts: (a) Convention for the Protection of Cultural Property in the Event of Armed Conflict, Regulations for its Execution, Final Act and Resolutions; (b) Protocol for the Protection of Cultural Property in the Event of Armed Conflict, signed at The Hague on 14 May 1954, *M.B.*, 16 November 1960.

protecting such cultural property in general. Also, these authorities helped raise awareness among Belgian military personnel on the protection of cultural property (courses given by the Red Cross in particular, dissemination of international texts and circulars, affixing distinctive red and green signs to monuments and natural sites in military domain, etc.) or among civilians responsible for ensuring the construction of refuges for property threatened in the event of war.

Furthermore, the Committee for the Protection of Cultural Property in the Event of Armed Conflict decided in 2013 to grant the status of "reinforced protection" to three Belgian sites listed as UNESCO World Heritage Sites: the house and workshop of architect Victor Horta, the Neolithic Flint Mines from Spiennes to Mons and the Complex House-Ateliers-Museum Plantin-Moretus in Antwerp. This follows recommendation enshrined in the Second Protocol to implement additional safety measures in peacetime.

Finally, Belgium widely uses the distinctive sign of the blue shield.

Despite the lack of direct effect, the Hague Convention and its two Additional Protocols have had a certain influence on the Belgian public authorities, encouraging them to take measures for the protection of cultural heritage in the event of armed conflict that they would not necessarily have taken in the absence of these international obligations. It is not always easy to make the armed forces aware of the need to protect the heritage, nor to train them to distinguish between properties worthy of protection, as has been shown in several cases in recent conflicts (wars in Yugoslavia, civil war in Syria, etc.). Moreover, it is far from simple to prepare for the worst and to envisage extreme situations where heritage would be squandered, even if it is essential.

On a diplomatic level, Belgium plays an active role in the implementation of these rules, having chaired the Committee for the Protection of Cultural Property in the Event of Armed Conflict from December 2012 to December 2014.

2.2 *The Fight Against Illicit Trafficking in Cultural Property*

UNESCO responded to growing looting and theft of cultural objects, notably in former colonised countries, by adopting the Convention on the Means of Prohibiting and Preventing the Illicit Import, Export and Transfer of Ownership of Cultural Property, signed in Paris on 14 November 1970 (2.1.). In addition to this public international law Convention, the Unidroit Convention on Stolen or Illegally Exported Cultural Objects was adopted in 1995, focusing on private law (2.2.).

The UNESCO Convention of 14 November 1970 Lacks Transposition

With 140 ratifications to date, the founding Convention for the Protection of Movable Cultural Property is the result of a compromise between the interests of countries exporting and importing cultural property, even though the distinction between these two types of countries remains relative. Even though the text is deemed "less ambitious, but more realistic" (Fraoua, 1986), it should not diminish its importance. Even if the importing countries remain reluctant to the rules it establishes, this Convention was the result of a sincere desire to reduce illicit trafficking and was applied in good faith (P. J. O'Keefe, 2007, p. 8).

A pioneering figure in the fight against illicit trafficking in cultural property, the UNESCO Convention is built around three pillars comprising prevention, restitution and international collaboration (Kono, 2010). It is driven by a double objective. The aim is, on the one hand, to encourage each State to protect its national cultural heritage, mainly through the establishment of an inventory and through export and import control measures, and, on the other hand, to reduce international illicit traffic by calling for greater collaboration between States.

Belgium only ratified the Convention on 31 March 2009,[2] which is not that late compared to some neighbouring countries (Germany in 2007, The Netherlands in 2009 and Luxembourg in 2015, but France in 1997 already). This delay is partly due to the distribution of powers under Belgian law, which requires the consent of all the competent federated States (regions and communities) before the Federal State can ratify the international text in question. This process significantly slows down the immediate implementation of a text into domestic law, especially if a federated State refuses to adopt an assent law or decree, effectively blocking any possibility of binding the State internationally.

As the Convention has no direct application, Belgium has yet to adopt certain legislative measures transposing the obligations contained in the Convention.

If the absence of direct applicability weakens the Convention, its influence—even before its final ratification—is nevertheless already perceptible. Even before ratification, the federated States have been encouraged to take measures to protect movable cultural heritage. Ratifying the Convention might have helped to alleviate Belgium's bad reputation as a hub for illicit trafficking in cultural property.

Although the competent federated States have already adopted transposition measures providing general protection for movable cultural property, there is still a need for a structural instrument to coordinate and harmonise the collaboration of the various entities in order to have a coherent policy against illicit trafficking in cultural property. To this end, a Consultative Committee, composed of the competent entities (communities, regions and the Federal State) set up by decision of 16 January 2009 the official platform "Import, Export and Restitution of Cultural Property". This platform has contributed significantly to the preparation of a draft law to implement the Convention in 2012, which, however, has still not been completed, although it should have been taken over by the Federal Government in 2015.

[2] Act of 13 May 2003 approving the Convention on the Means of Prohibiting and Preventing the Illicit Import, Export and Transfer of Ownership of Cultural Property, adopted in Paris on 14 November 1970, *M.B.*, 19 June 2009. Belgium added a declaration upon ratification: "For Belgium, the expression 'cultural goods' shall be interpreted as being limited to the objects listed in the Annex to Council Regulation (EEC) No 3911/92 of 9 December 1992, as amended, on the export of cultural goods and in the Annex to Council Directive 93/7/EEC of 15 March 1993, as amended, on the return of cultural objects unlawfully removed from the territory of a Member State".

In the meantime, the Senate has decided to move forward by drafting a report on the theft of works of art in June 2018, in which the complete transposition of the 1970 UNESCO Convention appears to be a priority (*Rapport d'information concernant l'optimisation de la coopération entre l'autorité fédérale et les entités fédérées en matière de lutte contre le vol d'oeuvres d'art*, 2018). Since then, the Federal Government has reportedly begun to work on a Preliminary Draft Law ("*Avant-projet de loi relatif à la restitution de biens culturels ayant quitté illicitement le territoire d'États ayant ratifié la Convention de l'UNESCO du 14 novembre 1970 concernant les mesures à prendre pour interdire et empêcher l'importation, l'exportation, et le transfert de propriété illicite de biens culturels*"), although no draft has yet been tabled in the House of Representatives. In fact, the federal government would appear to be assuming its responsibilities by having approved in the Council of Ministers on 16 November 2018 this preliminary draft law partially transposing, i.e. in matters falling within federal jurisdiction, the measures contained in the UNESCO Convention. As Prof. Bert Demarsin deplores, with the fall of the Michel I Government a few weeks later, this preliminary draft sunk into oblivion, distancing us from a finalised transposition with a view to the 50th anniversary of the Convention (Demarsin, 2019, p. 586).

The 1970 UNESCO Convention has therefore influenced cultural heritage policies in Belgium, mainly against the risks of theft and illicit export, but much still needs to be done. The European Union (see 3) and, to a lesser extent, the Unidroit Convention have also helped to make things happen and to add obligations in this respect.

The 1995 Unidroit Convention Refused Ratification

At the request of UNESCO, the International Institute for the Unification of Private Law (UNIDROIT) embarked on the ambitious task of providing a private law response to the gaps left by the 1970 Convention on Public International Law. The Convention on Stolen or Illegally Exported Cultural Objects was signed on 24 June 1995 in Rome. The innovative Convention strikes a balance between the collective interest of protecting cultural heritage and the prerogatives of the *bona fide* purchaser (Carducci, 1997; Groenen, 2018).

The starting point was a bitter observation that illicit traffic was steadily increasing and that the UNESCO Convention wasn't sufficient to combat the spectacular growth of theft, looting and other illicit exports in various parts of the world (Lalive, 1997; Prott, 2000).

In addition, national laws for the protection of cultural heritage are inadequate to respond to an essentially international problem since the theft of cultural property is often characterised by the crossing of borders.

The drafters of the 1995 Convention established a concise, simple and directly applicable text, unlike the 1970 Convention. However, while for the drafters and for most jurists the text constituted definite progress, for others it aroused only scepticism or hostility. The professional art world is often strongly opposed to this legal corpus granting subjective rights to the original owner and imposing a system of automatic restitution in case of theft. The strength of this lobby can be measured by the low number of ratifications of the 1995 Convention (48 up to date) but should not deter advocates of the multilateral treaty. Ratifications are progressing well and States are increasingly open to incorporating the treaty into their legal systems and are referring to it despite the lack of ratification by their parliaments (See Swiss case law: ATF 123 II 134 (*L. v. Indictments Chamber of the Canton of Geneva*), recital 7, c).

Moreover, the growing awareness of public opinion and its willingness to combat illicit trafficking is also prompting the authorities to act in favour of the text.

In 2012, the question was raised as to whether Belgium should ratify the Unidroit Convention through a study which concluded that "it is not clear whether or not Belgium should absolutely accede to the UNIDROIT Convention" (Haumont et al., 2012).

Consequently, on 25 June 2014, the Permanent Consultative Platform on the Import, Export and Restitution of Cultural Property issued the opinion that priority should be given to the implementation of the 1970 UNESCO Convention and the transposition of Directive 2014/60/EU of 15 May 2014.

Nonetheless, in its 2018 report on art theft the Senate explicitly encouraged the ratification of the Unidroit Convention, without mentioning the 2012 study though, maybe indicating a shift in policy. The Senate considered it to be one of the most successful instruments for implementing a coherent restitution policy.

2.3 *Thematic Protection of Cultural Heritage*

For a long time, national rules have been taken to protect cultural heritage, thematically, often starting with architectural heritage. Belgium adopted its first law for the conservation of monuments and sites on 7 August 1931 but already had scattered rules and administrative practice almost a century earlier. Later, legislation developed for other forms of cultural heritage (archaeology, intangible heritage…). International rules were mostly adopted in that second phase, starting after the federalisation of the Belgian State starting in 1970. Most of these international rules come from UNESCO, which drafted several conventions on cultural heritage, each one ratified by Belgium and having therefore an impact on Belgian national law.

The Active Implementation of the 1972 World Heritage Convention

After a first series of conventions and resolutions concerning cultural heritage in the event of armed conflict and the fight against illicit traffic, UNESCO adopted one of its flagship conventions, the Convention concerning the World Cultural and Natural

Heritage on 23 November 1972. Ratified by a record number of 193 countries—including Palestine—the Convention was only ratified by Belgium on 24 July 1996.[3] The reasons for this relatively late ratification would again be linked to the distribution of powers, which significantly slows down the process. The Convention is part of Belgian law, but requires domestic enforcement measures, which have no direct effect.

The Walloon Region is the only entity to have taken specific legislative measures for World Heritage, giving a separate place to this heritage inscribed on the list established by UNESCO and creating in 2011 a Walloon World Heritage Committee (CWAPAM) (see articles 4–8 of the Walloon Code for Heritage). However, the other two Regions have also made provisions for the protection of World Heritage, through their general heritage protection rules.

Since 1996, 12 Belgian cultural and one natural property have been inscribed on the World Heritage List[4] and 16 sites on the Tentative List (the list of potential candidates for inscription): 14 cultural, 1 natural and 1 mixed property. Applications for inscription are submitted by the various competent entities—in turn, according to the rules of representation established in the spirit of the cooperation agreement of 8 March 1994—and are then submitted by the Belgian delegation to UNESCO. Belgium thus has a considerable number of properties already inscribed on the World Heritage List compared to its relatively small territory.

The Federal Transposition of the 2001 Underwater Cultural Heritage Convention

In 2001, UNESCO adopted the Convention on the Protection of the Underwater Cultural Heritage, ratified by the law of 6 July 2013[5] and transposed by the law of 4 April 2014, giving it direct effect.[6]

---

[3]It was approved by the three Regions and entered into force in Belgian law on 24 October 1996 (*M.B.*, 6 November 1996).

[4]Belfries of Belgium and France (1999), Flemish Beguinages (1998), Cathedral of Our Lady of Tournai (2000), Complex Maison-Ateliers-Musée Plantin-Moretus (2005), Major residences of the architect Victor Horta (Brussels) (2000), The Grand-Place of Brussels (1998), The historical centre of Bruges (2000), The four lifts of the Canal du Centre and their site, La Louvière and Le Roeulx (Hainaut) (1998), The Architectural Work of Le Corbusier, an exceptional contribution to the Modern Movement (2016), Neolithic flint mines of Spiennes (Mons) (2000), Palais Stoclet (2009), Major Mining Sites of Wallonia (2012). The natural site of the Soignes Forest, part of the Primary Beech Forests of the Carpathians and other European regions, was inscribed in July 2017.

[5]*M.B.* 25 October 2013; After obtaining the following assents as it is again a mixed treaty: See the Decree of the Flemish Community/Flemish Region of 16 July 2010 (*M.B. of* 9 August 2010), the Decree of the French Community of 19 April 2012 (*M.B. of* 26 June 2012), the Decree of the German-speaking Community of 19 March 2012 (*M.B. of* 18 April 2012), the Decree of the Walloon Region of 26 April 2012 (*M.B. of* 22 May 2012) and the Ordinance of the Brussels-Capital Region of 4 September 2008 (*M.B. of* 30 September 2008—Ed. 5).

[6]Law of 4 April 2014 on the protection of underwater heritage, *M.B.*, 18 April 2014.

Underwater cultural heritage includes heritage discovered in the Belgian territorial sea, in the Belgian exclusive economic zone and on the continental shelf, except for wrecks and wreckage protected by the Nairobi International Convention on the Removal of Wrecks (2007). Territorial scope explains federal jurisdiction in this area, unlike maritime heritage, which falls under the jurisdiction of the communities.

The law innovates in the field of discoveries in the sense that it provides for different methods of hierarchical appropriation among them (see articles 11–13).

Another interesting aspect of this new law is the general prohibition on holding or selling illicitly obtained discoveries. This prohibition announces the legislator's intention to consider underwater heritage as part of the public domain and subject to its regime of inalienability.

The Early Implementation of the 2003 Intangible Heritage Convention

The 2003 Convention for the Safeguarding of the Intangible Heritage is another important heritage convention for UNESCO. Ratified by 172 States to date—and by Belgium on 24 March 2006[7]—it enjoys great popularity because it recognises an aspect of heritage often neglected by the Western and material vision of what cultural heritage should be, integrating the perspective and participation of "the communities, groups and, where applicable, individuals that create, maintain and transmit such heritage" (article 15).

[7]Flemish Decree of 10 February 2006 assenting to the Convention for the Safeguarding of the Intangible Cultural Heritage, done at Paris on 17 October 2003, *M.B.* 14 March 2006; Decree of the French Community of 17 February 2006 assenting to the Convention for the Safeguarding of the Intangible Cultural Heritage, adopted on 17 October 2003 and done at Paris on 3 November 2003, *M.B.* 15 March 2006; Decree of the German-speaking Community of 13 March 2006 approving the Convention for the Safeguarding of the Intangible Cultural Heritage, done in Paris on 17 October 2003, *M.B.* 10 April 2006.

The Convention was transposed into Belgian law by most of the competent entities: the French and Flemish Community, Brussels-Capital Region, but not yet by the German-speaking Community. This Convention influenced and initiated the adoption of Belgian legal texts in this area, even if some traces of folklore protection date back a few decades earlier (Dumont, 1996).

The decree of the French Community of 11 July 2002 is one of the first texts in Europe to draw up a legislative tool for the protection of the intangible cultural heritage, after being inspired by Japan and other Asian countries. This decree brings together the protection of movable and intangible heritage, which are perceived as complementary and inseparable, despite their different perspectives. In this respect, the Belgian experience proves that it is possible for a Western country to protect intangible heritage in the same way as for movable or immovable heritage (Genest, 2007). About the intangible heritage, Belgian experts have worked closely with UNESCO for elaborating the 2003 Convention. Consequently, the decree is also inspired by the concepts of the UNESCO programme for Living Human Treasures and the programme for Masterpieces of the Oral and Intangible Heritage, using almost the same terms (Ducastelle, 2013).

Unlike its French-speaking counterpart, the Flemish Community did not have a specific legislative tool dealing with intangible cultural heritage until recently. Indeed, on 24 February 2017, the Flemish Community adopted a decree on cultural heritage,[8] broadening and further specifying the scope of the decree of 2008 and then 2012 which it replaces. In this decree, the role of heritage communities is central. Cultural heritage is defined therein as follows in Article 3, 2: "cultural heritage: movable or intangible cultural expressions having common meanings and values within a current frame of reference and transmitted through the generations".

Like the French Community, the Brussels-Capital Region settles both the question of movable heritage (cultural property) and that of intangible heritage, in the same Ordinance of 25 April 2019.

Notwithstanding the current legal vacuum in the German-speaking Community, there are many attempts to protect and enhance the intangible cultural heritage. A good example is a regional development concept of the German-speaking Community that aims to promote cultural identity.

All these measures taken by the competent federated authorities for safeguarding intangible cultural heritage further specify their obligations, both at national and international level.

[8]Decree to support the exploitation of cultural heritage in Flanders (cited as: Cultural Heritage Decree of 24 February 2017), *M.B.*, 4 April 2017 and effective as of 14 April 2017.

The Lack of Influence of the 2005 Convention

The UNESCO Convention on the Protection and Promotion of the Diversity of Cultural Expressions of 20 October 2005 has been ratified by 148 countries to date and by the European Union and entered into force on 18 March 2007. Belgium ratified the Convention on 9 August 2013, the last of the Member States of the Union,[9] awaiting above all the assent of Flanders, which was given in 2011, four years after the other competent entities.[10] For some, this delay is explained by the reluctance in Flanders to agree to conventions on the protection of (cultural) minorities (Van Drooghenbroeck & Delgrange, 2002).

The Convention encourages Member States to take measures to establish cultural policies, thus opening the subject more broadly than just to the protection of cultural heritage. However, it is not clear to what extent the ratification of the international text has influenced Belgian legislators to act in one direction or another, or to take new measures in addition to those already taken previously.

The direct effect of the Convention has been the subject of some discussion, with some arguing that there is no direct applicability since the obligations are incumbent on States and do not create rights for individuals. For others, however, the fact that the obligations are addressed only to States and not to individuals in no way removes the possibility for individuals to directly invoke rights set out in the Convention. Moreover, some of the obligations contained in the Convention are sufficiently clear and precise for them to be directly applicable, but it will be for the judge to determine on a case-by-case basis which provisions would or would not be directly applicable (Romainville, 2014, p. 259).

3 The Council of Europe Heritage Conventions Without Direct Effect in Belgian Law

As soon as the Council of Europe was set up in 1949, the term "common heritage" appeared. It refers, in its intangible side, to the "spiritual and moral values" of the European peoples which are "the true source of individual freedom, political liberty and the rule of law, principles which form the basis of all genuine democracy" (Preamble of the Statute). As stated in Article 1 of the Statute of London, the safeguarding and promotion of this common heritage is necessary to achieve a greater unity between Member States.

---

[9] Act of 19 July 2013 assenting to the Convention on the Protection and Promotion of the Diversity of Cultural Expressions and the Annex, adopted in Paris on 20 October 2005, *M.B.* 30 October 2013.

[10] See Decree of the Flemish Community/Flemish Region of 6 May 2011 (*M.B. of* 15 June 2011), Decree of the French Community of 2 June 2006 (*M.B. of* 7 August 2006), Decree of the German-speaking Community of 30 October 2006 (*M.B. of* 4 January 2007), Decree of the Walloon Region of 10 November 2006 (*M.B. of* 28 November 2006), Order of the Brussels-Capital Region of 3 May 2007 (*M.B. of* 21 May 2007).

Alongside this idea of a common heritage, a sense of European cultural identity was born, always with reference to the values shared in Europe such as democracy and human rights.

The material side of the common heritage is referred to in the 1954 European Cultural Convention.[11]

For the regional organisation, heritage is part of the European construction, especially since the collapse of the Soviet system and the subsequent emergence of new democracies (Pickard, 2002). It plays a role in bearing witness to history through archaeological sites, monuments and other works of heritage, taking care not to discriminate against any cultural minority among the peoples of Europe.

The action of the European Council can be measured by large-scale projects, such as the European Heritage Days, but also by the adoption of legal texts.

Indeed, the leaders of the Council of Europe promote the protection of cultural heritage through conventions, resolutions, declarations, recommendations and other instruments that intervene along the "heritage chain" (de Clippele, 2014). Each of these texts focuses on a specific part of the cultural heritage:

- architectural heritage: Convention for the Protection of the Architectural Heritage of Europe, signed in Granada on 30 October 1985 (known as the "Granada Convention")[12];
- archaeological heritage: Convention on the Protection of the Archaeological Heritage (known as the "Valletta Convention") of 1969 was revised on 16 January 1992 in Valletta and entered into force on 25 May 1995[13];
- movable cultural property: Convention on Offences relating to Cultural Property, signed on 23 June 1985 in Delphi (the "Delphi Convention"), primarily aimed at combating illicit trafficking in cultural property. The Delphi Convention has been open for ratification since 23 June 1985 but has been signed (and not ratified) by only six Member States, four of which are victims of illicit trafficking. This lack of success is partly explained by the large number of international and European binding texts already in existence in the field. However, it has since been replaced by the eponymous Convention on Offences relating to Cultural Property, which was adopted on 3 May 2017 in Nicosia but has still not been signed by Belgium;

[11]European Cultural Convention of 19 December 1954 entered into force on 5 May 1955; ratification by Belgium on 11 May 1955 and entry into force on the same day.

[12]Ratified by Belgium on 17 September 1992, following the assent law of 8 June 1992 (*M.B.*, 29 October 1992).

[13]Ratified by Belgium on 8 October 2010 (entry into force on 9 April 2011), following the assent law of 23 June 2008 (*M.B.* 30 March 2011) and the decree of the Flemish Community/Flemish Region of 11 June 2010 (*M.B.* 19 July 2010), the Decree of the French-speaking Community of 17 December 2003 (*M.B.* 21 January 2004), the Decree of the German-speaking Community of 28 January 2008 (*M.B.* 22 February 2008), the Decree of the Walloon Region of 10 April 2003 (*M.B.* 4 March 2004 and 5 March 2004) and the Order of the Brussels-Capital Region of 20 May 1994 (*M.B.* 3 October 2002).

- cultural environment: European Landscape Convention, signed in Florence on 19 July 2000[14];
- intangible heritage and sustainable development: The Framework Convention on the Value of Cultural Heritage for Society, signed in Faro on 27 October 2005 (known as the "Faro Convention").[15]

Despite their mandatory nature in the event of ratification, most conventions contain few specific obligations vis-à-vis Member States and are rarely accompanied by concrete implementation mechanisms or monitoring bodies, diminishing its effectiveness.

Belgium has ratified almost all these European conventions (not the Delphi Convention nor (yet) the Faro Convention), but it is not always clear to what extent the conventions have influenced Belgian law or vice versa.

The 1985 Granada Convention has, for example, certainly inspired Belgian legislators to define the notion of monument and the concept of integrated conservation. The fact that the Convention is not directly applicable does not prevent it from being invoked in case-law and serving as a reference standard for national legislation (*Consorts Stoclet*, 2011; de Clippele, 2013).

Similarly, the European Landscape Convention—having binding force but no direct effect in Belgian law—has prompted many actors to act in favour of a better landscape policy, creating in 2011 a Belgian Landscape Award, the winner of which is presented to the European Landscape Award. However, it seems the implementation of the Convention greatly varies between the competent regions and communities (Leroy et al., 2004).

The Valletta Convention on the Archaeological Heritage was only ratified by Belgium in 2010, but several legislative measures had already been taken in this

---

[14]Ratified by Belgium on 28 October 2004 (entered into force on 1 February 2005), following the assent law of 15 June 2004 (*M.B.* 24 November 2004) and the Decree of the French Community of 19 December 2002 (*M.B.* 22 January 2003), the Decree of the Flemish Community/Flemish Region of 18 July 2003 (*M.B.* 5 September 2003—Ed. 2), the Decree of the German-speaking Community of 17 May 2004 (*M.B.* 30 July 2004), the Decree of the Walloon Region of 20 December 2001 (*M.B.* 30 January 2002), the Ordinance of the Brussels-Capital Region of 13 February 2003 (*M.B.* 5 May 2003).

[15]Not yet ratified by Belgium: the assents given to date are almost complete (the Federal State is missing): decree of the Flemish Region of 14 February 2014 assenting to the Council of Europe Framework Convention on the Value of Cultural Heritage for Society, signed in Faro on 27 October 2005 (*M.B.* 24 March 2014); decree of the Walloon Region of 2 July 2015 assenting to the Council of Europe Framework Convention on the Value of Cultural Heritage for Society, done at Faro on 27 October 2005 (*M.B.* 14 July 2015); decree of 2 July 2015 assenting, with regard to the competences of the French Community, the exercise of which has been transferred to the Walloon Region, to the Council of Europe Framework Convention on the Value of Cultural Heritage for Society, done at Faro on 27 October 2005 (*M.B.* 14 July 2015); Decree of 2 November 2015 assenting to the Council of Europe Framework Convention on the Value of Cultural Heritage for Society, done at Faro on 27 October 2005 (*M.B.* 2 December 2015); Ordinance of the Brussels-Capital Region of 11 May 2017 assenting to the Council of Europe Framework Convention on the Value of Cultural Heritage for Society, done at Faro on 27 October 2005 and signed in Strasbourg on 25 June 2012 (*M.B.* 30 May 2017).

field well before ratification, in particular with regard to the protection of excavations. Finally, the Faro Convention—not yet ratified by Belgium—also influences Belgian law, as Marc Jacobs, Director of FARO until September 2019 (Flemish Support and Liaison Point for Cultural Heritage [Movable and Intangible]) clearly notes (Jacobs, 2006). The Convention is very important as it broadens the notion of cultural heritage and gives it a fundamental dimension, recognising everyone's right to cultural heritage.

4 The European Union Rules with Partial Direct Effect in Belgian Law

Even though the European Union is showing a growing interest in the protection of cultural heritage (Cultural Heritage in the European Union, 2019), it has in fact only limited competence in the area, mostly related to the circulation of cultural goods (1), the rules of which apply directly in the national legal orders (2).

4.1 Limited Influence in Cultural Matters

The Union has subsidiary competence in cultural matters through Article 167 TFEU (Romainville, 2015). As such, it undertakes several actions in favour of European cultural heritage, developing a growing interest in this area, particularly in view of its impact on employment and the economy (*Cultural Heritage Counts for Europe*, s.d.). In its Council Conclusions on the participatory governance of cultural heritage (2014/C 463/01), the Council considers that "a people-centred and culture-based approach" linked to sustainable development should be followed. It calls on Member States to, inter alia, establish frameworks for governance and participation between stakeholders at local, regional, national and European level and to further develop digital opportunities to improve access to heritage.

In addition, the EU organised the "European Year of Cultural Heritage" in 2018 to raise awareness of the richness and potential of European heritage. The Union also supervises the European Capitals of Culture and the European Heritage Label. However, these various initiatives and projects remain relatively modest within the general framework of the Union's actions.

The Direct Effect of Certain EU Rules for National Treasures and Cultural Goods

Through its exclusive competence for the internal market and the movement of goods, the EU has nonetheless adopted measures to protect cultural goods and consequently to remove them from the principles of free movement. Article 36 of the Founding Treaty of the European Union (TFEU) admits exceptions to the free movement of goods in favour of "national treasures", which are to be interpreted restrictively according to the only European Court of Justice's ruling on the matter (*Commission v Italian Republic*, 1968); (See also: *Fachverband der Buch- und Medienwirtschaft v. LIBRO Handelsgesellschaft mbH*, 2009).

On the basis of this exception, Directive 2014/60/EU of 15 May 2014 adopts measures for the restitution of national treasures in the event of illicit intra-European exports, but without direct effect as they have to be transposed by the Member States (2).

Very recently, the EU adopted the EU Regulation 2019/880 on the import of cultural goods, which seems to change the situation (3).

Through its exclusive competence in customs matters, the EU has taken special and directly applicable measures for the export of cultural goods (a broader concept than national treasures) outside the territory of the EU (1).

While these measures have made it possible to make some progress in the area of movable heritage by adding effective burdens to the States—the obligations are either directly applicable or after transposition but under the supervision of the ECJ—to ensure the protection of national treasures and the control of cultural goods for export, they remain marginal in the general spectrum of the EU favouring a more commercial than cultural vision for these goods.

Regulation 116/2009 Standardises the Export of Cultural Goods Outside the EU

The Council Regulation of 9 December 1992, replaced by Regulation No 116/2009 of 10 December 2008 on the export of cultural goods, aims to standardise the control of exports of cultural goods outside the territory of the Union. This is a dual control, covering both the cultural goods specific to each Member State and cultural goods belonging to other Member States which might end up on the territory of the Member State as a result of the abolition of internal border controls.

This external aspect of the uniform measures makes it possible to avoid the risk of "cultural" *forum shopping,* where the author of the illicit export seeks the national legal system with the most liberal legislation on the export of a cultural object to a third State (Carducci, 1997, p. 100).

The Regulation establishes a system of export authorisations issued by the competent authorities of each Member State. The application for authorization is mandatory for cultural property as defined in the Schedule to the Regulations, but it does not have to be a national treasure.

On the other hand, the refusal of an export licence is only accepted "when the cultural goods in question are covered by legislation protecting national treasures" (Article 2, § 2, sub-paragraph 3), following Article 36 TFEU.

The relatively broad scope of application refers to an exhaustive list of cultural goods on the basis of two criteria: the age of the goods (more than 50 years) and the financial value of the goods (minimum value of €0 to €150,000 depending on the categories of goods concerned).

While EU law leaves the Member States free to determine their national treasures, it nevertheless attempts—by means of the EU's exclusive competence in customs matters and common commercial policy—to standardise the system for the export of cultural goods and thereby compels the Member States to comply with this policy.

Directive 2014/EU/60 to Return National Treasures Within the EU

Directive 2014/EU/60 on the return of cultural objects unlawfully removed from the territory of a Member State amends Council Directive 93/7/EEC of 15 March 1993 on the return of cultural objects unlawfully removed from the territory of a Member State. The first directive was transposed by the Belgian law of 28 October 1996,[16] and the amending directive by the law of 4 May 2016, which modified the law of 28 October 1996.[17]

The Directive provides for the implementation of cooperation mechanisms and judicial procedures for the return of cultural objects that have been unlawfully removed from the territory. Here, the spatial scope of application is more restricted than that of Regulation No 116/2009 as the Directive applies only within the territory of the Union.

The Directive removes the former condition of listing the categories of cultural objects and their thresholds in an annex (Lambrecht, 2014). If the good is considered as "national treasure" by the Member States, it falls within the scope of the Directive and may be claimed for return.

The limitation period for filing a claim is three years. An action for restitution is admissible only if the cultural object left the territory unlawfully after 1 January 1993 and is brought by a Member State.

Moreover, and quite importantly, the burden of proof is reversed and it is up to the possessor to exercise "due diligence" to obtain compensation and not the dispossessed owner.

All these aspects have been taken in the Belgian transposition law. The consultation platform for illicit trafficking in cultural property linked to the transposition of the 1970 UNESCO Convention must integrate these elements and develop a coherent policy on illicit trafficking.

---

[16] *M.B.*, December 21, 1996.

[17] Act of 4 May 2016 amending the Act of 28 October 1996 on the restitution of cultural property unlawfully removed from the territory of certain foreign States, *M.B.*, 23 May 2016.

Regulation 2019/880 on the Introduction and Import of Cultural Goods as a Game Changer

On 17 April 2019, the EU adopted its latest legal instrument in the fight against illicit trafficking: Regulation No 2019/880 of 17 April 2019 on the introduction and import of cultural goods. It is likely to have a considerable impact on the art market (Demarsin, 2020). The Regulation entered into force on 28 June 2019, but some parts will only enter into force later, spread over the next six years.

The key idea of the Regulation is to impose strict controls on imports of non-European cultural goods (i.e. cultural property that has not been either created or discovered in the customs territory of the EU) into the territory of the EU, prohibiting their entry if the goods have been illegally exported under the public law rules of the State of origin, or making their entry subject to the granting of an import licence or a declaration by the importer.

At the same time, the EU has been careful to maintain a balanced regulation, in particular with regard to the art market, international cooperation of museums and university research, by introducing exceptions to the import control rules. In other words, imports should not be requested in case of:

- temporary conservation of cultural property;
- temporary admission for educational, scientific, conservation, restoration, exhibition or digitisation purposes, in the field of the performing arts, in the field of research;
- temporary admission to art trade fairs;
- returned goods.

More specifically, the European legislator distinguishes between the *introduction*—any entry into the customs territory—and the *import*—release for free circulation or placement—of cultural goods (Articles 3 and Articles 4 and 5) (Demarsin, 2020).

The new regulation is being interpreted as a *game changer,* which will have positive and negative effects on the art market, both within and outside the EU (Demarsin, 2020).

On the one hand, the new European documentation requirements will influence other market players, who will find it difficult to circumvent the European art market, which is so important, even after Brexit. It is highly likely that the requirement to prove the provenance of cultural goods will force the entire art market to pay attention to this issue of identification and export documentation.

On the other hand, precisely in view of the overall effect of the Regulation, which is likely to require art market players from third countries to meet the administrative conditions for entering the European market, the market is likely to suffer as a result. Some art fairs may decide to relocate their events outside the EU, thereby impoverishing the antiques market in particular. On a wider scale, the circulation of a whole range of cultural goods would be frozen, as these goods would be damned if they were to remain in the country in which they were located when the European import regime came into force (Demarsin, 2020).

Through this import control regime, the European legislator assumes that the laws and regulations of the country in which the cultural property was created or discovered determine whether the export is legal or illegal. The regulations therefore recognise foreign public law, which is quite novel. For instance, the DRC has an Ordinance-Law No. 71-016 of 15 March 1971 on the protection of cultural property, which prohibits the definitive export of protected cultural property (Article 29), meaning that the import of such cultural property into the Union would be blocked under Articles 3.1 and 4.4 of the Regulation. This does not mean, however, that the Congolese heritage located, for example, in the Belgian Africa Museum must be returned to Congo. On the contrary, the Regulation ensures that new import applications arriving on European territory can be blocked in the event of illicit export from Congolese territory.

5 Conclusion

Even though the amount of UNESCO and Council of Europe conventions Belgium ratified is considerable, indicating their importance in Belgian law, they lack direct effect. They bind Belgium on the international scene, but without granting a subjective right which a claimant can directly invoke before courts.

Moreover, these conventions are lacking in concrete implementation mechanisms and often have few binding monitoring bodies. The obligations are not always precise, giving some leeway to Member States for their implementation.

Once implemented through national legislation, these rules become of course much more effective. Some of these implementation measures may then imply the recognition of subjective rights for the recipients.

In any case, international cultural heritage law has generally exerted a certain influence on Belgian legislators when drafting their own legal rules and strengthened the obligation for public authorities to protect cultural heritage in its multiple forms.

By contrast, the EU rules concerning the circulation of cultural goods are directly applicable, except for the Directive on the return of national treasures. They form a more binding legal framework for Belgian law than other international sources.

Nonetheless, this multitude of sources creates a fragmented legal landscape where the effectiveness of the system may be marred. Even if "there is no reason to be afraid of the normative conflicts inherent in the development of international law, especially in such recent and sensitive fields as the protection of cultural heritage" (Sartori, 2014), States can more easily escape from their obligations to implement this dispersed set of rules.

Indeed, it is quite clear that for illicit trafficking of cultural goods, Belgium is lagging behind in implementing international rules (no ratification of the UNIDROIT 1995 Convention, no implementation of the UNESCO 1970 Convention, no ratification of the Nicosia Convention…). It still suffers from its reputation as a central hub where art dealers trade illicitly trafficked objects (*Sur la piste du trafic d'antiquités en Belgique*, 2020). Having removed the Police Cell "Art and Antiquities" in 2015, the federal authorities give the impression they don't consider the policing of this issue to be a priority. This might however improve in the close future, seeing the renewed attention by the Belgian Senate and the draft proposal of the UNESCO 1970 Convention transposition law. The new EU Regulation on the import of cultural goods will also certainly heighten Belgium's obligations to fight illicit trafficking.

Also, Belgium still didn't ratify the Faro Convention (2005), recognising the fundamental right to cultural heritage. This illustrates yet another difficulty for the implementation of international law: the Belgian separation of powers for cultural heritage, requiring the assent of all competent regions and communities (and the Federal State) before being able to ratify conventions and treaties.

In this case, however, almost all authorities expressed their assent (not yet the Federal State). Furthermore, some national rules echoing the principles of the Faro Convention may be found, such as Article 23 of the Belgian Constitution, which provides the "right to cultural development" and already constitutes an important guarantee for the protection of cultural heritage (Romainville, 2014).

References

Bugnion, F. (2004). The Genesis of the Legal Protection of Cultural Property in the Event of Armed Conflict. *ICRL, 86*(854), 313–316.

Carducci, G. (1997). *La restitution internationale des biens culturels et des objets d'art volés ou illicitement exportés: Droit commun, Directive CEE, Conventions de l'Unesco et d'Unidroit*. L.G.D.J.

Casier, F. (2014). *Les régimes de protection en droit international humanitaire, les mesures de mise en oeuvre et leur application en Belgique* (p. 21). https://www.ismllw-be.org/session/2014-05-22-CASIER%20F-Texte%20final.pdf.

Commission v Italian Republic, C7/68 (European Court of Justice 10 décembre 1968).

Consorts Stoclet, 210.958 (Conseil d'État 2 février 2011).

Cultural Heritage Counts for Europe. (s.d.). Consulté 10 juillet 2020, à l'adresse. https://blogs.encatc.org/culturalheritagecountsforeurope/.

Cultural Heritage in the European Union: A Critical Inquiry into Law and Policy. (2019). In A. Jakubowski, K. Hausler, & F. Fiorentini (Éds.), *Cultural heritage in the European Union*. Brill Nijhoff. https://brill.com/view/title/36548. Accessed 5 July 2020.

de Clippele, M.-S. (2013). Quand l'art ouvre la voie au droit: Le palais Stoclet. *Journal Des Tribunaux, 4*(6506), 49–59.

de Clippele, M.-S. (2014). Quand l'équilibre devient art – Le Conseil de l'Europe et la balance des intérêts des propriétaires et de la collectivité en matière de patrimoine culturel. *Revue Trimestrielle Des Droits De l'homme, 3*(100), 913–935.

de Clippele, M.-S. (2020). Le patrimoine culturel immobilier en Région wallonne. *Guide De Droit Immobilier, 92*, 191–250. https://dial.uclouvain.be/pr/boreal/object/boreal:229400.

Demarsin, B. (2019). Verscheurd tussen koper en eigenaar—De kunst om de kloof in het goederenrecht te dichten. *Tijdschrift voor Privaatrecht, 2*, 493–606. https://lirias.kuleuven.be/retrieve/555518.

Demarsin, B. (2020). Recente ontwikkelingen in de kunsthandel. In VRG-Alumni (Éd.), *Recht in beweging—27ste VRG-Alumnidag 2020* (Gompel&Scavina, pp. 153–178). Gompel&Svacina.

Draye, A. M. (2007). *De bescherming van het roerend en onroerend erfgoed: Wet-, decreet- en regelgeving van kracht binnen het Vlaams Gewest/de Vlaamse Gemeenschap*. Larcier.

Ducastelle, J.-P. (2013). Le patrimoine culturel immatériel de la Fédération Wallonie-Bruxelles. In S. Cachat, *L'administration du patrimoine culturel immatériel en Europe. Organisation, réglementation et procédures* (pp. 80–91).

Dumont, H. (1996). *Le pluralisme idéologique et l'autonomie culturelle en droit public belge. 2: De 1970 à 1993* (Vol. 2). FUSL.

European Commission & Directorate-General for Education, Y., Sport and Culture. (2019). Illicit trade in cultural goods in Europe : Characteristics, criminal justice responses and an analysis of the applicability of technologies in the combat against the trade: final report. Publications Office of the European Union. https://data.europa.eu/doi/10.2766/183649.

Fachverband der Buch- und Medienwirtschaft v. LIBRO Handelsgesellschaft mbH, C-531/07 (European Court of Justice 30 avril 2009).

Fraoua, R. (1986). *Convention concernant les mesures à prendre pour interdirer et empêcher l'importation, l'exportation et le transfert de propriété illicites des biens culturels* (UNESCO Doc. CC-86/WS/40; p. 45). Unesco.

Genest, B. (2007). Le Patrimoine immatériel en Belgique francophone: Un modèle pour le Québec. *Rabaska: Revue D'ethnologie De l'Amérique Française, 5*, 47–70. https://doi.org/10.7202/019025ar.

Groenen, A. C. C. (2018). *UNIDROIT 1995: Tackling the illicit trafficking of cultural property through private law means: An evaluation of the appropriateness of the 1995 Unidroit Convention on Stolen or Illegally Exported Cultural Objects to Cultural Property Theft in comparative perspective* [Datawyse/Universitaire Pers Maastricht]. https://doi.org/10.26481/dis.20181002ag.

Hachez, I. (2008). *Le principe de standstill dans le droit des droits fondamentaux: Une irréversibilité relative* (1st éd.). Sakkoulas.

Haumont, F., Swennen, F., Tondreau, E., Kruger, T., Sanders, H., & Van Overbeeke, F. (2012). *Opportunité et conséquences de la ratification par la Belgique de la Convention UNIDROIT relative aux biens culturels volés ou illicitement exportés/Opportuniteit en gevolgen van de toetreding door België tot het Unidroit 1995-verdrag inzake gestolen of illegaal uitgevoerde cultuurgoederen* (p. 367). Direction du Patrimoine Culturel - Kunsten en Erfgoed.

Jacobs, M. (2006). Een nieuwe sleuteltekst voor erfgoedbeleid in de 21e eeuw. De kaderconventie van de Raad van Europa over de bijdrage van cultureel erfgoed aan de samenleving (Faro, 27/10/2005. *Mores, 7*(1), 11–13. https://www.academia.edu/3638829/Een_nieuwe_sleuteltekst_voor_erfgoedbeleid_in_de_21e_eeuw._De_kaderconventie_van_de_Raad_van_Europa_over_de_bijdrage_van_cultureel_erfgoed_aan_de_samenleving_Faro_27_10_2005.

Kono, T. (2010). The impact of uniform laws on the protection of cultural heritage and the preservation of cultural heritage in the 21st century. Martinus Nijhoff Publishers. https://doi.org/10.1163/ej.9789004180444.I-786.

Lalive, P. (1997). La Convention d'UNIDROIT sur les biens culturels volés ou illicitement exportés (du 24 juin 1995). *Revue Suisse De Droit International Et Européen, 1*, 13–57.

Lambrecht, L. (2014). Over reizende violen, music performance, digitale antifonaria, en hoe het recht dit allemaal bespeelt. In D. Arts (Éd.), *Mundi et Europae civis: Liber amicorum Jacques Steenbergen* (pp. 93–130). Larcier.

Leroy, I., Godart, M.-F., & Metalidis, I. (2004). *La mise en oeuvre de la Convention européenne du paysage et l'organisation du Prix du paysage* (pp. 67–70).

Négri, V. (Éd.). (2014). *Le patrimoine culturel, cible des conflits armés: De la guerre civile espagnole aux guerres du 21e siècle*. Bruylant.

O'Keefe, P. J. (2007). Commentary on the 1970 Unesco Convention (Second Edition). Institute of Art and Law.

O'Keefe, R. (2010). *Protection fo Cultural Property Under International Criminal Law*. Melb. J. Int'l L., 13, 339–392.

Pickard, R. (2002). *European Cultural Heritage—Volume II*. Council of Europe Pub: A review of policies and practice.

Prott, L. V. (2000). *Biens culturels volés ou illicitement exportés: Commentaire relatif à la convention d' Unidroit (1995)*. Organisation des Nations Unies pour l'Éducation, la Science et la Culture.

Rapport d'information concernant l'optimisation de la coopération entre l'autorité fédérale et les entités fédérées en matière de lutte contre le vol d'oeuvres d'art (N° 6-357; p. 56). (2018). Sénat de Belgique.

Romainville, C. (2014). *Le droit à la culture, une réalité juridique—Le régime juridique du droit de participer à la vie culturelle en droit constitutionnel et en droit international.* Bruylant.

Romainville, C. (Ed.). (2015). *European law and cultural policies: Droit européen et politiques culturelles.* P.I.E: Peter Lang.

Sartori, C. (2014). La restitution internationale des biens culturels: Analyse de l'efficacité d'un système fragmenté. *Annales Droit De Louvain, 4,* 557–642.

Sur la piste du trafic d'antiquités en Belgique. (2020, février 19). parismatch.be. https://parismatch.be/actualites/societe/371865/sur-la-piste-du-trafic-dantiquites-en-belgique.

Toman, J. (1994). *La protection des biens culturels en cas de conflit armé, Commentaires de la Convention de La Haye du 14 mai 1954.* Éditions Unesco.

Van Drooghenbroeck, S., & Delgrange, X. (2002). La signature de la Convention-cadre sur la protection des minorités nationales et les mesures de protection des minorités contenues dans les lois spéciales. *Administration Publique, 26,* 273–287. https://dial.uclouvain.be/pr/boreal/object/boreal:125700.

Cultural Heritage in International Law: (Still) Looking for a Definition? The Taxonomy of Cultural Heritage Across the Spectrum of UNESCO Conventions and Beyond

Alessandra Lanciotti

Abstract The growing interest in the protection of cultural heritage has stimulated the production of a multifaceted body of law that includes several conventions, protocols, charters and declarations, promoted by UNESCO and other international Organizations. Each multilateral treaty that forms part of this *corpus juris culturalis* describes some elements, often listed by categories, as being part of its scope. Each text refers to different elements that vary depending on their nature (movable/immovable, tangible/intangible), location (on land or underwater) and context (peace/wartime); it defines the term 'cultural heritage' or similar terms for its own purposes. Hence, from a normative approach it is hard to find a general definition of what forms part of the internationally protected cultural heritage. The definition is multifaceted and somewhat fragmented, besides it is interrelated to that of cultural property. This paper argues that, despite the 'fragmentation' in the definition of cultural heritage, a set of general principles, that are acknowledged by all States independently from their consent to be bound under specific treaty provisions, can be identified. These principles underpinning the *corpus juris culturalis* can assist in enforcing cultural heritage protectionist rules and in enhancing the return of lost and looted artworks.

1 Introduction

In the last decades, the increasing interest in the protection of cultural heritage demonstrated by the International Community has stimulated intense law-making activity. Such activity has produced a hefty body of law that includes several conventions, treaties, protocols, charters, directives, as well as soft law declarations and resolutions, promoted by UNESCO and by other organizations. This multi-faced body of law, or *corpus juris culturalis,* has gradually expanded the scope of cultural heritage protectionist rules at both international and national levels, far beyond the original

A. Lanciotti (✉)
Department of Law, University of Perugia, Perugia Via A. Pascoli 33, 06123, Italy
e-mail: alessandra.lanciotti@unipg.it

O. Niglio and E. Y. J. Lee (eds.), *Transcultural Diplomacy and International Law in Heritage Conservation*, https://doi.org/10.1007/978-981-16-0309-9_13

conception of cultural heritage encompassing only tangible artistic and monumental expression of such patrimony. Cultural heritage is a concept borrowed by other academic disciplines,[1] and is in constant evolution (Cornu, 2016: 46). Indeed, the definition has considerably expanded since I first broached the issue (Lanciotti, 1996: 5). Therefore, from a purely normative approach, it is hard to find a general definition suitable for use in different contexts. This paper examines the use of the expression 'cultural heritage' in a variety of multilateral conventions currently in force at both universal and regional levels and notes that several definitions of cultural heritage can be found in international treaty-law, each of which relates to the purpose of a specific legal instrument alone.[2] Then, this study tries to detect whether, beyond the multiplicity of conventional definitions, it is possible to find a set of universally accepted general principles regarding the regulation of cultural heritage protection. Notably, a few core principles, a sort of 'least common denominator' underpinning the vast and multifaceted body of treaty-law rules, that are valid for, and acknowledged by all States, independently from their consent to be bound under specific treaty provisions, and from whether the States concerned have accepted a broad or rather narrow definition of cultural heritage in their domestic legislation.

2 Defining Cultural Heritage in International Treaty-Law

Each convention which currently operates to protect 'cultural heritage' describes some elements—often listed by categories—as being part of the notion.[3] Sometimes the description is accompanied by adjectives, such as '*great*',[4] '*significant*'[5] or even '*outstanding*'[6] to better qualify the level of 'importance' of the protected elements. The qualifier is attached to the notion in order to identify the 'cultural' components that fall within the material scope of the convention. It thus creates a scale of relevance

[1] Archaeology, ethnology, history, prehistory, religion, literature, science, anthropology, environmental science and management, among others, are necessarily intertwined with cultural heritage law.

[2] Definitions contained in the many resolutions and declarations regarding cultural heritage are not commented here, as it would require a larger study, beyond the limited space and scope of this paper.

[3] The categorization system provides a general description of the elements that fall within the scope of the treaty and are thus entitled to international protection.

[4] Article 1, lett.(a), and Article 8, Convention for the Protection of Cultural Property in the Event of Armed Conflict (The Hague, 1954); Article 10, lett.(a), Second Protocol to this Convention of 26 March 1999.

[5] Article 5(3), lett.(d), UNIDROIT Convention on Stolen or Illegally Exported Cultural Objects (Rome, 1995).

[6] According to the Preamble and Articles 1 and 11 of the UNESCO Convention concerning the Protection of the World Cultural and Natural Heritage (Paris, 1972), the '*outstanding universal value*' is a condition for the inscription in the World Heritage List. The meaning of it is specified in the UNESCO Operational Guidelines for the implementation of this Convention, at para. 49, http://whc.unesco.org/en/guidelines/.

that seems to be valid for the purpose of that convention alone (Lanciotti, 1996: 9). Obviously, there can be some overlap, but a full correspondence in the definition from one text to another can hardly ever be found. Furthermore, the fact that the notion of cultural heritage has recently expanded, so as to include also manifestations that do not assume a tangible form, has made it even more complex to find an all-encompassing definition of such an elusive concept (Scovazzi, 2012; Bendix, 2011: 99). This enlargement has allowed the recognition of the *intangible* cultural heritage that had been ignored for a long time but, on the other hand, it has been envisaged as the opening up of a Pandora's box of difficulties, making the crafting of an all-embracing legal definition even more challenging (Logan, 2007: 33; Silberman, 2012: 245).

The difficulty in providing a uniform and generally agreed determination of the interests and values protected when dealing with cultural heritage has been underlined by a number of writers (Graham, 1987; Przyborowska-Klimczak, 1989–1990; O'Keefe, 1999; Blake, 2000; Francioni, 2007b; Scovazzi, 2008; Vecco, 2010; Lixinski, 2019). Some prominent scholars have also analyzed whether there is a difference between the notion of cultural heritage and that of cultural property (Prott, 1989: 222; Prott & O'Keefe, 1992; Frigo, 2004; Zagato, 2006; Fincham, 2011; Lixinski, 2019: 27). The two notions are certainly interrelated, and in some legal instruments both terms are used.[7] However, they never appear simultaneously as complementary notions in the same conventional text (Frigo, 2004: 367; Zagato, 2006: 130).

The first multilateral treaty in this domain refers to the term *cultural property*, while the expression *cultural heritage* appeared in International treaty-law only at a later stage. The merit of introducing the notion of *cultural property* as an autonomous category is attributable to the 1954 UNESCO Hague Convention for the Protection of Cultural Property in the Event of Armed Conflict. Previous international conventions applicable in times of war contained only a vague and somewhat empirical reference to objects of historical, monumental or humanitarian interest that should be spared from the violence of the belligerents. The term 'cultural property' has been retained in subsequent treaties promoted by UNESCO, such as the Second Additional Protocol of 1999 to the Hague Convention and the Convention on the Means of Prohibiting and Preventing the Illicit Import, Export and Transfer of Ownership of Cultural Property (Paris, 1970), which applies in peacetime. The same expression is used in the European Convention on Offences Relating to Cultural Property drafted by the Council of Europe (Delphi, 1985).[8] The latter treaty never entered into force,

[7]Both terms are used in the Preamble and Article 1, lett.(a) of the Convention for the Protection of Cultural Property in the Event of Armed Conflict (The Hague 1954); in Article 10, lett.(a) of the II Protocol to that Convention; in Article 1 of the Convention on the protection of archaeological, historical and artistic heritage of the American Nations (San Salvador, 1976). See also Preamble and Articles 2, 5 9, 10, 12 and 14 of the Convention on the Means of Prohibiting and Prevention the Illicit Import, Export and Transfer of Ownership of Cultural Property (Paris, 1970).

[8]ETS No. 119. In this convention, "cultural property" is only defined by reference to the categories of objects described in Annex II. The 1985 Convention has been repealed by a new version adopted in 2017 (ETS no. 221).

whereas the former two have been accepted by a considerable number of States, including many culture-rich countries as well as some important market States, thus contributing to the diffusion of this expression into domestic legislations by means of incorporation of treaty-law provisions into municipal law.

The somewhat different expression '*cultural objects*' has been adopted by the Convention on Stolen or Illegally Exported Cultural Objects (Rome, 1995), promoted by UNIROIT, although its French version sticks to the expression '*biens culturels*'.[9] Also EU Council Directive 93/7/EEC and Directive 2014/60/EU speak of *cultural objects* (unlawfully removed from the territory of a Member State).[10] On the contrary, the EU Regulation No. 116/2009, enacted to control the export of cultural items outside the EU territory, refers to '*cultural goods*' to circumscribe its scope, albeit it encompasses the same categories of 'cultural objects' listed in the abovementioned Directives.[11] In so doing, the Regulation follows the interpretation given by the EU Court of Justice that 'cultural property' is to be considered as 'goods' as long as it can be evaluated from an economic point of view within the scope of the EU Treaties.[12] Apparently, this interpretation, which emphasizes the commodification aspect of cultural items is in line with the principle of free movement of goods that led to the establishment of the EU single market. In this regard, it is worth mentioning Article 36 of the Treaty on the Functioning of the EU (TFEU) which refers to '*national treasures* possessing artistic, historic or archaeological value' when dealing with restrictions or prohibitions to import and export that can derogate from the principle of free movement of goods. Thus, Article 36 TFEU adopts yet another expression, at least in some of its linguistic versions, while in others it uses the somewhat different and broader expression of '*patrimonio artistico, storico e archeologico nazionale*; *patrimonio artístico, histórico o arqueológico nacional; nationalen Kulturguts von künstlerischem, geschichtlichem oder archäologischem Wert*' (on diverging translations, Lanciotti, 1996: 67; Frigo, 2004: 370–375; Stamatoudi, 2011: 117).

---

[9]According to Article 2: "For the purposes of this Convention, *cultural objects* are those which, on religious or secular grounds, are of importance for archaeology, prehistory, history, literature, art or science and belong to one of the categories listed in the Annex to this Convention" (emphasis added).

[10]Council Directive 93/7/EEC of 15 March 1993, repealed by Directive 2014/60/EU of the European Parliament and of the Council of 15 May 2014 on the return of cultural objects unlawfully removed from the territory of a Member State and amending Regulation (EU)1024/2012 (Recast). According to its Article 2, 'cultural object' means an object which is classified or defined by a Member State, before or after its unlawful removal from the territory of that Member State, as being among the 'national treasures possessing artistic, historic or archaeological value' under national legislation or administrative procedures within the meaning of Article 36 TFEU (see Sect. 3, below).

[11]Regulation (EEC)3911/92 of 9 December 1992 on the export of cultural goods, repealed by Council Regulation (EC)116/2009 of 18 December 2008 on the same topic. Both Regulation and Directive describe the categories of items falling within their scope in a separate annex.

[12]European Court of Justice, Judgment of 10 December 1968, Case 7/68 *Commission of the European Communities v. Italian Republic*, on the compatibility of Italian export tax on art treasures with the EEC rules on the free movement of goods.

The transition from the concept of *cultural property* to that of *cultural heritage*—the latter intended as a term encompassing multifaceted manifestations of human creation—came only at a later stage of codification. The reference to cultural heritage appears in the title of three very famous universal 'cultural conventions' promoted by UNESCO, namely: the Convention on the Protection of the World Cultural and Natural Heritage (Paris, 1972), the Convention on the Protection of the Underwater Cultural Heritage (Paris, 2001) and the Convention for the Safeguarding of the Intangible Cultural Heritage (Paris, 2003). Also, the 'old' 1954 UNESCO Hague Convention contains a reference to the notion of cultural heritage in the wording of Article 1, when it obliges States parties to avoid damage to 'movable or immovable cultural property of great importance for *the cultural heritage* of every people'.[13] Within the scope of the Hague Convention, however, the expression 'cultural heritage' means nothing more than the sum of the movable and immovable *tangible* elements considered worth to be spared from the violence of war for historical, artistic or cultural reasons. In its ambit, the definition 'cultural heritage' shares with that of 'cultural property' the limit of physicality of the object of reference, while ignoring completely those values and elements that have subsequently enriched the definition, such as folklore, dance, traditional skills and other manifestations of human creativity (Zagato, 2006: 130). Finally, the UNESCO Convention on the Protection and Promotion of the Diversity of Cultural Expressions (approved in 2005, fifty years after the 1954 Hague Convention, adopts a very flexible definition proclaiming that 'cultural diversity is made manifest […] through the varied ways in which the *cultural heritage* of humanity is expressed'.[14]

To conclude this survey on the taxonomy of cultural heritage across the spectrum of UNESCO Conventions and beyond, at least four different legal definitions of cultural heritage can be found: *world heritage* (cultural property of outstanding universal value); *underwater* cultural heritage (objects that have been underwater for more than one hundred years); *intangible* cultural heritage (traditions, folklore, original craftsmanship, music and even food preparation); *cultural diversity* (as a source of exchange, innovation and creativity, including a variety of cultural expressions) (Vadi, 2014: 18). Furthermore, the '*indigenous cultural heritage*' represents a separate category that partially overlaps with the former ones but involves peculiar issues which cannot be dealt with here. The novelty of such a broadening of the concept is that cultural heritage is now protected not just as a *res* endowed with its own intrinsic value—be it aesthetic, historical or archaeological—but because of its being associated with a social structure of a given cultural community (Francioni, 2012a: 16).

[13]Article 1, lett.(a) (emphasis added).

[14]Article 4(1) and Preamble, para. 1 (emphasis added).

3 The Meaning of 'Cultural Heritage' in Regional Treaty-Law

At the regional level, the expression cultural heritage appears in the title of four conventions concluded under the auspices of the Council of Europe. Namely: the European Convention for the Protection of the Archaeological Heritage (London, 1969 then revised at La Valletta in 1992)[15]; the Convention for the Protection of the Architectural Heritage of Europe (Delphi, 1985)[16]; the Framework Convention on the Value of Cultural Heritage for Society (Faro, 2005)[17] and the European Cultural Convention adopted in 1954 (Lanciotti, 2015: 125). The latter in particular refers to a '*common cultural heritage of Europe*'.[18]

Interestingly, while seeking a definition, the abovementioned treaties restrict their scope by adding a geographical specification.

The same geographical qualification is retained in EU law. Besides the reference to 'national treasures' in Article 36 TFEU (at least in some of its linguistic versions), the TFEU has another provision specifically dedicated to 'Culture': Article 167. This provision provides the legal basis for the EU's action in several fields related to culture, including that of 'conservation and safeguarding of *cultural heritage of European significance*'.[19]

This very expression had been introduced into EU law in 1992 by the Maastricht Treaty, and has since been maintained in the subsequent amended versions of the Treaty (Barrero Rodriguez, 1994: 232; Triggiani, 2019: 1670).[20] It seems to suggest the overcoming of a conception of 'cultural heritage' of exclusive national interest. It also indicates that the European 'Community' (now the Union) as such has an interest in enhancing the most significant material components of the 'European' culture, which undoubtedly are part of the 'common cultural heritage' mentioned in the first paragraph of Article 167.[21] This provision seems to be in line with the statement contained in the Preamble of the Treaty on the European Union (TEU), that the signatory States drew 'inspiration from the *cultural*, religious and humanist

[15]Convention for the Protection of the Archaeological Heritage (revised), La Valletta, 16 January 1992 (ETS No. 143), it updates the original London Convention of 1969 (ETS No. 66).

[16]Convention for the Protection of the Architectural Heritage of Europe, Granada 3 October 1985 (ETS No.121).

[17]Under Article 2 of the Framework Convention on the Value of Cultural Heritage for Society (ETS No. 199), "cultural heritage is a group of resources inherited from the past which people identify, independently of ownership, as a reflection and expression of their constantly evolving values, beliefs, knowledge and traditions. It includes all aspects of the environment resulting from the interaction between people and places through time".

[18]Article 1 and Article 5 of the European Cultural Convention (ETS n. 018).

[19]Article 167(2) TFEU (emphasis added).

[20]The wording of Article 167 TFEU corresponds to that of former Article 151 of the Treaty of Amsterdam and to the original Article 128 of the Maastricht Treaty.

[21]Article 167(1) TFEU: "The Union shall contribute to the flowering of the cultures of the Member States, while respecting their national and regional diversity and at the same time bringing the *common cultural heritage* to the fore" (emphasis added).

inheritance of Europe'.[22] However, it must be stressed that the concept of *cultural heritage of European significance* has not yet gained its own specific meaning. By way of contrast, the same concept does not seem to correspond exactly to that of '*national treasures possessing artistic, historic or archaeological value*' mentioned in Article 36 TFEU as a ground for limiting the free movement of goods within the internal market. The latter expression can be regarded as partially overlapping the notion of 'cultural heritage of European significance' in those situations in which a cultural object belonging to the patrimony of a Member State—thus qualified as a 'national treasure'—is also considered part of the yet-to-be-determined 'cultural heritage of European significance'. This being the case, such an object is entitled to a double level of protection: at the domestic level and, failing that, at the European level, considering that the EU action in the field of 'culture' is governed by the principle of subsidiarity as remarked in Article 167(2) TFEU (Cornu, 1993; Psycogiopoulou, 2008: 25).

In conclusion, both the Council of Europe and the European Union have sought to recruit cultural heritage in so far as it can reflect a pan-European characteristic as a vehicle for the construction of a European identity. However, even in this perspective, the choice of terminology does not seem to correspond to a specific theoretical approach.

4 Cultural Heritage and Cultural Property: Two Complementary Notions

Against this complex background of not well-coordinated sources of law, it is almost self-evident that the concept of 'cultural heritage' encompasses a much broader range of possible elements than that of 'cultural property'. The former expresses the idea of inheritance to be cherished and bestowed by one generation upon another, adding a further set of notions to its meaning (Prott & O'Keefe, 1992: 307; Vadi, 2015: 54). This concept is clearly expressed in the Preamble of the Convention on cultural diversity (Paris, 2005). Behind the rhetoric of international law texts, this idea is central to the potency of the term 'cultural heritage' in legal language (Blake, 2000: 69).[23] Conversely, the term 'cultural property' is more related to the notion of ownership and does not necessarily incorporate the concept of a duty to protect and preserve (Prott & O'Keefe, 1992: 319). It is often perceived as an essentially Western concept with commercial connotations that has a direct reference to property rights and disputes over restitution (Hardings, 1999: 301; Roussin, 2003–2004: 707; Yupsanis, 2011: 341). Although the two terms are sometimes used interchangeably,[24] the latter expression seems to have a more limited scope; it is mainly used in treaties aiming at preventing illicit export and theft of tangible property. In that

[22] Preamble, para. 2 TUE (emphasis added).

[23] On the notion of common heritage of mankind, see Sect. 7 below.

[24] See n. 12 above.

context, cultural property is generally accorded legal protection in so far as it can be ascertained to which (national) cultural heritage the 'cultural' property in question is assumed to belong (Frigo, 2004: 337).[25]

Moreover, if we compare the definition of cultural property to that of cultural heritage, we note that the former pertains only to a limited part of what falls under the label 'cultural heritage'. Hence, there is not a mere overlap or interchangeability between the two, but rather a relationship of complementarity, from species to genus. Such a relationship is without prejudice to the specific subgroup of items included in the notion of cultural property.

When looking at the description contained in the conventions that adopt the list method to define their material scope,[26] it can be observed that the definition of cultural property encompasses anything that bears witness to the artistry, history and identity of a particular culture. Such definition includes objects that are 'cultural' by nature as well as objects which have been rendered 'cultural' by reason of time and evolution of beliefs (Stamadoudi: 5–6). From this perspective, the definition of cultural property merges with that of cultural heritage in many areas. The two legal definitions are in fact strictly interrelated. Consequently, there is no 'battle of concepts' between them (Frigo, 2004). On the contrary, the inseparability of the notion of cultural heritage—covering a broader range of matters—from that more restrictive of cultural property is an emerging trend in current International law. As it has been pointed out (Blake, 2000: 64), 'the range of meanings encompassed by the term cultural heritage as used now in International law and related areas has grown far beyond the much narrower definitions included on a text by text basis'.

5 Is There an All-Encompassing Definition of Cultural Heritage?

The definition of cultural heritage codified in the main international conventions is multifaceted. It encompasses elements that vary depending on their nature (movable/immovable, tangible/intangible), location (on land or underwater) and context (peace or war time). Each situation is governed by a different set of International law rules, including rules dedicated to the conservation of indigenous peoples' cultural heritage. The existence of multiple definitions—each of which relates to the scope of a given treaty—gives rise to legal uncertainty as to the existence of a general, all-encompassing accepted definition under international law (Vadi, 2014: 42; Casini, 2011: 373).

[25] See the wording of the Preamble and Articles 2, 5, 9, 10, 12, 14 of the 1970 UNESCO Convention; Article 1, lett.(a) of the 1954 Hague Convention and Article 5 of the UNIDROIT Convention.

[26] Namely, the 1954 Hague Convention, the 1970 UNESCO Convention and the UNIDROIT Convention, but also the EU Regulation 116/2009 and Directive 2014/60 (footnotes n. 10 and 11 above).

In this scenario, it can be useful to ascertain whether, beyond the multiplicity of conventional definitions, it is possible to find a set of universally accepted general principles that stand at the core of the *corpus juris culturalis* and can offer a stable support in regulating cultural heritage protection. Such investigation is of some interest considering that, in the domain of cultural heritage law, there remains to be identified a truly comprehensive set of international principles governing practices and procedures comparable to that which has been recognized as customary rules in other areas of international law, such as human rights or environment protection Francioni, 2012a: 5). Besides, unlike other fields of International law, cultural heritage law does not have specific mechanisms of control that can ensure the consistent application of the relevant rules by all the recipients, nor has it a general and effective system of dispute resolution (Chechi, 2013: 185–186). The lack of control mechanisms shifts the responsibility for the effective implementation of international cultural heritage law to State actors, notably national courts, governmental agents and also private actors and institutions (Francioni, 2012b: 726). In this context, the identification of a core of shared common principles may contribute to strengthen the protection accorded within the domestic legal orders of different States. This is particularly true in those States in which implementation of treaty-law obligations into municipal law is absent or inadequate.

6 Principles Governing the Preservation of Cultural Heritage in Time of War

The first general principles that can be extrapolated from the interaction of the plurality of instruments devoted to the protection of cultural heritage are the principle *to respect* and the principle *to safeguard* tangible elements of cultural heritage. Those principles, embodied in the 1954 Hague Convention and enhanced in its II Protocol,[27] have gained universal recognition and now correspond to customary International law. Nowadays, both principles apply not only in inter-state situations of armed conflicts, but also in purely domestic situations. In particular, after the unanimous adoption of the UNESCO Declaration Concerning the Intentional Destruction of Cultural Heritage in 2003, the condemnation of the intentional destruction of

[27] The principle to respect is affirmed in Article 4 of the 1954 Hague Convention and Article 6, 1999 Hague II Protocol. The principle to safeguard is codified in Article 3 of the 1954 Hague Convention and Article 5 of its II Protocol. The basis for the development of such principles are to be found in Articles 27 and 56 of the Regulations attached to the IV Hague Convention of 1907 on the laws and customs of war on land and in Article 5 of the IX Hague Convention of 1907 concerning bombardment by naval forces in time of war; these principles were subsequently declined in the two Additional Protocols to the 1949 Geneva Conventions on the protection of the victims of armed conflicts.

cultural heritage has become general (Francioni, 2004: 1213; Francioni & Lenzerini, 2003; O'Keefe, 2004: 189).[28]

As regards the protection of movable cultural property during an armed conflict, there is a general *consensus* to recognize the customary nature of the principle prohibiting the plunder of artworks, either public or privately owned, and of the ensuing obligation of restitution at the close of hostilities, as well as the prohibition on retaining cultural property as war reparations (Chechi, 2013: 184, but a different opinion Zagato, 2008: 363). In addition, it has been argued that the rule on the prohibition of war booty has been gradually transforming into a broader principle related to the nonexploitation of the weakness of another subject to make a cultural gain (Scovazzi, 2009: 6, 15).

The universal recognition of those principles as general principles of international law paved the way for the establishment of a specific form of 'responsibility to protect' with respect to cultural heritage endangered by armed violence. Such responsibility is incumbent upon each and every State. Significantly, on 24 March 2017, the UN Security Council unanimously adopted Resolution 2347 that is the first dedicated exclusively to condemn the destruction and trafficking of cultural heritage in situations of armed conflict in general and at the hands of terrorist groups. The Security Council had already expressed concerns and condemnations with regard to those issues in past resolutions (Scovazzi, 2020: 3), but Res. 2347(2017) is unique as it is the first dedicated exclusively to the destruction and trafficking of cultural heritage (Jakubowski, 2018).

7 Individual Criminal Responsibility for Offenses Against Cultural Heritage

The increased sensibility on the preservation of cultural heritage from the effects of armed violence has contributed to the progressive development of a set of principles that aims to specifically protect cultural property, because of its intrinsic value and importance for humanity. This intention is proclaimed in the famous passage of the Preamble to the 1954 Hague Convention, at para. 2: 'damage to cultural property belonging to any people whatsoever means damage to the cultural heritage of all mankind, since each people makes its contribution to the culture of the world'.

In this context, individual criminal responsibility is added to the 'traditional' responsibility of the State for the violations of the *jus in bello* rules.[29] In line with this growth in consciousness, a principle expressly recognizing the accountability for

[28] See para. 6 of the UNESCO Declaration Concerning the Intentional Destruction of Cultural Heritage of 17 October 2003.

[29] See footnote n. 30 above.

offenses against the integrity of cultural heritage has progressively emerged.[30] Cases decided by the International Criminal Tribunal for the former Yugoslavia (ICTY)[31] and more recently by the International Criminal Court (ICC)[32] have demonstrated that penal sanctions can be imposed on those individuals responsible for deliberate attacks against cultural heritage (Frulli, 2005: 195; Brammertz et al., 2016: 1143).[33] Recent situations, such as the conflict in Iraq, Syria, Mali and elsewhere, have shown that cultural property is not simply at risk from incidental harm, but is being intentionally targeted as part of cultural cleansing campaigns. Some heinous acts against cultural heritage may not only fall within the category of war crimes, but also within that of crimes against humanity, if certain conditions are met.[34] For example, an act of destruction to the detriment of cultural heritage, if committed with discriminatory intent toward a culturally distinct group, infringes the fundamental human rights of the targeted group and may amount to a form of persecution as a crime against humanity (Mucci, 2012: 289–294).[35] In line with this approach, the crime of persecution could play an important role also in prosecuting offenses committed in peacetime and also offenses against *intangible* cultural heritage (Frulli, 2011: 212). Furthermore, actions deliberately carried out to destroy religious sites, religious objects and other cultural property that has great meaning to a particular group of people bound by a national, ethnical, racial or religious tie, may be considered in court as evidence of the *mens rea* in the crime of genocide.[36] In such a situation, the interaction between the principles to safeguard cultural heritage and to respect fundamental human rights becomes very close (Schaier, 2001: 59).

[30]It is enshrined in Articles 15–17, 1999 Hague II Protocol. It represents the rationale of Article 53 and 85(4), lett.(d) of Additional Protocol I and of Article 16 of Additional Protocol II to the 1949 Geneva Conventions.

[31]See footnote n. 38 and 39 below.

[32]*Prosecutor v. Ahmad Al Faqi Al Mahdi* (ICC-01/12-01/15), Trial Chamber VIII, Judgment and sentence, 27 September 2016, at www.icc-cpi.int/mali/al-mahdi. The prosecution of this case marked the first time that attacks against cultural heritage constituted the principal charge in an international criminal case. The accused was found guilty of the specific war crime committed during a non-international armed conflict of intentionally directing attacks against historical and religious building forming part of the cultural heritage of Mali. He was convicted to nine years' imprisonment under Article 8(2)(e)(iv) of the ICC Statute.

[33]Acts against elements of cultural heritage may constitute a war crime under Article 3, ICTY Statute and Article 8(2)(b)(ix) and 8(2)(e)(iv), ICC Statute. They are criminalized under Articles 15–17, II Hague Protocol.

[34]According to Article 7 of ICC Statute, "crime against humanity" means any of the following acts when committed as part of a widespread or systematic attack directed against any civilian population, with knowledge of the attack.

[35]This reasoning has been applied in *Prosecutor v Kordic and Cerkez* (Judgment, 26 February 2001—Case No. IT-95-14/2-T, https://www.icty.org/en/case/kordic_cerkez.

[36]ICTY, *Prosecutor v. Kristic*, Judgment of 2 August 2002 (Case No. IT-98-33-T, at https://www.icty.org/en/case/krstic).

8 Principles Governing the Preservation of Cultural Heritage in Time of Peace

In peacetime, the protection of cultural heritage can no longer be regarded as a matter of domestic policymaking of the State alone. As far as immovable cultural heritage is concerned, the universalistic idea expressed in the Preamble of the 1972 UNESCO Convention that 'parts of the cultural heritage of outstanding interest need to be preserved as part of the world heritage of mankind as a whole' is not completely new in International law.[37] The suggestion of a common heritage belonging to the whole of humanity operates in other fields of international law governing spaces and resources beyond national jurisdiction, entailing a formal prohibition of appropriation which is specified in the relevant treaties, such as those on the moon and other celestial bodies[38] and on the oceans' floor.[39] Undoubtedly, the provisions of those treaties have some rationale in common with the protectionist rules on cultural heritage of 'outstanding value': the action in defense of a general interest of humanity; the need for a joint effort by the International Community; the tendency to institutionalize protection through the establishment of a supranational authority[40] (Przyborowska-Klimczak, 1989–1990: 58–63). However, the concept of heritage of mankind, in the ambit of cultural heritage, has mainly an emphatic value (Lanciotti, 1996: 20–21; Frigo, 2015: 104; Vadi, 2014: 43). In fact, the similarities indicated above do not suffice to deprive the territorial State of its sovereign powers to control all elements belonging to the cultural heritage (of mankind) placed within its jurisdiction. The inclusion of a monument or site in the World Heritage List requires the consent of the State in whose territory the cultural heritage in question is located.

In other words, international norms proclaiming a cultural heritage of all mankind do not expropriate the State of its sovereignty over the cultural heritage components located in its territory, they simply impose some limits on its exercise. Accordingly, a State's sovereignty must be exercised in such a way as to be functional for the purpose of conserving and protecting the enlisted elements of cultural heritage in the general interest of humanity. Even when international cooperation is required by the territorial State, such State remains uniquely placed in protecting its heritage (Francioni, 2012b: 725; Vadi, 2014: 43).[41] It follows that the concept at issue necessarily assumes a different meaning in the cultural sector, given the lack of some features that characterize the regime of common heritage of humanity in other contexts—namely, non-appropriability and compensating inequality (i.e. an equitable sharing of benefits derived from the exploitation of resources)—and the

---

[37]Preamble, para. 6 (emphasis added).

[38]Treaty on Principles Governing the Activities of States in the Exploration and Use of Outer Space, Including the Moon and Other Celestial Bodies, 27 January 1967; Agreement Governing Activities of States on the Moon and Other Celestial Bodies, 17 December 1979.

[39]Convention on the Law of the Sea, Montego Bay, 10 December 1982, Part XI.

[40]In the case of Cultural heritage this function is carried out by the World Heritage Committee.

[41]See Article 4 and 6(1), 1972 UNESCO Convention; see also Article 1, lett.(h) of the Convention on Cultural Diversity. F. Francioni, *op. cit. supra* n. 53, at 725; V. Vadi, *op. cit. supra* n. 27, at 43.

different configuration of others, such as the so-called 'institutional internationalism' (i.e. the establishment of an 'Authority' or Committee for the management of the common heritage). Indeed, the said regime of common management of the resources has been excluded even with regard to cultural heritage found in marine areas beyond national jurisdiction (Mainetti, 2008: 587; Lanciotti, 2019: 175).

In sum, the notion of *world heritage of mankind* must be intended in a nontechnical sense, otherwise its use would be inappropriate, as it would mean that States have agreed to abdicate their sovereign rights over cultural heritage located in their territory (Frigo, 1986: 303). In any case, although with a different meaning, the use of this concept in the domain of international cultural heritage law has a positive effect: it serves to consolidate the *opinio juris* that the safeguard of cultural heritage is a common concern of humanity, at least when cultural heritage of outstanding universal value is at stake (Kiss: 229).

9 Principles Regulating the Protection of Movable Cultural Property

When it comes to the protection of moveable property, the International Community's main concern is to prevent thefts, spoliations and illegal exportation that may impoverish the State of origin's cultural heritage. The relevant treaties have a rather limited scope (Scovazzi, 2019: 1637),[42] but they have contributed to the affirmation of the principle that all States—not just States parties—are under an obligation to cooperate in the fight against illicit trafficking. In spite of this, the existence of a principle imposing the restitution of cultural heritage unlawfully removed in peacetime remains doubtful (Coulée, 2000: 375; Francioni, 2007a: 31). It can be argued that the application of said principle should be the basis for repatriation also in peacetime, at least in case of artworks stolen from public monuments, museums or archaeological sites. However, if we consider States' practice, we note that outside the personal and material scope of the abovementioned conventions (or of EU Directive 2014/60), the obligation of restitution is barely perceived as a general principle, for it would imply the recognition and enforcement of foreign laws protecting public interests when the preservation of another State's cultural heritage is at stake (Gordley, 2013: 110; Lanciotti, 2019: 184).

Lacking a general recognition of the State of origin's legislation, in cases not falling within the *ratione materiae, ratione personae* and *ratione temporis* scope of

[42]The 1970 UNESCO Convention imposes only a general duty to procure the return of stolen property (Articles 7 and 13), but it is not self-executing and operates only under certain conditions. A more stringent approach is adopted by the UNIDROIT Convention. Under Article 3(1), automatic restitution applies when the dispossessed owner, whether a public institution or a private person, proves that a theft has occurred. As for objects belonging to the national heritage transferred abroad (even by the rightful owner) in breach of the rules governing export, return can be obtained, as long as it can be proved that the removal significantly impairs one or more of the 'cultural' interests listed in Article 5.

the relevant conventional provisions, the requesting State has to rely on claims of ownership before foreign civil courts, rather than contend the return of its own cultural heritage on the basis of a recognized general principle. Consequently, unless uniform rules imposing restitution (such as those laid down by the UNIDROIT Convention or the EU Directive) apply in the specific case, the result of a dispute over restitution will finally depend on the requested State's conflict of law rules. Those rules shall determine which law regulates the transfer of title (Siehr, 1993; Lanciotti, 1996, 2012; Jayme, 2005: 218; Frigo, 2015: 158–212; Kowalski, 2001: 218). In those cases, the principles of cooperation and *in situ* conservation can assist the court in finding an equitable solution that takes into account the cultural interest at stake. It can be argued that said principles may become part of the *ordre public* of the forum State, if that State is a party to the relevant multilateral conventions.

Another issue is related to the circumstance that, generally, treaty-law provisions do not apply retrospectively.[43] It follows that, even in the presence of a specific obligation to return stolen or looted cultural objects, the enforcement of the non-retroactivity rule may represent an obstacle to repatriation. However, the strict application of this rule can be tempered by putting into operation of emerging principles of transnational justice. Particularly, the acknowledgment of the principle of non legitimization of past wrongs and acquisitions obtained with the use of force.[44] Following this approach, lost and looted artworks could be successfully returned as a form of relief, as in Holocaust-related disputes and in cases of cultural property removed as a result of colonial or foreign military occupation (Chechi, 2013: 186; Francioni, 2012b: 724; Roodt, 2013: 301). In this perspective, it has been argued that the return of cultural properties is not only the consequence of the duty to refrain from exploiting the weakness of another subject to get a cultural gain and of the duty to cooperate against illegal activities, but also the manifestation of the need to preserve the integrity of cultural contexts (Scovazzi, 2009: 30). This need is deeply rooted in the nature of cultural heritage and forms the core of another principle of International law. The principle of preservation of the integrity of the cultural context applies in particular when dealing with underwater cultural heritage.[45] Besides, the same principle can also be envisaged as a tool to ensure respect for cultural diversity.

---

[43] According to Article 7, the 1970 UNESCO Convention applies only to cultural property illicitly removed after its entry into force for both the States concerned. The 1995 UNIDROIT Convention follows the same rule in Article 10.

[44] A rule of this kind is embodied in Article 10(3), UNIDROIT Convention.

[45] In Article 2(5) of the Convention on the Protection of Underwater Heritage, States parties have agreed that *in situ* preservation is the best option to ensure the protection of submerged heritage.

10 Concluding Remarks

In international law, difficulties persist in the quest to reduce the notion of 'cultural heritage' to a common meaning and to organize a unified system of protection operating at the supranational level. The legal definition provided for by the multiplicity of treaties devoted to the safeguard of cultural heritage is multifaceted. This study has highlighted the polarization and inconsistency in the use of the expression 'cultural heritage' in the variety of multilateral conventions currently in force at both universal and regional levels and concludes that there is no uniform, universally agreed definition, rather a plurality of definitions, each of which is functional to the scope of the treaty that specifies it, which is devoted to the protection of some particular 'cultural elements' embodying the key values that are considered worthy of preservation through international cooperation. Legal uncertainty as to the existence of a general, all-encompassing accepted definition under international law can be mitigated by the detection of a set of general principles applicable in the field of cultural heritage protection that the international community has managed to recognize and accept.

These principles may be of some guidance when looking at the way in which international obligations on the protection of cultural heritage are executed in practice; it can also become a tool for increasing the uniform interpretation and application of the relevant rules in the effort to prevent damage to, and pauperization of cultural heritage, in both situations of peace and armed conflicts. These principles constitute the foundation of the so-called international *corpus juris culturalis* and can be invoked in relation to: (a) the safeguard of cultural heritage of great importance in wartime; (b) the conservation of immovable heritage of outstanding value; (c) the resolution of disputes on the return of stolen or illicitly exported cultural objects, particularly of objects removed in situations of colonial or military occupation.

Some of them, such as the prohibition of destruction of tangible cultural heritage in time of war and of heritage of particular significance for humanity as a whole, are already sanctioned by customary law (Vadi, 2014: 42; Francioni & Lenzerini, 2003: 134). Conversely, others, such as the principle that embodies the obligation of restitution to the Country of origin of items belonging to its national heritage stolen in peacetime and the principle of cooperation in the fight against illegal trafficking have not yet reached that status. However, they have experienced constant progress in practice, so their evolution into customary law on the basis of the progressive development of existing treaty-law is soon expected.

All in all, at the core of the *corpus juris culturalis* lays the uncontested recognition by the international community of the public interest in preservation of cultural heritage to prevent the risk of destruction and dispersion, or excessive commercial exploitation. Then, a 'least common denominator' that underpins this multifaceted body of law can be identified: the opinion that the cultural heritage of any country, of any people, of any place constitutes the essence of the international community's shared interest in conservation and fruition, independent of the public or private regime to which it is submitted (Frigo, 2015: 112). It has been argued that the respect of this principle has become an *erga omnes* obligation (Francioni, 2012b: 25; Triggiani, 2019: 1663).

The various fields in which this fundamental principle displays its effects are to be determined by the relevant agreed definition(s) of 'cultural heritage'. Then, the shifting of the approach to cultural heritage protection from a sovereignty-based idea of property to a fuller and more complete perception of its human dimension—as highlighted by the most recent UNESCO Conventions[46]—contributes to the consolidation of said principle and enables the evolution of cultural heritage law into an essential component of contemporary general international law.

References

Barrero Rodriguez, M. C. (1994). El nuevo precepto europeo en defensa del patrimonio cultural. El artículo 128 del Tratado de la Comunidad europea. In M. Chiti (Ed.), *Beni culturali e Comunità europea* (pp. 221–242). Paris: Editions de la maison des sciences de l'homme.

Bendix, R. (2011). Héritage et patrimoine: de leurs proximités sémantiques et de leurs implications. In C. Bortolotto (Ed.), *Le patrimoine culturel immateriel. Enjeux d'une nouvelle catégorie* (pp. 99–121). Paris: éditions de la maison des sciences de l'homme.

Blake, J. (2000). On defining the cultural heritage. *International & and Comparative Law Quarterly, 49,* 61–85.

Brammertz, S., et al. (2016). Attacks against cultural heritage as a weapon of war: Prosecutions at the ICTY. *Journal of International Criminal Justice, 14,* 1143–1174.

Casini, L. (2011). Italian hours: The globalization of cultural property law. *International Journal of Constitutional Law, 9,* 369–393.

Chechi, A. (2013). Plurality and coordination of dispute settlement methods in the field of cultural heritage. In F. Francioni & J. Gordley (Eds.), *Enforcing international cultural heritage law* (pp. 177–205). Oxford: Oxford University Press.

Cornu, M. (1993). *Compétences culturelles en Europe et principe de subsidiarité*. Bruxelles: Éditions Bruylant.

Cornu, M. (2016). Réflections autour de la définition juridique en droit d'auteur/copyright and en droit du patrimoine culturel. *Revue de droit de l'Université de Sheerbrooke, 46,* 359–389.

Coulée, F. (2000). Quelques remarques sur la restitution des biens culturels sous l'angle du droit international public. *Revue générale de droit international public,* 359–392.

Fincham, D. (2011). The distinctiveness of property and heritage. *Penn State Law Review, 115,* 641–685.

Francioni, F. (2004). Beyond state sovereignty: The protection of cultural heritage as a shared interest of humanity. *The Michigan Journal of International Law, 25,* 1209–1228.

Francioni, F. (2007a). Au-delà des traités: l'émergence d'un nouveau droit coutumier pour la protection du patrimoine culturel. *Revue générale de droit international public,* 9–42.

Francioni, F. (2007b). Des biens culturels au patrimoine culturel: l'évolution dynamique d'un concept et de son extension. In A. Yusuf (Ed.), *L'action normative à l'UNESCO, Élaboration de règles internationales sur l'éducation, la science et la culture*, 221–247.

Francioni, F. (2012a). The evolving framework for the protection of cultural heritage in international law. In S. Borelli & F. Lenzerini (Eds.), *Cultural heritage, cultural rights, cultural diversity* (pp. 301–326). Leiden: M. Nijhoff Publishers.

[46]The Convention on intangible heritage and that on cultural diversity, as well as the Faro Convention of 2005 (see footnote 17 above) show the interaction between cultural heritage norms and human rights norms.

Francioni, F. (2012b). Public and private in the international protection of global cultural goods. *European Journal of International Law, 23,* 719–730.
Frigo, M. (1986). *La protezione dei beni culturali nel diritto internazionale.* Milan: Giuffrè.
Frigo, M. (2004). Cultural heritage v. cultural property: A 'battle of concepts' in international law? *International Review of the Red Cross, 86,* 367–378.
Frigo, M. (2015). Circulation des biens culturels, détermination de la loi applicable et méthodes de règlement des litiges. *Collected Courses of the Hague Academy of International Law, 375,* 101–460.
Frulli, M. (2005). Advancing the protection of cultural property through the implementation of individual criminal responsibility: The case-law of the international criminal tribunal for the former Yugoslavia. *Italian Yearbook of International Law, 15,* 195–216.
Frulli, M. (2011). The criminalization of offences against cultural heritage in times of armed conflict: The quest for consistency. *European Journal of International Law, 22,* 203–217.
Gordley, J. (2013). The enforcement of foreign laws: Reclaiming one nation's cultural heritage in another nation's court. In F. Francioni & J. Gordley (Eds.), *Enforcing international cultural heritage law* (pp. 110–124). Oxford: Oxford University Press.
Graham, M. G. (1987). Protection and reversion of cultural property: Issues of definition and justification. *International Lawyer, 21,* 755–794.
Hardings, S. (1999). Value, obligation and cultural heritage. *Arizona State Law Journal, 31,* 291–354.
Jakubowski, A. (2018). Resolution 2347: Mainstreaming the protection of cultural heritage at the global level. *Questions of International Law-QIL, Zoom-In, 48,* 21–44.
Jayme, E. (2005). Globalization in art law: Clash of interests and international tendencies. *Vanderbilt Journal of Transnational Law, 38,* 928–945.
Kowalski, W. (2001). Restitution of works of art pursuant to private and public international law. *Collected Courses of the Hague Academy of International Law, 288,* 17–228.
Lanciotti, A. (1996). *La circolazione dei beni culturali nel diritto internazionale privato e comunitario.* Naples: Edizioni Scientifiche Italiane.
Lanciotti, A. (2012). The dilemma of the right to ownership of underwater cultural heritage: The case of the Getty Bronze. In S. Borelli & F. Lenzerini (Eds.), *Cultural heritage, cultural rights, cultural diversity* (pp. 301–326). Leiden: M. Nijhoff Publishers.
Lanciotti, A. (2015). Relaunching the economic activities through the promotion of cultural heritage in Europe: A legal survey. *European Lawyer Journal, XIV,* 123–138.
Lanciotti, A. (2019), Il Getty Bronze: prima un giallo archeologico, poi un rebus giuridico. Profili internazionalistici. *Archivio penale,* 175–190.
Francioni F., & Lenzerini, F. (2003). The destruction of the Buddas of Bamiyan and international law. *European Journal of International Law, 14,* 619–651.
Lixinski, L. (2019). *International cultural heritage law for communities: Exclusion and re-imagination.* Oxford: Oxford University Press.
Logan, W. (2007). Closing Pandora's box: Human rights conundrums in cultural heritage protection. in H. Silverman & F. Ruggles (Eds.), *Cultural heritage and human rights* (pp. 33–52). Springer.
Mainetti, V. (2008). Le principe du patrimoine culturel de l'humanitè: de la république des arts à un ordre public international. *La Salvaguardia dei Beni culturali nel diritto internazionale, Atti del Convegno XII Giornata gentiliana* (pp. 581–601). Milan: Giuffrè.
Mucci, F. (2012). *Le diversità del patrimonio e delle espressioni culturali nell'ordinamento internazionale, da ratio implicita a oggetto diretto di protezione.* Naples: Editoriale Scientifica.
O'Keefe, R. (1999). The meaning of cultural property under the 1954 Hague convention. *Netherlands International Law Review, 46,* 26–56.
O'Keefe, R. (2004). World cultural heritage: Obligations to the international community as a whole? *ICLQ, 53,* 189–209.
Prott, L. (1989). Problems of private international law for the protection of the cultural heritage. *Collected Courses of the Hague Academy of International Law, 217*(1989-V), 215–316.

Prott, L., & O'Keefe, P. J. (1992). "Cultural Heritage" or "Cultural Property". *International Journal of Cultural Property, 1*, 307–320.

Przyborowska-Klimczak, A. (1989–1990). Les notions des 'biens culturels' et du 'patrimoine culturel mondial' dans le droit international. *Polish Yearbook of International Law, XVIII*, 47–72.

Psycogiopoulou, E. (2008). *The integration of cultural consideration in EU law and policies*. Leiden and Boston: Martinus Nijhoff Publishers.

Roodt, C. (2013), Restitution of art and cultural objects and its limits. *Comparative and International Law Journal of Southern Africa, XLVI*, 286–307.

Roussin, L. (2003–2004). Cultural heritage identity. *Cardozo Journal of International and Comparative Law, 11*, 707–710.

Schaier, S. (2001). The intersection of human rights and cultural property issues under international law. *The Italian Yearbook of International Law Online, XI*, 59–99.

Scovazzi, T. (2008). La notion de patrimoine culturel de l'humanité dans les instruments internationaux. In J. Nafziger & T. Scovazzi, *Le patrimoine culturel de l'humanité - The cultural heritage of mankind*, 3–144.

Scovazzi, T. (2009, May 11–13). Diviser c'est détruire: Ethical principles and legal rules in the field of the return of cultural property. In *Study presented at the 15th session of the Intergovernmental Committee for promoting the return of cultural property to the countries of origin or its restitution in case of illicit appropriation, Paris* (CLT.2009/CONF.212/COM) Paris: UNESCO.

Scovazzi, T. (2012). The definition of intangible cultural heritage. In S. Borelli & F. Lenzerini (Eds.), *Cultural heritage, cultural rights, cultural diversity* (pp. 179–200). Leiden: M. Nijhoff Publishers.

Scovazzi, T. (2019). Meriti e limiti dei trattati multilaterali sulla restituzione di beni culturali illecitamente esportati 1633. *III Liber Amicorum Angelo Davì* (pp. 1633–1658). Naples: Editoriale Scientifica.

Scovazzi, T. (2020). International legal instruments as a means for the protection of cultural heritage. In O. Niglio & E. Y. J. Lee (Eds.), *Transcultural diplomacy and international law: Ethic, laws, and dialogue among cultures*, in this book.

Siehr, K. (1993). International trade and the law. *Collected Courses of the Hague Academy of International Law, 243*, 239–292.

Silberman, N. (2012). Heritage interpretation and human rights: Documenting diversity, expressing identity or establishing universal principles? *Intl Journal of Heritage Studies, 18*, 245–256.

Stamatoudi, I. (2011). *Cultural property law and restitution: A commentary to international conventions and European Union law*. Cheltenham: Edward Elgar.

Triggiani, E. (2019). I beni culturali per l'integrazione europea. *III Liber Amicorum Angelo Davì* (pp. 1659–1688). Naples: Editoriale Scientifica.

Vadi, V. (2014). *Cultural heritage in international investment law and arbitration*. Cambridge: CUP.

Vadi, V. (2015). Cultural heritage in international economic law. In V. Vadi & B. De Vitte (Eds.), *Culture and international economic law*. London: Routledge.

Vecco, M. (2010). A definition of cultural heritage: From the tangible to the intangible. *Journal of Cultural Heritage, 11*, 321–324.

Yupsanis, A. (2011). Cultural property aspects in international law: The case of the (still) inadequate safeguarding of indigenous peoples' (Tangible) cultural heritage. *Netherlands International Law Review, 58*, 335–361.

Zagato, L. (2006). Beni culturali e/o patrimonio culturale. In D. Goldoni, M. Rispoli, & R. Troncon (Eds.), *Estetica e management nei beni e nelle produzioni culturali* (pp. 121–134). Bolzano-Wien: il Brennero edizioni.

Zagato, L. (2008). La protezione dei beni culturali nei conflitti armati: riflessone sul rapporto fra diritto internazionale generale e diritto pattizio dopo il secondo Protocollo del 1999. *La Salvaguardia dei Beni culturali nel diritto internazionale, Atti del Convegno XII Giornata gentiliana* (pp. 340–376). Milan: Giuffrè.

Traditional Cultural Expressions (TCEs), Holder Communities and Conflicts with Central States: Policies for the Recognition of Intangible Cultural Heritage (ICH) and Intellectual Property (IP) Regulation

Carla Zuddas and Andrea Cocco

Abstract The paper will focus on the policies aimed at recognizing and protecting the ICH and TCE's endorsed by some international organizations, such as in particular UNESCO and WIPO. Hence, criticalities emerging from the relations between the international organizations and the central authorities of the States will be analysed. The central States are the signatories of the international conventions. In addition, both the State or the regional authorities can be identified by the same conventions as partners to the international organizations promoting the cited policies. However, when the holder communities of TCEs are in conflict with the State or regional authorities in whose territory the communities are located, there is a risk to compromise or limit the effectiveness of these policies, with damage to "moral" and economic interests of the community. Likewise, some critical matters related to policies based on the use of IPRs and *sui generis* protection rights, will be discussed, with specific regard to the difficulties in the identification of an owner as well as a work of authorship in a traditional context.

1 Introduction

Cultural Expressions related to traditions of a specific place or a specific population have been since long a subject of special interest from a legal perspective, both on a national/local and international level.

Legal language has defined such expressions in several ways depending on the typology of the expression analysed on a case-by-case basis or on the aim pursued

C. Zuddas (✉)
University of Cagliari, Cagliari, Italy
e-mail: carla.zuddas@unica.it

A. Cocco
University of Cagliari—Studio Legale Cocco, Cagliari, Italy
e-mail: avv.andreacocco@gmail.com

O. Niglio and E. Y. J. Lee (eds.), *Transcultural Diplomacy and International Law in Heritage Conservation*, https://doi.org/10.1007/978-981-16-0309-9_14

by law. According to the circumstances we talk about Traditional Cultural Expressions, Traditional Knowledge or Tangible and Intangible Cultural Heritage, etc. This paper focuses on the analysis of intangible expressions, namely those expressions not represented by artefacts, buildings or any other material shape.

Moreover, the terminology Traditional Cultural Expressions (TCEs) has been adopted, since on the one hand it appears to be the most comprehensive and on the other hand the most scientifically appropriate—for reasons that will be unfolded later.

It should be noted that, in some cases, such Expressions may include the knowledge at the basis of their creation, development and communication; since an intangible knowledge lies inherently at the foundation of the process of creation of tangible Expressions (Loffredo, 2003).

Our analysis will focus on the definition of such cultural expressions, taking into consideration the dynamics of their creation, re-elaboration, development, teaching and "communication to the public", starting with an anthropological reconstruction.

In the same perspective we will try to comprehend whether and to which extent it is possible to identify a subject or a community to which these expressions can be ascribed and that could lay claim to the ownership of such expressions as well as to any legal right concerning their use, management, tutelage and enhancement.

Moreover, it will be highlighted that the dynamics inherent to such expressions may be on occasion overlooked on a legal extent—one of the reasons probably being the fragmentation of such expressions on account of the specific objective pursued by the single law—which happens especially when such expressions are analysed and outlined through criteria and categories alien to them.

Such critical issues arise primarily in the process of identification of the object of protection.

As we will see throughout the debate, beyond the enunciated principles included in some legal norms analysed here, both the patrimonial policy and the tools of protection of cultural expressions tend to identify the object of regulation in single forms of individual expression, which are considered as works of intellect or more generally as a manifestation of the creative flair and of the collective knowledge belonging to a specific community.

Such an approach from a legal perspective, although not always to the same extent, is clearly related to the necessity to identify a specific object of protection. On the other hand, from an anthropological perspective it has been underlined that separating the forms of expression from the context in which they have been conceived (the context in anthropology being an essential factor of the process of creation, development and fruition of traditional expressions) appears to be from a scientifical point of view an inconsistent operation with potential risks concerning the protection, safeguard and enhancement of such expressions.

Other significant critical issues arise when taking into consideration the subjects: on a legal level we talk about "holders" or "holder communities" of traditional cultural expressions, although the identification of such subjects is less than undemanding.

From an anthropological point of view, it has been noted that there is no such thing as an autonomous and totally isolated community, even supposing the slightest outside contact; furthermore, when considering the phenomena of globalization and delocalization, which have been always present throughout history but are becoming more and more impactful, it is no longer possible to relate a single community to a specific geographical territory.

Nonetheless, conceded that a community is identified with sufficient accuracy, further issues arise when attempting to delineate an institutional body eligible to represent the interests of such community.

In fact, apart from the complexity of identifying a single community in relation to a specific territory, in many cases the current territory of national, ethnic and religious communities does not coincide with the territory subject to the rule of a single national or local authority, since those communities can have an origin prior to the political confinement of the territory in which they are currently located.

Moreover, such communities are frequently involved in conflict situations, more or less severe, with national and local authorities.

That been said, by assigning to such authorities the power of representation of the instances and interests of those communities as well as the right to rule and manage the tools of protection, safeguard and enhancement of their cultural expressions could result in contrast with the aim to promote and protect the interest of those communities as well as and moreover undermine severely such communities on a human rights perspective.

The aim of this paper however, is not to critically evaluate all the initiatives regarding TCEs enacted on a local, national and international level, but rather to examine the critical issues not only from a legal point of view, but also in the light of the dynamics of creation, fruition typical of such expressions, in order to comprehend whether and to which extent the tools so far prepared are appropriate for the pursuit of the ideal purposes at the heart of their foundation as well as to underline how neglecting such dynamics could hinder the pursuit of those same purposes.

2 Definition of the Field of Investigation

As already mentioned in the introduction, our analysis will start with a definition of TCEs and of their own dynamics concerning the creation and transmission as well as the definition of "holder community" and the identification of critical issues arising during such process of identification.

2.1 TCEs and Dynamics of Creation and Transmission

When talking about TCEs we normally refer to expressions related to the oral tradition. Generally speaking, the concept of oral tradition implies a form of transmission from the mouth of a sender to the ear of a receiver without the mediation of writing. However, from a practical perspective this mechanism is far more complex.

First of all, it must be made clear that the oral tradition is not necessarily in contrast with writing; they do not represent two parallel and alternative experiences and can coexist within the same social group on various levels.

It has been observed that in some cultures writing is mainly used on a linguistic level but, for instance, the musical practice is realized orally just like some cultures make use of music notation without knowing other forms of writing.

In this respect there is plenty of different situations related to numerous variables, as for instance the complexity of the social organization and the consequently different level of specialization concerning music and any other aspect of life (Molino, 2005).

Moreover, the advent of writing did not imply the disappearance of oral tradition, which continued to exist on various levels (Boynton, 2003).

The same is true for what concerns the western experience, where music (along with other forms of expression) was essentially transmitted orally before the advent of writing and oral tradition was never completely abandoned.

Likewise, the social hierarchy and the subsequent division in social classes influenced the fate of oral tradition and writing (Treitler, 1984; Molino, 2005; Shehan Campbell, 1989).

Beyond the relationship between oral tradition and writing, the concept of oral tradition itself shows extremely varied features. Ethnomusicology and anthropology have since long made clear that with regard to orality a fundamental role is played by the so-called "aurality": the transmission and learning is realized not only through the oral communication but especially by means of observation, listening, assimilation, memorization and imitation.

Such dynamics appear to be common to all cultures. They are surely traceable in less evolved cultures, where the above defined mechanism operates mostly unconsciously between the members of a social group; however, the same mechanism can be detected with similar features among more evolved cultures sometimes characterized by a very high degree of professionalization of artistic practice (Molino, 2005). The transmission from teacher to learner is realized in various ways but mainly through the mechanism of listening, imitation and those abovementioned related to "aurality" (Kwok-Wai Ng, 2011).

Alongside "aurality" in the proper sense it has been identified another type of aurality: the so-called "technical aurality" or "phonographic aurality" (Molino, 2005; Toynbee, 2006): since the introduction of technology and the diffusion of recorded performances in the musical tradition, the act of listening to such recordings has become common (and sometimes it has totally replaced) alongside the act of listening and imitating the teacher.

As it will be further explained, the difference is not merely practical, since this aspect has strongly influenced the dynamics of transmission.

Beside such dynamics of transmission and learning there is an important physical component related to the gestural memory of the performance.

(Rice, 1995; Lehmann, Sloboda, Woody, 2007).

Such aspect is clearly reflected by neuroscience research, since it is related to the identification of the so-called "mirror neurons", i.e. nerve cells which are able to create a "motor copy of an observed behaviour" which allows its reproduction as though the experience of such behaviour was not only visual and auditory, but rather physical (Rizzolatti and Fabbri-Destro 2010).

Memory plays a fundamental role in oral tradition not only during the learning phase, but also and especially during the fruition process.

The absence of a written text implies that the oral work is identified with its actual performance, by which the work becomes available to the public.

It goes without saying, that every performance of an orally transmitted work is inherently different; since variability appears to be an inherent factor of oral tradition, oral works are characterized by some elements with a certain degree of invariability whereas some others are affected by a constant variation and re-elaboration (Molino, 2005; Juhász, 2015; Treitler, 1984; Bronson, 1951).

Such variability can on the one hand be attributer to the performer's fallacious memory, on the other hand is deeply related to the role played by the context during its execution (Petrov, 1989).

In fact, the performer draws on a sort of "collective memory", consisting of linguistic, musical models from the tradition (and thus the result of previous re-elaborations) which are assembled following criteria belonging to that same tradition. Thus memory plays an active and creative role (Petrov, 1989) and each performance becomes a "collective re-creation" of oral works, whose collective aspect is identifiable in the use of traditional materials, which had already been re-elaborated by other performers sharing the same legacy (Molino, 2005; Boynton, 2003).

That being said, oral works appear to be not the permanent result of an original creation, but rather a model open to variation and re-elaboration, thus expressing a constant vitality (Molino, 2005; Toynbee, 2006; Goehr, 1994). As a result, oral works can be conceived solely when actually performed and their essence is embodied by their constant variation, which cannot be defined merely through the concept of "different versions" (Molino, 2005; Treitler, 1984).

2.2 TCEs "Holder Communities"

When talking about cultural tradition, legal language refers frequently to communities, from which such tradition stems; denominations like "bearers" or "holders" are common; their aim is to identify an entitled subject to represent such specific traditional expressions to be involved when discussing and applying protection tools.

That being said, it must be investigated whether it is actually possible to identify a community representing traditional cultural expressions (the analysis will be conducted drawing on the anthropological point of view in comparison with the legal definitions adopted at the international level).

Although herein the issue cannot be analysed in depth, it must be underlined that the concept of social groups (and their cultural expressions) as isolated and geographically localizable has been called into question, considering the migratory phenomena since the first half of the twentieth century.

The massive movement of individuals towards other countries has resulted in the displacement, sometimes to a dramatic extent, of such social groups.

Although some individuals were able to keep in contact with their national/original community, others lost gradually contact throughout the generations.

Furthermore, the introduction of new technologies has allowed the constant and immediate contact between individuals and cultures that previously had few opportunities to interact.

New "displaced" communities have been formed, while others have reorganized themselves, thanks to the use of new media, to such an extent that the most active centres related to some national cultures are currently located outside their original country (Fabietti–Malighetti–Matera, 2002).

Thus, defining a community on the basis of subjective and geographical criteria appears to be scientifically inaccurate, given that the requirements for being recognized as member of a community vary from society to society.

The concept of community (just like that of culture) appears to be vague and variable depending on the factor of "communality" taken into account.

In other terms, the same subject could belong to different communities depending on the adopted perspective; his/her religious point of view, ethnical origin or considering him/her as member of a specific cultural expression. (Rapport, 2010; Augé and Colleyn, 2006).

That is, it should be made clear that we are dealing not with "genetic" but rather with communities "of choice"—in which the members (1) legitimate each other on the basis of elements in common and (2) create their own "cultures" and "tradition".

In the latter case, it becomes even more evident how difficult it is to identify a "target community".

There is no such thing as a totally isolated social group, since each community is involved to a greater or lesser extent in what the anthropology doctrine defines as "cultural hybridization", a phenomenon describing the constant cultural exchange inside and outside social groups and that for obvious reasons makes the paradigm "community-territory-culture" even more complex (Augé and Colleyn, 2006).

With regard to legal language it is possible to detect some sort of opening towards a broader notion of "community". The UNESCO Convention for the Safeguarding of the Intangible Cultural Heritage (2003), although not offering such definition, does not exclude it entirely.

The *Framework Convention on the Value of Cultural Heritage for Society* (Faro Convention, signed in 2005 within the Council of Europe) introduces the concept of "heritage community" to refer to a group of «people who value specific aspects of cultural heritage which they wish, within the framework of public action, to sustain and transmit to future » . In the *Draft Provisions/Articles for the Protection of Traditional Cultural Expressions*, drafted by the WIPO Intergovernmental Committee on Intellectual Property and Genetic Resources, Traditional Knowledge and Folklore, the expression "cultural communities" is adopted—alongside that of "local communities"—in the former versions of the document. Such expression, although not being accurately developed, could have been intended as a sign of opening towards a definition of "community" disengaged from a geographical criterion. It has been however removed starting from the XXVII Committee Session (all the abovementioned documents will be further analysed).

De facto it must be underlined that all the abovementioned tools, even those who appear to offer a more comprehensive definition, are instruments of international law developed by national governments entitled to implement in their national law the regulations and principles expressed by such instruments.

Thus, it appears evident that the provisions deriving from an application on an international level can be applied solely in the territory belonging to the entitled country, not being able to take into consideration subjects geographically located in other countries, in spite of them being members of the same community.

Similarly, national governments own the power (1) to entitle subjects or communities as representatives of specific TCEs and (2) to consult such communities when drafting legal protection tools or the promotion of such expressions, of which such communities have been entitled as "holders".

Another element which seems to be undervalued in most of the international instruments (further analysed) is the fact that many specific TCEs—which are meant to be practiced as part of sacred rituals or to be kept secret outside their traditional reference framework—consist of a knowledge owned solely by members of a specific community, possessing a special status or role and thus belonging to an elite group (Molino, 2005), which in other words embodies a qualified subcommunity.

In the abovementioned *WIPO Draft Provisions* special attention is paid to such cases, which call for a differentiated discipline.

However, even by applying a more scientifically accurate approach when defining subjects and communities and when assessing their position towards TCEs, it appears to be inherently complex to override the limited concept of "territoriality", which is deeply related to the legal tools under examination in this paper (at least during their implementation).

As further explained, such critical issues arise when the "holder communities" of specific TCs are involved in conflict situations with national authorities as well as with local authorities subject to national power.

3 Traditional Cultural Expressions and Intangible Cultural Heritage in International and National Legal Instruments

The issue concerning the protection of TCEs is part of the wider framework regarding the protection of ICH both on a national and international level. A first (implicit) reference to TCEs is found in the *Berne Convention for the Protection of Literary and Artistic Works*, signed in Bern in 1886, in which the category of "works where the identity of the author is unknown" was introduced in order to include also the works of folklore, which was intentionally not mentioned explicitly due to the difficulty encountered by the member States in developing a shared definition of "folklore" (Galtieri, 1973; Nordemann et al., 1990; Ricketson and Ginsburg, 2006).

We highlight in this respect some significant steps: first of all, the Intergovernmental Copyright Conference (Geneva, 1952), during which the Yugoslavian delegation suggested the introduction of the "oeuvres de l'art national" among the protected works.

During a Study Meeting on copyright, held in Brazzaville in 1963, was adopted a recommendation inviting the member countries to provide themselves with the proper instruments towards the African folklore, in order to safeguard it from improper use.

The aim was to affirm the value of local CTs within a perspective related to the idea of creation and reclamation of a national identity.

One of the first official proposals aimed to the protection of ICH was promoted by Bolivia in 1973, which proposed an additional protocol concerning the protection of folklore to the Universal Convention on Copyright (from now on UCC).

In 1982 within the Conference of Mexico an initial definition of the concept of intangible heritage was conceived by the UNESCO member countries, which described ICH as the expression of the totality of spiritual works of humanity.

Since then Unesco and WIPO have integrated their efforts, each of them in relation with their specific mandate, focusing on the reflection upon the modalities of protection of ICH.

Another significant step was the Model Provisions for National Laws on the Protection of Expressions of Folklore Against Illicit Exploitation and Other Prejudicial Actions, emanated in 1982 within a joint project by WIPO and UNESCO, which was due to become a model for all countries interested in introducing in their national law specific regulation aiming to protect expressions of folklore (Gibson, 2004; Hughes, 2012). Interestingly enough by using the expression "folklore works" it was adopted theretofore a nomenclature coming from copyright terminology.

It was only with the Model Provisions that the phrase «expressions of folklore» began to be introduced. Such choice was related to the desire to underline the difference between the protection proposals included in Model Provisions—which were defined «sui generis»—and the concept of copyright, although not ruling out the possibility that the "expressions of folklore" could be embodied by "works".

However, the term folklore in the Model Provisions was not defined, in order to avoid potential conflicts with other definition possibly included in legislative acts of the countries (De Sanctis, 1967). Either way the reference is made both to expressions originated within a specific community and to those originated outside such community and subsequently developed, adopted and maintained over generations. It is considered irrelevant whether such expressions have been conceived collectively or individually.

The Model Provisions are inspired by the principle that when some uses of the expressions of folklore—such as their publication, reproduction, distribution and public performances—are made outside their traditional context, must be allowed (for a fee) by an authority entitled by the country in which the "bearer community" of such expressions resides. No authorization is compulsory when such uses are made within the traditional and customary context (regardless of their utilization for profit or non-profit), whereas it becomes mandatory when a member of the performs one of the abovementioned uses outside the customary and traditional context.

Particularly significant appears to be Chapter 13, which foresees that the protection introduced in the national legal act potentially inspired by the Model Provisions must not be interpreted as an obstacle for the common use and development of the expressions of folklore.

Another legal act is the Draft Treaty for the Protection of Expressions of Folklore against Illicit Exploitation and Other Prejudicial Actions (1984), which is the result of the collaboration between WIPO and UNESCO. It consists of a proposal for an international treaty which should have integrated the new laws inspired by the Model Provisions, in order to harmonize on an international level the legal protection concerning the expressions of folklore.

However, the Draft Treaty has not been very successful because of the nonuniform approaches on an international level. Such an instrument would have had a significant impact on national law for what concerns intellectual property. Thus, the path taken with the Draft Treaty has been abandoned shortly after.

In 1999 WIPO and UNESCO engaged in consultations (to which countries, supranational organs and some NGOs took part) on a local basis (Regional Consultations on the Protection of Expressions of Folklore); it emerged the necessity to create an autonomous organism connecting States with regard to the protection of the expressions of folklore. Such proposal was acknowledged by WIPO, which during the XXVI General Assembly session held in Geneve in 2000, ordered the establishment of the Intergovernmental Committee on Intellectual Property and Genetic Resources, Traditional Knowledge and Folklore (hereinafter "IGC").

Since 2004, the IGC has moreover undertaken the elaboration of a new model for an international tool of protection, divided according to subject areas (Traditional Cultural Expressions, Traditional Knowledge, Genetic Resources), which is adjourned on each new ICG session and which partially continues what was left unfinished by abandoning the Draft Treaty.

3.1 The 2003 UNESCO Convention and the Policies of Recognition of the Intangible Cultural Heritage

One of the most active organizations with regard to the safeguard of TCEs is the UNESCO, which after abandoning the joint project with WIPO on the protection of the expressions of folklore has followed another path.

The organization emanated in 1989 the Recommendation on the Safeguarding of Traditional Culture and Folklore, by which it suggested to the contracting States the adoption of a series of legislative measures aimed to the «safeguard of traditional and popular culture». Such Recommendation still includes references to some aspects concerning intellectual property related to the use of TCEs. It however clarifies that the initiatives «concern only an aspect of the protection of cultural and popular tradition» and that «a urgent adoption of distinguished measures in different fields is required in order to safeguard the cultural and popular tradition».

Such Recommendation was short-lived, especially because of «the excessive focus on the products and documentation at the expense of the producers and the process of production of intangible heritage» (Zagato, 2008). The doctrine also signalled that such instrument paid scarce attention to the bearers of the cultural expressions, not taking into account that the use of such expressions by a third party has to be allowed by the holder communities (Blake, 2001).

Such path was abandoned shortly after. However, in 1992 the UNESCO launched a new project under the name Intangible Heritage Program. It consists of a programme divided into thematic projects, the most important being listed in (1) the project Living Human Treasures, dedicated to subjects embodying specific traditional customs and knowledge, and (2) the project named Proclamation of Masterpieces of the Oral and Intangible Heritage of Humanity, dedicated to intangible cultural expressions, which led to the proclamation of the first nineteen in 2001 (Zagato, 2008).

The project was later implemented, supplied with the support of a bureaucratic framework and the adoption of the Convention for the Safeguarding of the Intangible Cultural Heritage held in Paris on 17 October 2003 during the 32nd UNESCO General Conference.

When the Convention entered into force in 2005, after being ratified by all the contracting States, the proclamations ceased and the expression «masterpieces» was abandoned, having arisen many perplexities especially from an anthropological doctrine perspective (Macchiarella, 2011).

The new instrument excluded the list of the so-called "Humanity masterpieces"—adopting a less emphatic formula—and prescribed the establishment of two representative lists: the Representative List of the Intangible Cultural Heritage of Humanity and the List of Intangible Cultural Heritage of Humanity which requires urgent safeguarding.

At the same time the Intergovernmental Committee for the Safeguarding of the Intangible Cultural Heritage was established, composed of the contracting States of the Convention, whose assignment consisted in establishing the two lists and elaborating the criteria for their adjournment and publication.

As can be noted the denomination of the Convention do not refer to folklore and its expressions but rather to a broader subject: the «intangible cultural heritage» (Stamatoudi, 2004), including «practices, representations, expressions, knowledge, skills—as well as the instruments, objects, artefacts and cultural spaces associated therewith—that communities, groups and, in some cases, individuals recognize as part of their cultural heritage». Moreover, pursuant to art. 2 «This intangible cultural heritage, transmitted from generation to generation, is constantly recreated by communities and groups in response to their environment, their interaction with nature and their history, and provides them with a sense of identity and continuity, thus promoting respect for cultural diversity and human creativity».

The same provision precises that, although concerning ICH in its broader sense, for the purposes of the Convention such heritage will be taken into account «consideration will be given solely to such intangible cultural heritage as is compatible with existing international human rights instruments, as well as with the requirements of mutual respect among communities, groups and individuals and of sustainable development».

Following a proposal from the contracting States, the expression of «intangible cultural heritage» practised within the corresponding territory can be a candidate for registration in one of the two lists (Bortolotto, 2012). Again on a proposal from the contracting States, upon approval by the UNESCO General Assembly, the Committee can select and promote periodically projects which are coherent with the purposes of the Convention as well as concede international support for the better pursuit of such purposes.

The Convention starts with the consideration of «the importance of the intangible cultural heritage as a mainspring of cultural diversity and a guarantee of sustainable development», as well as by underlining that «the processes of globalization and social transformation, alongside the conditions they create for renewed dialogue among communities, also give rise, as does the phenomenon of intolerance, to grave threats of deterioration, disappearance and destruction of the intangible cultural heritage, in particular owing to a lack of resources for safeguarding such heritage» . Based on such premises the Convention highlights the necessity of an instrument aimed at ensuring the safeguard of the so-called intangible cultural heritage. The art. 2 clarifies what should be intended with the term "safeguard", that is all «measures aimed at ensuring the viability of the intangible cultural heritage, including the identification, documentation, research, preservation, protection, promotion, enhancement, transmission, particularly through formal and non-formal education, as well as the revitalization of the various aspects of such heritage».

However, it must be noted how "doing an inventory" of such heritage is a less than undemanding process (Slattery, 2006). In particular, it has been observed how the same concept in terms of heritage of intangible cultural expressions appears to be scientifically inconsistent. Such concept lies at the foundation of a notion of culture since long exceeded from an anthropological perspective (Ciminelli, 2008; Dei, 2013), which revolves around a vision of culture as "reified", or in other terms composed of elements which can be considered singularly (Kurin, 2004). Such vision does not take into account the dynamics proper to cultural processes and the complexity underlying the related phenomena, with particular regard to their interdependence.

The lists appear to be a contradictory instrument with regard to the purposes of the Convention also from another perspective.

The inclusion of an element of intangible cultural heritage in such lists implies that such element must be identified and selected, in other words evaluated in order to establish what elements to recognize and thus creating a hierarchy of cultural expressions, although the Conventions states that each element must be given equal dignity and value.

Furthermore, although according to the Convention the bearer communities have to be involved, such involvement is merely marginal and at the discretion of the contracting States (Bortolotto, 2011). As a matter of fact the whole decisional is conducted by the States during the phase of presentation of candidates and later by the State delegates during the evaluation phase of such candidates.

In addition the involvement of scholars and experts appears to be more formal than substantial thus lessening the scientific rigour in the whole decisional process (Macchiarella, 2011).

The decisions themselves appear somehow to be inspired by reasons not related to the aim of promotion of cultural expressions, not to mention the fact that they can be perceived as being a top-down initiative (Ciminelli, 2008).

It should not be overlooked that some specific cultural expressions are diffused in a geographical area that does not coincide with a single national territory.

Although not excluding the possibility that many States in conjunction present a candidate, the Convention does not regulate such hypothesis: as happened with the inscription of the "Oral Heritage Gelede", attributable to the Yoruba-Nago community, currently distributed between Benin, Nigeria and Togo (http://www.unesco.org/culture/ich/en/RL/00002).

In such circumstances, which can be concretely detected within the representative lists, the attribution of a cultural expression to a single State would result in an act of dispossession of such TCE from its reference community, which is obviously in contrast with the general purposes regarding the protection of human rights, by which the Convention claims to be inspired. An example is represented by the case of registration in the first representative list of the language, dance and music of the Garifuna communities in 2008.

The registration was requested, and consequently attributed, to Honduras, Guatemala, Nicaragua and Belize, within whose territories, as reported in the explanatory guide, the Garifuna communities mainly live at the present time, although not exclusively (http://www.unesco.org/culture/ich/en/RL/00001).

Such contradiction becomes even more evident when considering that often the holder communities of specific TCEs face a conflict situation with the central government, the same government which is entitled to safeguard their heritage (Ciminelli, 2008) as for instance the Tibetan work which in 2009 was included in the first representative list assigned to China (Macchiarella, 2011).

Thus, considering that—apart from the proclamation per se—there is no other obligation with regard to promotion and protection neither for UNESCO nor for the States or local government involved, such proclamation does not grant any significant benefit to the bearer subjects of cultural expressions, except for a suggestive call for the States and local communities, which could claim one or more forms of UNESCO recognition within their territory (being the UNESCO brand seen as an «excellent "brand"»).

Some believe that the most of criticism regarding the Convention stems from a misperception of such 2003 UNESCO instrument, since it raises expectations which cannot be met considering the inherent nature of such instrument (Blake, 2014).

In this respect the real impact of the Convention must be seen not in its proclamation, but rather in generating ferment among the States and local communities, which have been stimulated to make an inventory of the cultural heritage concerning their territory with the aim to promote and revitalize it.

Even if, on the one hand, this is true, further considerations must be done.

First of all must be clarified that the introduction in one or more representative lists on a local level is one of the required evaluation criteria applied by the UNESCO with regard to the candidates: thus, such ICH inventories could merely derive from such aspect related to an atmosphere of competition among the States aiming to obtain as many proclamations as possible. Such second purpose should not be condemned, being seemingly a sort of virtuous competition.

What arises most of the criticism is the system of inventory: the inherent ineligibility of such system in embracing and representing the variety and complexity of cultural phenomena and in their mutual interaction appears to be a basic flaw: that being said it seems evident that an adequate safeguarding would not be possible without a righteous acknowledgement of the phenomenon at issue. In this regard, it has been noted that, in some cases of proclamation of traditional cultural expressions, the description of the characteristics of the proclaimed expression, as accomplished by UNESCO itself and communicated on its web page, is affected by approximations and inaccuracies such as to provide an erroneous representation of the phenomenon (Ciminelli, 2008; Macchiarella, 2011).

3.2 *Other Conventions and Projects Managed by UNESCO*

The UNESCO Convention on the Protection and Promotion of the Diversity of Cultural Expressions signed in Paris in 2005 is another international instrument aimed at TCEs. It is characterized by a broader scope compared to the Convention for the Safeguarding of the Intangible Cultural Heritage, since it makes reference to cultural expressions not individually but rather in their «manifold ways in which the cultures of groups and societies find expression».

In addition, although using a not entirely clear phrase, the Convention points out that «Cultural diversity is made manifest not only through the varied ways in which the cultural heritage of humanity is expressed, augmented and transmitted through the variety of cultural expressions, but also through diverse modes of artistic creation, production, dissemination, distribution and enjoyment, whatever the means and technologies used» So, it can be assumed that—as opposed to the 2003 Convention—it refers generally speaking to any cultural expression that can be valued with regard to its cultural "diversity" or, as stated in doctrine, that any type of expression corresponds to a cultural identity (Pineschi, 2008).

Such Convention establishes also the inclusion in its subject of TCEs.

Among the main features of such Convention on cultural diversity there are also the reflection upon the (double nature, economic and cultural) of cultural expressions and the recognition of the fundamental role played by the States (Zuddas, 2015) in implementing policies aimed to promote and to protect cultural diversity.

Likewise, the Convention on the Value of Cultural Heritage for Society signed in Faro (Portugal) within the European Council in 2005 (Faro Convention), revolves around cultural heritage, which entered into force in 2011.

4 The Faro Convention on the Value of Cultural Heritage for Society

The Faro Convention has had less impact compared to the UNESCO Convention on intangible heritage, due to the fact that it was ratified by a lesser number of member States of the European Council.

However, it is the first legal act to have directly correlated on an international level cultural heritage and human rights, by stating that «rights relating to cultural heritage are inherent in the right to participate in cultural life, as defined in the Universal Declaration of Human Rights» (Zagato, 2008).

Unlike the 2003 UNESCO Convention, which referred solely to intangible cultural heritage—being the tangible expressions analysed in a previous and separate act (Convention Concerning the Protection of the World Cultural and Natural Heritage)—the Faro Convention refers to cultural heritage in general terms, thus including both its tangible and intangible elements.

The art. 2 defines cultural heritage as «a group of resources inherited from the past which people identify, independently of ownership, as a reflection and expression of their constantly evolving values, beliefs, knowledge and traditions. It includes all aspects of the environment resulting from the interaction between people and places through time», and elaborates the concept of «heritage community to indicate «people who value specific aspects of cultural heritage which they wish, within the framework of public action, to sustain and transmit to future».

The contracting States affirm «the role of cultural heritage in the construction of a peaceful and democratic society, and in the processes of sustainable development and the promotion of cultural diversity» and recognize the existence of an individual and collective responsibility towards such cultural heritage in parallel with the right of each individual to its fruition (Vìcha, 2014).

In order to achieve such objectives and to realize such principles, the Convention obligates the contracting States to apply a series of measures aimed at promoting the respect for cultural heritage and its sustainable management, also by means of techniques and professionalities «based on tradition». In addition, such measures must take into account the potential of cultural heritage as one of the factors of a sustainable economic development; in this respect the States must enhance awareness with regard to such potential and simultaneously «ensure that these policies respect the integrity of the cultural heritage without compromising its inherent values» .

Finally, the Faro Convention requests that the contracting States develop innovative systems aimed at fostering the cooperation between public authorities and other stakeholders involved in the management and fruition of cultural heritage as well as fostering voluntary initiatives directed to an integration of the actions enacted by public authorities and the access to knowledge of cultural heritage, by encouraging its identification, study, research and protection, also by means of the participation of each individual to such process and promoting initiatives aimed at improving the access to culture, especially with regard to youngsters and disadvantaged people.

4.1 WIPO Projects and Instruments for the Protection of Traditional Cultural Expressions in the Field of Intellectual Property Rights (IPRs)

WIPO is the UN organization whose function is to promote the improvement of policies aimed at protecting intellectual property rights by means of an activity of cooperation and technical-legal support directed to the member States, it also performs the Berna Union administrative-executive duties, originally exercised by the Bureau Internationaux Reunis pour la Protection de la Propriété Intellectuelle (BIRPI).

Towards the end of the 1960s started an interesting collaboration between WIPO and UNESCO, with the aim to produce a joint study upon the cultural aspects concerning the safeguarding of folklore and the application of copyright and in general of intellectual property upon it (Ficsor, 1998; Janke, 1997).

From this interaction, as we have already underlined, originated: (i) the Model Provisions for National Laws on the Protection of the Expressions of Folklore against Illicit Exploitation and Other Prejudicial Actions, adopted by Unesco and Wipo in 1982 (ii) the Draft Treaty for the Protection of Expressions of Folklore against Illicit Exploitation and Other Prejudicial Actions in 1984; (iii) the Unesco Recommendation in 1989.

In 2001 the Wipo member States opened the work of the Intergovernmental Committee on Intellectual Property and Genetic Resources, Traditional Knowledge and Folklore (IGC).

In March 2004 the member States commissioned to IGC the elaboration of a new regulatory model, at first under the name of Draft Provisions and later Draft Articles, which contained the indication of the policy objectives and the main principles concerning traditional knowledge, folklore expressions and genetic resources. The Draft Articles are constantly adjourned according to the guidelines emerging on case-by-case within the Commission.

In July 2013 the IGC Commission presented a (second) revision of the Draft Articles with a different approach in comparison to the 2006 consolidated edition.

In such second version the base legal framework was completely called into question to such an extent that the majority of its articles show two separate options; one with a wider while the other a narrower range of application.

Such news approach, which is significantly more complex and bearer of hermeneutical ambiguities, is supposedly the result of the attempt to reconcile the different positions of the stakeholders.

Another issue regards the reading of the latter revision since includes lemmata characterized by a lexical ambiguity concerning their meaning and their translation and interpretation in the different languages spoken by subjects concerned.

The latter version of the Draft Articles regarding the protection of TCEs is included in the document WIPO/GRTKF/IC/40/5 22 March 2019 and published during the 17th–21st June 2019 session[1]

---

[1]https://www.wipo.int/edocs/mdocs/tk/en/wipo_grtkf_ic_40/wipo_grtkf_ic_40_5.pdf.

With regard to the object of protection it suffices to note that—although some limited differences in the definition—the notion of «folklore» (term which appears in the denomination made by the Committee and in the previous acts elaborated by WIPO) and that of «traditional cultural expressions», adopted in the IGC documents, are basically coincident.

The version of such text so far elaborated (Draft Articles) appear to be rather uneven, considering the different—and often irreconcilable—positions expressed by the member States. Each disposition, including those containing the definition of the object of protection and those expressing the main principles at the foundation of the future instrument of protection, offers many options, towards which so far has not been reached an agreement.

Generally speaking, the Draft Articles, similarly to the Model Provisions, state the principle of a prior approval by an authority entitled to represent the holder communities of the expression concerned and establish specific dispensation when such expressions are used not for profit or involve in various ways members of the holder community.

The Draft Articles show in this respect more awareness in comparison with the Model Provisions, and establish a separated discipline for those expressions related to sacred rituals, or that are meant to be kept secret outside their traditional reference context. Furthermore, such expressions appear not to be subject to the dispensations and restrictions abovementioned; in fact, even their utilization per se would result detrimental for their holder communities, regardless of the fact that the use could receive a financial benefit.

For what concerns the duration of protection, it can be limited, unlimited or defined by the States after prior consultation of the communities concerned.

Both the Model Provisions—which the WIPO has started to re-propose as part of a process aimed at the adoption of an international instrument—and the Draft Articles, establish forms of consultation with the holder communities. Nonetheless, both such instruments do not provide clear elements aimed at the identification of such communities; a task which will presumably be assigned to the States during the process of emanation of a national law on this subject and during the implementation of the prospective international instrument.

In general, considering the nature of such instrument and of the WIPO (as a supranational organization), each determining decision appears to be assigned to the States both when involved in negotiations of the conditions of protection in a future legal protection instrument (both on a national and international level) and when approving and implementing such legal instrument.

Without entering into further detail, it must be noted that such a solution—which as already underlined is in part related to the nature of the decisional process typical of international organizations like WIPO—appears to be problematic with regard to all the cultural expressions originated in communities or social minority groups or those facing a conflict with central authority; in such a situation, it would be legitimate to question whether any statal initiative on this subject would be inspired by the actual purpose to protect adequately the expressions concerned.

A reference to cultural traditions and their safeguarding through intellectual property instruments is in the United Nations Declaration on the Rights of Indigenous Peoples, approved by the UNO General Assembly in 2007. Such Declaration enshrines the right of indigenous people «to practise and revitalize their cultural traditions and customs», as well as «manifest, practise, develop and teach their spiritual and religious traditions, customs and ceremonies» and «maintain, protect and have access in privacy to their religious and cultural sites».

In compliance with art. 31, «Indigenous peoples have the right to maintain, control, protect and develop their cultural heritage, traditional knowledge and traditional cultural expressions, as well as the manifestations of their sciences, technologies and cultures, including […] oral traditions, literatures, […] visual and performing arts». The same article establishes that «in conjunction with indigenous peoples, States shall take effective measures to recognize and protect the exercise of these rights».

Several States have introduced in their national law dispositions relating to TCEs, sometimes within the regulation regarding copyright, sometimes following the example given by the Model Provisions, and finally adopting more or less innovative solutions for what concerns intellectual property rights.

It is possible to consult such dispositions on a database constantly adjourned by WIPO.

However, it must be taken into consideration that in the majority of the States the legislative competence on the subject of intellectual property—for reasons of legislation uniformity—is assigned to the central State whereas local authorities have limited autonomy.

Such aspect emphasizes the criticalities identified several times over the course of this paper, which are linked to the concentration of the regulatory power regarding in the hands of central authorities with regard to TCEs originating in minority groups or communities which often reside in regions that do not coincide with the geographical area of a single nation or that face a situation of conflict with such nations.

The adoption within the States of ad hoc-norms aimed at safeguarding TCEs—by making reference to intellectual property rights—practised within their territory (not overlooking all the criticalities identified with regard to a mere geographical profile), could partially mitigate the abovementioned critical issues.

If on the one hand the establishment of specific regulatory instruments reveals an increased awareness from the States concerned towards the demands raised by the cultural expressions and their holder communities; on the other hand it must be noted that such solutions could reveal themselves as inappropriate with respect to the stated purposes: first of all, although having the State the effective will to protect and promote such expressions, there is the risk that the regulation applied by the State is seen as a top-down initiative, especially when the holder communities are not involved in the process (Rahmatian, 2009); secondly, when the national authorities show less favourable intentions, the regulation of expressions coming from minority groups facing a conflict with the central State or its local branches could end up being a useful instrument of power and "misappropriation" of the TCEs subject to regulation.

5 Conclusions

In conclusion, it appears that the legal instrument herein analysed, although based on the statement of embraceable principles, show on a greater or lesser extent some difficulties in granting adequate protection to TCEs, especially when they can be referred to minority communities or communities not residing within the geographical area of a single State or facing a conflict with the central authority.

The biggest challenge is embodied by the inevitable necessity that the State itself is entitled to implement within its national regulation the norms of international law, including those concerning such subject.

Such criticalities are inherently related to the instruments herein analysed and they appear to be unavoidable. It is however possible to imagine that they can be somehow bypassed by changing perspective from the protection and safeguarding towards the promotion and enhancement of TCEs, perhaps by implementing the international law instruments (of course in terms of human rights but not exclusively) which allow to conceive such expressions not only as a group of heritage elements or works, but rather as a whole and in relation to their context of origin and fruition and not aiming at their protection and safeguarding but rather to promote their vitality in correlation with the subjects that use them traditionally not just as "objects" (perhaps endangered) but as simple manifestation of a lively culture in constant evolution.

References

Augé, M., & Colleyn, J. P. (2006). *L'Antropologia del Mondo Contemporaneo, Milano* (p. 59). Milano: Eleuthera.

Blake, J. (2001). *Developing a new standard-setting instrument for the safeguarding of intangible cultural heritage elements for consideration.* Paris: UNESCO.

Blake, J. (2014). Seven years of implementing UNESCO's 2003 intangible heritage convention—Honeymoon period or the "seven-year itch"? *International Journal of Cultural Property, 21,* 291ff.

Bortolotto, C. (2011). Le trouble du patrimoine culturel immatériel. *Le patrimoine culturel immatériel: enjeux d'une nouvelle catégorie. Maison des Sciences de l'Homme, collection «Cahiers d'ethnologie de la France»*. Paris.

Bortolotto, C. (2012). Gli inventari del patrimonio culturale intangibile – Quale "partecipazione" per quali "comunità"? In Scovazzi, Ubertazzi, Zagato (Ed.), *Il patrimonio intangibile nelle sue diverse dimensioni* (p. 75ff.). Milano: Giuffrè.

Boynton, S. (2003). Orality, literacy, and the early notation of the office hymns. *Journal of the American Musicological Society, 56*(1), 99ff.

Bronson, B. H. (1951). Melodic stability in oral transmission. *Journal of the International Folk Music Council, 3,* 50ff.

Ciminelli, M. L. (2008). Salvaguardia del patrimonio culturale immateriale e possibili effetti collaterali: etnomimesi ed etnogenesi. In Zagato (Ed.), *Le identità culturali nei recenti strumenti UNESCO. Un approccio nuovo alla costruzione della pace?* (p. 99ff.). Padova: CEDAM.

Dei, F. (2013). Da Gramsci all'UNESCO. Antropologia, cultura popolare e beni intangibili. *Parolechiave* (p. 131ff.).

De Sanctis, V. (1967). *La Conferenza diplomatica di Stoccolma della proprietà intellettuale*. IDA (Il Diritto d'Autore) (p. 303ff.).
Fabietti U., Malighetti R., & Matera V. (2002). *Dal tribale al globale. Introduzione all'antropologia* (p. 106). Milano: Mondadori.
Ficsor, M. (1998). Attempts to provide international protection for folklore by intellectual property rights. *UNESCO-WIPO World Forum on the Protection of Folklore, UNESCO/WIPO*, n. LXII (p. 215). Paris/Geneva.
Galtieri, G. (1973). Folclore e diritto d'autore. *Dir. Aut.* (Il Diritto di autore) (p. 379ff.).
Gibson, J. (2004). Intellectual property systems, traditional knowledge and the legal authority of community. *European Intellectual Property Review* (p. 280ff.).
Goehr, L. (1994). *The imaginary museum of musical works: An essay in the philosophy of music*. Oxford: Oxford University Press. Published to Oxford Scholarship Online: November 2003. https://doi.org/10.1093/0198235410.001.0001.
Hughes, J. (2012). Traditional knowledge, cultural expression, and the Siren's call of property. *San Diego Law Review, 49*, 1215ff.
Janke, T. (1997). UNESCO-WIPO. World forum on the protection of folklore: Lessons for protecting indigenous Australian cultural and intellectual property. *Copyright Reporter, XV*, 104ff.
Juhász, Z. (2015). A search for structural similarities of oral musical traditions in Eurasia and America using the self organizing cloud algorithm. *Journal of New Music Research, 44*(3), 196ff.
Kurin, R. (2004). Safeguarding intangible cultural heritage in the 2003 UNESCO Convention: A critical appraisal. *Musem International, 56*(1–2), 66ff.
Kwok-Wai Ng. (2011). Orality and literacy in the transmission of Japanese Tōgaku: Its past and present. *Ethnomusicology Forum, 20*(1), 33ff.
Lehmann, C., Sloboda, J. A., & Woody, R. H. (2007). *Psychology for musicians: Understanding and acquiring the skills*. Oxford: Oxford University Press. https://doi.org/10.1093/acprof:oso/9780195146103.001.0001.
LOFFREDO, E. (2003). Profili giuridici della tutela delle produzioni tipiche. *Riv. Dir. Ind. (Rivista di Diritto Industriale)*, I (p. 139 ss.).
Macchiarella, I. (2011). Dove il tocco di Re Mida non arriva. A proposito di proclamazioni Unesco e musica. *Ricerca Folklorica, LXIV*, 71ff.
Molino, J. (2005). Che cos'è l'oralità musicale. *Enciclopedia della Musica Einaudi* (pp. 367ff.).
Nordemann, W., Vinck, F., Hertin, P. W., & Meyer, G. (1990). Sub art. 15 BC, No. 6, 158, *International copyright and neighbouring rights law: Commentary with special emphasis on the European Community*. New York: Wiley VCH.
Petrov, K. V. (1989). *Memory and oral tradition*. Memory, Butler (Ed.), New York: Blackwell (p. 77ff.).
Pineschi, L. (2008). Convenzione sulla diversità culturale e diritto internazionale dei diritti umani. In Zagato (Ed.), *Le identità culturali nei recenti strumenti UNESCO. Un approccio nuovo alla costruzione della pace?* (p. 159ff.). Padova: CEDAM.
Rahmatian, A. (2009). Neo-colonial aspects of global intellectual property protection. *The Journal of World Intellectual Property, 12*(1), 40ff.
Rapport, N. (2010). Community. Routledge Encyclopedia of Social and Cultural Anthropology, Barnard–Spencer (Ed.). (p. 142ff.). London: Routledge.
Rice, T. (1995). Understanding and producing the variability of oral tradition: Learning from a Bulgarian Bagpiper. *The Journal of American Folklore, 108* (p. 266ff.).
Ricketson, S., & Ginsburg, J. C. (2006). *International copyright and neighbouring rights* (2nd edn, p. 513). Oxford: Oxford University Press.
Rizzolatti, G., & Fabbri-Destro, M. (2010). Neuroni specchio, *Enciclopedia Treccani*, http://www.treccani.it/enciclopedia/neuroni-specchio_%28XXI-Secolo%29/.
Ruesch, M. (2008). Creating culture: Protection of traditional cultural expressions and folklore and the impact on creation and innovation in the marketplace of ideas. *Syracuse Journal of International Law and Commerce, 35*(2), 369ff.

Shehan Campbell, P. (1989). Orality, literacy and music's creative potential: A comparative approach. *Bulletin of the Council for Research in Music Education, 101*, 30ff.
Slattery, E. K. (2006). Preserving the United States' intangible cultural heritage: An evaluation of the 2003 Unesco Convention for the safeguarding of the intangible cultural heritage as a means to overcome the problems posed by Intellectual Property Law. *DePaul Journal of Art & Entertainment Law, 5*, 201ff.
Stamatoudi, I. (2004). The protection of intangible property by means of the Unesco Convention on the safeguarding of intangible heritage and intellectual property law. *Revue Hellénique de droit International, 57*, 149ff.
Toynbee, J. (2006). Copyright, the work and phonographic orality in music. *Social & Legal Studies, 15*(1), 77ff.
Treitler, L. (1984). Orality and literacy in the music of the middle ages. *Parergon, 2*, 143ff.
Vìcha, O. (2014). The concept of the right to cultural heritage within the Faro Convention. ICLR, 14 (No. 1) (p. 25 ss.).
Von Lewinski, S. (Ed.). (2008). *Indigenous heritage and intellectual property, genetic resources, traditional knowledge and folklore*. Kluwer Law International: The Netherlands.
Zagato, L. (2008). La Convenzione sulla protezione del patrimonio culturale intangibile. In Zagato (Ed.), *Le identità culturali nei recenti strumenti UNESCO. Un approccio nuovo alla costruzione della pace?* (p. 27ff.). Padova: CEDAM.
Zuddas, C. (2015). *Strumenti e modelli per la tutela giuridica delle espressioni culturali tradizionali*. Napoli: ESI.

Heritage and Community

Cultural Diplomacy in India: Dispersal, Heritage Representation, Contestation, and Development

Rana P. B. Singh and Pravin S. Rana

Abstract India (Bhārat), being one of the oldest cultures with continuity of traditions has introduced cultural diplomacy in the ancient past, and constantly followed the path of cultural dispersal as illustrated with the diffusion of Buddhism during the fifth-century BCE—the CE twelfth century in southeast and east Asia. One such example was marriage of princess from Ayodhya (India) to the king of Gimhae (Korea). Of course, the orientation of these diplomacies and uses changed from one dynasty to another. These dispersal and interaction lead to 'heritage making' in different parts. With change in ideologies by the present ruling government, representation of heritage is now superimposed by Hindu nationalism, resulting to rejuvenate Hindu temples and converting them as a cultural hub for tourism, replacing spiritual environment and religious identities, as exemplified in case of Ayodhya and Varanasi. Since 2014, the new government under their missions of (i) Heritage City Development and Augmentation Yojana (HRIDAY), and (ii) Pilgrimage Rejuvenation and Spiritual Augmentation Drive (PRASAD), working to strengthen and promote the holy-heritage sites under pilgrimage-tourism in a sustainable way and befitting into the SDGs. However, only the time will give answer to the degree of success.

1 India-Bharat: Roots of Cultural Diplomacy (CD) and Issue of Dispersal

The concept of Cultural diplomacy, CD (in Hindi '*Sāṅkritik Rājanaya*') has been used in various contexts, purposes and cultural interactions, and reinterpreted in various time period. In ancient India (Bhārat), it was a common process and an ideology for the state polity, civility, conviction and its organisation and cultural integration—all depending upon the prevailing political conditions and the practising

R. P. B. Singh (✉) · P. S. Rana
Banaras Hindu University, Varanasi, India
e-mail: ranapbs@gmail.com

P. S. Rana
e-mail: psrana@bhu.ac.in

O. Niglio and E. Y. J. Lee (eds.), *Transcultural Diplomacy and International Law in Heritage Conservation*, https://doi.org/10.1007/978-981-16-0309-9_15

ideologies of the state. This is quite similar to a contemporary conception that narrates CD as a type of public diplomacy and soft power that includes the 'exchange of ideas, information, art, language and other aspects of culture among nations and their peoples in order to foster mutual understanding' (Lenczowski, 2009: 74). The oldest treatise on CD in India was a classic book of polity, viz. the *Arthaśāstra*, known as 'Science of Political Economy', by Kautilya (Chāṇakya), composed during the period of Chandragupta Maurya (reign: 317–293 BCE), the great king who defeated the Nanda kings (when several related kings trying unsuccessfully to rule India together), stopped the advance of Alexander the Great's successors, and for the first time united most of the Indian subcontinent in a sovereign empire (cf. Boesche, 2003: 10). All the cultural attributes and performances involved therein are conceived as processes of mutual cohesiveness and strengthening the power of the state. The most common framing was determining the cultural policy and ways and means of their implementation. This policy includes ideologies and jurisprudence, arts and performances, language and regional distinctiveness, culture icons like temple and sanctuaries, traditions and religio-ritual festivities, pilgrimages and holy sites, and so on. Of course, after passage of time, and perceived today too, they all are put under the broad umbrella of 'heritage'; however, in the Sanātan Dharma of ancient India these were eulogised in the purview of *dharohara* (heritagescapes). The frame of CD had also included expansion and diffusion of such cultural traditions in the neighbouring state and even far away states through pilgrimages, religious teaching, and cross-cultural discourses. Indian civilisation is among the oldest in the world, and what is unique in that respect is that the culture of the peoples still remains largely unchanged, with a strong thread of continuity through the ages, in spite of layers of superimposition, transformation, and absorption (see Basham, 2005). Here, heritage is conceived and narrated as the representative product of the long path of cultural diplomacy, and illustrated with some examples.

India was a home and hearth to two of the world's oldest surviving civilisations and religious traditions—Hinduism and Buddhism—that resulted to the ideological export of India's spiritual, artistic, and cultural impact in many parts of Asia and makes its soft power global. Indian ideas have travelled across the globe—from the peaceful spread of Buddhism across Asia historically to the Gandhian message through acceptance of non-violence in the twentieth century—enriching and exchanging other cultures but also absorbing and assimilating (Thussu, 2013: 45). Nevertheless, the interplay between the continuity of its civilisation—earliest urban cultures (Indus Valley Civilisation of 3500 BCE) to the *Vedas* (2500 BCE)—and the disruptions of invasions and early settlers means that the Indian knowledge system has been repeatedly rejuvenated and revitalised by constant exposure to other cultures and systems of thought from Islam to European modernity and has been able to communicate this through encounters and engagements with traders, scholars, monks, and pilgrims as well as emperors, and invaders (Thussu, 2013: 46).

In the second half of the first millennium BCE, Buddhism followed the trade routes, mostly over the 'Silk Route', across Southern and Central Asia and China, to Indonesia in the East and Alexandria in the West. As befitting its cultural philosophy and diplomacy, it was communicated by travellers—monks, traders, and scholars—carrying and translating scriptural texts; through artefacts—sculptures, cave paintings, and stupas, and by scholarly exchange at centres of learning—universities and monasteries and similar such institutions. As early as the first century CE, Buddhist monks made their way over the 'Silk Road' through Central Asia to China. By the seventh century, Buddhism had made a significant impact in China, interacting with the prevailing Confucian and Daoist cultures and ideas. By this time the tradition was also firmly established in Korea. In the CE sixth century, the Buddhist tradition was also introduced into Japan, where it developed within the purview of both Shinto and other indigenous traditions, resulting to develop an assimilating dharmic tradition. This form of Buddhism that first developed in India and later flourished in East Asia is known as the Mahayana, or '*Great Vehicle*'. By the eighth century, Buddhism was shaped by the Tantric traditions of northeast India, and spread to the high mountain plateau of Tibet. There, in interaction with the indigenous Bon religion, and with forms of Buddhism that had travelled to Tibet from East Asia, a distinctive and vibrant form of Mahayana Buddhism get transformed into another form, known as Vajrayana, the '*Diamond Vehicle*'.

In India, Buddhism began to wane in the sixth- and seventh-centuries CE when devotional Hinduism replaced Buddhism in the south and Hephthalite Huns invaded and sacked monasteries in the north. By the thirteenth century, repeated invasions by the Turks ensured that Buddhism had virtually disappeared. However, by this time Buddhism with its strong roots was flourishing in many other parts of Asia. As early as the third-century BCE the Indian emperor Ashoka, a convert to Buddhism, is said to have established the tradition on the island of Sri Lanka (Ceylon). After the passage of time, by the fifth-century CE Buddhism had spread throughout what are now Myanmar and Thailand. Thus, by the thirteenth century, one of the early Buddhist schools, called the Theravada, '*the way of the elders*', had become the dominant tradition of South and Southeast Asia. This way Buddhism reached to Japan and Korea in northeast by ca fifth to ninth-century CE, to Indonesia by ca seventh to ninth-century CE, and western Central Asia by fourth to fifth-century CE (see Fig. 1). This way by twelfth-century CE, most parts of south, southeast, east, and northeast Asia were predominated by Buddhism.

Throughout the Buddhist world, Buddhists have the 'Three Treasures' in common (the *Buddha*, the *Dhamma*, and the *Saṅgha*); to be a Buddhist means 'taking refuge' in the 'Three Treasures', i.e. to put one's trust in them and follow their rules. Buddhists see as central to their lives the Buddha as well as enlightenment in general, the teachings of those who are enlightened, and the community that follows these teachings. Of course, these 'Three Treasures' continue to provide inspiration to Buddhists, but they are not understood in exactly the same way everywhere, and also they are interpreted according to their local traditions.

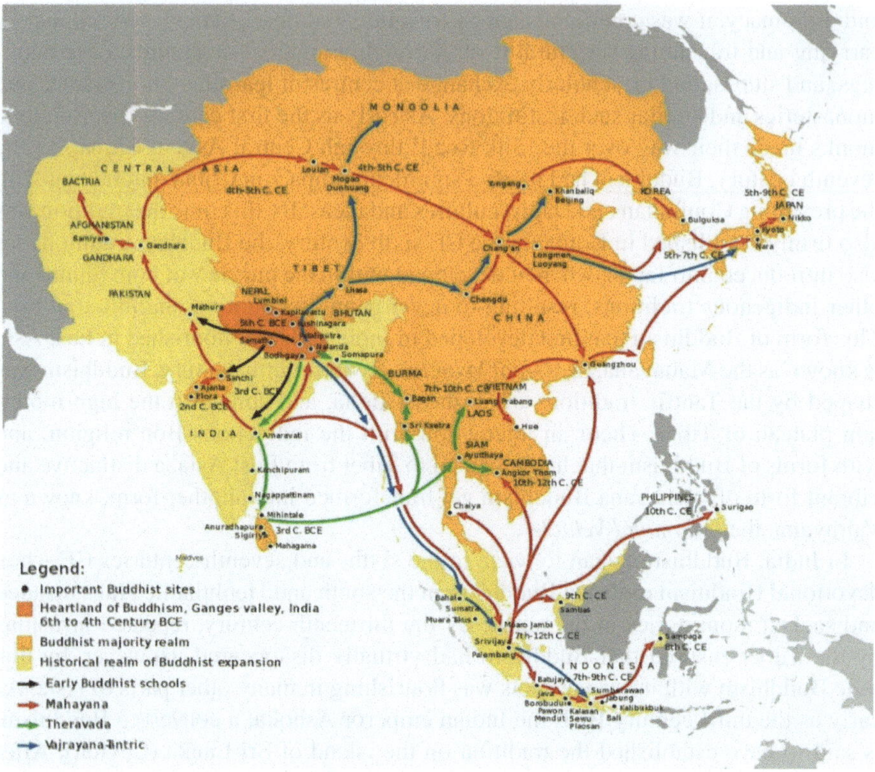

Fig. 1 Spread and dispersal of Buddhism in ancient period

2 Reviving Ancient Cultural Links: Ayodhya (India) and Gimhae (Korea)

After the decline of the Mauryan Empire (322–185 BCE), Kushan Dynasty descended from Yuezhi had ruled most of the northern Indian subcontinent and parts of Central Asia. Kushans belonged to the Yuch-chi tribe who lived in Chinese Turkistan. Because of pressure from other tribes they were divided into five branches, one among them was Kushans. Soon Kushans became powerful and invaded India in the CE first century. They occupied western parts of India after defeating Shakas and Parthians. Kushan Dynasty was one of the most interesting dynasties which ruled over Jammu and Kashmir, and under their cultural policy of assimilation they practised Zoroastrianism, Buddhism, and also Saivism (Singh & Kumar, 2019: 112–113).

The Kushan Empire (Ancient Greek: Βασιλεία Κοσσανῶν; Bactrian: Κυϸανο, Kushano; Late Brahmi script: Ku-shā-ṇa, Kuṣāṇa Sāmrājya; BHS: Guṣāṇa-vaṃśa; Chinese: 貴霜; Parthian: Kušan-xšaθr (Rosenfield, 1967: 5) was a syncretic empire, formed by the Yuezhi (Wolji), in the Bactrian territories from circa CE 30, to circa CE 375, until the advent of the Gupta Empire; they ruled around the same time as the

Western Satraps and the Satavahanas. It spread to encompass much of Afghanistan (Beal, 1906: 29 and 318–350), and then the northern parts of the Indian subcontinent at least as far as Sāketa/Ayuta (identified as Ayodhya) and Sarnath near Varanasi (Banaras), where inscriptions have been found dating to the era of the Kushan Emperor Kanishka the Great (Fig. 2).

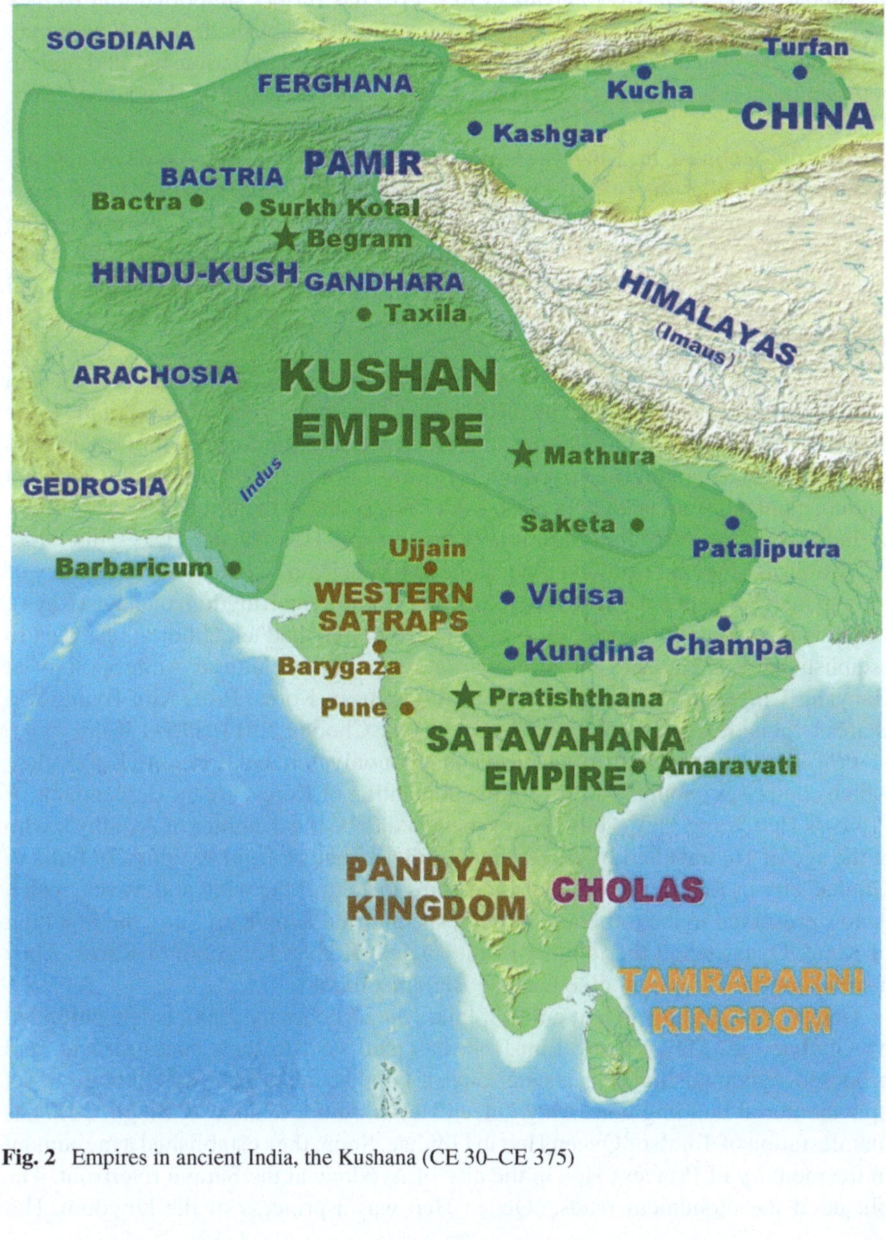

Fig. 2 Empires in ancient India, the Kushana (CE 30–CE 375)

Under the cultural policy of expansion and cross-cultural interaction, sea routes were already developed during the Buddhist period of fourth BCE–CE second centuries between India and the Fareast (China, Japan, and Korea); this is well described in the mass of literature describing boating and sailing (cf. Mukherjee, 1957: 53; Pathak, 2018: 82–83). The Buddhist literature of *Jātakas* have also vividly described the trade and commence through the sea routes (cf. Pathak, 2018: 84, also Majumdar, 1963: 37). Rhys Davids (1903: 116) has further supported that by 122 BCE the sea route between India and China was well established; that's how it may easily be speculated that during that period already trade relationship and sailing between India and Korea also get established (cf. Gupta, 2000: 168; Vajpayee, 1966: 71).

After the decline of the Maurya empire (322–185 BCE), Sāketa (Ayodhya) appears to have come under the rule of Pushyamitra Shunga (ca 187–151 BCE). The first-century BCE inscription of Dhanadeva suggests that he appointed a governor there (Bakker, 1986: 20). The *Yuga Purāṇa* mentions Sāketa as the residence of a governor, and describes it as being attacked by a combined force of Greeks, Mathuras, and Panchalas (Bakker, 1986: 18–19). Patanjali's commentary on Panini also refers to the Greek siege of Sāketa (Bakker, 1986: 19).

According to the *Samguk Yusa* ('Memorabilia of the Three Kingdoms', dated ca 1281, written by the monk Il-yeon of Korea), a Chinese-language memoir of the three kingdoms in Korea, Queen Heo Hwang-Ok (wife of King Suro) who founded the ancient Karak Kingdom (Geumgwan Gaya) was born in the city of Ayuta/Ayodhya (India), named Sāketa in ancient period. This refers that in the year CE 48 (27 July?), an Indian princess Suriratna/Shriratna (Korean name Heo Hwang-Ock/ 'Huh' 허황옥), who was 16-year old at that time, came to Korea from Ayodhya by the journey of sea and married with King Kim Suro of the ancient Korean Kingdom of Gaya (Kaya), which is now the Gimhae city (Kimhae city), and they had ten children resulting to establish Kim or Karak clan. A Professor Emeritus of Cultural Anthropology at Hanyang University and national archaeologist from Korea, Prof. Kim Byung-Mo shares a 'genetic connection' with Ayodhya (see Choong, 2011: 115–136).

Prof. Kim Byung-Mo firmly believes that not only him, but the entire Karak clan, which comprises about two-thirds of the population of Korea, are the descendants of Princess Heo Wang-Ock (Huh). Heo is believed to be the daughter of Ayodhya, who at the age of 16, travelled by sea in the CE fourth century from Ayodhya in India to Gimhae city in Korea, and carried stone-slabs to control the wind and waves, which is now preserved in the tomb area. There, she married King Kim Suro, the first king of Karak Dynasty and the founder of the ancient Korean Kingdom of Karak. They had ten children of whom nine became Buddhist monks.

Getting revived the ancient cultural links, on 27 February 2000, a delegation led by Gimhae city Mayor Song Eun-Bok, has paid visit to their ancestral site, and proposed Ayodhya (India) as a sister city of Gimhae and a plan was thought to set up a memorial building honouring Queen Heo in future (Kumar & Singh, 2017) as manifestation of Tomb of Queen Heo in Gimhae. Soon, they established a monument in the memory of Princess Heo in the city of Ayodhya at the Sarayu riverfront. The plaque at the monument reads, 'Queen Heo was a princess of the kingdom. Her father, the king of Ayodhya, on receiving a divine revelation, sent her on a long sea voyage to the Karak kingdom in southern Korea to marry King Suro'.

In continuation of bilateral cultural treaty, on 18 January 2001 Korean delegation, including the ambassador of Korea, has inaugurated a memorial stone-plate honouring their Royal ancestor Queen Heo. As followed up action, in the presence of hundreds of historians, and government representatives including the Korean ambassador to India on 6 March 2001 under the patronage of the Karak Clan Society, the memorial in the Park (Korean Park) was unveiled on the right bank of the Sarayu (Ghaghara) River at Naya Ghat, lying 750 m northeast from the Nageshvarnatha temple. At the Korean Park, every year hundreds of Korean pay visit and convey their tributes through ritual and festivities. Since last three years, in the month of March special delegation of Karak clan members uses to come here to pray tribute to their ancestral mother. Thus, opened a new window of transcultural tourism and the revival of ancient cultural links. The increasing cultural interaction with Korea, will also lead to promote Hallyu (the 'Korean Wave') by promoting cultural industries through cultural diplomacy (cf. Dhawan, 2017).

3 Heritage Representation: Cultural Diplomacy and World Heritage Sites

In ancient Indian tradition, heritage has been called ***dharohara***, which is a combination of two words, i.e. *dharā-* ('the mother earth, *Prithvī/ Bhūdevī*, Lord Vishnu who holds') and *-ihara* ('endeavour of identity through time'). This is mythologically described in the storey of a demon Hiranakshya, who dragged the Earth to the bottom of the sea, then Vishnu's incarnation Varāha ('Boar') took the form of a 'boar' in order to rescue the Earth and killed the demon (see *Vāyu Purāṇa*, 23.100–109), and finally he delivered sermon of spirituality and ways of conserving and preserving the Earth. Thus, metaphysically the deeper meaning of preservation is attached to the concept of '*dharohara*'. The word also carries the meaning of 'bearing' and 'preserving' the surface of the earth. Prithvī is also called *dharā, dhrī, dhartī, dhrithrī*, meaning that which holds everything (see *Shathapatha Brāhmaṇa*, a Vedic text, dated circa fifth-century BCE: 10.56.6, 10.59.25, 10.68.48). This is one way to explain it, i.e. in terms of the 'root' ('*shrota*') and 'identity' ('*asmitā*'). The word also signifies a framework of continuity of interconnectedness and a personality of culture; in terms of space it combines the microspace, site (*sthān*), the extended space, habitat (*paryāvāsa*, extended as dwellingness) and the regional projection, territory (*parikshetra*), and ultimately the link to the earth and the cosmos (*brahmāṇḍa*). Additionally, it also connotes the tangible, intangible, transitory and visual attributes. In other contexts, the word *dharohara* also refers to the spatial-functional symbol that links 'locality' and 'universality', consisting of four hierarchically covering layers, viz. *sthān* (site), *parikshetra* (defined territory), *sīmānta* (border transition), and *brahmāṇḍa* (cosmos) (Singh & Rana, 2019: 152).

Altogether the Indian word *dharohara* thus connotes a wide and expanded frame, therefore it should be better translated as *heritagescapes* (mostly in plural) and be explained in the purview of 'heritage ecology' in relation to 'deep-spiritual geography' (Singh, 1995: 197). It possesses the 'spirit' of spirituality and interconnectedness that has roots in the past giving messages, existing in the present promoting experiences, and envisioning the future in what is called *sanātana* ('***E****ssenceness-***B****eingness-***B****ecomingness*'), which in the passage of time and space represents eternity. This works in a unified totality for psychological well-being or soul and spiritual healing (see Singh, 2009). It is to be noted that the Sanskrit word *sanātana* denotes that which always is, and has neither beginning nor end, i.e. that which is eternal.

The word *dharohara* is also used differently in various regions of India in accordance to their cultural connotations and in contexts such as ascendancy, continuity of tradition, property rights, monuments, etc. It stands for wholeness, but also 'holiness' (referring to the sacred attachment and site of divine feeling) (see Singh & Rana, 2011). However, one should keep in mind that in Indian thought the life-ways have always been prescribed under the purview of *dharma*, the holistic philosophy of culture and realisation. *Dharma* denotes 'the natural way' of all kinds of objects and realities. For example, the *dharma* of wind is to blow, the *dharma* of water is to flow—the *dharma* of honey is sweetness—so the *dharma* of human being is to save the *dharohara* and sustainably transfer it to the coming generations. This is the *sanātana dharma*—the Eternal Natural Way of '***e****xistence-***m****aintenance-***c****ontinuity*'—a notion of cultural philosophy and diplomacy in the purview of sustainability (*saṅdhrita* and/or *saṁposhita*). In Eurocentric philosophy, however, such ideas are often projected and propagated as 'static, despotic, and irrelevant to world history' (Said, 1993: 198).

However, the context of cultural policy and representation of heritage and its preservation was introduced by the British rulers in the late eighteenth century. The history of cultural heritage and resource management in India started with an appeal made in 1774 by Dr. Samuel Johnson to Warren Hastings, the first Governor-General of Fort William, Calcutta (now Kolkata), 'to examine nicely the tradition and histories of the East, ... survey the remains of ancient edifices and trace the vestiges of its ruined cities'. After a decade, in 1784, the Asiatic Society was founded for enquiring among other things into the History, the Antiquities, Arts, Sciences, and Literature of Asia. From the early nineteenth century, various Governors-General acted to conserve and protect selected monuments and ancient buildings, although somewhat later under the administration of William Bentick (1928–1935), an unsuccessful move was made, in the early 1930s, to demolish the Taj Mahal for the value of its marble (Thaper, 1989: 165).

With the appointment of Alexander Cunningham (1814–1893) in December 1861 a systematic survey of the various regions of the country was started. However, only by April 1906, with the active involvement of Lord Curzon (1899–1905), was the Archaeological Survey of India (ASI) placed on a permanent basis, and John Marshall appointed as the Director General. Under the Act of 1904, the Government of India assumed all powers vested in the provincial governments. On 26 January 1950, the constitution of free India came into force. Under its provisions (7th schedule, Article

246) the allocation of function relating to archaeology was divided between the Union and the various state governments. At different stages necessary changes were made, the Parliament passed the Ancient and Historical Monuments and Archaeological Sites and Remains (Declaration of National Importance) Act 1951, by which all monuments previously protected under the 1904 Act were redeclared as sites of national importance. Furthermore, under Section 126 of the State Reorganisation Act 1956, over 450 additional monuments and archaeological sites were declared of national importance. The comprehensive outline of this legislation was enacted in 1958 (Singh, 1997: 103).

Presently almost all states have their own Department of Archaeology, and have enacted legislation largely patterned on the Act of 1958 and the Antiquities and the Art Treasures Act of 1972. Under the existing legislation nearly 5,000 monuments are looked after by the Central Government through the agency of the ASI and about 1,500 monuments by the states through their respective departments. In spite of this coverage, a number of monuments fall outside the purview of any of these agencies. Most of these monuments, archaeological and historic areas, and sacredscapes, are attached to urban areas thus comprising part of urban heritage (Thaper, 1989: 166–167).

Culture and heritage are one of the most significant of UNESCO's activities in India and include the safeguarding of India's cultural and civilisational heritage as reflected in the World Heritage List of UNESCO. Since its first meet, i.e. the World Heritage Convention of 1972 India has been an active member and for implementation of UNESCO's recommendations, works closely in cooperation with the Ministry of Culture and Archaeological Survey of India (ASI). As a member of the UN World Heritage Committee, India is currently seeking international recognition of several projects, both cultural and natural within the purview of her cultural diplomacy.

As a pluralistic, democratic, multi-ethnic, and multi-cultural state, the world's largest democracy, India while following its cultural policies and diplomacy has been and will continue to be a bridge between differing ideologies, cultures and civilisations as demonstrated in different periods of UNESCO's tumultuous history. India is currently a member of 19 of its UNESCO's Conventions, including those on natural and cultural heritage, education, and intellectual property rights.

The idea of creating an international movement for protecting heritage was realised after World War I, resulting to hold its first World Heritage Committee session in 1972 (Paris) concerning the Protection of the World Cultural and Natural Heritage developed from the merging of two separate movements: the first focussing on the preservation of cultural sites, and the other dealing with the conservation of nature. The forthcoming 45th Session is planned for 2021. Since its beginning India became member of the Committee, however only in 1983 the two properties were inscribed in the World Heritage List, viz. Taj Mahal and Agra Fort taking in view the 10-pont UNESCO WHL criteria for nomination.

Out of 1121 heritage sites in the world (869 cultural, 213 natural, and 39 mixed properties, as of 22 June 2020), 38 heritage properties (Cultural 29, Natural 8, Mixed

1, cf. Fig. 3) from India are included in the World Heritage List (cf. Table 1). Of course, there are 3,686 national protected monuments under Archaeological Survey of India (ASI). In addition, 46 properties from India are enlisted in the World Heritage Tentative List (15 April 2019). However, the Indian government has declared 150 places as national heritage sites on the basis of the criteria adopted by the ASI.

In India, the Archaeological Survey of India (ASI), the Indian National Trust for Art, Culture and Heritage (INTACH), and Indian Heritage Society (IHS) are the prime organisations responsible for protection, conservation and preservation of heritage sites; all these are linked to the Ministry of Tourism and Culture, Government of India. It is claimed that the ASI has not been maintaining traditional conservation

Fig. 3 India: UNESCO World Heritage Sites, 38 (July 2020)

Table 1 India: UNESCO World Heritage Sites, 22 July 2020 (cf. Fig. 3)

Se.	Category	No.	Heritage properties (year of inscription)
Cultural Heritage			
1.	Fort, Palaces, Tomb	9	Taj Mahal (1983), Agra Fort (1983), Fatehpur Sikri (1986), Humayun's Tomb, Delhi (1993), Qutb Minar complex, Delhi (1993), Red Fort Complex (2007), seven Hill Forts of Rajasthan (2013), Historic (walled) city of Ahmadabad (2017), 'Pink-Palace city' of Jaipur (6 July 2019)
2.	Monuments	5	Mahabalipuram (1984), Hampi (1986), Khajuraho (1986), Pattadakal (1987), Rani ki Vav (The Queen's Stepwell) at Patan (2014)
3.	Caves, ancient murals	3	Ajanta Caves (1983), Ellora Caves (1983), Elephanta Caves (1987)
4.	Buddhist Monuments	3	Sanchi (1989), Mahabodhi Temple Complex at Bodh Gaya (2002), Nalanda monuments (2016)
5.	Ancient temples	2	Sun Temple at Konarak (1984), Great Chola Temples: Gangaikonda, Airateshvara, Brihadishvara (1987)
6.	Archaeological Landscape	2	Rock Shelters of Bhimbetka (2003), Champaner-Pavagarh Park (2004)
7.	Mountain Railways	1	Darjeeling (1999), Nilgiri Mountain Railway (2005), Kalka-Shimla (2008). (*Counted as one group*)
8.	Church	1	Churches and Convents of Goa (1986)
9.	British Architecture	2	Chhatrapati Shivaji Terminus (formerly Victoria Terminus) (2004), Victorian Gothic and Art Deco Ensembles of Mumbai (2018)
10	Architectural astronomical observatory	1	Jaipur (2010; and also, at Delhi, Mathura, Ujjain and Varanasi, mid-eighteenth century)
–	Total	29	–

(continued)

practices and was exceeding its brief by setting up unnecessary structures, and that the comprehensive heritage environmental plan has not been taken into account.

In its projects, INTACH emphasises that India's living culture is becoming compromised somewhere along the way between India's historical continuity and India's acceptance of modernity. The planning strategy should therefore follow a middle path, maintaining the harmony of deeply implanted culture while at the same time taking into account future urban development. The connotation of terms like 'area conservation', 'heritage zoning', and 'heritage ecology' reflects this approach.

Table 1 (continued)

Se.	Category	No.	Heritage properties (year of inscription)
Natural Heritage			
1.	Natural Park	5	Keoladeo (1985), Nanda Devi and Valley of Flowers (1988), Sundarbans (1987), Great Himalayan National Park at Kulu, H.P. (2014), Khangchendzonga National Park in Sikkim (2016)
2.	Sanctuary	2	Manas Wildlife Sanctuary (1985), Kaziranga Wildlife Sanctuary (1985)
3.	Biological diversity	1	Western Ghats, ca 1600 km mountain range, consisting Sahyadri, Karnataka, and Nilgiri (2012)
–	Total	8	–
Mixed Heritage			
1.	Le Corbusier's works	1	Urban and Architectural Works of Le Corbusier in Chandigarh (2016)
–	TOTAL (all)	38	–

Source ASI Reports, collated by the authors; see https://whc.unesco.org/en/statesparties/in

All ancient and historical monuments and all archaeological sites and remains which have been declared by the Ancient and Historical Monuments and Archaeological Sites and Remains (Declaration of National Importance) Act, 1951, or by Section 126 of the States Reorganisation Act, 1956, to be of national importance shall be deemed to be ancient and historical monument or archaeological sites and remains declared to be of national importance for the purposes of this Act, and to be protected and taken care of by the ASI.

Formed under the umbrella of cultural diplomacy, the Advisory Committee on World Heritage (formed on Nov. 1, 2011) took lead in strengthening the cultural and administrative activities of State Governments 'to understand the tenets for achieving international heritage stature'. A total of 234 sites were submitted from states across India with short listing of about 56 properties by the Tentative List Working Group under the Advisory Committee. Among these 56 properties, 46 are already placed in the revised tentative list including some pan-India nominations such as "Satyagrah sites of non-violence freedom movement" which narrate the Indian story thus filling the previous gaps in typology, chronology, and unique cultural symbols, etc. (Jain, 2015). However, ten Natural Heritage Sites and transnational sites are pending since 2016. Cultural policy priorities of India include arts support, arts development, cultural heritage, arts education, cultural infrastructures, international cultural cooperation and exchange. In fact, the cultural policy and diplomacy have covered a range of complex, and often mutually contradictory, definitions, resulting to a lack of unitary cultural policy, which may corroborate with international norms. Additionally, given the need to be always alert to the political consequences of cultural policy, India has also to create a viable and functioning administrative mechanism through practical institutional segregation of responsibilities.

4 Heritage Making and Cultural Diplomacy: Heritagisation

In India cultural heritage is considered as one of the most visible representations of the existence and continuity of the traditions, performances, artefacts, and monuments, of course predominantly in the earlier days with religious denominations but subject to state's definition and practice of the cultural policy and diplomacy too. In World Heritage Committee, there appears a fair amount of critique on the viability of the world heritage concept, mostly referring to monumentation. Lowenthal (1998: 227–235) underlined that heritage is a private, non-public resource: 'Heritage is normally cherished not as a common but as private property. Ownership gives it essential worth. ... Claims of ownership, uniqueness, and primary engender strife over every facets of collective legacies'.

Cultural heritage, especially of religious built forms (as it predominates in India), has been historically important. However, beginning in the nineteenth century and continuing today, perhaps partially in response to 'modernity', cultural tourism has become more popular and explicitly reinforces the value, use, and conservation of religion; tourists who appreciate cultural developments increasingly comprehend the significant role of religious beliefs and practices in shaping local geographies through physical structures and associated rituals and performances. Political control, identity, hegemony, and social security are all religiously symbolised (see Harvey, 1979). Monuments and buildings are recurring testaments of successive generations, typically of the dominant community or a ruler's patronage, each in turn manifesting the then current understanding of the human place in and of nature (Singh, 2015: 2).

Cultural tourism plays a great role towards socio-economic changes and promotion of sustainability. According to Indian sentiment the pilgrim's centres or *tīrthasthāna* used to be visited by number of tourists to earn religious or spiritual virtue. As one of the largest industries, tourism is associated with many of the prime sectors of the world's economy; however, in India's domestic tourism pilgrimage-tourism predominates. Taking this view government is trying to promote pilgrimage-tourism in the purview of SDGs, taking in view 'heritage-making' ('*heritagization*' or '*patrimonialization*' in French). Pilgrimage defined as 'a journey resulting from religious causes, externally to a holy site, and internally for spiritual purposes and internal understanding' (Collins-Kreiner, 2010: 153); that's how pilgrimage-tourism will promote, sustain, and maintain economic and cultural sustainability, together with maintaining belief systems on the line of state's cultural policy and diplomacy. The majority of the pilgrimage cities (e.g. Ayodhya and Varanasi, discussed in the sequence) bear various interrelated common phenomena to which people are affiliated with belief system, faith, festivities and performances, and spiritual merits. This is also to be kept in mind that the sacred spaces vis-à-vis public spaces, in a way will serve as peace plaza and places of spiritual awakening having 'the potential for healing communal strife and reviving urban art, (*cultural*) and folk practices. Heritage conservation can thus "become an empowering tool for local communities and for the visitor an opportunity for spiritual growth" (Sinha, 2014: 60), which is one of the major aims of urban development under the present cultural policy of heritage-making' (Singh et al., 2020a: 201).

A recent study remarks that 'If the urban SDG is to prove useful as a tool as intended for encouraging local and national authorities alike to make positive investments in the various components of urban sustainability transitions, then it must be widely relevant, acceptable and practicable' (Simon et al., 2016: 60). This is valid in case of Indian holy-heritage cities, where one always faces the problem of linking locality and universality. Additionally, central to this task has been the challenge of determining how to benchmark and measure performance according to the SMART criteria (i.e. specific, measurable, assignable, realistic, and time-specific), based on specialist scholarship, the existing literature and practical experience of the site (see Birch, 2015: 228), taking into account demand, pressure response, and multifactor versus single factor, and also considering two metrics: the traditional dimensions of sustainability (equity, economics, and environment) and later forming the Liveability Principles of Partnership for Sustainable Communities (PSC), while making bridge between the age-old traditions and high-tech smart city plans.

In a recent meeting ICOMOS (2016) having discourses on 'Heritage as Driver of Sustainability: Mission and Activities for 2017-18', it has been noticed that the SDGs focussed on achieving representation of heritage in the major policy papers of Agenda 2030. Now that these policy papers are adopted at the highest, global level, and their goals and targets await being fulfilled, focus has shifted to 'implementation' through public participation and PPP (Public–Private Partnership). Therefore, the mission that ICOMOS has given its Focal Point for the SDGs in the new term is to 'steer a coordinated process of advocacy to advance the implementation of UN Agenda 2030- SDGs and Habitat NUA (New Urban Agenda) from the perspective of cultural and natural heritage, within the framework of the ICOMOS mandate and inputs from strategic partners'. The NUA, a framework laying out how cities should be planned and managed to best promote sustainable urbanisation within the purview of culture and cultural heritage will keep the vitality and image of holy-heritage cities (Singh et al., 2020a: 202).

Following the UN SDGs (Sustainable Development Goals) Target 11.4, focussing 'Transforming our World: The 2030 Agenda for Sustainable Development', cultural heritage and urban sustainability are now considered an inseparable part of holistic development. Religion had played a role for controlling power in Indian monarchy in the ancient past, and in contemporary India too it played a role in the formation of religious landscape and corporate identity of religious heritage under the umbrella of present government's cultural policy and diplomacy to reinstate, revive, and maintain the Hindu identity, through commonly using processions, pilgrimage, religious assemblies, religious fairs (*melā*), and rejuvenation of ancient temples those faced problem of destruction during the medieval period. Two such case studies of contested sites and the process of re-making through heritagisation are cited as examples. Newly introduced concept of pilgrimage-tourism will help to revitalise these sacred cities. Situated in the Ganga (Ganges) River basin Ayodhya and Banaras, both have been primarily ancient *tīrthas* (riverfront sacredscapes) and salvific cities that record settlement continuity since at least ca 1000 BCE. Under the patronage of cultural policy and diplomacy for holistic development and projecting them internationally, Government of India is promoting inclusive heritage sustainable development of heritage sites (cities), through active participation of stakeholders in the purview of SDGs and future development.

5 Rāma Janmabhumi, Ayodhya: Representation vs. Contestation

The city of Ayodhya (Urban Agglomeration, including merger of Faizabad) is situated on 26° 47′ North and 26° 80′ North Latitude and 82° 12′ East and 82° 20′ East Longitude in the state of Uttar Pradesh, on the right bank of the Sarayu (Ghaghara, a tributary of the Ganga) River in north India, and serves as the headquarters of the district of Ayodhya (cf. Fig. 4). In a recent agreement between the state government of Uttar Pradesh and the central ministry of culture—Govt of India (24 March 2017), Ayodhya is taken for special development programme for religious heritage and pilgrimage-tourism with a view to serving as nexus for global harmony.

With its general decline all over India from the sixth century onwards, Buddhism lost its position in Ayodhya too, and appears to be virtually extinct there after CE 1000. In CE 1193 Muhammad Ghori invaded north India, including Ayodhya. His army officer Makhdum Shah Ghori came to Ayodhya and destroyed the famous Jain temple of Adinātha in 1194. Since then under the Sultanate rule at Delhi and the Mughal rulers, the city of Ayodhya was invaded and destroyed many times. By order of the Mughal invader Babur, in 1528 his army chief Mir Baqi Tashkandi demolished the famous Rāma temple of Pratihāra and the Gahaḍavāla period at the birthplace of Rāma, and in the successive period of 15-month he built there a Muslim monument (mosque?) using the debris of the temple. Since its inception, this has been so controversial and sensitive a place that for centuries now, Muslims have never performed prayer (*namāz*) there, however the notion of being 'mosque' (*Maszid*) has been widely propagated. Since then it has also been a centre of Hindu–Muslim conflicts and riots, but the main site was always opened for devout Hindus till 23 February 1857 when the East India Company (Britain) made a separating wall and prohibited the entry of Hindus through the passage of mosque.

On 6 December 1992 a mob led by Hindu fundamentalists, the right-wing activist from World Hindu Congress (VHP), ultimately in their last attempt succeeded in razing the sixteenth-century Babri mosque in Ayodhya, which was already proved

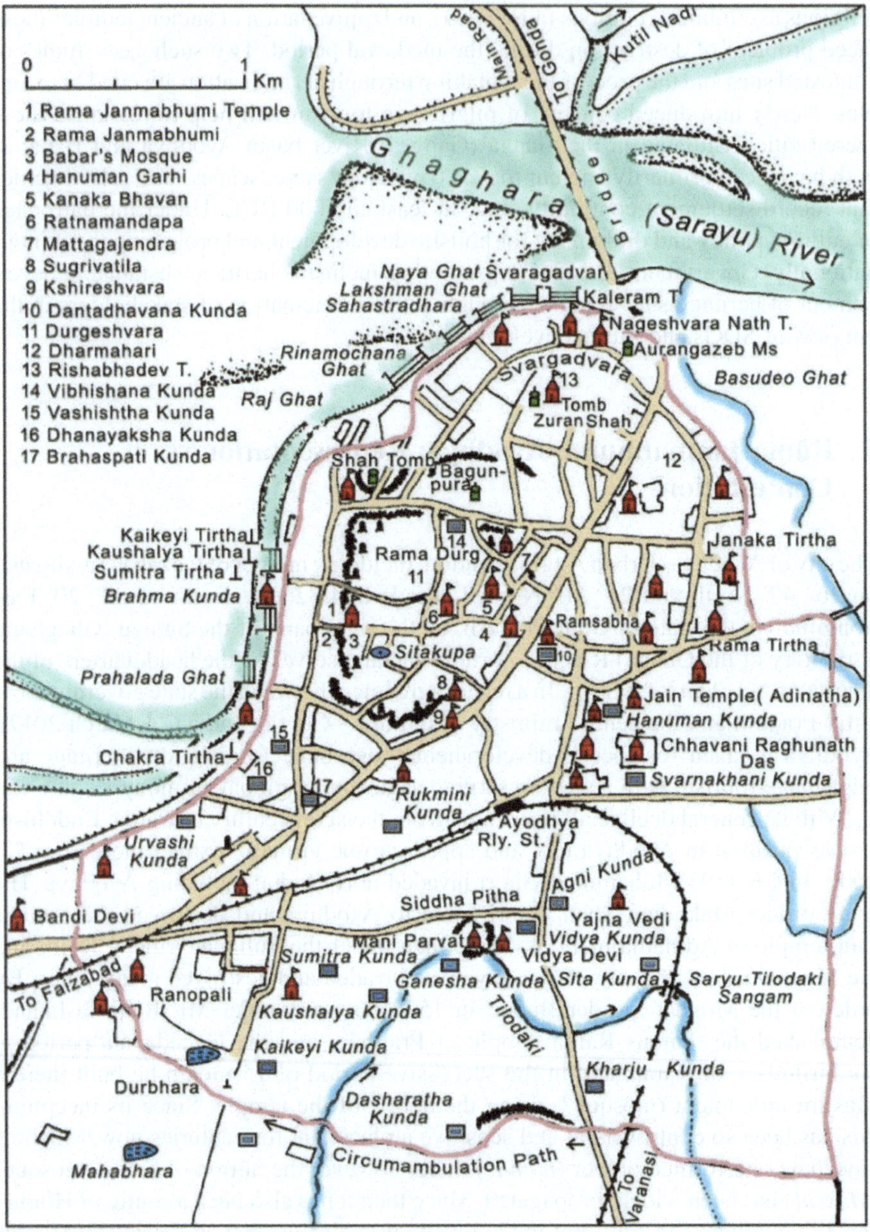

Fig. 4 Ayodhya (*Source* Singh & Rana, 2002: 302)

historically and archeologically as birthplace of Lord Rāma, and was a glorious site with lofty Vaishnavite Hindu temples in the early twelfth century, but converted into mosque after its demolition in the early sixteenth century (Singh, 2008: 131). During last 490 years there had been several attempts to remove the mosque through court, direct action, or planned attacks. After India's independence in 1947 the different religions and their monuments had largely coexisted side by side. The Ayodhya crisis must also be seen within the climate of increased tensions between India and Pakistan over the last few decades, and the fundamentalist groups between Hindus and Muslims within India itself (see Elst, 2002, 2003). Here cultural diplomacy could not succeed to resolve the issue. The VHP continued in extending their agenda for getting under their control several disputed mosques, strongly arguing for the important mosques in the holy cities of Mathura and Varanasi.

In the light of initiation of the newly formed pro-Hindu government, Bharatiya Janta Party, BJP (since 2014) using its cultural diplomacy and with the support of public awakening to preserve the historicity of the place, ultimately on 9 November 2019, the Supreme Court of India, has announced the verdict by vacating the previous court decisions and ordered that the land to be handed over to a trust to build the Hindu temple. In this continuity, on 12 December 2019 the Supreme Court has dismissed all petitions against the decision seeking review of the verdict in the light of scientific, archaeological, and historical evidences. On 5 February 2020, the trust named 'Shri Rāma Janmabhūmi Tīrtha Kshetra', consisting of 15 members, was set up by the state of Uttar Pradesh with the support of the Government of India and passed by its parliament to construct the Rāma temple in Ayodhya where once Babari mosque was existing. The trust was given the 2.77 acres (previously disputed) land as well as the 67.703 acres of surrounding land acquired under the Acquisition of Certain Area at Ayodhya Act, 1993; thus, in total 69.773 acres (28.24 hectares) will be now used for the temple compound (see Fig. 5). The present city area of Ayodhya is 69.76 sq km, but will be expanded to 872.81 sq km under the ongoing Master Plan for 2041, and the Rāma Temple will be the major landmark and a distinct symbol of Hinduism.

The first phase of construction of the Rāma Temple was scheduled in March 2020; however, the COVID-19 pandemic lockdown had caused a temporary suspension of the construction. But the temple construction has started with a grand ground-breaking ceremony on 5 August 2020, and attended even by the Prime Minister of India, Narendra Modi as a token of tribute and testimony to grant assurance to their cultural diplomacy and promises to the rejuvenation of the historicity of holy-heritage city of Ayodhya under the banner of Hindu nationalism. Anand's (2018: 112) remarks are noteworthy here, 'Reflections on the changing views of religious travel to Ayodhya offers an important new avenue to appreciate the tractability of place to renewal and reinvention—and the vulnerability of India's religious heritage to the agenda of Hindu nationalist politics'.

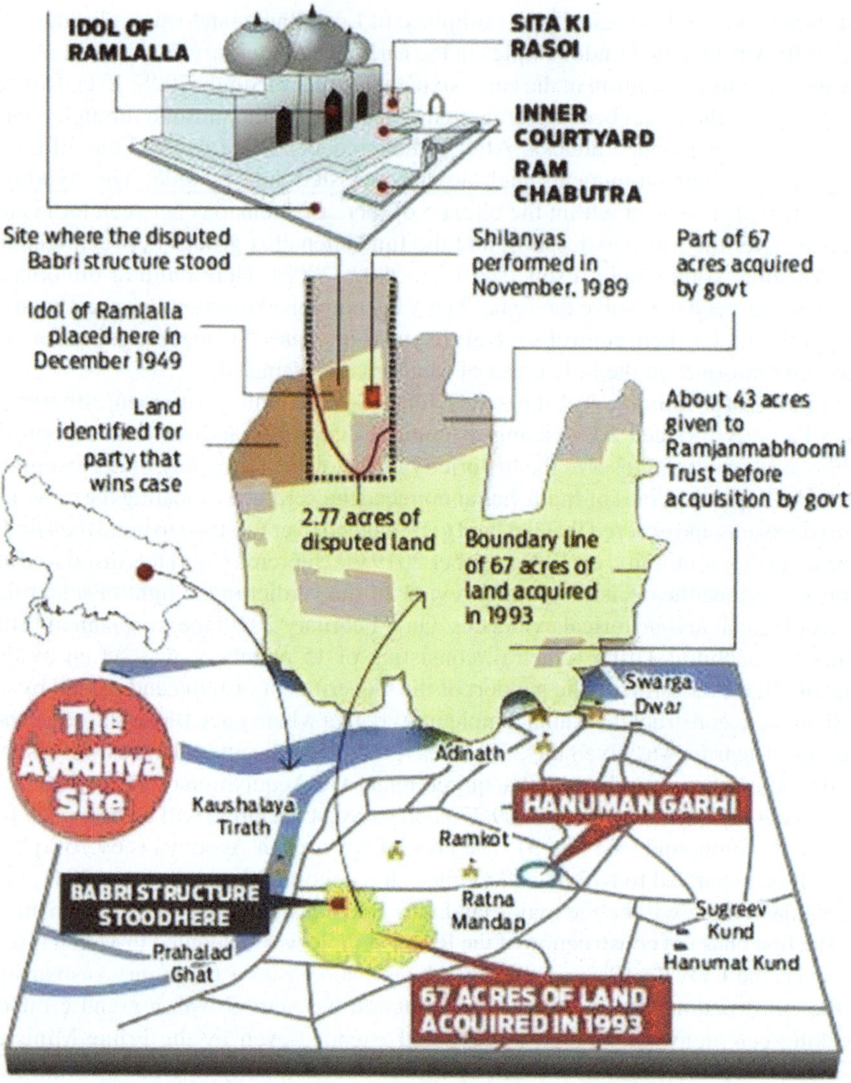

Fig. 5 Ayodhya, Rāma Janmabhumi; once contested, now under rejuvenation

6 Vishvanatha Temple, Varanasi: Representation vs. Contestation

The city of Varanasi, also called as Banaras and Kashi (25° 14′–25° 22′ lat. and 82° 56′–83° 03′ long., spread over an area of 83.60 sq. km, and populated with ca 1.6 million people), eulogised as the cultural capital and one of the seven salvific cities is known as the city of Lord Vishvanatha (Shiva), the patron deity. It is believed that the first temple of Avimukteshvara (later called Vishvanatha) was built around sixth century in the north-eastern part of the city, i.e. Rajghat, but in passage of time was completely deserted (Motichandra, 1985: 93). It again came to light in early seventh century (2nd site) that continued till CE 1194. During her reign Bibi Razzia (1236–1240) had built a mosque on the deserted site of Vishvanatha temple, which had been earlier demolished by Aibak in ca 1194. This mosque erected over the dismantled Vishvanatha temple, shows an act that effectively 'islamicised' a site particularly the most holy to the Hindus (Rötzer, 2005: 53).

By the end of the thirteenth century the Vishvanatha temple was rebuilt in the compound of ancient Avimukteshvara and existed till the next destruction (of course partial) under the rule of the Sharqi kings of Jaunpur (1436–1458). But in 1490 Sikandar Lodi completely demolished it. Only after a gap of about ninety years, in ca 1585–1590 with the support of Todar Mala, one of the senior courtiers of Akbar, the great scholar and writer Narayana Bhatta (1514–1595) had rebuilt it again, most likely on the structural plan of the previous temple of the thirteenth century (cf. Singh, 2009: 77). In 1669 even this temple was demolished by the order of the bigot Mughal emperor Aurangzeb, and today the Jnanavapi mosque stands on its site. As it would have been only a little additional trouble for Aurangzeb to order the demolition of the entire temple, one can only assume that the back portion was consciously spared as a warning and insult to the feelings of the city's Hindu population (Michell, 2005: 80). And, only a century later on 25 August 1777 by the patronage of Queen Ahilyabai Holkar of Indorethe present temple of Vishvanatha was completed (cf. Fig. 6). Ahilyabai's temple typifies the revivalist idiom that spread across north India during the course of the eighteenth century (Michell, 2005: 81). During late eighteenth century 'building fabric is being gradually dismantled and replaces with speculative multi-storeyed apartment blocks; [here] the clientele is affluent retirees, seeking absolution as well as modern amenities in Kashi [Varanasi]' (Desai, 2019: 75). Many shrines and temples have been built or re-constructed in the vicinity as a result of spatial transposition, and also several old ones revitalised under patronage of landlord and kings. Consequently, a mass of illegal encroachments and buildings grown up on the name of serving Vishvanatha, and within the houses shrines were constructed and folk mythologies superimposed to raise the image under upward mobility. The priests living there created and manipulated such stories and emotionally persuaded the devout and innocent pilgrims.

By nineteenth century the whole area surrounding Vishvanatha temple became a sanctuary of gods and godlings attached to Lord Shiva and his family, which to be broadly categorised into three groups, vis. historical-cultural old temples and shrines (including even some replicas) described in the *Purāṇas* dated up to ca seventeenth century, royal and patronised shrines and temples belonging to late eighteenth to nineteenth centuries and known for their architectural grandeur, and those built by private owners or priests and somehow added as part of the ancient glories (see Fig. 7).

From time to time, movements and confrontations were recorded to bring back the ancient glory and religious landscapes of Hindus, but could not be succeeded mostly due to suppression in the Mughal period and later in the British colonial

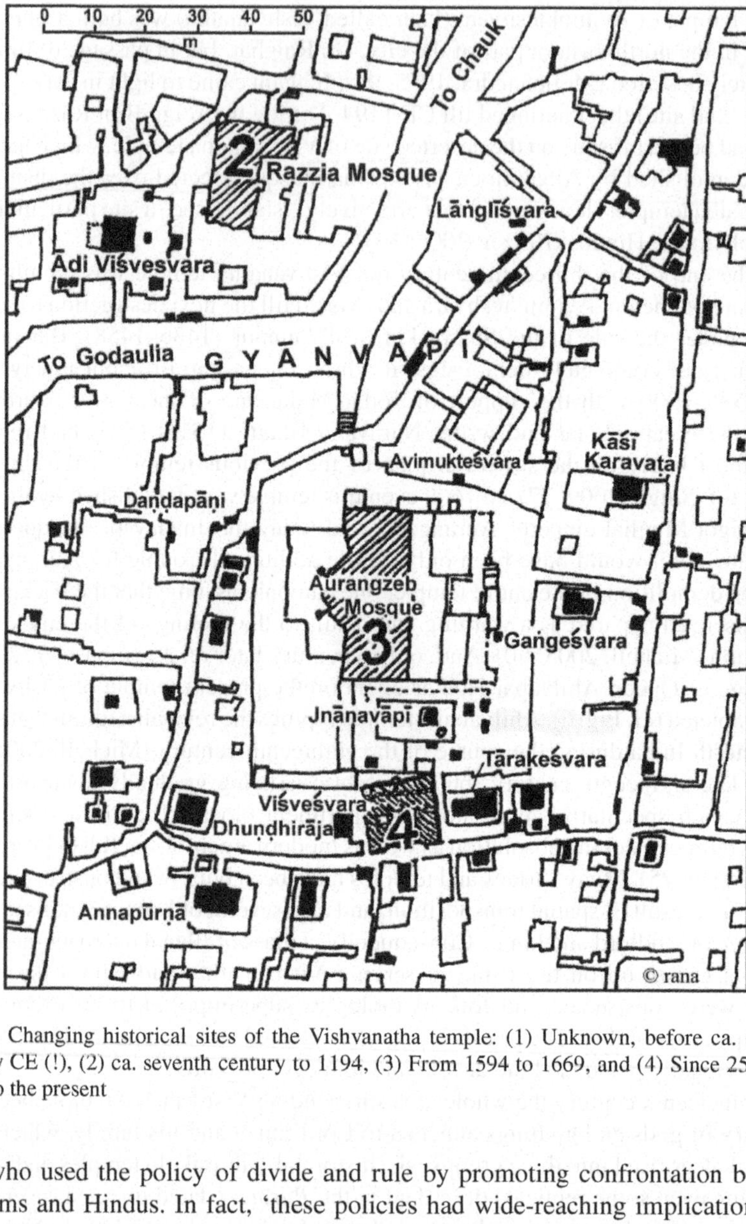

Fig. 6 Changing historical sites of the Vishvanatha temple: (1) Unknown, before ca. seventh-century CE (!), (2) ca. seventh century to 1194, (3) From 1594 to 1669, and (4) Since 25 August 1777 to the present

rule who used the policy of divide and rule by promoting confrontation between Muslims and Hindus. In fact, 'these policies had wide-reaching implications, and accounts by mid-nineteenth-century Indian visitors, such as Jadunath Sarvadhikari, who visited the city in ca 1854, reveal an affinity for exclusionary identities based in religious polarization' (Desai, 2019: 74). In Sarvadhikari's view, the Jnanavapi precinct, along with other religious sites in Varanasi, had once belonged to 'Hindus', and therefore had to be wrested away from 'Muslims', with the support of the colonial government (Sarvadhikari, 1915: 441). It is noted that immigration to Varanasi for

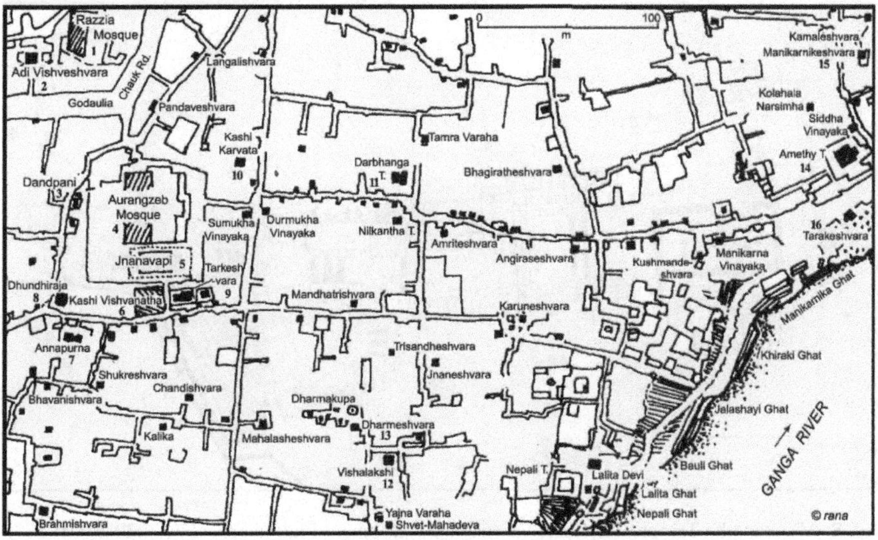

Fig. 7 Vishvanatha Temple and environs, Varanasi: as existed till 2017

religious and economic reasons has led to a marked heterodoxy of the city in general. It simultaneously provides a potential trigger for confrontation and at the same time, due to the sheer variety of backgrounds of the immigrants, a dilution of the potentially polarising communal solidarities (see Dumper, 2020).

After destruction of mosque in Ayodhya on 6 December 1992, the temple of Vishvanatha has caught attention to get its surrounding area cleaned and re-establish its prominence in the religious arena. This is strongly supported under the ideology of Hindu nationalism and cultural diplomacy. In the same vein, like Ayodhya, the present government planned to develop the Vishvanatha temple territory (*kshetra*) as a special area with modern facilities and open spaces, after getting cleaned the narrow lanes and congested and haphazard settlements (see Fig. 8, compare Fig. 7). Through the ambitious plan of promoting heritage tourism by replacing pilgrimage-tourism, under cultural diplomacy, a mega project of worth cost Rs 6 billion (equals to US Dollar 770 million) has been started with the approval of the state and the central governments on 8 March 2019, and projected as 'dream project' of the Prime Minister Narendra Modi under Smart City and Heritage Making programme. Under this project already 280 houses and shops were razed to ground, of course most of them rehabilitated but in a poor condition together with losing their identity, social interaction, and cultural harmony. The vision refers that 'the idea behind the project is similar to the ambitious redevelopment of many historical cities of the world like Paris [in the 19th century], where ghettos were removed'; however, it is completely neglected that the city and this area have been an unique image and personality of 'spirituality and pilgrimage'—no way tourism as almost all the domestic visitors are pilgrims or devout Hindus. All these developments are structured to superimpose

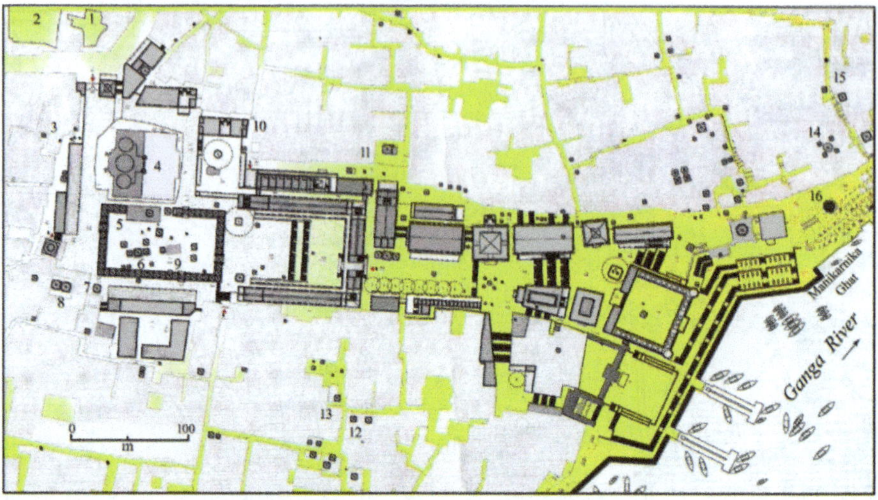

Fig. 8 Vishvanatha Temple Territory, Varanasi: Development Plan in progress, 2020–2021

'*heritagization*' through making a model of modernised Neo-Hinduism that will please the western tourists and rich neo-liberal Hindus.

7 Cultural Diplomacy and Development Missions

Under the premises of cultural diplomacy and revival of Hindu Nationalism, the Ministry of Tourism and Culture, and Ministry of Urban Development, Government of India, have recently conceptualised two appropriate national programmes of interfacing and counter-depending missions of (i) *Heritage city Development and Augmentation Yojana* (HRIDAY), and (ii) *Pilgrimage Rejuvenation And Spiritual Augmentation Drive* (PRASAD). These missions aim to strengthen and promote the heritage sites and centres of pilgrimage-tourism in making the environment green and sustainable while befitting into the roots of culture, traditions, and society. The three major sites selected at priority level, include Varanasi, Mathura, and Ajmer. Under the banner of new government in Uttar Pradesh (19 March 2017) an agreement between GOI Ministry of Culture and Tourism and the government of U.P. has been made on 24 March 2017 to develop and transform the twelve cities as special sites for heritage and religious tourism in India, including fives from U.P., viz. Varanasi, Ayodhya, Mathura, Gorakhpur, and Agra. Special plans are in process preparing conservation and rejuvenation of heritage and religious sites in these cities (Singh & Rana, 2019: 168).

The National mission on the '*Heritage city Development and Augmentation Yojana*' (HRIDAY), aims to conserving and preserving the distinct and unique characters of the *heritage cities*, those continued their traditions of heritage (tangible, intangible, transitory, and cultural landscapes). They would be used as a resource for sustainable development and ecological restoration on the line of achieving the SDGs (Sustainable Development Goals). The strategy of SDGs also includes cleanliness, planning, livelihood of the local people, economy, and cultural traditions.

Aiming to beautify and improve the amenities and infrastructure at pilgrimage centres of all faiths, a National mission on '*Pilgrimage Rejuvenation And Spiritual Augmentation Drive*' (PRASAD) has been announced in the Union Budget 2014–2015 and an amount of Rs. 1000 million (US$ 15 mill.) has been proposed for this initiative. Under PRASAD the old historical-cultural pilgrimage routes and associated sites would also be developed through pilgrimage-tourism as strategy for heritage awakening, deeper experiences, and transferring the religiosity into global humanism and spirituality (cf. Singh et al., 2020b: 78–79).

8 Concluding Remarks: Envisioning Cultural Diplomacy

The use of cultural diplomacy and related policies in India have a dubious history, of course, but it has been successful in cultural dispersal and making heritage representation, especially in southeast and east Asia. The recent in-practice India's 'Act East policy' is slowly becoming Act Indo-Pacific policy under the present government and successfully placed the Indo-Pacific at the heart of its engagement with the countries of south, southeast, and east Asia. Prime Minister Modi's philosophy of '*Sabkā Sāth, Sabkā Vikās, Sabkā Vishvās*' ('Together with all, Development for all, the Trust of all') is now the frame of cultural diplomacy on the path towards sustainability (cf. De, 2020). This philosophy is on the line of ancient cultural ethics that says: '*Udāra charitānām tu Vasudhaiva Kutuṁbakaṁ*' ('for open mind the whole world is a family', as in the *Maha Upanishad* 7.72, and the *Hitopadesha* 1.3.71, texts belonging to ca CE second to third century). In this sacred verse '*Udāra charitānām*' refers to the cultural diplomacy for welfare and peace to the whole world through realising the essence of interconnectedness of the world.

Under the umbrella of Universal Forum of Cultures 2007, emphasising the base of Developing Civility, Culture, and Sustainable Development is structured into three models, i.e. (a) Culture *in* sustainable development, (b) Culture *for* sustainable development, (c) Culture *as* sustainable development (Dessein et al., 2015: 29); here the role of cultural diplomacy and associated policies becomes vital. Let us think of cosmic integrity in the present era of 'Great Transition', as quite rightly expressed that 'We have explored seven evolutionary choices at the foundation of a future of Great Transition: *aliveness, consciousness, maturity, reconciliation, communication, community, and simplicity.* Taken together, these choices can take us along a pathway of healing and wholeness, enabling us to establish ourselves as an enduring species—civilization that can evolve into the deep future' (Elgin, 2020: 155).

References

Anand, D. (2018). Appropriating Ayodhya on "Valor Day": Hindu nationalism and pilgrimage as politics. In A. M. Pinkney & J. Whalen-Bridge (Eds.), *Religious journeys in India: Pilgrims, tourists, and travelers* (pp. 91–116). Albany: SUNY Press.

Bakker, H. T. (1986). *Ayodhyā: The history of Ayodhyā from the 17th century BC to the middle of the 18th century*. Groningen, the Netherlands: Egbert Forsten.

Basham, A. L. (2005). *The wonder that was India: A survey of the history and culture of the Indian sub-continent before the coming of the Muslims* (5th ed.). New Delhi: Picador India.

Beal, S. (1906). *Travels of Fa-Hian, The Mission of Sung-Yun and Hwei-S?ng* (Books 1–5). Kegan Paul, Trench, Trübner & Co. Ltd., London. Reprinted, Hill Publication, London (2009): pp. 29, 318–350.

Birch, E. L. (2015). Measuring U.S. sustainable development. *Cityscape: A Journal of Policy Development and Research, 17*(1), 223–232.

Boesche, R. (2003, January). Kautilya's Arthasastra on war and diplomacy in Ancient India. *The Journal of Military History, 67*(1), 9–37.

Choong, S. K. (2011). *Voices of foreign brides: The roots and development of multiculturalism in Korea*. New York: Alta Mira Press.

Collins-Kreiner, N. (2010). The geography of Pilgrimage and tourism: Transformations and implications for applied geography. *Applied Geography, 30,* 153–164.

De, P. (2020). *Act East to Act Indo-Pacific: India's Expanding Neighbourhood*. New Delhi: K.W. Publishers Pvt Ltd.

Desai, M. (2019). The Vishweshwur temple and Gyan Vapi mosque: Entangled histories in Banaras. In M. Dumper (Ed.), *Contested holy cities: The urban dimension of religious conflicts* (pp. 63–80). London and New York: Routledge.

Dessein, J., Soini, K., Fairclough, G., & Horlings, L. G. (Eds.). (2015, May 8). Culture *in*, *for* and *as* sustainable development: *Conclusions from the COST action IS1007 investigating cultural sustainability*. Jyväskylä: University of Jyväskylä. https://www.culturalsustainability.eu/conclusions.pdf. Accessed 21 June 2020.

Dhawan, R. K. (2017). Korea's cultural diplomacy: An analysis of the Hallyu in India. *Strategic Analysis, 41*(6), 559–570.

Dumper, M. (2020). Hindu-Muslim rivalries in Banaras: History and myth as the present. *His, power, piety, and people: The politics of Holy cities in the twenty-first century* (pp. 157–196). New York: Columbia University Press.

Elgin, D. (2020). *Choosing earth: Humanity's great transition to a mature planetary civilization*. Duane Elgin (personal), Woodacre, CA.

Elst, K. (2002). *Ayodhya: The Case against the Temple*. New Delhi: Voice of India.

Elst, K. (2003). *Ayodhya, the finale: Science versus secularism the excavations debate*. New Delhi: Voice of India.

Gupta, D. K. (2000). *Trade in ancient India* [*Prachin Bharat Mein Vyapar & Vanijaya Ka Vivechnatmak Adhyayana*]—From Indus Valley Civilization to Gupta Period College Book Depot, Kanpur. [in Hindi].

Harvey, D. (1979). Monument and myth. *Annals of the Association of American Geographers, 69*(3), 362–381.

ICOMOS (2016, November 24). *Mission and activities for 2017–18: Focal point for the UN sustainable development goals, agenda, and 'heritage as driver of sustainability'*. https://www.icomos.org/images/DOCUMENTS/Secretariat/2016/ICOMOS_Focal_Point_for_SDGs_112016/ICOMOS_FP_SDG_Memo_201611241.pdf. Accessed 3 May 2017.

Jain, S. (2015). *Determining India's role as a World Heritage Committee Member, UNESCO (2011–2015)*. Special lecture "Women in Architecture organised by SPA, New Delhi" on June 6. https://www.zingyhomes.com/latest-trends/world-heritage-committee-unesco-role-of-india-member/#:~:text=1%2C%202011%20was%20recognized%20as,2011.

Kumar, S., & Singh, R. P.B. (2017). Ayodhyā, the holy city of India: Riverfront and a Place of Indo-Korean interfacing symbolic Landscapes. *Sthāpatyam, Indian Journal of Architecture and Art, 3*(6), 61–74. ISSN: 2349-2368.

Lenczowski, J. (2009). Cultural diplomacy, political influence, and integrated strategy. In M. J. Waller (Ed.), *Strategic influence: Public diplomacy, counterpropaganda, and political warfare* (pp. 74–99). Washington, DC: Institute of World Politics Press.

Lowenthal, D. (1998). *The heritage crusade and the spoils of history.* Cambridge: Cambridge University Press.

Majumdar, R. C. (1963). *Hindu colonies in the Far East.* Firma K.L. Mukhopadhyay, Kolkata. Originally published in 1944.

Michell, G. (2005). Temple styles. In G. Michell & R. P. B. Singh (Eds.), *Banaras, the city revealed* (pp. 78–91). Mumbai: Marg Publications.

Motichandra. (1985). *Kāśī kā Itihās* (History of Kashi) (2nd ed.). Bombay. Vishvavidyalaya Prakashan,Varanasi.

Mukherjee, R. K. (1957). *Indian shipping: A history of the sea-borne trade and maritime activity of the Indians from the earliest times* (2nd ed.). Calcutta: Orient Longmans.

Pathak, M. (2018). *Commerce and boat-sailing in ancient India.* Faizabad: Shrinkhala Publishing House. [in Hindi].

Rhys Davids, T. W. (1903). *Buddhist India.* New York: G.P. Putman's Sons.

Rosenfield, J. M. (1967). *The dynastic art of Kushana.* Berkeley and Los Angeles: University of California Press.

Rötzer, K. (2005). Mosques and Tombs. In G. Michell and R. P. B. Singh (Eds.), *Banaras, the city revealed* (pp. 50–65). Mumbai: Marg Publications.

Said, E. (1993). *Culture and imperialism.* New York: Vintage Books.

Sarvadhikari, J. (1915). *Tirthabhramana ('Pilgrimage Tour').* Kolkata: Bangiya Sahitya Parishad. [in Bengali].

Simon, D., et al. (2016, April). Developing and testing the urban sustainable development goal's targets and indicators—A five-city study. *Environment & Urbanization, 28*(1), 49–63.

Singh, R. P. B. (1995, June). Heritage ecology and caring for the earth: A search for preserving harmony and ethical values. *National Geographical Journal of India, 41*(2), 191–218.

Singh, R. P. B. (1997). Sacredscape and urban heritage in India: Contestation and perspective. In B. Shaw & R. Jones (Eds.), *Contested urban heritage: Voices from the periphery* (pp. 101–131). Brookfield USA, Singapore, Sydney: Ashgate.

Singh, R. P. B. (2008). The contestation of heritage: The enduring importance of Religion. In B. Graham & P. Howard (Eds.), *Ashgate research companion to heritage & identity* (pp. 125–141). Aldershot Hamp. & London: Ashgate.

Singh, R. P. B. (2009). *Banaras, making of India's heritage city.* Planet Earth & Cultural Understanding Series, Pub. 3. Newcastle upon Tyne UK: Cambridge Scholars Publishing.

Singh, R. P. B. (2015). Heritage value of religious sites and built archetypes: The scenario of hinduism and illustrating the riverfront Varanasi. [A special address in the ICOMOS-UNESCO Conference, Seoul, Korea: 24 April 2015]. *Aatmbodh, the Journal of Knowledge of Self* (ISSN: 0972-1398), 12 (1), Spring: 1–23.

Singh, R. P. B., & Kumar, S. (2019). Interfacing cultural landscapes between India and Korea: Illustrating the memorial of Korean queen HEO in Ayodhya. *The geographer 66*(2), 109–120. (Aligarh Muslim University Geographical Society, Aligarh, India).

Singh, R. P. B., & Rana, P. S. (2002). *Banaras Region: Spiritual and Cultural Guide.* Varanasi: Indica Books.

Singh, R. P. B., & Rana, P. S. (2011). Heritagescapes of India: Appraising heritage ecology. In R. P. B. Singh (Ed.), *Heritagescapes and cultural landscapes* (Planet Earth & Cultural Understanding Series, Pub. 6 (pp. 87–128). New Delhi: Shubhi Publications.

Singh, R. P. B., & Rana, P. S. (2019). Visioning cultural heritage and planning: Banaras, the cultural capital of India. In V. Bharne & T. Sandmeier (Eds.), *Routledge companion of global heritage conservation* (pp. 152–176). Abingdon, Oxen, UK: Routledge, Taylor & Francis.

Singh, R. P.B., Kumar, S., & Rana, P. S. (2020a) UN SDGs and context of Heritage cities in India: A study of Ayodhya and Varanasi. In S. Sahdev, P. B. Singh, & M. Kumar (Eds.), *Geoecology of landscape dynamics*. Advances in Geographical and Environmental Sciences (pp. 187–206). Singapore: Springer Nature Pte Ltd.

Singh, R. P. B., Rana, P. S., & Kumar, S. (2020b). Intangible dimensions of urban heritage: Learning from holy cities of India. In K. D. Silva (Ed.), *The Routledge handbook on historic urban landscapes of the Asia-Pacific* (pp. 275–293). London & New York: Routledge.

Sinha, A. (compiled, ed.) (2014, December). *Ghats of Varanasi on the Ganga in India: The cultural landscapes reclaimed*. Urbana, IL, USA: University of Illinois.

Thaper, B. K. (1989). Agencies for the preservation of cultural heritage in India. In B. Allchin, F. R. Allchin, & B. K. Thaper (Eds.), *Conservation of the Indian Heritage* (pp. 164–168). New Delhi: Cosmo Publications.

Thussu, D. K. (2013). The historical context of India's soft power. In D. K. Thussu (Ed.), *Communicating India's soft power* (pp. 45–71). Series in Global Public Diplomacy. New York: Palgrave Macmillan.

Vajpayee, K. D. (1966). *Foreign trade in ancient India [Prachin Bharat ka Videsh Vyapar]*. Jaipur: Rajasthan Academy. [in Hindi].

Algeria and Its Heritage: Inventory of the Various Heritage Policies, from the Pre-colonial to Colonial and Post-colonial Times

Nora Gueliane and Kaouther Bouchemal

Abstract The question of heritage in Algeria is a crucial issue waiting to be addressed. For, despite its historical roots, Algerian heritage remains little known and valued. The first heritage policies emerged during the colonial period (1830–1962). After the country's independence (1962), a policy of oblivion/omission—and a rather selective one—was practised by the supporters of a conservatism that is still alive today. This manifested itself in the falsification of a secular identity, neglecting in some cases and overvaluing in others, to give more vigour to a particular ideology. The purpose of this article is therefore to examine the interest aroused by the question of heritage by addressing the various policies that have been implemented against it. In order to do this, we thought it appropriate to consider a plan that is articulated into two parts, according to a chronological order that starts from the pre-colonial and colonial period, to the post-independence era.

1 Introduction

The question of heritage in Algeria is a crucial issue to be addressed. Indeed, despite its historical roots, Algerian heritage remains little known. This is partly due to a policy of omission practised after independence (1962), during the socialist period. A period marked by a totalitarian regime with ideological references that saw to the Arabization of the land. The heritage policy of this period was a mixture of neglect and falsification in support of the dominant official policy. These practices are still alive today, which has caused the degradation of Algerian heritage (Guerroudj, 2000).

Algeria has been part of history since the earliest antiquity. It has known the accumulation of several civilizations: Amazighs, Europeans and Arab-Muslims. This is attested by a wealth of archaeological remains, literary, epigraphic and numismatic

N. Gueliane (✉)
Mouloud Mammeri University, Tizi Ouzou (UMMTO), Tizi Ouzou, Algeria
e-mail: nora.gueliane@ummto.dz

K. Bouchemal
Paris Nanterre University (Paris 10), Nanterre, France

O. Niglio and E. Y. J. Lee (eds.), *Transcultural Diplomacy and International Law in Heritage Conservation*, https://doi.org/10.1007/978-981-16-0309-9_16

sources, as well as numerous sites and monuments. The first texts describing Algeria, its landscape and monuments were written by authors of antiquity (Pliny, Strabo or Titus Livius) and from the eleventh century onwards by travellers and Arab authors of the Middle Ages (Ibn Hawkel, El Bakri, El Idrisi, Ibn Khaldun, Ibn Batutta). And even accounts of captives (evoking the description of cities and their monuments), and later maps of Algeria, drawn up by the Spanish and the French, evoked the presence of monuments located all over the Algerian territory. However, there were no precise descriptions of these monuments. It was only with the French colonization (1830) that the sources of a scientific historiography began to be available and an exploration of the country with a scientific concern was set up.

In our remarks, we wanted to examine the interest aroused by the question of heritage by addressing the various policies that have been implemented against it. Here we mean historical heritage. In order to do this, we thought it would be appropriate to consider a plan that is divided into two parts, according to a chronological order starting from the pre-colonial and colonial period, to the post-independence era.

2 Heritage and Its Management During the Pre-colonial and Colonial Periods

Before colonization (1830), the notion of heritage was understood in a different way than it is today. From 1830 onwards, the status of the colony and the organization of the Algerian territory into provinces, then into French departments, gave rise to legislation that was strongly inspired by that which prevailed in France—apart from that governing the individual status of the indigenous people. Consequently, the management of heritage, when it comes to historic monuments, has been moulded into the philosophy of French legislation.

Pre-colonial Algerian culture maintained a privileged relationship with memorials and funerary monuments dedicated to illustrious figures (heroes and saints)—for example, the tombs of Numidian kings, or marabouts such as Sidi Boumediène in Tlemcen—but gave little importance to all those who were not in phase with Arab-Muslim civilization. There was much more interest in heritage perceived through its spiritual aspect, based on the essence of objects, knowledge, genres and rhythms of life, than in objects as such. However, this certainly did not imply a total disinterest in the material heritage, since even at that time, care was taken to maintain the property of value to the community, such as mosques and the property of zawiyas (religious brotherhoods), which were given the status of habous or waqf (Mainmortal property).

In addition, the reuse of elements from earlier eras was commonplace. In pre-colonial houses, for example, it was not surprising to find a Roman capital or column. In fact, the reuse was not based on sensitivity to this heritage, but simply for purely aesthetic reasons. While bearing in mind that traditional societies generally had cultures, ways of life, which meant that preservation was not an issue. The desire to last over time, to transmit a heritage, of a value if possible equivalent to that received, was such that, barring disaster, the value of the heritage was maintained (Guerroudj, 2000). To say that the concept of heritage was therefore not in line with its modern-day meaning. As defined by Western society, the concept was introduced during the French occupation and underwent the same developments as in France. As such, Françoise Choay defines heritage—speaking of historical heritage—as "a fund intended for the enjoyment of an enlarged community with planetary dimensions and constituted by the continuous accumulation of a diversity of objects that their common belonging to the past brings together: works and masterpieces of applied fine arts, works and products of all human knowledge" (Choay, 2007: 9).[1]

With the colonization of the country (1830), the heritage policy met a different fate. Thus, given the heterogeneity that characterized that era, which began in 1830 and ended in 1962. It seemed to us judicious to spread the study over chronological phases, in order to better understand the heritage policies adopted.

2.1 Period from 1830 to 1880

During the first years of the conquest, the metropolis faced hesitations about the fate to be reserved for the new possession, especially about the status to be granted to it. It was a period of political instability that brought chaos, disorder and anarchy. Vandalism was perpetrated by the military and settlers. The administration, preoccupied with the demands of colonization, does not react to this situation. In spite of some reactions, such as the one noted in a report of the Africa Commission in 1833: "… since our occupation, 80 fountains have ceased to give water in the city, the pipes, so skilfully made and so carefully maintained under the Turks, have suffered the sad effects of indiscipline, of the taste of destruction of our soldiers, of the negligence of the administration…" (Oulebsir, 2004: 80). In the early years of the conquest, archaeological excavations were authorized for anyone who requested them. Individuals or groups of individuals, with no concern for the conservation of the pieces collected. The goal was to make a fortune. At that time, the word "antique relics" was not used by the administration—rather the word "precious objects" was used to designate treasures, medals, etc.Similarly, when excavations were organized, the first sketches, drawings and surveys were carried out by soldiers who had no experience in the field of archaeology.

The construction of a new French identity, a new way of life imagined, designed and adapted for and by the new masters, are elements that have been marked by a series of radical actions on space, on the fabric of the medinas and on ancient sites. These actions have materialized in destruction and reconversion. In a word: a radical

[1]"Un fonds destiné à la jouissance d'une communauté élargie aux dimensions planétaires et constitué par l'accumulation continue d'une diversité d'objets que rassemble leur commune appartenance au passé: œuvre et chefs d'œuvre des beaux-arts appliqués, travaux et produits de tous les savoirs des humains" (Choay, 2007: 9).

transformation of the urban heritage.[2] In this regard, we cite the work carried out in 1831 in Algiers by military engineers, and the reconversion in 1832 of the Ketchaoua[3] mosque to the Saint-Philippe cathedral. That of the use of ancient sites as quarries of inexpensive materials, such as the amphitheatre of Rusicade, which disappeared completely in 1845 and whose stones were used for the construction of the rampart of Philippeville in[4] 1839. These acts of vandalism were accompanied by deportation. For example, after his mission to Constantine in 1839, the Duke of Orleans, fascinated by the ancient remains of the region, recommended transferring a large part of them to the Louvre Museum in Paris. Among the remains transferred, the famous marine mosaic of the triumph of Neptune and Amphitrite stands out. Moreover, restoration, as a discipline, only came into being in Algeria late, around 1880, with the creation of the Department of Historic Monuments (Service des Monuments Historiques). Thus, the operations, at the beginning of colonization, were carried out by military engineers or by civil architects (Algiers appointed its first civil architect in 1832) who did not master restoration techniques, and without a sufficient budget.

In spite of the situation described, voices were raised to denounce acts of vandalism and to advocate measures for the protection and conservation of the heritage. But not just any measures. These are, essentially, the Roman remains of which the French settlers saw themselves as heirs. Concerning the heritage of the Moorish Middle Ages, its claim came a little later, around the 1880s.

This valorization started with the scientific exploitation of Algeria. In 1831, Captain Claude Antoine Rozet sent a letter to the President of the Academy of Inscriptions and Beautiful Letters of Paris "l'académie des inscriptions et belles lettres de Paris" to announce discoveries in Algiers. This prompted the Ministry of War and Public Education to collaborate with the academy and conduct research in order to get to know the country better. Thus, on 14 August 1837, the scientific commission of Algeria was created. A ministerial decision very soon officially instituted the commission in charge of research and scientific exploration in Algeria. The commission had scientific and artistic objectives, but also military intentions. The commission relied on works by ancient and Arab authors, and drawings by amateur soldiers. It followed the path of the army. Exploration extended over the period between 1840 and 1845. It focused mainly on the ancient, Roman and Byzantine remains, apart from some medieval religious buildings, which were of inestimable value. Two figures marked this commission, Amable Ravoisie and Adolphe Delamare. The work of the commission was sent to the metropolis, selected according to priority and sanctioned by a publication.

In addition to the scientific exploitation, other clues pointed to an awareness of heritage. In 1843, a letter from the Minister of War was sent to Marshal Bugeaud to give him instructions to bring the conservation of Algeria's ancient monuments into

---

[2]The cities most affected by these transformations are Algiers, Oran and Constantine. These have seen the space of their medinas shrink and give way to new buildings in the classical style.

[3]Built in the Ottoman period and protected by the convention of 4 July 1830, signed by Bourmont at the time of the capture of Algiers.

[4]French name of the town of Skikda, named after King Louis-Philippe.

line with the practices known in France since 1819. A first circular was issued by the marshal on 20 January 1844, asking for precautions to be taken in places containing antiquities. It was followed by another, dated 25 March 1844 and addressed to the various heads of services informing them of the new provisions for the conservation of ancient monuments, but unfortunately these decisions were not applied. In the same year (1843), the post of architect of the civil buildings of Algeria (Architecte des Bâtiments Civils de l'Algérie) and of the civil buildings and roads service (Service de Bâtiments Civils et de la Voirie) (1843–1872) was created. Its mission was the construction of new public buildings and the restoration of ancient monuments.

By decree of 12 November 1850, the government made other commitments, defining them as follows: "the construction, restoration and maintenance of monuments, buildings and public buildings of all kinds are the responsibility of the government, with the exception of diocesan buildings and edifices, the restoration and maintenance of state buildings and those of indigenous corporations, and the conservation and restoration of ancient monuments" (Oulebsir, 2004: 97). Tasks were reserved at the beginning of the conquest for the French army and military engineers. In 1845, the post of Inspector General of Civil Buildings in Algeria was created. The incumbent of this post was responsible for the conservation of historic monuments, identifying them and proposing guidelines for their conservation, organising local museums, reporting on excavations to be undertaken and inspecting building sites. The first to hold this post was Charles Texier.[5] A decree, issued on 12 October 1845, entrusted the custody and description of Algeria's monuments to the Inspector General of Civil Buildings. It is completed by the decree of 27 January 1846 which stipulates: "the research, observation and description of ancient monuments are placed within the remit of the Inspector of Civil Buildings without distinction of territory. In accordance with the decision of 12/10/1845, the conservation and restoration work of these monuments is carried out on civilian territories, under the direction and care of the Civil Buildings Service" (Oulebsir, 2004: 97). Finally, a ministerial circular, dated 31 December 1858, encourages the preservation of antiquities in their site of origin.

This period was also marked by the creation of learned societies. They are one of the consequences of the scientific commission of 1840–1845, which brought to the forefront of the rich heritage in Algeria. These societies became involved after noting the absence of the government concerning the preservation of historical monuments in Algeria. Initially, around 1841, it was the learned societies of the metropolis that designated one of their divisional members for Algeria. The decision was announced as follows: the council, considering that there exists in Algeria a large number of ancient inscriptions and debris, several of which have been mutilated and used in new constructions, and that it is important to seize any opportunities that may arise to stop such damage, decides that a divisional inspector should be appointed, and several inspectors to ensure, as far as possible, the conservation of such debris.

Proposals having been made to M. de Brix, inspector of the Norman association, newly appointed Advocate General at the Royal Court of Algiers, this honourable magistrate agreed to take on the duties of inspector of the society and to take, in

[5]The profile corresponding, in France, to the Inspector General of Historic Monuments.

concert with M. Berbrugger, librarian of Algiers, all the measures which will be necessary to obtain the conservation of the debris whose destruction is regretted every day (Oulebsir, 2004: 103). Later, several local learned societies appeared, as a sign of the reappropriation of the heritage by the colonists. As well as with the aim of creating a new identity, in the image of the learned societies of France. Their role was research, study and knowledge of monuments, their protection and, of course, the publication of research carried out, for example, the Society of Letters of Algiers (Société des Lettres d'Alger), the Algiers Science Society (Société des Sciences d'Alger) (1847), the Algiers Archaeological Society (Société archéologique d'Alger) (1848), the Constantine Archaeological Society (Société archéologique de Constantine) (1852), the Hippone Academy (Académie d'Hippone) (1863), the Algerian Historical Society (Société Historique Algérienne) (1856), the Society of Geography and Archaeology of Oran (Société de Géographie et d'Archéologie d'Oran) (1878).

Finally, this phase was marked by the creation of the General Inspectorate of Historic Monuments and Archaeological Museums of Algeria. It was entrusted to an inspector residing in Algiers, Louis Adrien Berbrugger, curator of the library and museum of Algiers. His role is to carry out regular inspections of Algerian antiquities in order to gain a better knowledge of the listed remains. He is responsible for indicating the localities that hold important vestiges, ensuring their protection, preventing ancient sites from becoming quarries for cheap materials, pointing out monuments to be protected from vandalism and proposing means for their conservation, as well as he acting as an intermediary between the various local museums.

We conclude that the first period of colonization is marked by a contradiction. On the one hand, there were acts of vandalism and a hesitation towards Algeria's historical heritage. On the other, a will to safeguard it thanks to efforts that were made, but weakened by the demands of colonization. Efforts marked by their punctual, selective and radical nature and not part of a general programme of the colonial administration. A large number of decrees and recommendations had no effect. As an example, one can point to the statement of Heron de Villefosse in 1873: "its loss [...] proves once again how useless are the decrees and ordinances of the general government concerning the antiquities discovered in Algeria" (Oulebsir, 2004: 217). On the other hand, the idea of heritage was very quickly integrated, especially among settlers wishing to settle permanently in Algeria. The latter wanted to build an "Algerian" identity, unearthed in the past and engraved on the monuments of this conquered land. This was done in total neglect of the indigenous population, dissociated from the Algerian landscape of the time. The seeds of the transformations appeared between 1860 and 1880, after Napoleon III's visits to Algeria. His instructions in favour of the heritage and the indigenous people favoured the emergence of a civil society.[6] It was during this phase that Algiers was transformed from a military city to an urban city. This was due to the proliferation of shops and the implementation of major projects, such as the Boulevard de l'Emtrice, which changed the face of Algiers. Likewise, special interest has been given to the natives and to Arab-Moorish art—it goes hand in hand with an interest in orientalism in the metropolis. This interest was further

[6]In 1870, a civilian Governor-General was appointed in Algeria.

strengthened by the mission of Edmond Duthoit,[7] who provided a deeper knowledge of the Moorish heritage.

2.2 *Period from 1880 to 1930*

A period characterized by relative stability and the founding of state institutions. Likewise, heritage became one of the main concerns of the local administration. Algiers, which was formerly under military rule, has become a civilian territory. As a result, it experienced increased development, both economic and urbanistic. The period was marked by the creation of the large schools (les Grandes Écoles). The Algiers Higher School of Fine Letters (L'École Supérieure des Belles Lettres d'Alger) (law of 20 December 1879), a high place of contact between Algerian institutions and those of the metropolis (Paris). The School of Fine Arts (École des beaux arts) (1881), directed by the architect Gaston Redon. As well as other institutions that saw the advancement of sciences, such as archaeology, drawing techniques and restoration processes, fields related to heritage management. In 1880 the service of historical monuments and the post of chief architect of the historical monuments of Algeria were created.

In addition, an operational heritage approach, programmed by the administration of fine arts, has been introduced. The influence of the Moorish tradition in the design of official architecture is well received. The clear desire to preserve the ancient and Arab heritage—expressed by the Ministry of Public Education and Fine Arts—has led to a heritage policy in Algeria on a par with that established in France. From 1896 to 1900, political reforms led to a certain decentralization; Algeria gained more and more autonomy, thanks to the law of 19 December 1900 which gave the country a civil personality and financial autonomy. Algeria sought to forge its identity based on local heritage references, in particular by adopting a local architectural style: neo-Moorish.[8]

It was during this period that the Department of Historical Monuments was created in 1880, it is based on the activity of the chief architect of historical monuments. It was marked by two figures: Edmond Duthoit, whose appointment took place in 1880, then Albert Ballu in 1889. This department was responsible for the classification of historic monuments of interest to Algeria, the adaptation to the local context of the principles of restoration applied in France, organising and directing excavation work, studying and consolidating monuments and proposing solutions for their restoration. An initial listing of monuments, the state of their conservation and the necessary

[7] Appointed in 1872 as an architect attached to the Historical Monuments Commission. His mission was to study the Arab monuments, their condition and the work to be carried out.

[8] An architectural style adopted in Algeria from the beginning of the twentieth century, under the rule of Charles Célestin Jonnart. It is based on the borrowing of elements belonging to Arab-Andalusian architecture: arches, domes, chiselled stucco, massive carved doors, earthenware and mosaics, Koranic inscriptions. The most emblematic monument of this style is the great post office of Algiers.

interventions were drawn up on the basis of the work of Duthoit and the proposals of learned societies and archaeologists.[9] The post of chief architect of the historic monuments of Algeria has held an important place in France since 1830. It was introduced in Algeria in 1880, far from the repairs and maintenance that marked the first decades of the conquest. Missions are entrusted to restoring architects using the most recent restoration techniques. The chief architect carried out his duties from the metropolis with an annual inspection in Algeria. It was not until 1927 that the chief architect carried out his duties from Algiers.

In addition, several museums were created after the conquest. The museum of Algiers which came to be in 1838, that of Constantine in 1852, of Tlemcen in 1857, of Cherchell in 1840, then those of Oran, Tébessa, Bône (Annaba). These museums only served the role of a simple depository for the objects found during the excavations. They are characterized by inefficiency, poor conservation conditions, lack of space, unqualified staff and repeated removals, which have facilitated the disappearance of objects and theft or simply the sale of objects by mayors. Similarly, the Algiers Museum, which played the role of a central museum, did not escape this situation. To this effect, Arsène Alexandre confides on the subject of the museum function in Algeria "… better the total absence of a museum than the existence of museums such as those in Oran and Philippeville" (Oulebsir, 2004: 184). For his part, the German archaeologist Johanne Schmidr also shares his impressions: "In the museum of Tébessa, I noticed the absence of a large number of inscriptions collated by Wilmanns […]. The museum in Bône […] is now in a state of complete disorder and dissolution […]. From what has happened so far, sending something to the Bône Museum is tantamount to destroying it. The most distressing spectacle is given to us by Constantine […], almost half of the inscriptions that were there before are certainly missing" (Oulebsir, 2004: 184).

This is due to the fact that, at the beginning of the conquest, the administration concentrated on the excavation and restoration of the monuments. While it gave less importance to the conservation of objects and the conditions under which museums operated. It was not until 1880 that the situation of the museums improved with the arrival of certain curators, such as Prud'homme at the Constantine Museum, William Marçais at the Tlemcen Museum, and the preparation of catalogue booklets—which became compulsory from 1880 onwards to avoid the loss of collections.

[9]Initially, the classification was done in metropolitan France, under the authority of the Ministry of Public Education and Fine Arts, on the advice of the service in Algeria. The governor subsequently acquired the possibility of classifying monuments by means of an order.

2.3 *Period from 1900 to 1954*

This period is characterized by the search for a new political and cultural identity and, at the same time, by a return to Algeria's Latin roots to justify its colonization by France. It is also a period in which the legal texts forcefully express the intentions of the government towards heritage.

The supporters of colonial power wanted to forge a new conception of colonial Algeria, a way of asserting the country's autonomy from the metropolis. They loudly proclaimed the achievements of the first half of the twentieth century, while alluding to a conciliation between natives and colonists: intensive development in all areas, with major construction sites and the expansion of trade. This is the image of a modern, young and united country that the colonial authority tried to give the world. The celebration of Algeria's centenary in 1930 was accompanied by major construction projects, by festivities in all fields and by the staging of the Algerian heritage and the achievements of the colonial administration in this field. Algeria's centenary "should show the work accomplished by France in a country that a century ago was abandoned to barbarism" (Oulebsir, 2004: 28). In the 1930s, heritage also became a symbol of "exaltations of Latin roots" and a support for an ideological discourse of "French Latin Algeria", an idea developed by Louis Bertrand, accompanied by a return to ancient heritage and its enhancement: "if Rome had its cradle in Italy, if it exercised its new strength there and founded its first splendours, it was in Roman Africa, in the first three centuries of our era, that it gave its greatest effort and found its full blossoming as a civilizing nation, in this country, which not only fuelled it with wheat and soldiers...but also provided it with administrators, scholars, orators and poets, it projected its enlarged reflection and perfectly realized its ideal of order, prosperity and peace" (Oulebsir, 2004: 283). Louis Bertrand evokes some great names, such as Saint-Augustin, and points out the similarities between Algeria and the other European countries of the Mediterranean (Italy, Spain and southern France). The aim was to link Algeria to its Latin roots, a way of legitimizing the colonial presence (the heirs of Rome). The moment of the centenary takes us away from the concerns of heritage management, but the archaeological excavations have not been stopped. However, at the same time, the Algerian intellectual class began to mobilize. An elite, who had been trained in French schools, tried to claim the rights of the indigenous people through political resistance until early 1954. Then came the outbreak of the war of liberation (1954) and with it the whole freeze on work in favour of heritage.

Turning now to the legislation that marked this phase. There are four texts. The law of 30 March 1887 relating to the conservation of monuments and objects of art of historical and artistic interest. This law is composed of two parts: on the one hand, the sacredness of private property that must be respected. On the other, its dispossession when the artistic and historical value of certain monuments and objects is confirmed. The classification affected much more the properties of the government. As the law is applied with caution to private property, classification is optional. The Historical Monuments Commission gives its opinions when applying the law. Article 16 of the law refers to its application in Algeria: "in this part of France, the ownership of objects of art or archaeology, buildings, mosaics, bas-reliefs, statues, medals, vases, columns, inscriptions, which may exist on and in the soil of buildings belonging to the State or conceded by it to public establishments or private individuals, on and in military grounds, is reserved to the State" (Oulebsir, 2004: 219).

The Historical Monuments Act of 31 December 1913, on the conservation of monuments and objects of art of historical and artistic interest. Its objective is to restrict the constraints caused by private property and to benefit the general interest in the preservation of objects and monuments. The innovation of this law lies in the classification of private property without the owner's consent. Article 36 advocates for Algeria "the adoption of public administration regulations governing the modalities of its application to this territory" (Oulebsir, 2004: 220). Made applicable in Algeria by decree 14 September 1925, this law made it possible to protect objects and buildings, even privately owned, from any inappropriate intervention, sale or transfer outside the national territory. Measures may be taken by the Governor-General—after advice from the Department of Historic Monuments—ranging from the temporary or definitive removal of an object considered to be under threat. The Law of 12 April 1906 on the Protection of Natural Sites and Monuments promulgated on 21 April 1906. Its Article 6 applies its various provisions to Algeria. It was through this Act that a commission for the protection of natural sites and monuments of an artistic nature was established and that several natural sites were classified. Lastly, the Act of 2 May 1930 on the protection of natural monuments and artistic, historical and picturesque sites. It is applicable to Algeria under Article 29. It provides for the possibility of classifying a natural monument or site without the consent of the owner. It also specifies the conditions under which a protection zone may be established around a historical monument or natural site (Oulebsir, 2004: 223).

3 Algerian Heritage Policy Since Independence (1962)

During the first three decades of independence (1962), the question of heritage was not taken into account in all its reality. It was perceived in a simplistic way. Indeed, the ideology that prevailed during this period removed several parts of the country's history from its discourse. In particular the history of Algeria before the Islamization of North Africa. Thus, and for political considerations, it gave more vigour to the supporters of Arab nationalism who always put forward the Arab-Islamist cultural referent. It was not until the 1990s, when the country made a liberal choice in its political system, that this rhetoric was given a rest. Thanks, among other things, to the dynamics set in motion by associations working in the field of heritage. Taboos were lifted and people "dared" to rehabilitate illustrious figures from antiquity, such as Saint Augustine, Archbishop of Hypone (Annaba), whose work revolutionized the Catholic Church, or Apuleius, a famous writer of Latin script. In any case, it is the legislative texts that provide the best information on how the question of heritage is dealt with by the public authorities.

During the first years of Independence, administrative services continued to be managed by texts resulting from colonization. Indeed, for reasons of continuity of operation, a law of December 1962 extended all laws drawn up by the French administration—when their provisions did not run counter to national sovereignty. The texts relating to the heritage fell within this framework. However, the management of the latter very quickly changed hands, insofar as the Direction des Beaux-arts, Monuments et Sites Historiques (Directorate of Fine Arts, Monuments and Historic Sites) was transferred from the Ministry of the Interior to the Ministry of National Education. The latter, as early as 1967, drew up the first ordinance relating to excavations and the protection of monuments, historic and natural sites. This was Ordinance 67–281 of 20 December 1967, relating to excavations and the protection of historical and natural sites and monuments. The basic ordinance is issued by ministerial order after the opinion of the National Commission for Monuments and Sites, and is based on French legislation that lays down the regulations concerning excavations and historic and natural monuments and sites. Thus, it announces the measures to be taken for the protection and intervention on historic and natural monuments and sites and determines the criteria and procedure for classification. It defines the modalities relating to the various forms of alienation of private property if it hinders the public interest. This ordinance was the only reference for cultural heritage management in Algeria until 1998.

Subsequently, the 1970s saw the emergence of a ministry dedicated to culture and information. It is the central body that hosted the Direction des Musées, de l'Archéologie et des Monuments et Site Historiques (Directorate of Museums, Archaeology and Historic Monuments and Sites). This directorate was later reorganized to bring together three sub-directorates: museums, archaeology and historic sites and monuments. In order to avoid the stagnation of centralized heritage management, the state has created several bodies spread throughout the national territory. However, they remained under the supervision of the Ministry of Culture and Information. They consist of National Parks, Offices, National Museums and Study Workshops. However, during a whole decade, a total disinterest in heritage, whatever its nature, has been noticeable. It is only from the year 1980 onwards that a renewed interest in it was perceived, notably through the proliferation of legislative texts. These include the decree of 17 May 1980 on authorizations for archaeological research. This decree prohibits archaeological research on the national territory without the permission of the Ministry of Culture and Information. They must be carried out with the participation of the services in charge of archaeology of the ministry in question and their results must be published in the scientific collections of the services in charge of archaeology or in other national editions. The 1983 Ordinance allowing for the protection of unclassified sites—until 1983, only the Kasbah of Algiers was the subject of a rehabilitation programme, thanks to the capital status enjoyed by the city where it is located- It offers the possibility of intervention in an urban area provided that it is adapted to urban functions. These interventions must be included in the Master Urban Development Plan (PUD).

We also have Decree 87 of 6 January 1987 creating the National Agency for Archaeology and Protection of Historic Sites and Monuments (l'Agence Nationale d'Archéologie et de Protection des Sites et Monuments Historiques). A public establishment of an administrative nature under the supervision of the Ministry of Culture. The decree that allowed its creation stipulates in its Article 3 that, within the framework of cultural development throughout the national territory, "the Agency is in charge of all the actions of inventory, study, conservation, restoration, enhancement and presentation to the public of the national historic cultural heritage" (Article 3 of decree 87 of 6 January 1987 in the Official Gazette). Act No. 90/09 of 4 April 1990 on the wilaya and Act No. 90/08 of 7 April 1990 on the commune, through which the Wilaya (State) and the Commune (Municipality)[10] are responsible for safeguarding the heritage and supervising rehabilitation, restoration and renovation operations. Thus, Article 83 of the wilaya code stipulates that the People's Assembly of the wilaya is called upon "to support the communes in implementing their housing programmes and, in this connection, to participate in renovation and rehabilitation operations in consultation with the communes" (Act No. 90/09 of 4 April 1990, Official Gazette, 4 April 1990). Article 93 of the commune code defines the tasks incumbent on the commune, in terms of the protection of the architectural heritage: "the preservation and protection of sites and monuments, because of their vocation and historical value. The safeguarding of the aesthetic and architectural character and the adoption of the homogeneous type of housing in built-up areas" (Law 90/08 of 7 April 1990 of the Official Gazette of 7 April 1990). In addition, Legislative Decree 94/07 of 18 May 1994 on the conditions of architectural production and the exercise of the profession of architect. This decree was promulgated in order to update Ordinance 66/22 on the profession of architect and to fill an important legal vacuum, particularly in the field of the protection of architectural heritage. Its Article 1 determines its objective: "The purpose of this legislative decree is to set the framework for architectural production and to lay down the rules for the organization and practice of the profession of architecture. It also aims to promote architecture and to protect and preserve the urban heritage and the built environment" (Article 1 of Decree 94/07 of the Official Journal of 18 May 1994).

Finally, Law 98/04 corresponding to 15 June 1998 on the protection of cultural heritage, considered as the ultimate legislative framework for national heritage policy since 1998 and a real revolution (Dekoumi, 2007; Aouchal, 2013). Based on Ordinance 67/281 of 20 December 1967 on excavations and the protection of historic sites and monuments, it updates its content by adapting it to a new cultural vision. Among the key elements of the law are the appearance of the notion of cultural property, movable and immovable and for the first time the notion of intangible heritage, as well as the creation of safeguarded sectors. Article 17 of the Act reinforces the interest in intangible heritage: "Historic monuments are defined as any isolated or grouped architectural creation that bears witness to a given civilization, a significant evolution and a historical event. This includes architectural monuments,

[10]Wilaya is an administrative division, usually translated as State. The commune is The Algerian municipality a decentralized territorial collectivity. According to Article 15 of the Algerian constitution: "The territorial collectivities of the state are the commune and the wilaya …". the official website of the Ministry of the Interior: https://www.interieur.gov.dz/index.php/fr/41-organisation-des-collectivites-locales/94-la-commune.html.

paintings, sculptures, decorative arts, Arabic calligraphy, religious, military, civil, agricultural or industrial buildings or groups of monuments, prehistoric structures, funerary monuments, cemeteries, caves, rock shelters, cave paintings and engravings, memorials, structures or isolated elements relating to major events in national history.

They are subject to classification by order of the Minister responsible for culture after the opinion of the national commission for cultural property, on its own initiative or that of any other person with an interest in the matter. The classification order extends to buildings, whether built or unbuilt, located in a protection zone which consists of a visible relationship between the historic monument and its surroundings, from which it is inseparable. The field of visibility, the distance of which is fixed at a minimum of two hundred (200) metres, may be extended in order to avoid, in particular, the destruction of monumental perspectives included in this zone" (Article 17 of Law 98/04 of the Official Gazette of 15 June 1998).

Law 98/04, whose implementing texts were published in 2003, allowed the transition from centralized management to a logic of deconcentration of the sector by creating a Directorate of Culture in each wilaya (DCW). As well as several bodies whose objective is to deal with heritage, such as the National Agency for Safeguarded Sectors and the Office for the Management of Cultural Property. It has given impetus to the preparation of a sectoral master plan for culture, which has been integrated into the national and regional land use planning schemes. This law was also at the origin of the institution of several management instruments, such as the permanent plan for the safeguarding and enhancement of archaeological sites and the plan for its protection. In 2006, it gave birth to the National Heritage Fund and, in 2012, to the Cataloguing Centre, which brings together all the data from the archaeological inventory.

Furthermore, in addition to laws, we raise the role of urban planning instruments in heritage policy. These are important in the urban and spatial planning of municipalities. They are of particular interest in the protection of historical and natural heritage sites. We mention the Plan Directeur d'Aménagement et d'Urbanisme (PDAU),[11] the plan d'Occupation des Sols (POS)[12] and the master plan.[13]

Concerning the actors of heritage policy and during the first three decades after Independence, only state institutions operated in the field of heritage. Today, civil society, through associations, has become a widely involved consultation body. The Ministry of Culture is the main operator in the field of cultural heritage with the bodies it has created—and are under its supervision. For the protection of heritage, it collaborates with the Ministries of Tourism, the Interior, Finance and Defence. For its policy, the Ministry relies on two directorates: la Direction de la Conservation et de la Restauration du Patrimoine Culturel (the Directorate for the Conservation and Restoration of Cultural Heritage) and la Direction de la Protection Légale des Biens Culturels et de la Valorisation du Patrimoine Culturel (the Directorate for the Legal Protection of Cultural Property and the Development of Cultural Heritage). The Directorate of Conservation and Restoration of Cultural Heritage is composed of three sub-directorates: the Sub-Directorate of Cultural Property Inventory, the Sub-Directorate of Conservation and Restoration of Movable Cultural Property and the Sub-Directorate of Conservation and Restoration of Immovable Cultural Property. The Directorate for the Legal Protection of Cultural Property and Enhancement of Cultural Heritage is composed of three sub-directorates: the sub-directorate for securing cultural property, the sub-directorate for research and enhancement of cultural heritage and the sub-directorate for legal control. In addition, there are a large number of bodies under the supervision of the Ministry of Culture. There are four research centres specializing in heritage (the Prehistoric, Anthropological and Historical Research Centre, the Arts and Culture Centre of the Palace of the Raïs, the National Centre for Manuscripts and the National Centre for Archaeological Research). Four offices specializing in tangible heritage (the Office for the Protection and Promotion of the Mzab Valley, the Office of the Ahaggar National Park, the Office of the Tassili National Park and the National Office for the Management and Exploitation of Protected Cultural Properties). Finally, 14 museums (the National Museum of Antiquities, the National Museum of Fine Arts, the National Museum of Popular

[11]PDAU is an instrument of spatial planning and urban management. It lays down the fundamental guidelines for the spatial planning of the municipality(ies) concerned. It defines the terms of reference of the land-use plan, taking into account all the development prospects of the municipalities. The fundamental orientations of the PDAU are based on principles of balance in the use of land (urbanization, activity…), but also of development and protection of certain spaces and landscapes, whether natural or urban (law n°90/29 of the official gazette of 1 December 1990 relating to town planning and development).

[12]The Plan d'Occupation des Sols (Land Use Plan) sets out in detail the rights of use and construction. It is based on the principle of dividing urban space into different land use zones. With regard to the protection and development of spaces and landscapes, it delimits particular sectors (districts, streets, monuments and sites to be preserved subject to special prescriptions, such as protection, renovation and restoration). (Law No. 90/29 of the Official Gazette of 1 December 1990, on town planning and development).

[13]The master plan is a new method of urban planning. It is used for the realization of projects that seem very important and complex, mainly in the field of urbanization and urban restructuring. An example is the master plan to restore the Medina of Constantine.

Arts and Traditions, the Bardo National Museum, the Cirta National Museum, the Nasr Eddin Dinet National Museum of Bou-Saâda, the Zabana National Museum, the National Museum of Setif, the National Museum of Illumination, Miniature and Calligraphy, the National Museum of Modern and Contemporary Art, the National Museum of Maritime Art, the National Museum of Tébessa, the Regional Museum of Chlef and the National Museum of Khenchela).

Alongside the actions undertaken by the state and fruitful cooperation with foreign partners, associations play an important role in preserving and safeguarding the tangible and intangible heritage. One example is the Bel Horizon association in Oran, which works to safeguard the historical heritage of Oran. L'association des amis du musée de Cirta (The Association of Friends of the Cirta Museum), in Constantine, which is active in the safeguarding and enhancement of Algerian heritage. L'association des amis de l'Ahaggar (The Association of Friends of the Ahaggar) which aims to enhance and develop the historical and cultural heritage of Ahaggar. The latter organizes every year the international festival of Tin Hinan (Antinéa) in Tamanrasset to celebrate the heritage of the Tuaregs.

4 Conclusion

In Algeria, the treatment of the question of heritage has evolved according to the different political circumstances that the country has undergone, from the French conquest to the present day. The colonial period was marked by the most far-reaching upheavals. The practices towards the Algerian historical heritage first resulted in massive destruction of the urban fabric by the conquerors in order to transplant the European architectural model. At the same time, vandalism was perpetrated here and there on sites of ancient history. As well as a relentless transfer of ancient art objects to France. But as the political situation became more stable, practices towards the heritage changed in character, and regulations and institutions, similar to those in the metropolis, were established for its protection, conservation and presentation. However, these actions have been accompanied by a desire to recover a certain identity, in the sense of reappropriation of Algerian heritage by the new arrivals. This was done in order to justify the conquest, by making the country's Latin roots prevail, and by setting aside all that was linked to the so-called indigenous population.

After independence, Algeria's policy towards its heritage was based on purely legislative criteria. Indeed, the Ministry of Culture relied on complex legislation to govern mainly tangible heritage. It was only in the 2000s, however, that renewed interest was shown in the intangible heritage. A heritage that has been greatly altered by changes in people's way of life. Some of its aspects have been banished from memory, while others are perpetuated: celebration of rites, music, singing, culinary arts and clothing.

References

Aouchal, H. (2013). *Pour une reconnaissance politique et sociale des valeurs des abords du patrimoine bà¢ti en Algérie. La basilique St-Augustin et ses abords à Annaba.* Université de Constantine 3, mémoire de Magistère.

Choay, F. (2007). *L'allégorie du patrimoine.* Paris: Seuil.

Dekoumi, D. (2007). *Pour une nouvelle politique de conservation de l'environnement historique bâti algérien: cas de Constantine.* Ph.D. thesis, Constantine, Constantine University.

Guerroudj, T. (2000). La question du patrimoine urbain et architectural en Algérie. *Insaniyat*, n.12, 31–43, https://doi.org/10.4000/insaniyat.7892. Accessed 5 July 2020.

Oulebsir, N. (2004). *Les usages du patrimoine: Monuments, musées et politique coloniale en Algérie (1830–1930).* Paris: La maison des sciences de l'homme.

The official website of the Ministry of Culture: https://www.m-culture.gov.dz/index.php/fr/textes-juridiques-patrimoine-culturel/loi-et-textes-d-application. Accessed 5 July 2020.

The official website of the Ministry of the Interior: https://www.interieur.gov.dz/index.php/fr/41-organisation-des-collectivites-locales/94-la-commune.html. Accessed 5 July 2020.

The official website of the official journal: https://www.joradp.dz.

On the Edge of Protection: Motives for Migration

Meltem Vatan

This chapter is dedicated to the people who had very difficult life experience ended up with a journey to the unknown, called a home land... The only desire was to protect their culture and identity...

Abstract Cultural identity can be influenced by migration movements that have a strong effect on the formation of a nation. Inevitably, the transformation of cultural identity as a result of immigration for both ends—immigrants and homeowners—is a clear truth. This study aims to explore the influence of migration on cultural identity as a psychological and social process. Particular attention is paid to the migration of the Turkish minority living in Bulgaria to scrutinize formative forces of identities and the motives of the migration process aiming at the protection of cultural identity. This study is especially concerned with immigration to "homeland" for the protection of cultural identity. In particular, migration activities in the 1970s and beyond as well as their causes will be explored. Immigration to Turkey of the Turkish population in Bulgaria, despite being a well-known subject, there is very little scientific research on this theme.

1 Introduction

"I picked up the stuff, I got the package,
I cried out and cried out,
This depart, yearning broke me up
Mountains, stones, homeland lamented for us,
All the vacant houses cried for us."
(Anonymous Bulgarian folk song with the theme of immigration)

M. Vatan (✉)
Faculty of Architecture and Design, Bahçeşehir University, Istanbul, Turkey
e-mail: meltemvatan@gmail.com

O. Niglio and E. Y. J. Lee (eds.), *Transcultural Diplomacy and International Law in Heritage Conservation*, https://doi.org/10.1007/978-981-16-0309-9_17

There is a mutual dependence between culture and identity which brings together tangible and intangible values to form a nation. Cultural identity can be influenced by migration movements that have a strong effect on the formation of a nation, although it is based on a common geographical location, history, culture, ethnicity, and so on. The mutual interaction of different communities and individuals as a result of migration brings metamorphosis for both ends—immigrants and homeowners. A new community is born with its cultural identity that has changed over the years based on mutual interaction.

Migration is defined by Erder (1986) as "all displacements realized over a meaningful distance and amount of time until effectiveness is realized." To find a better place, to find a new job opportunity, to escape from a conflict area or war, etc. there are many different motives and forms of migrations. While the intentions are different, the common basis of migration is to move from one place to another for permanent life. Therefore, without a matter of reason, it is obvious that individuals or communities who experience migration are affected spiritually and materially.

The Balkan Peninsula was one of the places that the Ottoman Empire ruled for hundreds of years. Therefore, migration between the Balkan Peninsula and the so-called Turkish land is part of the Turkish history. The Turkish nation has interacted with the Balkan Peninsula and its culture, which has had a strong influence on the formation of its cultural identity since the Ottoman Period for both ends. Tüzünkan (2019: 19) states that throughout its history, the intention of the Ottoman Empire was settling Muslim communities in the newly conquered lands where the minorities and non-Muslim people were allowed to live according to their traditions. Cultural interaction has become a reality as a result of sending natives to newly conquered places. Therefore, cultural identity was formed based on intercultural relationships. The Turkish population living in Bulgaria is one of the clear proofs of this cultural interaction and the creation of cultural identity.

The lands of so-called Bulgaria was ruled by the Ottoman Empire for almost 500 years, 1393–1878 (Lütem, 2000: 16). So, the conquest of Bulgarian land by the Ottomans is dated back to the late fourteenth century and the independence of Bulgaria is at the end of Russo—Turkish War (1877–1878). Cultural interaction between the Bulgarian and Turkish ethnic groups during the Ottoman rule in Bulgaria existed, although the Ottoman Empire did not force the Bulgarian people to change their religion or cultural traditions. Cultural interaction between two different populations was simply based on the share of daily life. After the independence of Bulgaria, most of the Turkish population moved back to so-called Turkey lands; however, approximately 10% of this population stayed in Bulgaria. Until the 1970s they were protected by law as a Turkish minority by having the right of their religion and language. After the 1970s the new political aspect was targeted assimilation of the Turkish minority (Şimşir, 1989; Crampton, 1989).

This study aims to discuss the status of the Turkish minority living in Bulgaria. Particular interest is given to the motives of immigration of Bulgarian Turkish population until 1984 and the dramatic change that took place in 1984–1989 period. The change of Turkish minority rights depending on the political decision and the political aspect of assimilation of cultural identity will be discussed as one of the main motives of immigration. Immigration to Turkey of the Turkish population in Bulgaria, despite being a well-known subject, there is very little scientific research on this theme. This study is especially concerned with the issue of cultural identity and immigration to "homeland" for the protection of its cultural identity. It aims to discuss the protection of cultural identity as the main motive of migration. The focus is migration movements of Turkish minority lives in Bulgaria (from Bulgaria to Turkey). In particular, migration activities in the 1970s and beyond and their causes will be explored.

2 Formation of Cultural Identity and Its Protection

There are a lot of studies and definitions about identity. However, the aim and the scope of this study is not about identities. However, the purpose and scope of this study are not related to identities. Culture and identity are important to understand the motives of immigration such as protection of cultural identity. Collective memory and ethnicity are two important characteristics of the identity phenomenon.

According to Eminoğlu (2019: 118) shared historical experiences in the common geographical region is defined as collective memory and it is connected to ethnicity. Therefore, the protection of collective memory is an act of protecting identity. This study is dealing with the demand for immigrating to protect cultural identity based on ethnicity. Ethnic identity and religious belief are two parts of key importance for cultural identity. Especially, the minorities in any country could preserve their identities within the limits of their rights and freedom of living their culture, speaking their mother language, and having freedom for their religion. This particular study is an example of thc results of assimilation actions to the Turkish minority in Bulgaria and the attitude of the minority people to preserve their identity. The loss of cultural identity is inevitable when a community is prohibited from speaking its language and having its original names. Halit Aliosman Dağlı (Köse, 2001) explains this with a short poem:

I didn't know in which language I would cry
In what language I would laugh
I did not know how to find my friends in memories.

This poem explains very well the feeling of Turkish minority people when speaking in Turkish was forbidden and their names were changed to the Bulgarian ones. They lose their dignity, culture, and, identity.

Massive migrations are very important for shaping cultural identity, especially, for the host country. Mutual interaction between immigrants and their host brings transformation on cultural identity which is an inevitable result even if the integration of the newcomers is at a minimum level. According to Tüzünkan (2019), the data from the Ministry of Interior Affairs shows that immigration since the second half of the nineteenth century played a significant role in ethnic changes in Anatolia as well as of cultural identity. In particular, migrations from Bulgaria during 1878–1989 effected on the Turkish population. A large part of the immigrants was educated and having a profession or occupying a craft. So, they had a strong effect on the development of the country.

3 The Case of Turkish Minority in Bulgaria

The Turkish population living in Bulgaria is part of the so-called Rumelia Turks. Due to the rule of the Ottomans for nearly 500 years, the Turkish minority in Bulgaria has always existed throughout its history. This study is dealing with the Turkish minority living in Bulgaria and it is limited to the independence from the Ottoman period and 45 years of the Republic of Bulgaria periods (1878–1989).

The administration of the Ottoman Empire was based on decentralization which means each state has its governorate (Tüzünkan, 2019: 21). Due to the large geographical spread, a multi-ethnic and multi-religious approach had been adopted in which not only Turks but also Bulgarians, Greeks, Albanians, Armenians, Jews, Arabs, and many other ethnic groups were settled. Kale (2014: 253) states that the settlements were formed by mixed Muslim, Christian, and Jewish ethnic groups, who were free in their languages, beliefs, and traditions. Besides, according to İnalcık (2001: 10), Turks from Anatolia were sent to newly conquered lands from the mid of the fourteenth century to support the expansion of the empire.

Bulgaria was conquered by the Ottomans in 1393 (Yıldırım, 2018: 28; Lütem, 2000: 16). In the fourteenth century, the population of Bulgaria decreased due to its history with many conflicts and battles. Therefore, the strategy of the Ottoman Empire was to send Anatolian Turks (natives) to newly conquered land to enhance security and safety in Bulgaria, which is on the road to Europe and close to Istanbul. Migration from Anatolia to Bulgaria took a long time with different accelerations (Lütem, 2000: 55). As a result in most of the Bulgarian settlements, from the sixteenth century to the nineteenth century, the Turkish population became more than half (Yıldırım, 2018: 30). Therefore, the interaction between ethnic groups lived in this area influenced the formation of their cultural identities.

As explained in the previous paragraphs, the rule of Bulgaria by the Ottoman Empire was during 1393–1878 and officially ended with the Russo-Turkish War (1877–1878). After its independence, Bulgaria established a principality and kingdom. The end of Russo–Turkish war can be expressed as the time when the speed of migration to Turkey by the Turkish minority living in Bulgaria has been increased. According to Tüzünkan (2019: 22) over a million Muslim Turks in Bulgaria immigrated to Turkey.

At the end of the war, the Treaty of Berlin was signed and the rights of Turkish minorities living in Bulgaria were mostly protected by this treaty. Turkish schools started to open again (Lütem, 2000: 57–58). After 1970 the Communist government imposes a program of cultural assimilation, whereby Turkish was no longer a tolerated language, Turkish instruction in schools was stopped, and it was not allowed to speak Turkish in public. A summary of the important dates and events related to the status and the rights of the Turkish minority to understand their social atmosphere, the mindset, and the desire to immigrate to Turkey as the homeland to protect their culture and identity is addressed in this sub-chapter.

A large part of the given data (about Turkish minority in Bulgaria) is based on the research and experiences of Ömer E. Lütem (2000), a Turkish ambassador in Bulgaria, who made a detailed study about the relationships between Turkey and Bulgaria during his mission (1983–1989).

3.1 Historic Review of the Rights of the Turkish Minority in Bulgaria

After the end of the Russo–Turkish War in the 1883s, Turkish schools belonging to the Turkish community in Bulgaria started to teach again and all their needs were provided by the fund of the Turkish community. The structure of Turkish schools was similar to the Ottoman ones and only Turkish was taught. However, the funding of the Turkish community decreased during and after the war, and it was even difficult to pay teachers' salaries and obtain the books. Over time, the oppression of the Bulgarian government on the Turkish community increased and in 1891 the Turkish schools started to be inspected by the government. Later on, in 1908 Turkish schools were forced to teach the Bulgarian language, history, and geography. On the other hand, getting a teaching position required Bulgarian citizenship and as a result transfer of Turkish native teachers from the Ottoman Empire was canceled. At the same time (1908), Bulgaria declared its independence which was ratified by the Ottoman Empire, and in 1913 mutual agreement between the two countries was signed. This agreement included the rights of the Turkish minority in Bulgaria (Lütem, 2000: 58–59).

With these formative forces on rights, the Turkish minority in Bulgaria has become more introverted and started to shape its community and the first signs of difficulty in protecting their cultural identity have been shown. At the same time, after the war (Russo–Turkish War), most of the educated and well-off part Turkish population immigrated to the Ottoman land (Tüzünkan, 2019: 28). To understand the conditions of the Turkish minority in Bulgaria important dates and circumstances regarding their rights and status are listed below.

- 1877–1878 the Russo–Turkish War: a large part of the Turkish population in Bulgaria immigrated to Turkey.
- 1878 Berlin Treaty: Turkish schools were opened and consequently the Turkish minority had the right to Turkish education.
- 1913 the treaty between the Ottoman Empire and Bulgaria. The Turkish minority had religious freedom.
- 1919–1934 government of Stamboliyski and his political party. The Turkish minority had the rights of Turkish education, Muslim religion, and traditions.

Although the Stamboliyski government was modest toward the Turkish minority, nationalist policies such as "Bulgaria belongs to the Bulgarian" emerged after the coup attempt (Tüzünkan, 2019: 28). As a result, the demand for immigration to Turkey increased (Yılmaz, 2013).

- 1925 the Treaty of Friendship and a Settlement Contract between Turkey and Bulgaria (Tüzünkan, 2019: 28). In this way, massive migration movements were avoided and the immigrants had the right to bring their goods and animals and to sell their immovable properties (Şimşir, 1986: 207). The treaty was signed as timeless which was the sign of endless peace and friendship between the two parties. So, according to Lütem (2000: 67) technically it still exists. Meanwhile, another agreement regarding residency and migration was signed and during 1923–1933 more than 100.000 people immigrated to Turkey.
- 1934–1944 the Fascist rule of Bulgaria. In this period, as the Latin alphabet was forbidden, Turkish rights were also ignored, and the Turkish people were forced to study with Arabic letters and religious education. Lütem (2000: 69) opinion on this decision is to suspend the Turkish minority from the modern Turkish Republic direction.
- 1944–1989 the Communism period. Turkish schools were connected to the Bulgarian Republic. One of the main consequences of this change for the Turkish minority was the revocation of the right to have its school, although the right to education in Turkish was revoked. Therefore, it can be said that the first signs of assimilation took place.
- With the increase of immigrations in 1947 Turkish government postponed the acceptance of massive immigration. However, the ones who had free immigrant visas were accepted and granted Turkish citizenship (Tüzünkan, 2019: 30).
- 1950–1951: as a result of the pressure of the communist government on the Turkish minority and the reduction of their rights, the Turkish population increased its demand to immigrate to Turkey. More than 150,000 Turks immigrated to Turkey and because of this large number of people, immigration was banned.
- 1946–1959: the number of Bulgarian classes in Turkish schools was increased and finally in 1959 Turkish and Bulgarian schools were united. Consequently, the Turkish population started to Bulgarian education including some additional Turkish classes (Lütem, 2000: 76).
- In 1968, based on the demand of the Turkish minority in Bulgaria to immigrate to Turkey, a special agreement was signed mutually between Turkey and Bulgaria. The main scope of this agreement was to define immigration conditions. Accordingly, only people who had relatives or siblings already immigrated to Turkey (before 1952) were allowed to immigrate. Migration activities based on this agreement proceeded until 1978.
- By the 1970s, assimilation politics was getting tougher. In 1971 the new constitution came into force where "the unified Bulgarian socialist nation" was addressed. In 1974, Turkish classes were assigned as electives and they could only be opened when there were enough participants. As a result, Turkish classes ended due to the insufficient number of participants (Lütem, 2000: 82).

- 1984–1989 period: the names of the Turkish population (even the names on the gravestones in the graveyard) were changed with the Bulgarian ones by force of the government. Turks who tried to resist were arrested or killed. Therefore, in many locations, clashes broke out between the Turkish population and the Bulgarian military forces (Köse, 2001). Consequently, to protect their cultural identity, the only way for the Turkish minority in Bulgaria was to immigrate to Turkey (Budak, 2010: 134).
- The last immigration from Bulgaria to Turkey took place in 1989 as the forced migration (Kirişçi, 2003; Tüzünkan, 2019: 31). People who emigrated were defined as Muslim Bulgarian citizens (the former Turkish minority) because since 1984 officially there were not any Turkish names in Bulgaria.

3.2 1984–1989 Period: Political Change in Turkish Minority Rights

1984 is the turning point of history for the Turkish minority living in Bulgaria. Since 1877–1878, Russo–Turkish war, the Turkish minority in Bulgaria had faced pressure and oppression regarding their culture and identity as part of assimilation politics. However, in 1984 the last step of this long process was done, the names of the Turkish population were changed with the Bulgarian ones, speaking in Turkish and living traditions of their culture were already banned. This decision was named "back to the race" (Lütem, 2000: 158–159). The Bulgarian government stated that there are no Turkish people in Bulgaria, only Bulgarian Muslims had changed their names voluntarily. Even though it was denied by the government, more prohibitions continued, such as changing names, restricting Turkish speaking, Muslim funerals, circumcising boys, and the like (Tüzünkan, 2019: 31). To demonstrate this denial common cemeteries for Turkish and Bulgarian people were assigned, ironically entitled as a cemetery of friendship. Because of the religious differences before the change of the names each ethnic group had its cemetery.

Taking the name of a person is to take his/her identity, culture, human rights… This was the feeling of the Turkish minority living in Bulgaria when cultural and identity rights were completely suppressed by the government in 1984. Many Turks who opposed the change were tortured, arrested, imprisoned (Belene), and killed. For this reason, each person of Turkish origin eventually got the new Bulgarian name, including the dead ones of their families.

One of the breakthroughs that have been made by the Bulgarian government was the new aspect of education. On one side, going to pre-school of all Turkish children was ensured to teach them Bulgarian language and to call them with their Bulgarian names. In the schools the scope was revised to include socialist and communist, Marxist-Leninist theories, patriotism, atheism, 500 years of Ottoman rule, praising Bulgarian culture and identity, and so on. In 1985, the new Family Code had ratified (Brunnbauer & Taylor, 2004) as the replacement of the previous one of 1968. The Bulgarian socialist model of the family as defined in this code.

Although rules and decisions were the same, their reflection and emotions were personal to everyone. Maybe the hardest part was for children, when the children went back to school they should be called by their new Bulgarian names. Understanding this condition is not easy for a child and as well as to be explained for the parents. The children were confused. Who am I? Am I a Bulgarian one or a Turkish one? If my parents say that we are Turks why I do not know to speak and read this language, why my teachers say that I should speak only in Bulgarian, otherwise I will be a bad child and my family will be badly punished?

So, it is obvious that the main target of assimilation politics were the children, they were like control of the adults. When a child feels fear it is very easy to control his/her family. Because none of the parents would take the risk for their children to traumatize them, the change of the names was enough tough. On the other hand, mostly Turkish people were interrogated individually with the claim that some of their close friends were messed up and they need to be careful to not contact them or to inform the militia about their action. The real meaning of these fake interrogations was everyone around you is suspicious, I am watching you, if you do not oblige to the new rules you will be tortured or imprisoned. Treat was the main tool of assimilation politics. Every Turk started to feel fear and to lose the trust of the friends and loved ones.

3.3 Forced Migration in 1989 and Adaptation to the "Homeland"

The reasons for the 1989 forced migration can be traced back to the 1950s where the change of political direction about the Turkish minority in Bulgaria has started. The first changes started with the decrease of Turkish classes, then the cancelation of Turkish classes, cancelation of Turkish schools, the prohibition of Turkish Speaking and living the traditions, doing religious rituals, and the last one was the change of the Turkish names forced by the government. This was the obvious showcase of assimilation politics.

Being considered as returning to the homeland, 1989 immigration to Turkey is a special case within migration types (Durmaz, 2019: 37). The president of Bulgaria, Todor Jivkov, made a call to the Turkish authorities (via national TV and Radio) to open the borders for Bulgarian Muslim citizens who wish to go to Turkey permanently or temporarily.[1] This speech was the flame of the last migration to Turkey in 1989. According to Lütem (2012: 145–149), within 2.5 months (June–August) in 1989 Turkey had experienced the densest migration in Europe since World War II (Tüzünkan, 2019: 31).

The daily life and integration of Turkish and Bulgarian people were rather far from the political decision, although 1989 immigration was forced by the Bulgarian

[1] Available at: https://www.youtube.com/watch?v=9Wgo1xmIEYo.

government and after 1984 the political aspect was changed dramatically in a negative direction to Turkish minority people living in Bulgaria. Turkish and Bulgarian people were living door to door together as neighbors. The friendship between two ethnic groups was proved almost by every immigrant. Bulgarian neighbors helped Turkish friends pack their belongings, proceed with their passport documents and other official requirements of the immigration process (Durmaz, 2019: 110). Some Turks also left their belongings to their Bulgarian neighbors hoping to come back and visit their friends again.

On the other hand, the condition and the process of immigration were quite different for all people. There was not any standard procedure. First of all, giving the passport for immigration was organized by the local governorates. So, it was a very personal decision. To have the right to sell the goods and properties and to collect money and take a piece of luggage, again was based on the decision of the local authority. Therefore, some of the immigrants were able to take their stuff and some of them arrived only in a suitcase (Durmaz, 2019: 111). The other side of the coin was the condition of the arrival at the Turkish border, also the process was based on the border forces. So, there was a mutual objective process of the immigration itself in both countries.

1989 migration was a forced migration. Therefore, people who experienced it had to leave their life, memories, friends, properties behind and to put all their stuff in a piece of luggage and straight ahead without looking back. When immigrants arrived in Turkey they were located in the immigrant camps or those who had some relatives or by their resources settled in temporal residences or were hosted as guests by the locals. Here, in this condition, the most important discourse is the adaptation process for both sides, the immigrant and the host. Although Turkish minority people from Bulgaria came to their homeland, there were huge differences between the two cultures. The reasons can be traced to the assimilation politics of Bulgaria, having different languages, being born in different countries and not having any contact before, and so on. Simply, there were two different nations and to trust each other, to accept each other was not easy. The local ones called immigrants as an immigrant, not with their names. So, the first border was constructed. This was the distance of communication and kind of discrimination which was an experience in all parts of life such as at the school, in the neighborhood, everywhere. Therefore, the experience of immigrants was to feel in between, to belong nowhere, and to be the other on both sides (Bulgaria and Turkey).

According to Durmaz (2019: 102), the noticeable fact of the results of assimilation politics of Bulgaria was the Turkish language capacity of the immigrants. Those who came in the 1950s could speak Turkish well and the new ones (1989) spoke Bulgarian very well, most of them knew some Turkish words very little, and especially the children did not know any Turkish word. Prohibitions and strong penalties regarding the Turkish language were the main reasons for the families to not use Turkish, especially after 1984, even in their homes. This fact can be defined as a deep trauma for people, to live the life in a fear of any penalty or more. Figure 1 shows an immigrant camp in Kırklareli (the personal experience of the author). In this kind of camp, the Turkish government assigned volunteer teachers to teach the Turkish

Fig. 1 Kırklareli immigrant camp–August 1989 (*Photo courtesy* Meltem Vatan)

alphabet and language to the newcomers, especially to the school children for being able to adapt to Turkey and to start school in the upcoming September. It is obvious that the first tool of communication is language, so knowing the language is a must.

4 Conclusion

Cultural identity is a strong connection and anchorage to be together and to feel unified for a certain group of people such as community, ethnic group, society, nation, and the like. Protection of cultural identity is based on a common shared base of languages, traditions, beliefs, religions, etc. One of the descriptive characteristics of cultural identity is the name given when a person is born. Blaga Dimitrova explains this as "…*Your given name!.. It is your face towards the world. The name of your father! Society acknowledges you with this name… Your last name (family name) is the one that connects you to your race (ancestors)… The ones who attempt to take your name and to change it with the new one assault your personality, your race, your dignity…*" (Köse, 2001).

Prohibition of speaking the mother language, living traditions, religion and beliefs, and finally the ban on own names are decisions that reveal the aspect of assimilation. Particularly, the statements of the Bulgarian government such as "the unified Bulgarian socialist nation" and "Bulgaria belongs to the Bulgarian" were the obvious pieces of evidence of this political direction. When these rights are taken from a population, there cannot be any community or cultural identity for that population. Turkish minority in Bulgaria has witnessed the history that cultural rights were banned every day (particularly after the 1970s) and there was not any other option than immigration to Turkey as the motherland for being able to stay as the one who they are, Turks. Therefore, continuous migration activities of the Turkish minority from Bulgaria to Turkey were based on the intention to protect cultural identity and ethnicity.

Immigration is a very hard decision for an individual or a group of people, to leave life and to start a new, completely unknown one… Migration brings mutual interaction for both ends because it brings tangible and intangible and material and spiritual cultural values together with the people. During the Ottoman Empire, people were free to live their ethnic origins and religions and lived together, depending on the administrative structure and political aspect of enlargement. The Balkan region included many different ethnic and religious groups. Based on this mutual interaction, the Balkan culture has been shaped for all communities such as Rumelia Turks. Therefore, the cultural identity of the Turkish minority living in Bulgaria was not as same as Turks living in Turkey.

The last immigration of the Turkish minority in Bulgaria took place in 1989 and it was an escape to freedom. The last generation of the Turkish minority in Bulgaria was born with Bulgarian names. The children did not know the Turkish language, and traditions, religious beliefs, Turkish culture were the history of a long time ago. These were clear results of Bulgaria's assimilation politics, although not accepted by the Bulgarian government. The purpose of this study is not to discuss politics or to criticize the Bulgarian regime. This study is only aimed at expressing the importance of speaking in the mother language, living traditions, having a religion, briefly having a culture… This paper is an intention to bring to the scene an own experience of the author to be an emigrant (from Bulgaria to Turkey—1989) and to discuss scientifically cultural identity and the fact of immigration to protect the culture of a community.

Although the main reason for the migration of some people belonging to the Turkish minority living in Bulgaria was to protect their culture and identity, this action has brought some other consequences to immigrants as well. Especially, there are many studies in the field of psychology and sociology such as attachment types, mentality and maturity, adaptation, etc.

As an immigrant, every person lives and feels their own experience, even though it is part of the same action such as forced migration. However, there are some common feelings for almost all immigrants. The case of this paper is immigration to Turkey as a motherland from Bulgaria to protect cultural identity. Although Turkey was defined as the motherland there were cultural differences between Turkey and Turkish people who emigrated from Bulgaria. These large differences can be explained in many different ways, here the personal opinion of the author is given.

- As a result of the Bulgarian assimilation politics, time and cultural characteristics for the Turkish minority people seemed to be frozen first, then completely ignored. In other words, the Turkish minority people in Bulgaria lived the life of the

Ottoman Empire, their spoken language, traditions, and religious rituals were based on the Ottoman period. Turks in Bulgaria were not aware of the development of the Republic of Turkey (because of the introverted administration of Bulgaria and prohibition for Turks to be in touch with Turkey), and the change in the language and daily life, expression of traditions and religious rituals, etc.

- Until the 1970s Turkish was not banned and consequently large part of this generation of Turkish minority knew the Turkish language and Latin alphabet. Religious rituals were known as well.
- After the 1970s the generations of the Turkish minority were not taught in Turkish and the Turkish language and religion were completely banned. So, disconnection from the origin and cultural identity was very clear. The generations born after the 1970s did not know the Latin alphabet, barely knew few Turkish words (inherited from the Ottoman period and heard from the family in secret), and nothing about religion was left.
- After 1984 by the change of the names (all Turkish people were forced to take a new Bulgarian name) officially there was not any Turkish ethnic group in Bulgaria. So, there was not any cultural identity of the Turkish minority.

The above-mentioned reasons were a brief explanation of the reason for immigration to protect the Turkish culture and identity of the Turkish minority living in Bulgaria. The other side of the coin is life, which is the beginning of the new life, when arrived at the motherland, Turkey.

- The journey to the unknown can be the best definition of immigration. To close the eyes and leave all the life behind for beginning the new one with the excitement of going to be Turk.
- Although the destination of the migration was the motherland and the main purpose was to protect culture and identity, because of the social, cultural, physical, and the like differences, Turkish emigrants who arrived from Bulgaria needed to structure their new cultural identity. In Bulgaria, they were defined as Turkish minority (at least before 1984) and in Turkey, they were defined as immigrants from Bulgaria. Therefore, for both sides, they were "the other." Integration to the existing place was an issue. To be accepted by society was another issue. Again, being a Turk needed time and the struggle for it.
- Being able to integrate into any new place or community communication is an inevitable requirement. So, a common language, a common base of traditions and culture are essential.
- Most of the immigrants (especially those born after the 1970s) needed to learn the Latin alphabet and Turkish language. Even the ones who knew some Turkish needed to adapt to the Turkish of the Republic of Turkey which is rather different than the one frozen from the Ottoman period and learned many years ago in Bulgaria.
- On the other hand, as in most cases, being accepted by the existing community was one of the major difficulties for immigrants who came to Turkey from Bulgaria. Immigrants from Bulgaria tended to settle in close neighborhoods to feel secure and safe and to support each other. Turks who emigrated from Bulgaria overtime

started to create their settlements, the first step in structuring the new cultural identity, a Turkish person who emigrated from Bulgaria.

To conclude, I can say that even for a very important and enthusiastic reason such as the preservation of culture, identity, and origin, I feel that being an immigrant is not belonging anywhere, it is to feel as "the other" everywhere. It is thinking all the time about how do I feel, where I belong which place has more impact on shaping my personality? and such that. I think these are the questions of all immigrants… The meaning of having a cultural identity and a mother land is very deep and invaluable. Only the ones who needed to struggle, to suffer, even to lose some of their loved ones for protecting their cultural identity can understand the meaning of motherland and the motivation to the journey of unknown (although they might not be welcomed by the whole when they arrived)… The best part of being an immigrant is feeling multicultural and to dignify human beings apart from their beliefs or cultures, learning this from the own experience while growing up in two different places.

References

Brunnbauer, U., & Taylor, K. (2004). Creating a "socialist way of life": Family and reproduction policies in Bulgaria, 1944–1989. *Continuity and Change, 19*(2), 283–312. Cambridge University Press. https://doi.org/10.1017/s0268416004005004. Printed in the United Kingdom.

Budak, Ö. (2010). Mübadele meselesi ve Lozan'da çözümü. *Karadeniz Araştırmaları, 26,* 129–142.

Crampton, R. J. (1989). The turks in Bulgaria, 1878–1944. *International Journal of Turkish Studies, 4*(2), 43–78.

Durmaz, A. (2019). *Endless Immigration: 1989 Bulgarian Immigrants Living in Immigrant Housing in Balikesir* (Bitmeyen Muhacirlik: Balikesir'de Göçmen Konutlarinda Yaşayan 1989 Bulgaristan Göçmenleri). Mimar Sinan University, Department of Social Sciences, Master Thesis (in Turkish).

Eminoğlu, C. (2019). Dispersion, diaspora identity and belonging: A case study on the Turkish Migrants in Copenhagen. In M. Khosrow-Pour (Ed.), *Immigration and the current social, political, and economic climate: Breakthroughs in research and practice information resources management association.* USA: IGI Global.

Erder, S. (1986) *Ghetto and turks in the welfare society* (In Turkish: Refah toplumunda "getto" ve Türkler). Teknografik Matbaacılık, İstanbul.

İnalcık, H. (2001). *The ottoman empire, the classical age 1300–1600.* Phoenix: China.

Kale, B. (2014). Transforming an empire: The ottoman empires immigration and settlement policies in the nineteenth and early twentieth centuries. *Middle Eastern Studies, 50*(2), 252–271. https://doi.org/10.1080/00263206.2013.870894.

Kirişçi, K. (2003). *Turkey: A transformation from emigration to immigration.* Retrieved from http://www.migrationpolicy.org/article/turkey-transformation-emigration-immigration.

Köse, H. (2001). *Bloody traces—Documentary stories of our martyrs* (in turkish: Kanlı İzler – Şehitlerimizin Belgesel Öyküleri) (2nd ed.). Publisher: Poligraf, Razgrad.

Lütem, Ö. E. (2000). *Turkish Bulgarian relations 1983–1989,* Volume 1: 1983–1985 (in Turkish: Türk – Bulgar İlişkileri 1983 – 1989, Cilt 1: 1983 – 1985). Balkan Araştırmaları Dizisi, Avrasya Stratejik Araştırmaları Merkezi.

Lütem, Ö. E. (2012). 1984–89 Dönemi Türkiye'nin Bulgaristan Politikası ve 89 Göçü, Ersoy. In E. M. Hacısalihoğlu (Ed.), 89 *Göçü. Bulgaristan'da 1984-89 Azınlık Politikaları ve Türkiye'ye Zorunlu Göç* (pp. 137–171). İstanbul: Balkar & Balmed.

Simsir, B. (1989). The Turkish minority in Bulgaria: History and culture. *International Journal of Turkish Studies, 4*(2), 159–178.

Şimşir, B. N. (1986). *Turks of Bulgaria* (in Turkish: Bulgaristan Türkleri). Ankara: Bilgi Yayınevi Publisher.

Tüzünkan, D. (2019). The international migration movements and immigrant policies from the ottoman empire—1299 to Republican Turkey 2016. In M. Khosrow-Pour 1(Ed.), *Immigration and the current social, political, and economic climate: Breakthroughs in research and practice information resources management association.* USA: IGI Global.

Yılmaz, S. (2013). Proceedings Book of 2nd International Conference of Lan-guage and Literature. *The Balkans and Turkish Culture through the Eyes of Yaşar Nabi Nayır* (Yaşar Nabi Nayır'ın Gözünden Balkanlar ve Türk Kültürü). Bedir University, Tirana-Albenia. 14–16 November 2013.

Yıldırım, B. (2018). *The existence and population of turks in Bulgaria* (in Turkish: Bulgaristan'da Türk Varlığı ve Nüfusu). Istanbul: İlgi Kültür Sanat Yayıncılık.

Defending the Sacred Valley of the Incas Against Misguided Tourism Development

Alberto Martorell

Abstract Sacred Valley (SV) of the Incas, the heart of the ancient Incan empire located at the river Vilcanota-Urubamba basin, is a rich cultural corridor. When Machu Picchu was inscribed onto the World Heritage List (WHL), ICOMOS recommended this declaration be extended to include the SV landscape in order to protect the entirety of the valuable cultural processes that have taken place within. However, the candidacy was never submitted. A dramatic change is now happening in the area due to the pressure of tourism developers with misguided conceptions. A project to construct an airport in the District of Chinchero, located at the center of the Valley, poses the greatest risk. The project has faced opposition for different reasons. Our focus is on the effects the project could have on the area's heritage, specifically on three particular world heritage sites: The Historic Sanctuary of Machu Picchu (HSMP), the Qhapaq Ñan (QÑ), and the City of Cusco.

1 Introduction

In this paper, we begin by presenting the site in consideration as well as the main archaeological sites that are likely to be affected by the airport project in the Sacred Valley (SV) of the Incas. We then discuss the effects of tourism services in the area. As a third point, we analyze the airport project, focusing primarily on the potential effects it could have on the location's heritage. Following the administrative process of the project, noticing that in 2019 UNESCO required a Heritage Impact Assessment for all World Heritage Sites (WHS) of the area. To understand the reasons behind this requirement, we analyze the relevant points of a previous Environmental Impact Study (EIS). We briefly reference the ICOMOS Guidance on Heritage Impact Assessment (HIA) for Cultural World Heritage Properties in order to establish a basis through which to locate the project's gaps and weaknesses, particularly in the aspects key to the conservation of heritage, which must have a territorial scope as a general

A. Martorell (✉)
Factor Cultura, Lima, Peru
e-mail: alberto.martorell@factor-cultura.edu.pe

O. Niglio and E. Y. J. Lee (eds.), *Transcultural Diplomacy and International Law in Heritage Conservation*, https://doi.org/10.1007/978-981-16-0309-9_18

landscape, and not partial studies. Finally, we introduce the planning stages in the area.

The Ministry of Transport began the first stage of the project work (ground-breaking). This has already had a negative impact on the landscape. The emergency caused by the coronavirus pandemic, however, has stopped all activity. Could this be the opportunity to find a better location, which would imply a new development pole?

2 The Location

The Sacred Valley (SV) located in the Cusco Region (in the Southern Area of Peru), is shaped by the Urubamba River course. Flanked by mountain peaks, it is a fertile agricultural landscape, and along its path, many small, Quechua-speaking villages can be found. A cultural laboratory for thousands of years, the Sacred Valley is one of the most amazing landscapes around the world. The most famous monument of the SV is the Historic Sanctuary of Machu Picchu—but it is far from being the only one of higher interest. In fact, in discussing the values of integrity among the sites based on the ICOMOS Evaluation (ICOMOS, 1983), the World Heritage Center (WHC) affirms:

> It is desirable to extend the property to encompass an even broader spectrum of human-land relationships, additional cultural sites, such as Pisac and Ollantaytambo in the Sacred Valley, and a larger part of the Urubamba watershed would contribute to strengthening the overall integrity. (WHC, n.d.)

Unfortunately, the Peruvian government did not submit the candidacy of neither the archaeological sites along the SV outside of the Machu Picchu area nor of the landscape in its integrity to the World Heritage List (WHL).

The SV played a very important, central role to the state of the Incan empire. Specialists sustain that this area was associated with royal estates, and there was a denser use of the space for local settlement (Covey, 1974). Agricultural productivity of the SV has always been very important for the economy of the region. Many structural changes, however, are affecting the value of the SV of the Incas.

The SV was declared cultural heritage of the nation by the RDN 988/INC-2006, which is meaningful in order to understand the value of the Valley, especially as per the "whereas" section (quoted by Dammert, 2007: 129). This section explains that the SV contains, between the districts of Huambutío and Piscacucho, the largest number of vestiges of the Incan civilization, including the archaeological parks of Pisaq, Chinchero, and Ollantaytambo, and more than 350 archaeological sites.

Another particularly important point underlined in the declarative text is that the peasant communities at the basin of the rivers Patacancha and Quitamayo, as well as the district of Chinchero, have a rich and wide, intangible cultural heritage. As we will discuss later, both the material and non-material heritage of the Valley are being affected by the initial changes the airport project has already caused.

This declaration, unfortunately, is not a clear or well-defined document. The area declared cultural heritage by the declaration only vaguely covers the locations in the provinces of Urubamba, Calca, Paucartambo, Anta, and Quispicanchis. The document fails to accurately establish limits and georeferenced data. Therefore, it is difficult to apply protective rules, which furthermore even implies some limitations to property rights. For practical reasons, in this paper we will focus on only some of the main elements that could be potentially adversely affected by the airport project. To define the area of interest, we use the "location of the project" information available in the official website of the Peruvian Private Investment Promotion Agency, which was in charge of the public tender process (Fig. 1).

It is important to note the situation of the first tender process, whose winner was the company Kuntur Wasi. We will not discuss in detail the administrative issues which led to this tender to be declared null. The company is thus no longer responsible for the execution of the project. There are currently open and pending legal cases by Kuntur Wasi against the Peruvian government.

Location of the Project

LOCATION		
DISTRICT	CHINCHERO	HUAYLLABAMBA
DEPARTMENT	Cusco	
PROVINCE	Urubamba	
AIRPORT LOCATION	29 Km from Cusco by road	
AIRPORT ALTITUDE	3, 712 m.a.s.l.	
DISTRICT ALTITUDE	3, 754 m.a.s.l.	2, 868 m.a.s.l.
DISTRICT AREA	94.6 Km2	102.5 Km2
DISTRICT POPULATION	9,422 inhabitants	4, 980 inhabitants

INFLUENCE AREA

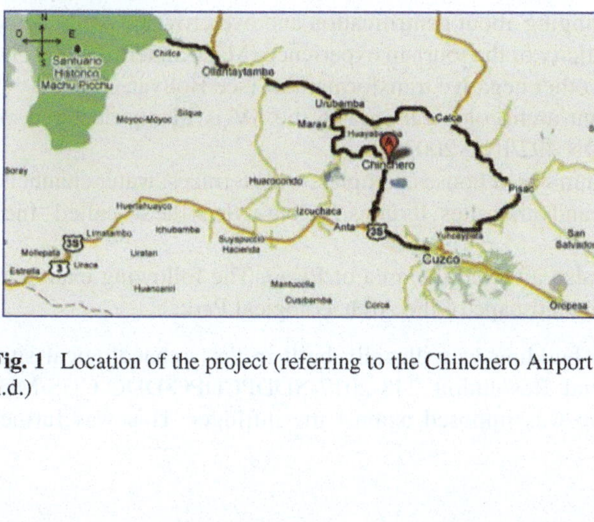

Fig. 1 Location of the project (referring to the Chinchero Airport Project) (*Source* Proinversión, n.d.)

It is also interesting to note that the SV has been included in the World Monuments Watch 2020 list of the World Monuments Funds. Such is a meaningful action. WMF explains that "Through the Watch we intend to continue the search for inclusive and equitable solutions to the development of the Sacred Valley" (WMF, n.d.).

3 The Main Archaeological Sites in the Sacred Valley Potentially Under Risk

There are many archaeological sites of significant value at the basin of the Vilcanota-Urubamba River (or, Sacred River of the Incas). We will briefly comment on the main sites in order to demonstrate the interest and importance of the whole area to Peruvian and universal culture.

Ollaytaytambo is located along the main road of the Valley and the railway from Cusco to Machu Picchu. The town is divided by the Urubamba River, marking the different areas. The town itself, known as Qosqo Ayllu, and the current archaeological area was a sacred space, with a ceremonial character called the Araccama Ayllu (Mujica, 1993). The space contains magnificent agricultural terraces with hydraulic systems that still work presently. Ollantaytambo was declared cultural heritage of the nation by National Directorial Resolution (RDN) 395/INC-2002.

The town is linked to the Sanctuary of Machu Picchu by the railway. One of the most important stations to access Machu Picchu has been established in Ollantaytambo. The short path for the most luxurious tourism trains begin there. Therefore, it is a crossing point for many tourists, most of who stay only just enough time to take the next train. This generates a temporarily overcrowded area, especially during times of departure and arrival of trains. The number of tourists who stay overnight is considerably less.

Negative effects of tourism can be discerned in the town. Coffee shops, restaurants, and handicraft centers surrounding the station have created their own "for tourism" style. In other areas, new buildings are under construction. These developments are affecting authenticity by bringing about gentrification and overcrowded areas. This, too, even affects the authenticity of the tourism experience (MacCannell, 1973). The town has seen a number of other negative transformations (see Bolívar, 2016).

Another highly important archaeological area in the SV is **Pisaq**, declared an Archaeological Park by RDN 492/INC-2002.

Pisaq is composed by a number of houses, temples, wide terraces, water channels, routes, bridges, a cemetery, and other sites. Its constructive style is the so-called "Inca Imperial."

False development has also affected the area of Pisaq. The following examples can explain the affect to the landscape of the Archaeological Park.

(a) In 2012, a five-level building was illegally built in the archaeological site. By Deputy Directorial Resolution 248-2017-SDDPCDPC-DDC-CUS/MC, an administrative fine was imposed against the infringer. This was further confirmed by Deputy Directorial Resolution 365-2017-SDDPCDPC-DDC-CUS/MC. However, no real sanction was executed because the procedure was, first, appealed, and afterward, declared under prescription. National administrative legislation establishes a one-year time-limit for execution of the resolution. As it was not executed, it expired.

(b) The same year (2012), a similar illegal construction (this time for a three-level building) was built in the same area. A similarly conducted administrative situation resulted in the revocation of the fine imposed—and these are only two of the many cases.

Another archaeological property of great importance is the **QÑ**. The QÑ has an area considered both national and world heritage. In fact, the methodology applied to inscribe the QÑ was to select representative areas that conjoin more evidently the "outstanding universal values" of the property. This includes an area that would be affected by the construction of the airport.

It is evidently clear that the question concerning the airport project is not limited to the immediate surrounding airport area. A greater number of visitors will have a wider impact.

For this reason, concern about QÑ includes both the sections in the closer area as well as the World Heritage section that is a halfway distance to Chinchero, too.

The complete road from Ollantaytambo to Lares is described in the Nomination file, including the:

> Patacancha micro basin twards Huacahausi, … the sub-basic of the Yanatile River, as well as micro-basic in the district of Lares and Amparaes, in the province of Calca. It then goes down the sub-basin of the Mapacho River… (Republic of Argentina et al., 2013: 443)

Some paragraphs after add:

> Six Areas of Maximum Protection were selected in this section, comprising total of 62.30 km of remains of the Inca road associated with nineteen archeological sites of Outstanding Universal Value. (Idem)

These areas are all specified in the *Archaeological Sites in Nominated Area* Charter, which contains the six areas of maximum protection. Ollantaytambo is not directly considered part of the selected sites.

3.1 Archaeological Sites Nominated Areas

There is no doubt that the main archaeological areas of the Sacred Valley, directly linked by natural reasons to Cusco, were connected by the most advanced roads, which can be identified in any other area of major interest in the Tahuantinsuyo reign (Fig. 2).

The Nomination file expressly underlines that structures and habits are basically the same as in the rest of Vilcanota and Urubamba basins, even when these areas contain the most elaborate features of the Incas, especially in the Sacred Valley

NOMINATED AREA	SITE CODE	NAME OF SITE	LOCATION			FUNCTIONALITY
			UTM COORDINATES			
			East	North	Altitude	
SEGMENT: HUACAHUASI - TAMBOHUAYLLA (PE-OL-26/CS-2012)	QÑ-OL-012	Panteon Moqo	823882	8546283	2936	Residential
SEGMENT: CHOQUECANCHA - KILLA KHAWARINA (PE-OL-28/CS-2012)	QÑ-OL-017	Choqecancha	821479	8556838	3025	Ceremonial
	QÑ-OL-020	Inca Acequia	820642	8550055	2977	Productive
SUBSECTION: PAUCARPATA - ICHUKA (PE-OL-29/CS-2012)	QÑ-OL-022	Umacalle	823227	8561327	3272	Not specified
	QÑ-OL-023	Samanapata	825330	8583250	3033	Associated with the Road
	QÑ-OL-024	Qoyllotamba	174820	8563567	3681	Residential
	QÑ-OL-025	Pumaqocha	176950	8567662	3928	Residential
	QÑ-OL-026	Inca Tambo	175035	8571558	3605	Associated with the Road
SUBSECTION: TAWIS - PUENTE OLLANTA (PE-OL-21/CS-2012)	QÑ-OL-031	Inkaraqay	824051	8588780	3784	Administrative
	QÑ-OL-034	Llaqtapata (Qellomayu)	828407	8593234	3597	Productive, Administrative, Residential

Fig. 2 Republic of Argentina et al. (2013: 444)

(Vilcabamba) of Urubamba, where the most characteristic Incan settlements are found, from Machu Picchu, which has become a type of icon of elegant Cusco architecture, to Pisaq, and of course, Ollantaytambo, Chinceros, Huch'uyqosqo (Uchuy Cusco), and other minor sites. In all these areas, roads are also special and very carefully elaborated, including those going to Choqek'Irau, a very beautiful sanctuary on the Apurimac Canyon (Republic of Argentina et al., 2013: 766, 788).

The Nomination File states that "the main road started in Haucaypata and continued on to Tococachi (San Blas), Amaro Marcahuasi, Abra Corao, Pisaq, Paucartambo, Tres Cruces, Pilcopata, and Cosñipata Valley" (Republic of Argentina et al., 2013, 983).

Within the national scope, other routes of the QÑ in the area are recognized and studied.

One of them namely, is the Chinchero–Urquillo–Q'espiwanka route (Proyecto QÑ Cusco, 2011), which is part of the Chinchaysuyo (North) road starting in Cusco city. The path of the route links Cusco, Chinchero, and Maras, and after this there is a bifurcation through Urquillos, Yucay, and Urubamba (Ministry of Culture, 2011; Dammert, 2007).

The fact that the airport project exerts a potentially negative influence over the QÑ in regard to both its WH sections as well as its national ones is clear. For this reason, the Heritage Impact Assessment (HIA) made by Román (2019) includes a special section that takes this issue into consideration.

Another area that could be impacted if the Chinchero airport project were realized is the most famous Peruvian archaeological site, the Archaeological Sanctuary of Machu Picchu. For this site, we consider it unnecessary to dedicate a larger selection of text to further explain this. The possible effects of the airport project over Machu Picchu are discussed in the following sections.

The primary aspect to consider, which has already been under discussion for a very long time, is the real capacity of charge of the Historic Sanctuary of Machu Picchu. We must make mention of the situation of this famous Peruvian site due to the coronavirus pandemic. As any other archaeological site in Peru, Machu Picchu was closed during the legal quarantine regulations established by the Peruvian government. After the lockdown, the government made many announcements regarding its reopening. However, as far as any available information indicates, Machu Picchu remains closed until July 29, 2020.

The case of the site of **Chinchero** is a matter of special consideration. The official governmental position to this matter is that the area that would be affected by the airport has no archaeological interest. After several different unclear administrative situations, the Peruvian Ministry of Transport has assumed the execution of the project. The only advancement that occurred before the general lockdown was the groundbreaking.

Two initial observations must be noted. First, the area of Chinchero is not an isolated area, as it is part of the whole landscape of the SV. The authenticity of the Valley depends on the authenticity of, at least, its main elements. Chinchero is one of them.

Chinchero was an important estate of the Inca Topa Inca Yopanqui. It is mentioned in the Chroniques of Juan de Betanzos and Petro Sarmiento de Gamboa (Dammert, 2007; Proyecto QÑ, 2011; García, 2018a).

From an architectural point of view, Chinchero included structures and squares from different typologies. At the same time, it was an urban and administrative center, a politic-administrative unit, a military place, and a commercial point (Alcina, 1976, as quoted by García, 2018a).

We will conclude our quick overview of the main archaeological sites in the Sacred Valley surrounding Chinchero by mentioning the case of the concentric terraces of **Moray**. Archaeologists have several different theories about this place but have not discovered with precision the functional aspect of the giant circular terraces. Moray is close to the Salt Mines of Maras, and both are located in the district of Maras. The proximity of the airport to these sites implies a deeper risk.

Considering the high values of the archaeological assets of the SV, we are limiting the description of examples to this category. Notwithstanding, the colonial and republic heritage of this area is also of great importance, and should also be considered in any conservationist planning (see Gobierno Regional Cusco - Per Plan Copesco, 2011).

4 Tourism and Its Effects

The idea that tourism and development necessarily go together is assumed by most governments and countries as an absolute truth even when talking of "cultural tourism." Of course, tourism is a useful tool for development, depending on the sustainability of the tourism management system implemented.

The main, troubling issue we detect is the wrong order of priorities created around tourism activities almost all around the world, with greater and deeper incidence occurring in less-developed regions. All systems seem to be designed to generate higher conditions of commodity to visitors. We are not against or opposed to the good service standards that are a must to protect and guarantee a good experience, but the system and the standards surrounding it must also generate a better quality of life for the local people.

Are cultural tourists themselves the type of visitors a country desires? Does quantity matter? If one tourist is surely someone to offer friendship to, how many friends would a local have when there are thousands of people arriving to his/her place by a number of planes each day? Undoubtedly, there is interest in tourism generating development and increasing the level of income of the local people. But, is it really the majority of the local population that benefits from tourism, or the few powerful companies that obtain the larger share of the generated income?

We will not give an answer to these questions. We only underline that at the center of the question is not the tourism per se, but the type of tourism, which, as a metaphor, I am calling here, "good tourism." It is the territory itself and its resilience which can give us the shape of "good tourism" for each specific territory. In general terms, the idea is to develop sustainable activities and avoid those which negatively impact the destination. Sustainability must be understood integrally, including social and identity sustainability, cultural and environmental sustainability, and economic and productive sustainability.

There are many indications that should alert how tourism is driven in the Sacred Valley. Being a privileged area for both natural and cultural reasons, the SV is an interesting tourism destination. Furthermore, it is an obliged path when traveling to the most desired destination in Peru: Machu Picchu.

For the last 20 years, the landscape of the SV has been changing, and in some aspects, dramatically. A recognized phenomenon in many tourism destinations is the creation of sceneries that respond more to what the visitor is willing to see than what the site actually is. Such was explained during the last decade of the twentieth century by Ashworth and Tunbridge (1990: 54) as the "*reduction of the complexity and richness of the (urban) heritage to a few simple recognizable and markable characteristics.*"

This quotation is perfectly applicable to the case of Chinchero studied by García (2018a: 161), who explains an alchemy that arbitrarily imposed new physical and symbolical limits to the population of the town.

Esta alquimia se había conseguido mediante una visualidad construida de acuerdo con las reglas de la perspectiva occidental, la cual producía un espacio luminoso, coherente y objetivo. El espacio "abstracto" resultante era físicamente limpio y visualmente despejado; pero también estaba desprovisto de misterio, era fácilmente empaquetable y consumible y había sido vaciado de significado cultural y religioso (Hertzfeld, 2006: 138; Lazzari, 2011; Lefebvre, 2013 [1974]).

We must state that we truly trust the potential of tourism in the creation of a healthy development model. It is a fact that tourism has had a positive influence on the economy in general terms. The question is how to create a balance between the conservation of the resources attracting visitors and the effective use of the site in order to guarantee sustainability, including ways to share the positive economic effects with the wider and poorer population.

We agree with Llorca-Rodríguez et al. (2012: 77) who, analyzing this issue in Cusco, state that "*The potential negative effects of tourism could be avoided and the entire society could be profited by modifying the tourism development model with the cooperation of the local population.*"

It is necessary to re-establish priorities between locals and visitors, where the permanent values of the territory must be the focal point in the planning and execution of tourism activities. As such, the proposal of Knight (2015: 143–144) analyzing the tourism in the SV of Cusco is useful:

When local accounts suggest that tourism has created or increased certain deprivations (measured through local accounts of restricted or undesirable functioning), strategies may be considered to address those deprivations through slight or drastic forms of institutional reconfiguration.

5 The Airport Project

There are many specialists concerned about the airport project itself. The project has been criticized for technical reasons regarding the conditions of the location for the functioning of an airport. It is necessary to have clear information of and about the Peruvian authorities and companies in charge of the project.

In order to establish a general idea of the project itself, we will briefly report the developments of the administrative process.

On October 11, 2001, the Law number 26578 created the Special Project International Airport in Chinchero, which was declared of public necessity and utility. Nevertheless, the first government to make a formal decision concerning the airport was that of Morales Bermudez, the president who approved the Decree Law 23028, establishing the engagement of a company to draft the technical studies for the construction (López, 2017a).

In the annual Tourist Market Trends 2002 (WTO, 2003: 315), the Ministry of Tourism of Peru reported the "access" as a positive fact, that the feasibility study for the Airport in Chinchero was ready, and they were discussing the best options for granting the concession. The results were announced on June of 2002.

However, it was not until February 2, 2010, that the Ministry of Transport and Communications gave authorization to the Public Commission for Investing Promotion (Proinversión) to call for tenders as public request to grant the concession of work for the airport. On April 25, 2012, the consortium Kuntur Wasi was granted concession. However, after controversial political affairs and corruption accusations arose, the concession was declared null and void in 2017. More importantly, before this occurred, the Law 29908 approved the expropriation of the lands for the construction of the airport. After difficult negotiations (see García, 2014, 2017, 2018a, 2018b, 2019a, 2019b; Knight, 2015; López, 2017a, 2017b), the government paid $20 dollars per square meter for the main land and "affected" community of Yanacona.

Researchers and writers underline the effects that the project has already had, even though construction has not really started. The money received by the "comuneros" (people of the local communities) generated what Lopez qualifies as a constructive "boom." Many new buildings arose in Chinchero with serious negative impacts on the landscape (López, 2017b).

As it used to be in Peru, social interest has become an issue of political populism, and this new illegal urban space is now a matter of "regularization" by the regional and local governments. The following image taken from the official Facebook page of the Municipality of Chinchero further clarifies this point.

Returning to the topic of the administrative process—no new formal project to grant a new concession was made. Contrarily, the government declared that the initial work was going to be directly carried out by the Ministry of Transport.

More interesting to our analysis are the Ministry's goals.

The main goal of the Ministry is to improve the airport infrastructure of the Cusco region, and in doing so, increase the flux of national and international visitors to Cusco and the rest of the country. As an additional consideration, the text also states that it must promote the development of the region (Proinversión, 2013a).

This view seems to respond to the previously criticized, simplistic ideas that tourism per se is synonymous to development and consequentially the main goal is to increase the number of visitors.

Among the specific goals stated, the third one establishes that the new airport should be a territorial structuring project, dynamizing the local economy of the SV and, in a broader scope, the departments of Cusco, Puno, and Apurimac (Figs. 3 and 4).

The necessity of an airport is not under discussion. The question is a matter of finding and creating the better option that would result in wider services and the least amount of negative effects possible, including its location.

Realistically, it might seem that the decision to construct an airport in Chinchero is a done given. However, our opinion is that it is a mistake and a lost opportunity to generate tourism elsewhere, where it is weak and not actively present. The South of Peru and the territories in the Region of Cusco offer many options.

It is possible that the deep economic crisis the coronavirus pandemic has caused may have created one last chance for reconsideration of this airport project. The pandemic has stopped all projects in their entirety, including the airport of Chinchero. Can this moment of stillness onset by times of quarantine offer us a fresh, new perspective?

If indeed, however, the project, which has already been initiated after all, continues toward full execution, we then raise the issue of how to convert it into a sustainable project by minimizing its adverse effects.

Point 1.6. of the pre-investment study calculations (Proinversión, 2013b) demonstrates the priority given to the economic numeric benefits that should amount to S/. 27,701 million as incremental net profit benefits due to the number of passengers; and S/. 881.1 million for the time economy of users.

More important to our study, the document includes "other benefits," among which we find a serial of aspects: to consolidate the leadership of Cusco in airport regional services, to contribute to improvements in quality of living in the region, to

Fig. 3 Official Facebook page of the Municipality of Chinchero, announcing the installation of basic services to the occupation called "Nuevo Yanacona" (Municipality of Chinchero, 2015)

create new direct and indirect places of work, to reduce aviation accidents and incidents, to generate environmental improvements, to improve the operational technical capacities of the international airport of Cusco, to improve the airport image, and to contribute to the development of tourism in Peru.

We think that there is a serious lack of consideration of the social and cultural aspects of the project. The proposal should consider propositions that strengthen the

Fig. 4 "Las Lomas." New urbanization in the landscape of Chinchero (Author Britzehida Callañaupa)

identity and traditional styles of life at the same time as accessing modern development. Local inhabitants of Chinchero and the SV must be first in the line of beneficiaries of the project. Measures to avoid and prevent negative effects on the archaeological, urban, and natural spaces of the SV due to the increment in the number of visitors are also critical.

Finally, in order to contribute to the development of tourism, a careful evaluation of the project is needed. Examples of overcrowded spaces with negative effects can be found in many cultural properties all over the world.

One of the sources that can be used to analyze the airport construction impacts is the concession contract (a version is available at Proinversión's website. See http://www.proyectosapp.pe/modulos/JER/PlantillaProyecto.aspx?ARE=0&PFL=2&JER=5379&SEC=22) and the considerations concerning its impacts. This is only a general indicator on how this issue was conceived, because the concession contract was, as previously stated, canceled. Considering the document was designed to regulate the contractual relationships between the Peruvian State and a private company, it could be adequate that consideration of the impacts are limited to those directly linked with the construction and operation of the airport. Point 12.3.1.1. of the contract limits the responsibility of the operator to the area of concession and the area of influence. If there is an impact outside of the said area, the concessionary will be responsible only if there is a probed direct or indirect responsibility. The described situation should be considered normal in contractual terms, if there were a public entity in charge of the necessary steps to have a regional study of the effects. An EIS must reach the affected primary area, the area of influence, the cultural landscape of the SV in general, and the broader influence area.

In any case, the responsibility to undertake other studies, including the Environmental Impact Study (EIS) is derived from the concessionary (i.e., the company

Kuntur Wasi). From this formal point of view, this company fulfilled the requirement of submitting the EIS for the airport in the year 2015 (see Kuntur Wasi, 2015).

We will briefly review some principle aspects. Item 4 defines the service area (SA) of the project. In general terms, it considers two divisions of interest. The first is the direct service area (DSA), defined by the cultural and natural elements directly impacted by the construction work for the airport. It includes the central working areas and its adjoining terrains. Directly linked to our thematic interest, it includes the Archaeological Park of Chinchero.

The second division of interest is the indirect service area (ISA). The Service Area is delimited, according to the document, and considers physical, biological, socioeconomic, and cultural environments. The main factor delimiting the ISA is the existence of natural and/or cultural areas impacted due to the various dynamics originating in the DSA.

From our point of view, it is even more important to consider the ISA because the territory will necessarily change, first, due to the different dynamics generated during the construction, and later, due to operations during the functioning period. The document clarifies that the factors taken into account to draft the ISA are the hydrographical basins and main roads and the political limits of implied districts.

The stated factors above are of interest but could not be accurate enough. Potential changes in the flux of tourism is a factor that should be added to this evaluation. Furthermore, the cultural elements attracting visitors are key to understanding their territorial spread, and thus need also be considered.

We will analyze item 5.3, Socio economic baseline. By our consideration, the fact that this aspect is limited to the DSA is a weakness of the project. It is necessary to create a broader evaluation of the project in terms of socioeconomic effects that are not limited to the inhabitants of the DSA. There are three peasant communities in the Chinchero district: Yanacona, Racchi Ayllo, and Ayllopongo.

The EIS includes a large number of tables concerning different aspects under evaluation. Table 239 (Kuntur Wasi, 2015: 508) presents the housing typology in the town and area of Chinchero (corresponding to the DSA). There is no special consideration for the heritage type of houses. This is a meaningful factor due to the nature of the project.

Item 5.3.6.8. is titled "Cultural Analysis." The content is limited to a list of the traditional festivities of the communities in the district. It far from includes all the aspects that need to be analyzed from a cultural point of view.

Item 5.3.6.13 contains a descriptive relation of the Archaeologic sites of the area. There is no specific study, evaluation of the state of conservation, or analysis of the values of the area. The text simply refers the archaeological problem to the archaeological monitoring plan (PMA) approved by the Regional Cultural Institute of Cusco (now replaced by the "Dirección desconcentrada de Cultura."). This kind of study is developed parallel to the constructive works.

However, the national legislation demands a previous study to determine the existence (or non-existence) of archaeological remains in the area (called the Certificado de inexistencia de bienes arqueológicos). The study was not conducted. This is one of the main discussion points.

In theory, the PMA goal guarantees the existence of the archaeological assets of the area. However, it would be during the moment of project work execution that such cultural goods would be identified, recuperated, preserved, conserved, and eventually, restored. Furthermore, considering we are speaking of the exact location of the new airport, it would only be possible to conserve moveable goods. A possible relocation of an unmovable good could be discussed only in cases of extreme value. This possibility is difficult to trust.

The dossier of the EIS was complemented by an annex containing a socioenvironmental plan and a plan for environmental observation, among others. None of these plans include any consideration about either the mitigation of the tourism effects on the area, or the effects on heritage assets.

Flaws such as those discussed in the previous paragraphs motivated the General Director of the World Heritage Center of UNESCO to express the entity's formal concerns. By means of document CLT/WHC/LAC/CMT/LP/2897 dated July 1, 2015 and addressed to the permanent representative of Peru in UNESCO, this institution requested from the Peruvian government information concerning the construction of the international airport in Chinchero and the impact it should have on the WHS of the area, namely the City of Cusco, the Historic Sanctuary of Machu Picchu, and the QÑ WH sections. UNESCO also asked the Peruvian government to undertake a wide and extensive evaluation that included an Environmental Impact Study (EIS) and a Heritage Impact Assessment (HIA).

We have already commented on an EIS previously approved by the Peruvian government. The second does not have a specific regulation in Peru, therefore, it could be classified as a non-mandatory study. Nevertheless, it is necessary to appeal to the general principles of Law, which in this case, include the principle of preventive conservation, used by heritage specialists of the environmental law systems. By this principle, any instrument that is positive and helps improve conservation must be incorporated in the protecting system. There is an international document drafted by ICOMOS to guide these kinds of studies, especially WH cases in particular. In fact, the most widely accepted guidelines for such studies are the ICOMOS Guidelines on Heritage Impact Assessment for World Heritage Properties (ICOMOS, 2011).

More importantly, the letter written by the WHC director, Dr. Metchild Rossler, dated July 2019, speaks of the necessity to undertake both EIS and HIA. For a moment, there was the 2015 EIS approved by the Peruvian government. However, it was part of a cancelled process (i.e., the Kutur Wasi concession). In any case, this document surely did not fulfill UNESCO requirements.

6 The Guidance on Heritage Impact Assessments for Cultural World Heritage Properties: Brief Analysis of the Methodology

ICOMOS is one of the advisors to the WHC for the application of the WHC (Art. 8.c WHC, 1972). In this quality, ICOMOS developed the Guidance on HIA for WH properties "in order to evaluate effectively the impact of potential development on the Outstanding Universal Value (OUV) of properties." The goal of the document is to attend to the necessities of the WHS "through considering them as discrete entities and evaluating impact on the attributes of OUV in a systematic and coherent way" (ICOMOS, 2011: 3).

Before analyzing HIA Guidance, there are some necessary notes to make:

(a) The HIA as presented by ICOMOS is an instrument to protect the OUV of the WHS. It responds to the international interest to protect them as the sustaining values of heritage inscribed on UNESCO WHL. It must not be considered as an instrument inapplicable to national goods. All of the WH system has the final objective of improving the conditions of conservation of the natural and cultural heritage of humanity in general terms. Therefore, the HIA that the Peruvian State is obliged to prepare should not be limited to the specific WHS, but rather include the heritage values of the SV landscape. This is very important, considering the characteristics of the area under risk.

(b) After an initial negative reaction, the Peruvian government formally accepted to undertake the HIA. At the same time, political actors declared that there was no compromise to implement the results of this study. As it is not included in Peruvian legislation, the project should continue despite the results. However, the realization of an HIA exercise is not simply a formal act to fulfill UNESCO requirements. It is a tool to guarantee the compromises already assumed by Peru as a State Party of the WHC, fully applicable to the three WHS in the area. Following the acceptance, the study was executed by Román (2019) and Rodríguez (2019), commissioned by the Ministry of Transport. The dossier was remitted to the Ministry of Culture for its formal approbation and it was denied. This implies that there is clear opportunity to undertake an accurate HIA considering both WHS as UNESCO demands and national sites as Peruvian interests.

Pereira and van Roers (2012) consider that the ICOMOS' Guidance include ten obligations:

- "The (broadness of the) HIA team" implies two aspects. On one hand, the team in charge must have the necessary specialists that the site demands. Pereira and van Roers recommend "to inventory the composition of HIA teams, as well as their affiliation to help determine their degree of impartiality" (106). On the other hand, there must be a broader team including various relevant stakeholders (i.e., the State Party, regional or local government, local community representatives, and the public). It is important to establish the necessity of a good determination of who the stakeholders are as a key aspect. We recommend an open-minded selection. When desirable, WHC and its advisors should be included.

- "The (early consultation with) relevant parties."
- "The (training of the) involved parties." ICOMOS recommend "an adequate training on HIA of the stakeholders involved with WH properties" (107).
- "The (appropriateness of the) commissioning of the HIA process." Pereira and van Roer underline the 16 stages established by ICOMOS to apply the HIA. The methodology implies to follow these stages and scope included in Appendix 2 of ICOMOS Guidance (2011).
- "The (full and effective) use of HIA output." Of course, the main reason to undertake an HIA is to implement what the results of this exercise indicate. According to Pereira and van Roer, it is a call for a comparative analysis of the application of the output or similar tools.
- "The (transparency of) HIA reports." The results of HIA must describe the attributes keeping the values of the place, sustaining "their individual and/or collective condition, importance, inter-relationships, and sensitivity, and possibly also an indication of capacity for change" (ICOMOS, 2011: 14). When potential damages are identified, the report should propose principles, and when possible, methodologies to avoid or mitigate them. Another very relevant issue that ICOMOS recommends to include in the HIA report, is to propose "other options for the development."
- "The (feedback into) the design process." The "results of data collection and evaluation should be fed back into the design process for the development or proposals for change or for archaeological investigation" (ICOMOS, 2011: 11). The report should identify the risk situations and propose solutions that should be fed back and implemented to avoid negative impacts on the OUV, the authenticity, or the integrity of the site. If that is not the case, alternative scenarios and what Pereira and van Roers call "what's if" options can be provided.
- "The (adequacy of) the HIA tools." "ICOMOS strongly recommends to gauge the adequacy of HIA tools in relation to the complexity of the property and the resources available to invest, operationalise, and maintain such tools" (Pereira and van Roers, 2012).
- "The (good) understanding of the WH property, its significance and OUV, its attributes and its content." Of course, the team in charge of IEA must understand the site and its values in its integrity. We consider that the *Statements of Outstanding Universal Value (SOUV),* the declarations on the authenticity and integrity, and the previous evaluations of the site are the basis for this work.
- "The baseline data about the WH property and its condition." In order to be accurate with the studies, data collection, comparative analysis, historic evolution of the site, and other relevant aspects are of greater interest to determine the current process of conservation/changing of the site, and how the site would be impacted because of the evaluated new arrangement.

The manner in which the team in charge is composed, as well as the extent to which the real stakeholders are considered, is relevant to making the next steps of the process viable. We will now analyze the HIA reports drafted by Román (2019) and Rodríguez (2019). It is convenient to note that both documents were submitted to the author by the Ministry of Culture of Peru by means of answering a legal application through the Transparency and Access to Public Information law enforced in Peru.

7 The HIAs Under Question and the Necessity of a New Process

As stated previously, the Ministry of Transport, which was put in charge of the airport project, commissioned the execution of an HIA concerning the three WHS, as requested by UNESCO. The results of the HIA were evaluated by the Ministry of Culture, due to serious considerations on the suitability of the document. The analysis made by the Ministry of Culture is clear, and we will consider its main aspects. We add some observations concerning the conception of the process, and we uphold the reasons because a complete evaluation of the impacts is necessary, including a new EIS. In our opinion, the EIAs under analysis do not fulfill the minimal requirements. For this reason, a real, focused, and specialized EIA is necessary.

As previously stated in the last section of this article, the composition of the team in charge of the EIA is specifically considered in the ICOMOS Guidance. In our opinion, this encompasses the first weakness of the discussed EIAs. This is an important point to make because the Ministry of Transport announced a new call for the realization of the EIA following UNESCO requirement, so we must emphasize the proficiency of the newly selected team.

The EIA concerning the QÑ and Cusco was placed under the direction of an archaeologist and a team that primarily included two other archaeologists and one anthropologist. Another archaeologist also supported the team, and an engineer served as a collaborator. The EIA concerning Machu Picchu had a similar team composition.

Due to the wide scope of the necessary studies required, we believe that both teams were limited, and did not fulfill the considerations of the ICOMOS Guidance. Anecdotally, the people involved were the same group of people. The only difference was that the chief on one team was just a member in the other, and vice versa. This point, which could be considered a relevant detail, demonstrates that there were no technical criteria to determining the team composition. The nature of a historic sanctuary, a cultural route, and an ancient city are all clearly very different. It is not right to propose the same team for all three WHS.

The HIAs to be conducted for this second opportunity must be limited to comply solely to the UNESCO requirements. It is not acceptable that the Archaeological Parks of Chincero, Ollantaytambo, and Pisaq, as well as the national sections of the QÑ not have an HIA. This point must be directly assumed by the Peruvian government in order to demonstrate minimal responsibility by our own history.

The justification for the point that the new HIA must be more centered and focused and not limited to WH cases can be found in the ICOMOS report concerning Machu Picchu, quoted in the introduction to this article. For this task, the team in charge must include professionals of Archaeology, Anthropology, Architecture, Urban and Rural Planning, Economics, Sociology, and Transportation Engineering, as well as Environmentalists, Risk Specialists, and Tourism Specialists, among others. A territorial approach could be the best one to take. As such, the HIA should include the SV landscape.

The analysis of the HIA of Machu Picchu and QÑ/Cusco, submitted by the Ministry of Culture to the Ministry of Transport is very clear. The next citation summarizes the scope of the arguments given to disapprove both of the HIAs (Fig. 5).

El EIP debe identificar los impactos patrimoniales y las acciones para la protección, la conservación, la mitigación, la salvaguardia y el sostenimiento de los bienes declarados e inscritos en la Lista del Patrimonio Mundial de UNESCO, principalmente por la naturaleza del Valor Único Excepcional (VUE) de los bienes a proteger. En ese sentido el análisis debe ser multisectorial y multidisciplinario con participación activa y programada concertadamente de todos los actores que resulten involucrados, que lleven a un diagnóstico holístico de los Sitios Patrimonio Mundial, que se encuentren inmersos en el desarrollo previsto del proyecto (Ministry of Culture, 2020).

We must comment that beyond formalities, to limit the HIA to the OUV of the WHS will not conduce desirable results.

Fig. 5 View of the QÑ in Chinchero (Author Britzehida Callañaupa)

8 Development and Urban Planning

The discussion concerning the airport project in Chinchero made it evident that it is necessary to have a wider vision of the developmental process in the SV cultural landscape and the different urban, archaeological, and environmental elements needing to be conserved. There are already some planning documents that should be evaluated in order to realistically prevent the adverse effects of the airport of Chinchero.

The concern is that the influence of an infrastructural intervention at the level of an airport implies a magnitude that in turn implies a general change in the planning of the whole region. Because of this, the general previous studies must include a wide vision of the scope of area influenced by the project, prior to making any kind of decision regarding the execution of the project. We are afraid that these kinds of preventive actions have not been undertaken and that the planning system, including old and new documents, has proven insufficient to justify the stage at which the project is currently at.

The matter at hand is to draft technical documents that would serve to evaluate the airport project through an objective lens. The scenery that needs comparison is the landscape of the SV with and without the airport. We are afraid that documents such as the recently approved Development Plan for the city of Chinchero (Municipal Law 002-202-MPU as of January 20, 2020) are planned purposefully with the intent to forge the ideal conditions for a general development model that favors the airport's construction, without any consideration to preventing the negative affects it could cause. Even the simple decision to use the word "city" to refer to the rural town of Chinchero carries a hidden meaning.

Keeping and preserving the rural values of the SV would form the cornerstone needed to make it sustainable. These local and landscape values that attract the imagination of humanity must be preserved. General planning created for the SV must have all material and non-material heritage and natural values as its sustaining columns. Authenticity, unicity integrality, and the enhancement of these values must be considered of the upmost level for the planning in the region.

9 Conclusions

- The SV is an exceptional cultural landscape and as such, its management must be focused on keeping it alive within the conditions of authenticity and integrity. The OUV of the WHS in the area are of higher importance but must also be considered in their interaction with the other sites carrying heritage value in the region. Any HIA developed must consider the integral panorama of the region. This point should be further evaluated in order to comply with the ICOMOS guidance.
- The conditions necessary to proceed with the execution of the airport project do not exist. The 2015 EIA, although approved, is not complete or accurate enough to justify the airport. Formal completion of the HIAs are still pending. As of now,

the UNESCO requirements concerning HIA studies for the three WHS of the region have not been completed.

- It would be desirable for the Peruvian government to seriously reflect on and consider other available location options for the new airport. To locate the airport in an area where the infrastructure and dynamics of an airport serve to create a new economic developmental pool could overall, produce more positive results. The SV is not one of the poorest regions neither of Cusco nor of the South of Peru. Moreover, the SV is one of the most visited areas of Peru. To generate a larger concentration of tourists in the same area would negatively impact both material and non-material heritage. Living communities native to the region need to create their own model open to modernity while simultaneously respecting traditional values. Such a task is only possible under a locally generated development approach.

References

Ashworth, G., & Tunbridge, J. (1990). *The tourist-historic city*. London: Belhaven Press.

Bolívar, W. (2016). Diagnóstico y cambios espaciales en el Parque Arqueológico de Ollantaytambo. *Arqueología y Sociedad, 32,* 451–476.

Covey, A. (1974). The imperial settlement patterns in the Sacred Valley. In A. Covey (Ed.), *Regional archaeology in the Inca Heartland: The Hanan Cuco survey* (pp. 175–191). Ann Arbor: University of Michigan.

Dammert, M. (2007). *La red de parques arqueológicos. El apogeo del Tawantinsuyo y el desarrollo regional del Cusco*. Lima: INC.

García, P. (2014). *Blessing or curse? The Chinchero airport*. Cultural survival. https://www.culturalsurvival.org/news/blessing-or-curse-chinchero-airport#sthash.K8DEMQLd.dpuf. Accessed 12 July 2020.

García, P. (2017). From folk history to empathy: Contesting heritage values in Chinchero, Peru. *International Journal of Heritage Studies, 23*(4), 335–346.

García, P. (2018a). *En el nombre del turista. Paisaje, patrimonio y cambio socia en Chinchero*. Lima: IEP.

García, P. (2018b). Weaving for tourists in Chinchero, Peru. *Journal of Material Culture, 1*(17), 23–26.

García, P. (2019a). Indigeneity in the air: The case of Chinchero Airport in Cusco, Peru. *Bulletin of Latin American Research, 39*(2, Special issue), 157–171.

García, P. (2019b). Desarrollo turístico e identidad indígena: Cuzco y el nuevo aeropuerto de Chinchero. *Revista andaluza de antropología, 17,* 64–85.

Gobierno Regional Cusco - Per Plan Copesco. (2011). Plan de Acondicionamiento Territorial 1ra etapa. Provincias De Calca Y Urubamba - Diagnostico. https://www.academia.edu/29678466/PLAN_DE_ACONDICIONAMIENTO_TERRITORIAL_1RA_ETAPA_PROVINCIAS_DE_CALCA_Y_URUBAMBA_DIAGNOSTICO. Accessed 12 July 2020.

ICOMOS (1983). Advisory Body Evaluation (ICOMOS) / Évaluation de l'organisation consultative (ICOMOS). https://whc.unesco.org/en/list/274/documents/.

ICOMOS. (2011). *ICOMOS guidelines on heritage impact assessment for world heritage properties*. https://www.icomos.org/world_heritage/HIA_20110201.pdf. Accessed 12 July 2020.

Knight, D. W. (2015). Tourism, poverty, and development: Local perceptions, empowerment, and strategies for change in Peru's Sacred Valley. Doctoral thesis. https://mountainscholar.org/bit

stream/handle/10217/167015/Knight_colostate_0053A_12981.pdf?sequence=1&isAllowed=y. Accessed 12 July 2020.
Kuntur Wasi. (2015). Estudio de impacto ambiental detallado. "Mejoramiento del servicio aeroportuario de la Región Cusco mediante el nuevo aeropuerto internacional de Chinchero, Cusco". Informe Final. https://portal.mtc.gob.pe/transportes/socioambientales/estudios_impacto.html.
Llorca-Rodríguez, C. M., Casas-Jurado, A., & Soler-Domingo, A. (2012). Development of the Cuzco region: The tourism contribution. *Ambiente y Desarrollo, 16*(31), 77–89.
López, M. (2017a). Reubicación y expectativas de modernidad: el caso de las familias campesinas de Yanacona y el proyecto Aeropuerto Internacional de Chinchero (Cusco). *Debates en Sociología, 44,* 67–90.
López, M. (2017b). El proyecto del aeropuerto internacional y el "boom" de la construcción en Chinchero. *Revista Argumentos, 11,* 20–25.
MacCannell, D. (1973). Staged authenticity: Arrangements of social space in tourist settings. *American Journal of Sociology, 79*(3), 589–603.
Ministry of Culture of Peru. Regional Direction of Cusco. (2011). Parques arqueológicos del Cusco. Guía Informativa. Cusco: DDC.
Ministry of Culture of Peru. (2020). Document 0021-2020-VMPCIC/MC from January 22, 2020.
Municipality of Chinchero. (2015, December 15). Nota de prensa nº 075-2015/RRPP/MDCH. [Municipality of Chinchero announces the instalations of water supply improvements for the members of the peasant's community of Yanacona "affected" by the expropriation process] Facebook. https://www.facebook.com/MunicipalidadChinchero/posts/554218181394629. Accessed 7 June 2020.
Mujica, E. (1993). Ollantaytambo, urbanismo Inka. *½ de construcción, 84,* 19–23.
Pereira, A., & van Roers, R. (2012). Editorial: Guidance on heritage impact assessments: Learning from its application on world heritage site management. *Journal of Cultural Heritage Management and Sustainable Development, 2*(2), 104–114.
Proinversión. (2013a). Contratación de un Consultor Integral para el Concurso de Proyectos Integrales para la entrega en concesión al sector privado del Aeropuerto Internacional de Chinchero – Cusco (AICC). Estudios de Preinversión a nivel de Factibilidad del Proyecto. Informe 9a – estudio de preinversión a nivel de factibilidad. Volumen 0. Aspectos generales e identificación, Lima. http://www.proyectosapp.pe/RepositorioAPS/0/2/JER/SA_CHINCHERO_ESTUDIOS_PRE_NIVEL_PERFIL/Perfil_Aeropuerto_Chinchero.pdf. Accessed 17 July 2020.
Proinversión. (2013b). Contratación de un Consultor Integral para el Concurso de Proyectos Integrales para la entrega en concesión al sector privado del Aeropuerto Internacional de Chinchero – Cusco (AICC). Estudios de Preinversión a nivel de Perfil y Factibilidad del Proyecto. Informe Nº 5.A y anexos (Tomo I). http://www.proyectosapp.pe/RepositorioAPS/0/2/JER/SA_CHINCHERO_ESTUDIOS_PRE_NIVEL_PERFIL/Perfil_Aeropuerto_Chinchero.pdf. Accessed 12 July 2020.
Proinversión. (n.d.). *Location of the project*. http://www.proyectosapp.pe/modulos/JER/PlantillaProyecto.aspx?ARE=1&PFL=2&JER=5897. Accessed 12 July 2020.
Proyecto QÑ Cusco. (2011). Proyecto de promoción y difusión camino Chinchero– Urquillo–Q'espiwanka. Chinchero-Cusco. http://biblioteca.culturacusco.gob.pe:8080/bitstream/ddccusco/687/1/Promoci%C3%B3n%20y%20difusi%C3%B3n%20camino%20Chinchero%20Urquillo%20Q%C2%B4espiwanka.pdf. Accessed 12 July 2020.
Republic of Argentina, Plurinational State of Bolivia, Republic of Chile, Republic of Colombia, Republic of Ecuador, & Republic of Peru. (2013). *QÑ Andean Road System*. http://whc.unesco.org/uploads/nominations/1459.pdf. Accessed 11 July 2020.
Rodríguez, L. (2019). *Evaluación de impacto al patrimonio (EIP) del Santuario Histórico de Machupiccu por el proyecto de nuevo aeropuerto internacional de Chinchero – Cusco. Document officially remitted to the author by the Office in charge of institutional transparence of the Ministry of Culture of Peru, in application of the Law 27086*. Lima: Ministry of Culture of Peru.
Román, N. (2019). *Evaluación de impacto al patrimonio (EIP) del QÑ – Sistema vial andino (Secciones Ollantaytambo – Lares – Valle de Lacco, Vitkus – Conquequirao y la plaza Inka Hanan*

Huacaypata – Cusco) y la Ciudad del Cusco, por el proyecto de nuevo aeropuerto internacional de Chinchero – Cusco. Document officially remitted to the author by the Office in charge of institutional transparence of the Ministry of Culture of Peru, in application of the Law 27086. Lima: Ministry of Culture of Peru.

WHC. (n.d.). *Historic Sanctuary of Machu Picchu.* http://whc.unesco.org/en/list/274.

WMF. (n.d.). *Sacred Valley of the Incas.* https://www.wmf.org/project/sacred-valley-incas. Accessed 12 July 2020.

WTO. (2003). *Tourism market trends 2002—Americas.* https://www.e-unwto.org/doi/pdf/10.18111/9789284405565. Accessed 18 July 2020.

Heritage and Conflicts

Intangible Heritage in Colombia in the Midst of Armed Conflict and Unreached Peace

César Augusto Velandia Silva and John Jairo Uribe Sarmiento

Abstract After sixty years of armed conflict in Colombia, the wounds have left very deep marks within the representative social groups and their cultural manifestations. War impacted vulnerable populations, especially those rich in indigenous and black heritage. The chapter explores the case of the El Salado massacre in the region of Montes de Maria, Colombia, in which between February 16 and 22, 2000, a group of paramilitaries executed 66 people, including men, women, and children while the victims were forced to play their traditional music or the killers played the instruments after each brutal murder or rape. The chapter discovers how international and national legislation reached out late but finally recognized the brutality of one group against another, and how from the cultural heritage a community strives to forget and to prepare its next generations for the future, based on reconciliation and revaluation of its intangible cultural values.

1 Introduction

Between February 16 and 22, 2000, a paramilitary command (illegal army at the service of the ultra-right-wing promoted by the State) perpetrated the death of 66 people among men, women, and children, using the members of their community to play their traditional music or, the killers playing their instruments after each murder or brutal rape.

Colombia's cultural heritage, originally a legacy from indigenous peoples and black slaves, is the basis of the traditional structure of knowledge and know-how that underpins cultural manifestations. The drums, shawms, and songs that are still not recognized by the Representative List of the Intangible Heritage of Colombia (MCC, 2017; Andrade, 2013), were beaten with all the force of the conflict in the most savage

C. A. Velandia Silva (✉)
Facultad de Humanidades, Artes y Ciencias Sociales, Universidad de Ibagué, Ibagué, Colombia
e-mail: cesar.velandia@unibague.edu.co

J. J. Uribe Sarmiento
Facultad de Derecho y Ciencias Políticas, Universidad de Ibagué, Ibagué, Colombia
e-mail: john.uribe@unibague.edu.co

O. Niglio and E. Y. J. Lee (eds.), *Transcultural Diplomacy and International Law in Heritage Conservation*, https://doi.org/10.1007/978-981-16-0309-9_19

and bloody way, supported by the strengthening of the political arm of the ultra-right-wing, supported by paramilitary and military forces, and encouraged by the rhetoric of "Democratic Security policy" from the Alvaro Uribe Vélez administrations: regional (Antioquia Governor 1995–1997) and national (President 2002–2006 and 2006–2010). (Comisión Colombiana de Juristas, 2009; Reliefweb-OCHA Services, 2015; Tribunal Superior de Medellín, 2017; VerdadAbierta.com February, October, 2019).

According to Article 10 of Colombia's culture law (MCC, 2019), intangible cultural heritage (ICH) has a symbolic value: a good has symbolic value when it expresses ways of seeing and feeling the world. The symbolic value has a strong power of identification and social cohesion. It maintains, renews, and updates desires, emotions, and ideals built and internalized that link times and spaces of memory. This value refers to the linking of the good with processes, practices, events, or activities that are significant for the memory or constant development of the community, as well as with manifestations of the community's ICH (MCC, 2019). It was this value that the massacre attempted precisely, continuing a historical practice between rival societies, in which during the process of annihilation of one social group over another, their symbolic values are destroyed, from motherhood attempted by the systematic rape of women, to the heritage values that are the most intimate, deepest and rooted in the cultural essence of a people, which overcome the attack on what can be recovered, such as property, land, houses, and crops. The execution of people to the sound of drums undermined the immaterial cultural manifestation.

On the other hand, despite the legal recognition that the victims have of integral reparation through Law 1448[1] and the Agreement[2] signed between the government and the Revolutionary Armed Forces of Colombia (FARC), cultural issues have remained in the background, even among scholars. However, initiatives such as that of the Semana Foundation in the Montes de María (Revista Semana, 2018) and the *cantaoras* survivors of the Bojayá massacre (Revista Arcadia, 2011), aim both at recovering the memories of the victims and at rebuilding their identities and heritage. As some authors have pointed out from a feminist perspective (Confortini, 2006; Theidon, 2006; Posada & Carmona, 2019; Paarlberg-Kvam, 2019), they have played a crucial role in the construction of new identities for the victims in the country.

The chapter aims to reveal the implications for the future of the social and collective reconstruction of the intangible heritage of the cultural manifestation of El Salado, used during violent acts against the population, in the form of violence most raging in the Montes de María region of Colombia. The implications allude both to the responsibility of the Colombian State and the possible support of the international community, but it is not limited to reparation for the victims but is pointed out in

[1]Law 1448 of June 10, 2011, "By which measures of attention, assistance and integral reparation to the victims of the internal armed conflict are dictated and other provisions". http://www.centrodememoriahistorica.gov.co/micrositios/caminosParaLaMemoria/descargables/ley1448.pdf. Accessed: 27 July 2020.

[2]Final Agreement for the End of the Conflict and the Construction of a Stable and Lasting Peace. November 24, 2016.

https://peacemaker.un.org/sites/peacemaker.un.org/files/Colombia%20Nuevo%20Acuerdo%20Final%2024%20Nov%202016_0.pdf. Accessed: 27 July 2020.

terms of the complex processes for the reconstruction of the cultural manifestation itself that will make reconciliation and peace possible in a long post-conflict process.

The premise is to broaden the discussion in the critical context of the Colombian conflict and take the theories of peacebuilding as useful for analyzing how the Colombian conflict devastated a manifestation of cultural heritage, taking as a case study the massacre of El Salado. At the same time, this chapter reviews Colombia's position and responsibility as a State Party to UNESCO and its subscription to international law, based on the Hague Convention in 1954, and which commits to a complex discussion as part of soft law, to so-called nonbinding international law or recommendations without the necessary obedience to the legal autonomy of each nation, although it is evident that human rights are reinforced through work on world heritage (García, 2005; Logan & Reeves, 2008; Logan, 2012; Ekern et al., 2012; Alatalu, 2020; Larsen, 2020).

2 Background on Political Violence in Colombia

Political violence between liberals and conservatives dates back to the mid-nineteenth century. After several civil wars, the country experienced relative calm until the so-called liberal hegemony in the 1930s. During this period, the liberals in power used the State apparatus to persecute, banish, and even murder conservatives in some areas such as northern Boyacá and southern Santander (Gutiérrez-Sanín, 2016). The war against Peru (1934) put this internal dispute in the background, as the parties united to defend the country. A decade later, the conservatives in power have their revenge and pursue their enemies, who take refuge in some regions such as the eastern plains, the Sumapaz moorland, southern Tolima, north-western Huila, north-eastern Cauca, and eastern Valle del Cauca. Communist party members also arrive in these areas. In these territories, armed groups are organized to protect themselves from the attacks by the so-called *Chulavita* police, "Los Pájaros" and conservative organizations that massacre their political enemies with the support of the local police and some members of the army. This period is known as "The Violence". By 1953, General Rojas Pinilla staged a *coup d'état*, and a military dictatorship was established, offering amnesty to armed groups in exchange for the laying down of arms. Many of these groups heeded this offer. Others developed criminal activities and became known as bandits. Others kept their distance, as they did not trust the promises of peace (González, 2016).

This whole process of political violence was juxtaposed with different conflicts over land. In fact, during the first half of the twentieth century, many landowners appropriated the settlers' lands, as well as the work of tenants, who either organized themselves or moved to new places (colonization). So, as the confrontation between liberals and conservatives, with the so-called National Front (a pact of political alternation between the two parties), these conflicts are added to the "closure" of the political system, because they do not find in the traditional parties or institutional spaces, a possibility of expression. In fact, the two traditional parties share power (which has reduced political violence), and they carry out social and development policies, even managing to reduce inequality in the country. However, they maintain a hard line against social mobilizations in the framework of the so-called national security (of anti-communist nature) promoted from the United States (Gutiérrez-Sanín, 2016).

Thus, in the 1960s, revolutionary guerrillas emerged that fed on the imaginary of the Cuban revolution. The FARC takes up the experience of the communist groups of southern Tolima (which were confronting both the government and the liberal groups with which they had allied themselves around 1950), which after living through bombings in Marquetalia, Riochiquito, and El Pato, decide to transform themselves into an agrarian movement. The People's Liberation Army (EPL) and the National Liberation Army (ELN) emerged in Santander. The former begins military activities in the area of Urabá and Magdalena Medio, with a Marxist-Leninist orientation. The second initiates its activities in Santander (Magdalena Medio) and is characterized by its radical orientation. Subsequently, the 19 April Movement (M-19) emerged as a response to what was considered electoral fraud during the election of Misael Pastrana (within the framework of the National Front) in 1970. By 1990, the EPL (90% of its members) and the M-19, as well as other guerrillas that had emerged (Quintín Lame, Worker's Revolutionary Party [PRT]), demobilized. In 2016, the FARC laid down its arms. While the ELN continues to be active in its military action.

On the other hand, there are reports of armed groups by landowners on the Atlantic coast who, at the beginning of the twentieth century, used violence to get their employers to control their land and resolve any threats (Ocampo, 2015). As mentioned, by 1960, a confrontation broke out between liberal (so-called "clean") and communist ("common") groups that led to the emergence of paramilitary organizations in southern Tolima (Barros & Uribe, 2019). But it was in the 1980s that armed organizations (linked to drug trafficking) emerged, with the capacity to confront the guerrillas and provide security. This was the MAS (*Muerte A Secuestradores*—Death to Kidnappers), a group that had the Magdalena Medio as its axis of action and that was created and developed from the Medellín cartel, headed by Pablo Escobar. However, given the struggle that the "extraditable" began with the purpose of abolishing extradition (which produced thousands of deaths, as well as car bombings, assassinations of judges, journalists, and massacres), the Colombian State (in collaboration with various U.S. agencies: DEA, CIA) lined up its forces to catch the capo. In this fight, the PEPES (Persecuted by Pablo Escobar) emerged, a group of drug traffickers who became enemies of the head of the Medellín cartel and who collaborated with the forces that pursued him.

After Escobar fell, the criminal groups sought to cleanse their fortunes. They filled the void left by him and integrate themselves into legal life. This process apparently led to the creation of the Security Cooperatives, armed groups that protected landowners and, among them, drug traffickers.[3] These groups, which had "recycled"

[3]This was not, therefore, the first time that the creation of private security forces was promoted in Colombia. In fact, according to Gutiérrez-Sanín (2016), this was a practice deployed since the beginning of the twentieth century to control agrarian conflicts.

the members of the PEPES, began an intense counter-insurgency activity that grew during the last decade of the twentieth century, even when they were declared illegal. By that decade, the FARC had reached its highest capacity and had taken over military bases and even a departmental capital (Ávila, 2019). Between 1998 and 2002 a negotiation process was developed between this guerrilla group and the Colombian government. This negotiation not only failed but also promoted the intensification of struggles between paramilitaries, the State, and the guerrillas. In fact, the ELN almost disappeared, while the *Autodefensas* and the FARC grew stronger, to the point that by 2001 there were hundreds of massacres, thousands of homicides, and tens of thousands of displaced persons (Ávila, 2019; Barros & Uribe, 2019).

Between 2003 and 2006, the main paramilitary structures were demobilized. However, this demobilization took place after an intense "purge" among the ranks of the Self-Defense Forces. So real confrontations developed between different paramilitary groups, for example, between the Cacique Nutibara Block and the Metro Block in the streets of Medellín.[4] It is worth mentioning that the paramilitary groups did not articulate themselves as an organization with a central command, so despite the emergence of the United Self-Defense Forces of Colombia (AUC), each group had autonomy and its own history. Thus, some groups were closely linked to drug trafficking, while others originated as a response to the guerrilla siege and therefore articulated in another way with local and regional elites (Aguilera, 2014; Beltrán, 2015; Ocampo, 2015; Ávila, 2019).

It is important to underline the existence of profound regional differences in the development of the conflict and in the construction of the State. It can be said that Colombia has more "modern" regions in the political, social, and economic sense. That is, these are areas that have a certain amount of bureaucracy and public planning and management processes dominated by technicians and specialists (which does not mean that practices such as clientelism have disappeared), areas that have development projects of a certain magnitude such as Bogotá, Medellín, Cali and, probably, Barranquilla. Other regions are linked to the national political dynamic through "clientelistic" logic. These are regions where the State is the main employer and where political intermediation is a tool of power (Ocampo, 2015; González, 2016; López, 2016).

In this way, a kind of balance has been consolidated between the regions and the center of Colombia, in which local/regional clientele networks are deployed, while national projects and the interests of the country's elites are developed in the central areas. In both cases, the latter have found ways of coexisting and reproducing their privileges (González, 2016). Thus, the traditional parties operated as articulating axes of the elites (networks of bosses and electoral chiefs) from which the nation and the State were built (López, 2016; González, 2016). Besides, there are areas of colonization where the conflict has been fought with greater intensity and that were precariously articulated to the traditional parties, as occurred in southern Tolima,

[4]A testimony of this process can be seen in the documentary "La Sierra", directed by Margarita Martínez Escallón and Scott Dalton in 2004. It can be seen at: https://www.youtube.com/watch?v=F3ENEjvzIrA&has_verified=1.

where the communist party held an important area (Aponte, 2019), as well as in the isolated areas of the Caribbean region, as in the Montes de Maria.

So, the armed groups developed their strategies from both access to resources not controlled by formal institutions, and the development of their war plans, always in tension with the strategies of their enemies. In this way, the different regions became areas controlled by one actor or became as places of dispute (Kalyvas, 2010; González, 2016; Arjona, 2017).

The Montes de María, for example, became a zone controlled by the EPL around 1970–1980 (with incursions by the FARC and the ELN). Given its strategic position for access to the Caribbean and the Pacific and its importance for the trafficking of illicit goods, this region was intensely disputed by the *Autodefensas* de Córdoba and Urabá, since the late 1990s. Thus, the massacre of El Salado can be interpreted as a typical action of the scorched earth strategy implemented by paramilitarism in the country (Ávila, 2019). Finally, this territory was controlled by these groups and their successors.[5]

Another fact to take into account regional differences refers to how the illegal groups were related to and/or confronted to the State. In general, the guerrillas made an effort to destroy legal institutions, preventing the work of mayors and public officials (Aguilera, 2014; Beltrán, 2015), while the paramilitaries made an effort to co-opt and to control the State apparatus (Ocampo, 2015; Ávila, 2019).

The guerrillas managed the most integrated territories as spaces for looting resources through extortion and kidnapping (for example, central Tolima and the central areas of the Caribbean region), while they used other areas as places for growing and processing cocaine (such as Putumayo, Caquetá, and Vichada) and used some isolated areas as strategic rearguard locations (such as southern Tolima). Furthermore, the illegal groups not only exploited resources such as coca crops, gold, or oil revenues but also developed various strategies to control legal economies such as coffee or bananas. Rettberg et al. (2018) have built an analytical framework to address the political economy of the conflict from the analysis of various regional economies. They argue that there are resources that can "motivate" the actions of illegal actors, given their strategic nature (coal, gold, oil), while others are "complementary" in that they allow them to add new income to what they usually have through the control of royalties or extortion and kidnapping logics (such as bananas or ferronickel). Other economies can be "isolated", that is, they are not affected in the same way (bananas, emeralds, or flowers).

As noted, the Colombian conflict is expressed very differently in the regions. These differences are due to the degree of integration with national dynamics, the type of resources available, as well as the strategies of the competing armed actors. It is worth remarking that violent actions are not due to the sheer barbarity of the actors in the conflict. Their activities were calculated within the framework of strategies, ultimately, the calculations that each actor makes about its situation, its possibilities,

[5]After the demobilization of the different paramilitary groups, so-called Criminal Gangs (Bacrim) appeared, organizations that "picked up" some structures that did not demobilize. These groups have evolved so that some call them "neo-paramilitary" (Ávila, 2019) and/or "narco-paramilitary".

and its risks (Kalyvas, 2010; Arjona, 2017). This turns the population into a military target: their suffering becomes a message sent to the enemy, their bodies are means of communication, building symbols of the power that each one is capable of exercising.

> I regret that situations like this arise. Above all, I believe that a greater evil is being avoided with an incursion like this. Tough, yes. Strong, yes. It is hard for the country to understand. It is not accepted in any way, but I think that the things that are prevented with actions like this are many in the long term[6]

As we can read in the words of Carlos Castaño, the chief of the self-defense forces who ordered the massacre of El Salado in 2000, the death and torture of the population became a way to avoid a greater evil, an action of the war.

3 The Massacre of El Salado in the Montes de María

The geographic region of Montes de Maria is vast. It is located in the Colombian Caribbean, between the departments of Bolivar and Sucre. It follows the Serranía de San Jacinto and has a total area of 6466 km2. It is confirmed by 15 municipalities: 7 in the department of Bolivar (Carmen de Bolivar, Marialabaja, San Juan Nepomuceno, San Jacinto, Córdoba, El Guamo and Zambrano) and 8 in the department of Sucre (Ovejas, Chalán, Colosó, Morroa, Los Palmitos, San Onofre, San Antonio de Palmito and Tolúviejo) (Ideaspaz, 2011; Andrade et al., 2019).

Located between the economic centers of Valledupar-Bucaramanga (to the east) and the Caribbean Sea (to the west), and linked to the regional corridor that connects Cartagena-Barranquilla-Santa Marta (to the north) and the Momposina Depression Transversal Highway, which connects Sucre, Cordoba, and Antioquia with the Magdalena and Cesar (to the south), the Montes de Maria region managed to develop important commercial and settlement dynamics of economic activities and population that gradually turned it into a strategic pole of many interests on the land, and the abrupt changes in the extensive exploitation of cattle and oil palm. The region reached a population of 867,821 in 1986, but due to the violence that displaced the population (3197 selective murders and 117 massacres were recorded between 1985 and 2017 (CIPDH, 2020). The population is estimated to be approximately 438,119 inhabitants in 2011 (Ideaspaz, 2011) (see Fig. 1).

The region has been the target of several events in the framework of the armed conflict in Colombia. As acts of war, in this region, in the town of El Salado, there have been armed incursions by the FARC and paramilitary groups. It should be clarified that paramilitarism is the fruit of the State's strategy for an alliance between State agents, illegal armed groups on the ultra-right-wing (paramilitaries), cattle ranchers, landowners, and regional politicians, including senators and parliamentarians sitting

[6]Taken from the documentary El Salado: Face of a Massacre. Directed by Tony Rubio. Produced by the National Center of Historical Memory (CNMH) and published on Youtube in 2012. https://www.youtube.com/watch?v=OrSbzIt0-Us.

Fig. 1 Location map of Montes de María region in northern Colombia (*Source* Creative Commons Attribution-Share Alike 4.0 International license)

in the Congress of the Republic, with the main aim of defending the interests of the appropriation, expropriation, and plundering of the land of peasants.

According to Andrade et al. (2019) in the Montes de María region, there are 8 periods in its historical process: (I) 1958–1981: peasant struggle and Montemarian armed repression; (II) 1982–1990: the period of the insurgent incursion and the self-defense structure in Montes de María; (III) 1991–1994: adaptation, reaccommodation and strengthening of paramilitary and insurgent groups in the region; (IV) 1995–1998: Dispute and territorial settlement between the insurgency and paramilitarism in Montes de María; (V) 1999–2001: Regional war: between violence and displacement; (VI) 2002–2005: consolidation and demobilization of the AUC, the State security policy and guerrilla subsistence; (VII) 2006–2009: Defeat of the insurgency, territorial recovery and presence of new armed actors; and (VIII) 2010–2016: consolidation of post-demobilization groups.

According to the above, the events occurred in the fifth period (Regional War 1999–2001). Andrade (2019) states the Rito Antonio Ochoa Front of the AUC was operating in the area. This front was subsumed by the Héroes de Montes de María block, which marked its arrival in that territory with the El Salado massacre (CNRR, 2009: 76). The area already had a paramilitary background, so the abrupt spread of paramilitarism was 1997 when a series of paramilitary massacres began in those areas where the guerrillas were active, such as the one carried out on 23 February 1997, in El Salado, where a group of 50 paramilitaries arrived at this village with a list in hand and killed five of its inhabitants. This first massacre in El Salado was the result of confrontations between the FARC-EP (People's Army) and the paramilitary group in the area, known as Los Méndez.

Meertens (2010) asserts that the paramilitary offensive developed during this period was called the Route of Death, where only in 2000 there were 135 fatalities, being the massacre of El Salado part of this escalation of violence in the region, where they killed 52 men and 8 women both within this town and in its vicinity. This village in the municipality of El Carmen de Bolívar has been considered a guerrilla town since the guerrilla incursion in the mountainous part of the region. This stigma became the central argument for the development of one of the most atrocious massacres in the history of Montes de María (Guzmán et al., 1988; CNRR, 2009).

At this point, it is necessary to highlight the relationship demonstrated between members of the Public Force and paramilitary groups in the El Salado massacre. The Marine Infantry Battalion No. 5, which had territorial and military jurisdiction in the area, did not interfere and allowed the paramilitary advance because the presence of that body in the territory had changed months before. This battalion had received orders from the Command of the First Marine Brigade to carry out operations in the municipalities of Córdoba and Zambrano, which implied a transfer of its military competence over the territory to the 31st Counter-Guerrilla Marine Battalion, which in turn changed its military position on 15 February 2000, that is, the day before the beginning of the massacre (CNRR, 2010). What turned out to be a recurrent fact in paramilitary massacres in Colombia: the prior knowledge, the withdrawal of troops, the deliberate lack of timely action-reaction and the consequent opening of spaces for the operation of paramilitary groups to execute massacres against the civilian population (e.g. Mapiripán, 1997 and those in the region of Montes de María: Macayepo, Chengue, El Salado, Mapuján in 2000, among others) (Andrade, 2019: 139; CNRR, 2010).

El Salado was a strategic rearguard for the FARC-EP since its position "allows an operational deployment to all the cardinal points in the region, in Córdoba, Zambrano, Ovejas and Carmen de Bolívar itself" (CNRR, 2009: 189). This town was at the time the most important *corregimiento* in the municipality of Carmen de Bolívar. It also supplied the logistical needs, provision of food, the transit of livestock, stolen vehicles, kidnapped inputs for the attacks, and was the focus for the recruitment of young people (Guzmán et al., 1988; Andrade, 2019).

The El Salado Massacre was committed in the Colombian town of Villa del Rosario-El Salado in seven days between February 16 and 22, 2000, although other sources speak of the massacre lasting two weeks. The mass murder was executed by the AUC's Bloque Norte and Bloque Héroes de Los Montes de María, which was commanded by Rodrigo Tovar Pupo (alias "Jorge 40"), and Rodrigo Mercado Pelufo (alias "Cadena"). The criminal action consisted of torture, slitting of throats, decapitation, and rape of an as yet undetermined number of defenseless peasants, including a six-year-old girl and a 65-year-old woman; initially there was reported over 30 and 60 people being killed, but in June 2008 the Attorney General's Office determined that there were more than 100, claiming that it may have been the largest paramilitary massacre in their history. The massacre was perpetrated by at least 450 men who also destroyed the houses and businesses of the population. It is considered one of the AUC's most bloodthirsty actions. At least 14 of the bodies were found in four common graves in a lot after being tortured and their throats slit in the town church, others were massacred on a table located in the local football field. According to witnesses, the paramilitaries dismembered and tortured the villagers with chainsaws, screwdrivers, stones, and wood while drinking liquor looted from the shops, raping women, hanging young people, beating up old people and pregnant women while listening to loud music. The massacre resulted in the displacement of at least 280 people, including men, women, and children (Periódico El Heraldo, 2019).

The chronicle "The Carnival of Sadness" (Restrepo, 2019) mentions that after the occupation of the village, some paramilitaries entered the house of culture and appropriated the musical instruments to later celebrate the death of the inhabitants. In this regard, the testimony of two women:

> Here there were drums and accordions, here there was a gaita group. The instruments were for the boys to start practicing, they took all that over. In this court, when death fell, they played, they played, they played drums, they played accordion and everything, So they loaded boom boxes, because in the houses there were good boom boxes and they even took the boom boxes, and they played the music [...] When that killed, they played, that was a party for them. That was for them. A party.

As a result, we know that this massacre not only cost lives and displacements, but also a transformation in the way the surviving victims relate to their culture or, more specifically, to their music:

> They [the paramilitaries] used their perversity to violate that essence of music. They did know that hitting the heart of the people would be more painful, that memory and that memory of hearing a drum would be more forceful, says Soraya Bayuelo, a victim of the armed conflict. The rhythms of Vallenato, Porro, and Cumbia would sound very different after the massacre. The drums, gaita, and accordion stopped being instruments to make music and became cruel tools to remember suffering and torment. (Restrepo, 2019)

4 The International and Colombian Legal Framework of the Conflict, Culture, and Heritage

The Convention for the Protection of Cultural Property in the Event of Armed Conflict and Regulations for the Implementation of the 1954 Convention (UNESCO, 2015, 2017) was adopted by the Colombian State on 18 June 1998.[7] This convention emphasizes that the Member States have the primary responsibility to protect their cultural heritage and that efforts to protect it in the context of armed conflict should be carried out in conformity with the Charter, including its purposes and principles, and international law, and should respect the sovereignty of all States. It invites in this regard the United Nations and all other relevant organizations to continue to provide the Member States, at their request and by identified needs, with all necessary assistance (UNESCO, 2017: 4). It urges the Member States to introduce effective national measures at the legislative and operational levels, where appropriate, and under their obligations and commitments under international law and national instruments, to prevent or counter-trafficking in cultural property and related crimes, such as considering the designation of activities that may benefit organized criminal, terrorist or other groups as serious crimes by Article 2 (UNESCO, 2017: 5). It also encourages the Member States to take preventive measures to protect, in the context of

[7] https://en.unesco.org/countries/colombia/conventions. Accessed: 18 July 2020.

armed conflict, their nationally owned cultural property and other cultural property of national significance, including, as appropriate, by documenting their cultural property and consolidating it in a network of "safe places" within their territories to protect their property, while taking into account the cultural, geographical and historical particularities of the cultural heritage in need of protection, and notes the draft UNESCO plan of action, which contains several suggestions to facilitate such activities (UNESCO, 2017: 6). In particular, Article 19 states that in the event of an armed conflict not of an international character, which has arisen on the territory of one of the High Contracting Parties, each of the parties to the conflict shall be bound to apply, as a minimum, the provisions of this Convention relating to respect for cultural property (UNESCO, 2003).

Previously, the Convention on the Prevention and Punishment of the Crime of Genocide, adopted by the United Nations General Assembly on 9 December 1948, and which entered into force on 12 January 1951, rejected the concept of cultural genocide and linked the *actus reus* of the crime to the physical destruction of a national, ethnic, racial, or religious group as such (Francioni & Lixinski, 2017: 12).

According to the report on the implementation in Colombia of the 1954 Hague Convention for the Protection of Cultural Property in the Event of Armed Conflict and its two protocols (1954 and 1999) (UNESCO, 2015), the Colombian State accepted the "Convention for the Protection of Cultural Property in the Event of Armed Conflict" and its "Regulations for the Implementation of the Convention", the "First Protocol" (Hague, 14 May 1954), in approval Act No. 340 of 26 December 1996, with constitutional revision in Constitutional Court Ruling C-467/1997 and finally adopted on 18 June 1998.

The "Second Protocol to the Hague Convention of 1954 for the Protection of Cultural Property in the Event of Armed Conflict" (The Hague, 26 March 1999) was approved by Law 899 of 21 July 2004, with constitutional revision in the decision of the Constitutional Court C-400/05 and finally adopted on 24 November 2010. From the moment of accession, the Convention and its two protocols have represented a great opportunity for Colombia, as they promote the effective and adequate protection of property that guarantees the effective enjoyment of other rights of the civilian population, which is vulnerable to the effects of the armed conflict. The implementation of the Convention has also been a great challenge for the Colombian Government, taking into account the special situation of Colombia and its internal armed conflict, which has left innumerable humanitarian consequences and has led to the destruction of civilian, educational and cultural property. Furthermore, Colombia is going through a post-conflict phase, which includes social, economic, cultural, and cultural aspects.

Likewise, Resolution 2347 of 2017 adopted by the United Nations Security Council was approved by the Colombian State at its 7907th session, held on 24 March 2017 (UN, 2017). Taking note of resolution 38 C/48 of the General Conference of UNESCO, in which Member States adopted the strategy for the reinforcement of their work in the protection of culture and the promotion of cultural pluralism in the event of armed conflict, recalling its resolution 1373 of 2001, which requires all States to prevent and suppress the financing of acts of terrorism and to refrain from providing any form of support, active or passive, to persons, groups, undertakings, or entities involved in the commission of such acts, deplores and condemns the unlawful destruction of cultural heritage, stresses that Member States bear the primary responsibility to protect their cultural heritage and that efforts to protect it in the context of armed conflict should be carried out in conformity with the Charter, including its purposes and principles, and international law, and should respect the sovereignty of all States; it urges Member States to introduce effective national measures at the legislative and operational levels, where appropriate, and in accordance with their obligations and commitments under international law and national instruments, to prevent or counter-trafficking in cultural property and related crimes, such as considering the designation of activities that may benefit organized criminal, terrorist, or other groups as serious crimes. It also encourages the Member States to take preventive measures to protect, in the context of armed conflict, their nationally owned cultural property and other cultural property of national significance, including, as appropriate, through documentation of their cultural property (UN, 2017: 2–6).

In addition, Colombia signed the Convention for the Protection of the World Cultural and Natural Heritage signed in Paris, 16 November 1972 (UNESCO, 1972). In addition, the country has been a State Party to the UNESCO World Heritage Convention since 24 May 1983.[8] Specifically, the Committee shall establish, keep up to date and publish, whenever circumstances so require, under the title "List of World Heritage in Danger", a list of properties inscribed on the World Heritage List whose conservation requires major operations and for which assistance has been requested under this Convention. The list may include only those properties of the cultural and natural heritage which are threatened by serious and specific dangers, including the outbreak or threat of armed conflict.

It should be noted that the preservation of the plurality and diversity of cultures is thus becoming a major concern for the international community, as witnessed by the adoption of the 2005 UNESCO Convention on the Protection and Promotion of the Diversity of Cultural Expressions adopted by the Colombian State on 19 March 2013.

Universal support for the 1972 World Heritage Convention, which embodies the spirit of representativeness of the most outstanding examples of the world's cultures, is also evidence of international concern for the identification and preservation of the diversity of their material expressions (Francioni & Lixinski, 2017: 13).

For its part, the 2003 Convention for the Safeguarding of the Intangible Cultural Heritage adopted by the Colombian State on 19 March 2008 aims, in its Article 1, at safeguarding the ICH; respecting the heritage of the communities, groups, and individuals concerned; raising awareness at the local, national, and international levels of the importance of the ICH and of ensuring mutual recognition thereof; and providing for international cooperation and assistance.

---

[8] https://whc.unesco.org/en/statesparties/. Accessed: 18 July 2020.

The ICH is manifested in domains such as oral traditions and expressions, including language as a vehicle of cultural heritage; performing arts; social practices, rituals, and festive events; knowledge and practices concerning nature and the universe; traditional craftsmanship (UNESCO, 2003; MCC, 2011).

The Colombian State is a State Party[9] to the Convention and a member of the Intergovernmental Committee for the Safeguarding of the Intangible Cultural Heritage (2016–2020), and is therefore obliged to adopt the necessary measures to ensure the safeguarding of the ICH present in its territory; among the safeguarding measures referred to in Article 2.3, it is required to identify and define the various elements of the ICH present in its territory, with the participation of the communities, groups, and relevant nongovernmental organizations (UNESCO, 2003; MCC, 2011). The definition of heritage contained in the 2003 ICH Convention states that consideration will be given only to ICH compatible with existing international human rights instruments (Francioni & Lixinski, 2017: 12).

For its part, Colombian legislation has established the framework of the Culture Law (Law 397 of 1997), the definitions of heritage and intangible heritage from Article 4 which was amended by Article 1 of Law 1185 of 2008. This law included intangible heritage as one of the elements that constitute the Cultural Heritage of the Nation. This consists of all tangible goods, intangible manifestations, products, and representations of culture that are an expression of Colombian nationality, such as the Spanish language, the languages and dialects of indigenous, black, and Creole communities, tradition, ancestral knowledge, cultural landscape, customs, and habits, as well as material goods of a movable and immovable nature to which special historical, artistic, scientific, aesthetic, or symbolic interest is attributed, among others, in areas such as plastic, architectural, urban, archaeological, linguistic, sound, musical, audiovisual, film, testimonial, documentary, literary, bibliographical, museological, or anthropological (RCC, 2008).

Recently, Decree 2358 of 2019 redefined the concept of ICH. In Article 2.5.1.2, it states that ICH is composed of the practices, representations, expressions, knowledge, and techniques, together with the instruments, objects, artefacts, cultural and natural spaces that are inherent to them, as well as oral traditions and expressions, including languages, performing arts, social practices, rituals and festive events, knowledge, and practices related to nature and the universe, and craftsmanship, which communities, groups and in some cases individuals recognize as part of their cultural heritage. ICH includes the people who are the creators or bearers of the manifestations that make up this heritage (MCC, 2019).

For the purposes of this decree, only ICH that is compatible with existing international human rights instruments and with the imperatives of mutual respect among communities, groups, and individuals for sustainable development will be taken into account (MCC, 2019).

Article 2.5.1.4. states in accordance with Law 397 of 1997, modified by Law 1185 of 2008 and within the limits, parameters, and procedures established therein, the entities that make up the National System of Cultural Heritage have the responsibility

[9] https://ich.unesco.org/en/states-parties-00024. Accessed: 18 July 2020.

to promote the safeguarding, sustainability, and dissemination of heritage with the purpose of serving as a testimony of the national cultural identity in the present and in the future. The Ministry of Culture of Colombia, in accordance with Act No. 1037 of 2006, approved the 2003 UNESCO Convention for the Safeguarding of the Intangible Cultural Heritage, in coordination with its affiliated entities, territorial bodies and the bodies of the National Cultural Heritage System, will support community initiatives for the documentation, research, and revitalization of these manifestations and legally empowered promotion programs (MCC, 2019).

Article 2.5.2.4. establishes the fields of the scope of the Representative List of Intangible Cultural Heritage. This list may be integrated with manifestations corresponding to one or more of the fields such as languages and oral tradition; traditional normative systems and forms of social organization; traditional knowledge about nature and the universe; traditional medicine; traditional and own production; techniques and traditions associated with the manufacture of craft objects; arts; festive and recreational events; traditional religious events of a collective nature; traditional techniques associated with habitat; culinary culture. It also includes ICH associated with cultural spaces; traditional games and sports; ICH associated with everyday events (MCC, 2019). Along with this legal basis, public cultural policy on intangible heritage has evolved (MCC, 2010a, 2011).

5 Theoretical Points About the Construction of Peace

Briefly, it can be stated that much of the research on peace in Colombia focuses on the dynamics of victimization, that is, on the logic of the conflict. In fact, the series of the National Centre of Historical Memory (CNMH) is based on this perspective, even though they have referred to strategies of local resistance and mention numerous cases of peacebuilding in the midst of war. Peace is then defined as a process of disarmament, reintegration, and reparation. However, other readings are emerging that emphasize the capacities of local communities to support, negotiate, and even oppose armed actors (Uribe & Salamanca, 2019).

Toward this line, peacebuilding has been analyzed as a process that involves the transformation of power relations and conflicts that emerge once the guns are silenced (Mac Ginty, 2008, 2010; Roberts, 2011). This perspective opens up spaces for conceptions that go beyond the so-called "statization" and "securitization" of peace (the control of internal threats that could destabilize the country).

Indeed, local actors raise the need to build peace with the territory, with the environment, between genders, ethnicities, and diverse social groups. This is not an effort to make the "State reach" the regions most affected by the conflict, but rather to build it. It is about rebuilding social, economic, political, cultural, and environmental relations, which obviously include but are not limited to the State issues. It is not a question; it must be stressed, of peace built from above, but of attempting a peace mobilized from below, from the territories.

Unlike the conflict centered perspective that conceives local actors as victims, the one that focuses on resistance and survival highlights local capacities and tries to give an account of the traces that these have left in the territory, as well as their accumulated potential to shape the peace that is at stake.

Sanz (2010) analyzes models of peacebuilding. According to him, several of these models have been developed from the 1990s to the 2000s and can be classified according to the vision they assume regarding the role of the State and civil society in peacebuilding. His criticism of many of these is directed at what could be called the "liberal consensus", that is, agreement on the need to generate a market democracy (liberal democracy, the market economy, and ethnic-cultural pluralism) in war-affected societies. A second criticism is directed at the Statist vision of social reality, i.e. a vision that is unable to conceive of a society outside of State relations, regardless of its position with regard to the restrictions that should be imposed on the State. The presentation of these criticisms is discussed in more detail below.

Also, the so-called "liberal peace" includes several subtypes: the conservative, the orthodox, and the transformative, among which there are differences and continuities. The differences and continuities are articulated according to three axes: (1) That of the concepts of sociocentrism and State-centrism; (2) The "bottom-up" and "top-down" visions, and (3) The tension between the strengthening of State institutions or their reduction in societies that are in transition from a state of war to one of peace. In other words, sociocentric perspectives refer to the fact that it is the visions of classes, pressure groups, the masses, civil society that constitute political relations, and the State. State-centric perspectives privilege relations within the State (elites, institutions, laws, armies) as constituents of social reality.

Transformative peace corresponds to the sociocentric perspective, which is inclined to construction from the bottom-up, concretely tending toward the strengthening of civil society.

Conservative peace, on the other hand, has a "top-down" vision that favors processes oriented by State-run institutions and aims at building a strong State that is capable of guaranteeing a market democracy. This form has its main impulse during the first decade of the twenty-first century, after the events of September 11th during the administration of George W. Bush. Orthodox peace shares the mistrust of the State presented by transformative peace. However, in the face of these forms that liberal peace takes, Sanz (2010) mentions two critical perspectives that seek to repoliticize and historicize peace-building processes and the concepts linked to them. He questions the vision of the State as a natural and legitimate institution per se, as well as the depoliticization of peace-building processes.

So-called post-liberal sociocentrism is nourished by post-structuralist ideas, emphasizing the historicity of concepts such as the State, civil society, governance, etc., criticizing liberal-conservative discourses that claim the existence of a single model of State and society. It uses terms such as governmentality, disciplinary regimes, or resistances and proposes the overcoming of liberal peace through concepts such as post-liberal peace, hybrid orders, and subaltern resistances.

Critical State-centrism emphasizes the central role of strong states in the construction of liberal societies but criticizes the fact that these processes have been inherently violent. It questions the post-liberal sociocentric view, arguing that since the State is the main arena of political contestation, a view that focuses exclusively on society can be depoliticized. The problems in post-war societies and the challenge for peacebuilding from this perspective are found in issues such as territorial sovereignty, global economic structures, or autonomous development. However, critical State-centrism is anti-statist.

According to Courtheyn (2018) "State-centered" peace (liberal peace) reproduces racism and patriarchy, making alternative notions of peace invisible. He argues that peace is not a utopia; it is a pluralistic spatial and political/discursive process. For him, liberal or modern peace does not always achieve positive results, it can be the expression of the victory of one actor (and of course, the destruction of others), or it can become repression for dissidents who fight for justice and to transform patriarchal hierarchies, racist or otherwise.

Courtheyn (2018) raises the question of authority and legality by posing the following question: Is it the disruption of order that constitutes a violent action, or is it the order itself (with the protective mechanisms it employs) that founds the violence? The question then remains: who exercises violence over whom, for example, is racist violence, or does someone who fights against it exercise violence?

Here we propose that peace has been a concept imbued with racism that maintains the privileges of whites against blacks and indigenous people. Modern peace perpetuates certain hierarchies. So, the question of which peace, is also the question, is peace built at the expense of what or of whom? Is perpetual, warlike (Roman) peace a racist structure? These questions and situations justify the need to create a normative structure that allows the multiplicity of peace to be evaluated. In this direction, the author argues that violence should not be limited to physical harm, nor should all physical harm be equated with violence. An analysis of power relations is required to distinguish between legitimate and illegitimate violence. At this point, the author suggests that there may be violence associated with emancipation.

On the other hand, Courtheyn (2018) points out that peace for one group may not be a good situation for another, as it happens in the Palestinian-Israeli case: peace may become a form of oppression and destruction. So what is peace? According to this author, the coexistence of groups in conditions of domination should not be understood as such. He constructs a concept of peace as "radical trans-relational".

It is the one that raises the ecological dignity created through networks of social movements of solidarity. Since liberal peace focuses on personal and national security, it has nothing to say about ecology. Trans-relational peace is opposed to anthropocentrism, for example, by taking up the notion of peace in Burkina Faso: peace is fresh air, that is, breathing in harmony with the divine breath. Courtheyn (2018) highlights other conceptions of peace in this same direction: as fertility, as interconnection with all beings. For example, peace understood as *Ubuntu* refers to the idea *I am because we are.* These definitions break with the defense of the liberal subject marked by fear and violence. Courtheyn (2018) speaks of trans-relational peace to highlight geographical solidarity (geography of solidarity) as well as the relational character of ecology to which he attributes certain autonomy within the framework of peace movements. In this sense, he clarifies that the prefix "trans" does not mean "beyond", it is "through" which refers to community resistances. In this way, it aims to gather contributions from feminism that focus on social movements and insist on analyzing peace from different scales, questioning the racial and gender dimensions.

Courtheyn (2018) offers several definitions of peace that from other cultures contribute to problematize the concept and that go beyond the State-centrism–socio-centrism debate pointed out above: the Scandinavian term *Fridr* refers to peace as fertility, both from agriculture and from human beings; *thaq*, in Quechua, means peace as cosmo-ecological harmony. Dietrich (2012) organizes the definitions of peace in four categories: (1) energetic peace (fertility, harmony with the cosmos); (2) moral peace (social justice according to the parameters of a community, salvation); (3) modern peace (security guaranteed by the State); and (4) post-modern peace (many peace). Peace thus articulates spiritual, personal, and sociocultural dimensions. Dietrich (2012) has shown that modern peace is a "peace without peace", given two conditions: (a) imposition of State security on individual citizens; and (b) promotion of a monotheistic morality that emphasizes peace in the afterlife, with one god and a life of suffering and salvation. Thus, the paradox of Roman peace is maintained in modernity: peace is the result of the defeat of the enemy.

Courtheyn (2018) raises the question of authority and legality by posing the following question: Is it the disruption of order that constitutes a violent action, or is it orders itself (with the protective mechanisms it operates) that found violence?

Here we propose that peace has been a concept imbued with racism that maintains the privileges of whites against blacks and indigenous people. Modern peace perpetuates certain hierarchies. So, the question of which peace, is also the question, is peace built at the expense of what or of whom? Is perpetual, warlike (Roman) peace a racist structure? These questions and situations justify the need to create a normative structure that allows the multiplicity of peace to be evaluated. In this direction, the author argues that violence should not be limited to physical harm, nor should all physical harm be equated with violence. An analysis of power relations is required to distinguish between legitimate and illegitimate violence. At this point, the author suggests that there may be violence associated with emancipation.

Courtheyn (2018) points out that peace for one group may not be a good situation for another, as it happens in the Palestinian-Israeli case: peace may become a form of oppression and destruction. So, what is peace? According to this author, the coexistence of groups in conditions of domination should not be understood as such. He constructs a concept of peace as "radical trans-relational". It is the one that raises the ecological dignity created through networks of social movements of solidarity. Since liberal peace focuses on personal and national security, it has nothing to say about ecology. Trans-relational peace is opposed to anthropocentrism, for example, by taking up the notion of peace in Burkina Faso: peace is fresh air, that is, breathing in harmony with the divine breath. The author highlights other conceptions of peace in this same direction: as fertility, as interconnection with all beings. For example, peace understood as *Ubuntu* refers to the idea "*I am because we are*". These definitions break with the defense of the liberal subject marked by fear and violence.

Courtheyn (2018) speaks of trans-relational peace to highlight geographical solidarity (geography of solidarity) as well as the relational character of ecology to which he attributes certain autonomy within the framework of peace movements. In this sense, he clarifies that the prefix "trans" does not mean "beyond", it is "through" which refers to community resistances. In this way, it aims to gather contributions from feminism that focus on social movements and insist on analyzing peace from different scales, questioning the racial and gender dimensions.

Courtheyn (2018) recognizes that the idea of a radical trans-relational peace centered on ecological dignity arises from social mobilization, and is inspired by the Colombian peace community processes, a conception that opposes the accumulation by dispossession that is characteristic of the global trend.

In a similar perspective, Moola (2006) proposes that top-down peace-building programs fail because they are unable to recognize gender-based inequity relations. This author understands positive peace as the absence of indirect structural violence, while negative peace refers to the absence of violence at a personal level. Moola (2006) mentions that peacebuilding was born in 1992 when the UN General Secretary proposed an agenda for peace that aimed to solve post-conflict problems in the world. The liberal theory defines peacebuilding as participation in the processes of economic and political liberalization, thus both democracy and the expansion of the free market are prescribed as the remedies for civil conflicts.

Moola (2006) takes as a central position the feminist idea that women are creators of life and caregivers within the framework of cultural norms so that they play a central role in shaping society and protecting their own families. This orients them toward nonviolence since they are socialized into peace-building skills from an early age. Women are therefore the cement of society. Even when they have been victims of sexual abuse and have asked their children, brothers, parents, and partners, they have become activists for peace and social justice. However, many women act as supporters in the development of conflict-related violence. In any case, by becoming a support for civil society amid war, they become the object of labor exploitation and the target of control by armed actors.

Moola (2006) considers it necessary to develop a bottom-up approach to dimension the participation of women in peacebuilding, an approach that in her opinion is not recognized by agencies such as the UN. However, she recognizes that this approach (bottom-up) can be complementary to traditional actions (top-down). For the author, this last type of approach presents a narrative that (following Freire) as "narration sickness", that is, the actors confronted and the victims are understood as "sick", or "wrong" who require "help". So NGOs and agencies often impose their vision and do not focus on transforming mentalities or generating power scenarios from and for women.

In general, international agencies privilege the constitution of negotiation tables between male warring elites, under the assumption that it is the men of war who can stop it. They forget that negotiations only support and that greater participation (especially of women) is required to build peace. Women's participation both at the negotiation tables and in subsequent processes is limited and/or subordinated. For example, in Macedonia, women's organizations are making important efforts for reconciliation and are lobbying NGOs and international agencies, but they do not have access to decision-making spaces. On the other hand, negotiations between elites end up favoring the global system and have little impact on the factors that generate poverty and exclusion. Nevertheless, the rhetoric of women's participation deployed by agencies and many NGOs often becomes a façade that tends to reduce women to the role of victims and does not recognize their important role in the agency of the required social transformations. It is worth emphasizing this point: women are agents of change, not just victims.

On the other hand, the participation of some women in political and/or negotiation and decision-making arenas does not automatically transfer resources and power to other women who may continue to suffer political, economic, and social exclusion. The security committees that accompany peacebuilding end up privileging the association between the public sphere and the role of men, leaving aside community and domestic tensions that also require attention.

For Moola (2006), peacebuilding has its roots in the theory of modernization of the 1950s–1960s, a theory that assumes the existence of a natural evolution that leads people toward democracy and the market, toward the West. But the imposition of electoral democracy and the market can exacerbate conflicts because it does not contribute to transforming poverty or inequality. On the other hand, the division of labor produced by liberal peace has not changed in favor of women and has instead added new burdens to their shoulders.

Moola (2006) raises the need to strengthen support for women's organizations, which often work in very precarious conditions. She also argues the need to strengthen the position of women to access the highest levels of decision-making. In this direction, she notes that some women in privileged positions end up assuming male positions to remain in existing power structures. Besides, the feminization of poverty is observed, as the labor market for women has stagnated as a result of the liberal prescription of peacebuilding. For example, South Africa has adopted a policy of integration into the global economy, which has led to women bearing the brunt of this, and so they are employed in the informal market. Thus, women's employment in the global economy is unequal and contradictory, while some manage to develop their prospects, others are excluded from technological and information networks, especially rural women. In this scenario, local knowledge is relegated. A culture based on individualism and consumerism is privileged, while African culture privileges the collective and the wisdom of the elders.

For Moola (2006), women's greatest challenge in building peace is the universal prescription of democracy, human rights, governance, and market liberalization. Indeed, the Westernised model of life is only achieved at the expense of those with fewer economic, cultural, and political possibilities, generally women.

Finally, it is worth mentioning that Moffett (2016) questions the conception that converts victims into passive actors within the framework of the dynamics of reparation that is characteristic of transitional justice, articulated from the perspective of so-called liberal peace. The author problematizes reparation processes based on the distinction between different types of victims. He recognizes the existence of what he calls "innocent victims" (those who did not participate in any action of harm to others in the context of the conflict) and "complex victims" (those who had some type of participation in victimizing acts). Moffett (2016) argues that it is necessary to develop a reparation structure capable of recognizing the nuances and realities of all victims in order to generate conditions that prevent new processes of violence. In fact, Moffett (2016) argues that the adequate treatment of complex victims requires overcoming the stereotype that makes victims into passive subjects, and recognizing all forms of suffering in a framework that is flexible enough both to identify responsibilities and to generate the corresponding reparation actions according to those responsibilities.

A key point of their analysis refers to the fact that, in transition processes, the recognition of victims is a controversial issue that involves identity dynamics related to the recognition of pain and responsibilities of armed actors, legal, illegal, as well as different State apparatuses and private actors. It is worth noting that reparation is a transitional justice mechanism and that different tensions are developing related to the definition of who is a victim and who is not, tensions that are deployed among others in political discourses related to the way in which each actor involved justifies its own actions and condemns those of others. Among them, the cultural aspects, specifically in relation to heritage.

On the other hand, in political conflicts, the distinction between victims and perpetrators is not clear and, in many situations, they can be both. Moffett (2016) questions the simplistic discourse that reduces victims to defenseless and passive subjects in order to consider the ways in which complex victims can participate in reparations to avoid future violence. The article analyzes the way victims are conceived; specifically, the way victimology evades the issue of the responsibilities that can be attributed to some of them, all in order to legitimize certain discourses, actors, and processes.

Moffett (2016) also argues that while international legislation focuses on human rights, political discourses during transitions continue the narrative of violence by different means (i.e. this is evident in Colombia with the discourses that promoted voting "No" in the plebiscite. Uribe et al., 2019). In any case, such legislation separates victimization and responsibilities related to facts of the conflict, so that the responsibilities of some victims have been insufficiently treated in relation to the type of violence typical of internal conflicts.

However, the label of the victim can be used to elicit sympathy, praise, or to justify individual benefits in recognition of suffering. In other words, the notion of the victim, as well as the type of institutions that recognize and repair them, are social constructions that assume ideals and stereotypes, so that these "ideal victims" may be represented as passive and vulnerable, unable to help themselves or contribute to the development of political or legal processes. However, the violence associated with conflict makes things more complex. For example, belligerent actors may portray themselves as collective victims in order to appear as "good guys" and arouse sympathy (this is reminiscent of both guerrilla and paramilitary discourses in Colombia). In Northern Ireland and Palestine, perpetrators appeal to collective victimization to justify their actions. In any case, in these power games certain cruel acts are made invisible (which in turn makes certain victims who suffered them invisible) and they even manage to justify violent action. The author raises the need to understand the victims in his agency and act accordingly.

Ignoring the potential responsibilities of some victims perpetuates a universalistic definition of victims that assumes that every person was victimized equally. In this direction, the author notes that the traditional idea of passive victims can lead to the idea that "we are all victims" (hiding some perpetrators), thus blurring their agency and making it impossible to recognize the differential needs of victims. A more nuanced perspective involves recognizing that individuals can be one and the other to apply a pluralistic perspective that allows for the establishment of appropriate mechanisms according to the conditions of the context. Failure to recognize complex victims can contribute to: (a) perpetuating stereotypes that lead to the idea that the victim "deserved" what happened, and (b) avoiding the application of reparations to marginalized groups.

Reparation plays a key role in the proper balance of the concession packages offered in the demobilization and reintegration processes. Thus, reparation is a key in the justice process because adequate recognition of suffering leads to actions by those responsible to remedy the pain caused. Reparation has purposes related to transparency (visibility, recognition, and reparation of victims), reconciliation, and peacebuilding, but these purposes can become tense when the corresponding actions are carried out. A key issue is how victimization and eligibility for reparations are established both in terms of procedures and outcomes.

Besides, reparation measures send messages about the values a society seeks to uphold, as well as a measure of the value of certain people in that society. The law organizes a scheme of responsibilities by establishing problematic notions of victims, prioritizing responses for certain victims, and making others invisible. A large number of victims creates a logistical challenge in defining victims and effectively redressing them. These problems can reveal the asymmetries of the law, as well as its limits for acting adequately. According to the author, "reparative" institutions serve more as devices for social control of suffering than as a way of recognizing and repairing it, as in the Argentine case. In this country, the receipt of money was understood by the victims as a way of legitimizing the State's narrative of anti-subversive struggle and minimizing their responsibilities for human rights violations. Reparations can "offend" innocent victims, not complex ones. In light of economic constraints, the latter are the first to be excluded. According to the author, in transitional justice, victims are generally defined simplistically without taking into account the complexity of their needs or the complexity of their identities in the context of conflict, so the complexity of their visions and experiences are equated in transitional justice. The absence of complex victims in reparation mechanisms can be explained (in part) because in many countries' reparation programs were built around the atrocities of authoritarian regimes in Latin America and Africa.

The State-centered approach to human rights has dominated reparation, assuming international standards, which, despite promoting "non-discrimination", leaves little room for establishing the accountability of non-State actors. In this scenario, the institutions in charge of identifying the victims, inquire about State responsibilities, but in terms of an abstract and autonomous apparatus, so that the civilians who supported their actions are dismissed (especially in Argentina and other authoritarian regimes in Latin America). Yet, from a transitional justice perspective, complex victims can come into conflict with other victims or with social perceptions. This makes them invisible and their suffering is not socially accepted. In this sense, reparation is more accepted if it does not compromise social values.

From a transitional justice perspective, victims are offered reparation, while for perpetrators, demobilization and judicial processes are offered. In both cases, the population is homogenized. Thus, legal categories constitute opposing entities that can inhibit reconciliation and limit sustainable peace. In this scenario, there has been evidence in some cases of the development of "transactional" justice in which the victims receive reparation while the perpetrators receive amnesty.

The ability to distinguish and assign responsibility is related to legitimacy, in fact, in cases where State forces can claim redress; they can also evade examination of their obligations. This can reinforce a hierarchy of victims, with some being treated as deserving of suffering. The nonrecognition of complex victims can limit reconciliation processes by excluding many victims who also suffered the violation of their rights. Furthermore, these exclusions represent a double standard, as where complex victims are excluded, State forces are often excluded from their responsibility.

Reparation programs are developed more as government programs than as the result of judicial processes. For this reason, they acquire a political character that should not be overlooked, so that the identification of victims is linked to the dominant political narrative and, therefore, their inclusion in compensation programs, their visibility, and public recognition end up being articulated as conflictive processes.

The discussion that has taken place up to this point highlights the need to understand the constriction of peace from a plural perspective. On the one hand, it is necessary to recognize that local actors have developed capacities to survive and even to oppose armed actors. These capacities are related to the possibility of transforming power relations related to the exploitation of territories, gender inequalities, racism, exclusion, and environmental deterioration.

On the other hand, the need to recognize the victims as active subjects alludes to the way in which they reconstruct their social and political identities. Indeed, victims in Colombia are in a complex tension regarding the meaning of their pain, for example, regarding discussions about memory (Acevedo, 2010), the way they should be repaired, the way they relate to the perpetrators (for example, about whether they deserve forgiveness, or not, in which cases, why). But just as important (perhaps even more so), around the victims an intense and complex discussion unfolds about their place in society, about their present and their future: is economic compensation enough, how to "repair" the destroyed social relationships, and if they cannot be repaired, what "new" relationships can they promote? As has been suggested, reparation policies tend to silence their voice, that is, they are not recognized as actors capable of devising and developing their own social and political programs.

6 On the Commitments and Measures of Response by the State

In order to comply with the "Convention for the Protection of Cultural Property in the Event of Armed Conflict", the initiative of the "Strategy for the Protection of Cultural Property in the Event of Armed Conflict" was proposed, led by the "Subsystem of International Humanitarian Law and Armed Conflict", in coordination with the Ministry of the Interior, the Ministry of Defense and the Presidential Program for Human Rights and International Humanitarian Law. Actually, the Presidential Advisory Office for Human Rights, which acts as its technical secretariat.

In addition, the Ministry of Culture, the Ministry of Foreign Affairs, the Historical Memory Centre, and the Central Bank of the Republic, among others, are involved. The strategy proposal is governed by the following specific considerations:

a. The establishment of priorities and the definition of strategies for assets covered by the special protection of international humanitarian law.
b. Without prejudice to the responsibility of the parties in conflict, to protect all types of property protected by International Humanitarian Law in the course of hostilities (This process goes beyond identification and marking).
c. To ensure that the absence of marking does not in any way exempt the parties to the conflict from obligations under the rules for the protection of this type of property (UNESCO, 2015).

In UNESCO report (2015) the Government of Colombia recognized that it is at an early stage of full domestic implementation of the Convention for the Protection of Cultural Property in the Event of Armed Conflict. For this reason, it considers that before evaluating the possibility of international assistance from the Fund, it will be necessary to continue building the strategy for the protection of cultural property in the event of armed conflict, and the creation of the Intersectoral Committee for the Convention for the Protection of Cultural Property in the Event of Armed Conflict.

Its Article 30 calls, inter alia, for the strengthening of appreciation and respect for cultural property, the dissemination of the Protocol, and the establishment of means of military instruction, training, and communication, as well as describing the measures taken in relation to the above-mentioned obligations.

The Ministry of Defense, in the context of its functional and mission-related competencies and general human rights policy, has repeatedly issued a large number of ministerial control directives and circulars, related to the care of victims:

- Directive 9/2005 introducing prevention and protection measures, humanitarian assistance in the event of emergencies, and socioeconomic stabilization of the displaced population.
- Directive 60/2006, which establishes the sectoral policy for the recognition, prevention, and protection of indigenous communities, mainly with regard to their autonomy, culture, territory and special jurisdiction; among other instructions, it requires respect for the special places of spiritual and cultural practices that make them sacred, previously defined in each community.

- Directive 7/2007, on the strengthening, promotion, and protection of human rights in communities of African descent, *Raizal*, and *Palenquero*, and emphasizing their collective rights, such as autonomy, territory, culture and special jurisdiction.
- Directive 48/2008, issued by the Army High Command, which gives instructions to strengthen the policy of prevalence, guarantee, and respect for the rights of children and adolescents, and establishes, among other things, that the Armed Forces should not occupy places protected or frequented by children, such as schools and hospitals.
- Permanent Directive 19-MD-CGFM-CARMA-ITAR-DDEHU-25.11/2010, of the Directorate of Human Rights and International Humanitarian Law of the Navy, which deals with the obligation to protect civilian property, including cultural property.
- Circular 033-MD-CGFM CARMA-ITAR-DDEHU-13/2014, from the Directorate of Human Rights and International Humanitarian Law of the Navy, issuing orders and instructions to protect civil and cultural property.

  Also, information bulletins on the protection of persons and civilian property, as well as those for extracurricular training for army units and officer training schools, are produced, which include these topics (UNESCO, 2015: 11).

The UNESCO report (2015) obviously does not recognize the involvement of State forces in the lack of action by omission despite prior knowledge of the planning of the El Salado massacre, seriously failing to meet the obligations undertaken.

As for specific and concrete actions in the work with communities, if they can be called as part of symbolic reparation, we can mention among others the activities of the program of the Ministry of Culture of Colombia in the region of Montes de Maria.

Since 1999 the Music Area of the Ministry of Culture of Colombia began the implementation of the Traditional Music Project as a pilot experience in the municipalities of Montes de María in Bolívar and Sucre, […] The process prioritized the formative work with children, young people, and teachers in these municipalities and the strengthening of their schools. With the implementation of the National Plan of Music for Coexistence, this project achieves coverage in all departments of the country, taking into account the particularities of traditional music in each region or sub-region, in a proposal of Axes of Traditional Music. The axes allow for the identification of traditional music in relation to a territory that has produced it as a priority and where it generates strong social roots and, therefore, a special identity; furthermore, they make reference to instrumental formats and the most representative genres.

In the region of Montes de María it is representative of the territory of whistle and drum music (departments of Atlántico, Bolívar, Córdoba, Sucre, and part of the Magdalena) in the formats of *gaitas, pito atravesa'o, tambora, baile canta'o, pelayera* band, and others; with music (rhythms) of *cumbia, bullerengue, porro, fandango* and others (Valencia, 2004) (see Fig. 2).

Fig. 2 *Gaitero* (Gaita player) (*Source Colombia Festiva.* Retrieved from https://www.radionacional.co/noticia/las-notas-transformadoras-montes-maria)

Currently, following this vision, the regions of Colombia respond to Sonorous Territories.[10] The region of the Montes de Maria belongs to the territory of the Chants, Whistles, and Drums.[11] At the same time, another initiative of Sonorous Territories has an archive of conversations around research, processes, audiovisual production, and accompaniment of the victims of the conflict (CNMH, 2019).

This stems from the Musical Routes of Colombia Program, now called Sonorous Territories (MCC, 2010b) based on the recognition of the country's cultural flows in order to consolidate the spaces of the music schools as a protective and transforming fabric of traditions. Stimulating creativity and the recreation of memory, promoting social and organizational networks, meetings of music teachers, researchers, instrument makers, festivals and regional managers, and the concerted formulation of Strategic Plans for the Development of Music in the Regions are alternatives for citizens to identify the needs, aspirations, and challenges of the music field.

Music, singing, and dance schools are spaces for knowledge, practice, and enjoyment, they are nourished by research and experimentation with new pedagogical models. Schools are centers of memory, creation, and production. Schools foster decentralization, autonomy and local relevance, respect for diversity, and the promotion of intercultural dialogue. This program has contributed to the integration and strengthening of the Cultural System of the territories, by generating greater value and recognition of cultural goods, services, and manifestations. In the Montes de Maria, it is hoped that the work of regional talent will continue to be a driving force for the reconciliation of the community with its heritage.

Recent processes have evolved into projects such as Sonorous Body, a proposal that has evolved from the recognition, appropriation, and enjoyment of art, heritage, and cultural assets, considering that the actions are undertaken to guarantee cultural rights make an essential contribution to the comprehensive development of early childhood and are fundamental to the protection and guarantee of other human rights.

[10] http://territoriosonoro.org/. Accessed: 26 July 2020.

[11] http://cantospitosytambores.blogspot.com/. Accessed: 26 July 2020.

Since 2011, this project has strengthened the processes of strengthening and qualifying the pedagogical practices carried out with early childhood by promoting workshops with the purpose of enriching and strengthening emotional ties with children, as well as contributing to their comprehensive development and the recognition of their cultural, social, and personal characteristics, based on promoting the enjoyment of all languages and artistic and aesthetic expressions, experienced through the senses, the body, movement, sound, play, and exploration. From the cultural, social, and personal recognition and the creative potential of the participants, new ways of growing, relating to each other, and thus advancing in the national commitment to building peace (MCC, 2018) are founded.

Between 2016 and 2019, the Ministry of Culture carried out the Sensory Expedition,[12] a set of coordinated activities for the implementation of research-creation laboratories; training in dance and music; provision of traditional music instruments and dance costumes; promotion of productive initiatives and cultural strengthening by the community on issues of community tourism, traditional cuisine, music, festivals; workshops and meetings in training for the formulation of projects, production of events, costume design, maintenance of instruments, artistic makeup, computer graphics of festivals, meeting of young leaders in the region. In addition to the results: the record production "Masters and Minstrels of the Montes de María"; the collective creation "Mako: Return without fire"; the exhibition "Where the owls squeak: Reflections of the Sensory Expedition"; the documentary "Sensory Expedition".[13] The book "Sabedores: Memory of the Montes de María" is the result of research into the sound practices of the Montes de María.

7 Conclusions: Refounding the Intangible Cultural Heritage as a Future for Peace

> The notion of community participation in heritage management is largely derived from human rights principles. The idea of promoting community participation, while difficult to enforce and apply, corresponds to the notion of a human rights approach to heritage management and governance. (Francioni & Lixinski, 2017: 11)

Finally, the connection or congruence of heritage concepts with human rights is visible, which is why heritage management in countries like Colombia cannot be dissociated from them. According to Francioni and Lixinski (2017: 17), the debates around the human dimension of international cultural heritage law seem to suggest that a similar erosion is also possible in the field of cultural heritage, precisely because of the influence of international human rights law and practice. This process of transformation began with a shift in the idea of "cultural heritage" from the tangible connotation of "cultural assets" and "cultural objects" understood as tangible assets

[12] https://www.mincultura.gov.co/areas/artes/expedicionsensorial/Paginas/montes-de-maria.aspx Accessed: 26 July 2020.

[13] https://www.youtube.com/watch?v=d_APYncn97g. Accessed: 26 July 2020.

of artistic, historical, and archaeological value to the intangible notion of heritage, which coincides with the tradition and living practices or manifestations of a cultural community. The concept of "cultural property" was inaugurated with the 1954 Hague Convention. The definition covered only monuments and tangible objects, in accordance with the prevailing Western tradition and understanding of art and culture. The scope of this notion was expanded with the 1972 World Heritage Convention, which included natural heritage and a new notion of cultural heritage as representing the variety of significant and distinct cultural traditions of the world (Francioni & Lixinski, 2017).

In this sense, Francioni and Lixinski (2017) argue the 1972 Convention is an antecedent to the 2005 Convention on the Protection and Promotion of the Diversity of Cultural Expressions. The decisive step toward international recognition of the human dimension of cultural heritage was the launch by UNESCO of the Living Human Treasures and Masterpieces of Oral and Intangible Heritage programs, which eventually led to the adoption of the 2003 ICH Convention. While the "dematerialization" of cultural heritage and the broadening of the scope of international protection to cover living heritage, culture, and "intangible heritage" have the potential to enhance human culture resulting in competing rights and entitlements.

Following Francioni and Lixinski (2017), one of the means by which heritage law can be enforced is international criminal law, an area similar to international human rights law. This shows the intersection between culture and human rights as a relative lag in the development of international law. The studies of international law have long neglected the connection between the protection of cultural heritage and gross violations of human rights. It took the descent into total barbarism of the Yugoslavian war of the 1990s and the subsequent infamous destruction of ancient art and heritage by the Taliban in Afghanistan—later replicated in Mali, Syria, and Iraq—for scholars and public opinion to realize the link between attacks on culture and human rights violations. Much of the cultural destruction of monuments, religious buildings, libraries, and historical sites in those wars was not the collateral effect of the conduct of hostilities, but the result of the deliberate selection of cultural objects for the purpose of "cleansing" the attacked territory not only of any human presence but also of the symbols and cultural traces of the life and presence of the enemy in the territory.

International conflicts have provided ample evidence that attacks on culture and cultural heritage have become a systematic method of conducting war by other "means" and extending the brutality of ethnic cleansing to cultural persecution and extinction. Over the past two decades, the link between attacks on culture and serious human rights violations have emerged at the level of international law and has acquired precise legal connotations in the form of international crimes. In 2003, the UNESCO General Conference unanimously adopted the Declaration concerning the Intentional Destruction of Cultural Heritage, which reaffirms the principle of State responsibility and individual criminal responsibility for deliberate acts of destruction of the cultural heritage of great importance for humanity (Francioni & Lixinski, 2017: 24–25).

Although adjudication of violations of individual cultural identity is by no means the only way in which heritage law and human rights can be put into practice. In the area of community participation, access and participation rights can be very useful, and human rights standards can be used to adjudicate and enforce this type of participation (Francioni & Lixinski, 2017; Ekern et al., 2012).

In conclusion, several elements can be highlighted from this whole journey through the Colombian conflict and some theories on peacebuilding:

a. The victims are not mere passive actors waiting for recognition. It is important to recognize their capacity to decide what they want, who they want to be, and how to achieve it. These heritages, these capacities, are part of their heritage, their past, their present, their way of building a future for themselves.
b. The victims were military targets of the armed actors, not a mere accident or mistake.
c. The capacities of the victims in Colombia also develop a political action that not only focuses on overcoming what happened but also demands justice, as well as social and cultural transformations. Here, heritage has not only a decorative value but is installed as a tool for building an identity with a profound political character that we must be able to recognize.

Finally, given that heritage and human rights are debated is a field in dispute (Francioni & Lixinski, 2017; Logan & Reeves, 2008; Ekern et al., 2012; Logan, 2012; Alatalu, 2020; Larsen, 2020), it can be said that these tensions are exacerbated in periods of violence and intense social conflict. Indeed, López De la Roche (2014) has documented and analyzed the effort of former President Uribe's administrations (2002–2006 and 2006–2010) to "rewrite" history, rethinking the role of the guerrillas, the way they emerged, as well as the role of the State in containing them. In that direction, he assigned the national army the label of "heroes of the fatherland" and turned the FARC into the number one enemy of the Colombian people. This type of process took the counter-insurgency struggle to new horizons, turning it into a strategy to reject the political pretensions of these groups, never recognizing their right to belligerence and thus gaining support for the State. Based on this perspective, statues and monuments were erected, books were published and the press was mobilized. But these logics were not limited to actions in the mass media and social networks. Actions were developed in the disputed territories through processes of "territorial consolidation" (Aponte, 2019), through which a military strategy was articulated to recover the areas that were besieged or controlled by the guerrillas, with a dynamic of building a "culture of legality" aimed at having citizens accept authority and reject illegal activities. In addition to this strategy, an effort was made to have the police and mayors occupy all the country's municipalities, to militarize the roads for the passage of land-based tourism, as well as to invest in roads and social services (health, education, and social security) known as "democratic security".

The peace process itself raised serious questions about its legitimacy and content, especially concerning the political participation of ex-combatants and the planned system of truth and reparation (Uribe et al., 2019). These authors argue that a series of strategies were developed in the country to "manage" the hatreds and fears against the agreement, that is, a series of activities in the media aimed at exacerbating these feelings through tweets and false news, for example, arguing that the agreement promoted homosexuality, or that the ex-combatants would receive astronomical amounts of money when they laid down their arms.

However, the demobilized combatants are also trying to present their version of the conflict and legitimize their decision to lay down their arms, to join legal life, and to transform their political work. Thus, in La Fila (a concentration site for ex-combatants in the municipality of Icononzo (Tolima), some 150 km south of Bogotá), they have tried to create a museum to tell their story and communicate their perspective to others. Others have published books about the history of the commanders and pioneers of their struggle: Pedro Antonio Marín (aka *Tiro Fijo*, founder of the FARC and the most iconic figure in the organization), Ciro Trujillo, another of the founders (Trujillo, 2017), among others.

On the other hand, the visibility of the victims is also a problematic issue. For example, Firchow (2017) points out that some massacres have achieved greater resonance in the media, while others have not received the same treatment, despite being as bloody as or more so than the former. This has led to the former receiving greater attention from both the State and NGOs, which in turn leads to the memory (the telling of what happened and the actions of reparation and reconciliation required) of the latter being pushed into the background. In this direction, as has already been established, it is necessary to consider the victims as active subjects, overcoming the traditional conception that reduces them to subjects without agency and without the capacity to respond to the circumstances in which they live. The victims in Colombia claim to be actors with a social, cultural, and political perspective and demand recognition, not only of their suffering but also of their capacity to contribute to the peace and development of the country (Acevedo, 2010).

As has been suggested, the construction of heritage, i.e., of those traditions that social actors rescue from the past as a symbol of identity, as well as those present customs from which they build a common future, are deeply strained by multiple interests, practices, and strategies that demand further analysis.

Therefore, it is fundamental to deepen the work of the heritagization of the cultural manifestation, in the case of the music of *Gaitas*, *Pitos*, and *Tambores* of the Montes de María, which despite having been savagely attacked, is key to generate new narratives of peace and to generate a corrective memory of the past. This corrective memory is a way of remembering the past through a new shared set of values and ethics (Huang & Lee, 2018). Where conflict continues to erupt or remembrance remains cruel, heritage conservation activities in such circumstances can usefully become tools of conflict management helping to build a shared sense of identity (Logan & Reeves, 2008).

Places of pain and shame need to be remembered for affected communities, not for tourism (Logan & Reeves, 2008). In 2008, the Itinerant Museum of Memory and Identity of the Montes de María (MIM) was created to remember the victims of the armed conflict, proclaiming justice, truth, and reparation, and demanding guarantees of non-repetition of the crimes committed against its population. The MIM is led by the Montes de María Communications Collective (CCMMLa21) and several national and international organizations have cooperated in setting up and making it visible, including the Ministry of Culture of Colombia, the National Centre for Historical Memory (CNMH), the Corporation for Development Solidarity (CDS), the Latin American Institute for an Alternative Society and Law (ILSA), the Movement for Peace (MPDL), the Spanish Agency for International Development Cooperation (AECID), the French Embassy in Colombia and Ibermuseums.

The Museum defines itself as a platform of symbolic reparation where the public and political voice of the affected communities is recovered. The Museum is itinerant and participatory; its light wooden structure makes it possible to move around. Inside it houses the "tree of life" from which 1400 leaves with the names of the victims hang; there are also testimonies of the conflict. Through various audiovisual sources, tools have been developed that are proposed to the community for the construction of their narratives and testimonies (CIPDH, 2020).

Later, in El Salado, *La Casa del Pueblo* (People´s House) was built with the participation of various entities (under the coordination of the Semana Foundation), is a key space for the construction of these processes:

> From pre-existing structures with a high symbolic value, such as the sports field where the massacre occurred, the remains of the buildings affected by the attack and the trees in the area, appreciated for their shade and as a meeting point, the proposal for the new center of El Salado began to take shape. In a process of resignification, the sports field was named Campo de la Memoria (Court of Memory), in which the cleaning of the floor was an act of care, affection, reflection, and generation of a new meeting place. The Culture Field emerged around the Cocuelo tree, remembered for its antiquity and large size, with new buildings for the community: the library, which transcends the mere activity of reading to become a meeting space; three ranches, for the activities of different members of society, and the Solar Tree, where the services and photovoltaic cells for the operation of the complex are concentrated. The landscaping and public space that weaves the parts of the new center for El Salado were based on the use of the shade generated by trees and eaves of the buildings, under which the community meets to play, talk, dance, and live with dignity. (Hosie, 2016)

However, the conditions of poverty in the region have not been overcome (Gómez, 2020). Young people do not find opportunities and migrate to the cities, despite the attention they have received from the public and private entities and NGOs. This territory, like many others in the country, continues to be marginalized, precariously linked to Colombia's social, political, and cultural life. As mentioned in a newspaper report, 20 years after the massacre (Noticias Caracol, 2020):

> It was two nights and three days of horror until the Marines arrived, while the paramilitaries disappeared, never to be seen.
>
> The only donkey that was left alive was heard braying because even the dogs were killed there.

This abandonment has also been forgetting of the pain experienced by its inhabitants:

> Yirley, who is now a leader, says that when it comes to repairing El Salado, they did the job the other way around: "Excellent road, excellent health center, half-assed school, and the social thing?..." The wounds are open: a lot of sadness. (Noticias Caracol, 2020)

And since January 2019, as has happened with many leaders like her, they began to threaten her. According to Indepaz (2020a) "from the signing of the Peace Agreement in 2016 until July 15, 2020, 971 social leaders and human rights defenders have been murdered". At the time of writing this chapter, 166 social leaders and 36 former FARC-EP combatants who signed the Peace Agreement (Indepaz, 2020b) have been murdered during the course of 2020.

Violence against the inhabitants of El Salado continues.

References

Acevedo, A. Ó. F. (2010). *Geografías de la memoria: Percepciones de las víctimas en Colombia en el período de justicia transicional (2005–2010)*. Bogotá: Editorial Universidad Javeriana.

Aguilera, P. J. M. (2014). *Contrapoder y justicia guerrillera: Fragmentación política y orden insurgente en Colombia (1952–2003)*. Bogotá: Penguin Random House.

Alatalu, R. (2020). Dignity of the heritage and the heritage communities. *Journal of Cultural Heritage Management and Sustainable Development*, vol. ahead-of-print no. ahead-of-print. https://doi.org/10.1108/JCHMSD-06-2019-0064.

Andrade, B. O. D., et al. (2019). *Entre paramilitares y guerrillas: la desposesión territorial en los Montes de María. Dinámicas históricas y territoriales del conflicto político, social y armado 1958–2016*. Instituto de Estudios Interculturales. Cali: Pontificia Universidad Javeriana. https://www2.javerianacali.edu.co/sites/ujc/files/node/field-documents/field_document_file/montes_de_maria_1.pdf. Accessed 15 July 2020.

Andrade, M. (2013). ¿A quién y qué representa la lista representativa del patrimonio cultural inmaterial de la nación en Colombia? *Boletín de Antropología, 28*(46), 53–78. http://www.erigaie.org/wp-content/uploads/2014/10/Andrade-2013.-A-quien-representa-la-lista-representativa-de-PCI.pdf. Accessed 19 July 2020.

Aponte, G. A. F. (2019). *Grupos armados y construcción de orden social en la esquina sur del Tolima, 1948–2016*. Bogotá: Fundación Centro de Investigación y Educación Popular-Programa por la Paz (CINEP-PPP)- Educapaz-Pontificia Universidad Javeriana.

Arjona, A. (2017). *Rebelocracy: A theory of social order in civil war*. Working paper document, Kellogg Institute for International Studies 422. https://kellogg.nd.edu/sites/default/files/working_papers/422_0.pdf. Accessed 15 July 2020.

Ávila, A. (2019). *Detrás de la guerra en Colombia*. Bogotá: Planeta.

Barros, N. N. I., & Uribe, S. J. J. (2019). *La retaguardia en disputa*. Ibagué: Ediciones Unibagué.

Beltrán, V. M. A. (2015). *Las FARC-EP (1950–2015): Luchas de ira y esperanza*. Bogotá: Ediciones desde abajo.

Centro Internacional para la Promoción de los Derechos Humanos-Categoría II Unesco [CIPDH]. (2020). *Museo Itinerante de la Memoria y la Identidad de los Montes de María*. https://www.cipdh.gob.ar/memorias-situadas/lugar-de-memoria/museo-itinerante-de-la-memoria-y-la-identidad-de-los-montes-de-maria/. Accessed 26 July 2020.

Centro Nacional de Memoria Histórica [CNMH]. (2019). *Territorios Sonoros, los diversos caminos que nos llevan a construir la memoria*. Podcasts. http://centrodememoriahistorica.gov.co/podcasts/territorios-sonoros/. Accessed 14 July 2020.

Comisión Colombiana de Juristas. (2009, April 27). Las responsabilidades en la masacre de El Aro: una verdad por desentrañar. Boletín No. 34. Retrieved from: https://www.coljuristas.org/documentos/boletines/bol_n34_975.pdf. Accessed 15 November 2020.

Comisión Nacional de Reparación y Reconciliación [CNRR]. (2009). *La masacre de El Salado: esa guerra no era nuestra*. Grupo de Memoria Histórica, Colombia: Fundación Semana-Editorial Taurus. http://centrodememoriahistorica.gov.co/wp-content/uploads/2020/02/3.-La-masacre-de-El-Salado.pdf. Accessed 26 July 2020.

Comisión Nacional de Reparación y Reconciliación [CNRR]. (2010). *La tierra en disputa. Memorias de despojo y resistencia campesina en la costa Caribe (1960–2010).* Grupo de Memoria Histórica, Colombia: Fundación Semana-Editorial Taurus. https://reliefweb.int/sites/reliefweb.int/files/resources/la_tierra_en_%20disputa.pdf. Accessed 12 July 2020.

Confortini, C. (2006). Galtung, violence, and gender: The case for a peace studies/feminism alliance. *Peace & Change, 31,* 333–367. https://doi.org/10.1111/j.1468-0130.2006.00378.x.

Courtheyn, C. (2018). Peace geographies: Expanding from modern-liberal peace to radical trans-relational peace. *Progress in Human Geography, 42*(2), 741–758. https://doi.org/10.1177/0309132517727605.

Dietrich, W. (2012). *Interpretations of peace in history and culture.* London: Palgrave Macmillan.

Ekern, S., Logan, W., Sauge, B., & Sinding-Larsen, A. (2012). Human rights and world heritage: Preserving our common dignity through rights-based approaches to site management. *International Journal of Heritage Studies, 18*(3), 213–225. https://doi.org/10.1080/13527258.2012.656253.

El Heraldo, P. (2019). *Tribunal ratifica omisión del Estado en masacre de El Salado.* https://www.elheraldo.co/bolivar/tribunal-ratifica-omision-del-estado-en-masacre-de-el-salado-686725. Accessed 26 July 2020.

Firchow, P. (2017). Do reparations repair relationships? Setting the stage for reconciliation in Colombia. *International Journal of Transitional Justice, 11,* 315–338. https://doi.org/10.1093/ijtj/ijx010.

Francioni, F., & Lixinski, L. (2017). Opening the toolbox of international human rights law in the safeguarding of cultural heritage. In A. Durbach & L. Lixinski (Eds.), *Heritage, culture and rights challenging legal discourses* (pp. 11–33). Oxford-Portland: Hart Publishing.

Fundación Ideas para la Paz [Ideaspaz]. (2011). Análisis regional de los Montes de María. Resource document. http://ideaspaz.org/media/website/MontesdeMariaweb.pdf. Accessed 13 July 2020.

García, F. J. (2005). La UNESCO y la protección del Patrimonio Histórico Universal. *ARI*, 144. http://www.realinstitutoelcano.org/wps/portal/rielcano_es/contenido?WCM_GLOBAL_CONTEXT=/elcano/elcano_es/zonas_es/lengua+y+cultura/ari+144-2005. Accessed 23 July 2020.

Gómez, A. J. I. (2020). El Salado: a 20 años de un hito de violencia. Periódico Digital UN. http://unperiodico.unal.edu.co/pages/detail/el-salado-a-20-anos-de-un-hito-de-violencia/?fbclid=IwAR0597t5nh0iYkR3Ie3I6VnBCjkKJqaAireM2vdYpxbMaOPUwmwlaJTCYTQ. Accessed 24 July 2020.

González, G. F. (2016). *Poder y violencia en Colombia.* Bogotá: ODECOFI-CINEP.

Gutiérrez-Sanín, F. (2016). *El orangután con sacoleva: Cien años de democracia y represión en Colombia (1910–2010).* Bogotá: Universidad Nacional de Colombia—Debate.

Guzmán, C. G., Fals, B. O., & Umaña, L. E. (1988). La Violencia en Colombia. Estudio de un proceso social. Tomo I. 206–207. Bogotá: Círculo de Lectores.

Hosie, S. S. (2016). La Casa del Pueblo: Nuevo centro de El Salado. El Salado, Bolívar, Colombia. *Dearq, 19,* 104–111. https://revistas.uniandes.edu.co/pb-assets/multimedia/dearq/19_Elsalado-1534454933627.pdf. Accessed 22 July 2020.

Huang, S., & Lee, H. (2018). Difficult heritage diplomacy? Rearticulating places of pain and shame as world heritage in Northeast Asia. *International Journal of Heritage Studies, 25*(2), 143–159. https://doi.org/10.1080/13527258.2018.1475410.

Instituto de Estudios para el Desarrollo y la Paz [Indepaz]. (2020a). *Informe sobre el homicidio de líderes y defensores de derechos humanos en Colombia.* http://www.indepaz.org.co/wp-content/uploads/2020/07/Informe-Especial-Asesinato-lideres-sociales-Nov2016-Jul2020-Indepaz.pdf. Accessed 25 July 2020.

Instituto de Estudios para el Desarrollo y la Paz [Indepaz]. (2020b). *Líderes sociales y defensores de derechos humanos asesinados en 2020.* http://www.indepaz.org.co/paz-al-liderazgo-social/. Accessed 25 July 2020.

Kalyvas, S. (2010). *La lógica de la violencia en la guerra civil.* Madrid: Akal.

Larsen, P. (2020). Modern conflict, emergencies, and cultural heritage: Exploring the relevance of cultural rights. In Protecting cultural property: International conference on the 20th anniversary

of the 1999 second protocol of the 1954 Hague Convention. Unesco. Retrieved from: http://archive-ouverte.unige.ch/unige:140520.
Logan, W. (2012). Cultural diversity, cultural heritage and human rights: towards heritage management as human rights-based cultural practice. *International Journal of Heritage Studies, 18,* 3. https://doi.org/10.1080/13527258.2011.637573.
Logan, W., & Reeves, K. (2008). *Places of pain and shame: Dealing with 'difficult heritage'*. Key issues in cultural heritage. London: Routledge. https://doi.org/10.4324/9780203885031.
López, C. (2016). *Adiós a las FARC ¿Y ahora qué?*. Bogotá: Debate.
López De La Roche, F. E. (2014). *Las ficciones del poder: patriotismo, medios de comunicación y reorientación afectiva de los colombianos bajo Uribe Vélez (2002–2010)*. Bogotá: Penguin Random House.
Mac Ginty, R. (2008). Indigenous peace-making versus the liberal peace. *Cooperation and Conflict, 43*(2), 139–163. https://doi.org/10.1177/0010836708089080.
Mac Ginty, R. (2010). Hybrid peace: The interaction between top-down and bottom-up peace. *Security Dialogue, 41*(4), 391–412. https://doi.org/10.1177/0967010610374312.
Meertens, D. (2010). El empoderamiento de las mujeres como elemento estratégico en la prevención del desplazamiento: políticas y prácticas en Montes de María. In C. Churruca & D. Meertens (Eds), *Desplazamiento en Colombia: Prevenir, asistir, transformar cooperación internacional e iniciativas locales* (pp. 219–248). Medellín: La Carreta Social Editores.
Ministry of Culture of Colombia [MCC]. (2010a). *Compendio de políticas culturales.* Bogotá: Ministerio de Cultura. https://www.mincultura.gov.co/ministerio/politicas-culturales/compendio-politicas-culturales/Documents/compendiopoliticas_artefinalbaja.pdf. Accessed 14 July 2020.
Ministry of Culture of Colombia [MCC]. (2010b). *Territorios Sonoros*. Resource document. https://www.mincultura.gov.co/areas/artes/musica/territorios-sonoros/Paginas/default.aspx. Accessed 26 July 2020.
Ministry of Culture of Colombia [MCC]. (2011). *Patrimonio cultural inmaterial en Colombia.* https://www.mincultura.gov.co/areas/patrimonio/publicaciones/Documents/C-Convenci%C3%B3n%20y%20pol%C3%ADtica%20de%20salvaguarda%20del%20PCI.pdf. Accessed 14 July 2020.
Ministry of Culture of Colombia [MCC]. (2017). *Representative list of intangible cultural heritage.* https://www.mincultura.gov.co/areas/patrimonio/patrimonio-cultural-en-Colombia/lista-indicativa-de-candidatos-a-bien-de-interes-cultural/Paginas/Lista-Representativa-del-Patrimonio-Cultural-Inmaterial.aspx. Accessed 19 July 2020.
Ministry of Culture of Colombia [MCC]. (2018). *Cuerpo sonoro: expresiones artísticas y primera infancia.* https://maguared.gov.co/wp-content/uploads/2018/10/cuerpo-sonoro-basico-v1.pdf. Accessed: 14 July 2020.
Ministry of Culture of Colombia [MCC]. (2019, December 26). Decree number 2358 of 2019, by which decree 1080 of 2015 is modified and added to the regulations of the culture sector, regarding tangible and intangible cultural heritage. *Official Journal N° 51.178.* https://diario-oficial.vlex.com.co/vid/decreto-numero-2358-2019-831282865. Accessed 12 July 2020.
Moffett, L. (2016). Reparations for 'guilty victims': Navigating complex identities of victim-perpetrators in reparation mechanism. *International Journal of Transitional Justice, 10*(1), 146–167. https://doi.org/10.1080/10130950.2006.9674759.
Moola, S. (2006). Women and peace-building: The case of Mabedlane women. *Agenda: Empowering Women for Gender Equity, 20*(69), 124–133. https://www.tandfonline.com/doi/abs/10.1080/10130950.2006.9674759. Accessed 24 July 2020.
Noticias Caracol. (2020). *Sobrevivientes de El Salado hacen la cronología de una masacre que, 20 años después, sigue doliendo.* https://noticias.caracoltv.com/informes-especiales/sobrevivientes-de-el-salado-hacen-la-cronologia-de-una-masacre-que-20-anos-despues-sigue-doliendo. Accessed 22 July 2020.
Ocampo, G. I. (2015). *Poderes regionales, clientelismo y Estado: Etnografías del poder y la política en Córdoba, Colombia.* Bogotá: ODECOFI-CINEP.

Paarlberg-Kvam, K. (2019). What's to come is more complicated: feminist visions of peace in Colombia. *International Feminist Journal of Politics, 21*(2), 194–223. https://doi.org/10.1080/14616742.2018.1487266.

Posada, Z. I. C., & Carmona, P. J. A. (2019). Devenir lideresa en el conflicto armado en Colombia: un tránsito de víctima a reclamante de justicia. In J. A. Carmona Parra & F. Moreno Martín (Eds.), *Reconstrucción de subjetividades e identidades en contextos de guerra y posguerra* (pp. 230–246). Manizales: Fondo Editorial Universidad de Manizales. http://ridum.umanizales.edu.co:8080/xmlui/bitstream/handle/6789/3507/Reconstruccion_de_subjetividades_e_identidades_en_contextos_de_guerra_y_posguerra.pdf?sequence=1&isAllowed=y. Accessed 24 July 2020.

Reliefweb-OCHA Services. (2015, October 16). *Álvaro Uribe, las Convivir y los ejércitos paramilitares*. Retrieved from: https://reliefweb.int/report/colombia/lvaro-uribe-las-convivir-y-los-ej-rcitos-paramilitares. Accessed 15 November 2020.

Republic of Colombia Congress [RCC]. (2008, March 12). Law 1185 whereby Law 397 of 1997 is modified and added general law of culture. *Official Journal N° 46.929*. http://www.secretariasenado.gov.co/senado/basedoc/ley_1185_2008.html. Accessed 17 July 2020.

Restrepo, G. A. (2019). El carnaval de la tristeza. Resource document. Universidad de Antioquia. http://udea.edu.co/wps/portal/udea/web/inicio/udea-noticias/udea-noticia/!ut/p/z1/vZXfT9swEMf_lfGQR9fX2EncvWWsA3Ut7bQWiF-Qk7qpt8QOiWk3_vo5AgmVDaoJGT_4l86fu-_ZOmOOrzHXYqdKYZXRonLrjMc3bHQaDlMKU4hpDGm8oFESnpHlJeCrQwMG7Auk35bTMV3NAOYR5q-fv8Qc80Lbxm5x1pjWiupuLUUAojtcbU0tH-Z9_0EbqwolugAKo63Uam16q6dt0yjtNAQgK1SI1qkSFVpLVAlkW9VZeS96102h1jjLSUIoowlKWCwQJYygPI6GaESShOU5GYVs81zq31p6qfBCS_tU8WfZ-DqMXLLGi4vl_HTxeRI-GrzCyFwMyUsxEKD4aqfkHq-0aWt3fd__U-L5UQ_RGz0cwSde8WehX_zQL554xbPYL97vy2F-X86c-sX7zT2FN-Inx8q4-yfUj9tbnrpi3tfjXxZfv3c1d0GWlckffq1U54SVmLdyI1vZDu5at721tuk-BhDAfr8flMaUlRwUpg7gX0e2pnMqDi1xU69qRn6jn5vZmNBssrv_dIGODdPNzEbZyR9FuMfY/dz/d5/L2dBISEvZ0FBIS9nQSEh/?page=udea.inicio.udea.noticias.noticia&urile=wcm%3Apath%3A%2FPortalUdeA%2FasPortalUdeA%2FasHomeUdeA%2FUdeA%2BNoticias%2FContenido%2FasNoticias%2FOpinion%2Fel-carnaval-de-la-tristeza. Accessed 18 July 2020.

Rettberg, A., Leiteritz, R., Nasi, C., & Prieto, J. D. (2018). ¿Recursos diferentes, conflictos distintos? Un marco para comprender la economía política del conflicto armado y la criminalidad en las regiones colombianas. In A. Retberg, R. Leiteritz, C. Nasi, & J. D. Prieto (Eds.), *¿Diferentes recursos, conflictos distintos? La economía política regional del conflicto armado y la criminalidad en Colombia* (pp. 3–45). Bogotá: Ediciones Uniandes. http://dx.doi.org/10.7440/2018.05.

Revista Arcadia. (2011). *Cantaoras, el alma de un pueblo*. https://www.revistaarcadia.com/agenda/evento/cantaoras-alma-pueblo/24668. Accessed 20 July 2020.

Revista Semana. (2018). *¡Resucitó El Salado!* https://www.semana.com/nacion/articulo/el-salado-la-recuperacion-de-un-pueblo-que-sufrio-una-de-las-peores-masacres/565283. Accessed 20 July 2020.

Roberts, D. (2011). Beyond the metropolis? Popular pace and post-conflict peacebulding. *Review of International Studies, 37*(5), 2535–2556. https://doi.org/10.1017/S0260210511000234.

Sanz, E. (2010). Estadocentrismo, sociocentrismo y estatismo en la construcción de paz. Resource document. Escola de Cultura de Pau-Universitat Autònoma de Barcelona. https://ddd.uab.cat/pub/estudis/2010/71728/post.dis.01.07.2010.sanz.estadocentrismo.pdf. Accessed 15 July 2020.

Theidon, K. (2006). Género en transición: sentido común, mujeres y guerra. *Cuadernos de Antropología Social, 24,* 69–92. https://doi.org/10.34096/cas.i24.4409.

Tribunal Superior de Medellín. (2017, November 24). Sentencia que ordena investigar a exgobernador al expresidente Álvaro Uribe Vélez y al excomandante de las Fuerzas Militares por masacres de El Aro y La Granja. Medellín, Colombia. Retrieved from http://www.derechos.org/nizkor/colombia/doc/jmvalle1.html. Accessed 13 November 2020.

Trujillo, C. (2017). *Ciro: Páginas de su vida*. Bogotá: Fuerza Alternativa del Común Editores.

UNESCO. (1972). Convention concerning the protection of the world cultural and natural heritage. Resource document. https://whc.unesco.org/en/conventiontext/. Accessed 18 July 2020.

UNESCO. (2003). Text of the convention for the safeguarding of the intangible cultural heritage. Resource document. https://ich.unesco.org/en/convention. Accessed 18 July 2020.

UNESCO. (2015). Report of the Colombian implementation of the 1954 Hague Convention for the protection of cultural property in the event of armed conflict and its two (1954 and 1999) protocols. Resource document. http://www.unesco.org/new/fileadmin/MULTIMEDIA/HQ/CLT/pdf/Colombia-1954Convention-2015.pdf. Accessed 13 July 2020.

UNESCO. (2017). Armed conflict and heritage: States parties database. Resource document. http://www.unesco.org/new/en/culture/themes/armed-conflict-and-heritage/convention-and-protocols/states-parties/. Accessed 14 July 2020.

United Nations [UN]. (2017). Resolution 2347. Adopted by the Security Council at its 7907th meeting, held on 24 March 2017. Resource document. https://undocs.org/pdf?symbol=es/S/RES/2347(2017. Accessed 16 July 2020.

Uribe, S. J. J., Romero, V. M., Mejía, J. M. C., & Salamanca, S. M. (2019). Gestionar los odios para obtener la paz: paradojas de la construcción de la paz en Colombia. *Revista Alteridades, 58,* 31–45. https://alteridades.izt.uam.mx/index.php/Alte/article/download/1117/1127. Accessed 15 July 2020.

Uribe, S. J. J., & Salamanca, S. M. (2019). Aprendiendo a ser fuertes y emprendedoras: Estrategias de supervivencia en mujeres desplazadas víctimas del conflicto armado. In M. Gutiérrez & Á. M. Olarte (Eds.), *Derechos Humanos y Violencia: Gobierno y gobernanza: Desplazamiento forzado, análisis para la prevención y la restauración de los vínculos sociales rotos* (pp. 49–77). Bogotá: Universidad Externado de Colombia.

Valencia, R. V. (2004). *Pitos y tambores: Cartilla de iniciación musical.* Bogotá: Ministerio de Cultura de Colombia. https://www.mincultura.gov.co/proyectoeditorial/Documentos%20Publicaciones/Pitos%20y%20Tambores/Pitos%20y%20TamboresWeb.pdf. Accessed 12 July 2020.

VerdadAbierta.com. (2019, February 8). Restitución en Montes de María, entre la ilusión y el miedo. 2011. Retrieved from https://verdadabierta.com/restitucion-en-montes-de-maria-entre-la-ilusion-y-el-miedo/. Accessed 2 November 2020.

VerdadAbierta.com. (2019, October 8). *Bloque Metro, el fantasma que ronda a Álvaro Uribe Vélez.* Retrieved from: https://verdadabierta.com/bloque-metro-el-fantasma-que-ronda-a-alvaro-uribe-velez/. Accessed 15 November 2020.

The Protection of the War Cultural Heritage in the Valencian Community: Analysis of the Shelter Cervantes (Alcoy)

Francisca Ramón Fernández and Cristina Lull Noguera

Abstract This study analyzes the regulation and protection of cultural heritage of war in the Valencian Community, after the adoption of Law 9/2017, of April 7, amending Law 4/1998, on Valencian Cultural Heritage. The objects that are protected and their legal regime are mentioned, considering that their importance for heritage comes from the relationship that they had with the Spanish Civil War. Along with this, special attention is given to shelters that nowadays are preserved and visited, especially that of Alcoy (Alicante), and their enhancement for the visitor who wants to know these spaces.

1 Introduction

When we talk about cultural property in the war field, reference should be made to the international instruments that regulate and support them.

According to the Convention for the Protection of Cultural Property in the Event of Armed Conflict with Regulations for the Execution of the Convention 1954, signed at The Hague, on May 14, 1954, the term cultural property shall cover, among others:

> […] movable or immovable property of great importance to the cultural heritage of every people, such as monuments of architecture, art or history, whether religious or secular; archaeological sites; groups of buildings which, as a whole, are of historical or artistic interest; works of art; manuscripts, books and other objects of artistic, historical or archaeological interest; as well as scientific collections and important collections of books or archives or of reproductions of the property defined above.

The Treaty on the Protection of Artistic and Scientific Institutions and Historic Monuments or Roerich Pact was signed at Washington, on April 15, 1935, and its first article affirms that:

F. Ramón Fernández (✉)
Department of Urbanism, Universitat Politècnica de València, Valencia, Spain
e-mail: frarafer@urb.upv.es

C. Lull Noguera
Higher Polytechnic School of Gandia, Universitat Politècnica de València, Valencia, Spain
e-mail: clull@upvnet.upv.es

O. Niglio and E. Y. J. Lee (eds.), *Transcultural Diplomacy and International Law in Heritage Conservation*, https://doi.org/10.1007/978-981-16-0309-9_20

> […] The historic monuments, museums, scientific, artistic, educational and cultural institutions shall be considered as neutral and as such respected and protected by belligerents. The same respect and protection shall be due to the personnel of the institutions mentioned above. The same respect and protection shall be accorded to the historic monuments, museums, scientific, artistic, educational and cultural institutions in time of peace as well as in war.

The Convention Concerning the Protection of the World Cultural and Natural Heritage was adopted by the General Conference of the United Nations Educational, Scientific and Cultural Organization at its seventeenth session, meeting in Paris from October 17 to November 21, 1972. Article 1 of this Convention mentions that the following shall be considered as cultural heritages:

> […] monuments: architectural works, works of monumental sculpture and painting, elements or structures of an archaeological nature, inscriptions, cave dwellings and combinations of features, which are of outstanding universal value from the point of view of history, art or science.

The Abu Dhabi Declaration concerning heritage at risk in the context of armed conflicts was adopted at the close of the International Conference on Safeguarding Cultural Heritage in Conflict Areas (December 2–3, 2016). The Abu Dhabi Declaration determined that:

> We need to ensure respect for universal values, in line with the international conventions of The Hague of 1899, 1907, 1954, and the latter 1954 and 1999 Protocols, which require us to protect human life, as well as cultural property in times of armed conflict.

The updated set of principles for the protection and promotion of human rights through action to combat impunity, of 2005, in its Principle 3, referring to the duty to remember, indicates that:

> A people's knowledge of the history of its oppression is part of its heritage and, as such, must be ensured by appropriate measures in fulfilment of the State's duty to preserve archives and other evidence concerning violations of human rights and humanitarian law and to facilitate knowledge of those violations. Such measures shall be aimed at preserving the collective memory from extinction and, in particular, at guarding against the development of revisionist and negationist arguments.

In Spain, the Law 1/2017, of April 18, on the return of cultural objects unlawfully removed from the Spanish territory or from another Member State of the European Union (Spanish Official State Gazette—BOE—No. 93, of April 19, 2017), was approved in order to prevent the loss of heritage, as well as the regulation of plundering that may have been executed. This Law incorporated the Directive 2014/60/EU of the European Parliament and of the Council of May 15, 2014 into the Spanish legal system and was commented by Ramón (2017).

2 The Protection of the War Cultural Heritage in the Valencian Community

In the Valencian Community, the Law 4/1998 of the Regional Government of Valencia, of 11 June, regulates the Valencian Cultural Heritage (BOE—No. 174, of July 22, 1998; Ramón, 2012). The Law 4/1998 was amended by Law 7/2004, of 19 October (BOE—No. 279, of November 19, 2004), by Law 5/2007, of 9 February (BOE—No. 71, of March 23, 2007), and by Law 9/2017, of 7 April (BOE—No. 112, of May 11, 2017).

The Law 9/2017 gives recognition to the protection of the war heritage; it should be considered that the protection of civil and military constructions from the Spanish Civil War was not contemplated until that moment.

The spaces and constructive groups (Ramón, 2016) that are protected by Law 4/1998 amended by Law 9/2017 have a great patrimonial value, for being part of the memory of the war (Valero, 2014), witnesses to history, as well as being an integral element of the historical and cultural heritage.

Different groups such as architects, workers, carpenters, stonecutters, union volunteers, prisoners, and replacements of the so-called fifth bag ("quinta del saco" in Spanish) participated in the construction.

It should be stressed the importance of the archeological remains of the Spanish Civil War as instruments of recovery from past events and knowledge of future generations, who fortunately did not experience the Civil War, but they will be able to know the facts and vestiges of it.

These elements are related to the territory and are linking with other elements of the landscape, history, or archeology that enhance the place by having great value for tourism, and contribute to the consolidation of the culture of peace.

This will be the starting point for the publication and dissemination of an inventory that ensures protection and thus enhances cultural tourism, both from the point of view of landscape and history.

Law 9/2017 mentions that since the advent of democracy the recovery of the cultural heritage of the Spanish Civil War in the Valencian Community is a historical demand of numerous social agents. It also states that there is a great number of initiatives from civic, cultural, and environmental associations, and various parliamentary actions related to the protection of the heritage of the Spanish Civil War in the Valencian Community.

Along with this, the Law 14/2017 of the Regional Government of Valencia, of 10 November, on democratic memory and for the coexistence of the Valencian Community (BOE—No. 311, of December 23, 2017), should also be considered. The seventh additional provision of Law 14/2017, indicates that the inscription of a property in the General Inventory of Valencian Cultural Heritage will not be an obstacle to its inscription in the catalog of places and itineraries constituting the democratic memory of the Valencian Community, in attention to the different protected heritage values. It also mentions that the departments with competence in matters related to Valencian cultural heritage and Valencian democratic memory, in order to establish an adequate procedural harmonization, will establish collaboration mechanisms regarding the assets registered in the instruments mentioned above.

3 Protected Items

The Law 9/2017 mentions that the Valencian society, as a sign of democratic maturity, attends to the awakening of an awareness of respect for all vestiges of the Civil War and toward the people who one day, forced or volunteers, worked, fighting, and, an important part of them, died in those places now forgotten. The result of this awakening is the legitimate aspiration to the fact that the war heritage of the Valencian Community acquired the normal status that it has in other European countries, achieving a recognized patrimonial entity so that it fosters the reconciliation of all Valencians with our historical past. It is time to intervene and recover a heritage that is a historical and social reference for future generations, as an example of what should not happen again in Spain, and for a culture of peace.

After the modification of the fifth additional provision of Law 4/1998 by Law 9/2017, the following categories of architectural elements will be considered as locally relevant real estate, and with this name must be included in the respective catalogs of protected objects and sites: the historical and archeological civil and military heritage of the Spanish Civil War in the Valencian Community, in addition to the unique relevant and historical spaces of the Valencian capital, like all those buildings that were used as the headquarters of the government of the Republic, in addition to the spaces relevant that used important figures in our history during the war period from 1936 to 1939. All these properties must have been built before 1940. In relation to this historical and archeological heritage of the Civil War, without prejudice to its legal recognition as a property of local relevance upon the entry into force of this law, the Ministry responsible for culture, with the collaboration of the Board of Valuation of Assets must carry out a specific inventory of these assets in which there would be an explicit differentiation between protected assets and assets only to be documented, according to their relative patrimonial importance. As well as the places of memory, which will become documented due to their historical importance.

The provisions of Decree 184/2018, of October 19, of the Regional Government of Valencia, which approves the regulation governing the Board of Valuation of Assets of the Valencian Cultural Heritage (Valencian Official State Gazette—DOGV—No. 8414, of October 31, 2018), must be considered.

As the Preamble of Law 9/2017 indicates, the following assets will be included for reasons of both historical and cultural importance:

a. Aerodromes;
b. Shelters;
c. Simple or compound trenches;

d. Simulated trenches;
e. Parapets;
f. Powder kegs;
g. Puller and mortar trenches;
h. Communication channels;
i. Observatories;
j. Command locations;
k. Armored elements of resistance (nests of machine guns, marksman's places, casemates, bunkers, or pillboxes);
l. Rafts for refrigeration;
m. Troop coats;
n. Underground warehouses;
o. Underground galleries;
p. Shelters;
q. Memorials;
r. All those constructive elements related to the military architecture of this conflict.

4 Shelters: The Case of Alcoy, Alicante (Spain)

The Shelter Cervantes is one of the Spanish Civil War anti-aircraft shelters of the more than 25 shelters that were used by the population of Alcoy (Alicante, Spain), to protect themselves from aircraft attacks during the Spanish Civil War. Nowadays, the Shelter Cervantes is a museum that can be visited (Figs. 1 and 2).

It is an underground space of more than 100 m long (Fig. 3) where data and aerial photographs are shown documenting the attacks by the Italian Savoia 79 bombers.

The museum has an interactive screen, as well as various military objects (Fig. 4).

The museum also has different images of the city of Alcoy during the Civil War, since this city was one of the targets for its bombing, being bombed seven times, during September 20 of 1938 and February 11 of 1939 (Figs. 5 and 6) and a video with testimonies of people who lived through that period. Successive bombers caused more than fifty casualties. More than 50,000 kilos of explosives were used and factories and buildings were destroyed.

The first bombers were without warning, but later an alarm siren was installed to warn the population and go to the shelter.

From a patrimonial point of view, it is interesting to highlight the underground construction that was carried out for the purpose of defense by the population, and which is not only unique to the city of Alcoy, but also carried out in many other cities, and therefore we are interested, in the Valencian Community, not only in Alcoy, but also in Valencia, among others.

Fig. 1 Shelter Cervantes, Alcoy, Alicante (Spain)

Fig. 2 Interior image of the Shelter Cervantes, Alcoy, Alicante (Spain)

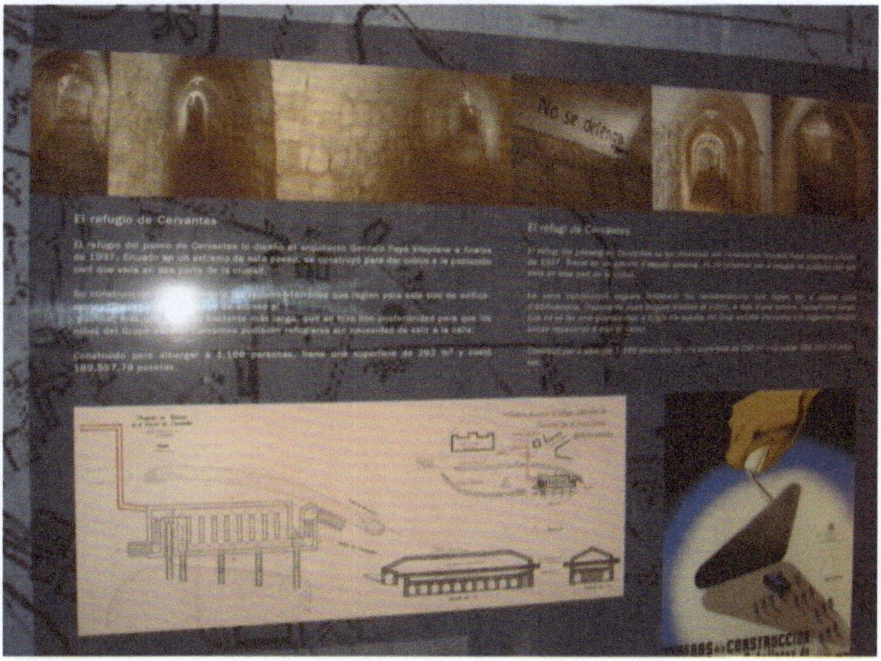

Fig. 3 Structure of the Shelter Cervantes, Alcoy, Alicante (Spain)

5 Conclusions

Air raid shelters are part of the heritage of a city (Cutillas & Gómez, 2017), and as such must be considered for their protection. Heritage also has an educational aspect, and many of the assets that have been protected, especially through their display in museums, such as collections, are part of the work of knowledge for citizens (Calzado, 2015; Jaén, 2015).

In the case of the shelters, they are also part of the urban landscape of the city (Collado, 2017), and after Law 9/2017 their enhancement has begun (González, 2016), since in the Valencian Community we find several of them (Moreno & Muñoz, 2011; Taberner & Broseta, 2015; Taberner, 2016; Moreno & Sapena, 2017), with the great exceptionality of the Shelter Cervantes, from Alcoy, Alicante, which has already been valued since 2006, which remains open to the public, as a museum (Rubio, 2009a, b; Soler, 2010), with a high rate of visits.

Fig. 4 Bomb image of the Spanish Civil War. Element exposed in the Shelter Cervantes, Alcoy, Alicante (Spain)

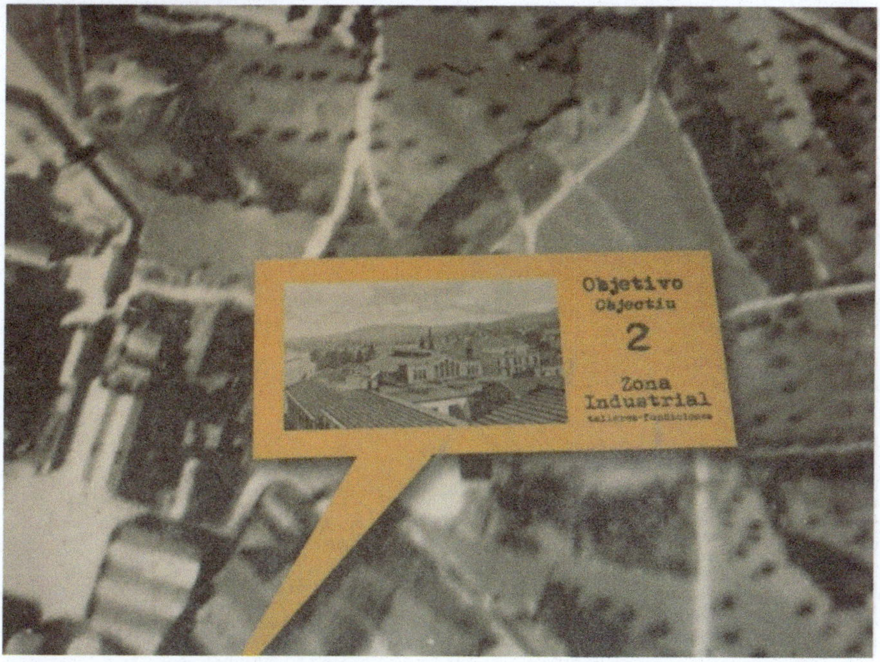

Fig. 5 War objectives in Alcoy during the Civil War. Documentation exposed in the Shelter Cervantes, Alcoy, Alicante (Spain)

Fig. 6 Image of Alcoy during the Spanish Civil War. Documentation exposed in the Shelter Cervantes, Alcoy, Alicante (Spain)

References

Calzado, A. (2015). El patrimonio bélico de la Guerra Civil en el País Valenciano: Una herramienta didáctica infravalorada. In *Pensar con la historia desde el siglo XXI: actas del XII Congreso de la Asociación de Historia Contemporánea* (pp. 5161–5173). Universidad Autónoma de Madrid. Available in: https://libros.uam.es/?press=uam&page=catalog&op=view&path%5B%5D=10&path%5B%5D=10&path%5B%5D=375-1. Accessed 20 Mar 2020.

Collado, F. (2017). Refugios antiaéreos de la ciudad de Valencia: estudio, propuesta y desarrollo como paisajes culturales urbanos. *Espacio Tiempo y Forma. Serie VI, Geografía, 10,* 79–101. Available in: https://revistas.uned.es/index.php/ETFVI/article/view/18725/16019. Accessed 16 Mar 2020.

Cutillas, B., & Gómez, M. M. (2017). Los refugios antiaéreos de la guerra civil española: arqueología contemporánea como un patrimonio más de las ciudades. In *Conviviendo con la arqueología: las capitales de las grandes potencias mediterráneas en la Antigüedad, una mirada alternativa: PHICARIA: V Encuentros Internacionales del Mediterráneo* (pp. 189–201). Available in: https://www.um.es/arqueologia/wp-content/uploads/2016/01/Cap.-2017.-Los-refugios-antiaéreos-de-la-Guerra-Civil-Española.pdf. Accessed 20 Mar 2020.

González, L. V. (2016). Proyecto de puesta en valor de los restos de la Guerra Civil en la ciudad de Alicante. *DAMA. Documentos de Arqueología y Patrimonio Histórico,* (1), 207–220. Available in: https://rua.ua.es/dspace/handle/10045/59162. Accessed 16 Mar 2020.

Jaén, S. (2015). Los vestigios de la Guerra Civil Española: Espacios de interés para la Didáctica de las Ciencias Sociales. *Didácticas Específicas, 13,* 6–16. https://revistas.uam.es/didacticasespecificas/article/view/2675/2827. Accessed 10 Mar 2020.

Moreno, A., & Muñoz, À. (2011). Arqueologia de la memòria: els refugis antiaeris a la ciutat de València. *SAGVNTVM. Papeles del Laboratorio de Arqueología de Valencia, 43*, 177–192. Available in: https://ojs.uv.es/index.php/saguntum/article/view/326/1349. Accessed 16 Mar 2020.
Moreno, A., & Sapena, T. (2017). Air-raid shelters: Civil war heritage in Valencia city. *Debats. Revista de cultura, poder i societat*, Annual Review, *2*, 197–214. Available in: https://revistadebats.net/article/view/1835/2712. Accessed 16 Mar 2020.
Ramón, F. (2012). *El patrimonio cultural: Régimen legislativo y su protección*. Valencia: Tirant lo Blanch.
Ramón, F. (2016). Arquitectura, urbanismo y patrimonio: medidas para su protección. In *València, 1808–2015: la història continua* (pp. 255–268). Balandra edicions.
Ramón, F. (2017). El mercado del arte: La restitución de bienes culturales y la protección del patrimonio. A propósito de la Ley 1/2017, de 18 de abril y la transposición de la Directiva 2014/60/UE. *Revista General De Derecho Europeo, 43*, 326–348.
Rubio, X. (2009a). La guerra: investigar para museizar. *Hermes, 1*, 60–66. Available in: https://raco.cat/index.php/Hermus/article/view/314657/404815. Accessed 15 Mar 2020.
Rubio, X. (2009b). El patrimonio de la guerra en la enseñanza. *Cuadernos De Pedagogía, 394*, 60–62.
Soler, A. (2010). Análisis sobre la musealización de los refugios antiaéreos en España. In *Arqueología, discurso histórico y trayectorias locales* (pp. 61–70). Ayuntamiento de Cartagena.
Taberner, F. (2016). La defensa pasiva: notas sobre la construcción de los refugios antiaéreos en Valencia. In *València, 1808–2015: la història continua* (pp. 99–119). Balandra edicions.
Taberner, F., & Broseta, M.T. (2015). Los refugios antiaéreos de Valencia: del olvido a la relevancia local. *Arché, 10*, 399–406. https://hdl.handle.net/10251/85188.
Valero, J. R. (2014). Los lugares de la Guerra Civil, mucho más que patrimonio inmaterial. *Revista del Vinalopó, 17*, 13–31. Available in: https://rua.ua.es/dspace/bitstream/10045/51165/1/2014_Valero_Revista-del-Vinalopo.pdf.

Attacks on Tangible and Intangible Cultural Heritage: Human Rights Violations, Violations of International Cultural Heritage Law or a Threat to International Peace and Security?

Kalliopi Chainoglou

Abstract Tangible and intangible cultural heritage has come under the radar of the UN Security Council; attacks to on cultural heritage are now perceived as threats to international peace and security. The paper discusses whether attacks on tangible cultural heritage and intangible cultural heritage practices, artefacts, and cultural bearers, should be viewed as human rights violations, or violations of international cultural heritage law or as a matter necessitating the response of the UN Security Council; in the latter case, the question is when should the Security Council react and what measures it could adopt. The paper addresses these issues and critically assesses whether the Security Council took advantage of the momentum to address the impact of COVID-19 on cultural heritage.

1 Introduction

Cultural heritage encompasses various forms of heritage, predominantly tangible heritage, composed of structures and remains of historical, religious or cultural value, and intangible heritage composed of customs, beliefs, traditions, skills, languages, artistic expressions and folklore. The 1972 Convention concerning the Protection of the World Cultural and Natural Heritage (hereinafter "1972 World Heritage Convention") along with the 2003 Convention for the Safeguarding of the Intangible Cultural Heritage (hereinafter "2003 ICH Convention") present the two bodies of rules on the protection of cultural heritage (international cultural heritage law). The widespread support for both instruments demonstrates a general *opinio juris* on the need to preserve and safeguard both forms of cultural heritage. The wording in the text of 2003 ICH Convention does not explicitly refer to its applicability in peacetime or times of armed conflict. However, by analogy to the 1972 World Heritage Convention which does not cease to apply in armed conflict, there is room to presume that the 2003 ICH Convention likewise applies in armed conflict too in parallel to the rules of international humanitarian law (Chainoglou, 2017).

K. Chainoglou (✉)
Department of International and European Studies, University of Macedonia, Thessaloniki, Greece
URL: https://www.uom.gr/en/chainoglou

O. Niglio and E. Y. J. Lee (eds.), *Transcultural Diplomacy and International Law in Heritage Conservation*, https://doi.org/10.1007/978-981-16-0309-9_21

The 1972 World Heritage Convention creates a legal regime on the protection of natural and cultural heritage, for example structures and remains of historical, religious, or cultural value, of "outstanding universal value", while the intangible dimension of cultural heritage is covered by the 2003 ICH. The definition of "intangible cultural heritage" is offered in Art. 2 of the 2003 ICH as following:

> [...] practices, representations, expressions, knowledge, skills – as well as the instruments, objects, artefacts and cultural spaces associated therewith – that communities, groups and, in some cases, individuals recognize as part of their cultural heritage.

Intangible cultural heritage can be manifested in five broad domains with the possibility of including elements from multiple domains: (1) Oral traditions and expressions, including language as a vehicle of the intangible cultural heritage; (2) Performing arts; (3) Social practices, rituals and festive events; (4) Knowledge and practices concerning nature and the universe; and (5) Traditional craftsmanship (Art. 2 (2) of the 2003 ICH).

The 2003 ICH Convention does not aim at safeguarding every single ICH that exists out there; the rationale is that intangible cultural heritage bearers, i.e. communities and groups themselves, as the sole rightful holders and bearers of ICH practices, recognize the need to safeguard their intangible cultural heritage into the future.

The definition of intangible cultural heritage in the 2003 ICH Convention acknowledges two dimensions to intangible cultural heritage (Chainoglou, 2017). The temporal dimension relates to the fact that the intangible cultural heritage must be "transmitted from generation to generation" and be "constantly recreated"; therefore, intangible cultural heritage essentially has to meet the test of "time". The spatial dimension relates to the fact that the intangible cultural heritage must be recreated "in response to their [communities and groups'] environment, their interaction with nature and their history". Within this context, intangible cultural heritage is identified by its determining value for the relevant intangible cultural heritage bearers or holders, i.e. communities, groups, individuals, (as opposed to the "outstanding universal value" of tangible heritage) as they are the ones who can define what their intangible cultural heritage is and ensure its preservation into the future (Chainoglou, 2017). Ultimately, this intangible cultural heritage should provide communities and groups "with a sense of identity and continuity, thus promoting respect for cultural diversity and human creativity" (UNESCO, 2015a: 3).

The 2003 ICH Convention should be read in line with all the instruments of international human rights law; human rights have a cultural dimension that is increasingly acknowledged on a normative level and in scholarly work (Wiesand et al., 2017). Cultural heritage belongs to the human rights construct. As the UN Special Rapporteur in the field of Cultural Rights has said cultural heritage "is a human rights issue itself"; and it is indisputably "a fundamental resource for other human rights" (UN Special Rapporteur in the field of Cultural Rights, 2017). In the author's view, the safeguarding of intangible cultural heritage is premised on human rights, and specifically the right to life, the right to participate in cultural life, including the ability to access and enjoy cultural heritage and the right to participate in decision-making on heritage matters. The same rationale could also apply for the protection of tangible heritage. There is an umbilical cord between international cultural heritage law (the 1972 World Heritage Convention and the 2003 ICH) and international human rights law that can holistically underpin the protection scheme and regulatory framework of cultural heritage. This is a normative gestation of international cultural heritage law and international human rights law which is at its beginning phase. Admittedly, there may arguments in favour and against such theorizing (see Lixinski, 2016) but one has to bear in mind that only international human rights law can offer the human rights entitlements and enforcement mechanisms of legal claims that concern the enjoyment and protection of heritage, whether tangible or intangible. This line of thought seems to be progressively acknowledged by UNESCO (Blake, 2017) and the UN Human Rights Council with the latter having recognized that "...the destruction of or damage to cultural heritage may have a detrimental and irreversible impact on the enjoyment of cultural rights, in particular the right of everyone to take part in cultural life, including the ability to access and enjoy cultural heritage..." (UN Human Rights Council, 2016, preamble). Hence, the element of cultural heritage, especially in the case of intangible cultural heritage, is interlinked with the individual or the group/community and their entitlements, and, when the element of cultural heritage becomes obsolete, then the enjoyment of human rights is being irrevocably denied to the cultural heritage bearers or holders. In this sense, attacks on and destruction of cultural heritage are not mere violations of international cultural heritage law but also violations of international human rights law.

2 Attacks on Cultural Heritage

Attacks on cultural heritage usually take place in the context of an armed conflict rather than in peacetime. Recent armed conflicts as seen in the cases of Mali, Iraq, Syria and elsewhere have highlighted the multidimensional character of the many phases and forms of attacks on cultural heritage as they have ranged from the physical destruction of heritage to looting and trafficking of cultural property. During an armed conflict, whether international or non-international, it is observed that tangible heritage may often, if not always, fall victim to ongoing hostilities. Whether through deliberately targeting or incidental damage of tangible heritage, this is the one form of heritage destruction that is usually recorded and reported about by the media, humanitarian organizations, civil society actors, etc. Yet, what is often underreported is the attacks and the eventual destruction of intangible heritage. This may be happening for two reasons:

First, the relationship between tangible and intangible heritage is underestimated and sidelined usually in the context of an armed conflict; yet, we know for a fact that tangible and intangible heritage can be interlinked and when attacks on one are materialized they are usually accompanied by assaults or the same destructive force on the other. This means that any damage caused to tangible heritage is very likely to have severe impact on the intangible dimension of this cultural heritage. This has been acknowledged in the report of the Special Rapporteur on Minority Issues. (UN Special Rapporteur on Minority Issues, 2017: 16)

> […] While the destruction of specific cultural sites has been evident, the conflict itself has had a massive, destructive impact on whole cities and towns of deep historical, cultural and social significance to some ethnic or religious groups. One Yazidi community representative stated of Sinjar: "If liberation means total destruction, it means the end of our existence here. People are going to migrate. What is there to come back to?" This was a sentiment echoed by Shabak representatives and others, who conveyed a deep sense of loss of much more than mere buildings and infrastructure, but rather loss of their entire cultural and historical heritage.

Secondly, the scale and effects of attacks on cultural heritage in times of war can vary, as well as the predominance of the attacks on tangible over the intangible dimension of cultural heritage can vary too. In this sense, the destructive force on tangible heritage can be easily measurable as opposed to the destructive force on intangible heritage which in order to be measured (or at least substantiated) it has to be coupled with the killings of innocent civilians and the physical destruction of civilian property or cultural goods/property. As a consequence, it could be argued that the destructive force on intangible heritage is only post-facto realized, for example, in the post-conflict phase. This is because the threats and the attacks to intangible heritage (as opposed to the attacks on tangible heritage) are rarely dealt with during the conflict phase. In the post-conflict phase efforts for development, sustainable peace and respect for human rights are made in order to rebuild the confidence of traumatized and abused communities. Hence, it is only in the post-conflict phase that the impact of the damage to the intangible heritage may be assessed and potentially addressed through peacebuilding or transitional justice measures.

The responses of the international community following the recent examples of destruction of cultural heritage in armed conflicts provide the intellectual space to discern four issues which support the view that protection of cultural heritage is now moving to a direction of a global governance scheme building on the normative stock of international cultural heritage law and international human rights law:

1. Heritage is an integral element to the construction of identities and to the cultural preservation of individual or communities as heritage bearers, and a catalyst for social cohesion and economic growth. The regulatory framework for the protection of intangible cultural heritage in times of war has been erroneously overlooked in the past vis-à-vis previous armed conflicts.
2. The destruction of cultural heritage, whether tangible or intangible, can be peculiarly complex as it can have a destructive impact on the other (mainly intangible) dimension of cultural heritage, with various actors bearing responsibility for these acts (see Chainoglou, 2017). This means that there may have been numerous unreported or non-acknowledged (before national or international courts) incidents where intangible heritage, i.e. practices and rituals, along with and intangible heritage bearers, i.e. people who were performing them in a particular spatial, cultural or social setting, have become obsolete, i.e. they were physically destroyed in their totality, due to an armed conflict. As a

consequence, these incidents were never treated as crimes under international humanitarian law or international criminal law, or as violations of international cultural heritage law, or international human rights law, the perpetrators were never brought to justice for these acts, the states responsible for these acts never assumed state responsibility for their acts or omissions that resulted in the attacks and destruction of intangible heritage, and most importantly, the element of intangible heritage was lost forever.

3. The issue of impunity for attacks against intangible cultural heritage and intangible cultural heritage bearers is seriously left out of the agendas of policy-makers. However, in recent years there is an accumulated caselaw concerning individual criminal liability for attacks against tangible cultural heritage, including cultural/religious sites (Dubrovnik, Timbuktu) and there is hope that in the future attacks on intangible heritage elements and intangible cultural heritage bearers will be addressed before national or international courts.
4. Cultural heritage destruction has been advanced in the security agenda of the UN Security Council (Hausler, 2018; Jakubowski, 2019). Acts of cultural heritage destruction have been found not only to terrorize local populations but may result to the cultural annihilation of such peoples (Bokova, 2015), which could eventually lead to (cultural) genocide where cultural, physical and biological elements of genocide have all being pursued simultaneously (Luck, 2018). An ongoing process of "securitization" of the cultural heritage destruction and the protection of cultural heritage has been taking place through the prism of the fight against terrorism. The UN and UNESCO (see i.e. UNESCO, 2015b) have taken numerous steps to affirm that the protection of cultural heritage is a "political and security imperative" and have approved exceptional measures to this end, save for military intervention.

The latter is the most significant development as it coincides with the normative gestation of international cultural heritage law and international human rights law discussed above. As the protection of both forms of heritage is now linked to the international peace and security agenda of the UN Security Council, the question that arises is whether attacks on tangible cultural heritage and intangible cultural heritage practices, artefacts and cultural heritage bearers, should be viewed as human rights violations, or violations of international cultural heritage law or as a matter necessitating the response of the UN Security Council. This will be further analysed below.

3 Other Forms of Attacks on Cultural Heritage: The Impact of COVID-19

So far, the discussion has focused on attacks on cultural heritage in the context of an armed conflict or related to terrorism. Yet, the COVID-19 health crisis followed by the immediate strain on social and economic life has struck also cultural heritage. Due to the indisputable fact of the interconnectedness and indivisibility of human rights, the COVID-19 pandemic has displayed numerous and unfathomable dimensions of its impact on culture and cultural heritage. In such a brief time since March 2020, there are numerous examples of how cultural heritage has been put at risk due to the pandemic. For example, intangible cultural heritage bearers who belong to indigenous communities were one of the first vulnerable groups identified to be at risk. Because of the systemic socio-economic marginalization they have been experiencing in their countries, i.e. poor access to healthcare and essential services, sanitation, being subjected to extreme poverty, etc., they have significantly higher rates of communicable and non-communicable diseases and less chances of survival (UN Department of Economic and Social Affairs, 2020). As the UN Secretary-General noted COVID-19 presents "particular existential and cultural threats to indigenous peoples" (UN SG, 2020: para. 57).

The lockdown measures also endangered their food security and their access to and use of traditional lands. Their way of living and their cultural life, i.e. their large traditional gatherings to mark special events or the fact that they live in multigenerational housing, has put indigenous peoples and member of their families, especially the elders who are the keepers of their cultural heritage and custodians of a wealth of traditional knowledge and practices, languages and culture, at risk (see e.g. Assembly of First Nations Knowledge Keepers, 2020). So, it became apparent that the issue of the protection of indigenous peoples was not only a human rights issue "but also one of preserving cultural diversity and ancestral wisdom" (UNESCO, 2020a). One may think, for example, in the Amazon, "on Brazil's oldest indigenous reservation, the Xingu, guidance from elders is key to performing the Kuarup dance ritual that brings together the community's 16 tribes each year to celebrate life, death and rebirth…." (Garrison et al., 2020). During the pandemic indigenous peoples were shielding away their tribal elders in fear of the fact that if they die, their intangible cultural heritage, whether that may be cultural traditions, religious rituals, traditional medicine, etc., will die out too along with their cultural identity (Garrison et al., 2020).

Furthermore, the pandemic brought about a change to the humanity's common understanding of physical "cultural life". One of the immediate impacts of COVID-19 was to violently renegotiate how we define "cultural life". The emergency measures in many countries and social distancing rules, impacted communities everywhere; cultural minorities and indigenous people were not allowed to go through cultural practices that were embedded in the physical public cultural space, i.e. mourning rituals, etc.

The impact of COVID-19 has been experienced in other sectors of culture as well as tourism. The closure of heritage sites and cultural facilities, i.e. museums, theatres, cinemas, libraries, etc., and the disruption of cultural services were consequences of the lockdown measures across many countries. The access to such cultural institutions was prohibited for many months for public health reasons and states suffered from "a large decrease in user charges and fees resulting from the closure of public facilities (e.g. cultural, recreational, educational and sport venue …)"(OECD, 2020). This in effect jeopardized funding for the culture and cultural heritage sector, including the conservations of heritage places and had impacted on the livelihoods of local communities. The disruptive effect on the cultural sector has been evident also in the publishing and literature world. The production of films was halted. While the impact on performing arts was devastating. High rates of unemployment in the culture sector (cultural professionals and artists) were recorded in the totality of the countries across the globe. Furthermore, the security of cultural heritage sites was also an issue during the lockdown period (ICOM & INTERPOL, 2020).

But the pandemic offered also the opportunity to explore other forms of public cultural life, primarily through digital spaces, as well as to explore new possibilities and new cultural forms. It goes without saying that new forms of cultural heritage must have emerged during this time. Some of them may be still undetected.

While digital space is a multiplying force for access to culture and cultural heritage, it is still early to identify what kind of vulnerable groups have been created during these difficult times, i.e. due to lack of access to the Internet connection, or due to excessive measures allowing censorship, or even due to the lack of a shared, physical and public cultural life. On the other hand, other vulnerable groups, like persons with disabilities or elderly people might have been empowered in their access to culture and cultural heritage.

Furthermore, the pandemic is revealing a new picture of how the right to participate in cultural life and the ability to access and enjoy cultural heritage must be exercised in conformity with public health (United Nations Special Rapporteur in the field of Cultural Rights, 2020b). However, it is too soon to predict how the dynamic between public health and cultural heritage will turn out.

4 The Role of the Security Council in the Protection of Cultural Heritage

Under Article 24 of the UN Charter, the Security Council is the primary organ of the UN to regulate international peace and security matters. The protection of cultural heritage has been brought into the Security Council's normative sphere and a number of resolutions have been adopted even on the legal basis of Chapter VII of the UN Charter. For the past twenty years, the Security Council has adopted various measures to protect cultural heritage, ranging from calling for the return of looted objects (Resolution 1483) in the case of Iraq, to integrating a cultural component in the peacekeeping operation in the case of Mali whereby it mandated MINUSMA with assisting the transitional authorities in "protecting from attack the cultural and historical sites in Mali, in collaboration with UNESCO" and "to operate mindfully in the vicinity of cultural and historical sites" (Resolution 2100 paras. 16 (f), 32), and to custom-tailored measures in an effort to avert the iconoclastic destructive force of ISIS and its funding through the trafficking of "blood antiquities".

During the last decade, the Security Council repeatedly condemned the destruction of cultural heritage and connected it to a violation of international human rights law and international humanitarian law, as shown in the case of Iraq and Syria (Chainoglou, 2019). In Resolution 2139, the Security Council calls on "all parties to immediately end all violence which has led to human suffering in Syria, save Syria's rich societal mosaic and cultural heritage, and take appropriate steps to ensure the protection of Syria's World Heritage Sites", "strongly condemns the widespread violations of human rights and international humanitarian law by the Syrian authorities, as well as the human rights abuses and violations of international humanitarian law by armed groups", "demands that all parties immediately put an end to all forms of violence, irrespective of where it comes from, cease and desist from all violations of international humanitarian law and violations and abuses of human rights, and reaffirm their obligations under international humanitarian law and international human rights law, and stresses that some of these violations may amount to war crimes and crimes against humanity", "stresses the need to end impunity for violations of international humanitarian law and violations and abuses of human rights, and reaffirms that those who have committed or are otherwise responsible for such violations and abuses in Syria must be brought to justice" (paras. 1–2, 9, 13). In Resolution 2170 the Security Council acting under Chapter VII condemns "the indiscriminate killing and deliberate targeting of civilians…persecution of individuals and entire communities on the basis of their religion or belief…destruction of cultural and religious sites and obstructing the exercise of economic, social and cultural rights, including the right to education, especially in the Syrian governorates of Ar-Raqqah, Deir ez-Zor, Aleppo and Idlib" and "emphasizes the need to ensure that ISIL, ANF and all other individuals, groups, undertakings and entities associated with Al-Qaida are held accountable for abuses of human rights and violations of international humanitarian law" (paras. 2–3).

With Resolution 2199 the Security Council condemns the destruction of cultural heritage, whether incidental or deliberate, and including religious sites and objects, in Iraq and Syria and notes that "ISIL, ANF and other individuals, groups, undertakings and entities associated with Al-Qaida, are generating income from engaging directly or indirectly in the looting and smuggling of cultural heritage items from archaeological sites, museums, libraries, archives, and other sites in Iraq and Syria, which is being used to support their recruitment efforts and strengthen their operational capability to organize and carry out terrorist attacks" and decides "that all Member States shall take appropriate steps to prevent the trade in … Syrian cultural property and other items of archaeological, historical, cultural, rare scientific, and religious importance illegally removed … from Syria since 15 March 2011, including by prohibiting cross-border trade in such items" (paras. 16–17). With Resolution 2249 the Security Council notes that the "eradication of cultural heritage and trafficking of cultural property…constitutes a global and unprecedented threat to international peace and security" and condemns "in the strongest terms the continued gross, systematic and widespread abuses of human rights and violations of humanitarian law, as well as barbaric acts of destruction and looting of cultural heritage carried out by ISIL" (para. 3). Resolution 2249 also "calls upon Member States that have the capacity to do so to take all necessary measures, in compliance with international law, in particular with the United Nations Charter, as well as international human rights, refugee and humanitarian law, on the territory under the control of ISIL also known as Da'esh, in Syria and Iraq, to redouble and coordinate their efforts to prevent and suppress terrorist acts committed specifically by ISIL…" (para. 5). Security Council Resolution 2253 further condemns "the destruction of cultural heritage in Iraq and Syria particularly by ISIL and ANF, including targeted destruction of religious sites and objects"; and recalls "that all Member States shall take appropriate steps to prevent the trade in Iraqi and Syrian cultural property and other items of archaeological, historical, cultural, rare scientific, and religious importance illegally removed … from Syria since 15 March 2011, including by prohibiting cross-border trade in such items, thereby allowing for their eventual safe return to the Iraqi and Syrian people" and expanded the mandate of the 1267/1989/2253 ISIL (Da'esh) and Al-Qaida Sanctions Committee and the Al-Qaida Sanctions List to include monitoring on the trade in cultural property (Resolutions 2253, preamble and Annex I). This Resolution further encourages states to engage in public–private partnerships to implement sanctions effectively.

In 2017, the Security Council unanimously adopted its first Resolution focused exclusively on cultural heritage. Resolution 2347 is an extremely important instrument as it provides for a holistic scheme of protection, prevention and accountability of crimes related to cultural heritage in the context of armed conflicts, introducing thus the mentality of "R2P" (the responsibility to prevent, the responsibility to react and the responsibility to rebuild) in this subject area (Weiss & Connelly, 2017). Arguably, this means that the original framework of R2P is now expanded to include the destruction of cultural heritage. It will be reminded that the original purpose of R2P concerned flagrant violations of human rights, war crimes, crimes against humanity and genocide, all of them being crimes against the right to life. What Resolution 2347 achieves is that it acknowledges and cements the link between the protection of cultural heritage and the human rights sphere, in particular the right to life, under a global governance scheme and with tools that simultaneously create synergies among various actors from the political, legal and technical domains, and ultimately contribute to the maintenance of international peace and security.

Resolution 2347 condemns the unlawful destruction of cultural heritage, including the destruction of religious sites and artefacts, and the looting and smuggling of cultural property from archaeological sites, museums, libraries, archives and other sites, in armed conflicts, notably by terrorist groups. Resolution 2347 affirms that states have the primary responsibility for protecting their cultural heritage within their borders and to advance the protection of cultural heritage, if requested, with the assistance of relevant UN agencies. Because this is essentially an R2P formula, this means that it is not only states that bear the responsibility to protect their cultural heritage but also the international community as a whole that bears the responsibility to protect cultural heritage. Furthermore, states bear the responsibility to protect cultural heritage towards both their people and the rest of the international community.

Under the responsibility to prevent, Resolution 2347 galvanizes member states and other international organizations to cooperate in data collection and conservation efforts, for example by "improving cultural heritage local and national inventory lists, through digitalized information when possible", "establishing procedures and where appropriate databases devoted to collect information on criminal activities related to cultural property and on illicitly excavated, exported, imported or traded, stolen, trafficked or missing cultural property", "taking appropriate steps to inventory cultural property and other items of archaeological, historical, cultural, rare scientific and religious importance which have been illegally removed, displaced or transferred from armed conflict areas, and coordinate with relevant UN entities and international actors, in order to ensure the safe return of all listed items", etc. (Res 2347, 2017: para. 17). Furthermore, states are encouraged to consider the use of safe havens for "their nationally owned cultural property and their other cultural property of national importance in the context of armed conflicts endangered cultural property" (Res 2347, 2017: para. 16), without though excluding the establishment of such havens in third countries. As it has been noted, this is another step of the Security Council to contribute to a "global, multi-faceted collaborative governance to safeguard cultural property in situations of armed conflict and/or terrorism", with the involvement of other partners, such as museums, etc. (Jakubowski, 2019, p. 183).

Under the responsibility to react, Resolution 2347 calls upon states to take measures in the legal sphere in order to condemn and criminalize the large-scale destruction of cultural heritage and to prevent ISIS from developing new means of financing activities: for example, states have to ratify the Convention for the Protection of Cultural Property in the Event of Armed Conflict of 14 May 1954 and its Protocols, as well as other relevant international conventions; to adopt "effective national measures at the legislative and operational levels where appropriate, and in accordance with obligations and commitments under international law and national instruments, to prevent and counter trafficking in cultural property and related offences", to "develop, including, upon request, with the assistance of UNODC, in cooperation with UNESCO and INTERPOL as appropriate, broad law enforcement and judicial cooperation in preventing and countering all forms and aspects of trafficking in cultural property and related offences that benefit or may benefit organized criminal groups, terrorists or terrorist groups", etc. (Res 2347, 2017: paras. 17, 20). The measures herein also strengthen the international efforts aimed at halting the trade in cultural property which were already tested with Resolution 2199 (2015). Furthermore, states are called to bring to justice the perpetrators of attacks "against sites and buildings dedicated to religion, education, art, science or charitable purposes, or historic monuments" as these attacks may constitute a war crime. It will be recalled that the original R2P concept allowed room for non-consensual interventions in the case of mass violations of human rights, such as sanctions and military force. However, the wording of this Resolution seems to close the door to any possible discussions for the use of force on the basis of intentional large-scale destruction of cultural heritage. With Resolution 2347, the Security Council has upgraded the mandate of peacekeeping operations to include a cultural component where cultural heritage is at risk (para. 14) along with the creation of a task force of experts for the protection of cultural heritage. As a consequence, Resolution 2347 brings forward the institutionalization of cultural peacekeeping complemented with the obligation of the establishment of safe havens and the transfer of movable cultural heritage property at risk to safe havens (see also UNESCO, 2015b).

Finally, under the responsibility to rebuild, Resolution 2347 calls member states "to support preventive and emergency operations, and to …undertake all appropriate efforts for the recovery of cultural heritage, in the spirit of the principles of the UNESCO Conventions" (para. 15). The reference to "the principles of the UNESCO Conventions" is placed to dissuade any states from resorting to forcible measures when recovering cultural properties. Lastly, under the responsibility to rebuild, Resolution 2347 invites states to financially contribute to the UNESCO's Heritage Emergency Fund and the International Alliance for the Protection of Heritage in Conflict Areas (ALIPH). It is reminded that the aim of the ALIPH is to prevent destruction, restore destroyed sites and fund a network of safe havens to temporarily store endangered cultural heritage outside the country of its origin.

Resolution 2347 offers measures that are chronologically correct; states must take preventive measures to guarantee the safeguarding of cultural heritage within their national borders; if they fail, then the next option is to react to protect what remains of the cultural heritage; if they fail, then the destroyed cultural property has to be eventually rebuilt. But the process does not identify who should be responsible for rebuilding the damaged cultural heritage. Nonetheless, the UN Secretary-General in his first report on the implementation of Security Council Resolution 2347 noted that institutional changes have already been taking place, for example, in the form of creation of specialized units in central and local administrations, designing tools and training for customs and law enforcement dedicated personnel and public prosecutors, and the creation or improvement of procedures or databases to collect information on criminal activity related to cultural property and its illicit trade (UN Secretary-General Report, 2017). In this context and as the momentum builds around protection for cultural heritage in armed conflicts, heritage organizations, such as ICOM and ICOMOS have feverously reminded states of their obligations to comply with the relevant legal instruments on the protection of cultural heritage during an armed conflict or even "political upheavals". The latter term denotes a lesser scale of violence that may not be conducive to the existence of an armed conflict—at least in the sense that it is defined so by the Geneva Conventions and the Additional Protocols—yet it is understood that both ICOM and ICOMOS have presumed the occurrence of "political upheavals" to be an equally destructive environment for targeted actions against cultural heritage whereby the 1954 Hague Convention should apply. Furthermore, ICOM and ICOMOS treat any forms of attacks on cultural heritage with the same gravity; also the intention behind the attacks is irrelevant. The attacks on cultural heritage may be carried out with the purpose of financing terrorist activities or warfare or "to affect the identity and the confidence of adversaries" (ICOM & ICOMOS, 2020). In a statement that was released on 6 January 2020, ICOM and ICOMOS have expressed their support to the existing legal framework on the prohibition of deliberate targeting of cultural heritage in armed conflict and they called upon states "to respect the international agreements that rule armed conflicts, and to protect the world's cultural heritage wherever it is, regardless of religious beliefs or political intentions"(ICOM & ICOMOS, 2020). These two heritage organizations have also expressed their support to the newly set up by the Security Council Resolution 2347 regulatory framework. From this perspective, it would be interesting to observe in the future the role of these heritage organizations in sustaining and upholding the Security Council Resolution 2347 regulatory framework. As with other regulatory frameworks that have been created by the Security Council, i.e. the framework on Women, Peace and Security that was initially set up by Security Council Resolution 1325, there is a constant need for other actors, such as intergovernmental and non-governmental international organizations, civil society actors, etc., to contribute to the viability of these frameworks. Without them, such frameworks may turn out to lose their credibility or relevance to states, or even turn out to be dysfunctional or obsolete. To put it simply, these actors need to remind states of their obligations concerning the protection of cultural heritage and to stress the need for the states' accountability and the ending of impunity by bringing the perpetrators of deliberate attacks on cultural heritage to justice.

5 Conclusion

The question of the sustainability of the Security Council Resolution 2347 Security Council regulatory framework is very much relevant to the expected role of the Security Council in the COVID-19 pandemic as much as in the post-pandemic world. Even though health matters fall predominantly under the mandate of the World Health Organization, the Security Council has set precedent, as in the case of Ebola (Security Council Resolution 2177 and Security Council Resolution 2439) and of the HIV/AIDS epidemic (Security Council Resolution 1983), to include global health emergencies under the international peace and security mandate. It was understood right from the beginning that COVID-19, much alike other contagious diseases, could essentially pose a threat to international peace and security as it was a global issue with an international nature.

On 11 March 2020, the World Health Organization had classified Covid-19 to be a global pandemic. On 23 March 2020, the UN Secretary-General called a global ceasefire which by June 2020 has been endorsed by 114 Governments as well as regional organizations, civil society groups and 16 armed groups (UN, 2020a: Annex, para. 7). However, as soon as states started taking emergency measures in March 2020 and while having the World Health Organization tackling the pandemic amidst criticisms and serious misconduct allegations, it was evident that there was a need for the Security Council to step in the forefront, to unite all states for international cooperation in order to counter the effects of this crisis and to adopt measures that would ease the handling of the pandemic while maintaining international peace and security. Unfortunately, the Security Council remained silent for many months while the UN Secretary-General, the General Assembly and other UN agencies tried to respond as effectively as they could under the unprecedented circumstances. Despite the organizational problems and political issues that arose at the time, the UN General Assembly managed to adopt on 2 April 2020, Resolution 74/270 in view of mobilizing a coordinated global response. With this Resolution the General Assembly is calling "…upon the United Nations system, under the leadership of the Secretary-General, to work with all relevant actors in order to mobilize a coordinated global response to the pandemic and its adverse social, economic and financial impact on all societies" (para. 1) and calling for "intensified international cooperation to contain, mitigate and defeat the pandemic, including by exchanging information, scientific knowledge and best practices and by applying the relevant guidelines recommended by the World Health Organization" (para. 5).

The efforts of the UN to make states align their COVID-19 responses with their human rights obligations have been best displayed through the enthusiastic work of the UN Secretary-General, the UN Human Rights Council and the UN Special Rapporteurs. The UN Secretary-General released in April 2020 a report highlighting how human rights could and should guide COVID-19 response and recovery. As of July 2020, the UN Special Rapporteurs had issued 90 press releases, 12 guidance and other tools and 16 reports to HRC/GA were planned or presented (United Nations, 2020b). By 30 April 2020, the UN Human Rights Council had convened an online meeting with the Coordination Committee of the Special Procedures on the human rights implications of the COVID-19 crisis and many of them acknowledged that the COVID 19 crisis proves the interconnectedness of all human rights and requested that states uphold economic, social and cultural rights in both the emergency response and the post-crisis recovery phases (UN Human Rights Council, 2020a). On 27 May 2020, the President of the UN Human Rights Council issued a statement that was later adopted by the UN Human Rights Council and which categorically affirmed states' obligations "to ensure that all human rights are respected, protected and fulfilled while combating the pandemic, and that their responses to the COVID-19 pandemic are in full compliance with their human rights obligations and commitments" (UN Human Rights Council, 2020b: para. 3). However, despite the commitment of the UN Human Rights Council and the Special Rapporteurs to emphasize that the COVID-19 crisis was also a human rights crisis, they refrained from alarming the international community on the dangers to cultural heritage and cultural heritage bearers. This was a task that was successfully assumed by UNESCO which capitulated on this momentum to develop tools for compiling information concerning the impact of COVID-19, including on living heritage (UNESCO, 2020b) as well as response trackers (UNESCO, 2020a).

The health crisis proved to be catalytic for the polarization of the Security Council and brought it to a stalemate; it will be remembered that for quite some time, the USA and China squabbled over whether the resolution should refer to the World Health Organization. Resolution 2532 was finally adopted on 1 July 2020, one hundred days after the initial calling for a global ceasefire by the UN Secretary-General (Pobjie, 2020). Resolution 2532 recognizes right from the beginning that "the unprecedented extent of the COVID-19 pandemic is likely to endanger the maintenance of international peace and security" (preamble). The brief and much-awaited text of the Security Council following months of negotiations are essentially aiming at the cessation of hostilities to allow states to tackle the COVID-19 pandemic, and a humanitarian pause for at least 90 consecutive days in order to enable humanitarian assistance and medical evacuations, in accordance with international law, including international humanitarian and refugee law as applicable. In addition, the Security Council requests the Secretary-General to "instruct peacekeeping operations to provide support, within their mandates and capacities, to host country authorities in their efforts to contain the pandemic" (Resolution 2532: para. 6). This could be interpreted to include also the cultural component of peacekeeping with regard to the protection of cultural heritage as set out in Resolution 2347. But with regard to the protection of cultural heritage, the text does not go further than that. Even though Resolution 2532 was adopted unanimously in effort to display or affirm solidarity in order to face the COVID-19 pandemic, it is evidently inadequate in bringing together a list of measures that were widely expected to deal with the multidimensional implications of COVID-19. After all, as a matter threatening international peace and security, COVID-19 is admittedly having a negative impact on states' economies and world economy as well as the human rights situation across states and regions. But even though Resolution 2532 acknowledges the "disproportionate negative impact of the pandemic, notably the socioeconomic impact, on women and girls, children, refugees, internally displaced persons, older persons and persons with disabilities" (para. 7), it falls short of introducing concrete measures or tools in measuring how states can prevent the deterioration of human rights situations related to the COVID-19 emergency measures, including for example cultural rights or the right to participate in culture, how states can effectively adverse the negative impact on cultural heritage given the fact that it is itself a matter of international peace and security as acknowledged in Resolution 2347, and how states can better support the critical role of women in an adequate and sustainable pandemic response efforts by encompassing the cultural dimension of human rights, including the right to access and enjoy cultural heritage.

Through the study of the documents adopted by the various UN organs, one notes that there is a piecemeal approach which heavily calls for the respect of human rights, including economic, social and cultural rights. One also further notes that there is a common request for addressing the adverse social, economic and financial impact of COVID-19 on all societies and especially the disadvantaged and most vulnerable people. The Secretary-General's Report is also shedding light on the vulnerability of cultural heritage bearers coming from the indigenous communities (UN SG Report, 2020). But there is not a single reference in the texts of the General Assembly or Security Council Resolutions which would directly or indirectly require states to give the attention much deserved to cultural heritage as a human right issue itself or cultural rights. And this is disappointing given the fact that cultural heritage is a fundamental resource for all human rights and it should be a priority at this time. Despite cultural rights' normative grounding and despite the repeated calls from the UN Expert in the field of Cultural Rights to recognize cultural rights as "human rights with the same standing as other rights", cultural rights were greatly misplaced having received neither adequate support nor appropriate protection during the pandemic (UN Special Rapporteur in the field of Cultural Rights, 2020a). Except for UNESCO and some regional organizations' initiatives on mitigating the impact of COVID-19 on culture and cultural heritage, the documents that have been adopted by the UN

General Assembly and the UN Security Council display at best a lack of attention to the cultural dimension of human rights, i.e. the rights of everyone to take part in cultural life without discrimination, freedom of artistic expression, the right to access and enjoy cultural heritage, the right of everyone to benefit from scientific progress, cultural rights of particular groups, such as indigenous, refugees, LGBTI persons, persons with disabilities, etc., and to the devastating impact of COVID-19 on cultural heritage and cultural heritage bearers.

In conclusion, the protection of cultural heritage has its indisputable normative grounding on both international cultural heritage law and international human rights law (and international humanitarian law wherever applicable). In 2017, the Security Council adopted the emblematic Resolution 2347 which created a global governance scheme devoted to the protection of cultural heritage under threat from armed conflict and terrorism; hence, cultural heritage became tied to the international peace and security agenda of the Security Council. This governance scheme displays particularities, such as (1) synergies that are promoted with UNESCO and other international organizations and bodies, civil society actors and professionals from the heritage domain, (2) the institutionalization of cultural peacekeeping and (3) and the establishment of safe havens. These particularities serve as a guarantee for the sustainable protection of cultural heritage. Yet, as it has been shown with the case of the pandemic, cultural heritage may be endangered by other, non-violent or non-conventional, threats to international peace and security, including pandemics. For this reason, it is felt that the pandemic offered a momentum for the Security Council to bring the protection of cultural heritage and cultural heritage bearers under its COVID-19 responses' agenda. But it failed to do so. In essence, the Security Council failed on the one hand, to expand, and on the other hand, to support the existing normative and regulatory governance scheme on the protection of cultural heritage that the Security Council had built itself with Resolution 2347. Admittedly, this is a time in which we struggle with many challenges but the protection of cultural heritage is a global imperative on which the Security Council needs to act on without succumbing to political excuses.

References

Assembly of First Nations Knowledge Keepers.(2020). *COVID-19 message.* https://www.afn.ca/assembly-of-first-nations-knowledge-keepers-covid-19-message/. Accessed 30 July 2020.

Blake, J. (2017). Development of 2003 UNESCO's convention: Creating a new heritage protection paradigm? In P. Davis & M. L. Stefano (Eds.), *The Routledge companion to intangible cultural heritage* (pp. 11–21). London: Routledge.

Bokova, I. (2015). Fighting cultural cleansing: Harnessing the law to preserve cultural heritage. *Harvard International Review, 36*(4), 40–45. https://www.unesco.org/new/fileadmin/MULTIMEDIA/HQ/BPI/EPA/images/media_services/Director-General/Fighting-Cultural-Cleansing-Harnessing-InternationalHarv.pdf. Accessed 18 Sept 2017.

Chainoglou, K. (2017). The protection of intangible cultural heritage in armed conflict: Dissolving the boundaries between the existing legal regimes? *Santander Art and Culture Law Review, 2*(3), 109–134. https://doi.org/10.4467/2450050XSNR.17.017.8426.

Chainoglou, K. (2019).Destruction and reconstruction of cultural heritage in eastern Mediterranean: From cultural genocide to War crimes and crimes against humanity. In S. Litsas & A. Tziampiris (Eds.), *The new eastern Mediterranean: Theory, politics and states in a volatile era* (pp. 113–138). New York, NY: Springer. https://doi.org/10.1007/978-3-319-90758-1_7.

Garrison C., Lammerty, M., & Boadle, A. (2020). Latin America's indigenous shield elderly 'cultural guardians' from Coronavirus. *Reuters*. https://www.reuters.com/article/us-health-coronavirus-latam-indigenous-f/latin-americas-indigenous-shield-elderly-cultural-guardians-from-coronavirus-idUSKBN22N1BO. Accessed 24 June 2020.

Hausler, K. (2018). Cultural heritage and the security council: Why resolution 2347 matters. *Questions of International Law*. https://www.qil-qdi.org/cultural-heritage-security-council-resolution-2347-matters/. Accessed 17 July 2020.

ICOM & ICOMOS. (2020). *Statement on the threats to cultural heritage in armed conflict*. https://www.icomos.org/images/DOCUMENTS/Secretariat/2020/ICOM-ICOMOS_Statement_on_threats_to_cultural_heritage/EN_threatstoculturalheritage_FINAL.pdf. Accessed 24 June 2020.

ICOM & INTERPOL. (2020). *Ensuring cultural heritage security during lockdown: A Challenge for museum professionals and police services: Recommendations*. https://icom.museum/wp-content/uploads/2020/04/ICOM-INTERPOL-Recommendations.pdf. Accessed 30 July 2020.

Jakubowski, A. (2019). International protection of cultural heritage in armed conflict: Revisiting the role of safe havens. *Indonesian Journal of International Law, 16*(2), 169–190.

Lixinski, L. (2016). *International Human Rights Law and International Cultural Heritage Law: Cooperation, conflict or cooption?* ESIL—International Human Rights Law Symposium. https://www.ejiltalk.org/esil-international-human-rights-law-symposium-international-human-rights-law-and-international-cultural-heritage-law-cooperation-conflict-or-cooption/. Accessed 24 June 2020.

Luck, E. (2018). *Cultural genocide and the protection of cultural heritage*. J. Paul Getty Trust Occasional Papers in Cultural Heritage Policy. https://www.getty.edu/publications/pdfs/CulturalGenocide_Luck.pdf. Accessed 8 June 2020.

OECD. (2020). *Policy responses to COVID-19: The territorial impact of COVID-19: Managing the crisis across levels of government*. https://www.oecd.org/coronavirus/policy-responses/the-territorial-impact-of-covid-19-managing-the-crisis-across-levels-of-government-d3e314e1/. Accessed 17 July 2020.

Pobjie, E. (2020). *COVID-19 as a threat to international peace and security: The role of the UN security council in addressing the pandemic*. https://www.ejiltalk.org/covid-19-as-a-threat-to-international-peace-and-security-the-role-of-the-un-security-council-in-addressing-the-pandemic/. Accessed 30 July 2020.

UNESCO. (1972, November 16). *Convention concerning the protection of the world cultural and natural heritage*. 1037 UNTS 151.

UNESCO. (2003, October 17). *Convention for the safeguarding of the intangible cultural heritage*. 2368 UNTS 1.

UNESCO. (2015a). *Report on the preliminary study on the advisability of regulating internationally, through a new standard-setting instrument, the protection of traditional culture and folklore*. Doc. 161 EX/15. https://unesdoc.unesco.org/images/0012/001225/122585e.pdf. Accessed 3 Mar 2020.

UNESCO. (2015b, November 2). *General conference: Thirty-eighth session, resolution 48*. Reinforcement of UNESCO's action for the protection of culture and the promotion of cultural pluralism in the event of armed conflict, UNESCO/Res/38C/48.

UNESCO. (2020a). *Culture and COVID-19: Impact and response tracker*. https://en.unesco.org/sites/default/files/issue_10_en_culture_covid-19_tracker-2.pdf. Accessed 24 July 2020.

UNESCO. (2020b). *Living heritage experiences and the COVID-19 pandemic*. https://ich.unesco.org/en/living-heritage-experiences-and-the-covid-19-pandemic-01123. Accessed 30 July 2020.

United Nations. (2020a, June 23). *Letter dated 22 June 2020 from the permanent representative of Germany to the United Nations addressed to the secretary-general*. S/2020/571.

United Nations. (2020b). *COVID-19 and special procedures*. https://www.ohchr.org/EN/HRBodies/SP/Pages/COVID-19-and-Special-Procedures.aspx.

United Nations Department of Economic and Social Affairs. (2020). *Indigenous peoples and the COVID-19 pandemic: Considerations*. https://www.un.org/development/desa/indigenouspeoples/covid-19.html. Accessed 30 July 2020.

United Nations General Assembly. (2017, January 9). *Report of the special rapporteur on minority issues on her mission to Iraq*. A/HRC/34/53/Add.1.

United Nations General Assembly. (2020, April 2). Resolution No. 74/270. A/RES/74/270.

United Nations Human Rights Council (2020a, April 30). *UN human rights council discusses human rights implications of the COVID-19 crisis with its special procedures mandate holders*. https://www.ohchr.org/EN/HRBodies/HRC/Pages/NewsDetail.aspx?NewsID=25853&LangID=E.

United Nations Human Rights Council. (2020b, May 20). *PRST 43/...Human rights implications of the COVID-19 pandemic*. A/HRC/43/L.42.

United Nations Human Rights Council Resolution No. 33. (2016, October 6). A/HRC/RES/33/20.

United Nations Secretary General. (2017, November 17). *Report of the Secretary-General on the implementation of Security Council resolution 2347*. S/2017/969.

United Nations Secretary General. (2020, April). *Report "COVID-19 and human rights: We are all in this together"*. https://unsdg.un.org/resources/covid-19-and-human-rights-we-are-all-together. Accessed 8 June 2020.

United Nations Security Council Resolution No. 1325. (2000, October 31). S/RES/1325.

United Nations Security Council Resolution No. 1483. (2003, May 22). S/RES/1483.

United Nations Security Council Resolution 1983. (2011, June 7). S/RES/1983.

United Nations Security Council Resolution 2100. (2013, April 25). S/RES/2100.

United Nations Security Council Resolution 2139. (2014, February 22) .S/RES/2139.

United Nations Security Council Resolution 2170. (2014, August 15) .S/RES/2170.

United Nations Security Council Resolution 2177. (2014, September 18). S/RES/2177.

United Nations Security Council Resolution No. 2199. (2015, February 12). S/RES/2199.

United Nations Security Council Resolution No. 2249. (2015, November 20). S/RES/2249.

United Nations Security Council Resolution No. 2253. (2015, December 17). S/RES/2253.

United Nations Security Council Resolution No. 2347. (2017, March 24). S/RES/2347.

United Nations Security Council Resolution Security No. 2439. (2018, October 30). S/RES/2439.

United Nations Security Council Resolution No. 2532. (2020, July 1). S/RES/2532.

United Nations Special Rapporteur in the field of cultural rights. (2020a). *Interactive dialogue statement—Human rights council, 43th Session*. https://www.ohchr.org/en/NewsEvents/Pages/DisplayNews.aspx?NewsID=25877&LangID=E.

United Nations Special Rapporteur in the field of cultural rights. (2020b, April 22). *Culture is the heart of our response to COVID 19*. #BeyondTheOutbreak: Cultural rights during and after the pandemic. https://www.ohchr.org/Documents/Issues/CulturalRights/BeyondTheOutbreak-online2020-KBspeech.pdf. Accessed 30 July 2020.

UN Special Rapporteur in the field of Cultural Rights. (2017, July 7). *Speech—Karima Bennoune—Inter-sessional seminar on cultural rights and protection of cultural heritage*. https://www.europanostra.org/speech-karima-bennoune-inter-sessional-seminar-cultural-rights-protection-cultural-heritage/.

Weiss, T., & Connelly, N. (2017). *Protecting cultural heritage in armed conflict zones*. J. Paul Getty Trust Occasional Papers in Cultural Heritage Policy. https://www.getty.edu/publications/pdfs/CulturalCleansing_Weiss_Connelly.pdf. Accessed 30 July 2020.

Wiesand, A. J., Chainoglou, K., Sledzinska-Simon, A., & Donders, Y. (2017). *Culture and human rights: The Wroclaw commentaries*. Berlin: De Gruyter. https://doi.org/10.1515/9783110432251.

Terrorism and the Loss of Cultural Heritage: The Case of ISIS in Iraq and Syria

Antoine Dib and Milagros Aurora Revilla Izquierdo

Abstract Since 2014, ISIS (Islamic State in Iraq and Sham) has committed many terrorist crimes, which is considered serious international crimes such as crimes against humanity, genocide and war crimes; they claimed the lives of thousands of civilians and military personnel, demolished places of worship and destroyed antiquities and historical sites in the areas that controlled. Indeed, Iraq and Syria were the most affected countries. In this chapter, a definition of the legal status of the territorial power IS (Islamic state) under International Law will be presented, especially that IS declared itself a state without the recognition of other states and it dissociated itself from the body of international law. Along with a brief review of the tangible cultural heritage loss, the ideology of ISIS behind this systematic destruction of historical sites and objects will be clarified. Moreover, the research will put light on the international actions applied by other states to limit such cultural crimes. Based on the previous definitions and the achieved experiences and results, the chapter will be ended by proposing a mechanism of transitional justice to avoid future rising feelings of revenge, which may lead to new crimes that destroy societies and cultural heritage.

1 Definition of ISIS and its Legal Status

Before defining the legal status of ISIS, the name itself of this jihadist "state" passed through different variations and it is worth to put light on the meaning of each one. The most common acronym is ISIS (used between 2013 and 2014) which stands for "Islamic State in Iraq and Syria" or "Islamic State in Iraq and al-Sham". The term al-Sham describes the Levant or all territories limited by Egypt, the Mediterranean,

A. Dib
Universidad Nacional Autónoma de México, Mexico City, Mexico
e-mail: adib@iingen.unam.mx

M. A. R. Izquierdo (✉)
Milagros Aurora Revilla Izquierdo Pontificia Universidad Catolica del Peru, Lima, Peru
e-mail: revilla.milagros@pucp.pe

O. Niglio and E. Y. J. Lee (eds.), *Transcultural Diplomacy and International Law in Heritage Conservation*, https://doi.org/10.1007/978-981-16-0309-9_22

Anatolia in Turkey and Euphrates in Iraq or more precisely Greater Syria formed by Syria, Lebanon, Israel, the Palestinian Territories, Jordan and including part of south-eastern Turkey. The English name is a translation of the Arabic name DAESH or DA'ISH (Dawla Islamiyya in "Iraq and Sham" (where Dawla means state). The Arabic acronym is not associated with a real word in Arabic but the combination of the sounds has an unpleasant sound impact and may be connected to the Arabic verb "to crush something", which goes in coherence with the objectives of this jihadist group. Another alternative used widely by UN and US officials is ISIL, an acronym of Islamic State in Iraq and the Levant. The group itself shortened its name in June 2014 to "Islamic State" or "IS" reflecting its expansionist ambitions outside the area of the Levant and Iraq (Irshaid, 2015). ISI or Islamic State of Iraq was used between 2006 and 2013, succeeding other names that referred to different terrorist groups like Al Qaeda, Al Jihad and Al Tawhid (Abd et al., 2018; Singer, 2015).

What pays the attention between all the acronyms: IS, ISI, ISIS and ISIL, is the presence of the word "State". Was ISIS really a state as their supporters declared themselves? And how is a state defined legally under international law?

In the textbooks of international law, three elements are essential to give a definition of a state: territory, population and governmental authority. Referring to the Convention of Montevideo on the Rights and Duties of States of 1933, a fourth element can be added which is the capacity to enter into international relations (Tomuschat, 2015). No need to develop in depth the applicability of the fourth point on ISIS because the only relations that developed through the years of their imposed regime were intellectual and organizational association with jihadist group in Afghanistan, East Asia, West and Central Africa, the Boko Haram group and Ansar Beit Al-Maqdis (Kaisi, 2020).

Regarding the first three elements, doubts arise about each one of them:

1. Territory: ISIS seized big territories in Syria and Iraq, 50% of Syria and 42% of Iraq (Kaisi, 2020), but all the conquests have no fixed borders, only a frontline that changes depending on the gains or the losses by the battles. Moreover, ISIS'S "territories" are not recognized by Iraq and Syria and they constitute occupied territories within the integral part of the concerned states.
2. Population: ISIS could not impose its power without the support of some people and followers where money was the biggest factor in encouraging young people to volunteer in the Iraqi-Syrian border areas under its banner. The poor social and economic conditions were the result of the absence of social justice, the dominance of the ruling regimes, the corrupt and favouritism practices among government leaders and the tendency towards importing foreign systems and values, excluding cultural and societal particularities (Revkin, 2016).
   Some volunteers might feel ideologically close to the IS, others received strong financial and social support (Kaisi, 2020) and some opponents found the Islamic State's legal system more efficient and effective than the available alternatives (Revkin, 2016). However, many others, especially minorities and opponents, felt like objects treated mercilessly and without any regard for their personal wishes and preferences (Tomuschat, 2015). Indeed, ISIS's members carried out

prominent crimes against large number of people: the kidnapping and trafficking of women as "spoils of war"; evacuating some Yazidi villages completely from their population; killing innocents like in the Camp Speicher massacre where between 1000 and 17,000 non-Sunni militiamen were killed; separating children from their mothers and taking them to locations in Iraq and Syria and were forced to convert to Islam and undergo religious and military training (Abd et al., 2018). All the above-mentioned ISIS crimes correspond to many forms of crime of Genocide with the objective of "purifying" the territory by eliminating national, religious or racial human group, in whole or in part and this is inconsistent with what was stated in Article II and III of the Universal Declaration of Human Rights of 1948, which states that "Everyone is entitled to all the rights and freedoms set forth in this Declaration, without distinction of any kind, such as race, colour, sex, language, religion, political or other opinion, national or social origin, property, birth or other status" and "everyone has the right to life, liberty and security of person" (Nations, 1948).
As a consequence, the self-declared state had not populations but only supporters and followers. It is true that populations must not be asked one by one or a referendum should be done, but, while an armed conflict is ongoing, the population of an occupied territory cannot be imposed to religious and political edicts and transformed by force into the people of that territory (Tomuschat, 2015).

3. Governmental Authority: Some administrative functions were performed in the occupied territories, especially in Raqqa and Mosul (Tomuschat, 2015). The Islamic State had developed, as any modern legal system, three features: police, courts and prisons, responsible for the protection of the Islamic State's legal system which is the Islamic Law or *shari'a*. The system appeared at the end shaky and difficult to be sustained under the shadows of corruption and extra-legal violence (Revkin, 2016). At the end, ISIS could not show a consolidated governmental authority, which, under the continuous fighting against international alliances guided by the United States, could not resist to declare a legal authority (Tomuschat, 2015).

It can be concluded that ISIS could not be considered a legal state as the International Law describe it. "State" was a mere self-declaration and the security council in the Resolution 2170 of the year 2014 defined "ISIL, also known as ISIS, and Al Nusra Front" as "extremist groups and movement of terrorists" but not a state (Council, 2014).

Considering that ISIS does not constitute a state and does not have the elements of the state, therefore, the armed conflict of the two legal states, Iraq and Syria, with that organization cannot be classified as a conflict between different states, hence the conflict is not considered an international conflict (Abd et al., 2018).

2 The Ideology of ISIS

Given the abundance of what has been written about ISIS issue during the last years, there is a great difficulty in writing about some of its aspects, particularly the aspects related to the reasons for the emergence of ISIS and its ideology. The difficulty here does not arise from the organization itself, its bloody regime, and the evidential terrorism and anti-humanitarian acts, but rather it arises from the different writings that have been written on this or that point, especially its indeterminate agenda and ideology.

Speaking generally, religious parties are rivals to political power and they try to organize every aspect of the life of their followers. The first interests of such organizations are in resolving religious or philological interpretation of religious problems. In a second phase, after gaining a certain degree of confidence and popularity, they extend their spheres of influence to other social aspects. Last, they set their sights on definitive social control through political power (Merari, 2007). This pass is pretty similar to the strategy of ISIS. From what it was written, it can be concluded that ISIS declared itself as a new defender of the Sunni Muslim faith, it constituted an armed revolutionary movement and then controlled big territories in Iraq and Syria and fight against the correspondent legal authorities.

As a "state", it rejects laws created by courts, legislatures or any human institution that oppose to divine laws. Its legal system purports to strictly apply the divinely revealed body of Islamic law known as shari 'a (Revkin, 2016). More precisely, the lectures of Abu Alaa al-Afri, a leader of ISIS in Syria, the archive of Abu Musab al-Zarqawi, the founder of Jama'et al.-Tawhid wal-Jihad in 1999 and the writings of Abu Muhammad al-Maqdisi, one of the most prominent theorists of the Salafi Jihad movement and a spiritual mentor of al-Zarqawi. Al-Maqdisi was influenced by Sheikh al-Islam Ibn Taymiyyah (1263–1328 CE), Ibn al-Qayyim (1292–1350 CE) and Sheikh Muhammad bin Abd al-Wahhab (1703–1791 CE), were an intellectual reference for the organization and they formed a basic internal and guiding system for them (Kaisi, 2020).

The Islamic State has always claimed that there is an Islamic legal basis for every act they perpetrate. Hence, theological motives may verify the ISIS's devastating campaign of destruction of the cultural heritage, as the same religious reasons were behind other world cultural crimes such as the blowing up of Buddha statues by Taliban in 2001, carved around 1700 years ago into a cliff in Afghanistan (Singer, 2015).

However, aniconism and the opposition of the use of icons to depict religious figures and living creatures in Islamic art does not explain the extent of extra-legal violence and genocide administered by ISIS or any other organization against cultural and human heritage. Historical sites, antiquities and monuments including icons and figures that dated back to different civilizations before the appearance of Islam and presented in ISIS's domain, were left intact during the times of the Umayyad, Abbasid caliphates and all Islamic governance that came afterward. Moreover, the

Sunni leading religious authority based in AL-Azhar, Cairo, described ISIS's actions as "a major crime against the whole world".

Even more, not only non-Islamic priceless sites and artefacts were destroyed by this terrorist organization; books of Islamic studies that contain materials different or in contrast with ISIS narrative were not spared; libraries housing invaluable manuscripts were burned out (Singer, 2015). They even destroyed religious architecture belonging to Islamic societies that do not follow their radical Sunni interpretation of Islam. Graves traced by names, dates and considered as a witness to the settlement of particular communities were wiped out by bulldozers. What shocks the most is the Fatwas launched by their lawmakers on the demolition of Islamic Sunni Religious sites such Al-Aqsa Mosque, the Dome of the Rock. In addition to that, there were many readings among these groups that it is permissible to demolish the tomb of the Prophet Muhammad in al-Madinah and thus destroy the Prophet's Noble Mosque because it contains the grave of the Holy Prophet (Daher, 2016), (CNN, 2016).

The later Fatwas were not new in the Islamic word; Sheikh al-Islam Ibn Taymiyyah, he influenced al-Maqdisi as it was mentioned before, forbidden to visit the grave of the Prophet; Ibn al-Qayyim was more forthright than his mentor Ibn Taymiyyah and advised that the dome of the Prophet's tomb must be destroyed and that the tomb must be removed from the mosque (Al Alam, 2016); the Baqi' al Gharqad Cemetery, near Al-Madinah in Saudi Arabia was destroyed in 1805 CE by the Wahhabis (Mohammad, 2016). This cemetery contained shrines of a large companion of the Prophet's family and the four Imams. However, it was rebuilt again after the fall of the Wahhabi state, and in 1926, Saudi authorities destroyed again this mausoleum, shortly after taking power in the city in the prior year (Singer, 2015).

The conclusion that can be obtained is that IS wanted to settle themselves as the eternal rulers of their territories through changing the existent religious landscape, destroying the society, erasing the collective memory of different existing cultures and the cultural assets that reflect the identity of the "others". This strategy of distancing between their regime and the past of the dominated areas can make the next generations, deprived of any experience outside the ISIS's social circle and ideology, less tolerant and respectful towards others.

3 Selling and Trafficking in Looted Artefacts, Damaging and Destruction of Historical and Cultural Monuments in Iraq and Syria

ISIS is a terroristic organization, and terrorism is a strategy based on psychological impact and can be defined as the easiest form of insurgency (Merari, 2007). A leader of ISIS, Taha Abd Arrahim al Ghassani, known as Hajji Naser Kardash, confessed in his jail that media was their most important weapon, their strategy was based on "Electronic Jihad" (Kaisi, 2020).

If the media was the main tool to spread their doctrine, the materials presented were based on terrorist deeds, intimidation and provocation. As this chapter is concerned only about cultural heritage, three main acts of ISIS's violence against people and places of religious and cultural importance will be presented. All these crimes, many of them documented by videos, failed to attract national and international support and they are considered part of crimes against humanity (Abd et al., 2018); they were framed in the process of ethnic cleansing (van der Auwera, 2012) and gained terrific publicity in accordance with ISIS's strategy (Merari, 2007).

3.1 Damaging and Destruction of Historical Sites and Cities:

ISIS was not a state in the legal meaning of the word, hence, it did not respect the international community and international laws, including international laws about conservation of cultural heritage. On contrary, armed with the interpretation of religious teachings, but more interested in income than ideology, it bulldozed intentionally its way through the cultural heritage of Iraq and Syria and they destroyed and damaged many of them; the visual recording video of this acts of destruction gained international publicity. ISIS's members did not spare any layer of the existing culture in Iraq and Syria: Assyrian, Roman, pre-Christian Christian, Sassanid and even Islamic sites went under attack. The destruction targeted churches, monasteries, historical sites, museums, libraries, even mosques and shrines. In the sections to follow, the most representative and shocking cultural terrorist actions are listed, even though the list is way longer. ISIS attacks against cultural property were classified by some researchers (Ristoldo, 2017) into two types: type one is the attacks on local minorities' cultural property, and type two is the attacks on UNESCO world heritage.

In Iraq, The Tal Afar Citadel, an Ottoman citadel located in Nineveh Governorate used by ISIS as a prison for women and then, northern and western walls were extremely damaged in December 2014 by ISIS's members (Lynch, 2014), (ASOR, 2017). In 2015, the ancient Assyrian city of Nimrud, flourished between 900 and 612 B.C and nominated to be placed on UNESCO's list of world heritage sites, located north of Mosul, was attacked by ISIS's "militants" with sledgehammers and then was blew up using explosives (Martinez, 2015). Few days before, a video recorded the intent destruction at Mosul Museum, Iraq's second-largest museum, of various ancient original artefacts, fortunately about half of them in the video were copies (Curry, 2015). Always in Mosul, the terrorist organization has burned and stolen thousands of books and rare manuscripts from many places, among them the Central Library of Mosul, the Mosul Museum Library, etc. (Curry, 2015). Few days after the destruction in the Mosul Museum, the ancient Assyrian capital of Khorsabad, one of three cities that served as an Assyrian capital (Guralnick, 2011), northeast of Mosul, had been destroyed and 19 priceless monuments lost in conflict. The Assyrian palaces in Khorsabad were characterized by the "stylistic innovations, the preservation of paint on its reliefs, and the extensive ancient written documentation concerning the organization of the building project" (Cullinane et al., 2015). Same time, the destruction of the ancient site of Hatra was a turning point in the terrible strategy of cultural cleansing. It dated back to 300 B.C., founded by the successors of Alexander the Great, conserved Parthian, Roman and Persian Sassanid Empires (Singer, 2015; Cullinane et al., 2015).

Many videos memorized ISIS while detonating Jonah's tomb, or the prophet Yunus. The holy site was inside a Sunni mosque in Mosul. The attack of prophet Jonah's tomb, said to be swallowed by a whale or the Judeo-Christian and Islamic traditions, is considered an attackon the Abrahamic religions (Curry, 2015). Another religious sites were demolished like the Monastery of the Martyrs Mar Behnam and Marth Sarah, built in northern Iraq in the fourth century that was heavily damaged but then restored (Camurat, 2017); Saint Elijah's Monastery, founded in the late sixth century and belonging to the Chaldean Catholic Church, was demolished in 2014 (McNeill, 2016); a tenth-century church in Tikrit, the Church of Saint Ahudemmeh (Hann, Dabrowska, & Townsead-Greaves, 2015), was also destroyed by IS "militants".

They destroyed religious places and shrines belonging to Sunni and Shiite followers, among them the Minaret of Anah that dated back to the Abbasid era; the Great Mosque of al-Nuri that has more than 850 years of history (Ingber, 2018), the thirteenth-century shrine of Imam Awn al-Din was destroyed as well and it was one of the few structures that survived the thirteenth-century Mongol invasion (Novacek et al., 2017), and the list continues.

The situation in Syria was not better than in Iraq. World Heritage and historical sites have suffered considerable and sometimes irreversible damage and the "rich tapestry of cultural heritage is being ripped to shreds" (Ki-Moon et al., 2014).

Despite ISIS's reporting that their intention is not destroying Palmyra, a UNESCO site, the terrorist organization demolished several statues including the ancient Lion of Al-lāt. It had blown up the first-century Temple of Baalshamin, demolished the Temple of Bel, destroyed seven ancient tower tombs including the destruction of the second-century AD Tower of Elahbel, called "the most prominent example of Palmyra's distinct funerary monuments". The famous Arch of Triumph and part of the Roman amphitheatre were also blown up. And finally, when the city was retaken by the Syrian forces in 2016, retreating ISIL fighters destroyed parts of the thirteenth-century Palmyra Castle, known as Fakhr-al-Din al Ma'ani Castle, causing extensive damage (Conti, 2018).

The Monastery of Saint Elian, a Syrian Catholic church in central Syria was destroyed in august 2015 by ISIS's members. Parts of the monastery date back to around 1500 years ago and housed a fifth-century tomb (Gutteridge, 2015).

They bulldozed also the two Assyrian statues of lions located in the city centre of Raqqa, originally from an archaeological site near Aleppo, dated back to the eighth-century BC (Lehr, 2020) and they demolished more than 70 per cent of the Parthian/Roman city of Dura-Europos in the east of Syria, nicknamed "the Pompeii of the desert", founded in 300 B.C (Christian, 2019).

ISIS's members did not spare the eighth-century Great Mosque of Aleppo and the eleventh-century Crusader castle, Crac des Chevaliers (Cullinane et al., 2015) among others.

3.2 *Illicit Trading in Artefacts and Cultural Properties*

When the Islamic State dominated over some parts of the rich archaeological territories of Mesopotamia, they use the cultural heritage as a sustainable financial resource and an intense propaganda factor based on psychological impact (Al-Azm & Paul, 2018). Theft and trafficking of stolen antiquities was not a pure idea of ISIS. It was consolidated a long time ago in the world and in the Middle East; but ISIS, during its bloody reign of terror in some zones of the "Cradle of Civilisation", took black-market trade in cultural property to an unprecedented level. The sale and purchase of antiquities are done with huge sums of money, under a military protection provided by the extremist organization (Al Kadi, 2015). Not only trafficking was done in traditional black markets, but they took profit also from the facility of selling priceless items through internet and social media, such as Facebook which made their illicit trade easier. It is not easy to know the real number of masterpieces stolen and sold in the black market and that went in private collections; even though, websites make it easier somehow to prove the existence of illegal activities; For example, Prof Amr Al Azm said that researchers are monitoring over 120 Facebook groups, the largest of them had around 150,000 members in 2019 and more than 437,000 in 2020. Maybe the recent increase can be explained by the economic crisis caused by the COVID-19 pandemic, but this was not just due to the increased number of impoverished to sell antiquities to make a few dollars (Swann, 2020). It is worth to remember that, in parallel to the looters affiliated with ISIS which were the most stolen for the Syrian and Iraqi antiquities, other terrorist organizations and parties, as well as opportunistic individuals, have illegally excavated areas in Iraq and Syria taking an opportunity of the presence of ISIS and the environment of disorder (Al Kadi, 2015; Melito, 2016). The sale of rare antiquities seized in the conflict became a large-scale efficient business operation and its proceeds are linked to financing terrorism (Singer, 2015; Melito, 2016; Ristoldo, 2017).

3.3 *Intimidation of People*

One tactic of the psychological strategy of terrorism is to spread fear in the enemy's ranks. They start by intimidating through kidnapping, assassinating or maiming the selected categories of people, especially popular faces, such as judges, journalists, scientists, that stand for their values and they do not give up even if their lives are jeopardized. Usually, every government official or employee or those who cooperate with the authorities or criticize apparently such crimes and refuse to assist terrorist, are punished. This coercive terroristic tactic is sometimes generalized and is applied to the general population (Merari, 2007).

One clear example of this intimidation policy is the murder of Khaled al Asaad who has become a symbol of resistance against terrorism, and a great defender of the city of Palmyra and its heritage, a UNESCO World Heritage site. This ISIS's victim, one of the most important pioneers in Syrian archaeology in the twentieth century, was the head of antiquities at the ancient city of Palmyra, (BBC, 2015). He did not leave the city, and before ISIS captured him, he said his famous words: "I am from Palmyra and I will stay there even if they have to kill me". His courage was fatal to him so he was killed with a wild way, because he did not give a legitimacy to their power in Palmyra, ISIS's response was a message of revenge as well as to terrorize the people in Palmyra. Terrorizing people was not the only cause of beheading him, but because he refused to say how to reach the stores of gold in the city where the hidden golden treasures are, which is a big lie that has been rumoured in Palmyra on their arrival (Abdulac, 2016).

Other ISIS victims that did not benefit from this sad fame of the "martyr of Palmyra" include more than 12 employees, 5 of them in their workplaces and one of them was murdered at the hands of the terrorist organization in Deir Ezzor, because he provided the Antiquities Department with information about the mafias of antiquities trafficking (Al Kadi, 2015). Abdallah al Humaid, an Iraqi guardian of a site on the edges of the Euphrates slain for staying on his workplace; an Imam in Al-Mufti Mosque in Mosul that opposed ISIS's order to remove all decorative elements from mosques in Mosul, even those contained Quranic verses, was shot to death (Rashid, 2015) and lawyer Samira Salih al Nuaimi was another example of intimidation (Abdulac, 2016). The later was a rights lawyer in the Iraqi city of Mosul. After posting messages on Facebook criticizing the militants' destruction of religious sites in Mosul, she was seized from her home on the 17th of September 2014, tortured for five days before the militants sentenced her to "public execution". In ISIS's self-styled Islamic court or "Sharia court", Al Nuaimi was tried for apostasy or abandoning Islam (Press, 2014).

4 National and International Actions that were Applied to Limit the Systematic Lost and Destruction of Antiquities and Cultural Heritage

The strategy of ISIS based on propaganda by deeds reached its desired goal, especially the use of the destruction of cultural heritage as an essential weapon in their war crimes and genocide. Different communities, states, individuals and institutions understood that the protection of the peoples of the territories affected by the conflicts and the protection of their heritage cannot be separated. They understood that the destruction of cultural heritage is not simply a collateral threat to heritage or an ordinary act of discrimination or a crime against property. It can be ranked rather as an attack against the human cultural memory in general, and to the identity and cultural and spiritual existence of certain human groups and their right to enjoy their cultural identity in specific (Thake, 2017). Moreover, the destruction and looting heritage sites affect directly and permanently the economic circle of the related individuals and states, and worse, the incomes of the sale of looted historical artefacts fund terrorist activity.

On the light on the forgoing, many activities have been taken by governmental and non-governmental entities, nationally and internationally, to protect and save Iraqi and Syrian cultural properties affected by the terrorist conflicts.

4.1 Awareness and Volunteering Protection

A first important action to limit the loss of cultural artefacts, through stealing, selling, damaging and destruction, is not a juridical or technical action, but it consists of implementing in the society the power of knowledge based on education and awareness of valorizing the importance of historical buildings (Della Torre, 2003). For instance, in a territory of conflicts and fear, under the absence of legal authorities to protect lives and assets, a minimum of volunteering wise decisions and fast actions can change drastically the destiny of thousands of inestimable artefacts. For this reason, around 2011, before the rise of ISIS and after 2003 Iraqi war and 2011 Syrian war, the Smithsonian Institution and US agencies have undertaken some activities to protect cultural properties of both countries. Among many activities, the Department of State (State), the government of Iraq and others established an archaeological and cultural management training facility in Erbil, Iraq (Melito, 2016). However, taking actions in a time of "peace" is totally different than acting while the missiles are above your head. In what it follows, an example puts light on the importance of individual actions during wars and conflicts:

When a big part of the city of Deir Ezzor in Syria was under the domination of ISIS, a cultural rescue operation took place on the 2nd of August 2014 which will be always remembered as honourable and heroic. To avoid the sad destiny of the patrimony of the city of Mosul in Iraq two months before, the stakeholders took a decision to transfer 13,000 artefacts from the city. Ya'reb al Abdallah, the former director of the monuments of Deir Ezzor, who is the current director of the National Museum in Damascus, said that with two colleagues, they blew everything up within a week and put them in a freight car before it came under heavy artillery fire, then they deposited the boxes in a warplane, among dead and wounded soldiers. The operation was but at least they succeeded. (Al Kadi, 2015).

Dr. Ma'moun Abdel Karim, the General Director of Syrian museums and antiquities since 2012, mentioned that 99 per cent of museum holdings have been saved, thanks to the dedication of 2,500 salaried employees, including those who still live in areas under the control of opposition forces. Despite that more than 300 sites of human value were subjected to destruction, damage and looting during the 4 years of the Syrian conflict, 300 thousand pieces and thousands of manuscripts distributed to 34 museums in Syria, including 80 thousand from the Damascus Museum alone, are kept in secret hideouts immune to fire, missiles and floods (Al Kadi, 2015).

4.2 International and National Laws to Protect Cultural Heritage

When Lemkin first coined the term Genocide in 1944, he included three forms of genocide: physical, biological and cultural. Unfortunately, cultural genocide was met with great opposition. Since then, the cultural genocide has survived only on Lemkin's draft but regrettably, was not admitted by the General Assembly (Thake, 2017). The intentional destruction of cultural heritage is a crime against humanity, not solely a crime against property, so a gap was existing between international criminal legislation and the reality. Fortunately, in March 2017, the UN Security Council adopted the Resolution 2347 for the protection of heritage which was the first-ever resolution adopted by the Security Council focusing on Cultural heritage. After the systematic cultural cleansing of ISIS, they finally arrived at the conclusion that destruction of heritage is a war crime and it is a tactic of war (Resolution 2347, 2017). Two years before, in 2015, the UN Security Council adopted the Resolution 2199 which condemns the destruction of cultural heritage in Iraq and Syria, and notes that such terroristic groups are "generating income from engaging directly or indirectly in the looting and smuggling of cultural heritage". It was mentioned in a following point that all Member States shall take appropriate steps to prevent the trade in Iraq and Syrian cultural property" […] "by prohibiting cross-border trade in such items, thereby allowing for their eventual safe return to the Iraqi and Syrian people" (Resolution 2199, 2015).

Under this Resolution, all Member States were obliged to take steps to prevent terrorist groups in Iraq and Syria from benefiting from trade in antiquities. For instance, to close a loophole in American law, the Senate voted, after months of delay and debate over the legislation, to ban the import of looted and stolen artefacts from Syria in order to discourage illicit trafficking of antiquities by terrorist groups including ISIS (Myers, 2016).

4.3 Social Media Bans Artefacts Trade

Nowadays, social media are aware of their big responsibility towards users and societies. After an investigation lead by BBC News team and a campaign by academic researchers on how artefacts and cultural items looted from Syria and Iraq are sold on Facebook, the later has banned users trading in such historical items on the site (Swann, 2020) The new guidelines of banning any content that encourages or attempts buying, selling, trading, gifting or soliciting all historical artefacts will be also apply to Instagram owned by Facebook (Facebook, 2020). The new guidelines of June 2020 were added to a previous rule of buying or selling stolen gold. The automated system is based on user reports, keywords and images identification through artificial intelligence.

4.4 Reconstruction of Damaged and Demolished Historical Sites and Artefacts

The huge amount of damage and destruction committed by ISIS reflects from one part the barbarity and intolerance of their extremist groups, and from another part shows the solidarity, sense of responsibility and fraternity between people from different races, religions, countries and believes. The destruction of cultural properties reunited somehow the humanity to save the cultural memory of the humankind. Directly after the retreat of ISIS from some occupied zones, citizens, authorities, non-governmental organizations and specialists starts to implement projects of restoration and reconstruction of damaged buildings, especially historical monuments. The first axiomatic action is to expect intervention from the governmental authorities to safeguard their national cultural heritage. This is the example of the Iraq Government which announced a ten-year $100 billion reconstruction plan as a response to the destruction of the Northwest Palace of the damaged city of Nimrud. The project involves collaboration with international cultural institution which the Smithsonian Institution in Washington. Of course the first phase will involve mainly documentation, mapping, screening of the damage. The reconstruction will be at the second phase by repairing broken artefacts and creating 3D-printed replicas of artefacts that are missed or cannot be repaired (Bassem, 2017).

The unprecedented damage and destruction of ISIS to cultural properties were followed by an unprecedented cooperation between nations. The agreement signed by Iraq, United Arab Emirates and the United Nations in 2017 reflects this cooperation. The UAE will donate $50.4 million for restoring the Great Mosque of al-Nuri and the leaning minaret. The estimated amount to repair the crumbling homes and streets is a minimum of $2 billion, but at least the restoration of cultural landmarks will generate employment and help to conserve the memory of the city (Ingber, 2018). Another example of collaboration between foreign states and local cultural entities is the annual funding provided by the United States to support several projects to inventory museum and archaeological sites, in countries where cultural property may be at risk (Melito, 2016).

International collaboration is including famous museums as the above-mentioned Smithsonian, and the British Museum which used an Ancient Sumerian Structure in Iraq to train two groups of female archaeologists in the necessary skills to restore the ravaged heritage (Beaumont, 2018).

Some restoration works are based totally on volunteers and local habitants; an illustrative example is the restoration of Mar Behnam Monastery in Khidr. Eight local workers and a team of free of charge professionals reconstructed the mausoleum to its original look which means that communities can meet again in it bringing down the walls of fear built by ISIS (Camurat, 2017).

A pioneering initiative of reconstruction was the restoration of the Lion of al-Lat statue from the city of Palmyra in Syria which reflect the important role of UNESCO in conserving cultural heritage. UNESCO sent a Rapid Assessment Mission to Palmyra after "a decision unanimously adopted during the 199th session of UNESCO's Executive Board concerning the Organization's role in safeguarding and preserving Palmyra and other Syrian World Heritage sites". The project was "funded by the European Union with the support of the Flemish Government and Austria", with collaboration of entities like the International Centre for the Study of the Preservation and Restoration of Cultural Property and the International Council on Monuments and Sites (UNESCO, 2017).

Of course, the mentioned actions were not the solely ones applied by different entities, organizations, individuals, but they are deeply appreciated even though the destroyed or heavily damaged monuments, sites and items will never be the same. More necessary actions should be taken and they are listed in the following section.

5 Future Necessary Actions to be Applied to Avoid Intended Cultural Damage and Establish a Transitional Justice

The frequently observed scenes of the intentional destruction of cultural properties of historical monuments and religious sites in Iraq and Syria by ISIS terrorist members are painful and unforgettable. Their actions are attempts to obliterate civilization history and culture, based on their dark terrorist ideology and they did not only target minorities, but as well all international community.

The rise of terroristic group, like ISIS, could not have place if the countries in which have been flourished were not divided by religious believes and ethnical subdivisions and the governmental authority was decayed by corruption, nepotism, favouritism and bribery. From here comes the importance of establishing a capable governmental authority based on social justice and equality. It is also necessary that the government understand the values and cultural background of all the groups and ethnicities within its territories and do not try to impose imported systems and rigid ideologies. The spirit of belonging to one nation should reunite all the people and this should be their first objective; then the problem of the establishment of new extremist groups or the rebirth of former similar organizations and all what it follows as cultural properties destruction will be eradicated from its roots. However, the question of how to establish social equality and capable authorities is beyond the scoop of this chapter and in what it will come next, tangible and consistent actions related to national and international legislation, technical and social decisions that seem to be the most important and relevant for the authors of this chapter and not treated in the previous section will be presented.

As it was identified in Sect. 1, ISIS is not a state, hence, the conflict with other states is not considered an international conflict. As a consequence, the armed conflict between the joint Iraqi and Syrian forces from one part and the ISIS terrorist organization from another one, falls within the framework of national armed conflict, but not international conflict, and therefore the Iraqi and Syrian criminal law are the laws to be applied to crimes committed by that organization, including cultural crimes. In the case of applying Iraqi Penal Code No. 111 for the year 1969 (Abd et al., 2018), it is important to amend it to suit the severity of the crimes committed by ISIS and other terrorist groups which reach the level of genocide and war crimes.

Moreover, the crimes committed by ISIS were defined by the Article 4 of (Resolution 2347, 2017) as a war crime, pursuant to international law and the correspondent perpetrators must be brought to justice. However, a limitation of the prosecution of the International Criminal Court (ICC) of the war crimes in Iraq and Syria may arise here, because both countries are not Member States of the Rome Statute, the treaty that established the ICC. The ICC could only obtain jurisdiction only if Iraqi and Syrian governments ratify the 1998 Statute of the International Criminal Court or accept the exercise of jurisdiction by the court through a declaration with respect to the crimes in question (Rome Statute of the ICC, 1998).

Regarding illicit trade and trafficking in artefacts and cultural properties, concerned states are required to: (i) improve and increase training on cultural property investigations and set an inventory of all existent items and artefacts of historical and cultural importance for use by law enforcement and market participants to track items at risk of being looted; (ii) implement national measures at legislative level and designate cultural property smugglers as terrorist financiers especially if organized criminal groups, terrorists or terrorist groups are benefiting from the returns and in case the cultural property items come from conflict zones; (iii) improve the border protection between states and require travellers and importers clarifying information of each artefact such as certification of provenance and a document of legitimacy; (iv) Increase national government's support of public–private partnerships and create an inventory of all customers of antiquities dealers by reporting information on antiquities transactions; (v) establish a heritage administration with the aim of discovering and retrieving stolen artefacts from abroad through collaboration with foreign governments and international organizations; (vi) create an anonymous website, application or hotline to report suspicious cultural property sales and purchases; vii) international collaboration to ban artefacts trade through all the giants of social media and any website specialized in selling and purchasing online.

The amount of damage and destruction left by ISIS in Iraq and Syria is huge and reached an unprecedented level of intentional destruction and devastation. Many of the damaged sites went or are going under reconstruction and reparation operations, but many technical and financial problems are facing such projects. Hence, regarding that affected structures dated back to a broad interval of time, constructors should deal with different building techniques and materials. Hence, a huge number of specialized workers are needed in the projects of reconstruction and it is the role of local engineers, architects, researchers and other professionals, with international collaboration, to translate their information into practical knowledge (Elisabethe & Cervantes, 2016). It can be an opportunity to educate and train local labours on developing and applying traditional techniques and modern or innovative methodologies, respecting the native identity of the site, and Venice and ICOMOS Charters without looking for cheap solutions or applying a blind copying of ready to use strategies.

Weapons, funding and laws are not the only solutions to defeat terrorism and specially, cultural crimes. It should be noted the importance of education, culture, prevention and the transmission of heritage from generation to generation in building peace. In the Iraqi and Syrian ambience, the rise of ISIS, as it was mentioned in paragraph 1, was due to poor economic conditions and the acceptance of the extremist ideologies. This fact puts lights on the power of religion and religious thoughts in Levantine countries, like Iraq and Syria. Therefore, to avoid future cultural heritage damage, the prevention and education steps should start from clergy. Clergy including Imam of mosques, priests of churches, mosques, churches and religious temples from all denominations, should spread among the believers the spirit of tolerance, peace and love and explain the danger of extremist ideas that call for hate and disrespecting others. Moreover, all religious places should be monitored periodically by competent authorities; authorities should ensure as well that religious sermons are free from arousing sedition and hate among people. States should invest as well in specialized centres to study the strategies of terrorist organizations and suggest theoretical and practical ways to combat the terror of such group and to avoid the flourishing of any future similar organization.

References

Abd, M. M., Hamzah, Q. M., & Khalil, N. A. (2018). Legal description of DAASH organisation crimes. *Majalat almuhaqiq alhilmi lil 'eulum al qanunia wal siyasia*, 476–507.

Abdulac, S. (2016). KHALED AL ASAAD ou l'itinéraire exemplaire d'un grand palmyrénien. In D. Syria (Ed.), *The martyr of Palmyra Khaled Al Asaad* (p. 50). Damascus, Syria: Directorate General of Antiquities & Museums.

Al Alam. (2016, July 5). Did IS intend to blow up the grave of the Prophet? *Al Alam Tv*. https://www.alalamtv.net/news/1835404/.

Al Kadi, K. (2015, March 27). Specialized in tracking stolen antiquities: The looting of syrian sites near the Euphrates began before Mosul. *Asharq Al Awsat* (13268). https://aawsat.com/home/article/322196/. Accessed July 10, 2020.

Al-Azm, A., & Paul, K. (2018, August 14). How Facebook made it easier than ever to traffic middle eastern antiquities. *World Politics Review*. https://www.worldpoliticsreview.com/insights/25532/how-facebook-made-it-easier-than-ever-to-traffic-middle-eastern-antiquities. Accessed July 5, 2020.

ASOR. (2017). *Incident report feature: Tal Afar Citadel*. Alexandria: American Schools of Oriental Research Cultural Heritage Initiatives. https://www.asor.org/chi/reports/incident-report-feature/Tal-Afar-Citadel. Accessed July 12, 2020.

Bassem, W. (2017, August 7). Iraq steps up efforts to restore lost heritage at ancient Nimrud. *Al-Monitor*. https://www.al-monitor.com/pulse/originals/2017/08/iraq-nimrud-archaeology-isis-reconstruction.html. Accessed July 12, 2020.

BBC. (2015, August 19). Syrian archaeologist 'killed in Palmyra' by IS militants. *BBC News*. https://www.bbc.com/news/world-middle-east-33984006. Accessed June 18, 2020.

Beaumont, P. (2018, Aprile 1). UK archaeologists help Iraqis restore their Isis-ravaged heritage. *The Guardian*. https://www.theguardian.com/world/2018/apr/01/uk-archaeologists-help-iraqis-restore-their-isis-ravaged-heritage. Accessed June 28, 2020.

Camurat, F.-B. (2017, September 4). Restoration work has begun at the Mar Behnam monastery! *fraternite-en-irak*. https://fraternite-en-irak.org/restoration-work-has-begun-at-the-mar-behnam-monastery/. Accessed June 11, 2020.

Christian, R. I. (2019). *House, Church, or neither? The Dura-Europos house church as Christian*. Unpublished master's thesis, University of Calgary, Calgary, AB.

CNN, A. (2016, July 06). After the Saudi monarch performed the Eid prayer. The Sermon of Eid al-Fitr in the great mosque of Mecca: "Woe to the ISIS and those behind them". *CNN*. https://arabic.cnn.com/middleeast/2016/07/06/saudi-eid-al-fitr-khotba. Accessed June 18, 2020.

Conti, R. (2018). *Behance*. https://www.behance.net/gallery/66798899/The-Arch-of-Palmyra. Accessed June 10, 2020.

Council, S. (2014). *Security council adopts resolution 2170 (2014) condemning gross, widespread abuse of human rights by extremist groups in Iraq, Syria*. New York, NY: UN Meetings Coverage & Press Releases. https://www.un.org/press/en/2014/sc11520.doc.htm. Accessed July 18, 2020.

Cullinane, S., Alkhshali, H., & Tawfeeq, M. (2015, April 14). Tracking a trail of historical obliteration: ISIS trumpets destruction of Nimrud. *CNN*. https://edition.cnn.com/2015/03/09/world/iraq-isis-heritage/index.html. Accessed July 18, 2020.

Curry, A. (2015, September 1). Here are the ancient sites ISIS has damaged and destroyed. *National Geographic*. https://www.nationalgeographic.com/news/2015/09/150901-isis-destruction-looting-ancient-sites-iraq-syria-archaeology/. Accessed July 18, 2020.

Daher, Z. (2016, October 28). ISIS crimes against civilization ... who benefits and who is affected? *Almanar News*. https://almanar.com.lb/924867.

Della Torre, S. (2003). *La conservazione programmata del patrimonio storico architettonico: Linee guida per il piano di manutenzione e consuntivo scientifico*. Milano: Guerini e associati.

Elisabethe, N., & Cervantes, R. (2016). Aplicacion de estrategias de conservacion y manejo urbano en el contexto cultural mexicano. In A. Balandrano, V. Valero, & A. Ziccardi (Eds.), *Conservacion y desarrollo sustentable de Centros Historicos* (pp. 63–81). Mexico: PUEC, UNAM.

Facebook. (2020). https://www.facebook.com/communitystandards/regulated_goods. Accessed July 18, 2020.

Guralnick, E. (2011). The palace at Khorsabad: A storeroom excavation project. In D. Kertai & P. A. Miglus (Eds.), *New research on late Assyrian palaces* (pp. 5–10). Heidelberg.

Gutteridge, N. (2015, August 21). ISIS dig up and desecrate Saint's bones after bulldozing 1,600-year-old Christian church. *Express*. https://www.express.co.uk/news/world/599816/ISIS-Islamic-State-Mar-Elian-monastery-Homs-Syria-bulldoze-saint. Accessed July 11, 2020.

Hann, G., Dabrowska, K., & Townsead-Greaves, T. (2015). *Iraq: The ancient sites & Iraqi Kurdistan*. Bradt Travel Guides.

Ingber, S. (2018, April 24). Mosul's famed Mosque and 'Hunchback' Minaret, destroyed By ISIS, will be rebuilt. *NPR*. https://www.npr.org/sections/thetwo-way/2018/04/24/605230101/mosuls-famed-mosque-and-hunchback-minaret-destroyed-by-isis-will-be-rebuilt. Accessed July 18, 2020.

Irshaid, F. (2015, December 2). ISIS, ISIL, IS or Daesh? One group, many names. *BBC News*. https://www.bbc.com/news/world-middle-east-27994277. Accessed July 18, 2020.

Kaisi, A. (2020, June 05). This is ISIS: The truth of the state discovered by Kordash. *Irfaa Sawtak*. https://www.irfaasawtak.com/iraq/2020/06/05/. Accessed July 20, 2020.

Ki-Moon, B., Bokova, I., & Brahimi, L. (2014, March 14). *The destruction of the cultural heritage of Syria must stop* (UNESCO Report). New York, NY: UNESCO.

Lehr, D. (2020, July 28). *Theantiquitiescoalition*. https://theantiquitiescoalition.org/understanding-the-problem/before-and-after-series/cultureunderthreat-before-and-after-volume-i/.

Lynch, C. (2014, October 2). Women and children for sale. *Foreign Policy*. https://foreignpolicy.com/2014/10/02/women-and-children-for-sale/. Accessed July 1, 2020.

Martinez, M. (2015, March 6). ISIS bulldozes ruins of ancient Assyrian city of Nimrud, Iraqi ministry says. *CNN*. https://edition.cnn.com/2015/03/05/world/iraq-isis-destroys-ancient-city-nimrud/index.html. Accessed May 21, 2020.

McNeill, S. (2016, January 20). Iraq's 1,400 year old St Elijah's Christian monastery destroyed by Islamic state militants. *ABC*. https://www.abc.net.au/news/2016-01-21/iraqs-st-elijahs-monastery-destroyed-by-islamic-state/7103224. Accessed July 18, 2020.

Melito, T. (2016). *Cultural property protection of Iraqi and Syrian antiquities*. Washington, DC: United States Government Accountability Office. https://www.gao.gov/assets/680/679061.pdf. Accessed July 18, 2020.

Merari, A. (2007). Terrorism as a strategy of insurgency. In G. Chaliand & A. Blin (Eds.), *The history of terrorism from antiquity to Al Qaeda* (pp. 12–51). Berkley, CA: University of California Press.
Mohammad, H. J. (2016, July 16). Remembrance of the demolition of the shrines in Al-Baqi. *Markaz Al Furat, FCDRS*. https://fcdrs.com/religion/489. Accessed June 18, 2020.
Myers, S. L. (2016, April 13). Senate votes to ban imports of Syrian art and antiquities. *New York Times*. https://www.nytimes.com/2016/04/14/world/middleeast/senate-votes-to-ban-imports-of-syrian-art-and-antiquities.html. Accessed June 23, 2020.
Nations, U. (1948). *The universal declaration of human rights*. New York, NY: United Nations Department of Public Information.
Novacek, K., Muhl, S., Fobbe, S., Matthews, R., Kolinski, R., & Nieuwenhuijse, O. (2017). *The intentional destruction of cultural heritage in Iraq as a violation of human rights*. Munich: RASHID International e.V. https://www.ohchr.org/Documents/Issues/CulturalRights/DestructionHeritage/NGOS/RASHID.pdf. Accessed July 21, 2020.
Press, T. A. (2014, September 25). ISIS kills Iraqi woman activist in Mosul. *Al Arabiya*. https://english.alarabiya.net/en/News/middle-east/2014/09/25/ISIS-kills-Iraqi-woman-activist. Accessed July 18, 2020.
Rashid, K. H. (2015, April 2). Islamic state forces Mosul imams to remove frescoes from Mosque walls. *TASS*. https://tass.ru/mezhdunarodnaya-panorama/1876232. Accessed July 18, 2020.
Resolution 2199, S/RES/2199. (2015, May 5). United Nations, Security Council.
Resolution 2347, S/RES/2347. (2017, March 24). United Nations, Security Council.
Revkin, M. (2016). *The legal foundations of the Islamic state*. Washington, DC: Brookings.
Ristoldo, F. (2017). *Attacks against cultural property as a weapon of war: An exploratory case study* (Student Paper Series 34). Barcelona, Spain: IBEI (Institut Barcelona Estudis Internacionals). https://www.ibei.org/ibei_studentpaper34_105354.pdf. Accessed July 18, 2020.
Rome Statute of the ICC, A/CONF.183/9. (1998, July 17). International Criminal Court.
Singer, G. G. (2015). *ISIS's war on cultural heritage and Memory*. Buenos Aires: Centro de Estudios de Historia del Antiguo Oriente (CEHAO).
Swann, S. (2020, June 23). Facebook bans 'loot-to-order' antiquities trade. *BBC*. https://www.bbc.com/news/world-middle-east-53140615. Accessed July 18, 2020.
Thake, A. (2017). The intentional destruction of cultural heritage as a genocidal act and a crime against humanity. In *European Society of International Law* (Vol. 10, pp. 1–26). Naples: ESIL SEDI. https://doi.org/10.2139/ssrn.3163108
Tomuschat, C. (2015). The status of the Islamic state under international law. *Die Friedens-Warte, 90*(3/4), 223–244. www.jstor.org/stable/24868695. Accessed July 18, 2020.
UNESCO. (2017). *Restoration completed on Lion of Al-lāt statue from ancient city of Palmyra, damaged by ISIL*. New York, NY: UNESCO. https://en.unesco.org/news/restoration-completed-lion-al-lat-statue-ancient-city-palmyra-damaged-isil. Accessed July 18, 2020.
Van der Auwera, S. (2012). Contemporary conflict, nationalism, and the destruction of cultural property during armed. *Journal of Conflict Archaeology, 7*(1), 49–65. https://doi.org/10.1179/157407812X13245464933821.

Urban Recovery and Reconstruction Strategies for the Old City of Mosul After ISIL/Da'esh Occupation

Giovanni Fontana Antonelli and Tommaso Cossu

Abstract The paper deals with the strategic approach to urban recovery and reconstruction for the Old City of Mosul after the damage deliberately inflicted by ISIL/Da'esh to its cultural heritage in 2014, and subsequently the loss and damage aggravated by the liberation of West Mosul in 2017. The damage to cultural heritage intentionally perpetrated by ISIL/Da'esh during the three years of occupation of vast swaths of territory in north-western Iraq, e.g., the twelfth-century Al-Nuri Mosque and its Al-Hadba Minaret, and the multilayered spiritual site of Nabi Younis within the ancient city of Niniveh, is unprecedented in modern times. Several months of armed conflict for the retake of the city left behind a wasted urban landscape, punctuated by destroyed monuments, demolished houses, damaged buildings, massive amounts of rubble, and unprecedented level of contamination from unexploded ordnances. Circa 40 percent of the historic urban fabric has been severely affected, with significant loss of integrity within the historic core, especially along the Tigris River. The paper aims at illustrating the methodology for the restoration and critical reconstruction of the Historic Urban Landscape of Mosul.

1 Introduction

Mosul is the capital city of Ninewa Governorate, in northern Iraq. This is one of the oldest continuously inhabited areas in the world, where many different cultures layered up, met, and clashed. Mosul was founded in 1080 B.C. on the right (western) bank of the river Tigris, opposite the ancient Niniveh, the capital of the Neo-Assyrian Empire. Mosul later succeeded old Nineveh (which became part of Mosul's expanding geographic territory) in importance and reached its peak under

G. F. Antonelli (✉)
United Nations Senior Consultant (UNESCO, UN Habitat, 2013–2020),
Jordan, Syria
e-mail: gfontana@archimediatrust.org

T. Cossu
United Nations Consultant (UN Habitat, 2018–2020), Milan, Italy
e-mail: tcossu@archimediatrust.org

O. Niglio and E. Y. J. Lee (eds.), *Transcultural Diplomacy and International Law in Heritage Conservation*, https://doi.org/10.1007/978-981-16-0309-9_23

the Umayyad rule in the eighth century A.D. when it became one of the main cities of Mesopotamia. Due to its strategic location, it prospered during the Abbasid Era as an important trading center across the trade routes connecting India, Persia, and the Mediterranean—a status that went into decline only after the opening of the Suez Canal in 1869.

The city however regained its significance with the discovery of oil in the area in the late 1920s. Since then, it has been a nexus for transporting oil to both Turkey and Syria. Like the rest of Iraq, Mosul city and its surrounding areas have witnessed a growing wave of extremism, as well as sectarian and ethnic violence following the collapse of the former regime in 2003. The escalation of fighting, particularly between 2006 and 2008, has sparked a mass exodus of thousands of people from their hometowns toward safer areas and destinations. Mosul city itself has acted as both a receiving city of internally displaced persons (IDPs) and as a rejecting one. Enormous numbers of Muslim Sunnis, of both Turkoman and Arab origin, fled their towns and villages south and west of Mosul and sought safety in the city, among a predominantly Arab Muslim Sunni population. Conversely, a great number of Mosul's ethnic and religious minorities (Christians, Kurds, Shabak, Turkoman Shiaa, and Yazidis) fled to other areas, in some cases under direct threat of violence.

Contrary to many journalistic reports that portray the fall of Mosul city to Islamic State of Iraq and the Levant (ISIL, also known as ISIS, IS, and Da'esh) on June 10, 2014 to have been shockingly rapid, local inhabitants of the city agree that Mosul began to disintegrate long before that date. ISIL/Da'esh, they argue, did not invade Mosul in June 2014; in fact, they were already there. During the three years of occupation of Mosul, ISIL/Da'esh implemented a vast destruction operation targeting places of worship, antiquities, and libraries, especially those bearing cultural heritage values. The international community recognized this as "cultural cleansing," considered as an additional threat beyond the unprecedented humanitarian crisis that affected the population. Therefore, in February 2018 UNESCO launched the initiative "Revive the Spirit of Mosul," aiming at the restoration of the cultural and spiritual landmarks of the city, Al-Nuri Mosque and its Al-Hadba Minaret, at the creation of jobs and skills development, as well as fostering social cohesion and reconciliation.

2 Urban Heritage in Mosul and Its Regional Context

In order to fully understand and appreciate the significance of the urban heritage of the Old City of Mosul it is useful to frame it within its regional and historical context, as the city's richness and variety of cultures that inhabited the area left their traces not only in the built environment but also contributed to "shape" the soul of the city.

The region where Mosul is located is renowned for hosting a great number of archaeological sites, since the area has been continuously inhabited for more than 8,000 years. Within a radius of 30 km from Mosul there are several cities with significant archaeological relevance, such as Kalhu (today's Nimrud) and Dur-Sharrukin (today's Khorsabad), once part of Akkadian Empire and capital cities of the Assyrian

Empire. Today, Mosul City includes the ancient city of Niniveh within its urban fabric. Niniveh was built on the left bank of the river Tigris and inhabited since the late Neolithic period. The city of Niniveh saw the peak of its magnificence at the beginning of the seventh century B.C., when it hosted majestic palaces, colossal statues, and a massive collection of low-relief decorations. The archaeological site of Niniveh comprehends two mounds and the remains of the city walls, which are 12 km long and embrace an area of around 750 hectares. The site has been threatened not only by the violent actions of ISIL/Da'esh, but also by the uncontrolled expansion of the urban fabric which in some cases saw the development of informal settlements within the boundaries of the site. Niniveh saw its decline after the end of the Assyrian Empire, and was destroyed in 612 B.C., yet it was never fully abandoned (Dalley, 1975–1993). On the opposite bank of the river Tigris, another settlement was growing and succeeded Niniveh as bridgehead and stronghold on the road that connected the Assyrian region to Anatolia: it was the city of Mosul, which name in Arabic means “junction,” “connection,” proving the importance of the strategic location along the Silk Road. Mosul and the surrounding territories have been part of various empires that controlled the region, such as the Achaemenid, Seleucid, Parthian, and Sasanian Empires, before being annexed to the Caliphates in the early seventh century A.D.

In the following centuries Mosul flourished and became not only a commercial pivot for the region, but also a cultural center, due to the variety of ethnic and religious groups that inhabited it. As a result of this, the Old City was dotted with mosques, shrines, and churches. Among them, it is important to mention the Great Al-Nuri Mosque, built in the late twelfth century on the location of the old Umayyad Mosque, known as the first mosque built in the city in the first half of the seventh century. Al-Nuri Mosque is also famous for its iconic leaning minaret, a 45 meters high structure decorated with geometric brickworks called Al-Hadba (“the Hunchback”), which became one of the symbols of the city. The Old City of Mosul hosts many Christian churches: just 250 meters away from Al-Nuri mosque lies the Syriac Orthodox Church of Mar Toma (Saint Thomas), where relics of the Saint were found in 1964 (Patriarchate of Antioch and all the East Orthodox Syriac, 2017), built in successive phases over the seventh, eighth, and fourteenth centuries. The southwestern part of the Old City was home to the Chaldean Church of Shamoun Al-Safa, dedicated to Simon Peter (Saint Peter) and dated back to the nineth century. The Old City hosts many other places of worship, such as the Shrine of Nabi Jarjis and Imam al-Baher Mosque, respectively, built in the twelfth and thirteenth century, Al-Tahera Church and the Dominican Church of Our Lady of the Hour. The territory around the city hosted old monasteries too, such as Mar Mattai Monastery, founded in 363 and famous for its collection of Syriac manuscripts, Mar Behnam Syricac Orthodox Monastery, built in the fourth century, and the Chaldean Catholic Monastery of Rabban Hormidz, founded in the first half of the seventh century.

The extraordinary value of the heritage in Mosul is not only to be found in the multifaceted network of monuments and places of worship, but it also lies in the alleyways and beautiful houses of the Old City. The maze of narrow streets characterized by small drainage canals, where corners are rounded up to a couple of meters to facilitate the circulation of small carriages, creates a unique atmosphere. The opaque stone walls of the two or three-story buildings usually only have small windows at the upper floors, while decorated marble portals mark the entrances. A great part of the urban heritage of the city lies beyond those portals: a dark hall that acts as a filter leads to majestic courtyards, often covered with carved panels of the precious al-Faresh, a crystallized gypsum grey stone, known as the Mosul marble. Houses were usually built with blocks of al-Faresh stone and filled with rubble masonry, providing insulation of the interior spaces. Slabs were supported with vaults, often lightened through the use of empty jars. The destruction occurred in the Old City tragically torn it apart, like a wounded body allowing to see its guts.

3 The Intentional Destruction of Cultural Heritage as Cultural Cleansing: The Islamic State of Iraq and the Levant and the Liberation of West Mosul

ISIL/Da'esh took control over Mosul from June 2014 to July 2017, using the iconic Al-Nuri Mosque to officially announce the self-proclamation of its caliphate. The group enforced a systematic strategy to oust religious and ethnic minorities from the city, and in addition to that it implemented widespread operations aimed at erasing any building and artifact that was not compliant with the fundamentalist faith promulgated by ISIL/Da'esh. Churches and shrines, along with ancient mosques were destroyed with explosives and bulldozers, aiming at the disruption of their sacredness. The cultural cleansing included an attack to the Museum of Mosul, where the group vandalized and destroyed statues and artifacts. A granite statue of a Lamassu, an Assyrian deity shaped as a winged bull found at one of the gates of the ancient Niniveh and dated seventh century B.C., was hit with jackhammers to the point of erasing the face and the whole upper part. The attempt to culturally highjack Mosul's culture and history by ISIL/Da'esh also went through the burning of thousands of books. The Central Library of Mosul, together with great parts of the University of Mosul's library and Mosul Museum's library were attacked and set on fire. Collections of manuscripts hosted in monasteries around the city were targeted too.

The destruction of cultural heritage found its reasons not only in the will of physically remove "idols," but also in the pursuit of leaving a mark in history and provide a culturally featureless, clean platform on which building the group's proselytism. Yet it is very important to consider that many of the smallest items, including statues and precious books, have been looted. In contrast with the 1970 UNESCO's Convention on the Means of Prohibiting and Preventing the Illicit Import, Export and Transfer of Ownership of Cultural Property, looted antiquities were smuggled out of Iraq to be sold in the antiquities black market, in order to finance ISIL/Da'esh's operations.

In July 2017, after nine months of battle, the coalition forces announced the reclamation of the city, but the aftermath of the conflict was a ravaged city, and the Old City in particular looked like a dusty pile of rubble. After the retake of the areas surrounding the city and the eastern bank of the Tigris river, the last ISIL/Da'esh in

Fig. 1 Bird's eye view of the old city of Mosul after its destruction

the city were in fact besieged in the Old City and in neighborhoods north-west of it: at this point the coalition chose to stop the building by building fight and give a final hit, with intense bombing by airstrikes. The operation was successful, with some ISIL/Da'esh fighters reportedly rigged Al-Nuri Mosque and Al-Hadba minaret with explosives (Fig. 1), and the last squad fleeing along the riverbank, but it broadened the destruction of the Old City, especially for civilian houses and facilities like schools. Al-Maidan, the neighborhood facing the river Tigris where the last bombs were dropped, has been completely flattened out. Within the 250 hectares of the Old City, counting nearly 15,000 houses, almost 1,700 buildings were completely destroyed and more than 3,200 reported severe damages (Initial Planning Framework, 2019): both sum up to more than one-third of the total buildings (Fig. 2).

4 Learning from the Past. Comparing Case-Studies of Urban Heritage Destruction and Post-Conflict Reconstruction

In order to address the challenging situation, UNESCO joined forces with UN-Habitat and started developing an *Initial Planning Framework for the Reconstruction of Mosul* to support Mosul's local government and city institutions with the reconstruction and recovery of the city. The first question was the definition of a viable

Fig. 2 Street view of Al-Nouri Mosque and its Al-Hadba Minaret

methodological approach for urban recovery and reconstruction, taking into consideration the Iraqi context. UNESCO commissioned a research to collect references regarding a series of case-studies of urban heritage destruction and post-conflict reconstruction that were found appropriate and relevant to the case of Mosul.

Articles, papers, newspapers, interviews to art historians, architects, urbanists, and intellectuals, as well as images from post-WWII reconstruction of historic towns and their iconic buildings, were collected, bringing Dresden (Germany), Le Havre (France), Rotterdam (The Netherlands), and Florence (Italy) as case-studies. The destruction of Stari Most (the bridge of Mostar) and its surrounding historic town in Ex-Yugoslavia, was also analyzed as a recent example of post-war reconstruction, especially since an iconic and symbolic monument was destroyed by the conflict and reconstructed. Warsaw (Poland) and Beirut (Lebanon) reconstruction processes were added to the research at a later stage. Two additional cases of reconstruction of historic areas were utilized, notably the case of Venzone, a village in northern Italy flattened by a severe earthquake in 1976 and rebuilt "à l'identique," and the Chiado, a central quarter of Lisbon (Portugal), devasted by a fire in 1988 and critically reconstructed through a regeneration program led by world-renowned architect Alvaro Siza.

The lessons learned from these case-studies corroborated the idea that in more than 70 years the discourse over the reconstruction of the historic town is still very debatable. The initial proposals that were circulating in Mosul and more generally in Iraq in the aftermath of the liberation were vaguely mentioning Dubai as a good practice of urban development, to be proposed for the reconstruction of the (Old) City on the bank of the river Tigris. It is thanking the timely involvement of the University of Mosul and its Faculty of Engineering and Department of Architecture, gathered in the Engineering Consulting Bureau, that a thorough discussion took place in the city, involving the various stakeholders dealing with reconstruction, e.g., the Governorate of Ninewa, the Qa'em Maqamieh of Mosul and its Municipal services, the Department of Urban Planning of the Ministry of Housing and Construction, religious leaders of the Sunni, Shia and Christian and other Minorities Endowments, in addition to international actors such as UNESCO and UN-Habitat, among others.

The agreed methodology based its foundations on the assertion that "documentation" and "damage assessment" are non-negotiable points of departure for any intervention, and that a careful survey of the historic urban fabric after the bombardments should be the first indispensable step to well inform the restoration and critical reconstruction of the Old City.

5 Documentation and Damage Assessment of the Old City of Mosul

In view of the urban and architectural surveys, the situation analysis in the Old City represented a unique challenge, due to the context of extremely reduced accessibility. Surveys on the ground were hindered by the lack of safety caused by the presence of Explosive Remnants of War (ERW), mines, Unexploded Ordnances (UXOs) such as bombs, grenades, or ammunition, and Improvised Explosive Devices (IEDs) such as suicide belts or booby traps, still present in the rubble mounds and often concealed in the remaining buildings.

Therefore, the surveys were supported by Unmanned Aerial Vehicles (UAV) to carry out the first documentation and damage assessment in the Old City, which took place in various phases from February 2018 to January 2019. The full digital documentation of the 250 ha. of Mosul's historic urban fabric convened into an open-source GIS platform incorporating all data acquired through aerial and (limited) ground surveys. These surveys were key to inform the Initial Planning Framework for Reconstruction, being jointly devised by UNESCO and UN-Habitat. UNESCO contracted two specialized companied from France and Italy to carry out respectively the UAV survey, including data processing, and the creation of a web-based open-source GIS.

To facilitate the survey, the Old City of Mosul was divided into 15 zones, targeting a 3 cm resolution. Two zones (using five flights each) were tested before applying a protocol that would ensure the quality results of the entire area of the old fabric. For several areas, technical problems arose, and additional flights were necessary to complete their scan. All in all, 90 flights were necessary to scan the 15 zones of the Old City—leading to an average of 6 flights per area. Altogether, these flights account for 25,000 aerial pictures of the Old City, taken at 75 meter-high with the camera pointing down (one flight) and 60 meter-high with the camera tilting at 45 degrees (five flights). Each of the five flights was performed along the main compass directions to get a full scan of the vertical elements.

The survey produced an orthophotograph at 3 cm resolution, which was complemented by a vector Plan, as well as a 3D model reconstruction of the entire historic fabric. The 3D model was particularly helpful to understand the degree of destruction of each compartment of the old city, which presents a high degree of density and complexity.

Nine high-resolution 3D models of historic buildings (exterior and interior at 1 cm resolution) were also produced, along with an interactive 3D viewer accessible locally and online. Six buildings out of nine, notably the Al-Nuri Mosque, the Al-Hadba Minaret, the Al-Tutunji House, the Museum of Mosul, the Old Al-Tahera Church, and the Church of the Clock are currently under restoration through different projects led by UNESCO.

All the data gathered during the survey and processed were included in an open-source GIS platform. A single reference system and georeferencing all the data according to this system was set up, in spite of the absence of benchmarks on the ground. The system collected a series of available raster image data; in particular, satellite maps of different periods that visually indicate the transformation of the urban fabric over time; subsequently, all these data were georeferenced on the orthophoto specifically produced for this program. Acquisition of more than 14,000 single building units was gathered from the 2007–2008 urban fabric census and a new ID card system was developed. The ID cards component will benefit the survey of historic buildings, and their archival documents (maps, drawings, photographs, etc.). The system is being regularly updated by the insertion of new vector layers, already georeferenced on the system indicated in previous points, such as: the neighborhoods, the streets, the cadastral maps, etc.

The data deriving from the digital documentation enabled a first-level assessment, which took into consideration two key aspects: damage level and heritage value, which were interpolated in a bi-dimensional matrix. Damage assessment was defined in five grades, through the identification of primary features of the building. This classification is agreed upon by development actors working under the Shelter Cluster; an inter-agency coordination mechanism that supports humanitarian shelter. Heritage value assessment aimed at the classification of the historical and architectural significance of every building through references to documentation and site surveys, where possible. It was defined in four grades, from the highest value assigned to buildings and monuments with an outstanding aesthetic significance and a documented role in the history of the city, to constructions that took place in recent times and are not related to any specific practice or activity within a historical context, which are classified as "no heritage value."

The combination of the two features created a matrix, which led to a set of codes related to a specific type of intervention, so that each building could take advantage of a reference to tailored guidelines. In addition to that, the coding system represented a tool for the local administration's control over the different reconstruction activities in the Old City linking group of codes/interventions to three building permit tracks, envisioned to assist the inhabitants in the recovery and reconstruction. The three tracks included a standard route, for buildings with low heritage value and high level of damage, a fast track with simplified documentation for buildings with relatively low heritage value and light damages, and a heritage route for buildings with a significant historical and architectural value in need of heavy intervention, where applications should be approved by the local authority for heritage and antiquities.

6 Resource Mobilization in the Framework of the "Revive the Spirit of Mosul" Initiative: Skills Development and Job Creation as a Tool to Foster Urban Reconciliation

The implementation of a rapid and targeted self-reconstruction process for the returning residents of the Old City was considered of paramount importance. Self-build reconstruction aims to develop an active framework for rapid reconstruction with the participation of the local community. The process that is currently being developed is an urgent response to the needs of the displaced communities to reconstruct their homes, religious, educational, and public spaces. Setting up a self-reconstruction system for the Old City represents an attempt to overcome issues like the lack of availability of appropriate construction materials and expertise (Figs. 3 and 4).

The use of appropriate materials and designs, where practically feasible, is essential to the success of this endeavor and the revitalization of the Old City. Traditional building techniques must be fully understood and employed throughout the process, wherever practical. It is only on the basis of adhering to the above that the surviving structures within the Old City can hope to offer a glimpse of the former architectural and cultural glory.

The use of traditional materials and techniques to build specific typologies is not only crucial in order to preserve the city's physical appearance and to reactivate the local economy with new jobs and skills development, but it is also a way to obtain better performing buildings. Thick stone walls, introverted buildings with openings almost exclusively facing the inner courtyards and narrow alleys where houses shaded each other helped buildings to stay cool during the hot summer, in contrast to constructions made of cheap cement blocks. This concept is in some way following the "Build Back Better" approach. In the Old City of Mosul, it means to focus on the implementation of infrastructures such as water and electricity networks, sewage, and drainage, which were basically missing, yet it must take advantage of the knowledge coming from its rich history when dealing with this kind of architecture.

This approach is sustained by a remarkable initiative launched by UNESCO's Director-General in February 2018, called "Revive the Spirit of Mosul." Thanking to this cultural operation, UNESCO managed to raise circa 100 million US dollars for restoration and reconstruction purposes, with a focus on skills development and job

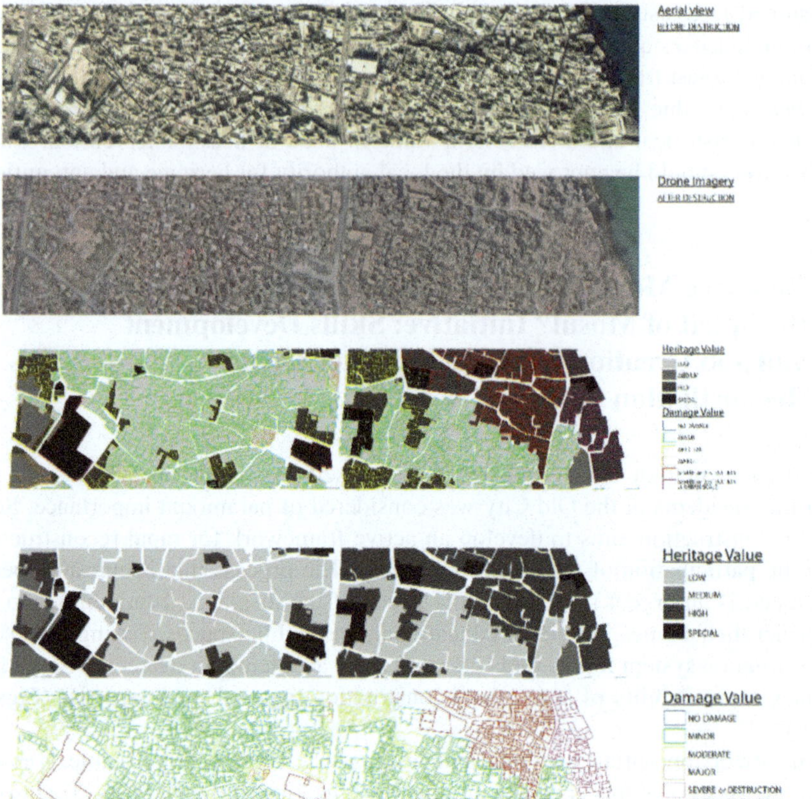

Fig. 3 Comparison of aerial and UAV photography of a portion of Mosul's historic urban fabric before 2014 and after (2018) the destruction, and graphic representation of the heritage values and damage assessment in the view of reconstruction (UNESCO & UN-Habitat, 2019)

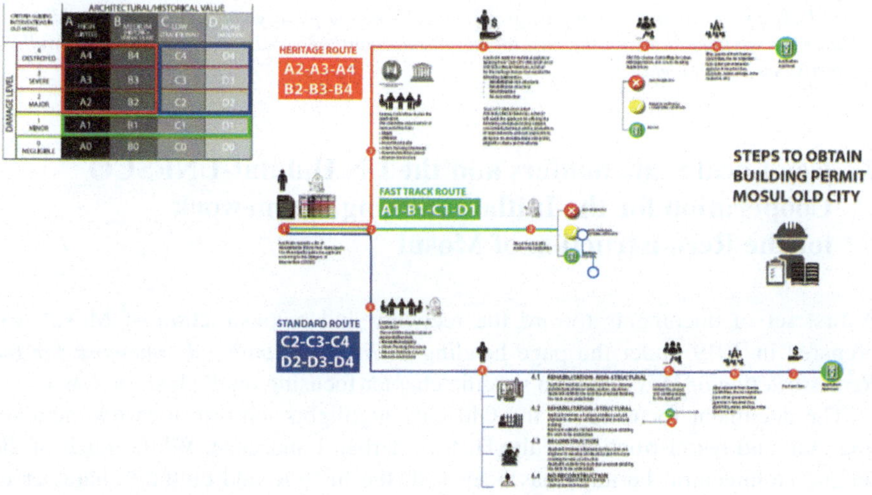

Fig. 4 Sketch showing guidance for reconstruction interventions

creation, especially for the urban youth of Mosul. In particular, the European Union-funded a project for *Urban recovery and reconstruction through a participatory approach to skills development and job creation to foster social cohesion and community reconciliation through restoration and critical reconstruction of Mosul's historic urban landscape and urban conservation in Basra,* while the United Arab Emirates contributed to the *Restoration and critical reconstruction of Al-Nuri Mosque and its Al-Hadba Minaret as a tool to foster social cohesion and community reconciliation,* as well as to the restoration of two iconic Christian sites, key for intercommunity reconciliation, namely, the Al-Tahera Church and the Church of Our Lady of the Hour, and the governments of Germany and Japan supported the reconstruction of other cultural, religious, and educational buildings.

The overall purpose of the proposed actions within the "Revive the Spirit of Mosul" initiative is to promote livelihood opportunities for youth in the liberated areas of Iraq and in particular among the communities of the Old City of Mosul and to contribute to the restoration of Mosul's Historic Urban Landscape while contributing to social cohesion and intercommunity reconciliation. Through these actions, the rehabilitation, restoration, recovery, and reconstruction of significant portions of the historic urban fabric of Mosul are supported, placing emphasis on job creation through Employment Intensive schemes and hands-on training for self-construction. An excerpt from a project document reads as follows:

> *The key objective is to establish a locally-driven mechanism - Old Mosul Self-Rebuilding Facility - for the promotion and support of a self-reliance methodology, fostering resilience and reconciliation. The proposed framework of the self-rebuilding facility is to be independent of any external workforce from outside Mosul. It relies on using local materials, including processed debris, labour and construction techniques. These materials are either the result of demolition or are easily available in the locality, which could be recycled, reused*

or developed for construction purposes. The self-rebuild facility contributes in rebuilding hope for the inhabitants of the city, taking into account their skills, craftsmanship, as well as historic urban identity.

7 Key Local Stakeholders and the UN Habitat-UNESCO Cooperation for the Initial Planning Framework for the Reconstruction of Mosul

A first set of documents toward the recovery and reconstruction of Mosul was prepared in 2019 under the page heading of *Initial Planning Framework for the Reconstruction of Mosul*, with a specific chapter focusing on the historic town.

The document focusing on the Old City highlights ten priorities for the safeguarding and reconstruction of the Historic Urban Landscape. While much of the unique architectural heritage has been lost, the historic and cultural character of the City—its soul—is still very much present. It is therefore imperative that the reconstruction, restoration, and conservation processes respect not only the tangible surviving elements of the historic urban fabric, but the traditions and techniques used in their original construction, and the associated practices. Key interventions in the Old City should adhere to specific rebuilding guidelines, being developed in conjunction with government stakeholders. These processes must be based on adequate research and documentation retrieval, to ensure that the rebuilt or restored structures, and at the same time a corpus of data on surviving building types, architectural elements, and material used, will be collated for reference.

In accordance with this philosophy, the document named *Mosul Old City: Reconstruction Priorities* is a summary of key recommendations and actions. It should therefore be seen in the context of the overall framework for all of Mosul, as many challenges that the Old City face are shared with the wider city. Multiple local government actors have expressed their concern that reconstruction without an overarching and holistic plan may be counterproductive to long-term sustainable development of Mosul and produce irreversible damage. The document provides the first priorities to be endorsed by the Prime Minister's Task Force for Reconstruction of the Old City to support the self-reconstruction process and prevent damaging recovery and reconstruction activities in the Old City. It draws upon earlier studies of the Old City; "Reconstruction of the Old City of Mosul Preliminary Study" (October 2017) and the "Reconstruction of Mosul Action Plan" (2018), both produced by the Engineering Consulting Bureau of Mosul University, as well as recommendations of Iraq's Engineering Union. Building on these reports, the following implementable actions are recommended:

1. Protect the heritage from further destruction
2. Recover the Old City through a block approach
3. Clear the city from debris and unexploded ordnances
4. Ensure reconstruction respects the city's historical character
5. Support the self-reconstruction process

6. Support the small-medium enterprises in commercial streets
7. Bring back schools to the Old City
8. Reconnect the Old City to the rest of Mosul
9. Assist Old City residents with property documents
10. Implement pre-crisis plans to build back-better.

References

Dalley, S. (1975–1993) Nineveh after 612 BC. *Altorientalische Forschungen, 20*(1), 134–147.

Initial Planning Framework for the Reconstruction of Mosul. (2019). *UN-Habitat and UNESCO.* http://unhabitatiraq.net/mosulportal/wp-content/uploads/2019/11/190408_Initial_Planning-Framework_Mosul-E.pdf. Accessed August 4, 2020.

Mosul University. (2017). *Reconstruction of the old city of Mosul preliminary study.* Engineering Consulting Bureau: Mosul.

Mosul University. (2018). *Reconstruction of Mosul action plan.* Engineering Consulting Bureau: Mosul.

Patriarchate of Antioch and all the East Orthodox Syriac. (2017). https://web.archive.org/web/20170623164839/, http://syrian-orthodox.com/readnews.php?id=530. Accessed August 6, 2020.

UN-Habitat & UNESCO. (2019). *Initial planning framework for the reconstruction of Mosul.* http://unhabitatiraq.net/mosulportal/wp-content/uploads/2019/11/190408_Initial_Planning-Framework_Mosul-E.pdf. Accessed July 30, 2020.

UNESCO. (2018). *Reviving Mosul and Basra old cities: Urban recovery and reconstruction through a participatory approach to skills development and job creation to foster social cohesion and community reconciliation through restoration and critical reconstruction of Mosul's historic urban landscape and urban conservation in Basra.* Paris.

The Role of Civil Society in the Application of International Law for Heritage Protection in Countries in Conflict in the MENA Region

Francisco J. Rufián Fdez, Isber Sabrine, and José Antonio González Zarandona

Abstract Throughout the Middle East and North Africa (MENA) region, there have been a myriad of conflicts of very diverse nature, which have had catastrophic consequences for its inhabitants. To this day, countries in conflict in the region have also experienced unprecedented instability in the area, which is having effects on a global scale and whose importance and influence in many cases are difficult to predict. Needless to say, such conflicts have also caused severe damage to the heritage of the affected countries. In an effort to mitigate such damage towards heritage in these countries, this chapter will examine the work of Non-Governmental Organization Heritage for Peace (HfP) in protecting cultural heritage at different levels (international, Islamic and domestic law), by showing how important is the role of civil society regarding the applicability of international law for the protection of cultural heritage. The chapter will present different examples carried on by HfP through a vast network of collaborations among the civil society in Syria, Iraq, Yemen and Libya.

1 Introduction

The MENA region has suffered a myriad of conflicts since the 1990s, which have shaped international relations. In addition, after the so-called Arab spring in 2011, these conflicts became even more complex, due to the inclusion of new parameters as well as the non-state actors, and the civil society. Even if non-state actors will be

F. J. Rufián Fdez (✉)
Member of a Law Enforcement Agency, Madrid, Spain
e-mail: francisco.rufian@gmail.com

I. Sabrine
Heritage for Peace, Barcelona, Spain
e-mail: esper.1985@yahoo.com

J. A. González Zarandona
History, CIDE, Mexico, Mexico
e-mail: antonio.gonzalez.zarandona@gmail.com

O. Niglio and E. Y. J. Lee (eds.), *Transcultural Diplomacy and International Law in Heritage Conservation*, https://doi.org/10.1007/978-981-16-0309-9_24

mentioned in this chapter, we will nonetheless focus the attention over civil society, because it was the main engine behind the movement related to the Arab spring.

Conflicts have been both a challenge, and at the same time, an opportunity to redefine the role of civil society in the MENA region. The civilian grassroots movements have also created an opportunity for Arab governments to forge new relationships with civil society actors, and for Civil Society Organizations (CSO) to exchange experiences in their respective areas of expertise (Vermeij et al., 2013). Likewise, the increase in conflicts and the emergence of 'non-state' actors in the MENA region presents both a challenge and an opportunity to think about the role of CSOs in responding to catastrophes related to heritage protection (Lostal et al., 2017).

This chapter wants to show the limitations in one of these areas of expertise, that is, heritage protection. We will show how civil society initiatives are filling the gaps that local authorities as well as International Organizations have left in this area, due to a lack of achievements in general (see for example Meskell 'The Future in Ruins') by training civil society members in heritage protection law.

2 The Concept of 'Civil Society'

The number of Non-Governmental Organizations (NGOs) has risen exponentially in Arab countries in recent times. The term NGO identifies private organizations founded under civil law, and free from any governmental influence to operate without aiming to make a profit. The notion is also included in the term Civil Society Organization (CSO) as 'civil society'. There are many definitions of civil society. For example, the United Nations Food and Agriculture Organization[1] defines civil society as '[a]ll groups working outside the framework of governments such as societal groups, nongovernmental organizations, labor unions and organizations that express the interests of social groups and raise awareness on major issues in order to influence public policies and decisions'.[2] This concept includes all range and types of organizations created under different laws, practices or traditions, such as community-based organizations (CBOs), or the traditional Islamic organizations in the MENA region. In this chapter, we will use the term Civil Society Organization to include all kinds of this organizational model.

It is characteristic of CSOs to be located in areas where they know the traditions very well and due to their fewer rigid structures (compared to other more traditional organizations), they respond better to emergencies in challenging operating environments. Also, they are the most effective tool to create and consolidate the response capacity in the region, as well as contributing to a resilient society. This means, for example, that a CSO can work for itself, or cooperate with another CSO, states, Intergovernmental Organizations (IGOs), or even, participating in international judicial

[1] www.fao.org.

[2] An analysis about the concept can also be seen in Karajah, 2007.

proceedings to fulfill their aims, which is why in some cases the definition of their international legal status is a problem.

Nowadays, the relevance of CSOs in the MENA region can be felt in different areas, such as human rights, climate crisis and international cooperation. As a result, their work on heritage protection is often associated with other related issues and with different levels of heritage protection, including local, Islamic and international law.

The CSOs movement in the Arab world focused on heritage protection, started with the threat to cultural heritage due to the many conflicts that have ravaged the region in the last three decades. As a result, some organizations, grouped into CSOs and social media initiatives, have been created to promote the protection of cultural heritage. This threat has also generated awareness of the cultural, economic and identity value of the MENA countries' cultural heritage which has spread among the local communities with great intensity (Brodie, 2015).

Civil society participation in the management of cultural heritage is essential in the MENA societies to address the different needs of the population (economic, social, health and cultural) that authorities cannot fulfill. In response, some governments have reacted negatively towards the work of these organizations, making their work even more difficult, while establishing very rigid legislations (Abdelaziz, 2017).

This participation not only permits the local population to access their heritage (particularly for those who live and work in heritage sites) but also allows protecting heritage at a local level. This is considered the best approach because CSOs bind communities together through cooperative work to preserve and promote the tangible and intangible cultural heritage. Such organizations are able to provide public programmes through which cultural heritage is shared: their role is crucial to build bridges between people and what they consider their cultural heritage. In doing so, they bypass corresponding authorities who cannot guarantee the safeguarding of this heritage due to lack of money, political interest or conflicts.

3 Understanding the Arab Concept of Civil Society

The concept of civil society in Arab culture is differently used in comparison to the concept used in western countries. References to the (Western) model mentioned above can be useful to highlight similarities and differences between them. However, to understand the term correctly we need to examine its meaning and how the concept has been applied in Arabic societies (Karajah, 2007).

In Arabic, the concept of 'civil society' is translated as 'al-mujtama' al-madani', but there are many meanings of the term, such as the various forms of the root *jama'* (to join, assemble), *umma* (community of believers), *ahl* (kin) and *asabiyya* (solidarity) (Browers, 2006). Therefore, in Arabic the literal translation is 'al-mujtama' al-madani' which means civil society, and 'mujtama al-ahli', which Islamists prefer, denotes a more indigenous civil and civic community, independent from the use that the state gives to the term. The latter term also includes schools and charitable organizations (Sadiki, 2009). Syrian philosopher Sadiq al Azm is one of the most important Arab thinkers who discussed the concept. He makes a similar distinction between 'mudjatama'a madani' and 'mudjatama'a ahli'—the former contains modern forms of civil society while the latter contains traditional forms of civil society (DRI, 2008). The establishment of organizations by voluntary citizens at the local level in neighbourhoods, towns or villages, grouped by common interests, is considered by Arab scholars the origin of civil society in the MENA region.

Civil society plays an important role in Islam. According to Hasan Hanafi, 'the importance of civil society derives from the need to balance the desires and needs of the individual with the will and needs of society' (Hanafi, 2002). In Islamic communities, civil society was always organized through the mosque and religious schools which dictated social rules for people to behave in accordance with Islamic tradition. In the Arab civil society, Islamic organizations play this role because they propagate the faith through the provision of charitable and social services (Hawthorne, 2005).

Hanafi believes that there is a need to have a civil society formed by a mix of both Islamic and Western conceptions. He actually considers that the Western conception of civil society is based more on rights, and less on duties, whereas in Islam, duties are given a higher priority over rights (Hanafi, 2002). Hence, civil society in the Arab context is still very connected to the Islamic organizations because the latter dictate the duties that people should follow, based on common objectives. That connection resulted in a non-strong civil society tradition, but the changes produced by the so-called Arab spring have confirmed that there is a vibrant society in the Arab world as well (Çakmak, 2017).

In order to articulate the connection between civil society and cultural heritage in the Arab countries, we will analyse two projects that HfP carried out in Syria, as examples of a collaborative network involving different entities. As we have shown above, the role that CSOs are currently playing is more and more important for Arab societies, but regarding cultural heritage protection, this role is even more necessary.

In itself, 'cultural heritage' is a western concept, but its significance and association with religion and ideology makes it a basic pillar of cultural identity, and a concept widely understood in general terms (obviously each region has its own particularities). As such, it has also provided many collaborative options to CSOs who want to engage with local communities. However, the role of civil society in preserving cultural heritage has not raised much interest, perhaps because culture is often regarded as a sphere of lower importance in the MENA region (Beliakova, 2019), or the initiatives began after the conflict began and basic necessities are more important.

4 Islam and Cultural Heritage

The rapid changes in the Arab world in the last decades prompt us to analyse and define cultural heritage through Islamic perspectives in an international level, the conference that grouped Islamic legal scholars (‘ulama’) in 2001[3] convened by UNESCO, ISESCO[4] and ALECSO[5] and hosted by Qatar was the starting point. That year was an inflection point in the region due to the destruction of heritage conducted in the Islamic Emirate of Afghanistan, and the attack in New York City.

In the proceedings of the conference, some important points were established on how the interpretation of heritage must be done by Islam practitioners. This particular interpretation connected the need to conserve with Islamic culture as the current protector of many previous civilizations and cultures that made the MENA their home. To understand correctly the religious Law of Islam or Sharīᶜah, we need to know and analyse its sources. These are the Qurʾān (the holy book of Islam); the Hadith (recorded sayings of the prophet Muhammad) and part of the Qurʾān; and the Sunnah (customs and practices of the Islamic Comunity) which is based in both previous sources.

The Qurʾān is the most important source of creeds, rituals, ethics and laws of the Islamic religion (Abdel Haleem, 2005). Thus it gives guidance for people to make tangible changes in their lives both individually and as a society. The Qur’ân does not initially draw the attention of its readers to the artistic manifestations of heritage as such. Instead, it concentrates on past lessons that can be used in the future as a clear reflection of the Islamic history in itself, which assimilated different cultures.

For example, the Qur’ân says: ‘There have been many examples before you. Roam the world and see what was the fate of those who disbelieved their apostles’ (The Imrans 3:137). Another example: ‘God desires to make this known to you, and to guide you along the paths of those who have gone before you in mercy. He is wise and all-knowing’ (Women 4:26). These examples suggest that to investigate past civilizations and examine their archaeological remains would result in learning lessons and gain insights into the lives of people who lived before the advent of Islam (Guessoum, 2001).

In the Qurʾān we can see how different methods are used to teach the positive role history and cultural heritage play in society. Mainly, it relies on three aspects.

The first is ‘Mithaal’ (an example and witness). There are straightforward and positive examples in the past that should provide guidance to us in our present decisions. There are, in their stories, instructions for men embedded with understanding. The second method is Ayeh (or signs). History is a series of signs that should be understood as instructions for mankind. Finally, the third method is Warnings, Nekal and Ebreh (to travel to derive knowledge). History is also full of warnings and cautionary tales.

Especially, looking at the work carried out by the main international Islamic organization in charge of cultural issues in the MENA region, ISESCO, in 2001 held the conference of Ulama on Islam and Cultural Heritage in Doha (now known as the Doha Conference). Involving a wide range of specialist experts on Islamic

[3]Proceedings of the conference are available here: https://unesdoc.unesco.org/ark:/48223/pf0000140834.

[4]Islamic World Educational, Scientific and Cultural Organization: https://www.icesco.org/en/.

[5]Arab League Educational, Scientific and Cultural Organization: http://www.alecso.org/nsite/en/.

Law such as senior religious clerics, heritage experts, judges and senior diplomats, they proposed a unified stance of Islam towards cultural heritage. Based on Sharia Law, these experts provided a definition of cultural heritage that insists on several of its aspects, such as its value, and included cultural, artistic and intellectual forms inherited from the early and recent past in the definition. For example:

- Archaeological monuments or artefacts discovered through excavations.
- Antiquities available in museums from different ages.
- Intellectual heritage drawing from the works of creative scholars and thinkers.

Unfortunately, the Quran has also inspired terrorists and Islamic fundamentalists to cite Quranic verses and Hadith[6] to justify their actions against heritage. A verse they commonly cite is 35:22 (Al Fatir, The Originator). This verse in the Qurʾān points out to the dead in the grave not having the ability to hear, and hence Ziyarah[7] and visitation, as well as seeking intercession, has no purpose because it could encourage idolatry.

Further evidence of the protection of places of prayer and other places which need to be protected from all harms, is the following fragment in the Quran:

> "The mosques of Allah shall be visited and maintained by such as believe in Allah and the Last Day, establish regular prayers, and practice regular charity, and fear none (at all) except Allah. It is they who are expected to be on true guidance". (Surat al-Tawba, "Repentance"; also known as al-Bara'ah, "the Ultimatum", in many hadith 9:18)

And yet, despite this clear verse, ISIS blew up the Grand Al Nuri mosque in Mosul in 2017, among other sites of prayer.

In conclusion, we can see that the Qur'ân teaches that there is always a lesson to be learned from historical artefacts, both tangible and intangible, and it is for this reason that we study history (Guessoum, 2001). The main subject to learn from Islamic teachings is the respect for Antiquities and for the culture which has created them.

5 Civil Society and Heritage Protection

The protection of cultural heritage is a phenomenon where International Law, International Humanitarian Law (IHL) and International Criminal Law (Bernabei, 2019) intersect, involving authorities at the global, national and local level, because they all interact to fulfil common cultural goals (Beliakova, 2019).

All these branches of international law have different effects in heritage protection. The confluences and interactions between them, however, have not been properly

[6]Record of the traditions or sayings of the Prophet Muhammad, revered and received as a major source of religious law and moral guidance, second only to the authority of the Qurʾān.

[7]Literally: pilgrimage. Refers to the act of visiting holy people, their graves or other holy places in order to show reverence for them and acquire spiritual blessings. Islamic extremists, such as Wahhabism, have banned this practice in order to discourage idolatry.

studied yet. Cultural heritage and forms of cultural expression are closely linked to human rights (Tünsmeyer, 2020), and for the same reason closely linked with civil society. Regarding International Law, UNESCO is the main international institution that oversees the protection of cultural heritage on a global scale. That protection is exercised through two regulatory mechanisms:

- Conventions, with normative value for all those countries which ratify them.
- Recommendations and declarations, without normative value, but which propose some actions.

There are many conventions and recommendations, and it is not the purpose of this paper to detail them. However, we would like to highlight some of the most important, and in particular those which are useful in conflict areas. The first one is the Convention on the Means of Prohibiting and Preventing the Illicit Import, Export and Transfer of Ownership of Cultural Property, signed in 1970, which is at present time the principal international instrument to fight the illegal circulation of cultural property (Manacorda, 2011). Although the Convention may rightly be regarded as a fundamental step towards international cooperation in combating trafficking, it should be noted that it was designed mainly to be used in the field of diplomatic cooperation, in the relation between the States, not CSOs.[8]

Later on, the difficulties to adjust national domestic legislation (Manacorda, 2011) to international legislation, prompted the *Convention on Stolen or Illegally Exported Cultural Objects*, signed in 1995 in collaboration with the *International Institute for the Unification of Private Law* (UNIDROIT), on demand by UNESCO. These two conventions apply to all illegal movements of cultural objects, whether the traffic began during armed conflict or peacetime (Gerstenblith, 2020).

IHL regulates the conduct of warfare and offers cultural heritage a regime of protection in armed conflict that goes beyond what is afforded to civilian objects (Lostal et al., 2017). In this sense, the 1954 Hague Convention for the Protection of Cultural Property in the Event of Armed Conflict and its 1999s protocol are still the most important legal tools to protect cultural heritage during times of conflict. The 1954 Hague Convention was promulgated as the first international treaty to address exclusively cultural property,[9] that established the term 'cultural property' as a legal category in international law and was subsequently adopted by national legislation implementing the Convention.

As a token in this legal framework, the same international penal jurisdictions, starting with Nuremberg and continuing with the ad hoc tribunals in the 1990s and the International Criminal Court (ICC), have recognized their competence to impose penal sanctions on acts serious enough to constitute international crimes

---

[8]https://ec.europa.eu/home-affairs/sites/homeaffairs/files/doc_centre/crime/docs/report_trafficking_in_cultural_goods_en.pdf.

[9]The Treaty on the Protection of Artistic and Scientific Institutions and Historic Monuments (Roerich Pact) (adopted 15 April 1935, entered into force 26 August 1935) 167 LNTS 289, was the first treaty drafted to address exclusively cultural property. However, it is of limited viability and was ratified only by States in the Americas (Gerstenblith, 2020).

(Manacorda, 2011). The creation of the ICC,[10] the International Criminal Tribunal for the former Yugoslavia (ICTY),[11] lasting from 1993 to 2017, and the International Criminal Tribunal for Rwanda (ICTR), opened in 1995, established an unprecedented international jurisdiction over individuals, at the same time that cultural heritage started to become an important target during armed conflicts. In that process, civil society also played an important role in protecting cultural heritage, by the continuing denunciation of the different destruction of heritage, which ended in an important step. In 2001, the ICTY stipulated, through an indictment, that intentional attacks against cultural property were crimes against humanity, thus drastically improving the legal framework.[12] In doing so, in 2004 this international tribunal condemned Miodrag Jokić, commander of the Yugoslavian Navy, to spend seven years in prison for ordering the bombing of the old city of Dubrovnik in 1991.[13] The resolution was the first sentence given by an international tribunal based on the charge of intentional destruction of cultural heritage. Likewise, in 2016, the ICC declared Ahmad Al Faqi Al Mahdi guilty for destroying in 2012 several sacred sites in Timbuktu, when he was leading Ansar Dine, a group associated with the terrorist organization Al-Qaeda.[14]

It is clear, however, that all these legal mechanisms have not been working as well as they should have, mainly because there is not a clear continuity between them which is applied during an armed conflict, and those that apply to the movement of cultural objects, primarily during peacetime (Gerstenblith, 2020). In the Arab spring, heritage destruction and the illicit traffic in cultural goods in the MENA region increased, and the consequences are visible still today (Brodie & Sabrine, 2018). The international responses to the problem have been inefficient and, in some cases, help came at a much later time, due to slow response and the inability of international organizations to sign agreements with formal states. As a consequence, vast regions in conflict areas have not received any aid during the conflict. In order to cover those necessities, the civil society organizes their work, and in some cases working on the ground in collaboration with international organizations, or with their own resources.

Later on, and due to the widespread destruction of cultural heritage in Iraq and Syria, international organizations tried to become permanent actors on the ground. For example, the creation of an Italian-led unit specialized in the protection of cultural heritage: the Carabinieri Command for the Protection of Cultural Heritage (NATO, 2018). This unit was also tasked with assisting in the fight against the illicit traffic of antiquities from countries in conflict. A year later, the governments of France and the United Arab Emirates, as well as other 40 countries, supported the initiative

---

[10] Adopted at a diplomatic conference in Rome on 1998, and began functioning on 1 July 2002.

[11] International Criminal Tribunal for the former Yugoslavia (ICTY): http://www.icty.org/en/about.

[12] https://www.icty.org/en/outreach/documentaries/dubrovnik-and-crimes-against-cultural-heritage and.

[13] https://www.icty.org/en/content/miodrag-joki%C4%87.

[14] https://trialinternational.org/latest-post/ahmad-al-faqi-al-mahdi/.

by establishing a change in international policy regarding heritage destruction in an international conference celebrated in Abu Dhabi.[15]

As a result of the pressure exerted by international organizations, such as UNESCO, to act in zones of conflict, the first time that a UN mission peacekeeping mission included the protection of cultural heritage in its mandate (NATO, 2018) was when the United Nations Multidimensional Integrated Stabilization Mission in Mali (MINUSMA) was established in 2013.[16] Within this context, the UN Security Council adopted on 24th March 2017 Resolution 2347,[17] to maintain 'international peace and security: destruction and trafficking of cultural heritage by terrorist groups and in situations of armed conflict', thus recognizing how important is the relation between heritage and peace.

In all these cases, the role that civil society played to account for the destruction of cultural heritage sites, as well as its work to highlight the importance to protect it, at a local and international level, contributed to the success in achieving such international normative.

6 SHELTr Project

In Syria, the role of civil society was practically non-existent prior to 2011 when the conflict started. In the last couple of years, however, the socio-economic landscape of Syria has dramatically changed (Khattab, 2017). The conflict was the catalyst for the creation of CSOs because they filled the gaps that were emerging in the fields where aid was needed. Some of them reacted in response to the catastrophic destruction and loss of Syria's heritage by the Islamic State and the Syrian conflict in general.

HfP was one of these CSOs,[18] and after years working together with other international CSOs, their members realized that legislations were being a problem for the CSOs working on the ground, due to the complexity of the law and the lack of knowledge about it. In collaboration with Save Muslim Heritage (SMH), HfP developed the SHELTr project,[19] which stands for 'Syrian's Heritage Law Training' project. Funded in March 2016 by the Gerda Henkel Stiftung, the project has a planned completion date of 2020.

The project started after surveying lawyers, imams, local council members, and archaeologists, and HfP designed a course that explains how cultural heritage destruction should be addressed. The results emphasized these key points:

---

[15] https://es.unesco.org/courier/2017-octubre-diciembre/resolucion-historica.

[16] Ibidem.

[17] Ibidem.

[18] For more information about HfP see: www.heritageforpeace.org.

[19] We would like to thank Joanne Dingwall McCafferty; Emma Cunliffe; Bastien Varoutsikos; Rene Teijgeler; Annis Turner; Hannah Skowronski; Elizabeth Mitchell; Marcela Szalanska; Tess Davis; Mahmoud Barakat; Abdullh Al- Masri; Zahra Kazemi (Save Muslim Heritage) and Saarah Bokhari (Save Muslim Heritage) for their work in the project.

- The large majority of the legal affairs in the opposition-held areas of Syria are handled by Islamic courts, or local courts, basing a large amount of their ruling on Islamic jurisprudence, while also including aspects of Syrian National Law on an ad hoc basis.
- An increased portion of staff courts lacks proper legal training, especially in matters on cultural heritage.

The project began with the objective of making more comprehensible the different laws regarding heritage protection in Syria, practised by Islamic court staff, heritage workers and government officials across opposition-held areas in Syria, to make the local Syrian population aware of the available law. The project has created an effective tool in the use of the different legislations to make the cooperation of CSOs easier.

It aims to assist those managing legal cases in the Syrian courts in the Idlib region to understand the legal obligations through a curriculum that address legal aspects of cultural heritage protection in the three legal frameworks relevant in Syria: Syrian National Law, Islamic Law and International Humanitarian Law (IHL). HfP has researched the intersections between these three branches of law relating to the safeguarding of heritage and has invited community leaders, heritage professionals and law officials to partake in e-learning training on the legal framework that forbids the destruction of heritage, looting and the illicit antiquities trade. Specifically, the project objectives are to:

1. Research the interactions between IHL and Islamic Law around the theme of cultural heritage, for application in Muslim countries worldwide, by considering the following aspects:
    a. In the Quran, what are the reasons why History is important to contemporary Muslims?
    b. What does Islam order in regard to cultural heritage?
    c. What is the role of heritage (historical remains) in the Quran, Hadîth and other tafsîr?
2. Promote the use and implementation of IHL and foster productive interactions with other existing legal frameworks such as Islamic law and Syrian National Law in courts in the opposition-held territories.
3. Remind local legal stakeholders about their duties regarding the protection of cultural heritage by
    a. Identifying ways to accumulate further evidence of damage.
    b. Identifying the relevant legal framework and relevant laws.
    c. Identifying strategies to strengthen prosecution strategies.
4. Reach out to community leaders and decision-making actors in the opposition-held territories to influence behaviours and good practices towards cultural heritage across Syria.

Through this programme, local legal stakeholders are better informed to advocate for and adjudicate on, the protection of cultural heritage. Ultimately, this project will improve the protection of cultural heritage and mitigate looting and the illicit antiquities trade in opposition-held areas through the participation of the community leaders and other decision-makers. While damage from the fighting and looting are still significant threats, today a large amount of damage is connected to heritage mismanagement and illegal development. The law courts in the Idlib region are currently faced with numerous heritage cases on a daily basis. Through this project, HfP trains court staff and heritage professionals to better handle these cases.

7 SHELTr Training

The training is divided into International Law (both humanitarian and heritage law), Syrian Heritage Law and Islamic Heritage Law.

7.1 International Heritage Law

The first part of the course introduces participants to the international conventions put in place to protect cultural heritage. This includes the 1954 Hague Convention and customary international law more generally. Other relevant international legal instruments are discussed together with the role of the ICC in prosecuting crimes against heritage. The course concludes with discussions on the relevance and the practical application of these legal laws within the local Syrian courts.

7.2 Syrian Heritage Law

The second part of the course looks at the role and structure of Syrian cultural heritage institutions, specifically, the Directorate-General of Antiquities and Museums (DGAM), and other international institutions, such as UNESCO, which operate in Syria. It covers the history of their work and the role they have played during the conflict. Specific focus is given to the current Law of Antiquities 222,[20] and its limitations. This leads to an analysis of the initiative for the new Syrian cultural heritage law.

[20] For more information about Syrian other Arab countries heritage legislation see: https://sherloc.unodc.org/.

7.3 *Islamic Heritage Law*

As Islam plays an important role in Syria, the third part of the course presents Islamic Law sections that are key in safeguarding cultural heritage in Syria. The key principles and concepts of Islamic Law are discussed, as well as its primary sources. This is followed by an explanation of cultural heritage in Islam and a discussion of law relating to movable and immovable heritage. Finally, extremist justifications of heritage destruction are considered, together with a brief consideration of countering these views using the religious texts of the Qurʾān and the Sunnah.[21]

Participants discuss and analyse these topics together with an emphasis on interweaving the principles of the three laws. Practical exercises after each course segment are key components of the training in order for the students to apply their theoretical learning into applicable situations they might experience on a daily basis.

Through the information collected and the work of the team, it has been possible to establish some work criteria to be applied in the confrontations between the various legal systems, and the different institutions involved—CSOs, the international organizations, and the religious and governmental institutions. As we have seen above, the application of the law is needed for a deep analysis that allows its application in the field.

Nowadays, that criteria, together with the information and the experience collected, has been utilized to create an online training package to learn about the different legal systems involved in the heritage protection in the Arab region. The training package will be available in late 2020.

8 Collaborative Initiatives from Civil Society

As a consequence of the different conflicts present in the MENA region, many CSOs started to diversify their work to address other issues as well. Today we can witness how civil society plays a significant role that advances legal tools such as the sentences handed by the ICC. Most of them are working in humanitarian law, initiatives such as the Coalition for the International Criminal Court,[22] for example, which involves civil society in 150 countries fighting for global justice against war crimes, crimes against humanity and genocide. Nowadays, the fields where the CSOs are working are as large as the unattended social needs.

In Humanitarian Law, civil society cooperation has become vital to collect significant information regarding crimes against humanity to guarantee future accountability. This form of cooperation is becoming quite standard between civil society and international organizations. For example, in December 2016 the UN General Assembly created the International, Impartial and Independent Mechanism to Assist in the Investigation and Prosecution of Those Responsible for the Most Serious

[21] Traditional social and legal custom and practice of the Islamic community.

[22] http://coalitionfortheicc.org/about/who-we-are.

Crimes under International Law Committed in the Syrian Arab Republic since March 2011,[23] signing a protocol of cooperation between the mechanism and 28 Syrian CSOs participating in the Lausanne Platform, on April 2018 (Burgis-Kasthala, 2019). This is an example of the work done by such organizations. Without their work, it would not have been possible to collect the victims' testimonies. Here we have an example of operational cooperation with a bilateral structure and regulated by national law or international private law, based on a contract between the signatories. However, most of the initiatives did not reach the objectives in the end because there is a fundamental need for capacity building among CSOs, particularly in a region that requires internal reform, changed management practices, financial viability and other assistance related to institution-building (Vermeij et al., 2013). The next step is thus to create a collaborative network between CSOs which would allow them to learn from each other, and to work together to increase their impact. In the next section, we will show what HfP is currently doing in this regard.

About the heritage protection and the different International Laws mentioned above, emphasis was made on the *in situ* protection of cultural sites and the recovery and return of stolen or looted cultural objects. But those initiatives have obviously failed to stop the plunder and illegal trade of cultural objects in Syria, as they have failed before in neighbouring countries (Brodie, 2015). Likewise, local communities in countries where conflict is ravaging their heritage have experimented a strong notion of the cultural, economic and identity significance that derives from their heritage. As a result, a growing number of volunteers are working on the ground in places such as Libya, Syria, Iraq and Yemen (to name a few in the MENA region) in zones where state authorities and the international organizations are unable to reach, thus contributing to the preservation of their heritage. The role of CSOs in countries ravaged by conflict is evident. However, its impact is mostly felt in the local regions where they operate and the areas of their direct influence.

9 Arab Network of Civil Society to Safeguard Cultural Heritage (ANSCH)

HfP also recognized that there is another gap in existing aid work in situations of armed conflict. Since international heritage law is mainly applicable to states parties, governmental and intergovernmental organizations can only work with heritage authorities that are supported by the recognized state authority, and with whom there are existing diplomatic relations (Sabrine & Ibáñez, 2019). Therefore, in situations of civil conflict, non-state actors may control heritage resources, but have no access to support or provide aid. One of the key differences between past and present-day armed conflicts is that today, most armed conflicts taking place in the world are non-international in character (Lostal et al., 2017). This issue makes collaboration between the civil society and International Organizations more difficult.

[23] UN Doc. A/71/L.48, 19 December 2016.

Looking to improve the opportunities for civil CSOs, HfP launched the ANSCH (Arab Network of Civil Society to Safeguard Cultural Heritage) as a collaborative platform to provide more resources and opportunities to CSOs operating in the MENA region. The initiative started together with ALIPH (International Alliance for the Protection of Heritage in Conflict Areas) and the Spanish Council for Scientific Researches (CSIC). They both launched this civil society network in Barcelona on 4 and 5 March 2020 at an event called 'Empowerment of civil society for the protection of cultural heritage in conflict areas'.

The event was attended by many representatives of CSOs from Syria, Libya, Yemen and Iraq, as well as members of the heritage authorities from these countries, who had the opportunity to present their work and discuss their needs, as well as experts from the University of Oxford, Blue Shield, the Syrian Heritage Archive Project, and University College London. The event concluded with the launch of the ANSCH website—Arab Network of Civil Society to Safeguard Cultural Heritage.[24]

To better know what are the needs of the CSOs, HfP developed a Needs Assessment: one for the CSOs, and one for the heritage authorities. The goal of the assessment is to collect information on heritage needs and analyse priorities, to identify helpful strategies and resources. The assessment asked:

- General questions that help us understand the background and employment of the people involved.
- Specific questions that provide us with detailed information on the professional needs and that of the organization in times of crisis.

In order to do the assessment, HfP designed a questionnaire, which was used as a tool to help evaluate the needs, assist in finding appropriate assistance and resources to meet the needs, and finally to help implement strategies to address the needs.

In the workshops developed in the event, some necessities were identified regarding the work of CSOs—most of them related to their capacity to access international funds. One point mentioned was the lack of training in law, and how the process of funding works. Thus, the priority for ANSCH is to facilitate those CSOs the access to international funding by organizing meetings between them and key funding institutions in Europe. As a result, more than 30 CSOs have now the opportunity to present their projects and to face the COVID crisis.

ANSCH is providing the knowledge exchange between the CSOs, looking to strengthen the links between them. One of the methods is to invite the CSO to participate as partners in the HfP projects. In that way, HfP is working in a collaborative network and developing the scope of the different projects which are currently underway.

[24]https://ansch.heritageforpeace.org/.

10 Conclusion

CSOs and grassroots movements in the MENA region need to learn how to expand the sphere of the legitimacy of their activities for sustainable and lasting success (Çakmak, 2017). One of the fundamental methods taken by HfP is the cooperation and the strengthening of collaborative networks. As we have shown in this paper, the difficulties to protect heritage in the MENA region are directly related to legislation and its applicability on the ground. Another difficulty is the bifurcation of international legal regimes between wartime and peacetime treaties that have severely hampered our ability as a CSO to protect heritage (Gerstenblith, 2020).

It is in this region where CSOs are playing an important role, based on the acknowledgement that heritage is significant, and its role in society must be emphasized. Thus, it is compulsory to understand correctly the different laws in which heritage protection is supported, in order to prevent further heritage destruction even more important during peacetime than conflict (Brodie, 2017).

The SHELTr project and ANSCH were created within the objectives and the work carried out by HfP in countries which are suffering armed conflicts. When the Syrian conflict began in 2011, it demonstrated that the international community was not prepared, or not willing, to protect cultural heritage during conflict. Indeed, the prevailing argument was that it would be necessary to wait until the conflict was over to send aid and salvage what was left.

Others felt, however, that it was clear that the international community needed to reflect on new ways of working and new measures of protection (Brodie, 2015). This is still the case today, despite the changes in international law and humanitarian practice. HfP was founded on the principle that it was vital to work before, during and after the conflict, rather than waiting until it was over. This stance directly contradicted many of the attitudes by international organizations and international CSOs.[25] Although now this stance seems so commonplace, it is easy to forget how quickly this has changed.

Recognizing that solutions must come from within these countries, this paper considers the important role that CSOs play in terms of cultural heritage protection. This is most evident in the work done on raising awareness; safeguarding collections, monuments and archaeological sites; documenting and monitoring heritage damage; and contributing to stop the looting and illicit trafficking of cultural heritage. As examples of some of the outcomes achieved by SHELTEr, we can mention:

[25] Although this statement is anecdotal and direct evidence is not available, knowledge of damage to Syria's heritage became widespread in 2012, when a report by the Global Heritage Fund was published (Cunliffe, 2012). The report was widely circulated in heritage circles (and picked up by news outlets in more than 16 countries). However, a review of the 2011–2014 HfP International Action report (Perini & Cunliffe, 2014) demonstrates that the vast majority of international work to protect Syria's heritage (rather than simply raising awareness about damage to it) did not begin until at least 2014—a year after HfP had already undertaken several projects to help Syrian heritage workers.

- To make the society conscious about the problems within the current law of antiquities, and the necessity of a new law in Syria.
- What should be the minimum content in a National Heritage Law.

We believe that heritage can serve as a key focus of dialogue between communities, nations and ethnic groups. Indeed, heritage can in fact, become a tool for peacebuilding (Walters et al., 2017). There is ample evidence to support the claim that heritage could be seen as a political and cultural challenge to sovereignty (Mackenzie & Yates, 2016; Mackenzie et al., 2020); a direct threat to religious identities (Isakhan & González Zarandona, 2018), and as a missed opportunity for society after an armed conflict or catastrophe devastates it (Viejo-Rose, 2013).

The correct understanding of the law is a compulsory element for a correct management of heritage, but as we have shown, not all the CSOs have the correct training in that matter. This chapter has only been an introduction to the relation between state duties, the international instruments on heritage protection, human rights treaties and the role of CSOs. The complexity of the subject and the continuous changes in law, makes compulsory to update and conduct more studies from different disciplines, to provide us with a wide perspective, while making more people conscious about the topic.

References

Abdel Haleem, M. A. S. (2005). *The Qur´an. A new translation*. Oxford University Press.

Abdelaziz, M. (2017). *The hard reality of civil society in the Arab World*. https://www.washingtoninstitute.org/fikraforum/view/the-hard-reality-of-civil-society-in-the-arab-world. Accessed 21 June 2020.

Beliakova, A. (2019). Role of civil society in preserving cultural heritage. *Journal of Governance and Politics: Civil Society Networks in Global Environment: Recent Trends and Developments, 1*(4). Available at: https://sgpjournal.mgimo.ru/2019-4/role-of-civil-society-in-preserving-cultural-heritage. Accessed 25 June 2020.

Bernabei, G. (2019). International courts and cultural heritage: Bridging the gap. *Art Antiquity & Law, 24*(2), 125–132.

Brodie, N. (2015). Syria and its regional neighbors: A case of cultural property protection policy failure? *International Journal of Cultural Property, 22*, 317–335. https://doi.org/10.1017/s0940739115000144. Accessed 25 June 2020.

Brodie, N. (2017). Protection not prevention. In J. Anderson & H. Geismar (Eds.), *The Routledge companion to cultural property*. Routledge Handbooks Online.

Brodie, N., & Sabrine, I. (2018). The illegal excavation and trade of Syrian cultural objects: A view from the ground. *Journal of Field Archaeology, 43*(1), 74–84.

Browers, M. L. (2006). *Democracy and civil society in Arab political thought*. New York: Syracuse University Press.

Burgis-Kasthala, M. (2019). Entrepreneurial Justice: Syria, the commission for international justice and accountability and the renewal of international criminal justice. *The European Journal of International Law, 30*(4), 1165–1185. https://doi.org/10.1093/ejil/chz065. http://www.ejil.org/pdfs/30/4/3021.pdf. Accessed 20 July 2020.

Çakmak, C. (Ed.). (2017). *The Arab Spring, civil society, and innovative activism*. Palgrave Macmillan. https://doi.org/10.1057/978-1-137-57177-9_1.

Cunliffe, E. (2012). Damage to the soul: Syria's cultural heritage in conflict. *Palo Alto: Global Heritage Fund: Report*. Available at: http://ghn.globalheritagefund.com/uploads/documents/document_2107.pdf. Accessed 25 June 2020.

Democracy Reporting International (DRI). (2008, February). Flawed by design: The 2007 Syrian Parliamentary and local elections and presidential Referendum. Post-election briefing no. 2.

Gerstenblith, P. (2020). The disposition of movable cultural heritage. In A. M. Carstens & E. Varner (Eds.), *Intersections in international cultural heritage law*. Oxford: Oxford University Press.

Guessoum, Abd-Ur-Razzak. (2001, December 30, 31). Islam and world heritage. In *Proceeding of Doha Conference of 'ULAMÂon Islam and Cultural Heritage: Doha/Qatar*. Available at: https://unesdoc.unesco.org/ark:/48223/pf0000140834. Accessed 4 August 2020.

Hanafi, H. (2002). Alternative conceptions of civil society: A reflective Islamic approach. In S. Chambers & W. Kymlicka (Eds.), *Alternative conceptions of civil society* (pp. 171–189). Princeton: Princeton University Press.

Hawthorne, A. (2005). *Is civil society the answer*? In T. Carothers & M. Ottoway (Eds.), *Uncharted journey: Promoting democracy in the Middle East*. Washington, DC.

Isakhan, B., & González Zarandona, J. A. (2018). Layers of religious and political iconoclasm under the Islamic State: Symbolic sectarianism and pre-monotheistic iconoclasm. *International Journal of Heritage Studies, 24*(1), 1–16.

Karajah, Sa'ed. (2007). Civil society in the Arab world: The missing concept. *The International Journal of Not-for-Profit Law, 9*(2). Available at: https://www.icnl.org/resources/research/ijnl/civil-society-in-the-arab-world-the-missing-concept. Accessed 25 June 2020.

Khattab, L. (2017). Re-imagining the 'State' in Syria during the first year of the uprising (2011–2012). In C. Çakmak, (Ed.), *The Arab Spring, civil society, and innovative activism*. Palgrave Macmillan. https://doi.org/10.1057/978-1-137-57177-9_1.

Lostal, M., Hausler, K., & Bongard, P. (2017). Armed non-state actors and cultural heritage in armed conflict. *International Journal of Cultural Property, 24*(4), 407–427. https://doi.org/10.1017/s0940739117000200. Accessed 29 June 2020.

Mackenzie, S., Brodie, N., Yates, D., & Tsirogiannis, C. (2020). *Trafficking culture: New directions in researching the global market in illicit antiquities*. Abingdon: Routledge.

Mackenzie, S., & Yates, D. (2016). Trafficking cultural objects and human rights. In L. Weber, E. Fishwick, & M. Marmo (Eds.), *The Routledge international handbook of criminology and human rights* (pp. 220–230). New York: Routledge. https://traffickingculture.org/publications/criminology-human-rights-and-trafficking-cultural-objects/. Accessed 30 July 2020.

Manacorda, S. (2011). Criminal law protection of cultural heritage: An international perspective. In S. Manacorda & D. Chappell (Eds.), *Crime in the art and antiquities world: 17 illegal trafficking in cultural property*. London: Springer Science.

North Atlantic Treaty Organization. (2018). The protection of cultural property in the event of armed conflict: Unnecessary distraction or mission relevant priority? *NATO OPEN Publications, 2*(4). Available at: https://www.act.nato.int/images/stories/media/doclibrary/open201804-cultural-property.pdf. Accessed 2 August 2020.

Perini, S., & Cunliffe, E. (2014). *Towards a protection of the Syrian cultural heritage: A summary of the international responses*. Volume I (March 2011–March 2014). Girona: Heritage for Peace. Report available online. http://www.heritageforpeace.org/wp-content/uploads/2014/04/Towards-a-protection-of-the-Syrian-cultural-heritage.pdf. Accessed 2 August 2020.

Sabrine, I., & Ibáñez, J. J. (2019). Sociedad civil y protección del patrimonio Sirio. *Afkar Ideas, 60*, 69–72.

Sadiki, L. (2009). *Rethinking Arab democratization: Elections without democracy*. Oxford: Oxford University Press.

Tünsmeyer, V. (2020). Bridging the gap between international human rights and international cultural heritage law instrument. In A. M. Carstens & E. Varner (Eds.), *Intersections in international cultural heritage law*. Oxford: Oxford University Press. https://doi.org/10.1093/oso/9780198846291.003.0014. Accessed 2 August 2020.

Vermeij, L., Troost, P., Elwan, S., & Wahab, W. A. (2013). Civil society and Arab transitions: A new beginning? *Norwegian Institute of International Affairs, Policy Brief*, 14. Available at: https://www.nupi.no/en/Publications/CRIStin-Pub/Civil-Society-and-Arab-Transitions-A-New-Beginning. Accessed 3 August 2020.

Viejo-Rose, D. (2013). Reconstructing heritage in the aftermath of civil war: Re-visioning the nation and the implications of international involvement. *Journal of Intervention and Statebuilding, 7*(2), 125–148. https://doi.org/10.1080/17502977.2012.714241.

Walters, D., Laven, D., & Davis, P. (Eds.). (2017). *Heritage and peacebuilding*. Woodbridge: Boydell & Brewer.

The Challenges Ahead of Iranian Natural Resources/Heritages Alongside the International Conventions in Upcoming Years

Hamidreza Solaymani Osbooei

Abstract As the key development strategy and planning instrument of the government, the Sixth Five-Year Development Plan 2016–2021 of the Islamic Republic of Iran is underpinned by three core pillars: Developing a Resistance Economy; Progress in Science and Technology and Promoting Cultural Excellence. Meanwhile, the United Nations Development Assistance Framework (UNDAF) 2017–2021 provides a strategic framework for cooperation and a broad guide to facilitate coordinated planning and implementation of specific UN agency work programs in partnership with the Government of Iran. Four main priority areas were identified in the UNDAF: Environment; Health; Resilient Economy, and; Drug Control. The objectives of the current article are to investigate the existing challenges ahead the Iranian natural resources/heritages to face the international conventions and/or the agreements. First of all, a vision of Iranian natural resources (Forest, Rangelands, and the internal water bodies) were explained, and then the confirmed international conventions/agreements described too. The relevant existing weaknesses and strengths discussed at the end.

1 Iran's Nature in a Glance

Iran is located in the southern part of the northern hemisphere on the arid belt of the world with a land area of 1.64 million km^2. Iran is bordered by Turkmenistan, Caspian Sea, Azerbaijan, and Armenia in the north, Afghanistan and Pakistan are on Iran's eastern border, the Persian Gulf, and the Sea of Oman in the south and Iraq and Turkey in the west. Two major mountain ranges affect its climate; the Zagros in the west and the Alborz in the north. Most humid clouds that come from the west are prevented from reaching central, eastern, and southern parts by these mountain ranges, so the central and southern lowlands and eastern parts of the country receive very little precipitation. As the result, approximately 65% of the territory has an arid or hyper-arid climate with the mean annual rainfall about 210 mm.

H. Solaymani Osbooei (✉)
Forest, Range, and Watershed Management, Organization of Iran—FRWO, Tehran, Iran
e-mail: hr.solaymani@frw.org.ir

O. Niglio and E. Y. J. Lee (eds.), *Transcultural Diplomacy and International Law in Heritage Conservation*, https://doi.org/10.1007/978-981-16-0309-9_25

The peculiar features and location cause the country to receive less than a third of the world average precipitation except the Caspian plain that receives more than 1000 mm of rain annually. Due to low and unevenly distributed precipitation in these areas, most rivers are seasonal, and their flows depend heavily upon the amount of rainfall. If rainfall is above average, flash floods are common. However, Iran's topographic and climatic variations and edaphical conditions has created different land uses and a unique collection of more than eight thousand plant species including shrub and tree species.

Iran is divided into eight major climatic regions. However, the humid climatic region may be further divided into six subregions thereby creating thirteen climatic regions in total. The diversity of climate allows for a variety of agricultural and aquatic products including the growing of citrus fruits, rice, and tea in large parts of the northern region and pistachios and dates in central and southern parts of the country as well as tropical fruits such as bananas and mangos. In cooler climates of the mountain ranges grapes, almonds, and apples are produced. There is a good potential for further development of agriculture and aquaculture in most parts of Iran, especially in the northern and southern regions.

Most of the lands of Iran are located in arid and semi-arid area; the wetlands of Iran are globally significant; large populations of migratory birds' winter at these wetlands or use them on their way. The complex and varied climates, topography, geological formations, and anthropological management of natural resources have led to a varied and unique biological diversity. In the Iranian ecosystems approximately 8,000 species of plants, 197 species of mammals, 535 species of birds, 227 species of reptiles, 21 species of amphibians, 160 species of freshwater fishes, and 710 species of marine fishes have been recorded. Iran is one of the most important countries in the Middle East and Western Asia for conservation of biological diversity. Habitat diversity in Iran allows for a wide range of animals to inhibit in Iran. With regards to ecosystem diversity of marine and coastal zones in the North and South of the country, it consists of 25 ecological types and units, in which the most important are coral reefs, bays, and small islands.

A detailed description of Iran's biodiversity status was provided in the forth (2010) and fifth national reports to conventional biological diversity (2015). A brief description of biodiversity is as follow:

The Islamic Republic of Iran contains a vast diversity of ecosystems, including two important mountain ranges, 10 Biosphere Reserves, 24 Ramsar listed wetlands and unique drylands and forests. Woodlands cover 12.4 million hectares and there are 10,000 hectares of Avicenna mangroves along the Persian Gulf. The number of species indicates biodiversity richness: 8,000 species of plants (of which 1,900 are endemic), 535 species of birds, 197 species of mammals, and 870 species of fish.

2 Existing Upstream Rules and Documents

Iran's constitution shows environment concept in three articles. Articles 45, 48, and 50 are the most important articles which show the approaches of constitutional legislator in Iran. Article 45 says: The following are under the control of the Islamic government: wastelands and public wealth, abandoned, or unclaimed land of deceased owners, mines, seas, lakes, rivers, and other public bodies of water, mountains, valleys, forests, marshlands, natural prairies, unrestricted pastures, inheritance without any heir, wealth without any identified owner, and public wealth that is confiscated from the usurpers. The Islamic government will treat these in accordance with the public interest. The law shall determine the detail and manner of utilization of each of them. Article 48 indicates: There should be no discrimination among various provinces and regions in the country in extracting natural resources and using national incomes, and in allocating economic activities to them. Each area according to its own needs and aptitude for growth should have access to the necessary capital and provisions.

Article 50 in Iran's constitution says: The preservation of the environment, in which the present as well as the future generations have a right to flourishing social existence, is regarded as a public duty in the Islamic Republic. Economic and other activities that inevitably involve pollution of the environment or cause irreparable damage to it are therefore forbidden. This article indicates three important elements of environment including Sustainable Development, The Right to Development and duty of people and government for preservation of environment.

On 19 March 2017, the "Law on the Sixth Five-Year Economic, Cultural, and Social Development Plan for 1396–1400 (2016–2021)" (the "Sixth Development Plan") was approved by the Iranian Parliament in 123 articles (IPoI, 2016). The development plan sets out the goals and objectives to be achieved by the country over the next five years. In a notable change to previous plans, the Sixth Development Plan places less emphasis on achieving hard targets and attempts to provide guidelines for the Iranian government (the "Government") to deal with certain shortcomings facing the country. Some of the key guidelines and goals for the various sectors as set out in the Sixth Development Plan are as follows: Financing and Investment Sector, Banking Sector, Government Guarantees, Legal Sector, Power Sector, Tourism Sector, and Water Sector. Theses sectors was also bolded by UNESCO (2017) in the relevant report about Iran's strategy.

In tourism sector, the government provides the necessary support to strengthen the tourism industry, increase the number of religious tourists, and provide financial incentives for the development of tourism industry in Iran's shorelines. The main objective in water sector: within the framework of the Iranian Constitution, the government is required to take the necessary steps to reduce consumption of potable water by 30% and by the end of the Sixth Development Plan to produce 30% of the required potable water for south Iran through desalination.

3 Iran and the Environmental Conventions

3.1 *Ramsar Convention on Wetlands*

The Convention's mission is "the conservation and wise use of all wetlands through local and national actions and international cooperation, as a contribution toward achieving sustainable development throughout the world." The convention entered into force in the Islamic Republic of Iran on December 21, 1975. The Islamic Republic of Iran currently has 25 sites designated as Wetlands of International Importance (Ramsar Sites), 25 covering sites with a surface area of 1,488,624 hectares.[1]

3.2 *United Nations Convention to Combat Desertification (UNCCD)*

Established in 1994, UNCCD is the sole legally binding international agreement linking environment and development to sustainable land management. The Convention addresses specifically the arid, semi-arid, and dry subhumid areas, known as the drylands, where some of the most vulnerable ecosystems and peoples can be found. In line with Article 23 of the UNCCD, the key function of the secretariat is to service the sessions of the COP and its subsidiary bodies. The 10-Year Strategy of the UNCCD (2008–2018) states that "Successful implementation of this strategic plan requires a strengthening of the core servicing, advocacy and agenda-setting and representation functions of the UNCCD secretariat—with commensurate capacity and resources—in order to support Parties, the COP and the subsidiary bodies of the Convention in fulfilling their respective roles." In tandem, Parties to the Convention further specified their goals: "to forge a global partnership to reverse and prevent desertification/land degradation and to mitigate the effects of drought in affected areas in order to support poverty reduction and environmental sustainability." All the Convention parties work together to improve the living conditions of people in drylands, to maintain and restore land and soil productivity, and to mitigate the effects of drought. The UNCCD is particularly committed to a bottom-up approach, encouraging the participation of local people in combating desertification and land degradation. The long term strategy of UNCCD secretariat facilitates cooperation between developed and developing countries, particularly about the knowledge and technology transfer for sustainable land management.

Iran joined UNCCD in 1995 and one year later ratified. Based on the decisions made by the NCCD (National Convention Combat to Desertification) the following nine strategies have been defined: (1) Integration of sustainable development concepts into ministerial and organizational programs, particularly any activities relating to agriculture, natural resources and the environment; (2) Emphasis on population

[1]https://www.ramsar.org/wetland/iran-islamic-republic-of.

control and family planning policies especially in rural and nomadic areas; (3) Priority for preventive measures in curbing desertification; (4) Development of technologies related to combating desertification through research and training programs with emphasis on indigenous knowledge and technologies; (5) Review of existing laws and enactment of the necessary regulations commensurate with sustainable development programs and anti-desertification activities; (6) Raising public awareness on the risks and consequences of desertification; (7) Increasing public participation in the planning, management and implementation of anti-desertification projects; (8) Directing financial resources toward the realization of NAP objectives in national development; (9) Developing measures for the expansion of applied research and integration of indigenous knowledge (FRWMO, 2004).

3.3 United Nations Framework Convention on Climate Change (UNFCCC)

The UNFCCC entered into force on March 21, 1994. Today, it has near-universal membership. The 197 countries that have ratified the Convention are called Parties to the Convention. Preventing "dangerous" human interference with the climate system is the ultimate aim of the UNFCCC. The UNFCCC is a "Rio Convention," one of the two opened for signature at the "Rio Earth Summit" in 1992. Its sister Rio Conventions are the UN Convention on Biological Diversity and the Convention to Combat Desertification. The three are intrinsically linked. It is in this context that the Joint Liaison Group was set up to boost cooperation among the three Conventions, with the ultimate aim of developing synergies in their activities on issues of mutual concern.[2]

UNFCCC stands for United Nations Framework Convention on Climate Change. The Convention has near-universal membership (197 Parties) and is the parent treaty of the 2015 Paris Agreement. The main aim of the Paris Agreement is to keep the global average temperature rise this century as close as possible to 1.5 degrees Celsius above pre-industrial levels. The UNFCCC is also the parent treaty of the 1997 Kyoto Protocol. The ultimate objective of all three agreements under the UNFCCC is to stabilize greenhouse gas concentrations in the atmosphere at a level that will prevent dangerous human interference with the climate system, in a time frame which allows ecosystems to adapt naturally and enables sustainable development.[3]

Iran joined climate convention and Kyoto protocol at June 14, 1992. Iran also joined the Paris Agreement on April 22, 2016. The first two conventions; Climate Change convention and the Kyoto protocol ratified July 18, 1996 and August 22, 2005, respectively. Iran submitted three national communication reports to UNFCC from at 2003, 2010, and 2017 which the third one has submitted December 2017.

[2]https://unfccc.int/process-and-meetings/the-convention/what-is-the-united-nations-framework-convention-on-climate-change.

[3]https://unfccc.int/.

The Third National Communication (TNC) report consisted of six chapters which are included: National Circumstances, National Greenhouse Gasses Inventory, National Greenhouse Gases Mitigation Policies, Vulnerability and Adaptation, Relevant Information and National Strategies and Action Plans on Climate Change from Chapter one to six, respectively. Vaghefi et al. (2019) shown that compared the base period of 1980–2004, to the period of 2025–2049, Iran is likely to experience more extended periods of extreme maximum temperatures in the southern part of the country, more extended periods of dry (for $\geq$ 120 days: precipitation < 2 mm, Tmax $\geq$ 30 °C) as well as wet (for $\leq$ 3 days: total precipitation $\geq$ 110 mm) conditions, and higher frequency of floods. Overall, the combination of these results projects a climate of extended dry periods interrupted by intermittent heavy rainfalls, which is a recipe for increasing the chances of floods (Abbasi et al. 2020).

3.4 The Convention on Biological Diversity (CBD)

In response, the United Nations Environment Program (UNEP) convened the Ad Hoc Working Group of Experts on Biological Diversity in November 1988 to explore the need for an. international convention on biological diversity. Soon after, in May 1989, it established the Ad Hoc Working Group of Technical and Legal Experts to prepare an international legal instrument for the conservation and sustainable use of biological diversity. The experts were to take into account "the need to share costs and benefits between developed and developing countries" as well as "ways and means to support innovation by local people." By February 1991, the Ad Hoc Working Group had become known as the Intergovernmental Negotiating Committee. Its work culminated on May 22, 1992 with the Nairobi Conference for the Adoption of the Agreed Text of the Convention on Biological Diversity. The Convention was opened for signature on 5 June 1992 at the United Nations Conference on Environment and Development (the Rio "Earth Summit"). It remained open for signature until June 4, 1993, by which time it had received 168 signatures. The Convention entered into force on December 29, 1993, which was 90 days after the 30th ratification. The first session of the Conference of the Parties was scheduled for 28 November–9 December 1994 in the Bahamas. The Convention on Biological Diversity was inspired by the world community's growing commitment to sustainable development. It represents a dramatic step forward in the conservation of biological diversity, the sustainable use of its components, and the fair and equitable sharing of benefits arising from the use of genetic resources.

Most of Iran is located in the Palaearctic realm and is considered the center of origin of many genetic resources of the world, including many of the original strains of commercially valuable plant species, such as wheat and medicinal/aromatic species. The southwest has some Afro-tropical features, while the southeast has some species from the Indo-Malayan subtropical realm. Iranian habitats support some 8,200 species of plants, of which 1,900 species are endemic. Woodlands cover 12.4 million hectares and Avicenna mangroves cover around 10,000 hectares along the

Persian Gulf. Studies indicate that there are over 500 species of birds, 160 species of mammals, 1,035 species of fishes (including 750 species in the Persian Gulf and Sea of Oman, of which nine are endemic), 100 species belonging to the Caspian Sea (10 endemics) and 185 species living in inland and fresh waters (15 endemics).

Ecosystem services arising from biodiversity in the country are particularly important for maintaining agricultural genetic diversity, however also important for soil and water quality regulation, fisheries (especially regarding sturgeon), reducing the rate of desertification and in regard to possibilities for developing ecotourism in the future. Iran ratified the CBD November 4, 1996 and submitted five national reports till now. The sixth national report will be submitted before the end of 2020.

4 Iran's Environmental Challenges

Water scarcity, land degradation, and pollution are three main threats on Iran's environment. Iran faces serious water shortages that are resulted in two main mechanisms: inadequate natural water resources supply and development of water infrastructures. Soil loss is related to salinization, sedimentation, soil erosion, desertification, deforestation, inadequate land-use planning, and overgrazing of the rangelands. In rapidly urbanized areas, air pollution originating from vehicle emissions and industrial effluents has become a serious environmental and public health hazard concern. The Dust Phenomenon or dust storms in recent years has taken on new dimensions in Iran and has changed from a local problem to a regional and national issue. The primary source of the dust storms that are regularly and negatively impacting Iran's air quality lies in the neighboring countries and internal sources partly.

Iran's environment is under a lot of pressure and faces many threats, such as: desertification, soil erosion, overgrazing, loss of traditional knowledge, lack of awareness, population pressure, unsustainable consumption/production levels, overexploitation, and high greenhouse gasses emission in urban and industrial areas. Coastal habitats and water resources are being polluted by oil, and industrial and agricultural activities. Overfishing is also a major threat for many fish species. Many projects have been put forward to halt the degradation of ecosystems, such as integrated fertilizer management, irrigation and inland water management, afforestation, as well as initiatives related to mountains (Shahchera, 2014).

Iran's growing environmental challenges have recently reached a crisis point. Water scarcity and air pollution, in particular, have not only caused sociopolitical and security problems inside the country but have also strained Iran's relations with its neighbors such as Turkey and Afghanistan for constructing new dams; and some Arab states such as Iraq, Kuwait, Jordan, Saudi Arabia as the main sources of sand storms that are impacted majority of Iran.[4]

[4]https://www.mei.edu/publications/growing-environmental-problems-strain-irans-ties-its-neighbors.

Tiany Lou et al. (2015) used an ensemble of climate models and socioeconomic scenarios, WRI scored and ranked future water stress—a measure of competition and depletion of surface water—in 167 countries by 2020, 2030, and 2040. They found that 33 countries face extremely high-water stress in 2040 that Iran's rank will be thirteen in the world till 2040.

5 Conclusion

Iranian authorities have been losing their war to adapt the climate change and combat environmental degradation for decades. Iran's forest cover declined highly from nineteen million acres in 1900 to fewer than fifteen million in 2012, dipping below twelve million three years later. In some parts of Iran, meanwhile, precipitation has declined by an average of 2.56 mm a year for the past forty years, contributing to desertification and water scarcity (Bodetti, 2019; Solaymani 2018; Solaymani and Gosain 2014).

The existing Iran's environmental condition needs urgent considerations. There are many factors to be addressed. The environmental conventions and the bilateral/multilateral agreements are the opportunities to move forward with the current situation on the environment. The first step should provide the common understanding of the concepts and then coverts all the benefits for all Iran's neighbor. The next steps will provide the constant economic and political national as well as international strategies that can be of help Iran to keep the international supports (technical, funding, and political) to survive the environment. The gap of the bilateral and multilateral corporation with the neighbors and the rest of the world, caused the uncertain situation to appear on the environmental development and protection.

References

Aa.Vv. (2010). *Fourth biodiversity national report*. Teheran: Islamic Republic of Iran.

Aa.Vv. (2015). *Fifth biodiversity national report (2015)*. Teheran: Islamic Republic of Iran.

Islamic Parliment of Iran (IPoI). (2016). *Law on the sixth five-year economic, cultural and social development plan for 1396–1400—Sixth five-year development plan (2016–2021)*. Management and Planning Organization (in Persian). https://policy.asiapacificenergy.org/node/3671. Accessed 16 Aug 2020.

Abbasi, H., Delavar, M., Bigdeli Nalbandan, R., et al. (2020). Robust strategies for climate change adaptation in the agricultural sector under deep climate uncertainty. *Stochastic Environmental Research and Risk Assessment, 34*, 755–774. https://doi.org/10.1007/s00477-020-01782-4.

Bodetti, A. (2019). Environmental degradation in Iran. *Inside Arabia*. https://insidearabia.com/environmental-degradation-in-iran/. Accessed 15 Aug 2020.

Forest, Range and Watershed Management Org. (2004). *The national action program to combat desertification and mitigate the effects of drought of Islamic Republic of Iran*. https://knowledge.unccd.int/sites/default/files/naps/2017-08/iran-eng2004.pdf.

Lou, T., Young, R. S., & Reig, P. (2015). Ranking the World's Most Water-Stressed Countries in 2040. *World Resources Institute.* https://www.wri.org/publication/aqueduct-projected-water-stress-country-rankings.

Shahchera, M. (2014), *A Model of Asset and Liability Management and Monetary Shocks (DSGE Model)* https://ideas.repec.org/a/mbr/jmonec/v9y2014i1p57-91.html Accessed 16 Aug 2020.

Solaymani, H. R. (2018). Applying partial order and SWOT analysis in water and land use planning to prioritize the adaptation strategies under changing climate. *Journal of Urban and Landscape Planning, 3.* https://www.julpreview.ro/files/JULP11_3_2018-HamidrezaREV_p61_68.pdf. Accessed 16 Aug 2020.

Solaymani, H. R., & Gosain, A. K. (2014). Assessment of climate change impacts in a semi-arid watershed in Iran using regional climate models. *Journal of Water and Climate.* https://doi.org/10.2166/wcc.2014.076 Accessed 16 Aug 2020.

UNESCO. (2017). *Country strategy for the Islamic Republic of Iran 2017–2021.* UNESCO Tehran Cluster Office. http://www.unesco.org/new/fileadmin/MULTIMEDIA/FIELD/Tehran/images/Iran.pdf. Accessed 16 Aug 2020.

Vaghefi, S. A., Keykhai, M., Jahanbakhshi, F., et al. (2019). The future of extreme climate in Iran. *Scientific Reports, 9,* 1464 https://www.nature.com/articles/s41598-018-38071-8. Accessed 16 Aug 2020.

The manufacturer's authorised representative in the EU is Springer Nature Customer Service Centre GmbH, Europaplatz 3, 69115 Heidelberg, Germany. If you have any concerns regarding our products, please contact ProductSafety@springernature.com

Printed and bound by CPI Group (UK) Ltd, Croydon, CR0 4YY
30/09/2026
02225324-0018